W9-AFN-848

Mixing, Recording, and Producing Techniques of the Pros, Second Edition

Rick Clark

Course Technology PTR
A part of Cengage Learning

COURSE TECHNOLOGY
CENGAGE Learning™

Australia, Brazil, Japan, Korea, Mexico, Singapore, Spain, United Kingdom, United States

COURSE TECHNOLOGY
CENGAGE Learning

Mixing, Recording, and Producing Techniques of the Pros, Second Edition
Rick Clark

Publisher and General Manager, Course Technology PTR:
Stacy L. Hiquet

Associate Director of Marketing:
Sarah Panella

Manager of Editorial Services:
Heather Talbot

Marketing Manager:
Mark Hughes

Executive Editor:
Mark Garvey

Project Editor/Copy Editor:
Cathleen D. Small

Interior Layout:
Jill Flores

Cover Designer:
Luke Fletcher

Indexer:
Broccoli Information Management

Proofreader:
Heather Urschel

For product information and technology assistance, contact us at
Cengage Learning Customer & Sales Support, 1-800-354-9706

For permission to use material from this text or product,
submit all requests online at **cengage.com/permissions**.
Further permissions questions can be emailed to
permissionrequest@cengage.com

Library of Congress Control Number: 2008932486

ISBN-13: 978-1-59863-840-0

ISBN-10: 1-59863-840-8

Course Technology, a part of Cengage Learning
20 Channel Center Street
Boston, MA 02210
USA

Cengage Learning is a leading provider of customized learning solutions with office locations around the globe, including Singapore, the United Kingdom, Australia, Mexico, Brazil, and Japan. Locate your local office at: **international.cengage.com/region**

Cengage Learning products are represented in Canada by Nelson Education, Ltd.

For your lifelong learning solutions, visit **courseptr.com**
Visit our corporate website at **cengage.com**

Front cover images: Top row (left to right): Emmylou Harris, Cookie Marenco and Jean-Claude Reynaud, Calexico's John Convertino. Bottom row (left to right): Calexico's Paul Niehaus, Osaka Pearl's Danielle Tibedo, producer Jim Scott (photo by Jimmy Stratton).

Back cover images: Top to bottom: Producer Jim Dickinson (photo by Tom Lonardo), producer Charlie Sexton and Clarence "Gatemouth" Brown, producer Brian Ahern. (All photos by Rick Clark unless otherwise noted.)

Printed in the United States of America
2 3 4 5 6 7 12 11

About the Author

Rick Clark grew up immersed in music in his hometown of Memphis, Tennessee, a place where rock, R&B, and blues were everywhere. His first records were Sun Records 45s by Carl Perkins, Jerry Lee Lewis, and Charlie Rich, as well as New Orleans Dixieland jazz by Sweet Emma and Her Preservation Hall Jazz Band and raw British Invasion albums by the Yardbirds and the Kinks. Clark regards his first concert, James Brown and the Famous Flames in 1966, as a life-changing event that inspired him to pursue a life in music. By high school, Clark was working in Memphis's main record shop, Poplar Tunes—a place where local artists such as Isaac Hayes and Al Green would sometimes hang, as well as every self-respecting band from England who made a pilgrimage there.

During the '70s and onward, Clark played live and in sessions, including projects with members of Big Star, Memphis Horns, and the seminal Memphis Power Pop scene.

Early on, Clark DJed his own radio show at WLYX-FM Memphis, and his enthusiasm for creating great road music mix cassettes earned him a reputation as a go-to guy for new and great sounds. He eventually started a successful business programming music for every genre in venues throughout the South and other parts of the country. Eventually, he wrote for numerous national publications, including *Billboard*, *Mix*, *Rolling Stone*, *Guitar Player*, the *All Music Guide*, *Goldmine*, and others. Over time, Clark began producing and compiling numerous major- and indie-label album releases, as well as writing liner notes for artists ranging from Ricky Nelson, Dave Edmunds, and Lynyrd Skynyrd to Leo Kottke, Jean-Luc Ponty, and Big Star. Clark also began working as a curator, music consultant, and independent A&R rep with clients ranging from museums, to magazines, to films and major label projects.

Clark's production work includes working with Death Cab for Cutie (music for the Band tribute album *Lost Highway* and the hit TV show *Weeds*), the Killjoys, Osaka Pearl, and Los Super Seven—an amalgam that included Calexico, Lyle Lovett, Delbert McClinton, John Hiatt, Raul Malo, Freddy Fender, Rodney Crowell, and others. Clark also produced 26 shows of Marty Stuart's *American Odyssey* for XM radio, directed two videos on Emmylou Harris for Warner DVD-Audio, composed and produced music for IBM's International Global Net, and had his photography featured in gallery shows, on record albums, and in ad campaigns.

Beginning in 1997, through a recommendation by the legendary producer Jim Dickinson, Clark began work producing, co-compiling, and doing all the legal clearance work for what would be the first seven volumes of the award-winning *Oxford American* magazine music CDs, featuring music ranging from legendary artists such as Bob Dylan, Randy Newman, and B.B. King to obscure blues, jazz, and Cajun music recordings.

As a film music supervisor, Clark's credits include work on Jason Reitman's *Up in the Air*.

Jim Dickinson

November 21, 1941–August 15, 2009

Jim Dickinson was a great producer and musician, a selfless mentor, and a devoted family man to his wife, Mary Lindsay, and his boys, Luther and Cody. I watched him grow his own family band with his gifted sons, who went on to become the North Mississippi Allstars. Jim and I grew up in Memphis and, though a number of years apart, we went to the same public school and had some of the same teachers. That said, one of my finest teachers was Dickinson himself. He was a fiercely passionate communicator and one of the greatest and funniest storytellers I've known. When there was something troubling you deep down, Dickinson was the cosmic "sin eater" who helped you get clarity. He loved Memphis and the Mississippi Delta and deeply knew how the culture and its tumultuous highs and lows were the lifeblood of the greatest music and art. The day he passed away was one of the hardest I can remember. I miss our long talks, his laughter, his thoughtfulness, and his generosity of spirit. He was one of the most important people who taught me to value where I came from and the importance of being true to your inner voice. As a result, I can attribute some of the best things that have happened to me in the last 20 years to Dickinson's support. This book is rooted in the spirit of mentoring, and Dickinson was one of the best. It's my hope that this collection offers you some of the enduring blessings Dickinson provided me. Thanks, Jim!

Left column top to bottom: Jim Dickinson (photo by Tom Lonardo) / Jim Dickinson, Studio B, Ardent, early 1970s (photo courtesy of Ardent Recording and John Fry), Jim Dickinson (photo courtesy of Steve Roberts) / Luther Dickinson, Cody Dickinson, Jim Dickinson (photo courtesy of Steve Roberts). Right column top to bottom: Ardent founder, John Fry, and Jim Dickinson at the studio's first commercial location on National Avenue in Memphis (photo courtesy of Ardent Recording and John Fry) / Jim Dickinson, John Eddy, John Hampton (photo courtesy of Ardent Recording and John Fry) / Jim Dickinson (photo courtesy of Mary Lindsay Dickinson).

Table of Contents

9   Dynamic Signal Processing   97

10   Evolution, Where We Are, Looking Forward, Giving Back, and Life Stuff   107

11   Field Recording and Film Sound   125

Introduction

First things first: This book wouldn't exist without the years of experience generously shared by the many producers, engineers, mixers, mastering engineers, and others who are featured in these pages.

I consider it a blessing to have met and learned from so many incredibly nice and talented people over the years. Many of those featured in this book have become good friends.

This book not only is an encapsulation of years of interviews I've done with hundreds of wonderfully gifted people in the recording industry, it is also a way I can sum up a huge piece of my life in one place.

The Sparks to the Heart

I fell into writing out of the pure love of music. It was the overflow from a life spent listening to, playing, writing, and recording music in my hometown of Memphis, Tennessee.

I grew up around the old Sun 45 records when they were new and came of age when Stax and Hi Records were making their mark in the world of R&B and soul music. Music was everywhere, and Memphis nurtured me down to my soul. It's a place that is inspiring and maddening, and I have loved it enough to hate it and love it all over again. I still travel there regularly just to keep myself properly fine tuned with its vibe and great barbecue.

Besides the great indigenous music, I grew up with a love of a wide variety of other musical genres.

My pre-rock musical loves were classical piano (Brahms' Second Piano Concerto is an all-time favorite), choral music ("Pilgrim's Chorus" from Wagner's *Tannhauser* and Bach's *St. Matthew Passion*), ragtime Dixieland (particularly Sweet Emma and Her Preservation Hall Jazz Band), and show music giants such as Gershwin, Cole Porter, Rodgers and Hart, and Rodgers and Hammerstein.

The arrival of the Beatles totally threw me into rock and pop, and the nights they performed on *Ed Sullivan* are events I'll never forget. I saw my first pop concert in 1965, which was James Brown and the Famous Flames. Every moment of that amazing show is etched on my mind. I bought my first three rock albums in one day in 1965: *For Your Love* by the Yardbirds and *Kinda Kinks* and *Kink-Size* by the Kinks. My first 45s were the Yardbirds' "Shapes of Things," the Kinks' "Till the End of the Day," and the Byrds' picture sleeve release of "Eight Miles High." I still listen to these records with the excitement I felt way back then.

Plugging In

Like many kids, it was only a matter of time before I would pick up an instrument and join a band. My first paid gig was in 1969, a few months after I had picked up my first bass guitar, which was a white plastic Hagstrom. We played at something like a Young Democrats backyard party and recorded it on an early stereo Panasonic cassette recorder. I still have that tape of us butchering Booker T. and the MG's, Pink Floyd, Blodwyn Pig, and Steve Miller. We even did an original number! It's a priceless document of innocence and joy. From then on, I played every chance I could get. By the mid-'90s, I had performed in every imaginable venue, from the pits of chicken-wire-around-the-stage redneck dives to huge arenas, either as a band mate or a sideman.

Magic in the Deep Grooves

While I loved playing live, it was always recorded music that captured my imagination. Listening to recordings has always been like hearing paintings, and I still feel that way.

Records were such mysterious things to me. You put a needle in a groove on a spinning vinyl disc, and this wonderful sound came out of the speakers. Often, I would become entranced by a certain song or part of a song and end up playing it dozens of times in one sitting. I memorized every instrumental part, every reverb or effect, and anything else that caught my ear.

When I wasn't playing in a band, I was working at Memphis's coolest record store, Poplar Tunes. It was also Memphis's only record store at the time, and in the late '60s and early '70s, it was a scene. Every week we had local people like Isaac Hayes, Al Green, and other legends, as well as artists from all over the world, such as David Bowie's Spider from Mars, hanging out in the store. What a time!

My vinyl fixation was made even more intense there, and by the time I left Poplar Tunes in 1973, I had already amassed a few thousand LPs.

Light My Fire: The First Sessions

My first studio session was in 1971 in Memphis at a place called Block Six. We were recording four songs—"Kansas City," "Light My Fire," Cinnamon Girl," and an original by the organist—that we were going to lip synch and fake our way through on a local television show called *Talent Party*, which was hosted by WHBQ-AM DJ George Klein, who was a member of Elvis's Memphis Mafia and the first man I ever met who wore a load of makeup. Anyway, I distinctly remember sitting under the huge Altec Voice of the Theater speakers and trying to play bass as the studio owner and engineer, Larry Rogers, told me that I was supposed to play the bass with a pick instead of with my fingers. For better or worse, I guess you can say that was the first time I was produced.

Shortly thereafter, I began spending time at two studios, Ardent Recording and Shoe Productions. At that time I met the guys in a brand-new band called Big Star and started working with Memphis power-pop artists Tommy Hoehn and Steve Burns. Warren Wagner and Wayne Crook, the owners of Shoe Productions, basically gave us the keys to the studio. We spent countless hours learning on a truly homemade console that looked like an automobile gasoline tank with slits cut in it for the faders and metal folding chairs for stands. We did everything wrong; it was all trial and error, and of that mostly error! There were no books or teachers around to tell us not to bounce guitars on a drum track or whatever. The whole concept of an educational program for rock and rollers was a pipe dream, and there was certainly no one around to mentor us. As the years passed, I continued gigging and recording in Memphis, and the friendship and support from people in the studio community has been priceless.

Putting the Passion into Words

I kind of fell into writing in the '80s, when Tom Graves, an editor of a new magazine called *Rock and Roll Disc*, asked me if I would write for their debut issue. I was busy as a producer, musician, and songwriter out of Memphis, and I figured that this would be merely something I did to channel my passion when I wasn't doing music. Little did I know that I would write in every issue for the life of that magazine, which turned out to be several years.

Dave Marsh and Peter Guralnick were part of this publication, which was supposed to be a compact disc equivalent to the *New York Times Book Review*. The writing came from the heart, and Tom was a good editor. I learned a lot and probably never made more than a hundred dollars for the total time I wrote for them. Lesson number one: You don't write for music publications if you think you are going to actually make money. Music writing is the literary world's equivalent to working in a record store. You are there because you love music. Unfortunately, publishers know this, too. Nevertheless, it put me in front of some serious readers.

Writing about music seemed natural, and by the time a couple of years had passed, I had been published in *Billboard*, *Rolling Stone*, *Details*, *Goldmine*, *Guitar Player*, *Music Express*, and a number of other publications. It was weird how it happened, because I never had this in mind as a career path.

I had played thousands of gigs, live and in the studio, had song cuts as a songwriter, and was focused on a career as an artist.

That said, I was one of those kids who voraciously read every music magazine and book I could get my hands on. There was a time when *Rolling Stone* was required reading, as was *Musician* during Bill Flanagan's time as editor. *Mix* magazine was another one I read cover to cover.

The Art of the Q&A

One thing I always loved was a good Q&A interview, and naturally I studied what made such satisfying reads. In fact, to this day, I would rather read a person's own thoughts than some writer's interpretation of them. It is largely the reason why I wanted this book you are holding to be a collection of carefully culled first-person lessons and reflections by a wonderful group of truly gifted people.

One book that I count as a serious influence was Bill Flanagan's thoughtful *Written In My Soul* (Contemporary Books, 1987). It was his *Musician* magazine interviews of artists discussing the creative process, all compiled in one great collection. I've read it dozens of times over the years. Flanagan's interviews reflected a kind of care and thoughtfulness that taught me a lot about treating subjects with dignity.

My first interview was in the early '80s, with jazz flautist Herbie Mann. He was in Memphis to perform and promote his latest album. He was a thoroughly charming man, and I realized that I enjoyed the process of getting people to talk about their passions.

Around that time, I had already been published enough to know that I didn't really enjoy writing features on some new hot act or writing reviews. I was acutely aware of all the work and dreams that went into making recordings, and I witnessed enough pain induced by uncaring, egotistical writers who should've known better. The only guideline I had in review writing was to make sure that I wrote it like I was talking to the artist face to face. That way, I had to be responsible for saying what I truly meant in a constructive fashion.

Finding My Groove

Even though I had written in many departments of *Billboard*, it was Thom Duffy and Paul Verna who opened the Pro Audio section up and allowed me to dive into writing about the recording world. It was the first time I really felt charged as a writer.

Generally, producers, engineers, mixers, mastering engineers, and others involved behind the glass don't have self-involved star mentalities. With few exceptions, most are low key, approachable, and generous about sharing their knowledge. In fact, they are often surprised that anyone would really want to interview them.

As someone who came of age in music before there were academic programs that taught about recording and the music industry, the idea of talking with those I admired for a magazine feature was like getting paid to have private tutorials.

A little more than 20 years ago, I began writing for *Mix* magazine. It was the beginning of a working relationship that I cherished. *Mix* editors Blair Jackson and Tom Kenny were always truly supportive buddies, and the others at *Mix* have been wonderful, too. Of all the magazines in which I've been published, I'm proudest of my association with *Mix*.

Mix magazine afforded me the chance to interview many of the people I've most admired in the world of recording. Besides feature interviews, *Mix* let me write numerous application features that showcased pros sharing their knowledge on various topics. It was from these features that the idea of this book began. Essentially, I returned to the original interview transcripts and intros for those features and expanded upon them for this book. I eventually went out and conducted many more new interviews for this latest edition.

The Process

Unlike many writers, I've always had a ridiculous need to completely transcribe every single interview. Over the years, I've transcribed thousands of pages featuring hundreds of conversations with people ranging from Chet Atkins, to John Fogerty, to Mark Knopfler, to Allen Toussaint, to Tony Visconti, to David Z.

Out of a 20-, 40-, or 150-page interview with one person, I might only use a small percentage for the feature at hand. That interview, however, would often contain a wealth of other great stuff that never made it into the magazine.

The interviews in this book range from being brand new to being ones I've done over the years. In some cases, those I approached chose to write out their thoughts on a subject. In every case, the generosity of sharing this hard-earned information has been a true gift. While technology is constantly changing, this book hopefully offers proven techniques, as well as creative ideas for producing, recording, mixing, and mastering music that are timeless.

Some Words on This Book

I've tried to mix it up so that there is something for everyone here. Some things might sound like nonsense or might seem tedious to one person and seem absolutely brilliant to another reader. Just as there are many genres of music, there is a diverse range of personalities represented here. Just check out the credits in the Appendix, and that should underscore how diverse the contributors who are represented in this book are. Then go check out their work....

As much as this book showcases the more technical applications of making music, I've made a point to make a lot of room for more philosophical musings. After all, this is about capturing creative sparks and paying attention to the space in between the notes.

To Those Who Made This Possible

There are many people who deserve my thanks: From my years gigging and recording in Memphis, I would like to specifically point out John Fry, Jody Stephens, John Hampton (an original Chew Head) and Skidd Mills from Ardent Recording, as well as Tim Goodwin of Memphis Sound Productions, Paul Zalesky of Stairway Recording, Steve Hauth and Ronnie Kietell for their endless hours at Steve's studio on Cleveland, and Larry Lipman and Richard Ranta of the University of Memphis' fine recording program. Jon Hornyak and the Memphis Chapter of NARAS have also supplied much valuable assistance over the years.

Other Memphis friends (some of whom have moved to Nashville) include George Bradfute, Steve Ebe, Robert "Bobby Memphis" Jordan, Joe Hardy, Keith and Jerene Sykes, Carl Marsh, Greg Morrow, Ross Rice, Rusty McFarland, Jack Holder, Johnny Phillips, Gary Belz, and Jesse Brownfield. Also special thanks to Norbert Putnam, a generous spirit who is joy to know as a friend.

Three people who did their best to provide support through thick and thin are Debbie Edmiston, Mary Truett, and Allison Black. I learned a lot during those years together. Thank you.

A true brother and partner in insane recording exploits at studios in Memphis and (particularly) Wishbone and Fame in Muscle Shoals is Mark Marchetti. We wrote loads of songs together and had a blast making music. Along the way, we even landed some song cuts and one that became a Billboard Top 20 Country hit. Thanks, Gail Davies!

One person who inspired and challenged me and was a true friend was producer, musician, and songwriter Jim Dickinson, who passed away on August 15, 2009. Jim, in more ways than he probably ever knew, held up a lens that helped me focus who I was in my culture from the Delta South and put a lifetime of feelings and understanding into something I could truly own and articulate with pride. He also was the first teacher who selflessly offered from the heart his feelings about the psychology of producing. Many of those things he shared fundamentally informed the way I viewed the creative process and honored the art of life around me.

The Nashville community has been incredibly nurturing. Trip Aldredge, Bob Bailey-Lemansky, Richard Dodd, Michael Wagener, Bill Lloyd, Brad Jones, Dan Goodman, Tony Brown, Bob Doyle, Lee Swartz, Richard Bennett, Lauren Koch, Chuck Ainlay, Justin Neibank, Jim Zumwalt, Benny Quinn, Denny Purcell, John Allen, Peter Cronin, Pete Langella, Joe and Marc Pisapia, Nichole Cochran, and Lisa Roy each have my gratitude for all the ways, big and small, where they made a positive difference.

A very special thanks goes to Brian Ahern, a dear friend and mentor. The thought and care I've seen Brian apply to artists, musicians, engineers, and anyone involved in his production projects has been a light on the path to achieving excellence, while treating others with dignity. He is a listener and concept architect who quietly contributes in usually unseen ways to pave the way to manifesting visions into realities. That's the mark of a true producer, in my book.

Between the spring of 2008, when the work on this edition of the book began, and its completion in spring of 2010, I had a number of wonderful people who assisted in typing out and going over several thousand pages of transcripts, organizing files and photos, creating progress charts, and doing all manner of other stuff that largely helped me maintain a semblance of sanity. With transcripts and contributions from more than 130 people, most of who made it into this book, there were stretches of time where I felt like I existed in some self-created blend of Barton Fink and an "All work and no play makes Rick a dull boy" version of Jack Nicholson in *The Shining*. Helping me push things along to a sane conclusion are the following:

One person who has been a total foundation and true support throughout the making of this book is Mary Ball. Her support of and patience with my creative process and endless crazy hours, plus her hours of proofreading, editing, and organizing consistently helped make order happen and goals become completed realities.

From Belmont University's intern program, special props go out to Wes Bailey, Brad Butcher, Kate Grom, Frank Serafine, Gabe Simon, Ben Trimble, and Stacey Wilson, who contributed many, many hours and months to this endeavor.

Middle Tennessee State University intern Crystal Potts also did loads of work with transcripts and photos.

In Santa Monica, I had the incredible help of Chris Vaughan and Nathaniel Shapiro. Both put in loads of work. Thanks guys!

Each of these people were a blast to hang with and work with. They went beyond being interns and became friends, and I'm grateful for their contributions.

Props to John Baldwin, who always has his hands full running his Nashville studio, engineering and producing cool bands, mastering at Georgetown Masters, and being the king of selling the best vintage audio gear on eBay. He somehow found the time to plow through chapter after chapter and provide factual corrections and tweaks. John, you always come through with the goods! Thanks buddy!

I owe a lot of gratitude to my editor, Cathleen Small, who was always upbeat, thoughtful, and supportive. Her follow-up questions and observations always clarified each page and made the book much better.

Also, super thanks to Mark Garvey of Course Technology PTR, who is probably the embodiment of patience and always believed this was a worthwhile endeavor.

I also want to give a shout out to Chris Fichera of Blue Sky monitors, A-Designs' Pete Montessi, and Dave Pearlman of Pearlman Microphones. All three of these guys provided a lot of help with introductions. Chris has always been good support, and I can honestly say that his company makes some of the best bang-for-your-buck speaker systems out there. They are the standard in the film/TV audio post world and are the reference speakers for all my music supervision work in Santa Monica. I've been a fan of A-Designs and Pearlman mics for quite a while, and I even featured A-Designs in a *Mix* magazine piece. Hanging out with them was a blast. They are like the pro audio Click and Clack with a lot of bad jokes.

Chris Vaughan (photo by Nola Carroll) / Nathaniel Shapiro (photo by Ed Massey) / John Baldwin / Ben Trimble. Row 2: Erin Manning / Brad Butcher (top) / Crystal Potts (photo courtesy of Crystal Potts) / Wes Bailey / Gabe Simon. Row 3: Belmont Interns (L to R) Stacey Wilson, Brad Butcher, Ben Trimble, Kaitlyn Grom, Gabe Simon. Row 4: Stacey Wilson / Frank Serafine (photo courtesy of Frank Serafine) / Rick Clark and Mary Ball. All photos by Rick Clark unless otherwise noted. Special thanks to Belmont University, Middle Tennessee University, and all these wonderful folks pictured above who gave a lot, helping with all the heavy lifting required to realize this book.

Bottom line: I feel blessed to be surrounded by such supportive people and hope this edition of *Mixing, Recording, and Producing Techniques of the Pros* makes everyone involved feel proud. To everyone reading this book, I sincerely hope you find a wealth of concepts, applications, and ways of thinking in these pages that prove priceless in your life's creative work in and out of the studio.

Rick Clark

April 2010

Producer Charlie Sexton & Clarence Gatemouth Brown / Michael Johnson. Row 2: Rick Clark (photo by Derrick Scott) / Bil VornDick (photo by Bil VornDick). Row 3: Rob Ickes and Tony Furtado / Marty Stuart & Porter Wagoner. Row 4: Ricky Skaggs / Keith Greeninger, Jean Claude Reynaud (positioning mic) & Dayan Kai. All photos by Rick Clark, except where noted.

Acoustic Ensemble Recording

There is nothing quite like the sound of the well-recorded musical interplay found in an ensemble of acoustic instruments. Long before "unplugged" became part of the pop-culture lexicon, Nashville was mastering the art of recording all of the great acoustic country and bluegrass groups that rolled through the town. Capturing the unique individual characteristics of each instrument and understanding how to present the chemistry of the overall band sound requires skill and sensitivity to the special dynamics of the players.

We gathered a handful of Music City's finest players and producer/engineers—Chuck Ainlay, Jerry Douglas, Brent Truitt, Mark O'Connor, and Bil VornDick—to discuss their thoughts on how to capture the sparks on tape. Special thanks also to Ellen Pryor and Elliot Scheiner for their supportive input.

Chuck Ainlay

Credits include: Mark Knopfler (solo and with Dire Straits), Trisha Yearwood, Vince Gill, Steve Earle, Lyle Lovett, Wynonna, and George Strait. See the Appendix for Chuck Ainlay's full bio.

For Vince Gill's album *High Lonesome Sound*, we used Alison Krauss' band for the title cut. They played on the country version with drums and everything, and we also did another version, which is bluegrass. Both versions are on the album.

If you are talking about bluegrass, the players really like to hear and watch each other. That is how they perform live. So when we did the bluegrass version, I basically used baffles laid out like a spoked wheel, where the baffles were radiating out from the center like spokes. This created compartments where each person could look toward each other in the center, and the mics would be back sort of closer to the center, pointing toward each player. That way, you could use the directional characteristics of the cardioid microphones to reject the instruments of the other players at other areas in the spokes. Cardioid is generally what I use. I rarely ever use omni microphones.

You don't want to get the mics too close to any sort of wall, because that would change the character of the microphone, too. So they are not right into the point of the pie, so to speak. I used baffles, because I wanted a real clean, tight sound without a lot of ambiance from the room.

Generally, for tracking the acoustic guitar, I'll usually use one mic sort of near the twelfth fret out maybe 6 inches from the guitar. Then I'll have another mic, generally shoulder height and out maybe 2 feet from the guitar, probably kind of above the bridge or the general vicinity. If I then decide to double the acoustic guitar, I usually go over the far mic because it is just too big. The doubling already gives you that extra warmth.

I love a Neumann KM 56 or KM 54 on an acoustic. That is usually my choice of a close mic. They have a nice top end, and the bottom end is rolled off pretty well on them. I will also use a KM 84 Neumann. For the second mic, the one that may be located about shoulder height, I would start with maybe a Neumann U 67.

On Vince's acoustic, I will use a 452 AKG because the isolation is better. The polar pattern is tighter, so I can get away with using that microphone and still use the tracking acoustics. The problem with those microphones on acoustics is sometimes that they can be too brittle-sounding, so you add some warmth to them in the midrange area. Yet you will need to roll out on the bottom, because when you have a vocalist, you have to mike close.

U 67s are great on acoustics if you are going for that bashing acoustic-guitar sound. If you are using a Gibson acoustic that is being played hard, you can take a U 67 and mike it farther away from the guitar, just straight out from the hole of the guitar, and get a great sound. Naturally, it all depends on what the player is doing.

The quality of the guitar also makes a lot of difference. For just pure strumming, a lot of guys have gone to kind of cheap guitars like Takamines because they don't have a lot of bottom end and a real rich character to them. What you are really looking for is a percussive strumming sound, rather than a filled-out acoustic sound.

I'm not a big fan of DIs, and I'm also a very big fan of uncomplicated sources. That is also why I say that I'm not a very big stereo miking fan. For fiddle, I really like the C 12. It works great. Mark O'Connor, who is one of the greatest fiddle players, always carried with him an AKG C 24, which is the stereo version of the AKG C 12.

Also, the Neumann M 49 is a much warmer microphone, and when you get them farther away from the instrument, they are going to sound very real.

For upright bass, I use two microphones. Usually there is one microphone about a foot and a half away from the double bass, about bridge height, and then the second mic is usually closer to the bass, maybe about 8 to 10 inches, looking at the left shoulder of the bass. That way you get the percussiveness wood plunk from the bass there. You get your bottom end from down near the bridge.

Sometimes, depending on the bass, you have to get it closer to the f-hole, though some basses will have certain notes that really stick out if you get too close to the f-hole.

Upright bass is one of the hardest things to mike. Your two microphones can cause some serious cancellation on bass because of the low frequencies. I still try and put the upright bass in a separate room because it is not a very loud instrument. You still want to have control, and you are going to get leakage with it.

For mandolin, I rarely mike with two mics. It is just too small of an instrument. Then again, I have actually used two mics. [Laughs] Again, it all depends on the mandolin. Some mandolins are richer and warmer than others. Generally the favorite position is near the f-hole. But getting too close to the f-hole can be too thick. If you are looking for that "woody" sound, that is where it comes from.

I don't think there is anything all that special that we do. I always like to point out that it comes from the musicians and the music. I can't tell you how many times I've sat there and pulled up levels, and it just sounded awful, and I'm tweaking knobs like crazy, trying to get it to sound good. Then all of a sudden it sounds good, but it isn't because I tweaked the knobs like crazy. It is because the performance came together, and all of a sudden everybody was listening to each other and they were playing tight. I think we are important people in not ruining this and making it comfortable for the musicians, but it still gets down to the players.

Jerry Douglas

Credits include: Alison Krauss, Emmylou Harris, Del McCoury, and Lonesome River Band, as well as many solo albums. See the Appendix for Jerry Douglas's full bio.

I like the live performance vibe and keeping everything as organic as possible going down on tape. I always do first takes, because that is when all the energy is up and it is the scariest for everybody. I don't erase anything. I don't punch into live tracks. I do adjacent tracks for instruments.

If we need to fix something, then great. But if there is a chance of leaking, then we do another take or another edit possibly. This is because you don't want the chance of "ghosts," which is what you get a lot in acoustic music. When you overdub, you run the chance of still hearing the old part off of someone else's track. So it is worth doing another take.

When you are working with a bluegrass act—like Del McCoury, for instance—whose band plays really dynamic bluegrass, I would try and cut live without much isolation and get some tight mics on everybody. I like to sit everybody around, so everyone can hear and see each other and not be completely dependent on headphones, but can use them if they want to.

For picking out the mics in this kind of situation, I would shy away from the bigger-diaphragm microphones. It is a give-and-take situation because I love the old big-diaphragm microphones for when these instruments are isolated, because they capture the whole sound of the instrument and not just a spot on the instrument.

We often use these big foam baffles. It is amazing how much isolation you can get from one of those things. Then it becomes easier to replace parts if something goes wrong.

Bass and fiddle are kind of hard to track in the room. Fiddle just takes off all over the room sometimes, and bass goes to the floor and shows up in the strangest places. I try to isolate the fiddle out of the room, like I would the vocal, too.

If we are going for a real live situation, I just do two takes and edit. But if we were trying to isolate everyone, I would put the fiddle in a different room and try and have an iso booth for fiddle and one for vocal.

Mark O'Connor

Credits include: James Taylor, Dolly Parton, Linda Ronstadt, Emmylou Harris, Michael Brecker, Yo-Yo Ma, and Nitty Gritty Dirt Band, as well as solo albums. See the Appendix for Mark O'Connor's full bio.

When I've done bluegrass recordings, often people will want the option to replace their solos and fix parts. Obviously, it is harder to do that in recording sessions when you are all playing in the same room. So when you do a democratic project, such as *Strength In Numbers*, you want to leave the studio knowing that you got what you wanted on tape. As a result, it made sense to be isolated. So before we were done with the song, we got the solo we wanted on there and we left, and that was it. End of story.

When I did *The New Nashville Cats* album, I put everybody in the same room and said, "Trust me. I'm going to edit together pieces from different takes."

I am a much greater fan of editing because [as the artist and producer] I can listen to takes and find out the parts that have the best musical energy. If the players got a really great solo section, but they completely botched the last head, then I can have the freedom to experiment with editing on a head from a different take, for instance. That kind of flexibility is actually more musical than overdubbing.

When you overdub, the other instruments are not playing with you anymore. They are playing to another solo. So what the soloist does on the overdub is not complete musical communication. So even though to a novice recording musician the editing might sound harsh in approach, it is actually more musical, especially if the tempos are fine and the energy and intensity match up. Then you can interchange between takes. That is what I do on most of the things that I do. It depends on how complex the music is. I think the more complex the music is, the more that you have to rely on editing.

I've recorded almost every solo performance I've done for years, trying to get better and better with it. When I finally realized that I was ready to record an album of these performances for real, I picked one of my favorite places I've performed solo—the old Shelton Hall in St. Louis, which was built in 1875. I rented it out and got the great mics up, my old M 49 Neumanns and the old AKG C 24, and played in front of a live audience and really did it right.

For the *Midnight on the Water* recording, I used my two old Neumann M 49s in a stereo configuration. The C 24 is very good for close miking, but not as much for accurate ambient miking, whereas the M 49s are almost like the human ear. So when I recorded my solo performance, I was actually achieving the instrument sound and the sound of the hall, the ambiance and everything all at one time with those two mics. It really worked out.

I also used the M 49s on my *Heroes* album, so I could have completely matched sounds between me and the other guest violinists. The only difference that you were hearing between the violin sounds was the actual player and the instrument, and not the way it was recorded. So each violin had one M 49, each of which was evenly matched from the same vintage year.

Temperature changes the sound and it changes the instrument. My violin is very sensitive to humidity. My violin sounds better in a warmer, humid climate. There are some violins that start to sound muddy or like they are stuffed with socks in a warmer, humid climate, where mine just sounds lush. Whereas when I get in too dry of a climate, it sounds too trebly and scratchy and squeaky, and it just drives me crazy.

As a matter of fact, one of the halls I considered recording in for *Midnight on the Water* was a beautiful hall in Aspen that is underground. When I performed my concert there a couple of years ago for the Aspen Music Festival, I loved everything except the sound of my violin. It was too dry. I thought about humidity problems and I went, "You know, I'm going to record this in the South during the summer in humidity," and so I did it in September in St. Louis at Shelton Hall. My violin sounds so rich on that recording, like it almost covers me. It sounds like it reaches out and embraces you. That is what I dreamed about. With humidity, I can make my violin sound like that.

That said, the humidity in this concert hall completely changed at night from the day. In some instances, it was as drastic as having an audience in there and not having an audience in there. It was that extreme. In most studios, you don't have to worry about that as much. But in concert halls, it's a consideration. So I realized that when I perform some of this stuff, I had to do it now in this time period, or I'd have to start all over. [Laughs] That was a little added pressure.

The biggest thing is to make sure that you can play your best. If the climate is changing, but you are in a place where you feel you can play your best, then that more than compensates for the problem.

Bil VornDick

Credits include: Alison Krauss, Charlie Haden, Jerry Douglas, Ralph Stanley, Bela Fleck, James Taylor, Doc Watson, Mark O'Connor, and Alison Brown. See the Appendix for Bil VornDick's full bio.

I pick the musicians for the song, instead of just working with a normal rhythm section. I like everybody to be going down on tape at the same time. I want as many pieces to the puzzle working with each other and playing off of each other as possible, instead of starting with a click track. I go for the overall feel of a take. I'm a guy who still believes that people buy records because they feel good.

A good example: I had a number-one song on a group called IIIrd Tyme Out, and the B string was out of tune. But the person who was singing the lead vocal was doing the guitar at the same time. That was his best performance, and we couldn't redo the guitar, because of the leakage. Maybe six or seven people have come up to me and said, "The B string is out of tune." I would say, "Yeah, we cut it quite a few more times, but the feeling and emotion weren't there." I went with the best-feeling performance that had the emotion within that helped sell the song. It still went to the top of the charts. There are some people, especially in Nashville, who would go redo the vocal and the guitar and do other things to deal with the B string on the guitar. I knew it was out of tune. Hey, it didn't hurt them. It was one of their biggest selling albums.

Currently, there is a now-successful acoustic artist whose roots were in bluegrass cutting tracks with a click and then going back and replacing everything. As a result, you've got all of the nuances that originally went on with the little inner licks and dynamics of the song disappearing in order to be precise.

Most of the albums I have done that have won the Grammys are all albums recorded on budgets between $10,000 and $20,000. These are not $250,000 albums. Alison Krauss' first Grammy-winning record, I think, cost $12,500.

I mike everything in stereo normally, so that within those two mics I have a depth perspective on each instrument.

I'm a pretty hardcore analog guy. I would much rather paint in oils than in acrylics. You get the whole waveform in analog, and in digital there are still quite a few overtones that the sampling rates are not catching. I can still hear them, but a lot of people don't care. I normally cut at 30 IPS with no noise reduction. If I can get into a facility that has Dolby SR, I like to cut at 15 IPS with SR noise reduction. Digital may be cheaper, but analog is still the art form.

Brent Truitt

Credits include: Dixie Chicks, Alison Krauss, Nitty Gritty Dirt Band, Dolly Parton, Riders in the Sky, and David Grier. See the Appendix for Brent Truitt's full bio.

For recording acoustic music, let me also say that hopefully the person sitting in front of the mic has a good instrument. Common sense tells you that if the guitar sounds bad and won't play in tune, a great mic isn't gonna help. If I'm producing a band that may not have any real studio experience, I make sure they have their instruments tweaked up and ready to go before we get into the studio.

Sometimes people have a hard time recording the fiddle. It's easy for a fiddle to sound shrill, especially going to hard disk. My favorite fiddle mics are KM 86s. I almost always use a stereo pair in cardioid and run them through a couple of APIs, smooth and warm. I usually place the mics on each side of the fiddle, maybe 10 or 12 inches apart. Try to leave plenty of room for bowing. In most cases I don't compress fiddle tracks going to tape. It seems to add that little extra harshness that you really don't want. Actually, too much compression on any acoustic instrument can be a bad thing. Use it sparingly going to tape.

As far as I'm concerned, the best mic for acoustic guitar is the KM 54, hands down. They aren't cheap or all that easy to find, but they are well worth searching out. I like to run a pair of these through a couple of Neves or APIs and then into a pair of Urei 1176s. I get great results with that signal chain.

If you can't get the KM 54s, get a couple KM 84s. Even the newer KM 184 will do a great job for you. If you don't have the Neves or APIs, the Avalon 737SP is a quality mic pre/comp/EQ that is affordable and really sounds wonderful on acoustic instruments. Mic placement on guitar is once again something to experiment with. I usually put one near the twelfth fret at an angle toward the sound hole, being careful not to get too much boom. The back mic position is almost never the same from one session to the next. Try moving the mic around while listening through the phones. The thing to watch out for is the midrange; sometimes that back mic can add an overly nasal quality to the sound.

Concerning the upright bass, this instrument is the reason my left eye twitches. It can be one of the most difficult beasts in the world to record, especially if it's not a very good bass.

By the way, there is a huge difference between a bass with gut strings and a bass with steel strings. Steel strings have more of point to the sound, more sustain, and definitely cut through a mix a little easier. But sometimes a gut-string bass, which usually has less point and more of a big bottom, is more fitting to certain kinds of tracks. For instance, I would probably go for steel string if the session were leaning more toward the progressive or modern side of acoustic music. But if the songs had more of an old-time or hillbilly vibe, I would probably lean toward a gut-string bass for that older sound.

I have been very fortunate over the years to have worked a lot with the late, great Roy Huskey, one of the greatest bass players ever. He was a gut-string man. Here are some details on how I cut his bass. I always used two mics on Roy. One of my favorite combos was a UM 57 [tube Neumann from the mid '50s] on the right side, or low E side, maybe 10 inches back from the f-hole. On the high side I put a KM 86 at about the area where he plucked the string and approximately 8 inches back. Both mics in cardioid and off-axis or pointed kind of off-centered from the sound source. Now here's where you can use some common sense. In case you don't have those mics, or that exact mic position may not sound good in your room, go out with headphones on and try moving the mics around the instrument until the sweet spot hits you. You'll know it when you hear it.

As far as mic preamps on Roy, I tried different preamps on different sessions, but I always used a Tube-Tech compressor at the end of the audio path. It always sounded great.

Another awesome bass player I've recorded is Todd Phillips. Todd is no stranger to anyone who knows acoustic music. He was a huge part of the early David Grisman sound. Todd is a steel-string man. We usually cut Todd's bass with a KM 184 on the high side, near the area he plucks, along with the UM 57 on the low side, kind of in front of the bridge and down a few inches. Both mics are in cardioid. From there we'll go into two Avalon 737SPs. The result is a very large and clear tone. Of course, Todd is a great player, giving me excellent tones to begin with, which makes it so very easy to record.

That's all great, but chances are pretty good that somewhere along the line you're going to end up recording a not-so-great bass. You might want to keep some pieces of foam handy to place in the tailpiece to help eliminate rattles and maybe some of the boominess. You might even try a small piece in the f-hole to help with the boom. Sometimes you're basically just going to have to hunt down some rattles and buzzes.

Jacquire King (photo courtesy of Jacquire King) / Leland Sklar (photo courtesy of Leland Sklar). Row 2: Glen Moore (bass) and Garrett Brennan at The Site / Mike Janas at RCA Studio B, April 2006 (photos by Rick Clark).

Analog versus Digital

The debate over the virtues of analog and digital has been long and furious. We decided to talk to a handful of legendary producer/engineers about their experiences with mixing up the two formats during recording. The questions were posed: If the situation presented itself to where you could have equal access to both analog and digital multitracks at a session, how would you go about utilizing the strengths of each in the recording process? Would you prefer cutting electric guitars analog or using digital for synths? Would you even bother with mixing it up at all?

What resulted was an interesting dialogue that covered the range of opinions. And as expected, the questions provoked strong feelings that increasingly focused more on the virtues of one format over the other. We would like to thank Tony Visconti, Nick Launay, and Jaquire King for their gracious input to this chapter.

Tony Visconti

Credits include: David Bowie, T. Rex, Iggy Pop, Moody Blues, and Morrissey. See the Appendix for Tony Visconti's full bio.

In 1967, when I started my career as a producer in London, I had a lot of ideas about engineering, mainly inspired by what the Beatles had accomplished in the way of shaping a specific sound for a specific song. *Revolver* just about blew my mind when I heard those sounds for the first time. They weren't guitars or pianos…or were they? Every sound on that album was a psychedelic pastiche of the instrument that was playing its part. Guitars were musical buzz saws, and pianos sounded as if the striking hammers were sledgehammers. I moved to London from New York to find out how the British made those sounds. It was some kind of alchemy, and I wanted to learn it badly!

Almost 30 years later, I'm hearing arguments about analog being warm and fat and digital being cold and clinical, and I have to laugh. Once I cracked the code (with the tutelage of many a great British engineer) of equalization, compression, gating, flanging, phasing, and ADT [automatic double-tracking], I considered myself lucky to get a reasonable facsimile of what I heard in the control room onto analog tape, *before* it was committed to tape. The tape in the late '60s and early '70s was pretty bad. The multitracks were laughable by today's standards. The end of a reel was often slower in pitch than the beginning of the reel, and lining up was a haphazard affair—sure the 1 kHz, the 10 kHz, and the 100 Hz read 0 VU, but if you dared to measure 30 Hz or 14 kHz, you'd see something on the VU meter that would make you lose your appetite.

Analog was so bad then that we were always craving for what is now digital to appear. A producer and engineer would work very hard "getting sounds" on the microphones and equalization. After that "magical" take was rendered by the group, I would enthusiastically ask them to come into the control room to listen. Why oh why was the snare duller on playback? Why was the kick drum playing back 6 decibels quieter?

After my first few disappointing collisions with the reality of analog multitrack, the engineer would have to return the drum kit through channel faders (instead of flat monitor returns) and desperately try to restore the live sound of the drums before they went down to tape with some fairly heavy EQ. Of course, the playback was never exactly the same sonic quality, but it impressed the musicians enough to have confidence that the sound was "ballsy," and then overdubs could safely take place. With the advent of 24-track [less width per track], the situation got worse; the kick drum and most transient-type sounds never played back even close to the original.

What so few engineers and producers of my generation are willing to admit is that they settled for second best and just made the most of the equipment and analog tape in those golden days of rock. Ironically, the very same records from that period make up the bulk of rock music played on radio today and are examined under a microscope by today's musicians, producers, and engineers. After hearing the Beatles, Zep, and the Stones for so long, there is a mental fix on the sound of that era as being the ultimate sound in rock. The sound of that period went through so many correctional phases before it hit the public that you can't pinpoint it to any one device that made that era so "warm and analog." My T. Rex mixes were very punchy when I finally did everything in my power to make them leap out of the speakers; compressors and equalizers were my friends, and the tape was my enemy. But then try to master those bombastic sounds to vinyl and watch the mastering engineer reach for the high-pass filter, the "low-end centering" button, and then drop the level for a drum fill. I came to accept that the public would never hear what we chosen few heard in the studio—until digital came along.

Now it may not be perfect, but the most accurate means of reproducing music we have, now available to the public, are digital products—disk and tape. My Bowie productions have been cleaned up by Sonic Solutions and zapped to CD. I can now hear reverbs that were lost in the scratches and the surface noise. But so can all the channels of stuff be heard that I put the sounds through to restore the sonic integrity in the first place, not counting the remastering added in the best interests of repackaging.

Rock music isn't and never was hi-fi. It was always a highly contrived sound coming out of domestic speakers, posturing as a very loud performance. The very same signal processors that were used to maintain some form of an exciting sound after it had been committed to analog tape are now the sound itself! What I'm saying is that even though analog was garbage in the good old days, we knew how to make it behave by a ton of sonic tricks. However, even after the great sounds were sorted out, analog tape used to—and still does, to some extent—eat them up.

Tape compression, although it is a reality that has become a romantic notion, is not an accurate means of compression and is unpredictable. If I am compressing and equalizing a kick and a snare, and I take a considerable time doing that, I don't want the storage system to change that hard work. Nevertheless, before digital came along, it did change my hard work, so I compensated for this in the mix or the submixes. [In the time before locking machines together, we had to submix the drum kit to make track room available.] The actual warm and nostalgic analog sound sought after today is not actually the tape itself. It was the total, sonic decisions of an engineer like myself, fighting down the long chain of production events, trying to restore the original punch of the instruments before they were committed to tape.

I want to add that I can still make a recording with that classic sound using modern equipment and modern digital tape—it doesn't depend on analog tape or equipment over 30 years old. Our filter tools from Neve, Focusrite, and Massenburg are superb tone shapers, and there are plenty of modern manufacturers making classic tube equipment, such as Tube-Tech and Manley. If you put fat, warm sounds onto digital tape, you will get fat, warm sounds on playback, for sure! With digital, what goes in also comes out.

The major tricks that make a great rock record are compression (the sound of rock), over-the-top EQ (the color of rock), and the many contrived echoes and reverbs, the phasing, the flanging, and the automatic double-tracking (the flavors of rock). And don't forget that invaluable tool that compiles a mind-boggling guitar solo from seven so-so tracks and allows a singer to sing a duet with himself—the multitrack tape recorder! Rock sound is, and has been, extremely manipulated since it began [remember Elvis' slapback?], regardless of what medium it was recorded on: analog, digital tape, or hard disk!

As long as an engineer and producer are proficient with their tools, the medium should be expected to reproduce exactly what is stored on it. Top-end studio analog and digital are so close now anyway, a blindfold test of the cleanest recordings possible would stymie many professionals. I have heard records made in this decade with vintage equipment and analog tape that sound horrible. I have heard records recorded on digital that sound fat and records recorded on analog that sound thin.

I think analog used intelligently can sound great, too. With analog, I am careful not to saturate the tape. Lining up at +9 on the latest high-octane tapes gives me plenty of headroom and very low noise. Nevertheless, kick drums and the like still don't sound satisfactory on playback to my ears.

The relatively low sampling rate of digital is a mistake, and the stuff lost above 20 Hz is somehow noticeable on high-end equipment, but not on most domestic. This is adequate for most pop music applications (cassettes, boom boxes, and mid-priced home stereos), especially when most pop fans are low-end freaks.

I especially like digital for having all 48 tracks at my disposal immediately, without locking up.

My one last point is this: If analog is so hot and this tape compression thing is so cool, why do some engineers get obsessive about purity in the signal path and then bang that pure signal down to 15-IPS 1/4-inch analog tape with Dolby SR and the VU meters glued into the "righteous red"? To me, that's as insane as betting on every horse in a race. You can't win that way.

Nick Launay

Credits include: Public Image, INXS, Kate Bush, Gang of Four, Nick Cave, Killing Joke, Yeah Yeah Yeahs, and the Cribs. See the Appendix for Nick Launay's full bio.

I think analog still sounds better than digital for many reasons, but a lot of it has to do with how you line the tape machine up and what tape machine you use. It's not just about renting any old Studer and throwing black and brown tape on it. You have to get the right Studer, and you have to line it up to the right tape. It really depends on what tape you use and what level you record the different instruments at.

I do, however, think that with digital we can be way more creative. Products like Pro Tools allow us to manipulate sound in the wildest ways we can imagine. So for me, it's a combination of both that makes for the best-sounding and most imaginative recordings.

With tape, I remember a lot of people were using GP9 Ampex tape for a while [which then became Quantegy]. I thought the GP9 was awful, absolutely terrible. The top end was distorted, there was no clarity to it, and it was almost saturated in itself. I thought the BASF 900 was the best. Ampex 499 was also great, which was the higher-level 456. It was essentially the same but just louder, so less hiss, and the top end was really clear. Now there are only two companies making analog tape: ATR and RMG, both of which sound amazing, I'm glad to say.

Nowadays, you'll find a lot of really good young engineers who know their Pro Tools, are killer with their plug-ins, and really have that whole thing down. They just have no idea about tape because they've simply never used it before, and when they put it up for the first time, they might do things wrong and go, "Well, I don't think analog is actually that good," and go back to digital.

When using analog for the first time, the most common mistake is to record hi-hats, bass drum, and snare really loud on tape. You can wind guitars and bass on really loud and it sounds great, but anything percussive has got high transients; you've got to leave a lot of headroom. I tend to record percussive things as low as −10 or even −15 VU. And I usually line up a 900- or 499-style tape at +6 above 185 NWB...not at +9.

There's a lot of misunderstanding, because there isn't that world of experience with analog anymore. I think it's going to get worse because this knowledge and training isn't getting passed down. It took me a lot of learning from people like Hugh Padgham and Steve Lillywhite to learn what levels to put on analog. Using analog tape is a whole art in itself.

Before digital came along, I obviously used to record all analog, sometimes having three 24-track machines synced up, giving me 69 recordable tracks. Things are very different these days. If today's dwindling budgets allow me to record as I prefer, I'll go all the way analog for the basic backing track. I'll record the band backing tracks, *i.e.* drums, bass, and main guitars, all at once with the band playing together in the same room, looking at each other, sometimes without headphones. I do whatever it takes to get the most energetic or moody performance. That will usually take up pretty much all 24 tracks on the tape machine because I use a lot of room mics. Then I will edit the 2-inch, old school–style with sticky tape. I'll often do lots of edits on the

2-inch. We might do 10 takes of a song and then decide that, say, Take 8 is the one but the middle section was better from Take 2. So I'll go back to Take 2 and edit that section into Take 8 and so on. On occasion, I've done up to 30 analog edits in one song. When the arrangement on 2-inch is the way I want it, I'll stripe it with code, sync it up, and bounce it to Pro Tools with the idea that we'll do all our overdubs on Pro Tools. So now we've got lots of extra tracks to do vocals and overdubs and go crazy with plug-ins if we want. Then at the end of the day, when it comes time to mix, I'll sync the Pro Tools back up with the original 2-inch so that the basic backing track is analog and the rest is digital, so both are used together in my mix. That's the most analog I'll do nowadays.

I just find that the whole thing of doing vocals on analog is so time-consuming. It is an absolute pain, and the band ends up getting bored waiting and waiting while I compile the best performances. The problem now is that budgets for records are about half what they were in the '80s and '90s, so you just don't have the studio time. You need to keep the flow. To be honest, I find that creating a momentum where the band isn't marching around twiddling their thumbs is really important for creativity.

Doing it completely analog, with no digital aboard, is getting into a romantic area. Because at the end of the day, it's gonna end up being on an MP3, and people are gonna be listening on their little iPod earphones. It becomes arguable that you can hear the difference. And nowadays, digital has gotten better; there's all these little plug-ins you can use to warm it up. And if you're mixing through a Neve or an API desk, it warms it up considerably.

I've never mixed "in the box" [in something like Pro Tools]; I always mix on an analog desk.

If the budget is really, really small, I figure that the best way of making albums is to not go to 2-inch at all. Instead, just rent some good A-Ds, like Prisms, for the multitrack recording, but do mix to 1/2-inch analog.

I will always mix to analog…always.

I sometimes have gone about recording albums in various ways. The biggest thing I find is that it's become a choice between things flowing really quickly in the studio or not. Analog absolutely sounds way better than digital, but digital allows us musical types to get what we imagine in our heads to come out of the speakers more quickly.

So it's all good!

Jacquire King

Credits include: Kings of Leon, Modest Mouse, MUTEMATH, Buddy Guy, and Tom Waits. See the Appendix for Jacquire King's full bio.

I love both analog and digital. For me it's about using them together. They're both extraordinary tools, each with great qualities. There have been times in the past where I was using only one or the other, but now for the last several years, I have a system of cutting the basic tracks to analog and then transferring to digital for all the overdubs through the mix. The typical setup is 16-track 2-inch analog tape patched straight into Pro Tools. That way I'm hearing the sound of the conversion the whole time I'm getting the sounds and the performances recorded. After that, the only sonic change that occurs is the sound of the recording coming back from tape, and I've never been disappointed by that. There is the romance of tape, and it's nice because you are getting the benefit of making the recording experience fun and comfortable. By creating that energy, some special things happen.

Recording on analog focuses everyone on listening to the playback. There isn't anything in the computer yet, and no one is looking at the music; they are just listening. There is a different pace because you have the rewind times, and things are a little bit slower, which allows a little bit of time for conversation about what everyone is hearing.

Another great thing about recording to analog is the limitation on tracks. It forces you to think about what is important in terms of how to mike up the instruments and capture them. Some of my favorite analog multitracks are the Ampex MM1200, MCI JH-16/24, any Studer, and the 3M M56. The M56 was what I used on the Kings of Leon's *Aha Shake Heartbreak*. I also used a TG console from Abbey Road on that album. Tom Waits' *Mule Variations* was an 80-series Neve with mostly 1073s. That tape machine was a Studer A80. Modest Mouse's *Good News for People Who Love Bad News* was similar but larger, and the tape machine was an Ampex MM1200.

I usually work at 15 IPS, but 30 IPS is the way to go when you're dealing with very dynamic instruments, such as acoustic guitars, strings, vocals, and performances, where there can be very quiet moments. I want to avoid collecting too much tape hiss and noise floor. Sonically, the best advantage to analog is that it has a really great shape to the transients. When recording with analog, I end up using a little less compression overall, especially on drums. It becomes more of a choice as opposed to a necessity. I love compression, but I'd rather use it more precisely in mixing and not have painted myself into a corner.

I can usually record a whole album with two or three reels of tape. After the desired takes of a song are recorded, they can be transferred to the digital medium. Then the tape is used to record another song. You can find some economy there. From that point on, all the overdubbing, editing together of takes, or fixing mistakes can be done in the digital realm. An advantage of digital is once the basic track is transferred, there is the opportunity to create a rough mix that can be stored along with the song for immediate recall. In future sessions, you can pick up right where you left off. Things like headphone mixes can be kept as recording work is completed throughout the overdub process.

I like to mix from Pro Tools in a hybrid sense, where I am using analog and digital together—submixing some tracks together in the computer and then using analog compression, EQ, effects, and summing that may or may not include a console. A great engineering lesson I've found in this method of tape before transfer to digital is that recording levels to digital shouldn't always be as close to 100 percent as possible. It was always said in the early years of digital recording that everything should be recorded as close to zero as possible. Recording to analog first you find that things like a bass guitar go to an analog tape machine pushing the VU meter into the red, but when it comes over to digital, its level is somewhere around –6 dB to –9 dB. Electric guitars are usually in the –6-dB range. Vocals will generally be peaking around −3 dB with only the very occasional peak near zero. The same holds true for drums. In terms of digital mixer architecture, if you have everything recorded at its highest possible level, when you try to get it all summed down to a stereo picture, you end up having to turn most of your volumes way down. By doing that you are throwing away part of what you have recorded anyhow. We're just talking about one or two bits of resolution. You want that headroom available in the math of the digital mixer architecture as tracks are processed with plug-ins and volume adjustments.

Digital is really great for overdubbing, especially when recording vocals. It's nice to be able to move fast. I can work at the singer's pace instead of having to wait for rewind times. I can easily collect six or eight takes and then pick and choose moments to put together. It gives me a lot of options. I understand not everyone is able to record with analog before working in a digital environment, but there are technical lessons and workflow ideas that can be adapted from working with analog to an all-digital process that will make for better recording craft.

Dylan Dresdow (photo by Dylan Dresdow) / Calexico Horns: Martin Wenk - trumpet, Jacob Valenzuela - trumpet, plus West Side Horns' Al Gomez (photo by Rick Clark). Row 2: Jim Dickinson / John Hampton (photos courtesy of Ardent, John Fry). Row 3: Jeff Powell & Wayne Jackson of the Memphis Horns (photo by Steve Roberts) / Wayne Jackson, Rick Clark, Tom Dowd, Jody Stephens, Susan Hesson (photos courtesy of Ardent, John Fry).

Bass is the primal meeting ground of melody and beat. It doesn't matter whether it's a classic Motown or Stax soul groove, a four-on-the-floor country roadhouse rave-up, Paul McCartney's orchestrated four-stringed counterpoints, or Lemmy's eighth- and sixteenth-note distorto hyperdrive for speed-metal band Motorhead, the bass is at the foundation of this experience we call music.

We've enlisted eight producers who have worked with a number of different kinds of basses: string bass, slap funk bass, rockabilly, 8- and 12-string basses, and more. Once we got these eight talking about it, it was apparent that a book could have easily been filled. Following are a few thoughts on keeping you grounded concerning matters of the bottom end.

Norbert Putnam

Production credits include: Jimmy Buffett, Dan Fogelberg, Joan Baez, John Hiatt, New Riders of the Purple Sage. Bass session credits: Elvis Presley, Henry Mancini, Roy Orbison, Linda Ronstadt, Al Hirt. See the Appendix for Norbert Putnam's full bio.

In the mid '60s, the only way to record a Fender Precision bass was through an Ampeg B-15 with the bass and treble turned off and a Neumann U 87 shoved up near the speaker cone. You had the treble knob and volume full out on the Precision bass and fixed the final output level on the front of the Ampeg. Most engineers then applied 2 or 3 dB of compression via an LA-2A or a Urei 1176. However, a few years later, almost all recordings were by direct box with the treble and volume still full out on the bass. I no longer had to haul a heavy amp. Yeah!

A little later on in the '70s, I had the Fender pickups wired directly to the output plug, bypassing the tone and volume pots. I thought this sound was cleaner and more hi-fi.

As for my acoustic bass, we recorded that two slightly different ways. One way utilized an RCA 44-BX [this was for a thicker, tubby sound] placed level with the bridge and sitting in the corner of two low-rise gobos. But my favorite miking technique was the ubiquitous Neumann U 87 placed higher up near the plucking finger, about 6 inches above the bridge. This gave you the added attack of a heavily callused finger and the ability to use all sorts of jazzy, buzzy sliding sounds. I used this placement on pop and rock sessions with Elvis, Henry Mancini, Al Hirt, and hundreds of lesser gods.

My daily complement of equipment [in the '60s] was carried in the back of a 1965 Ford station wagon. Instrument cartage companies were nonexistent in 1965. So, I personally lugged my Ampeg B-15 tube amp, my 1956 Fender Precision, and my

1925 Kay "plywood" acoustic bass to three or four studios a day. I had abandoned my 200-year-old German instrument because of resonant "hot spots." I also had handy a bow and some rosin just in case an orchestra appeared.

Note

A *hot spot* is a highly resonant note in an octave that registers and sounds much louder than the surrounding frequencies. In other words, *hot spots* means "some notes louder than others." Not good!

The ability to use the inexpensive Kay bass was due to enhanced low frequencies from the close proximity of the Neumann mic. Yes! That cheap old plywood Kay ate the hand-carved German instrument's lunch. Every note from the low E to the upper reaches of high G registered a zero level at the console. The engineers loved it! As a matter of fact, the level, clear sound of that old Kay helped me pluck many accounts from my richer fellow bassists with more valuable axes.

Jacquire King

Production and engineering credits include: Kings of Leon, Tom Waits, Buddy Guy, Modest Mouse, MUTEMATH. See the Appendix for Jacquire King's full bio.

The bass sound is hugely important to a recording. Oddly enough, though, it is simple to record based on getting certain aspects correct in the process.

I always like to record a bass amp. I typically use a microphone like a Neumann U 47, an FET 47, or an RE20. I also like the M 49 quite a bit. For the placement, I generally go anywhere from a few inches to as far as a foot—but not typically—off of the cabinet in order to let the low frequencies develop off the speaker before they get to the microphone. A DI [direct input] is also very important because the DI will capture some of the low frequencies you lose focus of as they come off of the amp into the air. When the recording is played back over a stereo, it's pretty much the first time those low frequencies from the DI have been released into an acoustic environment, and that can be very good for the low-end presentation.

In the relationship of placing a microphone that distance from the bass cabinet and the signal from the DI traveling to the speaker, they become slightly out of time with each other because of the time it takes the waveforms to develop at the microphone. Now, because of this time discrepancy and the wavelengths being so long, they won't line up well with each other, and you can get some frequency cancellation. What I will do then is run the bass DI through a higher-quality delay, like a PCM 41, and add a few milliseconds of delay. Usually about 3 milliseconds will line the DI up with the waveforms I'm capturing off of the bass cabinet. By doing this there is a more accurate phase picture. I don't usually like using tube DIs. I simply like a good old transformer, like a Jensen or a UTC. For whatever reason—and there are a few great tube direct boxes available for bass—I haven't found many of them that work for the sound I get. I've been jealous of other people and how well they've used them, but they don't usually work well for me for whatever reason. Although I have to say that the SansAmp Bass Driver direct works great into a tube mic pre. I like using a little compression on each signal, and old dbx 160s are usually my first choice.

I sometimes use a subharmonic synthesizer sent off the DI signal just after the compressor and then blend it with the DI to tape. I give the subharmonic synthesizer its own EQ and compression, often equalizing the signal before and after the subharmonic synthesizer. I have a great old dbx box that has four bands of synthesis and can really dial in the lows in relation to the key of the song.

Another thing that I like to do is put a bass through a Leslie cabinet or a Rotovibe pedal. With the cabinet, I usually unhook the wheel from the horn at the top so it's not rotating, and find some sonically interesting position for the horn to rest. I'll maybe put something like a SM57 on it. For the low end I usually like to use a pair of microphones a couple feet off, maybe four feet apart, looking at the lower rotating speaker. Most times I just record some doubling bass parts that accent certain parts of the song or section of an arrangement. It adds a wide "chorusy" sound to the bass and is a wonderful texture. A baritone guitar is another instrument where I have used this technique. It's a cool sound because it adds a performed effect layer to the production.

Leland Sklar

Bass credits include: James Taylor, Phil Collins, Randy Newman, Jackson Browne, Dolly Parton, Crosby, Stills & Nash, Linda Ronstadt, Neil Diamond, Rod Stewart, Barbra Streisand, Lyle Lovett. See the Appendix for Leland Sklar's full bio.

It is amazing to me that after 39 years of studio work, I still get totally excited to get in my car and drive to the studio to do whatever it is I am doing that day. Most of the time I do not know what the project is or what will be demanded of me until I arrive at the studio. It could be a record, a jingle, a movie, a cartoon, et cetera. That is part of the excitement that I feel. Hanging by your nails from the edge of the precipice.... It is the most wonderful feeling one can have, and then on top of that I get to play with the best musicians in the world. Does it get any better?

One of the downsides of the current technology is that there are fewer and fewer live *session* dates. There is an enormous difference between going to a guy's house, sitting in his bedroom, and overdubbing bass on pre-produced tracks and being in a room with other players and feeling the energy and excitement of ideas being tossed about like hot potatoes. The synergy of that is what made me love playing music in the first place. I am a "band guy."

So many of the great studios have closed and been torn down. They will never return. Real estate is too valuable now, and those spaces have become parking lots and strip malls. It's a sad state of affairs. But, not to be all doom and gloom, there are more sessions going on where they try to have full bands doing the tracking, which is wonderful.

When I go to work, I always show up early and am tuned and set up by the time the downbeat has been called for. A 10 a.m. call does not mean showing up at 10 a.m. It means that you are ready to play at 10 a.m. It is a work ethic that really counts in studio work. There is a lot of money at stake, and people's careers. It is fun, but *be professional*—this is your job!

I have always approached my work both as a bassist and as a cheerleader. Sessions are a serious event, but the more lighthearted, the better the performances will be. What a gig!

I show up with an assortment of basses. Usually my old standby Fender-ish four-string. It is a bass that was never an actual instrument, but rather pieces we assembled in the mid '70s, and *it worked*! Then my five-string Dingwall, five-string Yamaha fretless, Hofner Beatle bass, and a Washburn five-string acoustic fretless. I use an iAMP 800 combo by Euphonic Audio. I try to have the engineer take me both direct, using my old Tube Works DI, and the amp. I leave that up to the engineer, for he knows how many inputs he has, and usually the bass is the first to be sacrificed for an extra channel. Maybe we just don't whine loud enough. But I do love the combination.

I also, whenever possible, like to have the amp next to me. I have never been paranoid about leakage. It is like a condiment. I like the feel of bass, not just the tone. Bass is a visceral thing.

Once we get started, it is up to the artist/producer to direct what we are doing. There may be note-for-note charts, Nashville number charts, *no* charts, et cetera. The first thing I do is, if they have carpet on the music stand, take it off; otherwise, the first correction to the chart and your pencil goes right through the paper. Who the hell thought of that?!

If all goes well, we accomplish more than the artist hoped for. It is so wonderful when you get a group of musicians together with a little demo and leave with a complete, finished song. There is nothing less satisfying than not getting it. This rarely happens with the caliber of players I get to work with. Then it would be a problem between the artist and producer.

One of the things I do hate is when you have played a great chorus, and they say, "Great. We'll just cut and paste it in the other chorus!" I say, "The second and third chorus should evolve. Not the same as the first. Let me at least do it the way I feel it, and then after I leave, if you want to cut and paste it is your prerogative. Just let me leave feeling I have done my best job!"

The pleasure I get from this life as a musician is indescribable. I feel blessed every day I get to do it!

Jim Scott

Production, mixing, and engineering credits include: Tom Petty, Sting, Santana, Lucinda Williams, the Rolling Stones, Wilco, Foo Fighters, Red Hot Chili Peppers, Johnny Cash. See the Appendix for Jim Scott's full bio.

I always record an amp and a DI. I love having an amp. It doesn't have to be loud. It can be if you're going for that kind of a thing. There is just a dimension that comes out of a speaker that doesn't come out of a DI. DIs are great, and I'll always print one, but I'll always print both.

If I could only take one bass, I would take a Fender Precision bass and either an Ampeg flip-top or B-12 or a Fender Bassman with two 10-inches in the cabinet. What a great sound! Ten-inch speakers…it's the best guitar amp. I have a blackface, but the blondes were good. They had a presence knob, which was cool. My blackface is all muscle, tone, and umph. It's great for bass and great for guitar. I've also got an old SVT with two 15-inches. It sounds amazing, but those amps aren't easy to record.

For miking bass amps, I've had good luck with the RE20. I've also had good luck with the 47 tube mics on the bass cabinet. A 47 tube is a great mic, and people don't think about it for a bass cabinet. If it's not too loud, that mic will record a beautiful sound.

It can be a little dangerous because if the amp is too loud, you might damage the mic. I also use 47 FET on the bass cabinet. If I was going to take one mic for a bass cabinet forever, I would probably take the 47 FET. I put it right up on the speaker, halfway between the center of the cone and the edge of the speaker. That said, it's what's coming out of the speaker and whose fingers are on the strings.

Dylan Dresdow

Engineering and mixing credits include: Michael Jackson, Mariah Carey, Macy Gray, Herbie Hancock, Black Eyed Peas, Ice Cube, Coolio, Method Man, TLC, Christina Aguilera, Pink, Missy Elliott. See the Appendix for Dylan Dresdow's full bio.

I really like the Fender Precision and jazz basses going through Ampeg B-15 flip-top amps. I have never been disappointed with that amp and that rig. I also always, always use a DI on a bass. My favorite bass DI of all time is the A-Designs REDDI, which has a phenomenally great tube DI that has a thru output to send to the bass amp. It just sounds incredible. Anyone I've recommended it to who has checked it out has bought one. For miking the speaker, I typically use a U47 FET, which I seem to get a lot more detail out of the attack of the finger pluck of the bass sound than can be gotten out of the tube mics. If even more detail is needed, I'll typically just notch in maybe a dB of 1 kHz. It's very simple. I'll set a mic about 3 feet away. I want the bass amp to have enough room to physically reproduce a low-end waveform that's going to be big enough to sound good coming through the speakers.

Whenever I'm done and if I'm using digital, I will physically look at the waveform and nudge to line up. The reason I do this is because the amp signal is always going to be behind the DI signal. So if I move that forward and lock them up, that seems to be the best way for me to get the phase relationship tight between the DI and the bass amp signal. I monitor them individually, whenever the bassist is playing. Many times we just listen off the amp, then when we're done with the amp, I nudge it forward and then I can focus on making the sound as tight as possible. Because if I don't do that, especially when the kick drum lays down on the 1 and the bass plays a note on the 1, things can get a little bit fuzzy in there. That's the best way for me to get my bass clarity and ensure the musicians sound like they are playing as tight as they are.

For bass, I almost never record with compression. I say "almost never" because there are the times when I need to do it, especially if we're doing a funky slap-bass disco sound, which I will compress whenever we get that stuff. The Buzz Essence is great for this. But if it's just straight ahead, just finger plucking or even just plucking with a pick, I really don't use any compression at all.

For EQ, I like using the Pultec EQP1. There's also an API 500-series unit from A-Designs called the EM-PEQ, and that's basically a solid-state 500-series version of the Pultec. It has a tighter sound than the old-school Pultec tube units. One of the things that I like about using the API 500-series unit is that the EQs are consistent no matter what studio you're in. Many Pultecs—even though most of them do the same thing—have been recapped and re-tubed, and they are all going to sound slightly different from each other due to age, and that's a frustrating thing for me whenever I'm working and when I expect something to sound a certain way. If I try to dial it in, and it doesn't sound exactly like it should, then I start to get frustrated as an engineer because I feel like I am driving in the correct direction and just didn't get to the right destination.

The EM-PEQ is much easier to dial in, and I really like using the 60 Hertz for bass. I'll boost it up, but if it's getting a little bit too "subby," I'll actually turn the attenuator up instead of turning the boost down. That basically kind of mellows out the peak of the EQ curve. For the pluck sound, I'll basically boost at 3k. On the top end, I'll put the attenuator on 20k, and typically I'll attenuate anywhere from like 10 o'clock to 12 o'clock. I hardly ever go above that because that's getting kind of extreme. It just kind of seems to mellow out my top end and lets my bass focus on the low-end energy that I desire. If I'm having trouble getting it to translate on the low end, I'll pop it up to 100 Hertz instead of 60 Hertz, and most of the time that gives me much more translation to smaller NS-10 speakers than to my Augsberger mains.

David Z (David Rivkin)

Producing, engineering, and mixing credits include: Prince, Billy Idol, Fine Young Cannibals, Jonny Lang. See the Appendix for David Z's full bio.

Number one, there is nothing like a good bass with a good tone. It has got to have a pure tone. There is no substitution, unless you are going to use a synth bass.

Concerning bass recording techniques, when a bass player is doing popping and funky licks, it's good to take away the middle, like 1 Hz. That kind of gives it a warm pillowy sound, yet there is a lot of high end in there, so the pops can come out but it isn't too forceful.

I like to split the signal and use two different faders for the bass; one would be a tightly compressed signal with a lot of midrange to really sock it through, and the other would be very lightly compressed, but with a lot of bottom. I might have one with compression and one without. That way, I can EQ them totally different-ly. That way, I can combine the amount of each element to make it work on lots of different sets of speakers.

Anybody can get a bass to sound huge on a big set of speakers, but you have got to have it translate to all kinds of small speakers and really horrible speakers. I believe in the lousy speaker syndrome. For my home system, I have some big old KLH bookshelf speakers. They are really old and grungy, but I know what they sound like. I'm a bass fanatic; that is the thing I really fight to get right.

I love heavy bottom, but it can't be too heavy because it makes everything a mess. Sometimes I will cut the bottom off with a filter, like below 30 or 40 Hz. Then you can boost a little more without muddying up the super sub-lows. I would probably boost it around 100 cycles. You have got to be careful, though. If you are mixing a dance record for the dance floor, you almost need the subs in there. You have got to be kind of careful if it is going to end up in a club or on some huge speakers. You have got to translate to that, too.

I have to mix on a lot of different systems. The big system in the studio is for the sub-lows. Then I have to switch to lousy speakers to get the midrange right. Then I might have to switch to some good NS-10 midrange and high-end speakers to get the high end right. I have a pair of these Little David speakers that are super hyped in the high end and the low end, but you get a totally different picture than an Auratone or something like that. It is good to get it to sound right on every system you can. Bass is very elusive, and you want it have power and punch without vibrating the speakers until they rip. It is a fine balance.

Sam Taylor

Producing credits include: King's X, Galactic Cowboys, Atomic Opera. See the Appendix for Sam Taylor's full bio.

I view the bass and kick drum as the basic pivotal foundation of what you anchor all of the other sounds to. I tend to approach them as one instrument. Before I go into the studio and record, I start back in pre-production, making sure the bass player not only understands the concept of ensemble playing, but can play that way. If you have got four people in a band, it is not four different sounds. It is one sound. Everything has got to blend together. A lot of people don't know it, but their sound is based on the sound of everything around them. If they can figure that out, then you can come up with a really great ensemble.

For recording rock bass and drums, I like cutting 15 IPS analog with Dolby SR, because of the warmth and beefy sonic quality I can achieve in that medium.

For the powerful King's X 8- and 12-string bass sound [which was played by Doug Pinnick], I employed a multiple-miking setup that enabled the bassist to switch instruments for different parts of the song and ensured sonic consistency.

When Doug started bi-amping, there might be as many as three mics capturing the high end and two mics on the low end. Those mics, plus a direct, would all be running live into the board, where we would assign them or mix them together, depending on what was sounding correct with the ensemble. I would keep the high end and the low end and the direct separate. That way I would have more control over it in the mix. I would re-compress all of those when I would use them. We would always tend to boost the high mids.

Sometimes we might change basses in the middle of a song, for a particular section. Doug might be playing a 12 and then he would switch to a 4-string for another section. This setup would allow me to try and come as close to matching that, so you wouldn't feel that something had completely left.

A lot of times, with the 12- and 8-string basses, I would get Doug to double the 12- or 8-string part with his 4-string Hamer bass, which was one of the finest, cleanest basses I ever heard. It takes somebody who is really good when you start doubling the low end of an instrument, because the sound waves are so far apart that any variation in the attack or intonation is very apparent.

Recently, I have become a big fan of engineer/designer John Cuniberti's Reamp, which is a super-clean tape-recorder-to-instrument amplifier interface. The Reamp allows me to take a clean instrument signal [in this case, the bass guitar] and try out any number of amps and tonal settings.

The cool thing about the Reamp is you can plug the player in and he's ready, as long as he's got new strings on his bass and it is in tune. There is no need for any mics or need to EQ his amp; he's ready to go. A bass player would be smart to have one of these. When they do a session, he can just say that this is what he uses for a direct. He plugs it into the patch bay and goes. When the track is done, he can help with the sounds and the miking of the amp. The bass player is involved in the process of getting his own sound again, without having to stand around and play a part over and over again while someone else is tweaking it. After all, we are making this together.

Eddy Offord

Producing and engineering credits include: Yes, Dixie Dregs, Emerson, Lake and Palmer, 311. See the Appendix for Eddy Offord's full bio.

For the well-known Chris Squire bass sound that helped give Yes much of its distinctive sound in the early '70s, we put the bass through more of a guitar amp setup, which I think was a Sunn amp with either 10-inch or 12-inch speakers. I took it direct at the same time. On the amp, we went for lots of treble and distortion. I would just roll the bass end off of the amp, so it was all click and presence. I used the direct for the low end. I mixed those two signals together while making sure they were in phase. By balancing the two, I could bring out the lows or focus on the treble side. I would usually bring out the upper midrange, about four or five thousand, to bring out that gritty, trebly sound. By itself, the amp sounded like a piece of garbage, but when mixed in with the direct, it sounded great.

Chris was the first guy I knew of who really wanted a sound that became more of a lead instrument, almost like a guitar. Before that, bass guitar was just there to provide the bottom. I still use the same principle recording bass. Of course, that depends on the player and what he is looking for, too.

Whenever I can, I try to use the LA-2A tube compressors, which I think are really good. I compress the signal quite severely. For string bass, I prefer to have the player in an iso booth if the player is amenable to the idea.

I did an album with John McLaughlin called *Extrapolation*. I put one of those hypercardioid pencil condenser mics really close to the bridge so I could get the sound of the fingers on the strings. That way, I could get more presence and not so much boom. I usually place the mic an inch or two from the bridge, on the upper side of the bridge, pointing right at the strings.

Jim Dickinson

Producing credits include: Ry Cooder, the Replacements, Big Star, Toots Hibbert, John Hiatt, Mudhoney, Jason & the Scorchers, North Mississippi Allstars, G. Love & Special Sauce, Screamin' Jay Hawkins. Session credits: The Rolling Stones, Bob Dylan, Aretha Franklin, Primal Scream, Los Lobos. See the Appendix for Jim Dickinson's full bio.

For want of a better word, it is the mystery of the bass and the motion that I try and capture. Everyone says we are bottom-heavy in Memphis, and thank God we are, because I think that is where the beat is. I don't think that the bass sound should be overly articulate. I think the bass can afford to be mysterious.

The great players of the '60s and '70s were all very mysterious. The perfect example is Bill Wyman, who is now being dismissed by some as if he were some kind of unimportant musical figure. As far as I'm concerned, the exact opposite is true. The role that he played on the early Rolling Stones records can't possibly be overemphasized. With Bill Wyman, it is the motion of his notes, more than his actual articulation, that makes him special as a player.

It has been my good fortune, as a sideman and as a producer, to work with some of whom I consider to be the greatest Fender P-bass players of our generation, like Chris Etheridge, Tommy Cogbill, Duck Dunn, and Tommy McClure, who to me was the greatest. There was a certain mystery to all of those players. The bass part wasn't up your nose. It was kind of floating around between your ears and behind your head somewhere. That is still the sound that I go for.

For recording the bass, I prefer recording digital because of the medium's ability to capture a deep, punchy bottom end. I feel that, while analog is warm-sounding, it fails to capture deep bass frequencies. The issue of warmth is one that I address in other ways.

I find that the fewer times I record the ambiance of the room, the better. I will use an amp while tracking, just deferring to the bass player. I almost never use that signal. I take the bass direct through some kind of tube pre, just to warm it a hair, and then when I mix, I re-amp that signal in the room and print that directly to the master. I prefer using an old B-15 or B-18 flip-top Ampeg if I can get it. It is still my favorite. Unless it is like a recorded, processed sound you are after, the fewer times you record either the echo or the bass, the better off you are, as far as I'm concerned.

Another one of my preferences is to record the bass last in the control room, if the player is comfortable with the idea. I would rather record the bass last. Almost everybody overdubs bass right after the drum track. To me, if I can get a bass track I can live with while overdubbing, I keep it. Then I let the bass player overdub last.

There is a very different focus to the performance when you are tracking. It's a different set of motives. I always tell them not to play anything that doesn't help the drummer. I am after a different kind of performance when I track than by the end. I am definitely trying to "best" the performance of the track. That is what the record is about. Otherwise, it is just a documentary recording. Of course, I keep the live tracking bass, guitar, or whatever it is until I have bested it.

The idea of recording bass in the control room has to do with the distance between the speakers. The bass player can't hear the bottom end of his instrument through his phones anyway. I will always put the bass player in the control room if he is up for coming, because it is the only place that he is going to hear his instrument. There is just enough physical delay, because of space and time, between the speakers and your ears to put the bass player back in the pocket when the tempo is no longer an issue, because it is being dictated by the track you are overdubbing to, if you see what I mean.

With most music—R&B for sure—I want the bass player a little bit late, because I try to get the snare as dark as I can get it. If the bass player is dead in the pocket when we track, when I put him behind the big speakers in the control room, he's going to fall back in the pocket. I saw Sly and Robbie do the same thing, when I produced the Toots Hibbert record. As soon as the tracking was over, Robbie [Shakespeare] walked into the control room, turned his back to the speakers, and overdubbed every single bass part.

I understand the whole thing of having his back to the speakers. He was waiting for them. He simplified his parts when he overdubbed, which is one of my reasons for doing it later. With his own technique, he achieved everything that I tried to get in my process, which is to get simpler and further back and down in the pocket bass parts. By playing in the control room, you can hear your notes better and articulate your overtones and all the stuff you can't possibly do either with earphones or with a live amp in your face.

Dickinson understands that not all music should have the bass on the backside of the pocket. This was especially true when he produced the Replacements' classic Pleased to Meet Me. *Their bassist, Tommy Stinson, drove the band's groove by playing in front of the pocket. Stinson had a highly overdriven top end–heavy sound, which presented a different kind of production approach for Dickinson.*

Tommy Stinson played with his earphones on because he heard the note almost instantaneously. The whole Replacements groove was in Tommy being in front of the beat and Mars behind the beat and Westerberg in the middle.

Tommy played through a homemade 300-watt rig. I put the amp in the concrete equipment closet of the "B" studio in Ardent, and it was cranked all the time. I said, "Do you really need the 300 watts?" He said, "I've got 600 watts at home, man." He was trying to make that slapping roar, and we were just miking that room. The room was so small, it was compressing. You could hear it all over the building. In that case, I definitely used the amp sound, as opposed to re-amping.

For acoustic string bass, I think it is important to understand the value of finding the true bass tone out in the room.

People will jam stuff up in the bridge and up in the f-hole, and they will wrap microphones in foam and all that kind of garbage. On the bridge, all you get is this little midrange-y note. The big sound of the bass is coming out of the entire front and back surface. The thing people don't understand about miking an upright bass is that the sound is in the room.

A lot of the rockabilly slap-bass guys had Kay basses that were basically boxes of plywood and sounded like garbage. The closer you got with the mic, the more it sounded like a plywood box. If you had a good-sounding room and the bottom end was coming off the floor, the farther you backed off the mic, the better it got. The best bass sound you can get is from across the room, because the waveform is so long.

For the old Sun Records sound—think about how simple this is—you want the bass drum and the bass to have the same sonic space. Use the same microphone. Sam Phillips only had five microphones. He had one RCA Victor ribbon microphone in the sweet spot that was on the bass drum and the bass instrument. If he wanted more bass instrument, he got the bass player to move closer to the mic, in front of the bass drum. How easy can it be? Yet, can you get anyone to do that now? He was miking the room. All of his mics were open all the way around, sometimes with the exception of the vocal mic. He was mixing it all into mono, so there was no phase cancellation, and the sound of that room was wonderful.

Brass

There is nothing in popular music that can elevate a track to a new level of excitement or richness like the addition of a well-placed horn arrangement, solo horn punctuation, or lead ride. It would be hard to imagine many of the greatest pop, rock, and R&B tracks of the last 40 years without the key horn parts that drove them. Even though the title of this chapter is "Brass," I am also including a woodwind instrument like sax, because it is crucial in the sonic chemistry of a typical horn section.

This time out, we sought out two legendary horn players (Tower of Power's Greg Adams and Memphis Horns' Wayne Jackson) and four engineer/producers (Ken Kessie, Jeff Powell, Ralph Sutton, and Shelly Yakus) to offer their pointers on the matter.

Ken Kessie

Producing, engineering, and/or mixing credits include: En Vogue, Whitney Houston, Celine Dion, Tony Toni Toné, Herbie Hancock, Jody Watley, Tower of Power, Brownstone. See the Appendix for Ken Kessie's full bio.

Most of the horn section work I've done in the last four years has been recording the infamous Tower of Power horns. I've been lucky because these guys are so good that they make me sound great every time. Punchy, raw, and somehow still sophisticated, this group calls for a simple, high-quality recording method that just gets out of the way and lets the music speak for itself. This method was developed jointly with Maureen Droney, who actually recorded all the horns on *T.O.P.*, their 1992 Epic release. [Besides being the Los Angeles editor of *Mix* magazine, she records a fat horn section.]

The whole philosophy behind the Tower of Power horns is funk, funk, funk! This is accomplished by keeping the horns raw and live-sounding. We record as quickly as possible to keep the boredom factor down and the excitement factor up. Only slight compression is used—and only on one instrument—to retain live dynamics. All the horns are close-miked to retain that in-your-face attitude. Separate room tracks would be nice, but we never seem to have enough open tracks. Ambience can always be added later but is impossible to remove. Feel free to try this at home—but without the cats themselves and the impeccable arrangements of Greg Adams, you ain't gonna get the flavor.

The horns are always set up in a straight line, like they play on stage, and parallel to the control room window. The order from left to right is Lead Trumpet, Second Trumpet, Baritone Sax, Sax 1, and Sax 2. Any player who flubs during a take holds up his hand (or starts playing another song), and I can instantly back up and pick it up from before the mistake.

Mic choice is as follows: trumpets, Neumann TLM 170; baritone sax, Electro-Voice RE20; saxes, Neumann U 87s. I always kick in the mic pads because these guys are way loud. [Years of live on stage and bad monitors.] Mic pres are always Neves. I will use any Neve console preamps, but on any other console I'll rent 1073s. Neves seem to have the proper amount of musicality, richness, and just enough edge to keep things exciting. Using this combination, I'm able to cut without EQ. The only instrument that is compressed is the baritone sax. I only knock it down a couple of dB, just to keep it in place. A Summit tube compressor is my first choice.

Doubling horn sections is an oft-discussed issue. Usually, Tower of Power will double the trumpets and saxes on their own records. Sometimes inversion and notes are changed, sometimes not. The bari is never doubled, as that always subtracts from the "funk factor." However, on the blues and other old-school tracks, doubling sounds too slick and is avoided like the plague.

Solo horns are another story. Neumann U 67s sound great on the sax, what with the added "tube factor," although I've been known to use an 87 or even a 57 if I need a little more rock and roll. Solo trumpets, especially if muted, require a very dark mic. One really sweet combination is an RCA 77 with a Massenburg preamp. Other combinations that work well at my home studio: Use a Shure Beta 57 (!) and either a Neve, Mackie, or Aphex Tubessence preamp. Sometimes I'll throw a shirt (!!) over the mic to simulate a vintage RCA. I've never had to record a baritone sax solo, but if I did I would stick with the RE20. This mic adds the right funky mids to make all the bari notes stick out.

Remember to keep it simple. Keep the signal path short and get it on tape while the talent is fresh.

Greg Adams

Credits include: Tower of Power horns lead arranger and trumpet player. Session credits: Elton John, Santana, Eurythmics, Little Feat, Rod Stewart, Grateful Dead, Luther Vandross, Bonnie Raitt, Terence Trent D'Arby, Huey Lewis and the News, Michael Bolton, Phish, Linda Ronstadt.

There are tried-and-true microphones that work well with horns. My favorite mic for trumpet is an RCA 44...the big old behemoth. It is really warm, personal, and it expresses well.

On my solo record, *Hidden Agenda*, I played a lot of Harmon mute. We used an Audio-Technica version of a 57, and it sounded great. Ken Kessie, who is my producer, didn't even use the room sound for those parts. With a windscreen or foam pad in front, it was like I was pushing against the mic just to get all of that lip and the mouth noise. That was part of the whole performance. We are not talking about acoustics here. It was just about capturing the sensuality of the instrument itself.

I liked it because it sounded intimate, like the way some of the old Miles Davis stuff sounded. I think that the way we did it, we took it a step further and put it right in your face. When you listen to my record, it comes across almost more like a voice than a trumpet.

If we are performing in a really dry room, we will say, "Wet it up and get some reverb going on in the phones." We want to sound like we are making a record. It is role that we are playing, and we are adding to the whole tapestry of the song.

Even if you are recording in a nice, big, live room, and the engineer is using that room mic 10 feet above you, you may not be hearing that room sound in the phones. You may only be hearing the direct signal from the individual mics, which are like a foot or two away, and you are not getting much slap off of them. A little reverb goes a long way if you are not getting that from the room.

We will always ask for stereo phones, but inevitably, everybody will have the left or right side of the phones off just a little bit to hear the room. It always seems to be that way.

You depend on the engineer to give you a good balance of the horn section in the stereo phones, along with the track. You should be hearing enough keyboards or guitar for the pitch and drums for the time. The vocal is always important because that'll help you find a spot on the tape, if you have to stop and go back and punch in for a lyric cue or something like that.

There are engineers who stand out in my mind as really taking time to make it all work for horns. Ken Kessie, Al Schmitt, and George Massenburg are engineers who really take the time to do it right. Another engineer I like a lot is Russ Kunkel's son, Nathaniel. He has done the last two Lyle Lovett records, which I worked on. He is a brilliant up-and-coming engineer.

Probably my favorite room is Studio A at A&M in Hollywood. It is a big room, and there is a lot of wood. It has a great vibe, and I have worked there for years. It just seems to always be there. Capitol A, Skywalker, and Conway are great rooms, too.

Jeff Powell

Engineering and/or mixing credits include: B.B. King, Memphis Horns, Afghan Whigs, Bob Dylan, Primal Scream, Stevie Ray Vaughan, 16 Horsepower. See the Appendix for Jeff Powell's full bio.

Overall, I generally don't like compressing horns to tape. I know a lot of people do that, but if you are not very careful, you can thin out the sound and squash the dynamics, which I try and bring out as much as possible. I like the little things that are swelling in and out, going from inaudible to the mighty sound that they can have. I think it's very important to keep as much of that as possible, and you need to get as much of that to tape as you can.

I usually don't EQ the horns to tape either. I move the mics around until I get the sound I'm looking for. I basically go straight to tape with them, no compression and no EQ. I just keep my finger on the "trigger," on the channel fader, as it is going down. If I compress anything, that is how I do it. [Laughs]

The Memphis Horns are a lot of fun to work with, and they definitely have a formula on how they stack their parts. They usually do a pass with just the sax and the trumpet. Then they double that and either switch parts, do a harmony, or double a part. They do all head arrangements on the spot. Then Wayne [Jackson] adds a trombone to it. He usually plays the bari sax line or something similar to that. With the trombone, it is really the glue that holds it all together. It is really cool, and it is an instantly recognizable sound.

Typically, I would use a Neumann M 249 on Andrew Love's saxophone. It is an old tube mic, and it is really warm-sounding. It does a good job of capturing the air around it. I don't ever mike it directly coming out of the bell. I'll put it off the side a little bit, to the side where the keys are. It is also back a ways, about a foot and a half to 2 feet away.

On Wayne, I will use a Neumann U 87 or sometimes an AKG 414. I usually have to pad it with him because he is really strong. I don't usually compress to tape. But I usually keep my finger on the channel faders as it is going to tape, and I ride it to tape a little because they play very dynamically. I have worked with them so many times that I have a feeling when it is about to go up…or when I need to pull it back a little bit. That is kind of how I keep it within the realm and get it to tape at the right level. I don't like compressing them because it really squeezes the life out of the sound.

Sometimes, if I have the luxury of enough tracks, I will cut them each to their own track. If not, I will take the time to get the blend of the trumpet and the saxophone to one track, and then when we double, I will repeat the process and listen to the blend and ride it to tape, making sure I've achieved the correct balance. Horn players of this caliber work very fast, so you've got to be on your toes because they will do head arrangements.

They will hum out a part as they are listening, and it never takes them much more than a pass to come up with what they are going to do. They will get a lick going and they will vibe out. They will then go, "Okay, every time that appears in the song, let's do that now. Now let's go back and…"

They are really very good about vocalizing their opinions about whether or not something should go there. They will do whatever you ask them to do, but they are very helpful sometimes, like, "I don't know if that part needs to be there. I don't really think that we need to play there."

They will go through the song and say, "Let's do all of the choruses. Let's back up now and get all of the verses." You've got to make sure that you don't run into the other parts. It isn't like going from top to bottom with a song. You pretty much have to memorize the licks of the songs as they are playing them. [Laughs] It always helps to have a good assistant looking over your shoulder, saying, "They want the third *ba da bomp bomp*." You've got to be able to get back there and punch that one place.

Generally, I've had the most success when I have just used three tracks. They sound very full and definitely have their own sound. Their instruments sound great, too. Like anything you record, the quality of the player and the instrument make a huge difference. Those two guys are some of the best in the world.

From working with them so much, I have learned that you have got to capture that energy out front. They really project. To just stick a mic right on them, you don't capture the air and the blend of what is going on in the room. If you walk into a room and hear them playing together, it sounds amazing. Sometimes I will stick in an extra room mic farther back and get some extra ambiance. I might use a Neumann 67 or a 249.

For the trombone, I usually use a Neumann U 47 FET. I have that mic set up to the side, so Wayne actually points at the trumpet mic when he is playing trumpet; he sets it down and grabs the trombone and points at the trombone mic, off to the side a bit. He actually turns around sideways in his seat and plays pretty directly into the bell. Andrew and Wayne are very good at listening to each other and blending as well. They are among the very best at doing that. They know what is going on, and that helps a lot.

Wayne Jackson

Credits include: Al Green, Sam & Dave, Otis Redding, Elvis Presley, Aretha Franklin, Rod Stewart, Sting, Jimmy Buffett, the Doobie Brothers, Neil Diamond, Willie Nelson. See the Appendix for Wayne Jackson's full bio.

My philosophy is this: If it is not happening on the floor, it can't get on tape. If it is happening on the floor, then there is little you can do to screw it up.

The ambient room sound is important to me when we play. Andrew and I prefer to work in a live room that has a lot of ambiance or natural echo, so that to our ears, we sound wonderful.

A long time ago, there was one studio [not Stax, Ardent, or American] in Memphis that was as dead as a Kleenex box. It was very painful to play in there. There were no ambient frequencies. I guess it was good pitch training, because all you heard were the core pitches, but there was nothing else coming back at us.

If an engineer deadens something behind us, that is okay. It is what bounces back from the wall in front of us and above us that is probably what we hear the most.

Andrew and I prefer the Neumann U 87 microphone for trumpet and sax. That is the microphone that has been giving us the sound we like since back in the Stax Records days. It is a timeless microphone. For trombone, I like the old RCA ribbon mic. It gives it sort of a splatty sound, but not too much.

We have a technique that we have worked out for overlaying horns that involves overlaying three tracks in sequence...trumpet, tenor sax, then trumpet, tenor sax, and finally slide trombone. We do that very quickly.

We have to have an engineer who is attuned to the process that we use, because we will listen to a song and at any moment, either one of us may hear a part that needs to be in the track; we stop the tape, and we stack all three parts to that little section immediately. Then we go through the song and find all of the sections that are just like that and do all of the same parts, because we have the phrase fresh in our minds and we are hot on that phrase. So we do all of them at the same time.

We may come back and do the first one again, because by the time we reach, say, the fourth chorus, we are hotter than we were when we did the first one, so we will go back and redo the first one again. Then we will go through the song and find another part that we like—whatever pops out of either one of our minds—and do the same process. The intros and the endings are usually spontaneous and inspired.

Andrew and I are big on unison parts because unison is powerful. We do harmony parts, but normally, on the first track, we always do unison. On the second track, we put on harmony parts, and then the final harmony comes with the trombone track. Still, it all just depends on the song.

Ralph Sutton

Credits include: Stevie Wonder, Lionel Richie, the Temptations. See the Appendix for Ralph Sutton's full bio.

For the brass instruments, trumpets, trombones, flugelhorns, and the many other valved and slide brass instruments whose tone is produced by vibration of the lips as the player blows into a tubular mouth piece, I like large diaphragm for most applications. They do a great job of capturing the essence of the player and the instrument.

There are two factors in changing the pitch on a valved brass instrument: pressing the valves to change the length of the tubing, and the player's lip aperture, which determines the frequency of the vibration into the instrument, which is the sound of pushing air through a mouthpiece and their tongue and their teeth. All of those things play a important role in how it ultimately sounds.

With a large diaphragm, you can hear them before the note comes out—you'll hear the attack of the note. I like this sound. It adds player character to the recording. For brass sections, I use small capsule microphones, which help me control leakage, along with a stereo pair of large-diaphragm mics set to the omni position, in front of the section, mid left and right. I listen to the mic and make the necessary adjustments. Remember, you are using these mics for more than room mics—you are capturing the section as a whole so that you can bring life to the section and the recording.

The Neumann 47s, 67s, and 87s have been my brass staples for many years. I also like the sE 5600 and 3300 large diaphragms. I like the sE 5600 on the trombone; it gives me a good, round, articulate bottom with a coherent trombone top. Placement is 8 to 12 inches from the bell—that's a good starting point. I like the sE 3300 and sometimes the 87 on a trumpet, 12 to 14 inches from the horn. I like the sE 5600 on a flugelhorn, 8 to 12 inches away. The tube in the sE 5600 just sounds right on the sexy sound of this "big trumpet."

Brass can be broken up into two groups—valved and slide. With the slide group, the player uses the slide to change the length of tubing. The main instruments in this group are in the trombone family. However, valve trombones are occasionally used in jazz. The next group is the valved instruments, and this is the action group. This group has a lot going on. It includes all of the modern brass instruments: the trumpet, French horn, euphonium, tuba, cornet, flugelhorn, baritone horn, sousaphone, mellophone, and the saxhorn. If you have never recorded any of these horns before, start by listening in the room that you will be recording the player in. Ask the player to start warming up, and as he does, get close to the instrument. Then back away from the instrument and determine where the best sound or representation of the instrument is coming from. Once you've got it, place one mic and listen in the control room to make sure that you are capturing the best sound from the instrument for the recording being made. And by the way, start out with no EQ or compression. Get the best mic placement first and then use what you need to make it better.

Now, on some of these valved instruments, you may use more than one mic. These instruments are the tuba, sousaphone, cornet, euphonium, and baritone horn. The size and design of these instruments gives them areas that emit sound that can be helpful. For example, with the tuba, sousaphone, cornet, and euphonium, they all have long tubes that make up part of the sound of the horn. If you use a small-diaphragm mic in this section of the horn along with your other mic, that should be somewhere around the bell, capturing the essence of horn. Now blend those to taste, and you will be very happy you did. Remember mic placement, EQ, and compression techniques—brass has been known to add fire to any song and can be arranged in a way that brings excitement.

Shelly Yakus

Credits include: The Band, Van Morrison, Lou Reed, Tom Petty and the Heartbreakers, Bob Seger, Aretha Franklin, Blue Oyster Cult, U2, John Lennon, B.B. King. See the Appendix for Shelly Yakus's full bio.

You have to make sure that it sounds right when you are recording the horns, or you won't get anything worthwhile.

Recently, when I did Edgar Winter and the White Trash Horns, Edgar played baritone sax with two other players on tenor sax and a trumpet. Basically, what we did was record the horns in Edgar's house in a hallway that had a granite or marble floor. I went into the hallway and talked to Edgar and the guys and listened to my own voice. If my voice didn't sound right, I put a few small throw rugs on the floor in different places to try to make my voice sound more natural, as well as the other people talking. The key to recording anything is to have the instruments sound like they are supposed to sound, and not altered so much by the room.

We weren't trying to deaden the room down; we were just trying to make it a little less wild-sounding because of the hard floor and the hard walls in the hallway. It tended to make it a little too live and a little too ringing for the track.

We then positioned the guys in a north, south, east/T-shape kind of position in this narrow hallway. The sax player and the trumpet player were facing each other about 10 feet apart. Edgar was intersecting them in the middle, and he was back about five feet from the center.

We positioned that way because you couldn't put two people side by side in the hallway because there wasn't enough room, but it worked out great. The hallway filled up with sound when they played. The mics picked all of that stuff up, and it translated into a good, solid horn sound from bottom to top. It was one of the first times that I have recorded horns where it absolutely fit this raging track.

Usually you have to EQ them a little too much sometimes to get them through the track, and then they start sounding small.

We put a U 87 on the trumpet. Normally, once you put a pad on those mics, they are only good for banging nails in the wall. They are like blunt instruments. It kind of kills them, and they just aren't that great-sounding with the pads. But for trumpet, it sounds very good because they are loud instruments.

On a baritone sax, I prefer to use a tube mic, like an M 49 or a 47, but all we had to work with was the TLM 170, and it worked very well.

For trombone, I would use an 87. Trombones, even more than trumpet, tend to clip. They break up easily sound-wise. They seem to have overtones, and if you are not careful, the console will overload or the console or tape machine will clip. So I find that I have to use a mic where I can put a pad on the mic when I'm doing a trombone.

Sometimes, if you get the mic far enough away, you can use a tube mic on it, and they can sound really good. It just depends on what the player is playing.

If you were to put a bright mic on a bright horn, you are going to get a little sound. So I find that if I use an 87, it warms the horn up in the right way. I have tried other mics, and the 87—for me and my style of recording—seems to work the best on loud instruments—loud horns and stuff like that.

As far as positioning, I always pull the mics back quite a ways from the bell. I get it back as far as I can. I really believe that the sound doesn't become the sound until it is a few feet away. What I am looking for is the fullness. Typically, we were putting them all on one track.

When you pull that horn section down into the mix, if you don't get it right, all you are going to hear is the trumpet peaking through all the instruments, and you lose anything else. Everything is sort of in there, but it isn't in there loud enough. So by getting a lot of body on the instrument, you are more assured that when you pull the horns down into the track, you are going to hear everything that they are playing.

What I would do is limit the low horn, like the bari sax. Typically, when you drop the horns into the track, you are going to lose the lowest horn first. The brightest horn, in pitch and frequency, is the one that is going to stick out. So if you limit the low horn a little bit—or the low two horns, like the bari or the tenor—it holds those horns in a place on the track so that you are not going to lose them in the final mixdown.

I don't limit the trumpet because it just doesn't sound right to me. You also lose a lot of the dynamics. The trumpet being unlimited seems to make the other horns sound not limited, even though they really are.

Another reason why I leave limiting off the top horn is that it appears to give the whole horn section life. It is sort of an audio trick.

If you put the mic too close into the bell of the horn, the result may seem to be exciting-sounding, when you are listening to the horn soloed on the speakers at a loud volume, but when you drop it back into the track, it is going to be this little farty sound.

I find that if I take the mic and move it around to get what I am looking for on the horn, there are enough places I can face that microphone and get what I want.

Creative Production and Recording

Sometimes it is so easy to get in a rut and do what you know is going to produce predictable results. The elements of having too little time and relying on habitual recording methods, compounded with the ease of all manner of samplers, MIDI devices, digital workstations, and so on, have made it easy to work without ever really feeling like you need to make a journey into the land of fearless experimentation.

In this book we'll discuss compression, building mixes, and tuning rooms, as well as miking bass and brass. But this time, I decided to let a few bold souls share their less-than-correct methodologies in achieving desired production results. Some of the folks I approached were amused. Some wouldn't dare share production sickness secrets, preferring to stay in the closet.

Some of you might ask why this silliness is included here at all. But where would we be without the creative recording leaps by the Beatles, Beach Boys, Pink Floyd, and many others? They figured the music wasn't creatively "fixed" unless they took a chance at breaking convention.

Regardless, I know there are enough of the afflicted out there who just love off-the-wall ideas, so this chapter is for you.

Some of you may already be well immersed in the advanced stages of this kind of thinking and may find some of these anecdotes to be old hat. Just remember, the Mother of Invention is always looking for new victims.

What you'll find here are not only some great ideas, but also some outrageous stories that, hopefully, will inspire you to never forget what it is like to be truly playful while you're recording. After all, humor and playfulness are at the root of creative magic.

I would like to thank John Agnello, Roy Thomas Baker, Jim Dickinson, Eddie Delena, Marc Freegard, Paul Grupp, John Hampton, Joe Hardy, Bob Kruzen, Dylan Dresdow, Jacquire King, and Jeff Powell for their gift of time and knowledge, as well as Greg Archilla, Brad Jones, and Eli Shaw for their fine input.

Roy Thomas Baker

Credits include: Queen (including "Bohemian Rhapsody"), the Cars (their first four albums), Journey, Dusty Springfield, Nazareth, Foreigner, Alice Cooper, Ian Hunter, Be Bop Deluxe, Smashing Pumpkins, and Ron Wood. See the Appendix for Roy Thomas Baker's full bio.

My experimental years begin with Queen. There is a song on *Sheer Heart Attack* called "Now I'm Here." We wanted a long delay, and an Echoplex wasn't long enough, and there weren't any digital delays in those days. So we got two Studer

A80s, and we ran a tape loop to the second Studer two-track machine, which was about 10 feet away from the first Studer two-track machine. The distance was just far enough away for the delay to be in time with the music. To watch the tape go from one machine across a light fixture and down to a chair and over a table and then to the other machine was really funny. Because the Studers had double guides, and they wouldn't work unless they were both physically in action [otherwise, the machines would just stop], we had to gaffer tape the rotary guides down.

So we had Freddie's voice going into one of the tracks on the Studer multitrack, and we went out of that into the left-hand channel of the first two-track Studer machine, playing back off the left-hand channel of the second Studer 2-track machine, and that would go back to another channel of the multitrack as a delay. We would feed the left-hand output of the second machine into the right-hand input of the first Studer machine at the same time we were recording that on a separate track on the multitrack. Then we were playing back off the second Studer machine, on the right-hand side, and that would go into the third track on a multitrack.

So whatever Freddie sang, there would be a delay coming from his vocal. He would sing something like "Now I'm there," and then it would come out "Now I'm there" again, and it was all in time with the music. It was a really long delay, and Freddie was actually singing harmonies with himself. When he heard the repeat coming out of his headphones, he automatically sang the third above, and when he heard the third above coming back, he was then singing the fifth above, so it was a three-part harmony.

I'm located on the Mojave mountain range, overlooking the Colorado River. Since we are on mountains that are half-volcanic and half-granite, there are loads and loads of volcanic rocks around. They are the rocks with the holes in them.

We've got these solar tubes called Burke Tubes. I've got one that is like 6 feet long, and I stick it in front of the bass drum and seal the bass drum and the Burke Tube, which is the same width as the bass drum, and we fill it with all of these volcanic rocks. Then we put a couple of Shure flat mics inside. I think they are called the SM91s. That sounds really good. It livens up the sound but deadens some frequencies more than others. We end up with this huge low-end thud that comes from the bass drum. It is such a big, big sound, yet it is relatively short, because the weight of the rocks alone causes a lot of dampening. The sound doesn't go long like a normal bass drum. It actually makes a [high-impact dead sound] really loud.

Years ago, I did an album with Chris de Burgh over in Europe; he was always on tour, and he has his own fleet of airplanes. So while I was mixing in Metropolis Studio in London, we hooked up the stereo mix going from ground to airplane control via satellite, on two separate radios in his private airplane. He had one set of headphones on one radio and one set of headphones on the other radio, and he put one headphone from each set on each ear, so he could hear the mix in stereo as we were doing it, while he was flying from Ireland to Germany.

When the Cars first bought their studio in Boston and changed the name to Syncro Sound, we were doing the mixes of the fourth Cars record, and we weren't sure if the mixes were going to sound good over the radio, so we set up a link to the main rock radio station, and we played the mix over the air at 2 o'clock in the morning, while we were still mixing. We had it on automation, so the faders were going up and down. The radio station was playing the mix live on the air, and we would drive around in cars and wave at each other, listening to the mixes as they were going down on the radio. [Laughs] That way we could hear exactly what it would sound like as it came over the radio, through their compression and through all of their EQs and stuff…. We did that on the first mixes, just to see what it would sound like over those radio things.

Eddie Delena

Credits include: Stevie Wonder, Tom Petty, John Cougar Mellencamp, Mick Jagger, Black Sabbath, Kiss, Devo, Michael Jackson. See the Appendix for Eddie Delena's full bio.

We've made entire drum and percussion kits out of Michael [Jackson] sort of beat boxing and stuff. Michael would sing on a wooden platform, because during his singing and sometimes without singing, he would stomp on the platform, which would basically be the kick drum, and he would do all of the percussion with his hands and mouth. He'd clap and finger-snap and slap his thighs and make all of this beat boxing from his mouth. It was a cool sound effect. All of these sounds would be incorporated. At one point we sampled every one of them and made a whole percussion kit out of that, and he even wrote a song with that as the foundation of the song. One song was called "Stranger in Moscow," which was on *HIStory*. He does that on a lot of his records anyway. Sometimes you are not sure if it was a percussion instrument or him. He was really tremendous to work with, and that was a lot of fun to do.

During the mixing of *HIStory*, we did something that was the height of overkill. [Laughs] I don't know if it has been done before, but for mixing the song "HIStory," we hooked up two control rooms with four 3348 digital multitracks DASH-locked and both SSL computers running sync at the same time from different rooms at Larrabee North Studios. That was 96 tracks in each room. This was for one song. [Laughs]

Basically, in Room A, we had an 80-channel SSL, so we were using both large and small faders. That essentially had the basic tracks, like all the music tracks and lead vocals, et cetera, and Room B had an orchestra spread out, a choir, background vocals, Boyz II Men, and a bunch of other stuff. [Laughs]

The tracks in B Room, like the orchestra, were sent to the front bus, and the vocals, like the choir, were sent to the rear bus, which came up on four faders in the A Room. Then the entire stereo mix bus, from the A Room, was sent to an external monitor in the B Room, so you could actually adjust the levels in the B Room and listen to how everything sat in the entire mix. By changing which 3348 was master, you could run the mix in either room. [Laughs] Between Steve Hodge, myself, and a guy named Andrew Scheps, who kind of technically put it all together, we all worked on the ongoing song.

Joe Hardy

Credits include: Georgia Satellites, Steve Earle, Colin James, Jeff Healey, Carl Perkins, Tom Cochrane ("Life Is a Highway"), Jimmy Barnes, Merchants of Venus, the Replacements, the Hooters, ZZ Top. See the Appendix for Joe Hardy's full bio.

I just produced this female artist from Australia named Marie Wilson. For this one song, I wanted this acoustic guitar to sound sort of like a Leslie, but the problem is that when you run an acoustic guitar through a Leslie cabinet, it sort of destroys the acoustic-ness of it, because once you amplify the guitar, then it is no longer an acoustic instrument. It is an amplified instrument at that point. It may be a cool sound, but it is a different thing.

So to get a Leslie effect on the acoustic guitar, I miked the acoustic guitar by putting two wireless SM58 microphones on a ceiling fan. That is how I miked the guitar. So instead of making the speakers spin, as in a Leslie, I was making the microphones spin. It really does the same thing, but this way it really sounds like an acoustic guitar. There is a lot of Doppler and phase shifting going on, except it is all acoustic and not electronic.

There are many of these boxes out now trying to simulate the Leslie sound, but real Leslies sound great because there are so many weird things going on at the same time, like the Doppler and phase stuff and amplitude changes. The sounds are getting louder and softer and louder and softer. It is crazy.

The stuff I did with ZZ Top is the nuttiest, on the verge of being almost unbelievable, because they had money and time and Billy Gibbons, who is just insane. For example, on the song "Rough Boy," Gibbons had five different guitars tuned to the chords of the song, and he played them with an airbrush, so there was no impact. He was just nuts, and he could afford to have five guitars that were exactly the same.

On the song "Sleeping Bag," I bolted an EMT driver onto one of those gray metal utility shelves that you see in like anybody's garage, and we put that in the echo chamber at Ardent, and that is on every snare sound on that song.

On the last ZZ Top record, which is the best album they did in many years, there is a song called "Loaded." Billy wanted a guitar effect on the end that sounds like a shortwave radio. Since he was a kid, he would listen to these crazy broadcasts from Mexico, and he has always loved the way shortwave radios sounded.

The reason shortwave radios sound so oddball is because part of the signal gets there direct, but also part of the signal bounces off of the ionosphere, so it takes longer because it has to go farther. It phases with the original signal that was direct. Because the ionosphere changes so much, the frequency that it phases at changes really rapidly and in a really weird, random, fractal fashion.

We made a cassette of only the guitar part and sent it to a friend of his in Mexico, who broadcast it over his shortwave radio to Houston, where Billy had this crazy shortwave radio that was made in South Africa and doesn't use batteries or plug in. It has some weird internal generator, and you wind up the radio with the big wheel on the side, and it works for like 30 minutes. Then you wind up the wheel again.

So we recorded it off of Billy's wind-up radio in Houston and then flew it back into the track. So it is just a nutty guitar sound. Since Billy wanted it to sound like a shortwave radio, the easiest way to do it was to broadcast it over a shortwave radio. You see, instead of running it through a harmonizer that just happens to say "Shortwave Radio Effect" or something, we just did the real thing.

If you were across town and tried it, it wouldn't work. You need to be far away, because if you are close, there is not enough phasing. Plus, Billy insisted that it come from Mexico. [Laughs]

Jacquire King

Credits include: Kings of Leon, Tom Waits, Modest Mouse, MUTEMATH, Sea Wolf, Pictures and Sound. See the Appendix for Jacquire King's full bio.

I use a boom box or a cassette recorder as a microphone. The microphones that are built into them typically have great midrange. The line outputs will often pass the input signal without having to actually record on the unit. Putting a boom box in front of a drum kit and using it as a close room element blends in very well with the close mics. Most of these recorders also have built-in compressors, so it can add a lot of explosive excitement to the recording. I really like to light those things up sometimes, and it gives you a crazy blown-up sound of the drum kit.

Some artists have a harder edge to their vocal sound, or it's desired to just have a distorted vocal sound in the production. I've taken recorded vocal tracks and run them back through a microphone preamp or re-amped them through a guitar amp to achieve this. When re-amping a track, you can mike it close or far for some added ambience. Some singers perform through loud, awful PAs as part of their live show, and it ends up becoming a texture of their sound. Being able to create that in a recording is important.

When I know the final vocal will have a drier presentation, I like to record a slightly distorted amp sound with the clean vocal sound. I'll split off the signal with a mult before the multitrack and send it to a re-amp box. I use a small tube amp for guitar, like a Watkins or a Maestro, and go through a graphic EQ pedal before it to filter off some of the bottom end. Putting the voice through an amp gives you a great texture to blend in and that adds a grainy air to the sound of the voice. It fills in for something like reverb or delay and adds a lot of excitement to the sound. Sometimes while mixing, I like to use an old Blue Stripe 1176 very aggressively on the vocal. They have a distortion quality to them that really is quite pleasing and translates well to small speakers.

A unique piece I like to use while recording drums is a Sony portable tube two-track machine that I have. It came with a pair of little microphones that I like to stick into the kick drum or lay on the floor under the snare. I get a lot of level into the tape recorder and make the tubes saturate. It adds a very interesting sound to the drum kit. It always blends in really well with the drum picture. On the Tom Waits record *Mule Variations*, I placed those microphones at each end of the piano, where they added an element of murky, yet high-frequency excitement to the sound of the piano and voice. While combining the sound of those mics with the piano mics, a vocal mic, and some room mics, I had a total of seven sounds to play with and find a cool balance. It's great to have some sounds that are very near as well as farther away, but for really unique presentations, it's helpful to have sounds that have different qualities of clarity to blend in, too.

Another thing I would occasionally do on the Waits records is re-amp tracks through an SVT in a room where we had recorded. I would re-record the sounds at loud volumes to get the rattle and shake of the room. It added an element of danger and excitement into the mix. I also played back Tom's voice in a similar way and would capture the ambience of the room for use as a vocal reverb.

Mark Freegard

Credits include: The Breeders, Ride, Dillon Fence, Madder Rose, Marilyn Manson, Del Amitri. See the Appendix for Mark Freegard's full bio.

People are always a little surprised or concerned with the way I am using the equipment. There is a track on the Breeders' *Last Splash* called "Mad Lucas." There were times when Kim Deal would say, "How small can you make this sound?" She would keep saying, "That is still not small enough, Mark." Well, there is a guitar and a violin on that track that I managed to get pretty small.

At first, I would be winding out all of the bottom end, but finally, I ran it through a little Tandy speaker that I carry with me. It's a little mini-amplifier and speaker that is pretty hideous. It's not a personal computer speaker; it is worse than that. It is a tiny little plastic box that cost a couple of pounds in England and runs off a 9-volt battery. It works well for distortion or resizing a sound and sending it somewhere else. I put the guitar through that speaker, back through the board, and out through an Auratone, which I miked up in a toilet, recorded that, and filtered that over again.

The ambient properties of the toilet at Coast Recorders were useful for other aspects of *Last Splash*. We actually recorded quite a lot of the vocals in this toilet at Coast Recorders in San Francisco. Kim Deal really loved it in there. Anyway, it had a really good sound. I started recording more of the little speaker things in there, too.

I also use an Eventide 3500, which has a lot really cool distortion or Doppler effects that the 3000 doesn't have. Sometimes I find myself putting a signal through that and monitoring the return and not using very much source. I did that with a string section on an English band called Goya Dress. We had this one song where we put on strings, but we didn't think they were working very well. I just looked for a program on the 3500 that did something to the strings on the middle eight that took them to another place. The program made them become another instrument, certainly not strings.

I used the Roland Space Echo on the Goya Dress session. I changed the pitch of the tape loop by pushing my finger up against the pinch roller. I controlled the pitch of the sustain spin like that.

For a more unique ambient touch on the vocals, I found Coast's grand piano a useful tool for vocals. On the Breeders album, on a track called "Do You Love Me Now?" the vocal reverb on the intro is a piano. I had Kim sing into a grand piano. It is really quite useful, because there are all these resonances from the piano that make up the reverb. I just put a couple of mics on the soundboard. She was leaning over the front of the piano, singing into the soundboard. She got quite annoyed because I had to set the gain really high, and if she moved, we couldn't use it. It ended up being quite a special moment.

Paul Grupp

Credits include: Roger McGuinn, Little River Band, Rick Nelson, REO Speedwagon, Sammy Hagar, Quarterflash, Charlie Daniels, Pure Prairie League, Michael Murphy. See the Appendix for Paul Grupp's full bio.

There are hundreds of things that I have done, but most of them are not worth mentioning. They are stupid things, like back in the old days, we used to dissect the old analog synthesizers and patch them into everywhere they weren't supposed to go. Everyone did it, so it wasn't that big of a deal.

Lowell George taught me the trick for getting his slide guitar sound, when I was working with him on a project. He told me to align this old 3M 79 tape machine at +20 dB. So I did, and it sounded really wonderful. There was tons of incredible tape saturation and compression, distortion, and all of that stuff.

The next time I did a slide guitar, I did the same thing, and I burned up a head stack. As it turned out, when I did it the second time, I did it in stereo and used two adjacent tracks. I later found out that you had to put many tracks in between because it heated the heads up so much.

I should have used Track 1 and Track 24 or Track 1 and Track 16. What I did was put the information on Tracks 9 and 10. Since the two were right next to each other, there was nothing in between to dissipate heat.

I just basically melted down a $5,000 head stack, which the owner of the studio wasn't too thrilled about. It was at Westlake Audio. When he came to me, I said, "Well, it should take it." I went on about AGFA tape: "If you align it at +10, it should work out fine." Then I went on about the design of the machine and this and that, and he looked up at me and said, "I designed that machine when I was working at 3M, before I started this company. It is not designed to take that!" That was Glenn Phoenix.

For mono or stereo, if you do it carefully, you can definitely see how Lowell got this unique sound. You do everything else normally, like mike the amp and so forth. You just overdrive the machine well before you start hearing something. Normally, about +6 is where you start noticing pretty good distortion. At +12, it is history.

A lot of the desired noise and impact gets lost in the normal signal path. This method got it straight to tape. See, you would distort the console, and nothing in the whole recording chain would ever deliver it. It would clip the signal and prevent that level from ever getting to tape. You might get +10, but you would have this distortion from all of the electronics, rather than the tape. This way, it was a matter of sending a normal signal to the tape machine and then cutting it onto the tape +20 dB hotter.

I can tell you of one thing that I witnessed, but I didn't do myself. Lee Kiefer was a producer and engineer of the first Tubes records. He had this brilliant idea that he wanted to take a tinny 2- or 3-inch transistor radio speaker, connect wires to it, and hook it up to a microphone input. He took a couple of pieces of string, put a couple of holes in the speaker, and hung it from the tuning lugs of the kick drum. This speaker was hanging dead center in the back of the kick drum, where the head had been removed.

They used it as a microphone for the kick drum, and it recorded only the sounds that caused that speaker to really move. Where the speaker was efficient and moved, the sound would propagate down the line, and the ones that it couldn't reproduce or couldn't handle, it just didn't. When you did a final mix and played it back on one of those small radios, that kick drum really stood out. It practically ripped the speaker out that you were playing back on. On a big system, you didn't really notice any big deal. His whole idea was that on small radios, the kick drum was always lost. He wanted to figure out a way to get around that. It worked great.

John Agnello

Credits include: Redd Kross, Dinosaur Jr., Aerosmith, Earth, Wind & Fire, Alice Cooper, Son Volt, the Smithereens, Screaming Trees, Dish, Chainsaw Kittens. See the Appendix for John Agnello's full bio.

A microphone and a speaker are the same thing. They are transducers. One sucks and the other blows, as I like to say. When you wire the subwoofer as a microphone, it sucks. What it does is reproduce these signals out of the bass drum, which are sub-low frequencies. You can barely hear it, but you can feel it a ton.

My only real speaker of choice is a 15-inch subwoofer, as opposed to just a 15-inch speaker, which I've tried. It seems like the subwoofer, for some odd reason, catches the frequencies in different ways. At least that is true with some of the ones I have had. Of course, I might just be insane, and I am just convincing myself of this. However, at the times I've not had actual subwoofers and just had speakers, it seemed to me to be different.

If you have a guy with a small bass drum, it really helps to make it sound thicker or deeper. If you've got a guy with a big bass drum, you can hopefully make it sound even bigger. It is a matter of taste, but in optimum situations, it really works great. I use it all the time. People think I am crazy, but I do it.

Bob Kruzen

Credits include: Jerry Lee Lewis, G. Love & Special Sauce, Mojo Nixon, The Radiators, Live Aid, Hall & Oates, the Neville Brothers. See the Appendix for Bob Kruzen's full bio.

While recording the *Panama* album, which was produced by Dony Wynn, we were looking for ideas to make a couple of songs a little more extreme. I had this Shure mic that was really old, and it had this strange hollow sound to it that we liked. I mentioned to them that for a lot of the old-time sessions, people would sing into a bucket for an effect. Dony found a big old steaming pot for crawfish, and we put mics in the bucket and had the singer sing into it. It was a really nice vocal effect with a tone we couldn't have gotten any other way.

I've got a couple of compressors that are great for weird things. One of them is an old Altec 438A compressor. I've got it to where I have complete control over the attack, decay, and compression. I can almost make it work backward to where it is expanding instead of compressing. It has also got a nice distortion element to it.

The great compressor for doing really strange stuff is an Eventide Omnipressor, and a lot of people don't know about it. It has a knob on it that will do anything from extreme compression to reverse expansion with a gate, so it will actually make the transients louder and then cut off the low parts. It'll put dynamics into something instead of taking things out.

I have used it to de-compress over-compressed things. It is also a great device for drums, because you can stick a point on a drum that isn't there. You can make it inside out, so when you hit a drum, it'll go away and then suck up in reverse.

I've got a Telefunken V72, which I basically use to be a fuzz box. I know a lot of people use them for mic pres because they are usually looking for the Beatles' "sound." I think it is a good mic pre, but when I overload it and use it as a distortion box, it really adds a special quality. I like it especially on the bass guitar or drums. If I want something clean and quiet, I've got some Universal Audio things that I use for actual preamps. I just use the Telefunken V72 as an effect.

Another thing we have done is take a Rockman and patch it into the effects send of a console, like an SSL, and use it as a fuzz box. It isn't really made to run through a console, but when you patch it in, it really sounds pretty cool. The input/out works best, as opposed to using the cue send, because it has a really hot signal, and it overdrives everything. I've run vocals, guitars, and drums through it. In fact, a snare drum through a Rockman is quite a sound.

John Hampton

Credits include: the White Stripes, the Raconteurs, the Cramps, Robert Cray, the Replacements, Gin Blossoms, Travis Tritt, Marty Stuart. See the Appendix for John Hampton's full bio.

If you are looking for a total out-of-control effect, a lot of times you can go to the SSL Listen Mic compressor to achieve that. It is a total, 100-percent ass-bashing, trash-compacting compressor. It takes any dynamic range and reduces it to one level. If you hit a drum and then stop, the compression lets go, and the room tone gets as loud as the drum hit does.

Let's say we are doing this on mixdown. Generally, you use a regular echo send from a channel and send that to the Listen Mic input of the console. You kind of play with the echo send level and the listen mic input level to achieve the desired effect. This is done while in Listen Mic mode. Once you've done that, the only way you can get that to tape is to hit the Listen Mic To Tape button and put a track into Record. Be warned that you cannot control the level to your monitors, because the monitor volume pot is out of the loop now, as is the Cut button. In other words, you can't turn it off. The only thing you can do is unplug the speakers or turn the monitor amps off. The end result is messed up and great. You record it onto another track and add it into the mix when you need it. A lot of the Replacements' *Pleased to Meet Me* album was run through the Listen Mic compressor. I've used it a bunch.

Many things have been said about where the paths of excess lead, and I'm more than happy to relate one such experience.

Joe Hardy [ZZ Top, Tom Cochrane, Jeff Healey] and I used to do lots of stupid things. We once had an old Les Paul, and we were looking for an odd sound for a band called Photons on Line Records in Germany. The song was called "Idle Jets." For the hell of it, we ran the guitar through every piece of equipment in the room that we could get our hands on. The guitar ended up sounding exactly like an elephant charging. It was totally, completely messed up.

I know for a fact that we started off going through an Orban two-channel parametric equalizer. We went in one channel, maxed it out, and took the output of that channel into the input of the other channel of the equalizer. We maxed that out, too, took that through an EMT 140 plate, and took the output of the plate to a Langevin Passive Graphic. We took the output of that to a Lexicon Prime Time digital delay, went from that to a Pultec MEQ5, took the output of that through another Pultec MEQ5 and went into a rack-mounted MXR flanger, and then into an MXR phaser. We took the output of that into a Dolby unit on encode and took that into Pandora's Time line. We recorded that onto tape at +17 over 185 nW.

On the same song, we took the mix and ran the left and right channels through separate Fender Twins, out of the board onto a separate piece of tape. The Fender sound was very distorted.

As the song was ending, we would cut to the Fender amp recordings every four bars of the mix, and then to the normal signal straight out of the board, and we went back and forth every four bars. The desired effect was hi-fi/lo-fi. The end result was indeed very sick. Too bad I did all that stuff when I was younger, because nobody will let me mess up their records like that anymore.

Jeff Powell

Credits include: Afghan Whigs, Primal Scream, Alex Chilton, Lynyrd Skynyrd, the Allman Brothers, 16 Horsepower. See the Appendix for Jeff Powell's full bio.

One time, when I was working with a band on the Ardent label called Neighborhood Texture Jam, we basically needed a big disastrous noise on a track called "The Brucification Before Pilate." It was on an album called *Don't Bury Me In Haiti*. The song was in the key of E, and we borrowed a cheap old Fender Strat copy from a friend who didn't care what we did with it and strung it up with nothing but big low E strings. The band was so broke that it took all of the band's money to afford all of the E strings.

We put the guitar on a stand and ran it through a Marshall head with all the knobs turned up as far as they would go, and at the point in the song where we wanted this big noise, we cranked up a weed eater and ran it over the guitar strings above the pickup. The weed eater played the guitar for a few seconds before we really dug into it and blew it up. It took about eight seconds before the strings totally snapped and went everywhere. It was a really wonderful noise that was perfect for what we needed.

It took about 30 minutes to buy all those big E strings and string the guitar up, and it took about eight seconds to record it. It was definitely a one-take kind of thing. We added a little reverb to the sound, and I added a bit of EQ. It all came across on tape really well.

Dylan Dresdow

Credits include: Black Eyed Peas, will.i.am, Pink, Michael Jackson, Wu-Tang Clan, TLC. See the Appendix for Dylan Dresdow's full bio.

Once when I was at Record Plant, I saw analog tape machines gathering dust in the back of the room, and I freaked out and asked the assistant to get some shop tape for the 1/2-inch machines because I wanted to do an analog tape flange in the bridge of a song. Whenever I did it, he freaked out. He had never seen anything like that before. These are techniques and things that are really being lost.

Whenever I'm doing an analog tape flange, I'm really loose about it. I don't have to have my 1/2-inch machine aligned at +6 over 185 or +9 or, you know…Dolby SR or anything like that. Shop tape is fine for the majority of it, and sometimes even better because it is a little bit off.

There are a couple ways to do this, but I like to record a section of a song with some pre-roll and then play the two-track simultaneously with the DAW in record. I'd slow the two-track down by putting my thumb on the flange or using the deck's varispeed function, which gives it this deep sound like it's being sucked into a vortex. Then I'll VSO it up so it comes out exactly when I want it to. Whenever you do this, it's like you're playing gear like a musical instrument.

Nowadays, somebody would just put a flanger plug-in on the elements and automate the bypass and automate it. And while it's great and it's neat, there is a lost art form to a lot of the stuff with recordings we're doing, because major studios are failing. These techniques won't be passed on to the next generation of assistants if the major sound motels keep dying off. And I mean, you may only do an analog tape flange effect two or three times a year. Whenever you do those with a client in the room who has never seen or witnessed it before, they will be your client for life because they will really understand that you know what you're doing. If you know how to do that, you truly know how to EQ a kick drum, and you know all this stuff.

While it is a quite technical thing, you need to technically know how to do it— you need to do it and practice it and be proficient at it so that it actually sounds artful. Just doing it on a tape flange is one thing, but being able to pull it off so it sounds exactly like what you had envisioned before you could hear it…the room is high-fiving all around and experiencing each other because you pulled it off. You've added something to the song with that one production technique. If it sets up a section better than before, then you've done your job tastefully. But that's just one production technique.

Jim Dickinson

Credits include: the Klitz, Big Star, Ry Cooder, the Replacements, Toots Hibbert, Sleepy John Estes, Jason & the Scorchers, Mudhoney, Billy Lee Riley, Mojo Nixon and True Believers, the Rolling Stones, Bob Dylan, Arlo Guthrie, Flamin' Groovies, John Hiatt, Aretha Franklin, Primal Scream, Dan Penn. See the Appendix for Jim Dickinson's full bio.

I quit Ry Cooder in 1972 or early '73 to produce Dan Penn. Dan and I were going back and forth to Muscle Shoals a lot at the time. I was helping him get his first record, *Nobody's Fool*, mastered. I didn't have anything to do with that album, but on one of those trips to Muscle Shoals, he said, "Jimmy, why don't you produce me? I need to make another record. I think you ought to produce me." I said, "Dan! Right on!" So I started producing Dan's second record, which was called *Emmett the Singing Ranger Live in the Woods*. It's my greatest unreleased record!

We recorded quite a few songs for this project at Sam Phillips Recording [in Memphis] with Knox Phillips as the engineer. This is where we cut the session for this album with the two live Harleys. It was a song called "Tiny Hinys and Hogs." Yeah. "Tiny hinys and hogs, funky ladies love outlaws." It contains one of the greatest Dan Penn lines that I know of: "This chrome hog is a rollin' rocket. A two-wheeled Caddie with a highway sprocket." [Laughs] No one yet has written a motorcycle song at the level of a hot rod song, like "Little GTO." There is no motorcycle song that comes to that level. This song did, had we been able to finish the project.

Dan is the master of cutting a screwed-up demo, and he had this demo of "Tiny Hinys and Hogs," where he was slapping on his leg like this [imitates rhythm] and making the sound of a Harley-Davidson. Japanese motorcycles scream, but there is a rhythm to a Harley-Davidson engine. It goes ba-da-bump, ba-da-bump, ba-da-bump, and that was the rhythm of his hands. Not to be outdone, because Dan can come up with some crazy stuff, Dan had Gene Christman, a brilliant drummer, go in on the drum set and play this screwed-up hambone rhythm that Dan was doing.

I thought, "What we need now is some Harleys to play the percussion part, like bongos." So I got Campbell Kensinger and one of his other cronies from the family Nomads to bring their bikes into the studio. Campbell was an artist anyway. Campbell was in the center of the studio playing lead Harley. He had his buddy, who didn't really "get it," off in the corner playing rhythm Harley. Well the rhythm Harley was just playing. He just started the motor and let it run. Campbell was actually trying to get the motor on the beat. He was retarding the spark with his screwdriver to slow the engine down and giving it gas with the throttle to keep it from dying, so it was sort of choking out. Every time it would choke out, he would rev it up, and he was shooting like three feet of blue fire out of the exhaust. The whole studio was filling up with carbon monoxide. It was great! Eventually, Campbell got to the point where he was really playing the bike. Not only was he keeping this beat going, but when we got to this solo part, he was doing this saxophone thing. Dan was playing acoustic 12-string and playing on the floor, where he insisted on singing with the Harleys live in the vocal microphones.

Knox Phillips was engineering these sessions, and he was crazy as a rat at that point and willing to let me do anything. Knox is tight buddies with Mike Post, the Hollywood guy who does all the TV music, like *Hill Street Blues* and all that stuff. I had met Mike a couple of times, but we weren't what you would call "friends." Post had a session that was starting the next day at Phillips. There was another person from L.A. that was also with Mike who was a "somebody," too.

Anyway, they came in during the session, just as we were starting the bikes and all that garbage. Post was horrified by the whole thing, and he had to leave. The guy who was with him said, "No way in the world am I leaving. You go on. Just come back and get me later. I am going to stay here and watch this." [Laughs] Post was basically saying, "This is crazy. I know who these people are, and they should know better than this."

So Post returns a few hours later, and we are playing it back, and he says, "That's incredible. The motorcycle is playing the beat. It sounds like a saxophone." He just went crazy. I'm going, "Yeah, sure." I sort of had the attitude like the time to appreciate my genius is before I do it. You better believe I can do it. Of course the motorcycle is playing with the beat. Where did you think I was going to put it? Did you think I was going to bring them in here and have them play off the beat? I'm not going to bring some amateur to come in here and play the motorcycle! [Laughs] These men are professionals!

Everybody, when they hear the tape, thinks the bike is playing along with the instruments. Well, of course, what is happening is the instruments are playing with the bike. The bike is so hypnotic, and Gene Christman is such a brilliant drummer, that you hear Dan say on the tape, "Start your bikes, Campbell!" [Makes motorcycle sound] Then you hear the rhythm of the engine. Christman just played with the bike. It is so obvious, but nobody ever sees it.

Brian Ahern at Easter Island Surround. Row 2: Brian Ahern, Andrew Mendelson (owner/chief mastering engineer of Georgetown Masters), Doug Beal at Georgetown Masters / The McIntosh 275 amp used for headphones. Row 3: Emmylou Harris playing guitar for mic shoot-out between Neumann M 50s and Blue Bottle mics with capsules that emulate the M 50. Photos by Rick Clark.

Cue Mixes

Anyone who has ever recorded in a studio knows how crucial the proper headphone or monitor mix is to a good performance. For someone cutting on the floor, an unbalanced or distorted mix can blow the vibe of a session. Inheriting a bad set of phones will sometimes be enough to hang it up for the day.

Some players and singers want real hyped-sounding phones and mixes, and some couldn't care less. There are those who feel that phone volume works best at a relatively low level, while many gravitate toward turning their brains to oatmeal with wide-open volume.

Reading the dynamic of tastes and needs between different people is only part of the job an engineer has to deal with when setting up the proper phone or monitor mix to those recording.

For this chapter, we've enlisted six world-class engineers—Brian Ahern, David Briggs, Terry Brown, John Guess, Clif Norrell, and Jeff Powell—who have some very different takes on addressing the world of studio cue mixing.

Brian Ahern

Producing credits include: Emmylou Harris, Anne Murray, George Jones, Johnny Cash. See the Appendix for Brian Ahern's full bio.

I believe if musicians aren't hearing the best sound possible in their headphones, then they won't play the best possible. This is all part of extracting the best performance. It is one of the things you can do without saying anything. They seem to notice it and comment on it.

If you use tubes, you can work for long hours without fatigue. For my headphone mixes, I dedicated my McIntosh MC275 tube amps, which are relatively old, so the performers would get the best possible sound in their headphones.

Most studios just throw away the importance of this particular stage of the recording process, but that's where the performance of the artist starts...with what they're hearing. To me it's job number one—making sure everybody hears really, really well and can listen all day without fatigue. That is job number one, and then you move on to choosing and positioning your microphones and ordering lunch.

John Guess

Producing, engineering, and mixing credits include: Vince Gill, Suzy Bogguss, Reba McEntire, Patty Loveless, George Strait, Rod Stewart, Donna Summer, Kenny Loggins, Captain Beefheart, Funkadelic, Luther Vandross, Frank Sinatra, Jeff Beck, Stevie Wonder, John Fogerty. See the Appendix for John Guess's full bio.

With a cue mix, I like to create as friendly an atmosphere as possible. That usually means getting a good stereo mix of everything, except for the vocal. I like the musicians to be able to control that. Most of the studios that I work at in Nashville have the individual eight-fader cue mixers, made by Formula Sound, and that allows me to get a good stereo mix—along with six monos for individual controls, or what we call *more me's.*

With that stereo mix, I have a good mix of the band. There will be an individual one for the vocal. In the stereo mix, I will add reverb, with nothing too long or swimmy. That usually consists of some EMT 250 on one of the sends, and I'll use a Lexicon 480 on a small hall setting with a pretty healthy pre-delay. I will put that on another send. On the vocal, I just blend that with its own reverb, usually something like a Yamaha SPX-90, and feed it on its own fader.

What I usually do is set up the phones prior to the session with a preexisting basic track tape that has similar instrumentation. That puts me that much further ahead in the game when the musicians walk in. That way, I have a general setting of everything, and I can tweak it from there.

I'm fond of the small mixer-style of cue boxes that are often called *more-me boxes* in Nashville. They are called that because they allow the musician to customize the cue mix with individual faders, which enables each of the players to hear more of himself in his cue mix.

When I set it up, I will always leave the more me's down on the faders out on the floor in the studio. I will go around to each station and just bring up the stereo mix to where it is comfortable for me. I will then leave it up to the individual musicians to bring the more me's up to their personal taste.

The only thing that is scary about that is, after a session you can walk out and somebody will have his or her more me turned all the way up, and there will be nothing else on. You can usually discover that because that person will start having timing problems during the session. If all he is hearing is himself, he will start getting out of the pocket. I can usually tell him to back it down a little bit if we have a problem.

If you happen to be using a click track on one of the faders, and someone has it up too loud, sometimes it will bleed and you can't get rid of it later. Acoustic guitarists are famous for this. You just have to be aware of that.

For string bass sessions, it is a whole other matter. I prefer using single headphones if they are available. That allows players to hear what is going on in the room a little better, and then they can just follow the conductor. It gives them enough to "pitch" in the phones.

Every singer is different. Some adapt to phones easily and don't have any pitch problems. Then there is the other type who sings normally until he puts phones on. Then he drifts sharp or flat consistently. Each individual has to experiment and find out what works for him. He might need to pull one phone back a little bit to hear what is going on in the room.

When the "A" players come in, there is usually very little discussion about the phone mix. If there is something that needs to be adjusted, they will usually voice that right away. Since they have their own faders and pan pots, they can position that mono signal anywhere in the field they want to.

My headphone preference, even when I am mixing and just for comparison, is the old model Fostex T20. Not the newer ones. They are the old flat ones. I still prefer them over everything because they don't have that real hype-y high end, and they are pretty smooth.

I've found that some drummers will put little earplugs in their ears before they put their phones on, just to cut down some of the level. Larrie London had his own little earphone system that he put in his ears and then put those gun mufflers or sound mufflers over his ears. If they are professional drummers, they often have their own setup. They'll put on their small phones and then actually muffle outside sound with sound-deadening devices. That way, they can hear the sounds more immediately, without having to turn it up as loud.

If the session is an all-acoustic bluegrass recording, then you can often go without phones. The musicians will gather around and let the leakage happen and go for that. Most of the things that I do, however, are a more controlled situation. I usually have the drums out in the room by themselves, with maybe the bass player. Everyone else is pretty isolated.

A number of years ago, I did have a singer one time who was never satisfied with the cue system. He could never hear anything. One day he said, "I want to hear more highs in the lows." I said, "I'm not sure how to go about doing that." What I ended up doing was taking a stereo graphic equalizer and setting it up in front of him. I ran the cue mix through the graphic and said, "Here, have at it!" I let him EQ any way he wanted to. After the session I saw how he had set it, and it was pretty frightening. The level was even more frightening. Over the years, the consequences of playing phones too loud can be very alarming.

Jeff Powell

Producing, engineering, and mixing credits include: Alex Chilton, Big Star, Lynyrd Skynyrd, Allman Brothers, Afghan Whigs, Primal Scream. See the Appendix for Jeff Powell's full bio.

At Ardent, we have a system that uses an eight-channel submixer that our technical department designed themselves. These submixers have, on each of these channels, a separate panning control and a level control, as well as an overall volume control. They are on rolling stands with long cords on them, which makes them convenient to roll around anywhere in the studio. This means that each musician has the option to add to, take out, or mix all or none of the components that are sent down these lines.

I usually set up a stereo mix with the drummer as we are getting drum sounds and send that down the first two channels. I always make the sends pre-fader and globally select channel-safe mode, so I have complete freedom to listen to what I want in the control room without affecting their mix at all. For the rest of the instruments I will take a direct multitrack-out or tape-out feed into the corresponding channels of the cue amp. This gives them complete freedom for their cue mixes as well—not just from what I need or want to hear, but from what their band mates want to hear as well. I usually save back two modules—say 7 and 8— to set up an auxiliary stereo effects mix. In an instant, players are then able to add as much reverb or echo as they may want to hear on their vocals or instruments.

They can make it sound like they are in a bathroom or an airport hanger, or they can make it sound completely dry. This is my basic starting place during tracking sessions.

Usually the musicians are so happy to have the control over their own sounds that they don't ask for extra EQ, but I can provide extra if they want it.

In overdub mode, to make things easier, I will usually send a stereo mix down Modules 1 and 2, and I will give them what I call a *more-me* track.

If the lead singer is going to blow through four tracks of him doing a song and comp it later, I'll send him the stereo mix on 1 and 2, which includes his voice. If he can't hear himself over the mix enough, then he can turn up his voice in the more-me track and add that in.

Sometimes you might run out of the eight tracks, but we cut the Allman Brothers live with two drummers, two guitar players, organ, bass, percussion, and lead vocals, and it worked perfectly.

At Ardent, we use the Fostex T20s for phones. Sometimes drummers don't like them, especially ones who move their head around a lot, because the phones can fly off their heads.

The submixers have red overload lights. Sometimes I can go out on the floor, and they will be all lit up and the phones are completely distorted. So I will sneak out there and tweak it up a little bit, and all of a sudden they can hear. It amazes me how little importance some musicians place on headphone fidelity and mixes. The only thing I can think is that some of them are used to lousy headphone mixes.

We also have a Tascam 20-watt amplifier on top of each eight-channel mixer. We have two different rows of input holes that you can plug into. In fact, six headphones can run out of one box. It's great if you are doing a group vocal. Anyway, there are four top-row inputs and two bottom-row inputs. The top inputs are connected to this 20-watt amplifier. It can get so loud that it can practically melt the phones. I've had a drummer throw off the phones one time because they were burning his ears. He had them up so loud that they were hot as a firecracker. I've never had anybody say they weren't loud enough, even the deafest people. Drummers and lead vocalists seem to like it the loudest.

Back in my days as an assistant, I've seen engineers cop an attitude of, "Well, tough," or make feeble attempts to fix things. When you put phones on, you can immediately tell if something is distorting. I've always believed that if a musician says there is something wrong with the phones or the mix, nine out of ten times it's not because he is stupid, it is because there is something wrong that I can help him with. That is why I always have a headphone box by me in the control room, so I can hear exactly what they are hearing. It usually takes about two seconds to know what the matter is.

Clif Norrell

Producing, engineering, and/or mixing credits include: R.E.M., John Hiatt, the Replacements, Indigo Girls, Billy Idol, Widespread Panic, Tom Petty, Gin Blossoms, Jeff Buckley. See the Appendix for Clif Norrell's full bio.

About 50 percent of my projects use monitor wedges, as opposed to phones. This is primarily due to the fact that many of my projects are bands who need to have a gig atmosphere approximated, in order to capture the most natural performance of the band or artist.

It depends on the artist, but lots of times I will isolate the drummer, and he will be the only one with headphones on. I will have everyone else use floor wedges. I try to keep everything as live as possible, except for the drums. We can usually get away with not having to baffle off too many guitar amps. I just put close mics on the guitar amps and still have a live vocal and don't worry about leakage too much.

Concerning wedges, I basically don't have a preference. We usually use whatever rentals are available, usually JBLs or EVs. We just power them off of the headphone amplifiers and use auxiliary sends for those. I record on a lot of old consoles. The kind of board I'm using dictates how many sends they have, but I try to send a stereo headphone mix to the drummer and then use wedges for whoever else is out there in a live band situation, which is usually what I work on.

Oftentimes I will do a standard headphone mix for everyone, and I try to keep things fairly isolated when I do that.

Do I prefer using wedges over phones? I do and I don't. Sometimes the leakage gets a little critical. You have to have a good room to isolate the drums in and a big enough room to put everybody else in. You really have to have two good, decent-size rooms for that normally. It does work, and the bands seem to like it a lot more. It is more like a gig for them. They seem to be able to hear a little bit better. It works well if you don't have a whole lot of mixes to give to them and they can stand closer to their amps. It also makes the guitars sound a little bit different when they have some direct feedback to their amp and they can walk closer to it or do what they need to physically do to get in touch with their amps. Sometimes when they are off in another room, they are not going to get the kind of sustain and interplay with the amp that they need to.

I tend to do vocals in the control room sometimes. It just depends on what the artist likes and what he is used to and feels comfortable with.

With R.E.M., we generally used Sony MDR-V6 headphones for *Automatic for the People*, and they liked them quite a bit because they are a lot hypier. They have a lot more high end than most other phones. I tend to use those quite a bit, and I listen through those sometimes when I'm mixing as well, just to check the mix.

I also like the Fostex T20s. They seem to be able to get really loud, and a lot of bands like it really loud. They don't tend to blow up very often or clip out.

Even though we used phones for tracking on R.E.M., we cut some of the guitar and keyboard overdubs in the control room. Those were things where we would just put an amp out in the studio.

I recorded the Jayhawks, and we did lots of singing in the control room instead of using phones out on the floor. A couple of times we actually had them holding their own mics and singing in the control room with no headphones to the monitors. They could go where they wanted to; they loved that, and it seemed to work fine. They sang mostly through Shure SM58s and SM7s.

In that case, I allowed the bleed to become part of the natural mix. As long as you don't have anything on tape that is really loud, that you are not going to use, the leakage is really not a problem. I know a lot of people are probably afraid to do that, or they say, "You can't do that" or "You have to put the speakers out of phase." You can do that, but it sounds weird for the people who are singing or playing to the monitors. They can't hear as well. We usually just leave the speakers in phase and turn it up for them and mainly keep it from feeding back. That works quite a bit.

I find it can help singer's pitch quite a bit, because there is some kind of psychoacoustic pitch change that you get with headphones. I'm sure there is a technical explanation for it, but I think that it helps a lot of singers to sing with monitors.

When Amy and Emily of the Indigo Girls would sing together, we used floor monitors, and that worked quite well. We would have a baffle between them or have them looking at each other with a fairly directional mic for vocals.

I don't think [the bleed] makes it sounds better, but I do think that it makes the performance so much better that it doesn't seem to affect the overall sonic quality that much. You might get a cleaner recording by not having the wedges. You could probably isolate things a little bit more and get the exact sound on the exact instrument that you want without having to worry about bleed when you are using headphones, but I think the advantages from a production aspect of the performance far outweigh any kind of loss in overall sound quality.

Wedges work well for me. I think singers must feel a little uncomfortable at times with phones because they are not hearing their own voice. They are hearing it through all the electronics and whatever kind of effects you've got on it. They may be used to that, but some of them may not be. They may not be as in touch with the music as they could be if the music was coming out of the speaker, even from an overdub aspect. From the live band aspect, most bands prefer monitors.

If you are using headphones for a band session, and they have two guitar players, it seems to work a lot better to put them on stereo cues with them panned left and right to keep it from becoming a wall of mush in the phones. That way they can hear themselves playing.

I quite often work on old Neve consoles that don't have that many sends, and you've just got to make do on those. I don't usually work with the systems in some studios where you send a submix out and have the people do their own mixes. Generally, I do the mixes for them and go with what I generally think they need, and I go from their suggestions and change it when they need things changed.

I think the headphone mix is so critical that it is important to give the musicians and singers something that will inspire them, like a big-sounding stereo mix, as opposed to something that is all cluttered. I think it deserves more attention than it gets. You should get it right, ideally, before recording. It is as critical as spending time to get good sounds to go on tape. Getting the phone mix is critical to the session, especially when you are tracking. If things aren't happening, it can seriously cause problems. When it is right, the artist's mind is freed up, and you get a better performance.

I usually track a lot of people at the same time, and you need to make sure that everyone is happy with his own mix. I will generally start out with the drummer on one mix and everybody else on another mix, and then a vocalist on another mix. Hopefully, we can keep it that way. If someone still isn't happy with what they are getting, you can set up another mix for him.

Sometimes a musician will ask you to turn things up until all of a sudden you are wondering, "God, how can he listen to this?" So it is a good idea to go around in between takes and check his mix and make sure that everything is working right. Don't just use the control room headphones and flip through his mixes, because his phones might be flapping out or doing something strange. You need to hear what he is hearing.

Terry Brown

Producing credits include: Rush, Blue Rodeo, Klaatu, Cutting Crew. See the Appendix for Terry Brown's full bio.

Headphone mixes are such a personal thing. You can never really be sure that you are going to keep everybody happy. I did a production with a group that was really centered around a guy in the band who did all of his writing at home with headphones. As a result, his headphone mix had very specific requirements. I had to get him a power amp to drive his headphones, which were a pair of AKG Parabolics with double drivers in each earpiece. They were seriously loud.

We had a Takamine acoustic guitar with a DI and a little chorusing and live mics and vocals. He would cut guitar and vocals as a bed track with no click, and we built everything around that. Even though his requirements weren't very complicated in terms of other instruments playing, he had to have his mix exactly right, with the right kind of reverb and decay, and he wanted the guitar in stereo. It had to fit exactly, and he had to be totally comfortable with each tune, and things changed for each tune. That was a very specific thing. He could not record unless it was perfect.

Then there are situations in which you have a band and three or four different headphone mixes because everybody's requirements are so different. From isolating different instruments, it is very difficult to give everybody the perfect feed. The guitar player always wants more guitar, and the drummer always wants less guitar. With a band, you need at least three or four headphone mixes. Otherwise, it is totally impossible to keep everybody happy.

I find that with the volume that you naturally get off of drum kits, it is hard to give a drummer (especially in a very loud, ambient, warehouse-type room) a really good headphone mix on the drums. This is because you are hearing so much from outside of the headphones. The actual ambient volume of the drums is such that it is very difficult to create the right vibe inside the phones. In this situation, it is really a case of mainly putting hi-hat, kick, and snare in the phones and letting most of the other sounds just bleed into the phones. This problem is especially true when you are playing to clicks and you're running in sync.

You can only work at such a loud volume for an hour or two. The fatigue is dramatic if you are working at too high a volume.

Some players cannot work unless the phones are screaming loud. It can get dangerously loud sometimes. You can get a lot of distortion involved, and then you aren't hearing the signal properly. Volume is definitely something that has to be watched. It can be devastating listening to a click screaming loud in your phones for a period of more than eight hours. As the day progresses it get louder and louder, and the ears shut down. I'll sometimes set a limit on it and say, "This is it. You are not getting any more. You are going have to concentrate, or we are going to have to change the sound of the click."

Sometimes changing the sound of the click, such as making it sound like a cowbell, will fix things. Many drummers like to play with odd percussion elements in the phones so they can pick up on internal beats. I usually tailor those for the drummer and find something that the drummer is totally comfortable with.

With Rush, Neil [Peart] usually used a pair of AKG Parabolics, and he would listen to them at a fairly loud volume, but he always knew his limits as far as volume was concerned.

I think the more sophisticated the player you are working with, the less of a problem playing with headphones becomes. They usually have a good handle on what they are playing and how they are playing vis-à-vis the time on the click. Moving in and out of time with a click is not a problem for them because they have such a good internal clock that they can move around the click and always find their way back. With less experienced drummers, it can sometimes be a real problem because they are not players with the same level of sophistication. In order to give them that little more security, the click gets louder and louder. Eventually, they are fighting to stay with the click. Volume then becomes the only real substitute for lack of finesse. It is certainly not the answer, but that is the way it tends to go, I find.

I'm using this pair of Sony Professional MDR-7506s. I like those a lot. They have a really wide frequency spectrum with a very solid bottom end. I find they are great for vocalists. I don't think I would use them for drums. I did try them a couple of times, but they have such a wide frequency range that by the time you get the bass drum to a point where it feels comfortable, they are usually bottoming out. Then, of course, you end up turning them up a little bit louder and a little louder, and then it is not a workable situation. You need a brasher type of headphone for drums, more like the gold AKG models. I forget the number of them.

I do most of my work with three- or four-piece bands. Normally, I create my mixes at the console, using three, four, or five submixes created at the console.

The SSL has got a very convenient submix situation. With anything that is being done as a sort of final cut, if we are overdubbing, I'll send stereo mixes. But in terms of doing tracks, mono mixes are usually more than adequate.

The older Neves are a tough setup—the two-pot, four-button type of syndrome. It is very hard to give a number of separate mixes on a standard old Neve. I'll usually steal the reverb send for headphone mixes in those kinds of cases. At least then you can do another complete setup.

I use players in the control room so much that the headphone mix is not really a major concern of mine. Sometimes a guitar player will want to use phones so he can immerse himself in sound, rather than sitting in a room and being distracted by other sounds and people talking. Bands do get a little boisterous.

It's hard to find a headphone mix that will satisfy a guitar player who desires to be in the room with a big rig feeding back and so on. In that case, I think the AKG Parabolics are the way to go. They are more than loud enough for what you need.

Unless it is a specific situation where a guitar player needs to be in the studio with his amp, I would much prefer him sitting in the control room with me so we can communicate quickly. That way, we are hearing all the nuances in the playing that he wants to hear, coming out of the control room monitors.

Personally, I prefer having the drummer cut alone in the tracking room and having the other players record in the control room.

Hopefully, the band is well-enough rehearsed that it won't take all day to lay the tracks. That is a preferable way of doing things.

I like the idea of cutting the bass player later, as an overdub. It seems that bass finds the pocket better when played to the control room monitors than when the bassist is sitting in the room with the drummer and hearing drum bleed and drum signal conflicting with one another.

If you are going to cut in the room with the drums, one way to achieve a better connection to what's being played is to sit on your amp. Then you have a problem to consider, which is bleed into the drums. You are kind of stuck. Headphones for a bass player are a really tough call, especially when he is in the room with the drummer. More than likely, you are not going to really hear what you are doing. It's a rough version of what you are playing. You don't hear the fidelity of the bass. There is no headphone in the world that can complete with that. It is much nicer to do it in an overdub situation.

David Briggs

Producing and engineering credits include: Neil Young, Spirit, Royal Trux. See the Appendix for David Briggs's full bio.

Headphones are for *persona non grata* in my studios. There is no way in the world that you can put headphones on and work for eight hours. They are for people who want to lose the top end of their ears in about an hour.

Most musicians go into the studio, put their headphones on, do this and do that, and they putz around, and their energy and focus are history by the three-, four-, or five-hour mark. When you work like I do, which is without phones, I get 15 or 16 hours of playing a day out of bands, and they love to do it. They go right back out and play some more.

I set the band up and build it in such a way that everybody who is playing in the band has a sweet spot like you hear on stage. It's how big of a sweet spot you can get that is the name of the game. If you have a really active, physical band, like Pearl Jam or someone like that, who is bouncing all over the stage, there is not any way to cover and fill the whole stage. In most cases, however, when you take them into a studio, the physical stage movements come out of the performance, and they begin to work in a smaller area. If you put them in a sweet spot with no headphones and you get that P.A. to where it sounds great, then they don't have to work and scream their heads off. They hear everything. You don't get that feeling from phones.

I don't like wedges, but sometimes I use them for drums. Sometimes I may let the drummer use headphones. In truth, after five, six, or seven hours bashing with cymbals cutting through their heads, the drummer's top end is gone anyway. I like to use the big side fills and throw them in a big four-corner configuration, not in the room but around the band—two coming at them and two going past them, two fronts and two backs. I surround them with the vocal. I don't put the band into the P.A. I just put the vocal up in there, except for a little bit of the kick drum, so some people can hear a little better. It is such a great way to make a record. It is infinitely less fatiguing to your ears. It is a lot more supportive for the band because instead of having one guy out there in this lonely little dark room with his headphones and his one instrument, censoring and editing himself as he plays along, trying to attain the perfect part, he is out there with three or four of his mates, and they are all mashing and bashing. The end result is a whole different story.

Drum Teching

Drummers can make a glorious noise, but when a noticeable percentage of the sounds hitting tape are undesirable gear squeaks and creaks cluttering up the groove, it can help wreck the vibe of an otherwise killer performance.

Drums may be made to take a beating, but like anything else, there is a point where negligence or poor maintenance will not only cause your gear to sound bad, it'll cost you jobs. It's the old what-goes-around-comes-around routine.

As a result, most producers and engineers encounter situations in which it is necessary to troubleshoot drums that aren't producing optimum sounds.

We rounded up Steve Ebe, Pat Foley, Don Gehman, Robert Hall, Ronan Chris Murphy, and Craig Krampf to provide helpful tips to get the best results out of a kit, live and in the studio. In this chapter, they offer some great commonsense pointers and very creative problem-solving ideas that really work.

Steve Ebe

Credits include: Human Radio, Dixie Chicks, Kim Richey, Sonny Landreth, Shawn Lane, Duck Dunn, Little River Band, Al Kooper, Adrian Belew, the Box Tops with Alex Chilton, Marty Stuart, Rodney Crowell. See the Appendix for Steve Ebe's full bio.

The single most important thing is to have a well-maintained, professional-quality drum set with new heads. DW drums are some of the best, in my opinion. They are loud, punchy, clean, and easy to tune over a wide range. It's also nice to have some different sounds for different styles of music, so I have a variety of other vintage kits, such as Gretsch, Ludwig, and Camco.

I usually muffle only the bass drum, using the hourglass-shaped pillow made by DW. It attaches to the shell with Velcro, so it doesn't move around. It is low mass and low profile, so it's not soaking up any more volume than necessary.

If I find it necessary to muffle the snare, I use gaffer's tape in one of two ways. Either I loop the tape with the adhesive facing out or I fold two or three waffle-like creases in the tape before applying it near the rim. Moongel is also a handy product and a good way to muffle a drum.

Having a variety of sounds available is crucial. The drummer should always have a wide variety of sticks, brushes, and bass drum beaters. A variety of heads should be handy for last-minute tonal changes.

I use Remo Coated Ambassadors for the tops of snares and toms, Remo Clear Ambassadors for bottoms of toms, Remo Hazy Ambassador snare bottoms, and Remo Powerstroke 3 Clear for bass drums.

I have found that a handy way to carry the spare heads is to remove the center post from an old fiber cymbal case and place them in there. It is the perfect size.

I think a lot of people screw up by not paying much attention to the place where the cymbal sits on the stand. You should use the felt doughnut-shaped pads that are situated on either side of the cymbals, but don't screw them down too tight with the wingnut. There is also a nylon sleeve or surgical-tubing type of sleeve that goes over the metal post. A lot of drummers let those things wear out, or they don't use them at all. As a result, you have the cymbal touching metal, and that creates all kinds of rattles and sounds. I always keep a bunch of the sleeves in my stick bag, so when I go out and play on someone else's kit, I'm ready.

Pat Foley

Credits include: Slingerland Drums Director of Custom Products, Gregg Bissonette, Bernard Purdie, Faith No More, Los Lobos, Mötley Crüe. See the Appendix for Pat Foley's full bio.

Microphones have no preconceptions. They don't know whether you have a big drum or a small drum in front of them. A lot of people will say, "I want a really big drum because I want a really big sound." In fact, I have done a lot of records where I have used very small drums that just sound huge, because with a smaller drum you can generally tune the head lower and still maintain a little bit of tension on it. Because the bottom head responds quicker, you tend to oftentimes get a smaller drum to actually sound bigger. I think it would surprise a lot of people to see the kits that many of their "heroes" are playing are not nearly as big as they might suspect.

If you have a drum set and it isn't very big, I wouldn't assume that you are not going to get the sound you are looking for. A lot of times, nice, small, traditional sizes of drums, like 12-inch, 13-inch, and 16-inch, will sound extremely large in a recording studio. I wouldn't get preconceived ideas about, "You need to buy power toms to sound powerful." Those are marketing ploys, basically. [Laughs] That is a way to sell drums.

At Slingerland, we are sort of getting back to offering classic sizes and setups. The fact is that most of the great records that you and I grew up listening to, that we loved so much, were not made with "power" toms and all of these elaborate types of super-deep bass drums that drum companies offer nowadays. They were made with standard traditional-sized toms that evolved because they worked very well. It has only been in the last 10 years that everybody seems to think that drum purchasing is very complicated and that you have to be educated to all of the depths and diameters.

Ultimately, a drum set is one instrument. If I had to give one overall tip for tuning, I would say to think of them as one instrument, rather than a collection of instruments hanging together, and tune them accordingly. If you strike your 12-inch tom tom, and your 16-inch resonates a little bit, don't be quick to dampen down that 16-inch to stop that resonance. Just tune it in such a way that it rings sympathetically with the 12-inch, so that it enhances the overall sound of your set. You just want to be conscious when you tune drums of the harmonics that you are hearing, and make sure that when you strike one, and the one next to it rings a little bit, that it is basically ringing in tune. Then it all becomes one instrument and sounds much more musical than deadening and isolating the individual components.

Most people have their own techniques of choosing the intervals that they want to use, but the important thing in tuning concerns the relationship between the top and bottom heads of the drum. If I had to give someone a quick tuning lesson, I would say to tune the tom toms with a tension that feels reasonable on the top head; snug it up and then start with your bottom head matched to the sound of the top head, to where they are basically creating the same pitch. Then, once you've become tuned into what you are listening for, strike the top head, and you will hear a slight waver between the top and bottom heads. That is like a phasing situation because there is a slight delay before the bottom head responds. What I would normally do is have someone bang on that top head, while I just slightly detune the bottom head until I can hear those two pitches ring together. Then you will have a nice sustaining note.

Another thing that people do, if their drums don't have the sustain they want, or they don't have a big enough sound—they adapt their drums to the RIMS Mounting System. That is a trademarked product that happens to come standard on the drums we make here at Slingerland. It stands for *Resonant Isolation Mounting System*. RIMS is the most popular of these types of mounting systems. What is does is suspend the drums by the tension rods, in effect, so you don't have to place a mount on the shell, which tends to restrict the vibrations.

Don Gehman

Producer credits include: Tracy Chapman, R.E.M., John Mellencamp, Hootie & the Blowfish. See the Appendix for Don Gehman's full bio.

Drummers who usually play live often hit cymbals way too loud in relation to the drums. Generally speaking, it is my biggest problem in the studio as a producer/engineer. As much presence that you want to dig out of drum heads, you often wind up dragging a lot of cymbals in through the drum mics. Over the years, my problem is to try to figure out how to maintain a balance in the set where the cymbals aren't totally making noise all over the record.

DW drums are a solution. I haven't found anything that comes close. Most of that is because of sheer level. They are the loudest drums I have found so far. I have measured them on meters, and they just seem to be a good 6 dB louder. It is the same way with the kick drums. It is louder. That means you are ahead right off the bat.

I carry cymbals around with me, and if a drummer is an especially hard hitter, I will go for the thinner cymbals. Zildjian has got these cymbals that are thinner and quieter. Maybe they are called "A" customs. They are a little shorter duration, but more than anything they don't take up as much 2-kHz midrange in the area where I am boosting up the drums; I don't pull up quite as much of that on cymbals. It kind of works itself out in the long run.

Tuning tricks are hard to describe. I am the drum tech on my session, so I usually tune drums on most sessions for the drummer. The search on each drum to find whatever sweet spot it has got is the best trick I know. You should take them down all of the way and then start bringing them up, and you can feel the spot where the drum starts to come alive. You then work both heads around that sweet spot and try to get the drum to speak as clearly and loudly as you can.

I like drums that are real pitch curvy. I like snares that go "boing," as well as the toms. That usually means unequal tuning between the heads, top to bottom. Generally, I set up the bottom heads lower than the top ones, which I think might be upside down from what a lot of other people do.

I don't use any padding, except on kick drums. On kick, I will use those little DW hourglass pads. I use front heads with small holes, as small as I can get away with. I usually encounter trouble if I have the kick drum totally sealed up. It is hard to get the resonance of the drum at the right duration. That is my biggest problem with front heads, at least for the way I put the bottom end together. They seem to eat up space that I would like the bass [guitar] to have. Drummers love it, and certainly it adds a lot of tone and action, but it is right in the heart of where I would like to put a bass guitar. It is that 150-Hz to 200-Hz area that gets gobbled up when the front head is sealed.

Building tunnels is probably the fix that I use most of the time on drums that aren't DWs, to get the kick drum to work. I will build tunnels out in front of the kick drum to extend the front mic so that I can get more tone and also to get me more rejection, because the drums aren't loud enough.

I will take a piece of foam, mic stands, and blankets and basically extend the shell. The tunnel would be maybe 2 feet long. I do that with most drums because you wind up with so much stuff going into the kick drum.

I usually use a mic on the front of the head, as well as one inside. That allows you to move that mic more out in front of the kick, so you can affect the resonance of the drum.

Robert Hall

Credits include: Memphis Drum Shop (owner) custom drum and live/studio tech clients: R.E.M., Mickey Curry, Chris Layton, John Hampton, Jim Gaines, Joe Hardy, Jim Dickinson. See the Appendix for Robert Hall's full bio.

First off, new heads are the best thing you can do to get a great sound, live or in the studio. Heads go dead just like guitar strings do, but most people don't address that nearly as often as they do their guitar strings. Generally, the stuff that comes on drums when they are new is less than the best quality to begin with because that is a way they can keep the costs down.

The bottom or resonant heads really have almost as much to do with the overall sound of the drum as the head you are hitting on. Many drummers replace the top and still keep the bottom heads that came with the drum when they were new.

One of the most common unknowns concerns setting up the snare wires properly on the snare drum. If those aren't centered on the bottom of the drum, then it is nearly impossible to get rid of the extraneous snare buzz that goes on. It is most important to set up that snare drum with the snares (when they are engaged and tensioned up) an equal distance from each side of the drum on the bottom. If they are pulled to one side or the other, it is going to drive you crazy trying to get rid of that buzz.

When all of that is set up properly and you still have got some kind of sympathetic buzz going, you can detune the tension rods on either side of the snare wires themselves, the two closest to it on either side. You can actually detune a little bit, and a lot of the time that'll take the buzz that one of the tom toms is causing away.

A cool trick to get resonance out of a floor tom is to take the felt washers [like you use on cymbal stands], or you can take a little 2- or 3-inch foam square, and set them under the legs of the floor tom. By just getting it up off the ground, it doubles the resonant factor of the drum.

Concerning the bass drum, a lot of times you will oil the hinges but not realize that the spring itself, on the pedal, can be making a lot of noise. Sometimes newer springs and newer pedals make noise, and you can literally stretch them by pulling the beater forward a little bit and doing it back and forth before you ever put the pedal on the drum. You can stretch that spring, and it gets some of the kinks of the manufacturing out of it, and it'll quiet it up that way. That is without using any oil or anything.

When a drummer has a whole lot of ringing in his toms that he wants to get out, but duct taping on the heads seems to choke or take the sound away too much, you can drop three or four cotton balls inside the tom toms. When you hit the drums, the cotton balls kind of come off the heads and then they settle back down, and it is like this little natural muting system. It is kind of like if you were to hit the drum and then press it with your finger, only the cotton balls are doing it without you having to touch it. You still get a really nice, full, round drum sound, but then it stops the ring just a little bit after the note. Naturally, the larger the toms, the more cotton balls you can put in there.

When you are using a bass drum without the front head and using a lot of packing, you get a lot of attack and punch, but you sometimes tend to lose that low end that is desirable on your bass drum sound.

In the old days, we would take a '20s- or '30s-style marching band bass drum that was 26- to 28-inches in diameter with calf heads front and back, and set that drum in front of the drummer's bass drum and not only mike the kit bass drum, but also mike the front side of the big calfskin bass drum, which was acting like an ambient woofer. It added all of this low end that you could mix into the final sound and really give some low end to this otherwise just punchy kind of bass drum sound. That is a trick producer Jim Dickinson taught me about 25 years ago. I've used that so many times it is crazy, but it really works great. [Laughs]

If you leave that front bass drum head on, you really do get more volume, resonance, and more of everything out of the drum, if you can work it. From a drummer's perspective, sitting on the stool and playing, you can feel and hear so much more of the bass drum when you do that than if you have got that front head off. If you feel good about the way your drum sounds, then you play better. You can hear it and feel it better, and you are depending less on monitor mixes and playing more acoustically with other instruments.

Craig Krampf

Drum credits include: Alice Cooper, Santana, Alabama, Son Volt, the Church, the Motels, Kim Carnes. See the Appendix for Craig Krampf's full bio.

When I was younger, no one seemed to know anything about bearing edges. There weren't publications out like there are now for younger drummers to learn about certain things.

The bearing edge is where the head sits on the drum. If that bearing edge has lumps on it, or if it is rough in one area, or if that area is a little higher or lower than the rest of the bearing edge, then your head isn't seated on that drum properly.

I have known a number of people who, when they change heads, have become very fanatical about looking over that bearing edge.

If you are very careful, and you don't take too much off, you can use a little light sandpaper or steel wool and maybe smooth some rough spots out. Nevertheless, there are professionals out in drum stores who really have some great equipment and work on bearing edges. Those can always be straightened out. It's one of those little things that adds up to ensuring the high quality of your sound.

Around 1980, I went to using clear Remo Ambassador drum heads, and I went to using a Pro-Mark square felt beater. As a result, I am not denting my bass drum head. With round beaters you start denting the head and then it's like you start chasing your tail. For years, Dr. Scholl's foot pads were the famous thing to use to help prevent that problem. While I was growing up, no manufacturer made any sort of bass drum pads, so in the old days it was Dr. Scholl's foot pads. Nevertheless, the round beater would wear through that, and you would put another on, and you would just start chasing that 'cause you didn't want to dent or break your head. Now there are actual manufacturers out there who make special dots and special things that you can put on your head to prevent that damage.

Recording is like being under the microscope, and every little thing does matter in the studio. Any time anything is taped or stuck on top of a drum head, you are killing sound and certain frequencies. You are deadening your head. I was absolutely amazed when I went to that clear head with a square beater. My bass drum sound improved at least 60 percent. There were actual lows engineers could show me they were getting now on that drum that didn't exist before. Some people maybe have a little bit of trouble since the square felt beater weighs perhaps just a little bit more. The action isn't quite as quick, and maybe if you are a real "funk drummer" or "fusion drummer," you probably couldn't get the quick action out of it. Regardless, that is one of the tips for bass drum that works for me.

If I'm doing something live, I have always been in the habit to have a spare bass drum pedal and a spare snare drum sitting right behind me on stage. It's a wretched feeling to have your bass drum pedal go down or to break a snare head and not have a replacement. I was caught once or twice when I was very young. In the studio, I've got three pedals and usually seven to nine snare drums that come along with me.

Even if you're playing a dive club, and you feel it might not be the greatest gig in the world, you're still playing. You should still have pride in your instrument, and you should take preventative measures—just in case something would happen.

You should give the engineer enough time before the other players get there to get the drum sounds right. If you have the time, the studio is available, it fits in everybody's schedule, and it is not going to cost a fortune, I love to get set up the night before and have the time to just have you and the engineer there and take the time to experiment and find the best area in that particular studio and try different mics and things. More drummers—and musicians in general—need to be understanding of the engineer's position.

Nashville work is highly unionized, and there are certain start times, like 10 a.m., 2 p.m., and 6 p.m.: three-hour sessions with an hour in between. I've heard of certain drummers in town who will stroll in about 10 'til 10 a.m. That doesn't give the engineer time to get a drum sound. Other musicians do the same thing. Everyone is part of a team trying to work together and trying to have great sonics. People should be more giving with their time. The more time that I give, the better I am going to sound. It is for my benefit to come in an hour or two earlier for whatever is necessary.

Ronan Chris Murphy

Producer, engineer, and/or mixing credits include: King Crimson, Steve Morse, Terry Bozzio, Grupo Irakere, Steve Stevens. See the Appendix for Ronan Chris Murphy's full bio.

One of the big problems with drums concerns the fact that people will tune and perform drums in a way that isn't really directly related to what they hope would be coming out of the speakers. People often tune and play drums in ways that are inappropriate for the song. For instance, if you want really big, punchy "in your face" drums that are going to cut through big, thick guitars, it's just not going to happen if your drums are really resonant and have a lot of sustain to them. There are a lot of tricks we can try that might be able to mitigate that problem at the mix stage, but it's the kind of thing where, if you want your drums to make a hard cracking sound but they are actually making a ringing sound, you've really shot yourself in the foot in terms of getting to that "cracking" sound on the record. It's the same way the other way around. If you're doing an acoustic jazz record and you really want the drums to sing and sustain, but they're super tight or super dead, you've kind of shot yourself in the foot for trying to get to that end goal.

This is an extremely common problem that I run into, and I run into it with world-famous drummers and bands just out of high school. That said, you never run into this with great session drummers. They go, "Okay, we're doing that kind of tune," and they tune their drums, and you put one mic on the other side of the room, and it's practically there.

Calexico's John Convertino (photo by Rick Clark) / Steve Ebe (drums) and Garry Tallent (bass) (photo by Rick Clark). Row 2: Studio A, Ardent Recording - Lynyrd Skynyrd sessions (photo courtesy of Ardent Recording, John Fry) / Hunt Sales (photo by Rick Clark). Row 3: 1964 Ludwig "Super Classic" with a second rack tom added (photo by Jimmy Stratton) / Ronan Chris Murphy (photo by Roscoe Webber).

Drums

Great drum sounds have been achieved with everything from mega multi-miked setups to overly compressed single-source cassette jam-box recordings. It all boils down to capturing performance sparks that embrace the soul of the moment.

Check out all the great records in the history of popular music, from the swelling dissonant sea of cymbals and toms in the Beatles' "Tomorrow Never Knows"; to the thick, earthy immediacy of Al Green's "Take Me to the River"; or the relentlessly ominous attack of Peter Gabriel's "Intruder"; and the floating lyricism of Tony Williams' solos on the classic VSOP recordings. It is amazing to hear the range of sounds that have been derived from drum trap sets.

Any engineer or producer will quickly admit the importance of getting the appropriate drum sound down right from the start.

We enlisted a handful of the industry's finest, as well as two legendary session drummers, to offer some input for maximum percussive output. Along with Kenny Aronoff, Dave Bianco, Peter Collins, John Hampton, Roger Hawkins, Dylan Dresdow, Jacquire King, Nick Launay, Russ Long, Skidd Mills, Nile Rodgers, Elliot Scheiner, Jim Scott, Ken Scott, Ralph Sutton, and Dave Thoener, we would like to thank to Jim Dickinson and Jim Keltner for their assistance in helping put things together for this chapter.

Nick Launay

Credits include: Midnight Oil, Public Image, INXS, the Church, Kate Bush, Gang of Four, Talking Heads, David Byrne, Semisonic, Nick Cave and the Bad Seeds. See the Appendix for Nick Launay's full bio.

The first real recording studio I worked at was the Townhouse, Townhouse Studio Two, which had one of the best and most explosive-sounding drum rooms in the world at the time. Unfortunately, it doesn't exist anymore because EMI bought the building and stupidly rebuilt it into something ordinary!

When Virgin Records decided to build Townhouse Studio Two, it was originally going to be a mix room, but they had so much stone left over after using some for Studio One's control room that they ended up building this two-story room with stone floors and rock walls. It was much taller than it was wide, and it was quite a narrow room. It had this incredible sound, because it wasn't that big, so sound was tight and usable for percussive instruments. If you played drums in there, the sound ricocheted off the walls, which weren't that far away from each other, and you got this incredibly punchy, loud sound. It was an impossible space for cymbals. It would make them horribly loud and unusable, which is why the most famous recognizable drum recordings done in the stone room were played without cymbals.

Hugh Padgham was one of the in-house engineers there at the time, and he worked on Peter Gabriel's third album, which was produced by Steve Lillywhite. That album, which contains the song "Intruder," has no cymbals or hi-hats. It was an actual production decision not to do it, which obviously helped in getting that drum sound. This was around 1980.

Phil Collins came in to play on four songs on that album at the Townhouse Studio Two, and he liked that drum sound there so much that he even asked Hugh to co-produce his debut solo album, *Face Value*, which is the one that had "In the Air Tonight," which doesn't have any cymbals either. Without the cymbals, you could really wind up the top end on the drum ambience to get this kind of explosive air in the sound. On "Intruder" and "In the Air," these mics were then gated, which sounded even more powerful. [No reverbs were used.]

I was the assistant engineer on those albums, as well as XTC's *Black Sea*, so I was very inspired by that sound and learned how to get it. I did quite a few records there, including *Flowers of Romance* by PiL, *What's THIS For* by Killing Joke, *Release the Bats* by the Birthday Party, *To Hell with Poverty* by Gang of Four, and *10, 9, 8...* by Midnight Oil.

It's basically a blend of three mics that create that sound. Two are Neumann U 87s placed at about 4 meters away from the drum kit. Maybe a bit higher, on tall boom mics at quite a tall height in the room and pointing down at an angle. They were then compressed with the SSL compressors on the desk. That particular SSL desk in Studio Two at Townhouse was a prototype called the B series. It had these very vicious DBX compressors built into it, which were much more vicious than the ones that you find in later SSLs, such as E, G, J, or K series. With gates on each channel, you didn't need any outboard equipment; it was simply a combination of those two Neumann mics and overdriving the desk until it distorted in a good way.

The third mic used to get this sound was called the *Ball and Biscuit*, which was made by the BBC. The reason it was called the Ball and Biscuit was because it looked like a little biscuit—like a cracker, like a Ritz cracker—with a ball on top of it, and it was black in color. It would hang from the ceiling as a talkback mic, which went through an internal compressor in the SSL desk that was there purely for listening to the musicians. At the Townhouse, the maintenance staff made it possible to plug into the internal compressor so you could put it to tape. That's primarily how that sound was created.

I basically did all the early stuff in that room and became an in-house engineer, but not for long, because I quickly became a freelance producer.

Later on in the '80s, a lot of people developed this heavily gated drum sound where the kick drum was usually this very dry clicky sound, and the snare would be enormous with this gate on the reverb. That was very irritating to hear. The difference between what Hugh Padgham, Steve Lillywhite, and I did was we didn't use any reverb at all. It was a very natural-sounding room, but the whole room was gated, and the kick drum as well. As a result, the kick drum and the snare have the same feeling to them, so it feels more real. The fact that there's no digital reverb on it and it's real room sound means that every time the snare hits, it has a different tone to it. It's not "blanded" out by this digital sound that is the same on every hit.

Of course, people started using sampled snares, and that became a really bad thing during the later '80s, where people couldn't get good snare drum sounds, and it was much easier if you sampled one good hit and triggered it. I really didn't like that gated reverb sound. There was a setting on the AMS reverb called Non-Lin1 or Non-Lin2, depending on what model of AMS reverb you had. These came out in 1982 or '83. It was like a box that you could plug in that sounded like the Townhouse Studio Two, and it was developed by AMS with Hugh Padgham. Hugh helped them get that sound into that box, and it does do the trick and sounds very close to that sound, but people mistakenly thought that the box *was* that sound. People were like, "Oh, I want that Phil Collins drum sound on my dance record." They'd get the AMS reverb and dial in the Non-Lin and think that was it, and they put it just on the snare, but it's completely different to recording a live drummer in a very loud stone room with sort of mild gating on it, and the gating was done with some kind of artistic decision as to how long to make the beat work. It's a very different aesthetic. To me, the use of the Non-Lin or any of those gated reverbs was a bit like going to McDonald's. Here it is, in a box! Bang it on! There we go! Everybody's impressed? Not!

The way compression was used was not to bring down or even out the level; it was done because it was like using a distortion pedal. Especially that use of compression had nothing to do with limiting, and it had everything to do with making an explosive sound—a sound that sort of made you go, "Whoa!"

The other thing I find that's interesting about that particular drum sound is that even though it's aggressive, it seems to not come across to people as harsh. It's more organic and tribal. Women generally like that drum sound and find it emotional. I do think there are sounds that are very male in their aggression, but this isn't like that. A good example would be Kate Bush wanting that exact drum sound on her record. There's a few songs on *The Dreaming* that are really aggressive and over the top drum-wise, but the song underneath is really beautiful, and it works really well. She'd say, "I want the drums to sound like cannons," and she'd go out and play on the piano. The contrast was wonderful. Her piano playing is eccentric, and the combination of the two was just perfect.

Nile Rodgers

Credits include: Chic, Madonna, Peter Gabriel, Duran Duran, Power Station, Vaughan Brothers, Paul Simon, Al Jarreau, Sister Sledge, David Bowie. See the Appendix for Nile Rodgers's full bio.

My philosophy, when it comes to recording drums, is pretty simple. Depending upon the style of music, and depending upon the ultimate philosophical goal that we start out with—which is also subject to change a thousand times, before the record is finished—I look at the drums as the foundation of the record, the foundation of the groove, the foundation of the song, and the foundation of the mix. Everything is based around the drums.

I think of the drummer as an instrumentalist and a composer, so we are composing a drum part. We are not just playing the record. We are playing a composition with a beginning, middle, and end.

Most of the time, we all play together when we are cutting a rhythm track. Often, I'll say to the drummer, "You're the only person who counts right now. We are all subordinate to you because we can all change our parts."

When I'm recording drums, I'm expecting some unique, wonderful thing to happen on the drums that is going to inspire me to say, "What a minute! Let's make that a hook!" That was certainly the case with Madonna's song "Like a Virgin," on which Tony Thompson played drums.

I'm not sure that I gave Tony the actual [*sings the chorus drum fill*] pattern, but I sure know that when I heard it, I went, "Hey, I want you to do that every time at this point." It just became a hook.

In R&B music, putting hooks in the rhythm section used to be a very powerful trick. After all, when a person is singing your song, they never sing a lyric all the way through. They sing lyrics and then they sing some part of the groove.

Another song that jumps out at me is "Modern Love" by David Bowie. When we sat down and rehearsed the song, I said, "Okay, Omar, this is what your pattern is going to be." He played it, and we started grooving, and while we were playing the song, I noticed that he was changing the pattern. After we finished the performance, I liked what he did so much that we then went back and changed our parts to be more sympathetic with his parts. That is a perfect example of what I'm talking about. The arrangement that I had written and rehearsed with the band wasn't ultimately what went on the record. It was just because of the magic of that performance. After he made that performance, we didn't go, "Okay, let's cut another one and try and make it better." Instead I went, "That's the one! That's the drum performance!"

A drummer's ability to understand the beat and how to shift the feeling and vibe, to be on top of the beat or behind the beat, is incredibly essential to me in feeling comfortable with a musician. If a person doesn't understand the difference of interpreting a beat and interpreting swing feel and isn't able to rock and groove behind and on top of beats and all of that stuff, then it isn't a person I really want to play with. I feel uncomfortable with them.

When I think about those days with Chic, we played the songs like 10, 11, or 12 minutes at a pop with no click track. We just grooved like that. "We Are Family" has got to be like 10 minutes long. When you start the record "We Are Family" at the beginning, all the way toward the end, you don't feel like there is some big groove shift.

I grew up in a vibe that was like, "The only time you speed up when you are playing is if the conductor makes you speed up." But R&B bands were all about pocket and laying and sticking right there and being able to set your watch to the tempo. We were like metronomes. We would just practice grooving. You had to be able to play the same thing over and over and over again and be able to keep it there for an hour if you had to.

Nowadays, I use click tracks all the time because all the drummers I know are completely comfortable with them. As a matter of fact, I only started using click tracks when drummers I knew started requesting them.

Traditionally, it is older guys who have been playing in blues bands or more freestyle bands who have problems with click tracks. I've been a good enough coach with these guys to make them very comfortable with them. That is because I program something that feels musical to them. It feels like part of the arrangement, and they are not just playing to a [makes a metronome sound]. Instead they are playing to something that is swinging. [Laughs]

If you could go into every poker game and start every hand with two aces, you would feel pretty good. So every time I walk into a recording studio, I'm trying to get in there with as many aces as possible—a great engineer, great equipment, great musicians, and hopefully great songs. Then I try and make it as good as it can be.

Elliot Scheiner

Credits include: The Eagles, Fleetwood Mac, Jimmy Buffett, Aerosmith, John Fogerty, Billy Joel, Toto, Boz Scaggs, Stevie Nicks, Steely Dan. See the Appendix for Elliot Scheiner's full bio.

I go in with the attitude that I don't want the players to do what I want them to do. I want them to do what they do. Obviously, somebody saw something in them. In the case of a band, I feel that it is my obligation to capture what somebody saw. The whole trick with a lot of this is in placing the mics right.

Nine out of ten times, I find the same mics will work for almost any drummer's kit. On the kick, I normally will use a 112. Occasionally, I will find a bass drum that won't work with that mic. In that case, I will go to an RE20. It seems to be working in those situations where there is a drum that is tuned a little bit differently—usually a little lower—and where I'm not getting enough attack. The RE20 gets me a little bit more attack on the drum.

For snare drum, I use one mic and one mic only. It is on top, and I seldom use a bottom mic unless somebody insists on it. I have always used an SM57. It gives me the natural sound of the drum. They take a beating and they don't overload.

For the rack toms, I used to use 421s. The 421s worked great on just about anyone's toms. I did some live recordings for the Eagles, and 421s worked out fine. But when I worked for Fleetwood Mac, their front-of-house guy was using SM98s on Mick's toms. Since then, I've noticed that most of the live guys have gone to SM98s for toms. The live guys use them because you don't see them. They are teeny, and the front-of-house guy gets everything he needs out of them for live stuff, but I wasn't getting everything I needed out of them for recording.

I ended up putting ATM25s in there, and those worked out great. I close-miked each tom, and I didn't have to use any EQ. The 98s were already in place, and the front-of-house guy wasn't going to lose his 98s. So I had to position my mics pretty close to the 98s and pretty close to the heads. Those mics take a beating as well. I was surprised. I've been using the ATMs in the studio as well.

I never put mics underneath. I don't see the benefit. It is more phase shift that I have to worry about, and it doesn't add anything. I can usually get what I want out of the tom toms from right above.

For overheads, I've always used C 12s. I keep them up fairly high. I try and get more than just the cymbals. I try to get as much good leakage as I can from the rest of the kit. I usually place them right above the cymbals, anywhere from 4 to 6 feet, depending on how many cymbals there are. I will also angle them a bit.

For hi-hat, I will mostly use a KM 81, positioned away from the drummer on the back side of the hat. If you are looking at the drummer from the side, and the top of the hat that is closest to the drummer is at about 12 o'clock, then I will place the mic at about 4 o'clock, not too close to where his stick hits.

I've been using RE20s as room mics, and I bring them down to about chair level for somebody who is sitting down. Sometimes I will face the drums, and sometimes I'll face them away from the drums. Either way, I end up capturing what I want out of the drums, with very little EQ.

I really like big, live rooms to put drums in. I can always put baffles around the drummer, but I like to start with a very live room and then work down.

I've always felt that the drums and bass were the heart of the record. On most of the records I've mixed, the drums are fairly loud. With the exception of a few rock-and-roll records, where they are sitting back a little more, most of the records I've done are records where I can afford to keep the drums way up there, like the Eagles and Fleetwood Mac. John Fogerty loves loud drums. He had the drums louder than I have ever mixed them. I wouldn't have thought about mixing them that loud, but they definitely worked that way.

Jim Scott

Credits include: Tom Petty, Red Hot Chili Peppers, Santana, Wilco, Counting Crows, Foo Fighters, Ride, Sting, Dixie Chicks. See the Appendix for Jim Scott's full bio.

For recording drums, I like expensive mics a little bit farther away and cheaper dynamic mics right up close, because the cheaper dynamic mics can take the level and not break right when you are right in the middle of a fantastic track and the guy is riding the snare like quarter notes on the way out of the best rocking track he ever recorded. You don't want your condenser mic or your tube mic to give up. "I'm breaking now because he's hitting a little harder." You don't want that. You want the 57 to just take it, and it will. It will never let you down.

Put the most expensive mics that you have on the overheads and the other most expensive mics that you have as your room mics. I usually put my room mics close to the drums so that they are 6, 4, 3 feet—not very far, just to round out the sound. Just to give a little bit of a beautiful stereo spread, rather than a real specific, "That tom tom is there, that snare is there, that hi-hat is over there, that ride cymbal is over there" approach. If you want that left, right, center detail, you have to use close mics. If you want to soften that a little and give a little bit of breath to the room, then you put your own mics just far enough back so it's the size of the room you want, and that's the size of the room you have in your track. You can't dwarf everybody else with a Led Zeppelin drum sound if you don't have Led Zeppelin to play. You need just the right size for the right size music for the right size song.

In all the years that I was at Cello Recording in Studio 2, they had a great mic collection. I would use C 12s on the overheads with Neve pres—anything that had a purple knob at the top, 1073, 1081, 1079, or 1064. At the Record Plant we had APIs and SSLs. I love the APIs because they are tough and warm.

I like to use Neumann 47s up near the kick drum. Outside the shell, on the head, a few inches away. On the tom toms, I use dynamic mics like 421s or RE20s. Just make sure they are in tune.

Concerning EQs for drums, I know that the evolution of the modern drum sound is on the faceplate of the API 550 equalizer. If you want the modern kick-drum sound and you have an API 550, do +2 at 5k, −2 at 400, +2 at 100 or 50, and that's the sound. It's on the faceplate of the API 550. I know it. You can do that on the other equalizers that are kind of worse, but if you do it on the API, that's your drum sound. That's what everybody is trying to do, and that's what it sounds like. It kind of the same with snare drum.

Whenever you find good drums, buy them. Ludwigs from 1964, white shells, white on the inside are favorites of mine. I have five sets of them, and they are all great. They all speak and bark, and they have lots of tone. Gretsch drums are great, too. I have used a lot of Gretsch drums, but if I had to take one set, it would be a '64 Ludwig with a good fat 22-inch kick, 13-inch, 16-inch with white interiors. I have tried 24-inch kicks, but they just don't have the impact. Everyone's going to have an argument. I just figured it's good enough for Ringo, so it's good enough for me. It's the right size. Something has to be the bottom of the track. The bass? Maybe. The left hand of the piano? Maybe. Kick drum? Maybe. It's got to be one of them. It can't be all three of them. They will battle it out. Something has to be the bottom, something has to be next to the bottom, and something has to be above that. I have just found with those kinds of drum sounds, it's punchy, it's impacting, and it's rockin'. You can still get a bass guitar underneath it. And that's a good thing.

For cymbals, I prefer the Zildjians from the '60s because of their warmth and their sustain. I've got 40-year-old cymbals that get used every day in the studio, and they don't break. Choosing cymbals, however, depends on how hard the drummer is going to hit.

When I think of guys who actually hit the drums with love and play music and hit them for the tone and the love of it, Jim Keltner and Don Heffington come to mind. I've found that drums can be twice as big when they are hit half as hard. Cymbals, too. Cymbals can be really beautiful and luscious, or they can be irritating and noisy…same cymbal, depending on how you hit and who's playing it. That is just something you have to want to learn as drummer, and it is way more important than just keeping time. Keeping time is what they all strive for, but finding a sound and being inside of the drum sound is how the good drummers that I want to work with play.

Ken Scott

Credits include: The Beatles, David Bowie, Lou Reed, Supertramp, Mahavishnu Orchestra, Devo, Missing Persons. See the Appendix for Ken Scott's full bio.

The one thing that has changed very little over the years, when recording drums, is my miking technique and the EQ I use. What has changed is the sound in the studio. These days, you just get any sound in a studio: "Oh don't worry, guys. We'll use this plug-in, and we'll use that plug-in. It doesn't matter what it sounds like down there. We'll get it to sound great up here." These days, you just put thousands of plug-ins on, and you get a sound. It's not necessarily good or bad; it's just different. Whereas in the past, we'd get the drum sound in the studio. It's a much more organic way of doing it. You get the sound down on the floor, and then by the time it gets to the control room, you don't have to do that much.

When I finished working with Missing Persons in the '80s, I had discovered three new acts that I decided I was going to do demos with to try and shop deals. I decided the way to do it with each band was to do the basic tracks over the course of three days. I used the same mics on all three band's drums. On the first day, we'd have the first act come in, set them up, and do it. So I got everything together for the first band's drummer. I got the sound, EQ, got the basic tracks, and when we were done, I pulled the mics out of the first band's drums. That set would go out, and on the next day, the next drummer would come in, and the same mics would be put back in place. All the kits were the same size, so I didn't have to change any EQ whatsoever. It was exactly the same for all three bands those three days. In the end, all three sets had completely different sounds because the drums were all different, but the EQ I used and the mics were identical on everything. This approach all goes back to how limited the EQ was back at Abbey Road when I worked there. So for those three different drum sets on those three consecutive days, I used very similar EQs to what was available at Abbey Road back then. I don't move too far away from that because it's what I'm used to. It's what I learned to use right back then, and I know what it does, and it works for me.

During the '70s, the drum sounds were very dead. That's what was "in" at that time. It sort of came from Ringo, who had tea towels on everything. With Supertramp or Bowie's drummers, we used tape to damp everything down.

With Ringo, it was intentionally very dead. He had sheets, towels, or something over everything. Everything was completely covered and in the bass drum was a sweater that a fan had knitted for the Beatles. It had two arms but four necks, so they all could wear it at once, and that's what deadened the bass drum.

In the period between *Hunky Dory* and *Ziggy Stardust*, Woody [Woodmansey— Bowie's dummer] and I were talking, and he said how he wasn't particularly enamored of the drum sound on *Hunky Dory*. He said it sounded like a bunch of cornflakes boxes, as far as he was concerned, and he didn't want that sound again. So, on the first day of recording, I had the tea boy at the time and go out and buy as many different-sized boxes of cornflakes as he could get. Myself and the roadie set up a full drum kit, with no drums, made out of different-shaped cornflake packages waiting for Woody's arrival, so he'd feel nice and at home. When he walked into the studio, he fell about laughing!

I hated cymbals at the time I was doing those albums, so I would tend to mix them down. I just found them distracting. I don't know what got me off of them. Maybe there were a lot of records I heard at the time where I thought the cymbals were just way too loud and got in the way of everything else. All I know is for a long period of time I felt that way. Even today, there are times when I don't like cymbals, but sometimes they're very important, like with a drummer like Terry Bozzio. He uses cymbals in such an incredible musical way that you have to have them up there.

Around the same time I was working with Bowie, I started working with Billy Cobham on Mahavishnu Orchestra and his solo project. Because of the style he played, it was a much more open sound, and there was nowhere near as much damping on the drums. The one thing I always remember with Cobham was that he started off with the snare drum being live, and I'd say, "Can we just dampen it a bit?" He'd pull out his billfold, put it on the snare, and it was perfect-sounding every time.

With drums I always pan them like I'm the audience looking at the drummer, so the hi-hat will always be on the right-hand side. Low tom on the left and going across. The snare and the bass drum would be in the middle, unless there are two bass drums, and then it was half left and half right for those. If there are three toms, the high one would be on the right, the mid tom in the center, and the floor tom on the left. If there are more, then it just pans around accordingly. Whenever possible, I would have one or two ribbon mics for overhead, usually Coles 4038s or Beyer M160s. If the studios didn't have those, I'd use Neumann 87s or AKG C 414s, but I always find that ribbons are much smoother.

How far back I usually like to set the ribbons depends on the power of the drummer, the number of cymbals, and how they're set up. For instance, you may need to favor one over another because it's slightly quieter...that kind of thing.

I'd mike the snare with a Neumann KM 54 or a KM 56 about 4 inches from the center at the edge, placed as close as I could safely get it (without the drummer hitting it) and angled at about 45 degrees, aimed toward the center of the drum where he's going to hit it.

For the toms, I use Neumann U 67s and place the mics far enough away so that the drummer doesn't hit them, but they need to be angled toward the center of the head to capture the full attack.

In the early days, I would use an Electro-Voice RE20 for the kick drum. Another mic I like for kick is an AKG D 12.

Some drummers don't play with both heads on their bass drum. They're so used to either only having one head on or having two heads but a hole cut. It's important for things to be the way the drummer is most comfortable, but if the drummer is open enough to do it my way, then it would be with both heads on with the mic suspended by wires inside the kick, and the cable comes out through the shell.

The great thing is my miking technique hasn't changed over the years, so you can be pretty certain that most of what I'm doing now is the same as I did back then.

Ralph Sutton

Credits include: Stevie Wonder, Rick James, the Temptations, Mary J. Blige, Lionel Richie, Elton John, Eddie Murphy. See the Appendix for Ralph Sutton's full bio.

I like to think of myself as a drummer's engineer. The gentleman who spent the most time with me early in my career was Ken Scott [the Beatles, Mahavishnu Orchestra, David Bowie], and he no doubt was a drummer's engineer. I actually picked up a lot of the tips, tricks, and techniques that I use to this day from Ken.

With the drum kit, I like to mike each one of the drums itself, and then I use my overheads to fill in the gaps because a lot of times when you're doing tight miking you eliminate a lot of the bleed, and it kind of makes the drums almost sound sterile. There's a combination of the direct application of the close miking and then the ambience from the overheads and the room mics that, when you blend them just right, you get this really wonderful picture of the drums.

With snares, I like the 57 on the top and an AKG 451 or sE Electronics sE1 from the bottom, with the 10-dB pad maybe 6 to 8 inches away from the rattles [depending on the snare], and that seems to give me a nice full snare sound...almost that gunshot sound. I've been leaning more toward the sE1 now for quite some time, with the 10-dB pad.

I'll go out, set up, set my mics, come in, listen, go back out, kind of move them around until I hear what I'm listening for, and then I leave it alone and tighten up everything and tell the drummer, "If you bump anything, let me know." Between each take, I'll always stand up and look just to make sure nothing's been moved, because there's nothing worse than hearing a great track, and then you notice that the hi-hat mic has been swung all the way to the left.

The kick drum is another one of my favorite parts of the drum kit, where I use a Sennheiser 421 on the inside of the kick inside the shell. I literally point that diagonally directly up under the mallet, maybe an inch away from where the mallet is hitting that front skin. That gives me that mallet sound. Then on the outside of the kick, I use the sE Electronics Z3300.

I like a dead kick opposed to a very ringy kick. I typically pack the kick drum to get it nice and thick, with as little ring as possible. I then always cover the whole kick with a packing blanket. The Z3300, the 421, everything is then covered with a packing blanket. It gives me more isolation, and that's just my thing. I like that thick R&B kick, which I started doing when I was at Hitsville with Motown.

I've become a fan of the sE stuff, and I like that 3300. It gives me a good, round sound from the outside, and I like being able to blend that mallet with that "poof" from the outside of the kick. Once again, it's all about that balance or blend. When it is right, you get a good R&B kick that you can feel in your chest, and that's really important to me.

For the toms, I like 421s about an inch and a half off the top skin. Periodically, I will mike the bottom with a 421 as well, but I've found that most drummers don't really have a good concept of how to tune the top and the bottom skin. As a result, I typically shy away from doing the bottom skin.

The reason why I like the 421 is because it can handle a great deal of SPL, and that really is the key. I also like using 421s on the floor toms, too. I'd like to use 87s, but they just seem to collapse at about 110 SPL. In my past experience, I have successfully used 67s about 4 inches away from that bottom skin. Overall, I generally like large-diaphragm mics like 421s and 57s for drums.

When I mike the hi-hat, I like the KM 84 or the sE1. The KM 84 is my all-time favorite. The sE has some sizzle that I like in it, and it also gives me a good transient response.

I always pan the hi-hat to the right-hand side, as if you're looking at your drummer. Some people like drummer perspective. I like the listener's perspective because I always imagine the listener looking at a drummer. And the hi-hat would be on that side unless the drummer is a lefty. I position the hi-hat mic 6 to 8 inches away from the hi-hat itself, so if the drummer was hitting the hi-hat at the 6 o'clock point, the mic would be located at the 9 o'clock point and maybe 3 to 4 inches away from where the drummer is hitting it, and then a little off, almost on the lip of the hats themselves. I never direct the mic on top of the hat, just because it's too thuddy. I like to be able to hear the chiming and the clapping of the hi-hat. I find that when you're off, almost on the edge of the hi-hat, you can actually hear the clapping...the opening and the closing.

For overheads, I like the sE2, C 12 As, or 414s. It just really depends upon the drum kit itself and the way the player plays, the type of cymbals. All of those things factor into the microphone selections that I make for overheads.

The overheads and the room mics play a very important part in that mural, or that collage of sound that you're painting. One I get that tight, close-miked sound, we've got to "paint it out," because if I don't it just doesn't sound right. So you have to choose the right microphones to paint that ambience to where it's entertaining to the listener. I don't know if the listeners know what they're listening to, but they know when they don't hear it.

When you're doing drums, you want the listener to literally feel as though that drummer is in the room with them or there with them in their car. They want to hear the clarity and the nuances, the hi-hat dancing, and the backbeat and things of that nature.

When people have an opportunity to use a really good drummer, I find that those typically are sessions that go really quickly for getting great drum sounds.

The years that I was with Stevie [Wonder], we would set up the drums, dink around with them, and let them cure into the room, and then a couple of hours later, Stevie might say, "Okay, now let's listen to them." There is actually something that happens with drums after you set them where you want them to be and get the air conditioning where everybody is comfortable, which is typically around 72 to 73 degrees. If you let them sit for a bit, everything kind of settles, and you then re-tweak the tuning of them. They will sound better, but that's a very expensive proposition for some people to tie up studio time in that fashion.

Dave Bianco

Credits include: AC/DC, the Posies, Ozzy Osbourne, Henry Rollins, Teenage Fanclub, Tom Petty, Primal Scream, Mick Jagger, John Mellencamp. See the Appendix for Dave Bianco's full bio.

I think my big rule of thumb is simplicity and less phasing between microphones. I try to use as few as possible. It depends upon the acoustics. You have to figure it out. There are no rules. Lately, what I have been doing for drums is to try and find one microphone that will pick up the entire drum kit, like back in the day when you were working at Sun Records and recording Elvis. I try to find the best mono microphone that will get the entire kit. It should be able to get an equal amount of kick and snare. I usually put that in front of the drums. Sometimes I will use a stereo mic, like an SM69, or a tube mic, like a U 67. Occasionally, I will apply some light compression, usually with a Urei 1176.

When I worked on Mick Jagger's solo record, *Wandering Spirit*, there were a few songs that we wanted a retro-type sound on. I just used the one microphone for the whole drum sound in the mix. I used nothing else, and it was amazing.

With that being the core of the sound, I like futzing around the off-ceiling and the close mics. I will use D 112s on the kick or RE20s, or sometimes a 421, and outside the kick, maybe a 47 FET. Sometimes I will double up on that, but I don't do that often.

I usually use an SM57 on the snare drum. I like a 57 because it has the midrange peak, and it usually can take all the abuse of the sound pressure level and not break up. It is the handy dandy.

Recently, I will "Y" the snare microphone and record it that way, top and bottom. I put a pair, so you will have a top and a bottom, which can phase and sometimes doesn't. If it doesn't, I will put a phase reversal on the bottom. I find that having both microphones coming down one line makes an extraordinary full and fat sound on a snare. That is one trick I use.

For the toms, I normally use 421s, because I like the way they capture the low end and the attack, while having the ability to take intense sound pressure. SM57s also work well.

Sometimes I will let the 421s get the full attack and impact of the toms and get the overtone from an 87, pulled back maybe 6 to 8 inches above, or maybe in between two rack toms or above the floor tom. That way you get this decay from the condenser mic.

KM 86s are my favorite choice for overheads. However, if I can get my hands on some C 12s, I'll gravitate toward them.

C 12s are fun to use because they are so full-spectrum, punchy, and bright. They kind of set the tone of what the set is going to sound like at the top of the spectrum on down. The problem with those sorts of microphones, though, comes from the fact that they are so wide-pattern that you can get some phasing and can get into a little bit of a jam with them. If that is the case, then the 86s are the answer because they are a little tighter and clearer.

I often like to shoot the room mics underneath the cymbals. Sometimes, I will have them behind the drum kit and aiming at the center of the drum kit.

Experimentation is something that I really love to do, and I get much inspiration from hearing the raw-energy drum sound found on many home demos.

It is great to study about using this tube mic this and tube mic that and use the cool console and all of that, but if you listen to what kids are doing on home recorders, you would be amazed how much wild is being done with cheesy compressors and microphones in really funny places. The young kids are fearless, they don't know how things work, and they stumble upon things that are just amazing.

For the Motorcaster sessions, I re-amped a subgrouped section of the drums back into the studio for maximum energy. I just wanted the maximum resonance that I could get. We sent a mix of the kick drum, snare, and toms out in the room, through a PA that had a subwoofer and about a thousand watts of power. What it did was make the room resonate a bit more, and we got a bit of a better room drum sound with that. There is only so much that you can do before feedback happens, but we would get the sound just under the feedback mark, where you would hit the tom and wouldn't get a big over-ring.

We EQ'd the PA as much as we could to get that resonant sound out. Basically, we had more low end that way, and it really made for a great drum sound. I have done that on a few occasions. I think we had the most success here because of the shape of the Ardent "C" room. We were able to do enough dampening to it to make it work.

I took Motorcaster's drum sound a step further by drawing from the freewheeling home demo aesthetic. We had this SM58 above the drums, which we ran into a Boss guitar sustainer pedal. It is a compressor that has an input/output and a sustain control. It didn't work, going right to tape, so we put the signal back through the Yamaha cassette four-track that they recorded their demos with, and then went from the output of that to the tape recorder. I further compressed it to get it up to a level that the tape would like to see, and it gave us the most amazing sound.

In spite of all the playful experimentation of sound, I still maintain that the key to all really good drum sounds is having a good kit that is well tuned.

We have microphones that are very good at showing you what reality is, and if you have a good-sounding set of drums, you are going to sound good. If you have a bad-sounding set, it is the opposite. It seems obvious, but it is really the truth.

Dylan Dresdow

Credits include: The Black Eyed Peas, Michael Jackson, Ice Cube, TLC, Madonna, Christina Aguilera, will.i.am, Anita Baker, Nas, Macy Gray, Common, Bone Thugs-n-Harmony, Wu-Tang Clan. See the Appendix for Dylan Dresdow's full bio.

The first thing I do before recording anything is walk into the live room and listen to what the drum kit sounds like, because how else are you going to know what the thing is supposed to sound like unless you go out into the live room and listen to it? I will listen to the drummer play and go inside the control room, mimic the sound, and then try to make it sound maybe five percent better. But first I want to go for an accurate representation of what it sounds like live. A lot of this has to do with correct mic placement.

When I record drums these days, it is a pretty straightforward setup. I'll use my Stephen Paul modified Neumann U 47 FET on the kick in a blanket tunnel, as well as a Sennheiser MD421 or a Shure SM7B to try to really get the beat or attack. I stick the MD421 right inside of the kick drum or on the beater side of the kick drum. I try to get it tightly in there to where it's just picking up as much of the attack as possible, so it's pretty much dead-on pointed directly where the beater is going to hit the drumhead. Sometimes you just have to move that around a little bit to where it sounds good. If you don't have a good transient on your kick drum, you'll have problems translating to smaller speakers.

For the kick-drum mics, I really like using the A-Designs Pacifica mic pre on the beater side, and for the U 47 I like using the Neve 3405 mic pre. The Pacifica is a great all-around mic pre to have. It seems to capture the top end a little bit more accurately than some of the other mic pres on the market, and it seems a little darker with the pad in. So for the beater side, you get that clickiness out of it, and you get really good attention to detail whenever that beater really slams hard against that drumhead.

I typically stick the U 47 back maybe about a foot or two from the outside shell of the kick drum, so the kick gets a chance to reproduce the low end. Then I'll take a packing blanket and two mic stands and create a tunnel with it so that I get isolation from all of the toms, the cymbals, and everything else. I want an isolated kick-drum sound that has all of the low end and the beefiness to it that makes your speakers push air. When I do that, I can do a lot more things with the kick drum later down the line. It also helps me determine much more easily if the kick drum has a tight phase relationship with the overhead microphones, and that's really, really important because there's nothing worse than hearing a cymbal crash that just kind of comes in and out and rolls after the cymbal has been hit.

When I mix, I go to my Auratones, which are really small low-fidelity speakers, because they really let you know if stuff translates well. Whether you're on the phone on hold or in a department store, you still want to hear the kick drum. It's important for you to get a good attack out of it.

I always check the phase relationship between the U 47 and the SM7B, which can sometimes be weird. If it is weird, sometimes you aren't 180 degrees out of phase, so you're getting slight cancellation. Sometimes what I'll do is solo the U 47 and then solo the SM7, and if they sound great on their own but they sound weird together, you have to fix the phase relationship. Most people just move the mics around, but if they sound good where they are, I'll use the Little Labs IBP unit. It's basically like an all-pass filter, and instead of flipping it directly 180 degrees out of phase, you can do variants of anywhere between 180 to 90 or 45 or anywhere in between.

The IBP, which stands for *in between phase*, is a brilliant device made by Jonathan Little, who has been on the studio scene for years. The way that I use this is I flip it out of phase first and press the phase invert, and I sweep this with both of the tracks playing at the same time until it sounds most hollow. Basically, what I'm doing at that point is I'm trying to make it out of phase on purpose. Whenever it's the most hollow-sounding, I will pop the phase back in, then everything is going to sound most present, and all of the frequencies are going to enhance themselves as opposed to comb filtering or phase canceling themselves out.

Some people keep the phase regular and just sweep it around until it sounds good. For me, my method is how I can pinpoint the most tightly locked phasing relationship between the two microphones. I also commonly use this whenever I'm working on guitar cabinets. Another thing I see people do often on snare drums is do the top mic and the bottom mic, 57s from both sides. That said, I've really been getting much more into taking a single SM57 and miking the shell of the snare drum, and a lot of the time this ends up sounding more like a snare drum than taking two microphones and miking the top and the bottom. While you won't have the separation and be able to tweak the snare part versus the funky part of the top, it often captures a true and desirable snare drum.

If the single SM57 sounds wrong miking the shell of the snare, I'll do the top and bottom, and sometimes just the top. Of course, a lot of this depends on the drum kit and the drummer, as well as the way the drums sound in the room.

For the hi-hat, I use a Shure SM81 mic. On the hi-hat, I don't point the microphone toward where the person is hitting the hi-hat; I point it straight down to the floor above the outside part of the cymbals, so it's on the opposite side of where the drummer hits it with the drumstick. Sometimes if I have isolation problems, picking up too much of a crash that is close to the hi-hat, I will physically take copper insulation that plumbers use and cut it and wrap it around the microphone so it's only being sheltered from all of the other sounds that are coming toward it, so that I can get good isolation for my hi-hat.

Sometimes people just have too much hi-hat because the drummer plays it too loud, which makes it even more important for you to mike it, because you can use that miked hi-hat to trigger gates or compressors later on, or even just side-chain a de-esser so that you can get rid of the hi-hat later on in the mix if you have to. I recommend to tracking engineers that they always record the hi-hat, even if they don't think they'll use it, because if they don't, they're kind of screwing the mixer if they aren't the one mixing it.

For the toms, I'll use an MD421 or even an AKG 451EB, and then for the floor tom, sometimes instead of using a 421, I'll switch it up with something like a Shure SM7B.

On all of these 421s, there's an M and an S knob that you can turn in the base of them. The S stands for *speech*. The M stands for *music*. I always keep them all the way on the M. I've tried the speech setting several times, and it just doesn't work very well for me.

For my toms, I really like using these Neotek MicMAX mic pres or the Sytek MPX-4A. On Channels 3 and 4, it's very common to have the Burr-Brown modification, which basically just gives the mic a little bit more silkiness and detail, as opposed to the stock channels, which can sound a little bit more grungy and are really great for indie rock, for example.

For overheads, I will use Earthworks mics, typically the V77s. Sometimes I switch them out and use the TC25 omnis. If the room is super live, the cardioids tend to work better because when it's really live, I'm going to pick up most of the liveness from my room mics, not my overheads, and you're going to get a lot of it in your overheads anyway. If I have the cardioids, I can use them to focus on my cymbals.

For my overheads, I really like using mic pres that have a fast slew rate. The Audio Upgrades mic pre is stellar for this and was created by this guy, Jim Williams, who, as I understand it, uses video components to get these blistering fast slew rates. With the Audio Upgrades, I get to hear everything about that transient. I get really nice decay, especially on something like a really big ride cymbal. I get a nice ping, as the cymbal stands itself out. I get all of that detail.

If I didn't use the Audio Upgrades pre, I would probably use the NightPro/NTI—the PreQ3, designed by Clifford Maag, which is a really, really great mic pre for stuff that you want top end on. It just makes it great for overheads because it has an EQ in the circuit—there's basically a top and shelving EQ that you can set for more air in the sound. It actually goes all the way up to 40k, which is extremely high, and the result is a more open-feeling top end. If you're boosting 40k, if you really crank it, you're obviously going to be affecting the lower frequencies as well. I typically roll off my low end on my overheads because I don't want the kick drum and stuff like that in there. I want it to focus on the overall sound of the top-end portion of the kit, mainly the cymbals.

I usually don't decide on the live room mics until I've been in the room and heard what's going on. If it's a really, really great-sounding room, sometimes I will set up two microphones in mid-side configuration, but if the room doesn't sound good, forget about it. Sometimes I'll use a pair of 47 tube mics or the AKG C 12s, which have a much more brilliant top end. If I can I'll use a Decca tree made with Neumann M 50 microphones, which are extremely rare, and that just sounds fantastic.

I move my room mics, which are almost always set to omni, around wherever they seem to sound fit in the room. When the drummer is playing, I walk around the room bobbing and weaving, moving my head around until I find that point where I think the drums sound the best, because every room will have nodes and anti-nodes that are going to reinforce sound or get rid of them. If you don't know what that means, just play a 1k tone through the speakers and slowly walk around your room, and you'll hear places where the 1k tone is really loud and places where you can barely hear it all. Those are basically places where all the reflections are phase-canceling in that spot, and those are the places I try to avoid. In the places where it sounds loud, it's actually doubling up on itself, so you're kind of exaggerating the sound you're going to hear. Most of the time I try to move around until it sounds like the drums are most natural, and not twice as loud, because then the sound is exaggerated, and that's not something I want to do with my room mics. I want them to sound more natural and help me give the drums space if I need to mix.

A lot of times, I'll also set up one extra microphone, like a kind of a lo-fi chunky mic, which can be anything, and I'll run that through this Shure Level-Loc, which is this unit that takes microphone input and spits out line output. It was actually created for podium mics for speeches. It has these flip switches with a switch with settings for 6 feet or less, 12 feet, or 18 feet or more. When you switch toggle through them, it was supposed to be set up based on how close the person was going to be to the microphone when giving a speech.

The Shure Level-Loc was not designed for drums, but when you run drum signal through it, it just squashes and compresses the hell out of it, so it's really like a compressor, not a mic pre. It gives you this really crunchy, nasty squashed sound. Sometimes I'll just add that in under the regular drum signal to give it a little more beef and girth, but sometimes it's totally inappropriate for the track except for in something like a drum turnaround, and you mute all the other drums, but for that one bar you leave that in there so you get this really crunchy drum sound. When the other drums kick back in, you have a contrast of this lo-fi crunchy sound and then—BAM!—it kicks into this nice hi-fi sound where the drums are just pounding your chest. That's something I really love doing when recording drum kits. Standard Audio also makes a 500-series unit based on the Level-Loc.

Jacquire King

Credits include: Tom Waits, Modest Mouse, Kings of Leon, MUTEMATH, Archie Bronson Outfit, Buddy Guy. See the Appendix for Jacquire King's full bio.

At the source, drums can be a complicated acoustic instrument to capture in a recording. The kit has to be well tuned and the hardware in good working order. I've made it a point to know how to tune and get the sound I'm after. I have the philosophy about anything I record that the sound is at the source. I enjoy recording drums because you can do so many different things with them: You can deaden them down, muffle them, tune them loose, or tune them tight and ringing. I love putting thick paper over the snare to take the overtones out of it and make it all about the attack and the buzz of the snare wires.

There was something that I read in a *TapeOp* article or a thread of discussion about transformerless SM57s. I have now yanked transformers out of about half a dozen 57s and have left a trail of them at various studios. I have one at my studio now, too. I really think it's great on snare.

On hi-hats a lot of people use small-diaphragm condenser microphones. I have done that a lot too, and it can be very successful. It depends on the type of music, but what I have found to work really nice is using something like an SM57 on the hats. I get a nice, complementary sound with the overhead miking. My typical overhead mic choice usually has a very articulate top end for the cymbals, and the hi-hat is almost always a louder element of the drum kit. I'm going to get a lot of nice high frequencies in the overhead sound from the hi-hat, so using a mic that is more about upper midrange gives me some nice options for a more specific placement in the stereo image.

I've gotten away from miking the rack tom sometimes because of the mono technique I use for the overhead sound. I'll use only one overhead mic because it gets away from phase issues. It's usually over the rack tom and often gets the perfect sound on that drum. I also usually get enough additional wash of the ride cymbal in the floor tom mic to satisfy me, but then if the ride cymbal articulation is really important to the style of a player, I will put a microphone on it. In that situation I often use ribbon microphones, like RCA 77s, on the hi-hats and ride cymbal. That way I get good tonal spread with those mics in the drum image, and ribbon mics always EQ well in the upper frequencies. With drums I don't particularly care about a super-wide stereo image. I like to create an image with several mono elements, and I don't really care about stereo pairs of microphones all that much on drums. I'll place some mono mics in different positions that favor the kick, the snare, and an overall kit sound. When I pan those out a little in the stereo spread, I can create an image that has some width and depth but remains centrally focused.

Russ Long

Credits include: Dolly Parton, Sixpence None the Richer, Osaka Pearl, Gary Chapman, Swag, Michael W. Smith, Phil Keaggy. See the Appendix for Russ Long's full bio.

As far as drums go, you have to start with a great room. It's pretty tough to make it all happen if the room doesn't sound good, and I go into tracking with intention of recording sounds that can actually be used in the mix as opposed to replacing everything with Drumagog or SoundReplacer. My favorite tracking rooms are Omnisound Studios, Ocean Way, House of David, and Vibe 56 [all in Nashville], but I've had some great results recording in houses, rehearsal rooms, and even public storage spaces.

I love to tailor my drum sounds to each song. A lot of people prefer to get a good overall drum sound, knowing they can tweak all of the sounds independently in the mix. I think the entire recording process is far more inspiring to everyone involved when more time is spent being sonically creative during the initial tracking process. My favorite recording experiences have been the occasions when I've had the time to completely construct the drum kit sound from the ground up for each song.

Ideally, I'll go into a band tracking session with two or three kick drums, six or seven snare drums, a half-dozen toms, and at least a dozen cymbals. I have several of my own pieces that I always bring to supplement the drummer's gear, and if we come up short, we'll borrow or rent for even more options. I have a great-sounding 24-inch kick drum that I always bring to tracking sessions. It seems that a lot of drummers don't have 24-inch kicks because they don't necessarily translate that well in live situations, but I've had great luck with them in the studio. Mine is a 1970s Ludwig Vistalite, and it sounds enormous. I also have a few snare drums that provide some great sonic options. My favorites are my 5.5×14-inch 1960s White Pearl Slingerland and my 6.5×14-inch Tama Artstar. The Slingerland nails that Jim Keltner classic snare tone, and the Artstar is perfect for more aggressive stuff. I also carry a bunch of cymbals with me, mostly Paiste, but I have a few Zildjians and Sabians. I can't get enough of the Paiste Traditionals series. Ken Coomer turned me on to them more than a decade ago, and I still love them. They have a dark, intricate, and slightly trashy quality that fits well with most of the bands I record. I have 20- and 22-inch rides and several crashes from this line. Before each tune, the producer, drummer, and I discuss the musical direction of the song, and we'll put together a kit that matches the sonic vibe that we are trying to capture. This includes kit placement, room dampening, and mic selection.

I love to experiment with different mics, but my typical setup includes an AKG D 112 or a Heil PR 40 inside the kick, a Neumann U 47 FET just outside, and a Yamaha SubKick about an inch off the back head. The SubKick looks like a snare drum sitting on its side, but it is actually a giant mic that uses a shock-mounted 6.5-inch woofer as a diaphragm, and it allows you to capture subharmonic information in a way not possible with ordinary microphones. I use a Heil PR 20 or Shure SM57 on the snare top and a Heil Handi on the bottom. I like the Neumann KM 86i on the hats, or if they sound a bit brittle or harsh, I'll use the Royer SF-1 instead. I like Mojave MA-100s or Sennheiser MD421s on toms, and I use the Royer SF-12 for overheads. I always record several room options. I use a pair of Coles 4038s for stereo room, and I always record a couple of mono rooms—one with a Placid Audio Copperphone, which is one of the coolest mics I've ever heard, and one through something else, usually a Royer SF-1A.

I never use any gates when tracking because I don't ever want to lose a snare or tom hit if the drummer decides to hit a bit softer in a certain section of the song. Automation is so powerful now that if you are using Pro Tools, you can always automate the gate's threshold in the mix and make sure you don't lose anything. I do lightly compress the inside kick mic using a Tube-Tech CL 1B, the snare top using a dbx 903, and the overheads using a Manley Langevin Dual Vocal Combo, which funnily enough seems to work great for me on everything except for vocals. It's my signal path of choice for keyboards, too. I'll squash all of the rooms quite a bit using Distressors, RCA BA6s, or Fairchilds. It always varies a bit, but I like a Gordon or an A-Designs Pacifica mic pre on the kick drum. The Gordon has plenty of character but very little coloration, and the Pacifica is loaded with that classic '70s coloration. I usually use a Gordon, a Pacifica, or a Seventh Circle N72 on snare. Again, the Gordon has character without coloration, and the Pacifica has tons of character. The N72 is loosely based on the Neve 1073 and 1272, but when I compared it to a vintage Neve 1073 on snare, I liked the N72 better. It has all the impact and body of the 1073 with an additional high-frequency sparkle. I usually use Daking modules on the hat and toms. The Dakings are a copy of the Trident A-Range circuit, and they sound great on pretty much anything. All of this gear is my stuff that I bring to every session.

Even though I like to experiment, I always like to have a sonic foundation that I can return to if things just aren't coming together for some reason. With this said, if I'm tracking in a room with an API console, I'll usually use the console pres and EQs on a lot of the inputs because the API stuff just sounds awesome on all things drum. Besides getting the gear right, I always check the phase of all of the mics with a phase checker and by listening to make sure there aren't any phase issues.

Click is another big issue when recording drums. I typically track to Pro Tools, and I'll build my song map with all of the song's sections as quick as possible. I'll substantially drop the click volume anyplace the drummer is letting a crash ring out, and I'll mute it at the end of the song to make sure there isn't any unwanted bleed to come back and haunt us during the mix. This is also useful if we end up recording any acoustic instrument overdubs.

Skidd Mills

Credits include: ZZ Top, Spin Doctors, Killjoys, B.B. King, The Bar-Kays, Skillet, Third Day, Spacehog, Robert Cray. See the Appendix for Skidd Mills's full bio.

I take great pains to make sure that the components of the kit are the best they can be. I also like sampling an array of snares, cymbals, and other elements of the kit to ensure the most appropriate tonal setting for the production at hand.

I think that the most important thing, beyond having great-sounding drums to begin with, is to make sure that all of your mics are in phase. Sometimes you have to be careful. You can have a snare drum that is in phase, and if you start doing something like EQing your overhead mic, then that phase can change. You have to stay on top of it.

For my typical trap kit mic setup, I like SM57s, one on top and one on the bottom. Sometimes I'll use a 421 on the bottom. My favorite kick drum mic is the AKG ATM 25, while for toms I prefers 57s on the tops and 421 on the bottoms.

RE20s have become a mic of choice for hats unless I'm wanting a little more top, in which case I may choose a 451 or a KM 84, especially for a more pristine effect.

When I begin working on the drum sound, I usually start working with the overheads.

I think how good your overheads sound has a lot to do with the final overall quality and sound of the drums. From there, I will bring in my kick drum and everything else after that point. You have to have some frame of reference, however, so I usually use my overheads as starters. Again, you want to make sure that everything is in phase with each other. It makes all of the difference in the world.

Once that is all happening, I usually like to start concentrating on my room sounds. The room itself is probably the most important thing. As far as mics, there are about three different things that I will use. I will use Neumann KM 86s in front of the drum kit, maybe five or six feet back on each corner at about chest level. Depending on how much I like the sound, I will sometimes compress it to tape. My favorite is a stereo Fairchild. Other than the KM 86s, I will sometimes use Neumann 249s. Sometimes I will use two PZMs, tape them back to back, put them in the center of the drum kit, and stick them up pretty high. I will sometimes blend those in with either my 249s or my KM 86s to add some "zizz." It depends a lot on what the production style is and how much of a room sound you want.

My favorite overhead mics are 414s. Depending on what kind of a record it is, I will usually put them both in a cardioid pattern and have them placed with one taking care of the hi-hat, snare, and any cymbals over on the drummer's left side, and the other one taking care of the toms and the ride cymbal or any other cymbals on his right. That is your basic "H" pattern. I would probably have them about 3 feet apart and about 2 or 3 feet off the cymbals. Those heights may change, depending on phasing.

The other way I may deal with overheads is to use two AKG 414s in an M-S stereo pattern, which stands for *middle sides*. I use one cardioid mic that is suspended above center of the kit and pointing straight down on it. I then use another 414 butted right up and perpendicular to the first mic. The cardioid mic is assigned to two tracks, while the bidirectional is assigned to one track in phase, with the other signal assigned to the other track out of phase.

The whole trick to M-S is getting them decoded correctly. I have seen people decode by eyeballing the meters, which isn't going to give you a correct stereo picture. I've seen people decode off of the monitor faders, which is not really correct. The best way to do it is to decode off of the console busses. That way, you are basically listening to the output of the console while you try to get those two bidirectionals completely out of phase. That is what you are trying to do. Once that is correct, it is a great stereo picture.

David Thoener

Credits include: Billy Joel, John Mellencamp, J. Geils Band, Rosanne Cash, Aerosmith, Jon Bon Jovi, Jason Mraz, AC/DC, Matchbox Twenty, Meat Loaf, Kiss, Willie Nelson, Keith Urban. See the Appendix for David Thoener's full bio.

It's a real art, recording drums. Drums are among the most difficult instruments to record because there are so many drums you're encountering, and you're dealing with ways to get all those drums sounding exactly like they do in the room. When the drummer comes into the control room and listens, I try to get it to sound exactly like what he's hearing when he's out in that room—not only the sonics of the drums themselves, but the ambiance, too. If I can achieve that, then I'm very happy, and usually the band's very happy.

I often like to use a minimal miking approach at first. Nevertheless, I am careful not to limit my choices as the project unfolds. One rule I've learned over the last 20 years is that anything can work, and you can never dismiss any idea when it comes to recording anything.

Someone might say, "We'll just put a U 87 30 feet in front of the kit, and that's the only mic we're going to use." Immediately I may think that is not a good idea, but the artist or the producer is hearing it in a way that's hard to describe, and that's the best way they're trying to describe it. You have to take what you think they want and turn that into something that's viable on tape. Those people can change their minds, which often happens, as you start putting down overdubs, and the song turns into a beast of its own. You have to make sure that you've recorded the drums in such a way that if all of a sudden the arrangement has changed, you can still bend.

In other words, you've got five overdubs on the track, and all of a sudden that single-miked drum balance that was perfect in the basic track is not quite the same balance anymore. Everything affects everything. Nevertheless, I'm a minimalist in that I will record with as few drum mics as possible—even one mic, if I can get away with it.

At the Record Plant, we used to stick drums in this first-floor back area behind Studio A, where they used to put the garbage. It used to be a real drag for the drummers because they'd have to stay out there for eight hours a day, drumming with garbage around them. But everyone agreed that it was a killer sound because there was a lot of marble around and cement walls and stuff. You know, whatever you gotta do.

To me there are no rules whatsoever. I am open to everything. If someone says to me, "Let's put the drum at the bottom of this stairwell and mike it on the first floor," it's like, "Sure, sure." Maybe something amazing will happen that will cause us to look at each other and say, "That sounds great."

Kenny Aronoff

Credits include: John Mellencamp, Melissa Etheridge, John Fogerty, Iggy Pop, Neil Diamond, Joe Cocker, Joe Jackson, Bob Seger, Trey Anastasio, Santana, Rod Stewart, Elton John, Bob Dylan, Jon Bon Jovi. See the Appendix for Kenny Aronoff's full bio.

If I don't properly hear my cymbals, then I start selecting different-sounding cymbals with different personalities that will allow them to speak in the kind of room I am working in. When I am playing in a room that is really bright, I will go to a darker cymbal. The converse is true if the room is very warm or dead. In that case, I will go to brighter cymbal with more ambiance. It all comes down to what I am hearing through the speakers.

If my cymbals are getting lost in the overall sound, I address the situation by changing out cymbals that work in a frequency range that isn't shared as much by other instruments, particularly guitars.

The biggest components in getting a great drum sound are obviously the right drum equipment and the way the drummer tunes and plays his drums. That is what the drummer has control over.

Nevertheless, mic placement is everything, too. I just did a song on the new Melissa Etheridge album called "I Could've Been You" that had a real laidback bluesy feel. I used two snare drums. I played on a very small 4-inch wood drum very lightly in the verses. Hugh made that drum sound so deep and big. Then when the chorus came in, it was more aggressive-sounding, like Soundgarden. That was a 6 1/2-inch metal drum, and that drum sounded higher than the other one. The richness of that 4-inch wood drum was so amazing; of course, it was tuned pretty low.

Roger Hawkins

Credits include: Percy Sledge, Aretha Franklin, Staple Singers, Paul Simon, Bob Seger, Traffic, Etta James, Boz Scaggs, Herbie Mann, Laura Nyro, Jimmy Cliff, Leon Russell, Linda Ronstadt, Eric Clapton, James Brown. See the Appendix for Roger Hawkins's full bio.

It is very important for the drummer to like the sound of his drums. If he doesn't like the sound of his drums, then he isn't going to put out a maximum performance. Sometimes session drummers—and I am sure that a lot of session drummers can relate to this—have a great sound in the booth, but they aren't hearing it correctly in the phones. You just won't put out as much. It just isn't as possible to do, because suddenly you are fighting the drums instead of playing the drums.

It is important for the drummer and the engineer to communicate and for the drummer to not feel afraid to mention to the engineer that it isn't sounding the same to him in the phones as it is sounding in the studio. I don't think good engineers take offense to that. I think they know what I just said.

It is important for drummers to realize the effect of listening to the drums too loud in phones. The freedom offered by multi-channel personal headphone mix boxes also can lure drummers into setting up headphone sounds that unwittingly compromise their performances.

One of the things that was a little tricky to me was the multi-channel phone mixers, when I first started using them. Naturally, I turned myself up pretty loud. When I walked into the control room, I could tell that the drums weren't "singing." You are executing the parts okay, but the energy isn't there. That is something to be aware of for any drummer starting to use a multi-channel headphone mix. Keeping the level down a little bit and playing up to the music is one way drummers can approach the situation.

Ultimately, the engineer and drummer owe it to each other and the music at hand to have an open, respectful dialogue. If you are not hearing what you are playing, sound-wise and level-wise in the phones, then you are pretty much going to be a sterile player. A lot of times drummers are afraid to speak up, but if you speak up in the right way and you are serving the project, I think it is fine. It must be done that way.

Peter Collins

Credits include: Rush, Queensrÿche, Jewel, Indigo Girls, Brian Setzer, Elton John, Alice Cooper, Bon Jovi, the Divinyls, Tom Jones, Kenny Loggins. See the Appendix for Peter Collins's full bio.

Generally speaking, these days I like for the listener to be able to "see" the kit in its entirety, rather than split up over the stereo system, with each component cleanly separated. I'd rather be able to "see" the drummer sitting in the room with the kit, with the kit sounding like one instrument, than "see" a whole bunch of percussive elements. So when I'm recording, I want to have that vision at the end of the day.

I think that's found on most of my records over the last few years, particularly on the Brian Setzer record, which has a very natural, organic sound to it that isn't hyped up.

I'm a huge fan of pre-production, so that the drummer is totally prepared and we can nail it very quickly in the studio. I try and catch the early performances. They don't get better; they usually get worse. It is important to catch him while he is fresh and not "thinking." It is very important that drummers don't "think." Then you just get a natural flow of performance.

I usually like to use click tracks that are not metronomes, but actual tonal sequences that follow the chord changes. It is also helpful for everybody concerned, in terms of reminding them what the pre-production was. It gives everyone some room to breath around it because it isn't as rigid as a metronomic-type click.

For me, a personal landmark record was *Rites of Passage* by the Indigo Girls, which we recorded with Jerry Marotta over at Woodstock. We used Bob Clearmountain's mix room, which was normally not used for recording. We had Jerry in a booth in this small room, and the drum sound was extremely present. It is the complete antithesis of the stadium rock sound.

When I produced Rush's *Counterparts* and *Test for Echo*, I went for a much more organic, less-hyped sound. My philosophy with Neil's [Peart, Rush's drummer] drums has changed over the years. In 1985, when I first worked with him, they wanted an ultra high-tech sound, which was very fashionable in those days—the days of Trevor Horn, Yes, Frankie Goes to Hollywood, and all those British bands. Rush specifically wanted to be in that arena, which involved a very high-tech drum sound, if you like. It was not a particularly organic sound.

The engineer, James "Jimbo" Barton, was very much into that sort of thing—high compression on the drums and very clever use of reverbs that were very much larger than life. In those days, when we did *Power Windows* and *Hold Your Fire*, Jimbo's use of it was extremely effective. You listen to those records now, and they sound a little over the top. [Laughs]

At the time, Neil was triggering samples of African drums and all sorts of other odd things, plus he had a small kit behind him and a big kit in front there in the studio. Together, with all his toms and percussion stuff, he would spin around in the middle of a song and play the smaller kit and then come back to the big kit.

A very good example of understated drums is the drums on the single remake I did of Jewel's "Foolish Games," which was a Top Ten hit. The drums created a really cool momentum to the track, without you being very aware that they were there. Omar Hakim played, and it was a really beautiful subtle performance.

Overall, I think drum sounds today are so much better than they used to be. The standards are so much higher.

John Hampton

Credits include: The Raconteurs, the White Stripes, Lynyrd Skynyrd, Gin Blossoms, B.B. King, the Replacements, the Cramps, Toots and the Maytals, Alex Chilton, North Mississippi Allstars. See the appendix for John Hampton's full bio.

You want to know how to record drums? First of all, as everybody knows, you have to start with a good drummer. In my personal opinion, if you mainly are recording rock, you've got to find a guy who hits the drums pretty consistently and hard, because you want a solid backbeat.

The drums they are making today, like DW [Drum Workshop], Pearl, GMS, Noble & Cooley, Ayotte, and all those solid shells, are made to withstand high pressure, and they really sound better—more "rock"—when you hit them harder.

In the process of all this, you can get a little more help recording drums by using analog tape. That is because there is kind of a maximum that the tape can handle before it puts this nice, smooth little bit of compression on the drums themselves. You might say that analog tape has a true zero attack time, so you don't have to worry about little peaks getting through before the compression reacts. So I like to use analog tape, and I like to use good drummers and good drums. All that stuff helps and should be in place before you move microphone number one into the picture.

I like to go for a natural drum sound. The way a drum kit really sounds is probably the way they sound 20 feet away or so. Because the closer you get to them, you are so overwhelmed by the shock of the air molecules hitting your body that your concept of what that drum sound really is is pretty distorted. Even if you put your fingers in your ears, you are still feeling the drums against your body. It is not really what drums sound like.

So I tend to start with a good realistic stereo overhead picture, looking at the kit from the top. When you are doing that, you are not getting a lot of the kick drum, but it is a good place to start. When you look back at old pictures of George Martin and the Beatles, that is how everybody did it. You are looking from the top and adding the kick drum to it.

I like a fairly wide stereo picture. In that regard, I tend to shy away from X-Y stereo, and my personal taste heads toward M-S stereo, or mid-side stereo. That can give you a wider image than a normal X-Y and yet remain phase coherent. I like to use condenser mics that have a pad. I've used everything, but my favorites today are AKG 414s. They get the closest to capturing the body of the cymbal, as well as the high part of the cymbal. They usually will also give you a pretty good starting drum sound on their own, without any other microphones.

From there, I will start trying to put the kick drum into the stereo overhead picture. My choice today is the AKG D 112, but there are a lot of good kick-drum mics out there. I've used Beyer 201s and Audio-Technica ATM25s, which are good-sounding kick-drum mics. I've even used a KM 84 and blew it up. But it sounded good for a minute.

Getting that microphone to be phase coherent in your overhead picture is pretty much a matter of hitting phase switches. You try to get the kick drum as equal in level to how loud the kick is in the overheads. Then you start hitting the phase switch on the kick drum, and you'll usually find that one phase position yields a bit more low end than the other. That is the one you want to go with. Then you EQ to taste, like dump all the midrange but add a little 4 kHz.

My rule is W-A-R on 580 hertz, if you are using a Neve console. [Laughs] Dump it when you record it and dump it when you play it back. Why? Because if you do that, then the sound you get is the sound of rock. It is "that" sound. It is the sound you've heard on every great rock record on the planet. Midrange on drums, to me, just sounds like cardboard. It sounds cheap. Dumping midrange is a more high-tech sound.

Now we have to bring the snare drum into the picture. Normally, I will use a regular old Shure 57. I mike top and bottom. The bottom mic, for me, is optional. Sometimes you need it and sometimes you don't. It depends on how hard the person playing is hitting the drum. If the drummer is creaming it, you may need a little bit of that bottom mic because one of the physics principles of a snare drum is that no matter how hard you hit the drum, the snare rattle is always about the same level. So the harder you hit the snare, the quieter the sound of the bottom head relative to the top head. So the harder the drummer hits, generally the more I might need that bottom mic to get the whole sound of the drum.

Usually, a 57 is a little midrange-y in the 1-kHz range, and you want to get rid of some of that and add a little top to brighten it. So put in a little mid-dump and add top EQ to it and then bring that into the overhead picture and get it balanced in there about equal with the overheads, and you start doing the same thing with the phase switch. You will always find one phase switch that is a bit more robust than the other.

Over the years, I've received many projects to mix where whoever engineered failed to get the snare drum in phase with the overheads. All of a sudden, for the first time, people are hearing their snare drum in phase with their overheads, and they think I'm a genius. I'm not a genius. All I did was put your snare in correct phase.

Basically, what I just explained is what I do all the way around the kit. I do the same thing with the tom toms. I dump some mids and usually add a little in the 4-kHz range for stick attack, so it'll kind of cut through the wall of guitars you are going to end up with. And with all the tom toms, check the phase by putting each of them up equal in level to how loud it is in the overheads, and mess with the phase until you get it right. I usually use 57s on the toms, too.

Sometimes, some drums don't give you that 100-percent happy feeling in the resonance department. Adding a mic underneath the tom tom, usually out of phase with the top mic, adds back that boom boom you are so used to hearing. I usually use 421s for that, and I generally don't EQ. I just knock it out of phase. Knocking it out of phase will do a little bit of a natural midrange dump because of its distance to that top mic. A lot of times, that mid-dump is proportional to the size of the drum. What I mean by that is, the bigger the drum, the further those mics are apart, and the lower that canceling frequency is, which is about right for the bigger drums. You want to go down with the frequency with the mid-dump.

For some reason, whatever that cancelled frequency is between those two microphones, that seems to be a good frequency to cancel, and that frequency obviously becomes a lower and lower frequency the bigger the drum is, because that distance between those two mics has been increased. The wavelength of the cancelled frequency is longer because the microphones are getting farther and farther apart, because the drums are getting bigger.

So you've got the kick, the snare, and the toms in the picture with the overheads. At this point, I will get the guy to play for a while and kind of putz to get it to where I like it. At that point, you want to listen to the balance of the drums and make sure that the ride cymbal and the hi-hat are sonically in proportion to the kit.

A lot of times, when you lean on an overhead picture like this, the ride cymbal—just by virtue of the fact that the drummer generally keeps the ride cymbal lower and closer to the drum kit than a crash cymbal—sometimes needs a little help. So although it is totally against everything I know, I'll put another mic on the ride cymbal to help bring it into the picture. The more mics, the more of a headache it becomes to keep it all phase coherent.

Now I have the distance between the ride cymbal mic and the overhead mics to contend with. Sometimes you will find that if you talk to that drummer, you'll find out that he may be able to live with the ride in a place where it is more easily heard. A lot of drummers are like that. So the first thing I'll do is say, "Hey, can we scoot this over here?" If this doesn't cause a panic, then I will do that. If it does cause a panic I'll bring in another mic, because I don't want to ever mess with a player's comfort level.

A lot of times, you can bring in the other mic underneath the ride cymbal. This is a little helpful because the cymbal itself becomes a sonic barrier to the crash cymbals. It can actually help isolate the cymbal by miking it in from the bottom, although generally the ride sounds you are looking for come from the top, where the bead hits the metal. So in an ideal world, the extra mic would be on top, and you'd just live with it. Maybe you can squeak just enough of it in to where it is in proportion, and that is it. Don't try and get it too loud, or you will open a whole new can of worms.

For a lot of these drummers, when the hat opens and the cymbal plates are loose and banging into one another, you can't get the hi-hat low enough in the mix. Then when they tighten it up and start playing a little beat on it, you can't get it loud enough. It has always been a big headache. So I usually have a good condenser mic, probably a good KM 84 or a 451 or something that is a half-inch condenser with a 10-dB pad. It is on the top, above the hi-hat, not necessarily looking at where the stick hits the cymbal, but rather in a place where it is not letting the snare drum fall into the microphone's pickup pattern. Usually, you can take these mics and you don't have to aim the mic at the point where the stick hits the cymbal. You can aim it opposite the cymbal from there, and where the stick hits the cymbals, it is still within the good part of the microphone's pickup pattern, but the snare drum is not.

So I usually have that, but I like to keep it down unless I absolutely have to have it. Because, again, it brings in another little phase problem. The fewer mics the better.

A lot of times, in rock music especially, it kind of gets hard to keep that sound-stage picture clear, and I understand that a lot of people nowadays—you kids out there—don't necessarily want it to be clear. Fine! But in case you are one of those who wants to keep it a little cleaned up, usually the best way out of that is to put some of that super-high 16 or 17 kHz–type EQ on those overheads. It makes an artificially detailed drum picture, but it has a tendency to detail the drums in a place that is well above the smear of electric-guitar crunch stuff. The higher frequencies are not really in those guitar sounds. So those higher frequencies are a good place to go to pull the drum detail out of the guitar hash.

But then you may run into the problem of a hi-hat falling into the same frequency range of an "S" in the vocal. Now you've got a singer who is singing about "girls" instead of a "girl," and now he's got two girlfriends. That is because the hi-hat made it sound like there was an "S" after the word "girl." [Sings] "You're so fine girls. Ooohh, you're so fine girls." So the guy's girlfriend hears his song on the radio and knocks him upside the head, thinking he's got a bunch of girlfriends.

My favorite reverb is a natural room, and my *favorite* favorite reverb is the room the drums are sitting in. That is actually air molecules moving around in sympathy with the drum kit. When I do set up *room* mics, I like to set up room mics, meaning I don't mike the drum kit from the room; I mike the room. I usually have a tendency to use large-diaphragm condenser mics looking away from the drum kit toward parts of the room that sound good. I'm getting what's coming off the walls and floor and ceiling. I think the reason I like that is because it enables me to maintain a detailed drum picture and yet add a room sound to it.

If you put your room mic up looking at the drum kit, you will often encounter some problems with maintaining the clarity of the drum's sonic picture.

Let's just set up a typical scenario. The stick hits the ride cymbal. The sound gets to the overhead mics in, say, 2 milliseconds. Then that sound arrives to the room mic in 47 milliseconds. Now you have smeared the definition of the drum picture. And that is happening with all of the cymbals and all of the drums and everything. But if you are just getting the reflections off the wooden walls of the tracking space, the wood doesn't contain those higher frequencies, and therefore the walls don't have a tendency to smear the detail of the drums.

There are some pretty bright-sounding rooms out there, and Ardent's C studio is one of the brightest. But even our C studio doesn't ever get up to the point of smearing that detail. It gets pretty bright, but it doesn't do that. If I do end up mixing stuff where people had mics looking at the drum kit, I have a tendency to dump everything from about 3 or 4 kHz up out of those rooms. I then let the overheads serve as the providers of the detail, and not the room mics. That is often helpful.

Clockwise from top left: Sam Taylor (photo by Jimmy Stratton) / Jerry Berlongieri recording a plane (photo courtesy of Jerry Berlongieri) / Bill Schnee (photo courtesy of Bill Schnee) / Richard Gibbs with guitar and bat (photo by Keegan Gibbs) / Ben Cheah with mic (photo courtesy of Ben Cheah).

Dynamic Signal Processing

Depending on which engineer or producer you are talking to, the subject of when and how to use dynamic signal processing—compressors, limiters, expanders, gates—can raise a passionate range of opinions. If you say to the wrong guy, "Hey, I really like the sound of a compressor smashing the heck out of a room drum sound," you might have permanently discredited yourself. Someone else might get enthusiastic and excitedly share his methods in achieving new levels of sonic bizarreness.

When it comes down to it, almost everyone will admit that it's whatever works for your ears. Obviously, jazz or symphonic music requires a different sonic approach than rap, hard rock, folk, or country.

It is generally regarded that dynamic signal processing came into being during the 1930s, with Bell Laboratories designing equipment to control the amplitude characteristics of telephone signals. It was around that time when the film, broadcasting, and music recording industries picked up on this development, enabling users to have better control of excessive signal variances.

Basically, limiters kept extreme or sudden loud passages from going beyond a certain point, and compressors helped contain those loud sections while bringing up the volume of quieter passages. This enabled the signal to have more apparent loudness.

Early devices of note were the Western Electric model 1126A limiter amplifier, which was used extensively by the film world. RCA was another pioneer in dynamic signal processing. Their BM6A, which came out in the early '40s, was another classic that found much use in the film world.

Since then, there has been a truckload of signal processing devices introduced in the audio world. Most haven't endured, but names like Fairchild and Pultec elicit quite a cult of equipment personality reverence for many. As a result, the value of these vintage units has increased to phenomenal proportions. That said, most people these days rely on their plug-in processing tools.

For this chapter, I talked to Richard Dodd, Jim Scott, Michael Wagener, Michael Brauer, Ken Kessie, Bruce Swedien, Joe Hardy, and John Hampton, who generously gave their input concerning the gear they like best and how they use it in the studio.

Richard Dodd

Credits include: Tom Petty (solo and with the Heartbreakers), Dixie Chicks, Boz Scaggs, the Traveling Wilburys, Wilco, Robert Plant, the Connells, Clannad, Green Day. See the Appendix for Richard Dodd's full bio.

What I go after with compression is to purely emulate the ear and a perception of sound, because obviously what a sound is and how we perceive it are two different things. Does a tree falling alone in the woods make a sound? I don't know, but if it does, I imagine it to be one thing, and in actuality it might be something else. Have you ever heard a gunshot outside, as it were? It is nothing like what we hear in the movies. It's a perceived thing. I typically use a compressor or limiter to achieve my perceived envelope—to add excitement and sensitivity or presence or change or add perspective, much in the same way that some people use reverb.

Just because you have compressed something, you don't have to use it all. If you compress something to the extreme of any perceived tolerance, it is obviously exaggerated and probably of no use. But if you then mix that in with the unaffected sound, you have something very useful. People sometimes say to me, "You use compression so well. It is so compressed, but it doesn't sound like it is compressed." The trick is that I am using both. I will have one signal that is totally pure mixed with the desired amount of the compressed signal. There is now a phrase for this: parallel processing.

What has become readily available in the digital world is multilane compression. Basically, that is of more use than an equalizer in many cases. What it has led me to realize, of course, is that even the old-fashioned analog units are actually multilane compressors, inasmuch as their inefficiencies and deficiencies, as it were, change the tonalities. They do it in an irregular fashion, and in some cases that is wonderful, and in other cases it's a negative. The way to recover that is by mixing in either a completely unaffected signal with it or a partially effected signal to achieve the right thing.

In other words, I may go to the compression extreme to get the effect I want, and then I will analyze what it has done to the sound. If I need some of the purity back sonically, I'll add back some of the unaffected sound. It's no more difficult than that. [These options are always available during mixdown.]

If I am already committed in the digital world for a project, then I will happily use the digital plug-ins, rather than go back to analog just to use an analog compressor. The cost of conversion isn't always worth the gain. The digital multilane compressors seem to be more phase-coherent than using multilane analog equalizers. By effectively slowing down a band and thereby giving emphasis to another part of the sound, you can change the whole sound. By using a multilane compressor to do that, it's more like getting a sound like sticking your finger in your ear. An equalizer isn't like that. Not that an equalizer is bad, but it doesn't give that effect. All it does is change the tone. It doesn't change the envelope. If you are in the analog world and you want to do that, then there are other tricks to be able to do that, but it's more involved.

I love black 1176s, preferably with the serial number below 4,000. They are distorted in a nicer way, and they do that thing of changing the sound in a way that gives you an option, rather than in a way that you immediately hate.

Jim Scott

Credits include: Tom Petty, Wilco, Red Hot Chili Peppers, Black Sabbath, Sting, Barbra Streisand, Randy Newman, Santana, Rolling Stones, Foo Fighters, Weezer, Dixie Chicks. See the Appendix for Jim Scott's full bio.

When it comes to discussing compression, it is almost something that has to be two different conversations. There's the "before digital compression" conversation and the "after digital compression" conversation.

If we were to have had this conversation 10 years ago, I would have said an 1176 on the vocal and a snare drum just adds a sharpness and an excitement and an eyes-open, clean-breath, menthol kind of a sound to whatever you put it on. An LA-2A or a Fairchild 670 would give you a warm blanket kind of a sound on your kick drum or bass guitar or left hand of a piano. Compressors were musical instruments, and the old ones still are. I don't have a lot of modern newer ones. I think my newest stuff is a dbx 160X, which is probably 15 years old, and a couple of Distressors.

I like Distressors a lot, but they are a little dangerous because they are really powerful, and you think, "What an amazing sound that is," but a few minutes later you realize, "Maybe I hit that a little too hard, maybe that's a little small-sounding, maybe that's a little distorted, maybe…I'll use different mic." [Laughs]

Compressors were instruments that helped you create a sound and also helped you with your dynamics and protected the tape. A lot of compressors were used to protect the tape and keep the level from getting too loud…take it to a certain point and cut it off.

Now with digital compression conversation, I will say that I get sent a lot of Pro Tools files to mix. Inside those files are either the mix that I'm trying to beat (I'm remixing because they don't like what they had) or a rough mix of their last foot-print or where they were the night they sent me the file. I mean, I understand trying to create excitement with compression, but when you open those things up, they are usually just crushed beyond crushed. The war has been lost because everybody has a big gun, and we are standing 5 feet apart shooting at each other with the same big gun. It's not exciting anymore. It's exhausting.

Michael Wagener

Credits include: Ozzy Osbourne, Megadeth, X, Skid Row, Extreme, Alice Cooper, Queen, Janet Jackson. See the Appendix for Michael Wagener's full bio.

There are a few ways of using compressors other than the obvious automatic level control. For instance, a compressor with a sidechain access can be used for cleaning up your bottom end. Try sending the bass through the compressor and key [sidechain/trigger] it with the kick drum, so every time the kick hits, it pushes the bass back a little. Set the release time of the compressor so that the bass comes right back up after the kick sound stops. That's an easy way to control low-end buildup without losing punch. Just don't tell the bass player about it.

I also used to set up two compressor/limiters with a two-way frequency crossover in a way that I could send a bass or guitar, for instance, through that frequency crossover and then connect two different types of compressor/limiters to the output of the crossover—one to the low-end out and the other to the high out. The outputs of the two compressor/limiters are patched back to two line inputs of the console. That gives me the chance to use a limiter on the high end and a compressor on the low end with different attack and release times. Low frequencies don't like fast release times too much—you'll get distortion that way. On the other hand, I could ride the high fader on the console on clicks and string pops without losing the low-end content of the mix or the melody line of the bass, or I would brighten up the bass in the choruses even in the days before EQ automation.

If you happen to have one or two of the old 1176 Ureis, you can use them on the room mic(s). Push all four ratio buttons in. The compression will be immense. Patch an EQ before the 1176s, and that will take quite a bit of high end off [shelving] and then bring up a little low end—maybe 2 to 3 dB around 80 to 100 Hz— then set the attack time to a slow setting and the release to a faster setting. Then set the input level so that the needle goes back to at least −10 dB. Your drummer will not want to hear any other mics in the mix.

There are a whole bunch of different compressors out there. You don't always have to use the $30,000 Fairchild. In fact, some of the "cheap" compressors do a great job because you can hear them work. It's like with microphones—every single one has a different sound and can be used successfully on a variety of instruments. Experimenting is the secret.

Michael Brauer

Credits include: The Rolling Stones, Bruce Springsteen, Jackson Browne, Billy Joel, Luther Vandross, Stevie Ray Vaughan, Michael Jackson, Jeff Buckley, Tony Bennett, Eric Clapton, David Byrne, Coldplay. See the Appendix for Michael Brauer's full bio.

One of the most versatile compressors on the market is one designed by David Derr called the EL8 Distressor Compressor. It's the kind of compressor that can be really clean and gentle and warm and transparent. But if you want it to be vicious, there is no compressor that I know of that can get you up to 40 dB of compression, which is what it might take to get something really wicked. I always tell people to buy three, because you're going to end up using two of them in stereo, and you're going to use that third one for bass or vocal or whatever.

With this unit's ability to get 40 dB of compression, you can take a regular lousy snare drum and turn it into a John Bonham kind of snare. What that means is that if you want to create your own reverb without reverb, you can! You can absolutely pull the "room" out of your snare drum.

You take the snare drum or whatever sound you are working on and sub-group or mult it to two channels. On the first channel, the dry or source channel, apply more gentle compression with a slow attack. By "gentle," I mean around 5 to 10 dB of compression, which is a lot on other compressors but not on this one. The resulting sound will be this smack or really hard sound. The higher numbers on the attack knob are slower. Now, on the second channel, crank the compression up to 40 dB with a very fast attack and release. When you completely remove the attack, it brings up the room ambience. So now you've got this one sound with horrendous attack punchiness to it and another sound that captures the room reverb. You mix in the one where all the attack has been removed, you bring that up with the first fader, and you have a natural room without any reverbs, yet you hear the reverb from the snare. By the use of your compressors, you are creating your own reverb.

Now, if you are going to put in 40 dB of compression, you are going to want to crank the output gain up to make up for this extreme compression. When you crank up the output, it just becomes a different animal. That is a key function of this. With the Distressor Compressor, you won't get any buzzing or humming or giving out. It's amazing.

The Distressor Compressor also really does a great job on vocals. It has this setting, which I guess is a mid-band emphasis setting, that is really designed for vocals that get thin and harsh and hurt your ears and cause you to EQ that section every time they get into that range. When you hit this setting, it automatically attenuates that area and warms it up, so you have this warm vocal all the way to the top of the range, where normally it would get very harsh. If you are dealing with a really thin voice, you can also add this DIST2 harmonic distortion setting, and it adds warmth and a little fuzz to the vocal. Depending on the application, it just sounds great.

Here is another idea, this one based on the 1176. It is called the British Setting. If you are familiar with the 1176, you basically have two knobs, an in and an out, and you have four buttons. With those four buttons, you can select your compression ratio. What you do is press them all in. Depending on the vintage of the unit—because you can't do this on some of the newer 1176s—hitting these four buttons makes it freak. The compressor needle, or indicator, will slam over to the right. Normally, whenever there is anything going on, the needle does the opposite. This looks really weird, but as long as it slams over this way, you know that it's working. This setting gives the sound a certain sense of urgency. It strains it. It's great for a vocal that needs extra urgency. Of course, you are going to be able to control the amount of strain in the voice by the input level. In the beginning, the needle may not move at all, so you have to keep bringing the gain up until the needle starts slamming over to the left.

Here's the additional touch for this: The compressor is so wild in what it's doing with the vocal, [for example], that although you don't hear the vocal coming in and out, you are hearing this intense sound. That's the best way I can describe it. Then you start bringing that second channel up to where it would normally phase out totally. Because the compression is moving this sound around, it kind of goes in and out of phase. So you back it off, just before you get to it. You have to play with this, but what that can do—especially with a vocal or instruments—is make the sound explosive.

There's a sweet spot, and you have to play around to find it. If you feel that it's starting to phase out or it's disappearing, you might want to play with that second channel. Remember, if you bring the whole thing up out of phase, no matter what it is, it's going to disappear. But when you have that kind of compression going on, and you put it right before its cutoff—it's 180 degrees out—weird things start happening. It's pretty wild!

Obviously, it is not something you are going to want to do on a Tony Bennett record. He doesn't use any compression. It has got to be used for really aggressive rock and roll—something where you are not going to use much reverb anyway—but you are not going to create a certain intensity.

When people give me ideas and certain mix approaches for specific things like I just said, the first thing that I start thinking out is, "Wow, forget the vocal. How about doing this other thing?" There are always ideas that take off from there.

Joe Hardy

Credits include: ZZ Top, Georgia Satellites, Steve Earle, Jeff Healey, the Hooters. See the Appendix for Joe Hardy's full bio.

The term compressor, in and of itself, sounds pejorative. It's like, "You are compressing my voice? You are taking my big huge voice and squeezing it down to this?" It sounds like an evil thing, but compressors are our friends.

A lot of singers might get a nice thick tone, but when they go up to another note, their tone thins out a little bit. If they go up to another note, it is messed up. To a degree, compressors really help all that, because they even everything out.

Generally, I go for the slowest attack I can get and the fastest release I can get.

If the attack gets fast, it really starts crunching the transients. It makes everything sound non-raucous. You want to let all the transients come through, but if the attack time is too ridiculously slow, it never catches anything.

Compressors kill high end real fast. They can really dull stuff out, and it is because they start taking the transients out. If your perception is, "The cymbals don't sparkle as much as they used to," it is because you are not getting that first big spike that screams "cymbal" or "snare drum" at you. Pianos, acoustic guitars, all those things start getting duller when they just don't have that little spike on them.

Bruce Swedien

Credits include: Duke Ellington, Tommy Dorsey, Paul McCartney, Barbra Streisand, Nat King Cole, Donna Summer, B.B. King, George Benson, Mick Jagger, Muddy Waters, Michael Jackson. See the Appendix for Bruce Swedien's full bio.

I do a lot of R&B music. If the music doesn't have a lot of the primitive energy in it, then it loses a lot of its appeal. To me, compression kind of takes away that extreme energy and makes things sound a bit contrived. Limiters and compression in general will tend to remove high frequencies first. I would rather have peaks that go past the limits of what we should be doing and keep the primitive energy there.

Michael Jackson's classic 1979 dance hit "Don't Stop 'Til You Get Enough," which I mixed, has absolutely no compression.

The absolute opposite of that approach was "Jam," the opening cut of *Dangerous.* On that track there is a lot of individual channel compression on the SSL.

Among the compressors and limiters that top my list are the Fairchild, the Urei 1176 LN, and the Neve 2254, which I occasionally used slightly on Jackson's voice; it's a favorite for mixing. I also have a stereo pair of 165A dbx limiters, as well as four dbx 160s.

I found this Neve console in Toronto. In it were these Class A solid state 2254 Neve limiters. I had them pulled out and installed in my racks. I replaced the dbx 165As with the Neve 2254s. I didn't change anything else and made Michael [Jackson] a mix on a cassette. He called me the next day and said, "You've changed something on my voice, and I love it." If that isn't a testimonial, I don't know what is. It was precisely the same gain control and the same levels, in and out, but a totally different emotional response. It was warmer. It almost sounded like more low end, but of course, it wasn't. I would also use the adjectives *clearer* and less *fuzzy*.

The Fairchild is also a classy piece of gear. The one I have is an old tube two-channel mastering limiter. It is extremely warm and very gentle. I don't think you can even vary the attack or release. It's pre-set. If you have a choir image or something where the miking image hasn't been optimum, and you've got some tones or sounds that are a little woofy or will present too much level to your mix without adding any impact, then the Fairchild is a wonderful choice.

Unless I am going for the specific effect of a squashed sound during the mixdown process, I will almost never put a program limiter in the chain. I can remember a couple of instances, but not very often.

Ken Kessie

Credits include: En Vogue, Tony! Toni! Toné!, Brownstone, Vanessa Williams, Celine Dion. See the Appendix for Ken Kessie's full bio.

Creative compression is all about breaking rules and doing what you're not supposed to. If you've got a deadline, you've got to go for what you know works. But when you feel that urge to step out and break new ground, try these ideas.

I sometimes make a cool faux stereo sound out of a mono one, not by time manipulation with a delay or pitch changer, but by dynamics. If you mult a single sound source to two faders, process them differently with two compressors, and then pan them left and right, you'll get a sound with no additional time slop, but with space still in the center for a lead vocal. Try compressing one side really hard while barely touching the other. With any luck, there will be some motion across the speakers. This works great on hi-hats, snare drums, and other percussion instruments.

Another effective compression move involves the bass drum and bass. In a lot of the R&B mixes I do, the kick drum and bass often play at the same time. When in R&B-land, I always make the bass and kick huge—that's one reason I work a lot!—then always have a problem fitting them both in the mix. What I do is compress the bass with the kick drum. You need a stereo compressor with stereo linkage and attack and release controls. So far, the Drawmer DL241 is my favorite. Send the kick drum to Channel A and slave Channel B [the bass] to it. Every time the kick hits, it knocks down the gain of the bass, and by using the attack and release controls, you can get a perfect blend between the two. Settings vary for this, of course; use your ears rather than the meters.

When I'm working on an SSL board, I sometimes record through the stereo bus compressor. Here's the patch to access the compressor: In the SSL patch bay, find the section called Pre VCA and Post VCA. Using two patch cords, connect Pre VCA [top row] to Post VCA [bottom row]. This bypasses the stereo compressor and the master fader. Inputs to the compressor are Pre VCA bottom row, and the outputs are Post VCA top row.

Warning! This patch is possibly lethal to speakers or talent with headphones on. Only attempt at low volume in case of a disaster, and please note that the master fader is out of the circuit and cannot be used to lower the volume. It's worth it, though—this compressor sounds great, especially on acoustic piano.

Euphonix consoles have a dynamic filter preset called a *de-esser* in their dynamics presets. Since I don't over-EQ anymore—yeah, right!—I don't need de-essers as much, but I found that by lowering the frequency into those pesky cheap mids, the device can also act as a harshness filter, especially when there are lots of nasty midrange parts. I run it across the stereo bus and tune it to remove just a pinch of ugly midrange when the track gets loud. It has a very smooth-sounding effect on the mix.

Many guitar stomp boxes have lots of personality, punch, and, let's face it, horrible noise. Interface them with a preamp or DIs or just plug and overload. Not only are these great for alt-rock sessions, they are practically required for proper indie cred.

Look, we all know about short signal paths by now, but sometimes you've got to throw the book away. Sometimes it takes several compressors chained together to create the impact or smoothness needed for a standout sound. Sometimes one box acts as a peak limiter while the other works as a low-ratio compressor. There's no formula; just use your ears. And I do mean use your ears—compression meters are often misleading. Like Joe Meek said, "If it sounds right, it is right."

John Hampton

Credits include: White Stripes, the Raconteurs, the Replacements, Lynyrd Skynyrd, Gin Blossoms, Vaughan Brothers, the Cramps, B.B. King, the Allman Brothers. See the Appendix for John Hampton's full bio.

I generally put limiters, like a Fairchild, on musical instruments and compressors on voices. Usually I will break out a limiter on acoustic guitars or clean-sounding electrics that have a lot of dynamic range, especially when they have to compete with a wall of constant-level Marshalls in the mix. However, I don't like constricting the dynamic range that much.

I use slower attacks on programming in general, including the drums. A slow attack will hold down the overall level, but it lets the little transient things pop through, which to me is a more lifelike sound.

If you want "I don't hear it" compression that does a good job of controlling level, my preference is the UA 176B. A slow attack [such as 4:1 ratio] with a pretty quick release, but not totally quick, is almost perfect for a female singer who you don't want to notice a lot of compression. With the UA 176B, you can control the attack and release times, something you can't get from old Fairchilds. Generally, I like the artifact of compression and the way it sounds on a voice. Some people don't like it, but I personally do.

The SSL compressors are perfect for giving you a hard, agitated effect. If you don't necessarily want that, I will ditch the SSL from the program and use the Summit DCL-200. I'll dial the attack time and release on the Summit to where I'm kind of hearing a similar tone. Then, I'll A/B the SSL compressor to the Summit; most of the time it will be toned down a little bit and not quite as hard-sounding. The Summit definitely warms things up. I use that religiously on mixes, drum kits, and a number of things.

A transistor compressor that I like is the Valley 440. You can control all of the parameters on it—the ratio, release and attack time, threshold—and you can dial up just about any kind of compression on it quickly.

Expanders work well on voices that have too much noise on poor analog recordings. I will use an expander as a kind of single-ended noise reduction. They will let the voice come through, and as soon as the singer is done singing or in between words, it kind of closes things up a little to keep the noise down. It doesn't work quite as hard as a gate, which turns the signal completely off. There is an expander in the Valley 440 that I use. There are also expanders on the SSL console.

For really weird compression, hit Listen Mic to Tape on the SSL console and put any track in Record. Whatever is going through the input of that compressor is recorded on tape. It's this wild, crazy pumping, 60 dB of gain reduction thing that smashes everything to pieces. It's a real neat sound to add occasionally, when you are looking for a raved-up sound.

Gates come in handy for a lot of things, but I never automatically gate anything. Gates on kick drums with a fast attack and a pretty fast release can add a whole new dynamic envelope to the drum. A lot of times you can economize the amount of low end in your mix that way, which helps the bass guitar be more intelligible.

During the '80s, mainly in metal music, a lot of people only wanted to hear the stick on the head and then let the reverb become the rest of the drum, so to speak. For that effect, gates played a big role. As a result, you could have this little drum attack with the giant reverb attached to it. It's really no longer a drum. It's another animal. I don't know what it is. It's a thing.

I will use gates with slow attack a lot of times if I've got, for example, a real quiet passage, and I've got single-coil guitar buzz, and I want to eliminate it in between the parts the musician is playing.

I personally tend to not use any compression at all if there is something that has got its own natural attractive dynamic all by itself and it's not competing with too many constant-level sounds. Once the overall level of everything is set, I like to let the music have its own dynamic and then ride faders as needed. After all, there are definitely times where dynamic signal processing can work against you.

When you are trying to get a record approved by a record company, you might run the mix through a compressor so it will sound like it's on the radio. Sometimes that's what it takes for some record company people to visualize the commercial potential. I try to do it always, even when I am doing rough mixes, so people will kind of get an idea what it is going to sound like when it is finished. It's going to get smashed when it comes out of the radio transmitter anyway.

Greg Leisz at Village Recorders / Redd Volkaert, Los Super 7 sessions. Row 2: Producer Charlie Sexton at Ocean Way, Los Super 7 sessions. Row 3: Porcupine Tree's Steven Wilson (photo by Susana Moyaho) / Michael Wagener (photo courtesy of Michael Wagener).

Over the course of my interviews and the assembling of this book, there were times when I would be going over piles of transcripts, and there were things shared that really didn't have anything to do with recording a drum set, building a mix, or mastering. They didn't neatly fall into production or engineering philosophy, either. Nevertheless, I would read these sections and simply feel they were gifts offered by those I interviewed. Sometimes it came in the form of observations about the state of the industry, and other times it was just hard-earned wisdom and life understanding that always made me feel glad and gave me a little extra calibration when I read it. For lack of a better way to title this chapter, I've created a title that is sort of a net for these meditative odds and ends.

Wayne Kramer

Credits include: MC5, Gang War, GG Allin. Film/TV credits: Talladega Nights, Eastbound & Down, *Fox Sports Network themes, E! Network's* Split Ends. *See the Appendix for Wayne Kramer's full bio.*

Based on my experience, succeeding in life has more to do with character than it does job skill. Once you've figured you know what you're doing in the first place, it's then a matter of being who you say you are and understanding that anything you do in music is a collaborative process. I think this book could be useful because you're distilling all these experiences, techniques, and philosophies and making them available to other people. The idea that I can make a contribution and share what little I know is a relatively important thing to me. I was a taker for a long time, so I'm hoping to tip the scales a bit in the other direction now.

We are dealing with humans, and humans are notoriously messy with each other. It's like the Bob Dylan lyric, "We all have to serve somebody." I try to conduct myself in such a way to be thought of as a good person to have around and to be seen as the solution to a problem. My goal is that when someone has a music "problem" to solve, calling me to take care of it offers that person a feeling of excitement as well as security. It seems to me that the people who move forward are the ones who are conscious of the relationships between one another and from that point work from the basis of service.

The key is to understand the dynamic of these relationships and to know who you work for and what is at stake. Oftentimes in the work I do, there are serious people with a great deal of money on the line. There is a lot of pressure, and it's my job to actually help somebody else finish a job. That's very different from being in a band. It's a whole different mindset.

If I'm in my own band, my bandmates are helping me do what I want to do, and I write some songs, and I make the calls, and I'm the main man, and I call the shots.

But in the TV and film world, I am certainly not "the Man." Often the director is "the Man" or the producer is "the Man," and I've got to figure out which one is which in order to streamline the process.

I was once told that a composer has to figure out who is God on the movie, meaning who can fire you. Everybody on the film will have an opinion, and you can't abide by everybody's opinion, so you've got to know whose opinion matters the most. It's a lot of fundamental stuff.

An honest rule of thumb is never gossip and don't spend valuable time trying to entertain people with your thrilling tales of yesteryear. What I generally see on scoring sessions, from top to bottom, is that people are really making an effort to work together. This is true from the musician out on the floor, to the engineers, to the producer, to the composer, to the director. There is a great deal of respect and dignity about the process, and everybody is doing their best to be of good humor and trying to create a pleasant environment in which to work. These are things that shouldn't have to be talked about, but I think it's worthwhile to discuss because common sense isn't actually so common.

For instance, when you go to a meeting to talk to somebody about possible work, don't dominate the conversation. Let them talk. Learn how to listen to what other people have to say. Don't promote yourself. They already know who you are, and you will reveal who you are over the course of the lunch or over the course of the meeting. They'll get a sense of who you are, and that's why you'll get hired (or not). It's because they say, "You know, he's cool. I like working with him. He seems like the kind of guy I'd like to have around." People who are accustomed to collaborating have a radar, a sensitivity to one other.

We shouldn't have to talk about these things, but I think it's true. It's basic stuff like, "Go to a meeting clean. Take a shower, and for God's sake, brush your teeth. Compose yourself like a responsible adult."

I work with my wife, who represents me. She told me once early on that we had a lunch meeting with somebody who did music at one of the networks, and maybe there was a chance I could work with them. She said, "You know, Wayne, if the conversation isn't about you, you lose interest in everybody and everything." And I said, "That isn't true. You're crazy!" And she said, "No, I'm not crazy." But she was right, and I figured out that this attitude I had was a carryover from being in a band, being a rock-and-roll guy. Rock musicians often have a sense of entitlement that carries over into everything they do. That point of view that, "If we're not talking about Wayne, then Wayne's not interested." So I had to grow up. I had to learn how to attend a meeting and just be comfortable being myself and not promoting myself. I don't have to tell people, "I'm Wayne Kramer from the MC5." They already know that. And if they don't, it doesn't matter anyway! I want them to see today that I'm the type of guy they might want to have on their project. As a result, I've learned to be straight-ahead and give a straight considerate answer with good humor and some mutual respect and dignity for other people and my actions with them.

I think some people get buried in ambition, ego, and career climbing. There are a lot of incredibly talented people in my business. You'll see talented composers make a couple of movies, never to be heard from again. It seems to me that the reason you never hear from them again is because they're jerks. Word quickly gets around town, and soon nobody wants to work with someone who is actually going to make this already monumental task all the more difficult. Those considering hiring a composer are often honest about their experiences. "Yeah, he was a big problem on the last movie." As a result, they don't ever call that composer again. I want to be able to stay in business and have people call me and go, "Hey, we got another project next month. Would you be interested in that?" Hell yes! I want to work. I want to be productive. I want to participate and be in on it all.

This subject of character is the most important thing. When there's a deadline, it's important that I can prioritize and get the job done when it is supposed to be done. Sometimes this is a very high-pressure business, and it's certainly not easy. It's hard when people start busting your chops, and they don't like what you're writing, and they don't use it. I've sent cues over that I've worked hard on, and they go, "I don't know. It just didn't do it for me." And to my way of thinking, it was brilliant. But, you know, it ain't up to me. It is up to them, so I've got to swallow that quickly. I can't get hung up on the fact that they didn't like that cue. I've got to write another one, and I've got to figure out right away what it is they want from me. And I achieve that by actually listening.

It's a whole different world than being in a "band" world. You know, this is a very different paradigm. There are people who come out of music school who never played in a band. They just wanted to be a composer from the beginning. It's kind of like I got in the side door, because I was in a band that some people have heard of. That might have gotten me closer to the front of the line, but I have to carry my own water.

When it comes to anything in the arts, we are in the idea business, and our job qualification is being able to create something out of nothing. Sometimes there is money to be made at it, and sometimes there isn't. There is nothing wrong with succeeding and being compensated fairly for your work, but there is a lie about money and success, especially in the world of music and in all the arts. The lie is, if you do whatever you have to do to achieve success—whether it's a hit record, hit book, hit movie, TV show, or dance video—you will somehow, as if by magic, be delivered to a good life. This is a lie. The fact is that if there is something wrong with me before I achieve success, not only will success not fix that issue, it will make it worse. It's unfortunate, because most young people swallow the lie.

The odds of you becoming wealthy and internationally famous in pop music are about the same as they are in professional sports, which is about 100,000 to one. How many guys in your neighborhood played baseball as a kid, and how many of them ended up with careers in the big leagues? It's the same thing in music. How many people played the guitar years ago and ended up wealthy and internationally recognized? It's like a pyramid, and there's only room at the top for one Bruce Springsteen, one Sting, one U2, and one Beyonce. It's a very tough position at the pinnacle to sustain.

It kinda doesn't matter that I say these things, because young people are going to go for it anyway. No one could tell me. They're all going to do it anyway.

The first thing I tell young people is to learn music. Learn your job. Learn to read and write music. Go to school. Learn how to read a contract. Learn how to protect yourself. Learn what your rights are. Learn how get your own health insurance. Learn how to file your own taxes, because even if you get in a successful situation as a composer, musician, or producer, and the money is rolling in, and you have managers and agents, you probably can't trust them. They are only there as long as the money is there. Our industry is full of stories of people who lost fortunes because they didn't file their own taxes.

We're self-employed, and what I'm saying isn't being fanatical, it's just protecting yourself so that you can have a career in music and continue to work. My idea of success is being able to continue. If I can continue to do music for a living and work with people I like to work with, doing things that I think are important, then I've succeeded beyond my boyhood dreams.

Nathaniel Kunkel

Credits include: James Taylor, Lyle Lovett, Little Feat, Linda Ronstadt, Graham Nash, Neil Diamond, Billy Joel, Warren Zevon, David Crosby, Barbra Streisand, B.B. King, Van Morrison, Morrissey, John Mayer. See the Appendix for Nathaniel Kunkel's full bio.

For too many years, everyone has been trying to conform to this jive idea of living and dying by a hit record. It's a flawed concept, and now that the music business is basically going into a freefall, we're going to see a lot of people starting to tell the truth because there just isn't any reason not to. They should have been telling the truth all along.

Thank God Joni Mitchell didn't have to sell three and a half million records on her first album, or she would have gotten dropped. And thank goodness they let her make another record! Just think, we wouldn't have any of these amazing artists if the same standards were applied to them that are applied to artists these days. If something doesn't sell a million copies, does that mean it doesn't have any value? Art simply doesn't work that way.

You don't know what's going to work for people when you are making it. You're just trying to be true to what you are creating at hand. If you start out with the goal of trying to sell a commodity to 25 million people, it ain't art. Where those two realities butt heads is where the problems are coming from in the music business. We're trying to sell music like we're marketing hog jowls. They're totally incongruent.

If you're interested in making money, you should be in the petrochemical industry. You will make more money for less work.

We don't need more robber barons in the music industry. We need artists. And the people who are truly in the music industry for the love of it don't need to make millions and millions and millions of dollars. When that kind of success started to happen, it was cool, but that's not what motivates Bob Dylan to write songs. It's why that guy who runs Exxon runs Exxon. That's the problem! Understand the business you're in and what your goal is, and if we can make good money at it, then that's awesome. If we can't make money at it, we can't torpedo music just because it's not making us enough money. Isn't music more important than that? It seems to me like it would be.

My immense frustration these days is that we're not making records as good as we once were. Not only that, but they're not selling, and we still continue making them not as good. The definition of insanity is expecting a different response from the same action, and yet that's what most of us are doing.

It seems to me the thing we need to be focusing on the most is paying attention to the music, paying attention to the song, and being true to it.

There's so much fear in the music business, and the truth is that fear isn't going to be what brings about good change in the music business, and it's not going to be what brings about good music, either. What's going to bring about good music is exactly what Beck was thinking when he did his first record: "I'm doing it my way." And it was totally different! Of course, when it became successful, A&R people at the major labels said, "Hey, he made a record for $4,000, and it sold millions of records! Okay! All record budgets are $4,000!" It's like, "No! That was just what Beck did! That was only the process for his specific piece of art."

When people ask, "What should I do? What are we going to do in this economy with this industry tanking?" my response is always the same: When you're the best at something, you can make a living. People will seek out excellence. When I look around at the people who are really doing well, they do their thing uniquely better than anybody else does. I don't care what it is. If you do what you do better than anybody else, you're going to make more money than you could ever need.

How do you do something better than anyone else? You have passion about it! How do you have passion about something? You love doing it! In the end, if you do something you really, really love, you can't help but make money. The word will get out, and the people will find you. If you start thinking, "I want to make records and be successful, so I have to go make records like this, because that flavor is what everyone is buying," you're convoluting your destination with all these other parameters that you don't really feel in your heart. As a result, you're not going to be as good at your job, and no matter how far you go after that, you're just going to be another guy turning out productions and mixes that are okay, not inspired.

Really paying attention to what matters to you and making the art that you connect with is going to be the thing that gives you longevity, and other people are going to respond to it. You can sit and make something sound like someone else's record, but it's not going to be inspired. It's going to sound just like someone else's record, you know?

Tony Shepperd

Credits include: Madonna, Kenny Loggins, Take 6, Boyz II Men, Yolanda Adams, Lionel Richie, Flora Purim, Diana Ross, Michelle Williams. See the Appendix for Tony Shepper's full bio.

THE TECH BREAKFAST

During the late '90s, after some late-night session, I got into this great discussion with a couple of the friends of mine, Dave "Rev. Dave" Boruff, a saxophonist who was David Foster's right-hand man for years, and Stephen Bray, who once produced Madonna and was a production partner of mine for a number of years. The three of us, a musician, engineer, and a producer, were hanging out, and Stephen said, "Why don't we get together tomorrow in the morning and just talk tech?" So we met up the next morning up the street and had a tech breakfast, which would be the first of many to come.

When we started, it dawned on us that we're all stuck in our own separate worlds in our own studios, and nobody sees anybody anymore. There was a time when, if you were working at Ocean Way, for example, you could pop in to Studio A if you were working in B and say, "Dude, what ya working on? Play me some!" Well, now we have to go out of our way to do something like that, because everyone is in their own cubicle in their houses, and you don't see anybody else anymore. It's imperative, now more than ever, to reach out to each other and try to communicate.

Over time, Tech Breakfast has become this way for a bunch of engineers, musicians, producers, and manufacturers to come out and talk about the industry, what's going on and what's not, and see each other and be of real support.

We typically meet once every two months at 10 in the morning at the same place in Burbank, and we have guys as far away as Oxnard [California] drive in for these Tech Breakfasts. A lot of Who's Who in the industry show up there. Over time, it has also evolved into creating www.techbreakfast.com, so we could mentor people and have an active forum with a lot of industry pros. We also kind of open it up with the DVD series.

There are some things that separate the forum from other sites. One is you have to use your real name in order to post. That is a must, because so many people give misinformation. There was a kid who was on the site the other day wondering how Seal got the vocal sound on "Crazy." Steve MacMillan, who's active in Tech Breakfast and who engineered and mixed that song, was able to provide that information. It's great to see that. It's a chance for pros to reach out to the next generation, because let's face it, the days of having a second engineer in a studio are going, going, gone. Most of the engineers who are really worth their salt are not always working at the major commercial facilities. They've got their own rooms.

We are also creating videos with serious pros who do great work. For example, we went out with engineer/mixer Frank Wolf when he was getting ready to go out and do the *Hairspray* orchestral sessions. We sat in there for two days with him and just videotaped. I recently called Nate Kunkel and asked, "Dude, do you have a big session coming up and you need something documented? We'd love to send a crew down there, because we could interview you and the whole nine yards."

Tech Breakfast is one of those things that has been growing exponentially. I go around and do lectures at schools. These kids are hungry. It's like "teach us," because they're learning just the fundamentals at a lot of these places, and they are desirous of obtaining real-world knowledge from those in the industry.

THE MUSIC INDUSTRY AND REINVENTION

There was a time when there were true A&R talents who really sought out great artists and took a chance on them. They didn't think in the box. Eventually, you would see these great visionary A&R guys not get rewarded anymore. The record labels bought into this cookie-cutter vision. It's like, "We've got 20 cookies like this, and they are all the same, but we're just going to put a little different flavor on top." A number of these great record men and women grew tired of the cookie-cutter garbage and left or retired.

Jim Ed Norman was one of Warner Brothers' great record people. He was in Warner Brothers Nashville, the city that most people think only has country artists. He signed Take 6, an a cappella vocal group with roots deep into gospel, doo-wop, and sophisticated jazz-influenced singing. That signing was against the conventional wisdom of less creative music-industry types. That first Take 6 record cost $150,000 to make, including the video. That album to this day has sold over two million copies. Jim Ed was someone with a vision, and it paid off for years for him and the label, but the dynamic of the industry has changed, and I don't think it's ever going back. Around the end of the '90s, there was a sea change, and you could see it coming. You could see the whole industry starting to shift. It was very subtle at first, and then it became more violent.

I remember talking to a friend of mine at a major label in 1997 and saying to this person, "I don't think this label will be around 10 years from now." The reply was, "It has been here forever. It will always be here!" I said that I thought it would be a distribution company, but it wouldn't be a viable record company as they were at that time. That was in 1997, and there seems to be that concept of "We haven't hit rock bottom yet." In some ways it's good, and some ways it's bad.

I once took a project to a major label in hopes of it getting picked up. The A&R person said, "I'm not really interested, blah, blah." I said, "Sure. That's okay." Two years later this person got fired. At the time we really didn't know each other, but years later we became friends. This former A&R person admitted, "You know, when I think about all those people who came to me, I was so cavalier. I see all of them now, and I wish I had invested in real artists back then, because I would have had something to take with me when I left. Most of the artists were flavor of the month. Now the chickens are coming home to roost, and we deserve it because we signed junk, and we should have been signing quality artists and developing them. We were the gatekeepers, but we helped make our jobs irrelevant."

I have a friend who sold 7,000 copies of his first album, which he did all on his own and got everything that came through the door. He sold 11,000 copies of his second album. There was a major label that heard it, flipped out, and wanted to sign him to their jazz label. When his third album came out, the first on this major label, it sold less than a thousand copies. The label then dropped him; he went back to doing it his way and sold 20,000 copies of his fourth album. He knew his market and knew what he was doing. He knew what kind of record he should make and did it in such a way that it fed his soul, instead of what some major label wanted him to do, because they really don't know anymore. They're throwing something against the wall and seeing what sticks. There is a paradigm shift, and people are starting to say that they don't care what other people are doing. They're doing what they want to do.

Practically everyone I know is being hired by artists who aren't signed to major record labels and are out making albums they want to make. They are getting calls from indie artists who are saying, "I only have $20,000 to do this record. What can I do?" Now it's like, "Dude, let's make something cool, because I don't have to worry about going down and sitting there on the clock at some major commercial studio at $2,500 a day."

I really think the industry is on a slow upswing, because it's gaining knowledge from asking, "How did we get into this mess?" People are looking back to those times 30 to 40 years ago when studios were run by owner engineers, and you went to that studio because you wanted that sound. "I'm going to Nate Kunkel, because he can get me that sound I love! I'm going to Steve MacMillan's place, because he has the sound that I'm looking for." We're getting back to that now.

Big studios, commercial studios, have their place, but when I have more plug-ins and hardware, more IOs, more things that are going to make my life better here at my place, why am I paying you $2,500 a day? In the big picture of things, I think I'll just stay here in my studio.

When I'm approached by indie clients and certain producers who can't afford everything upfront, I give them the reduced rate and put them on a payment schedule. They don't get the sessions back, because I mix in the box in Pro Tools, but they get a WAV file with a couple of different versions, and they don't care that they don't have everything archived. They don't need that. They just need everything to sound great. It's fantastic for me, because I know at the beginning that I have one producer client who has four different artists he's working with. I set up an arrangement where I will mix their stuff and cut my rate by half, put them on a payment plan where they pay me a third now, a third next month, and a third a month from then. Like clockwork, I get my check. It's better than working with a major label! For the most part, these people are funding their projects themselves. It's not their day job. They're doing stuff trying to make ends meet, and it's hard work. They make a commitment to doing their project, and they want it done right, and they pay you like clockwork. I can't get Geffen or Warner Bros. to pay me within six months of a billing.

It's insane, because the labels want you to keep working for them, but this isn't a charity case. My mortgage company doesn't understand when I can't pay for six months. I wouldn't own a house anymore! They think they can not pay you for six months and everything is good. It's very frustrating, but the industry has shifted, and I've chosen to shift what I do with the realities of getting paid, because this is not a charity. I'm not here doing it for my health, and I have to sit back and say, "What's good for me and what will work for my family?"

A few years ago I worked on a Christmas album project for a major artist. The major label said the producer wanted me to go down and cut all of her vocals in another city. The label then added that if the artist didn't show, I didn't get paid. The producer told the label that I wasn't going to sit around and wait for this artist, who was notorious for not showing up. Sure enough, the producer went down there to the studio in that city 14 times and stayed over the course of a month and a half and never recorded a lick. I wasn't about to go sit around there and not get paid.

There was one time where I did three or four 16- or 18-hour days at Westlake Audio, and I just came home that fourth day, and I'm like, "Oh my God. I just can't do this anymore." I have four kids, and they are growing up without me. That experience was one of the last straws. I started to put together a room in my garage and began to get work there.

For me, working out of my home is fantastic, and now I'm finding these clients who say they'll cut me a check today and give me the drive, and I start mixing. I put the mixes up on the iDisk, and they download and listen to them and write me back and say what they need addressed. I now have ConnectLive and Connect Pro, and I connect directly to the clients that way.

I have one guy who is a producer back east who calls me up and will take his laptop to his favorite coffee shop in Virginia and sit there with his headphones on and have me stream the mix, which I play right out of Pro Tools. He'll make his notes with me on the phone. He might say, "The second word in the bridge she sings is a little hot. Can you pull it down a little bit?" I pull it down, send it back, and it's perfect. He does this whole thing at the coffee shop, and it's done in an hour. We'll tweak like four or five songs, and it's done. I'm working a new way. This is where things are going, and I have a lot of clients that I'm doing production with who are back east, and they can't really come out to L.A. They will send me mock-ups on MIDI. I'll go through and track guitar, piano, vocals with all the guys in L.A. I send them stuff every night, and they never have to leave their houses, and they approve stuff instantly. We're completely redefining the way this industry is working now, because we had to.

I have a friend who is a producer in Florida, and he has artists who live out here in L.A. The artist will take her laptop. She'll get the iChat going and stream everything out of Pro Tools and Chicken of the VNC over the Internet to control my system. Some of the PC programs, like GoToMyPC and InTouch with PC, are basically controlled from a remote station from my computer. So the producer is in Florida, and his artist is here. When I get the vocal sound right and ready, I look into the eyesight and ask him if he's got everything. I go into the house, and he'll call me and tell me everything is done and she's gone. The entire session was run from Florida punching in and out, controlling my Pro Tools from here, but he's in Florida. Then I send him the files of everything I've done, and he tweaks them, pops them back, and I mix it from my place. You just have to reinvent the way you are working, because the industry is completely changed, and it's never going back. All of this is now completely built into Connect Pro.

I was talking to Kenny Loggins about this, because he was trying to figure out what to do. Sony had dropped him after 30 years and many hit records. I told him that I thought it was a blessing in disguise. He already had a client base, including a fan club base that was 20,000 names big. Every fan that goes to a concert, you've got their email. Do a record and do it on a subscription-base service.

In the '50s they didn't do a whole album. They didn't do 10 songs. You put out a single that hit the charts, there was a B side to the single, and it went as far as it could. When they were done, they put out another single. I said, "If you use that as a model, say you're gonna record a single this month and create a subscription service, so all the fans who pay $50 a year will get a new song every month, backstage priority when it comes to shows, et cetera." There are all kinds of fan-club things that you'll get for that, and every month you'll get a free download. I told Kenny that if you've got 20,000 dedicated fans, then how much money did you just put in your pocket, right now this month? You can play games with a record label, but why would you if you've got enough money to fund your own recordings this way? What do you care? Why go to the label and have them fund it for you? Go in and make the record you want to make, release one new single a month, and at the end of the year you can package them all together and make a special album release. You can take orders and know exactly what you are selling before you even have to worry about selling it. The downloads cost you nothing except server time. You've already got your server because you are a dot-com. You know, it's taking some of the past and reinventing it and making it more relevant to the future of our industry. Because right now people are scrambling trying to figure out what to do, and this way really works.

I think it works not only for established artists, but it's working for artists who are really kinda out there gigging heavily. You have your fan base. They know what they want to do. Some fans will buy an album of their favorite group and listen to it night and day for two weeks, and then they are done with that record. But what if the group had dropped two songs this month and one song next month, and they dropped them as singles? You might be a little bit more interested. Who knows? I don't know, but certainly with fanatics of groups it's more reliable to say I've been a fan of Kenny Loggins for 30-something years. If Kenny drops a new song this month, I'm out there; I'm getting it. It's a buck download, but if you have paid the $50 a year for the subscription, not only do you get your fan base goodies, like getting to see Kenny backstage at special appearances, but you get the downloads for free because you've already paid for the year subscription to the service.

So, I mean doing things like that. The artist or band goes to guys like myself and makes deals, saying, "Listen, here's what we're gonna do. We're gonna work on this record. If you can reduce your fee, since I'm paying for it out of my pocket, I'll cut you in on a piece of the record. Let's find out a way to make this happen."

In some ways, the industry is just crumbling in on itself, but if you are looking for opportunities, there are new opportunities as engineers and producers to really find venues for us to still have our art become art and not have to sell ourselves to the lowest bidder and jump. It might seem like the worst of times, but it's really the beginning of the best of times, if you approach this with an open mind and some resourcefulness. I think there is something to be said about finding your niche in this industry, taking the tools you've developed over time, and reinventing it with something new. If you don't, then how are you going to make it? It can't be business as usual. You've got to do something different. If you can reinvent yourself as an engineer and producer, that's fantastic.

David Kershenbaum

Credits include: Joe Jackson, Tracy Chapman, Joan Baez, Cat Stevens, Peter Frampton, Duran Duran, Supertramp, Marshall Crenshaw, Kenny Loggins, Joshua Kadison, New Order. See the Appendix for David Kershenbaum's full bio.

I believe all of the arts, whether they are paintings, books, movies, or records, deal with playing on people's emotions. It's all about emotion. I think all of us are trained from a very early age to be appropriate and not really express emotion, so as a consequence, we've got our emotions kind of compartmentalized and kept behind our masks, and we rarely show our true emotions unless there's something traumatic or a catastrophic. As a result, we close ourselves off from a lot of our feelings, and when someone takes the chance to really come from a level of true feeling, it can connect with a lot of us in a way we'll never forget.

For instance, to this day, more than 20 years after Tracy Chapman's "Fast Car" was released, people will come up to me and say, "I know exactly where I was and who I was with and even what I was wearing the first time I heard that song." It was because that song connected so deeply with people on a real emotional level. Regardless of the style of music, I think that emotion plays one of the biggest parts in the communication of music.

I've found that great artists don't need anything to be who they are. They'll sit down with a piano and a guitar and open their mouths, and out it comes. And you go, "Wow! I don't need to hear anything else. This is great!" I think an artist who is not about throwing something together to try to make it big, but is committed to make something meaningful and well thought out and has real emotion, will cause word of mouth to spread about them, because I think great music reaches its own level. You can't stop it.

In the old days with the big record labels, you could actually manipulate things up to a certain point, and it wouldn't go any farther than that. I think that if someone makes a record that's meaningful, it will stand on its own. By doing the Internet steps of exposing it, creating a fan base, creating a live show, eventually getting booking and the management, they can, through their real artistry and smarts, create a durable career with real potential.

I tell artists to really weigh the considerations of what they may be giving away by doing a major-label deal versus being independent and making probably less in terms of sales but ending up with much more money. It's important to nurture that grassroots foundation thing and then get it so that you can keep stepping it up to the next level, until finally you go out into the major distribution. Once artists have got their name out there and established a base, they just need to keep their system running and put their music out, and people will find it and be interested in buying it. So, my feeling is that it's the best time for music. It's even great for Baby Boomer–age artists—artists who the big labels would've historically thought to be too old. There are no limitations now, if you take the right steps.

It used to be that you had to be 20 to 25, or you weren't going to get signed, and you had to do whatever flavor was happening in pop at the time. In the earlier days, the radio stations were the tastemakers, and that's how people found out about new music. It's different now.

Over the last 30 years, there really wasn't a whole lot of change in the way the record business operated, force-feeding music through a little tube, basically broadcasting to mega audiences with the hopes of selling 10 or 20 million albums. Unfortunately, what happened was that a lot of artists tried to fit themselves into the mold to run down that chute, and as a consequence, it got harder to be signed, the more they compromised themselves to get signed. I think a lot of the creativity and innovation went out the window as a result. Fortunately, that is way out the window today.

Today, the Internet offers not only an opportunity to get your music up and be heard instantly, but it also offers the opportunity of artist development, because you can take a number of shots until you get it right, and you don't have to necessarily fit into a mold. The sky's the limit as far as your creativity goes, and I think that's so exciting.

I think there's a huge opportunity for new artists, if they're focused enough. But even though the good news is while you can get your music up on the level playing field of the Internet in minutes, the bad news is that you're suddenly out there with a lot of mediocre, low-quality things. There are a few things that are amazing enough that you'll see a million hits, but they are few and far between.

A mission of mine has been aimed at trying to get people focused in their music to create things of lasting value. I get so many demo submissions, and one of the things I notice is that very few of them are even familiar with song structure. It's okay to break structure to come up with something innovative, but I think you need to know structure first, because structure in a song, in a production, is like a movie. It's tried and true. A movie has key structural turning points, and when it is good, it holds your attention. You can look at it overall as a dynamic map.

If you go into the studio with the production attitude of "I'm just going to make tracks and throw a bunch of stuff on and put a vocal and see what works later," you'll likely end up with something very unremarkable. It's important to think of the production in terms of the organics of the song form. Then it turns out to be a much more alive kind of experience. I've had people I've trained try it, and they're amazed at the results because it causes you to think in terms of the overall emotional picture rather than getting stuck in, "Gosh, this is a great bass drum sound."

I've produced a lot of great singers over the years, and the thing that I always try to do is start with the vocal and work backwards. I think most people start with the track and go forward, and usually the vocal ends up functioning like an extra added attraction. Then you figure out that your overdubs are conflicting with each other and there's no space for them, so then you have to start pulling out things.

We're dealing with emotion, and we're trying to disarm people by connecting them at the level of their spirit—not just with a lot of sound or something they can tap their foot to or sing or dance to, but something that is going to make a difference...something that is moving.

There's even a way of performing an instrumental solo part that actually pleads, begs, or congratulates...or whatever it is, that has the emotion of what the story-line is supposed to be. You can play it so you're just pulling the feeling out of it. But to get people to do that, and particularly with singing—because it's the most spiritual and the most difficult—they have to kind of become a conduit and just let it flow through them, rather than coming out of their head with it.

The best recording I found is when they don't know you're recording, because the minute the red light goes on, all of a sudden it's like do or die: "I'm going to be judged on this! This is my moment! This is my career!" I'm interested in methods and techniques we can use to disengage that potential for the performance to be undermined by fear and getting into the head as opposed to being in the heart, because I think that's what's going to make the difference in performance.

For whatever reason, I've found that the best artists seem to carry the most baggage. Their lives are a disaster, but they're able to express like nobody else, because they can't hold it in. They can't hide. It's just out there on the surface all the time.

With all the technology we have, you can micro-produce to the point that you can choke the living tar out of something by the time you get done with it. If you go back and listen to the great records, there are all kinds of imperfections and warts, but that's what made them charming and real.

When the producer gets into the same fear-based position of the artist—that fear that everything's at stake, and they had better make something louder and funkier and cooler than everybody else—the end result is not going to fly. I found I've done my best work when I was nowhere around, if you know what I mean. When I stepped out of the way, it just came through me. I wasn't even thinking about what I should do. It would just be obvious what the next move should be and what should happen next. I think we all have an inner voice that's broadcasting the correct instincts loud and clear if we listen to it.

When I was starting out, I was positive every record I made was going to last. Absolutely convinced of it! I soon realized that if I tried to do something similar to the popular commercial flavor of the moment, the result would sound stiff and forced. Yet, when I just did what I did and let the artist do what they did, I loved the results. When that happened, a moment of fear would step in and have me thinking, "Wow, is this going to work?" Over time, I learned that this is exactly what I should be doing as a producer. Every artist I've had success with was out of the pocket, a left-of-center artist that I brought back into the mainstream just by the fact that what they did authentically connected with people.

You've got to get to the point where there's nothing at stake. I realized that when I stayed true to that way of working, not only did I become very successful, but I was there because I loved what I was doing and not because this was going to pay the rent.

It was then that my work got to be really interesting. I could step on the gas or put on the brakes when I needed to. I could do whatever it was that I was feeling because I was attuned to healthy gut instinct, as opposed to fear.

I think fear often motivates producers to put too much on the tracks, because there is a concern the music isn't impacting enough or edgy or hooky enough.

Tracy Chapman's record [her debut album featuring "Fast Car"] is an example where I had to fight myself. I purposely kept it as simple as I could possibly keep it, because I needed for her to clearly come through. It's really important for a producer to not succumb to the fear of trying to outguess what's going to appeal to listeners and begin forcing something onto the project or recording.

You can get a vocal technically perfect. You can get a guitar part absolutely perfect. You can tune it and snip it in time. You can also do a session that puts everybody on edge and totally stressed, because they're all trying so hard to do the same thing. But at the end of the day, I think everyone in the studio, although they may not recognize it, feels that stress in the music. In the end, I think it shows and actual recording suffers, because stress and tension gets captured. It's all about projection.

If you're sitting in the studio and you're feeling something, there's a really good chance that most of the people who are going to listen to it are going to feel something.

Jerry Moss [one of the founders of A&M Records] taught me something that I'll never forget. He said, "It can just be a cello player playing in a room alone, but if the performances rips your heart out and makes you cry, that's it." Jerry was never one to say we had to follow any kind of paths or trails. He'd just go with the real stuff that people could go with. If you're sitting in the studio and you're feeling something, there's a really good chance that most of the people who hear it are going to feel something, too.

Richard Gibbs

Credits include: Oingo Boingo, Robert Palmer, Eisley, Korn, War, Tom Waits, Melissa Etheridge. Film/TV credits: Fatal Instinct, 28 Days, I Spy, Doctor Dolittle, Battlestar Gallactica, Say Anything, Dirty Work, Queen of the Damned.

There is a common sentiment floating around that file sharing is here to stay, that there is nothing that can be done about it. Let's lay that myth to rest right now.

The more accurate statement would be that there is nothing that *has* been done about it—at least effectively. The record companies took to suing individual file sharers, to no particular avail other than to destroy what little credibility they had left. But that is hardly the end of the issue. Technically, there is *plenty* that can be done to monitor, control, eliminate, or monetize file-sharing activities—the problem is that there has not been the political will to do it.

First, let's look at the ability of Internet service providers (ISPs) and governments to snoop into anybody's Internet interactions. If you really want a crash course on this subject, try typing a few Jihadist phrases, preferably in Arabic, naming dates and locations of an impending attack. Then prepare the tea and cookies for the Homeland Security visitors that will arrive any minute. Seriously, you all know there is massive monitoring of Internet activities at all times, worldwide.

Now let's talk control. Anybody remember the brouhaha that erupted when the Chinese government severely restricted the abilities of the journalists covering the Summer Olympics? Certain words and phrases were completely blocked. Google had to make many censorship accommodations in order to operate in China over a number of years because of political considerations and because the Chinese government is playing favorites with Baidu, a huge homegrown search engine. Clearly, games are already being played on a massive scale with Internet access there.

On a less draconian scale, there are many ideas that have been proposed and attempted recently in Europe and elsewhere to deal with copyright violators. One is a so-called "three strikes" rule. The way it works is if one is caught file sharing to any significant degree a warning is issued—strike one. Then a second warning is sent out if the copyright infringement continues—strike two. If the infringement continues unabated—strike three, you're out. Out, in this case, can mean a couple of things. The most extreme proposal is that your Internet access is cut off for three months and that you are listed as an infringer, making it so that you cannot simply change ISPs and continue your lawbreaking ways. A more reasonable proposal that has been gaining traction is to throttle your Internet connection speed so severely that all you can use it for is email and simple text. This is all being discussed heatedly in Europe right now. Why we aren't doing it here in the USA, the home of the entertainment industry, is beyond sanity. But obviously it can be done. Monetizing file sharing is the most rational and positive approach. It's simply a matter of will. It is not a matter of ability. The ability exists.

In 1998, the United States Digital Millennium Copyright Act was written to protect copyright holders while keeping an eye on the privacy rights of consumers. Currently, there are people developing business models that take advantage of the technological ability to physically locate copyright infringers via their IP address and the unique signature of each computer. Under privacy laws, ISPs are not allowed or required to identify their subscribers, but upon positive identification of copyright infringement, the ISPs are legally obligated by the DMCA to pass infringement notices on to their customers. Such notices are basically threats of a lawsuit that could cost each violator hundreds of thousands of dollars.

While I wholeheartedly believe that music has intrinsic value and that downloaders are breaking the law, I do not believe that a punitive approach aimed at the customer makes any sense whatsoever. The culprits are the ISPs, file-sharing sites, and search engines. They are all making major money providing free access to properties that they do not own. Going after consumers is a PR fiasco of the first order.

What is extremely interesting is this unintended loophole in the DMCA that presents a potential for gain for artists of all types. Check this out: Wouldn't it make good sense if artists were to use the DMCA notice to build a positive relationship with their fans? Instead of a threatened lawsuit, the essence of the notice could be along the lines of, "Hey, we see you have been downloading our music without paying." [It is required to call them on the infringement, or else the ISPs will not forward the notice.] "Glad you enjoy our music! Sign up here to have direct contact with us—we'll let the infringement slide this time because we are so happy to have you as a fan. Buy our songs directly from our site for 50 cents each. Plus, we have some bitchin' T-shirts and beanies…."

Also fascinating about this tech approach is that it could be used for incredibly targeted marketing. Let's say your band the Screaming Monkey Typists has released three albums' worth of material to date. You are getting ready to tour Europe for the first time. It's possible that you could see exactly where your biggest fans are located by looking at the download logs. Maybe you would have thought (and hoped) that Paris would be a goldmine, but it turns out that you could easily do a week in Bratislava, selling tons of tickets and T-shirts to your biggest fans. The French…well, not so much. You will not only know where your fans are, you will know what their favorite songs are. That should positively inform those set-list decisions, eh?

What I really like is that a positive and creative way of addressing file sharing could lift the veil of anonymity from it. I've always felt that most people who file share would not do it if they truly understood that (A) they are hurting the creators of the music/movies/games/applications/photos they love; (B) they were now doing it in full view; and (C) there was another viable, reasonable way for them to purchase what they desire. This technology could provide the missing link in a lucrative and fair distribution system for music, movies, photos, and all forms of intellectual property.

Now check out this scenario. Anytime someone downloads a song (or any identified copyrighted material), there could be an automatic micropayment tacked onto that person's ISP bill. Say a dime for a song, a buck for a movie. Doesn't matter where the material is downloaded from. It would be unavoidable, automatic, unequivocal, just as certain as your electric bill or phone bill. I doubt that too many people would complain too much about a system like that. Open, fair, accountable. The ISPs would take a small percentage for their troubles, both legalizing and incentivizing them, and the artists and creators could reap the rest.

Now, a dime per song doesn't sound too good until you look at the numbers. Most research shows that at least 97 percent of the music being downloaded every day is not paid for—not one red cent. iTunes charges a buck a track. (I know they now have different pricing structures, but let's keep the math simple for now.) Currently, for every hundred downloaded songs, iTunes collects $1 each for three of them, while 97 other songs are ripped without remuneration. Would you rather have 97 dimes to (mostly) pocket, or three dollars to divvy up with iTunes? Catch my drift?

Obviously there are some holes in my model here—not the least of which is that some people would most likely not download quite so much if they had to pay, even though we are only talking one thin dime per song. And clearly there would be considerable negotiations and fine-tuning necessary to make this work. But it could work, and work brilliantly, if only the dummies running the record companies and publishing companies would drop their antiquated business models or get the hell out of the way. All of the technology to make this happen exists right now. Today. We could be looking at a new golden era. What do you all think?

Rick Clark

As a final thought for the "Evolution" chapter, I'd like to take this on a more personal note.

Recently, I was at a pub called Boscos in Nashville's Hillsboro Village area with Neal Cappellino, a friend who is also a highly regarded engineer (Joan Osborne, Mindy Smith, Vince Gill). We talked about the balance of our work and our personal lives, and it dawned on me that I could probably fill a book with input from engineers, producers, and others in the local industry on this topic.

We devote so much energy to our studios, gear, and productions to serve this potentially transcendent thing called music, yet it is so easy to neglect to nurture the very priceless human relationships and experiences that inspire some of the greatest music.

Ever since I first rolled into Nashville, I've heard people in the music industry say, "It's a great place to raise a family," or, "The quality of life here is so much better than L.A. or New York." I've also heard Nashville called "L.A. with religion," but I can attest to the fact that Nashville is a great place to raise a family and enjoy a good quality of life. I also believe that no matter where you live, you are who you are, and in our line of work, it is just as easy to be consumed by the cave culture of studio life in Nashville as it is anywhere else.

"It seems to me that mainstream country really does understand the needs of personal life and family more than other genres," says Cappellino. "Anytime I do mainstream country, I'm usually home at a reasonable hour, because most of the people are in the same situation, and they respect it. Frank Rogers [Brad Paisley, Darryl Worley] is a producer I work with all the time. He's got two kids and he's got to get home, so he structures his day in a way so those gigs will honor that. Since he is the producer, he makes that call, which I appreciate."

However, plenty of other sessions fall into the trap of being all-consuming. "We love music and we care, no matter what kind of music we are recording, and it's hard to let stuff go if you think it can be better," Cappellino offers. "The sacrifice we make isn't always acknowledged, but we do it because we want to. It is almost a compulsion or an obsession. Your clients will love you for it while you are there because this is their project, and they want to burn the midnight oil. But we do this day in and day out, and something has to give. And often, if we aren't careful, it is our personal lives and our health."

I called up a couple more friends whose opinions I respect on things personal and musical. Richard Dodd, a producer/engineer/mixer/masterer who has amassed a huge list of credits, including Tom Petty, the Traveling Wilburys, Clannad, the Dixie Chicks, Wilco, and many more, is a devoted husband who, over the years, figured out a balance of home and work life that dignifies both.

"Separating work from personal life isn't easy," he says. "They are so interrelated. The first 10 years of my career, I wasn't married; I was married to my work. When you are not married, it's easy. The next 10 years, I was married in my first marriage, but my work was much more important than the marital relationship, and ultimately [was as much] an influence on the ending of that marriage as anything else.

"This time I've got it right," says Dodd, who's been married to his second wife, Carolyn, for 17 years. "I'm at a stage in my career where I do turn down work because it is the right thing to do. I don't go places because it is the right thing to stay with my family. Nowadays, it is becoming less and less necessary to travel because much of the work can come to us electronically."

I mention that some engineers and producers try to solve the problem with home studios, but Dodd cautions, "Don't do it! Now you are in that other part of the house that you call the studio, and you effectively have the doors locked and are a million miles away. Having a studio in your house is for lonely people or soon-to-be-lonely people.

"Engineers, producers, and artists can create something out of nothing, and then the real thing comes along, like a child," Dodd continues. "We then realize that we have done something incredible, but the child doesn't go off to mastering and get presented to the public and you make your money. It takes a lot of work to help that child be all it can be."

Memphis-based producer/artist and musician Jim Dickinson (Ry Cooder, the Replacements, Big Star, the Rolling Stones, Bob Dylan, and John Hiatt) was married for 44 years to Mary Lindsay, until he passed away in 2009. I always found their devotion and personal chemistry inspiring. Dickinson is proof that uncompromising commitment to music and to your family is not unattainable.

"When you're not at the studio," Dickinson explained, "you've got to really not be at the studio. You can't let it follow you home. You've got to make the most of the time you do have. Privacy is crucial to me. In my own situation, I poured the money that I made during my periods of success into my family rather than into my career.

"My wife, Mary, is the first person in my life who accepted me the way I was. She wasn't trying to fix me. She didn't think I was broke, and I was. And she actually defended me to other people. Her half-brother was a musician, and in fact, he was one of my inspirations. She watched him stop doing it and go off into straight life. She told me one day, 'I'm determined that's not going to happen to you.' Now that is a special person. I couldn't have gotten nearly this far without her."

Field Recording and Film Sound

Chapter
11

The world around us is full of sounds that we take for granted. Those of us who spend huge blocks of our lives in studios and listening rooms—analyzing the soundstages and wet and dry properties of particular musical recordings at hand—rarely take the time to focus our awareness and appreciation on the natural sonic richness that surrounds us every day.

Field recording for film and for ambient augmentation in musical settings requires much more than a mere documentary approach. An essential understanding of the gestalt of the cinematic or musical moment, in which the ambient recording is to be applied, is essential in conveying the proper tone. For example, if a scene is melancholy, then the audio environment around it should enhance that mood.

This chapter focuses on those who have spent a significant amount of time in the field capturing those sounds in every place imaginable. I enlisted Ben Cheah, Dennis Hysom, and Rodger Pardee for this chapter, as well as Christopher Boyes, who not only discusses some of his field recording adventures, but also his sound design, mixing, and other aspects of his film post-audio work. Each of these men has an enormous list of credits and has traveled the world in search of the exact sounds required for their projects.

Christopher Boyes

Credits include: Avatar, Titanic, Iron Man, *all* Lord of the Rings, *all* Pirates of the Caribbean, The Weather Man, Jurassic Park II & III, Mission Impossible, Terminator 2. *See the Appendix for Christopher Boyes's full bio.*

For *Jurassic Park II*, I flew down to Costa Rica, hired two guides for five days each, and went into jungles, both in the mountainous regions and down on the coastal areas. I recorded many hours' worth of tropical ambiance and everything that you can imagine, including volcanoes and alligators. It was a good trip.

Whenever I go off recording on that kind of scale, I like to capture every time of the day. Audio-wise, Costa Rica is really graphic. There is something different happening at every time of the day and night. In the morning, you get these incredible crickets that sound like a burst of a shower nozzle, but with articulation and brightness. They come in right as the sun is coming up. Sometimes, you get them at sunset. You only get a three- or four-minute period where this happens. It is the most incredible sound, and anybody hearing it would feel like they are in the most prehistoric place on Earth.

To get a really clean, articulate ambiance is really difficult. It taxes you creatively and physically because you have to find a place that can give you a beautiful natural ambiance, you have to get there at a time when you are not going to be adulterated by either motor sounds on the ground or planes in the air, and you have to have absolutely superb equipment to get a clean ambiance. Everything comes to bear in that.

The second hardest thing would be animal vocalizations, because unlike humans, they do not perform well. Typically, if they see a microphone, they will think it is a gun. As a result, they clam up, so you must have an amazing amount of patience. Tame animals are worse than wild ones. At one point, I wanted to record a hippopotamus, and I think I sat there for four hours before it gave one vocalization, but it was worth the wait.

I have invested a lot of money in microphones and equipment. While I hate to slam a manufacturer, I bought a Neumann RSM 191. On the first night out in Costa Rica, we were trying to record owls, and we somehow managed to pull a little bit on the cables going into the mic, and it came apart. We took it apart, and it was like jewelry inside; you breathed on the cables, and it looked like they could come apart. Luckily, I was able to fix it with my Swiss army knife and gaffer's tape. I think it sounds great, but I think it's not robust enough for the kind of stuff that we do.

Granted, not everyone tromps into the jungle, like I do, but from my point of view, every film should have a significant amount of new, fresh sounds that nobody has ever heard before. If someone is doing major sound effects for major films and *not* doing things like that, then you have to wonder if they are recycling effects. I am a really strong advocate of recording effects for the purposes of sound design for each film that are fresh and new.

I don't really like the idea of a broad mic for some ambiances. In the jungle, if you point in one direction, you are going to get a different sound than if you point the mic in another direction. I would rather get the ambiance in one location from two or three perspectives, as opposed to getting that whole ambiance from a 360-degree perspective. Then I can mix it as I like. For field recording, the most durable mic that I have used is the sister or brother mic to that Neumann RSM 191, which is the KMR 81.

In the jungle, it is amazing. You move you a mic 180 degrees, especially if it is a slightly directional mic, and the sound you hear is absolutely different than the sound you heard in the previous position.

This isn't to say that I wouldn't use a nice set of omnidirectionals for some ambiances. Certainly, some ambiances aren't that directionally sensitive, in terms of the quality of the sound. But when you are deep in the jungle, there are all different sorts of wildlife.

Field recording always seems to have its surprises that end up expanding the sound library with fresh elements.

At one point in Costa Rica, while I was waiting around to record any given ambiance, I noticed that the mud I was standing in, which was around 6 to 12 inches deep, made a very powerful sound. I started recording that. That turned out great, and the sound I captured made its way into *The Lost World* and *Volcano* in separate entities, for things like dinosaurs eating and for lava glops. You can be anywhere in the world, and you can be looking for one thing out in the field, and you can stumble across something else—and you will never know what you'll use it for.

Even though I love capturing great recordings of sounds out in the field, I also feel that mere documentary sound recording isn't good enough when you are trying to assist in capturing the impact or tenor of a specific scene in a film.

If you and the effects editor and sound designer were hired to work on a scene, like taking a situation where someone is swimming, you would say, "What is happening in this scene? What is happening in the film?" That would affect how you would address the sound. You wouldn't just say, "Okay, this is what she is doing. She is moving water." Your sounds would reflect some emotional content that would read on their own, to some extent, to anybody, what was the mood of that part of the story. If it is a melancholy moment, you might find that the water moves heavily and more slowly than you would expect it to in real life. A good sound person automatically applies that sort of principle, and it comes out in their work.

Often, a number of these sounds that I capture get compiled with other sounds to create some of the unique, memorable sonic statements in movies.

Fire is a very difficult thing to capture in any film. I believe that it is one of the more difficult things. I find fire to be very difficult to sound like anything other than a snap, crackle, and pop. It takes a lot of work, a lot of patience, and a lot of recording to create anything other than a rumble or high end. For *Backdraft*, the approach was to make the fire live and breath and talk. We actually used a lot of human and animal vocalizations as well.

I have to say that every film has a very challenging element. For the film *Volcano*, the biggest challenge on that were these lava bombs, where the director [Mick Jackson] asked for the lava bombs to be a cross between a screaming banshee, a Dopplered train whistle, and a Stuka siren. Of course, I immediately started working with those very elements, but it was a little hard to define what the screaming banshee was. [Laughs]

Not so long ago, I debated the merits of field recording with a DAT recorder over a Nagra. That was back when I was an assistant sound designer to Gary Rydstrom on the film *Jurassic Park*. So many things have changed since then, and yet so many things have remained the same. The visual FX side of making movies has reinvented itself many times over, and I'll bet anyone working in that field would say the same thing. We, as a group of people trying to be creative with tools of the trade, are constantly put in a place where we must chase the cutting edge of technology, while not forgetting the tried-and-true tools that still have value.

Years ago, the DAT machine was a real game changer for all of us working in audio. The tape was 1/8 the size of a roll of 1/4 tape. Also, as far as we knew, unlike 1/4, DAT wouldn't flake its oxide off and render itself unusable unless it was placed in a Suzy Homemaker oven. Not to mention that one could get up to 120 minutes on this little guy, unlike the 15 minutes at 15 IPS we would get out of the 1/4 tape. If you were sharp, you could carefully renumber the IDs at the beginning of each DAT recording and then produce a document that helped navigate someone to each place of interest in the 120 minutes of recording. Personally, I didn't trust such a small tape to 120 minutes and opted for the 60-minute DATs. If there was a section or two—and there always was—that I wanted Gary Rydstrom to avoid because the recording, for either technical or creative reasons, was unusable, I would label it NG for No Good. Gary, as a matter of course, would go there first and happily create a cool sound effect from the NG section.

As much as the DAT technology offered us, there was something we lost at the same time. First of all, the mic preamps built into these DAT machines, while usable, were vastly inferior to what was built into the analog Nagra machines. Also, digital sound itself was a bit of a strange world for those of us who grew up with analog. This 16-bit, 44.1-k signal had none of the hum and noise of analog, but it seemed to lose some of the sweetness as well. In a way, it felt as if this smooth, warm sound had been replaced with something very clean and precise in its image, but hard and shiny like a mirror. It was especially edgy sounding with loud sounds, like explosions. The DAT would hold the signal all the way to its technical limit, but then right at the peak, it would give way to a nasty "snat" that was unusable to anyone. The Nagra, of course, would sound great all the way through to the loud explosion. At that point, instead of providing unusable digital distortion at the peak, like the DAT, the Nagra gave you this amazing usable sound of apparent distortion, much akin to what the human ear itself will do when faced with such volume. This often provided us with a sound we could use in a way that conveyed loudness without actually having to be all that loud.

Randy Thom once said, "Distortion equals art," and emotionally he's right, although in the digital age, managing distortion for us as re-recording mixers is a whole different problem. As I pointed out, digital distortion is unusable, and creating pleasing analog distortion in a digital age is a challenge.

This is not intended as a treatise on analog versus digital; it's more a reflection on how the world of creating, editing, and mixing sound for film has changed over the years and why we—any working professional—will find it necessary to continually adapt new ways of working, while losing some of the old tools that came before.

What is expected of a sound designer or editor on a film of today has changed simply because technology has forced it to. For instance, as a young sound designer, I would create sounds often in my Synclavier for a client like George Lucas and need to get them to him by the next morning. I'd lay the sounds off to 1/4 tape and write the description on the back. Beau Borders, my assistant at the time, would be waiting at the door with a FedEx package addressed and ready to go. We knew, partially due to Beau's penchant for driving racecars, exactly how long it would take him to drive from Skywalker Ranch to San Rafael, where the main FedEx depot allowed us a 6:30 p.m. cut off. We almost always made it, but it was always too close. I would marvel to myself at how I finished this sound by 6:00 p.m., and George [Lucas] would have it in the morning! Contrast that to today, and it would be sent via the Internet in matter of minutes without the need for jet fuel. Years later, with the help of our producer, Barrie Osborne, I would print-master a reel of *Lord of the Rings: The Two Towers* in Wellington and have NT Audio laying it back to film hours later in Santa Monica. Today, that has just become common practice.

When I say technology has forced us to change, it's not, of course, only us. For any filmmaker these days, technology has opened new possibilities, and at the same time, it has increased the pressure on that filmmaker to manage many parts of his or her film all at once. Usually, for us in the "old" days, we knew that once we reached the final mix stage of our project, we had pretty much the undivided attention of our director. This isn't true anymore. Now they are often working insane hours approving VFX or color timing, as well as trying to put their stamp on the final mix. I understand the stress a filmmaker must feel with all the major elements of the film coming together so late with a looming deadline. I, as a mixer, need to make their time on the stage as smooth and productive as possible. Several films I've worked on recently have really used new paradigms to give the filmmaker time during the post process to make decisions *before* they hit the final mix, thus enabling us to use the final mix for what it was intended to be—fine tuning of music, dialog, and sound effects.

One way we have done this is to insert a sound person in the picture department when possible, as we did on *Pirates of the Caribbean*. Craig Wood [picture editor on *Pirates*] is one of many people who have told me he will often use sound to make a picture cut. Well, that said, I wanted to make sure he used my sounds whenever possible, if it were going to determine where he would cut, because a sound used in that way, if successful, will never likely change.

Peter Jackson said essentially the same thing on *The Lovely Bones*. On that film, we basically maintained a 5.1 for Peter to hear as he cut the film. In the initial stages, I was up in California while Brent Burge, Chris Ward, and their crew worked down at Park Road in New Zealand. So, with their help, I was able to lock up my Pro Tools to Peter's Avid via iChat. Since we had the same media on both sides of the planet, when they hit Play, we would both be looking at and listening to the same thing. I was able to see and hear Peter while he made comments as he watched the film. Once I got down to Wellington, New Zealand, Brent and Chris had the editors cutting in 5.1, and Brent maintained a 5.1 mix that was very similar to what we would start off with in the final mix. I'm not a fan of mixing in the box, but if used wisely, it has many plusses. In this case, Peter and Fran were able to comment and guide us so that when we reached the dub stage, many of the creative questions had been conquered, and we could focus on mixing.

On James Cameron's *Avatar*, we were doing a similar thing. The difference there was that Jim [James] himself likes to cut sound, and he's very good at it. At the outset, he really only wanted to hit a dub stage for four or five days. With the help of Steve Morris and Addison Teague up at Skywalker, we had built a platform that allowed me and my crew the ability to design, edit, and mix the track at Jim's facility in Malibu. We also had that automation carry forth exactly as he heard it in Malibu to the dub stage for the final mix. In the studio we built in Malibu, I could access four or five Pro Tools systems, lock them together, and sync all that to HD picture. If I like, I could lock my Synclavier into the loop as well. Of course, there had been many iterations in between and for everything; pre-dubbing and final mixing sound would be pumped through and mixed on a traditional console. This is important to me, because I don't believe any audio workstation can deliver the sonics of a traditional board. The main point, though, is that Jim was able to approve not just a sound or two, but a mix before it hit a dub stage, so when he arrived on that stage, his time was utilized as efficiently as possible.

There exists many ways an audio post team can choose to approach a picture, and no way is perfect. The challenge to me, however, is to use a method that supports your own creativity and gives the filmmaker the ability to make sonic decisions throughout the post process, rather than at the last minute.

Technology has indeed offered and forced new ways of working, but it's only really dressing up a well-laid path, one that started in the first days of sound for film. In the end the goal remains the same: We use sound, music, and dialogue in an emotional way to help support a story.

Ben Cheah

Credits include: The Wire, The Royal Tenenbaums, Sleepy Hollow, O Brother Where Art Thou?, The Big Lebowski, Men In Black I and II, Get Shorty, Fargo, Adventureland, I'm Not There. *See the Appendix for Ben Cheah's full bio.*

Part of making quality sound effects is recording the live, organic elements of those sounds. Without good original sounds, it is difficult to make original sound effects. It doesn't matter how simple or complex the sound is going to be; it all relies on the source sound that you have.

It is important to have original and organic source material in every soundtrack and to make things sound like they don't just come from commercial sound libraries. Otherwise, you find different sound editors from every sound house using the same sound effects libraries, and that really limits the amount of fresh material that is coming in.

Sometimes, when you are seeing a movie, it gets to the point to where you know which disc a sound effect comes from and the track number from which that certain sound originates. Believe me, it takes away from the movie. [Laughs] It happens all of the time.

When you are doing on-location recording, you are able to fine tune perspectives, whereas the people who are limited to just using commercial sound libraries are usually stuck to the one perspective that has been offered. When I record a sound effect, I'm really recording the space, and if moving, the object/person/vehicle's movement through that space.

Our job is highlighting drama in a scene, be it a very subtle moment or a very violent moment. We are trying to create more interesting elements and dimension through the use of sound. You are often overacting the drama with sound, but that is the way that you can translate things into telling the story. It adds a whole extra dimension to the scene. The emphasis is on drama and recording it in the correct situation.

For instance, when you are recording vehicles, the real thing usually doesn't sound big enough. If you find the right vehicle, and you drive it in and follow the action, it doesn't sound dramatic enough, so you have got to screech the car in and out to make it sound right. We have been known to drive vehicles at speed in second gear in order to get enough drama in the sound effect. Otherwise, the difference between reality and filmmaking falls apart, and the soundtrack doesn't live up to its job.

Dennis Hysom

Credits include: Apocalypto, Nature Conservancy *series. See the Appendix for Dennis Hysom's full bio.*

For environmental recordings, I have traveled from Alaska to Costa Rica and points in between to capture the desired ambiances. Most of the problems that you find in field recording can be solved if you are patient and persistent and if you plan carefully enough. If you have done your research, know where your species are, and have talked to all of the various park rangers involved in managing the wilderness areas, then you can pretty much locate what you want to record. So most of the problems can be avoided.

An extreme example of how a recording expedition can be interrupted concerns a recording trip I made in North Louisiana in a place called Kisatchie National Park. It happens to be near Fort Polk, I believe it is. The conservancy land where I was recording was nearby. I was trying to record this endangered species of woodpecker, called the Red-cockaded Woodpecker. This is a real fragile sound that this bird makes. All the trees are marked where the Red-cockaded Woodpecker has its nest.

The best times to record are very early in the morning or late at night. So I got there before dawn, and I was down in this culvert, and I waiting for the woodpeckers to start vocalizing. I heard this rumble, and it got louder and louder. I turned around, and there was this big tank from the fort, and there was a guy pounding on the top of the tank, screaming and yelling to the guy inside the tank, "Left, I said! Left!" I was over in the culvert, and I had my earphones on, and I had this microphone that had a windsock on it. It sort of looked like a gun. It had a pistol grip and everything. I was sitting there aiming it at this tree. The guys in the tank were 15 to 20 feet away, and they were oblivious to me. The gruff sound of the tank and the very quiet fragile sounds of the woodpecker were funny juxtaposition of sounds. I could probably use it, if I ever get to do a war movie or something like that. [Laughs] It was a very funny situation.

Sometimes what it takes to really capture a sound can place you in some pretty harrowing situations. While we were in Alaska, we went out for a couple of days to record Stellar sea lions. There were these small little islands all over the area where they gathered. The boat captain actually took me out on the bow of the boat, and he pulled up fairly close to the two colonies. Each colony of sea lions is looked after by an alpha bull, and both of them were warning me away with these really low belching sounds. I had this really great stereo recording of a bull on the right and a bull on the left warning me away from their harems.

We were floating in a rough sea, and the waves were making us move up and down extremely in the boat. I was up on the bow, trying to balance myself, holding the microphone, and it was frightening because the rail of the boat wasn't very high. It would've been very easy to lose equipment or fall over into the freezing water. It would've also been all over for me because of the rocks, which were everywhere. We were within 12 to 15 feet from the rock outcroppings. The boat captain constantly had to backpedal, because the water was pushing the boat toward hitting the rocks. It was pretty wild.

It is getting to be a very crowded world, and it is very difficult to get truly natural sounds for any length of time at all. The sensitivity of the gear can pick up a lot of human sounds, like machines, boats, saws, and airplane noises, as well. Consequently, I have to do a lot of editing.

For every hour I record, I may hopefully come up with a minute of sound that is not only quiet, but also interesting. You can sit out there in the field for eight hours at a time and not get anything, until something special takes place. In North Dakota, for example, I sat out most of the night, trying to record coyotes. Then, finally, there may be two or three cries right near you.

I traveled to the Dakotas several times throughout the year to get the seasonal variety of sounds necessary for the Badlands CD. One night in the fall, in North Dakota's Theodore Roosevelt National Park, I was with a park ranger and my assistant, recording elk. It was a moonless night, and all three of us had flashlights. We had been walking to areas where we heard elk, stopping to record, and then, of course, we'd hear the elk bugling where we'd just come from! They'd circled back around us. It was a good lesson for a field recordist. It's almost better to sit and wait than to chase a sound.

Anyway, we were walking back to the road, and my flashlight began to fade and just died. My assistant, Steve, turned his on, and it died. "Well, that's a little weird," I thought. Maybe a bad batch of batteries. The park ranger turned her flashlight on, and it died. None of us could believe it. Too strange. She said, "No big deal"; she knew where the road was. We weren't that far away, so we began slowly walking in absolute pitch-black darkness. We'd been walking about 10 minutes when I heard her whisper, "Wait." She was quiet, and then she whispered, "Ohmygod, ohmygod, back up, back up. Bison. Bison." I guess we had wandered into the middle of a herd of bison. I knew that bison can be dangerous if you get too close, and earlier she had expressed a fear of bison, mentioning that every year some fool gets too close and gets severely hurt by irritating a bison. I squinted and could barely make out these big black shapes all around me. We backed up and got clear, although I have no idea how. I think maybe it was a close call. She was shaken up.

I think my favorite place to record has been Central America. The variety of species and rich soundscapes is stunning. I was once contacted by a sound supervisor in L.A. looking for howler monkey sounds. I have some MP3 samples of howlers I recorded in Belize and Costa Rica on my website, and when Kami Asgar, the supervisor, did a Google search, he found the site and contacted me. It turns out it was for Mel Gibson's *Apocalypto* film. In the end, many of my rainforest ambiences and animal vocalization recordings were used in *Apocalypto*.

My field recording setup is a Tascam DA-P1 DAT recorder with a Sonosax preamp. I use the Sanken CMS-7 mic for my ambient recording. It is a wonderfully versatile and durable microphone. I have had it in rainstorms, steamy hot weather, and I've never had it fail. While I'd like to check out some of the new Flash recorders, this rig suits my purposes fine. I'm also using a Sony MZ-RH1 minidisc recorder as a backup unit. It's light and small, and I'm pleased with the quality of sound.

My favorite part of an entire production, from the concept planning stage to the final duplication mastering process, is scouting out a location and going in and recording. Even though it can get a little hairy once in a while, most of the time there is something very peaceful and serene about doing this.

All of the Nature Company projects I've done were created in co-partnership with The Nature Conservancy. The Conservancy received a percentage of the CD sales to promote further efforts to protect land. The overall concept was to record natural soundscapes on Conservany co-managed land, arrange each soundscape into an interesting ambient recording, and then compose music that, when mixed, would blend and become one interwoven fabric of music and natural sound. For example, one piece might be a morning at the La Selva Biological Station in Costa Rica. It might take several days recording from dawn to mid-morning to get enough audio to compile one perfect morning of sound. So, on the recording, after it's put together, a listener gets the best possible situation, where they are hearing a beautiful dawn chorus in La Selva. And those mornings do happen. You just have to show up enough to record them.

Rodger Pardee

Credits include: The League of Extraordinary Gentlemen, The X Files, Pacific Heights, Red Heat, Rambo III, Apt Pupil, Flight of the Phoenix. *See the Appendix for Rodger Pardee's full bio.*

I have recorded an awful lot of vehicles. It seems to be a kind of specialty. The first time I had to record cars was for *To Live and Die in L.A.* (1985). I filled up tape after tape, teaching myself how to do it. [Laughs]

There is no big trick to recording a car starting and driving away or a car driving by. The trick is for the shots where you are tracking alongside the car. It is not an interior sound. It is more of a mixture of the sound that comes from the engine compartment and also the exhaust and a little bit of tire work. That kind of sound doesn't always play well in a movie.

Basically, what I ended up doing was putting a mic under the engine compartment and another mic back by the tailpipe and mixing the two together. I used the term "onboard" to distinguish that from an "interior" sound.

An interior sound is distinctive, too, but it is not real exciting, in terms of drama, if you are just driving along in a car with the windows rolled up. You don't really hear a lot of engine, yet that is an element that you would like to have when you have got a shot of the good guy driving along inside the car.

So what I do is record a simultaneous onboard track and a stereo interior track using two synched recorders. That way, when you are inside of the car, you can play the interior and sweeten it with the onboard engine sound. We have used that technique with quite a bit of success.

For onboards, I tend to use stuff like dynamic mics, like RE15s, because they are very sturdy and can take a little bit of heat. You could put a condenser mic in the engine compartment, but it is not the best treatment for an expensive condenser mic.

Miking the engine compartment isn't hard, but miking the tailpipe gets tricky because of the wind noise when the car is in motion. After some extensive R&D, we designed some special wind noise attenuators. It's true that they look like old coffee cans lined with carpet, but that is only because we never got around to painting them. [Laughs] I tend to use an Electro-Voice RE15 or a Shure dynamic back by the tailpipe. We tend to have those pretty rigged.

I use Schoeps hypercardioid mics. For more rugged stuff, we have some EV RE15s that go back many years; they're practically indestructible. And I have some other mics I've accumulated, but rattling off equipment lists isn't that revealing. More important are decent mic placement and a sound source with character.

I've recorded some really nice effects using analog cassette decks and $40 mics; I just happened to be standing in a good spot during a good sound. You don't have to be an audiophile connoisseur. After all, you can take Madonna's voice and run it through some Art Deco preamp the size of a cinder block, but it's still going to come out sounding like Madonna. Personally, I'd rather hear some lo-fi recording of Billie Holiday.

There are guys waxing enthusiastic over certain mic preamps now, like they are some kind of fine wine. The gimmick is to have huge knobs and dials on everything. It is like a fad. I am sure they sound fine, but it sometimes strikes me as absurd and trendy. It is like, "Here is my rack o' gear." Yeah, I've got a rack o' gear, but how interesting is it to rattle on and on about what is in the rack? If having a rack full of the latest shiny gear gives you goose bumps, then go ahead. It's harmless fun. But I'm not sure it's that important. I'd rather hear sophisticated dialogue out of a crude sound system than the reverse.

When I teach intro film-sound classes, I like to reassure the students that they do not have to be engineering or computer wizards to do creative sound work. In a sense, you need to become just comfortable enough with the technology so that you can ignore it, because if you're busy thinking about SCSI drives and file management, then you're not thinking about the story and the feel of the sounds.

I like to start by playing a series of sound effects and getting people to discuss the feelings they evoke. Then you can start to analyze the causes of the feelings. Some sounds have subjective memories and associations linked to them—the clickety whir of a Lionel train set can trigger intense nostalgia in some baby boomers. Or you can look at the objective character of the sound—maybe one reason that gentle surf is so soothing is because it's analogous to the heavy regular breathing of someone sound asleep.

Once you start thinking in those terms, you begin to appreciate how even fairly mundane sounds like air conditioning can have character. In the end you ask yourself: Is the sound interesting? Is it involving? Does it do any good?

Game Audio

Game audio has come a long way since the days of *Pong, Space Invaders, Donkey Kong, Super Mario Brothers,* and *Pac-Man.* All the squeaks and squawks, blips, and doinks that accompanied the gameplay back in those days essentially served a purpose not much different from the attention-getting sounds manufactured by pinball machines. One of the first games that got my attention—that wasn't a shoot 'em up—was *Myst.* The thing that really made *Myst* (and its follow-up, *Riven*) less static was a totally immersive soundtrack and the various accompanying sound design elements that conveyed doors opening, the sound of water, or the movement of paper when a book was opened or closed— strange mechanical devices that would engage a new element in the game. It was the first game where I remember thinking, "This is a huge new world of opportunities for composers, sound designers, engineers, mixers—anyone in the world of audio." Not only has that become true, but game audio has evolved to the point where it seems to offer some of the greatest—the most challenging—opportunities for anyone with a creative soul who loves to work in audio.

These days, audio in games encompasses everything from the creation of music (ranging from cutting-edge hard rock to electronica) to major film score orchestrations, as well as major film-level ADR, foley, and sound design. Stereo is long gone, and surround mixing has been the standard for years. These days, the planning and skill set required to make this immersive world as believable as possible require some serious chops. Also consider this: When you compose a score for a film, it is a linear creation that follows a preset storyline. In the world of games, you not only have to compose the score, but that score has to be created in such a way that the motifs and the dynamics and flow of the piece are responsive to every move and decision the player makes. That's pretty heavy creative lifting, when you think about it.

For this chapter, I enlisted Greg Allen and Jerry Berlongieri, two longtime veterans in game audio who are highly respected in the field and have a list of game title credits that any longtime gamer would immediately recognize. Both of them generously shared from their many years of experience and offered a good introduction into their world, as well as offering some tips that anyone in the world of recording may find useful.

Greg Allen

Credits include: Creative director/founder of Apparatic LLC. Previously senior audio director at Electronic Arts, Sony, and C&G Entertainment and senior sound designer at Activation and Interplay. See the Appendix for Greg Allen's full bio.

The very first thing I say to anybody who is deciding to do audio for games is it really helps to have picked up a love for some type of instrument. The reason why I say that is that some of the best sound designers I know are amazing musicians who got into this field from making music. Along the way, they developed a real understanding about frequency spectrum, how instruments layer together, and how sounds in general fit together. Having played music can only help your understanding of doing sound for games.

It's important that you have a core understanding of audio basics before getting into sound design. What is compression? What is limiting? EQ? Expanding? How do all these things work together? How do you set up EQ and compression when you try to do dialogue? In games, you're dealing with music, with individual sounds, mixing surround, and I find most students or people wanting to get into game audio are lacking a true understanding of how to use those most basic audio tools.

Let's say I need to create the sound of breaking through a wooden fence for a scene, and let's say I'm just going to go pick up a bunch of breaking-wood sound elements from the sound library I have, so I'm not even talking about going out and doing any field recording. It's important to know how to use EQ and compression with all the different sounds I'm pulling together to create a cohesive sound. This is basically Sound Design 101. Just because I'm creating the sound of breaking through this wooden fence, it doesn't necessarily have to sound like I'm merely snapping boards. Maybe, to arrive at an emotionally effective sound, I use some tree branch movements and throw in some metal whining elements in there. Maybe I throw in some pig snarls and other stuff to create what I have in mind, because the whole job here is to make that sound memorable and bring out the emotion in that sound. It's not always the real thing—in this case, the literal sound of wood snapping—that provides the most effective result.

Sometimes I get sounds from someone that are wimpy. If I point out that it needs more presence, the person might say, "Well, turn up your speakers." My response is, "Why?" I should be able to play my speakers super low and still get the impact of the sound. There are a lot of techniques and tricks to be able to do those things. But the fundamental basic part of it is knowing how to use your EQ, your compression, and your limiting correctly and learning how to do the editorial selecting—by that I mean gathering the correct sound for the correct thing. Then once you've gotten to that point, you start assembling the sounds you've gathered. But you don't just merely stack those sounds. The process is to more or less stagger the sounds. What you're trying to do is create a performance. You have to pick one element that's going to be your low end, one that's going to be your body, one that's going to be your detail piece, and one that's going to be something else. If you were going to create the sound of blowing up the side of a hill here, you wouldn't have 15 explosions literally stacked on top of each other. You have a low-end sound and an impact sound, and you have debris, which is maybe like rocks and other stuff, plus a couple other elements to give the explosion a little bit more detail. To achieve the best effect, the staggering of each of these sound elements is a really important aspect as far as sound design goes. Obviously, it takes time to learn this stuff. That's why I say it is important for audio to have some music background. If someone has done any real work with playing and recording music, they will understand that sound design is just a different way of doing music. It's like mixing music instruments. You're not going to try to make a bass guitar eat up the same frequency range as that electric guitar, and you're not going to let a guitar float in all the bass range, either. They each have their specific areas, and that's how you have clean mixes. So sound design really comes down to knowing how to mix things appropriately. The better that you are at mixing in the individual sounds, the better the overall mix will sound.

Another big mistake often made by people trying to be sound designers is confusing the difference between what is loud and what is big-sounding. For example, I take an explosion that has this big kaboom on it, and then I go, "Oh! This other explosion has this little tighter sound on it, and this other one is also great!" So suddenly there are four or five explosions stacked together. "Oh! It sounds so big!" No, all you've done is just taken your 16 hertz, and you've multiplied it by four. If you take something that's sitting in the same frequency and you multiply it, yeah, it sounds louder, but it really doesn't sound bigger. There's a difference between big and loud. You have amplitude, and then you have the perception of something that's bigger, and learning that is a huge, huge benefit in the long term of sound design.

Once you really start to get a handle on using your audio tools, there are all sorts of tricks you can apply that are very helpful in drawing the listener's ear to the sounds you want to highlight.

When I was working at Interplay, we came up with a concept called *air compression*. I would find the cheapest lousy compressor that pumps a lot. I really liked the Alesis 3630 compressor, which was awesome at doing this. What I call air compression is this horrible pumping distortion sound that a bad compressor will do. Now, if you make two explosions sound bigger, you will take, for example, my Alesis 3630 and jam some explosion through it. It makes this unusual imploding effect at the end. Well, you take one of those sorts of pumping sounds, and you put it maybe 50 or 100 milliseconds right before the same explosion sound without that compressor, and all of a sudden, your ear will perceive that explosion as being louder and bigger than what it was before. This is because your ear first focuses on "What's that sound?" which has this imploding sort of effect. It's just this slight thing that's not even that loud, but your ear keys into it. Because your ear keys into that small sound, your mind doesn't expect the next thing. So procedurally, your mind will think that that sound is bigger because your mind has actually tuned into that sound first—and then boom!

Here's a good technique. It's kind of advanced, though. Let's say you have a sound, and you want that sound to cut through the mix so you can hear it. You've done EQ. You've done everything you can, but everything has chewed up your bandwidth, so you can't really hear what you've done. What I'm about to share is a procedural ear-tricking technique. Most people won't tell you these things, but it's used a lot, for example, in car chases, because car chases are just noisy, with guns firing and many other sounds. Let's say in this chase there are all these elements like skidding, engines going, gun shots, and all that, but you want the skids to cut through all the other sounds. What you do is you go in, and you actually chop out very fine little granular slots within that skidding sound, like a couple milliseconds to a millisecond. So if you soloed that sound by itself, it would actually sound like it's stuttering. But when you play it in the full mix, all of a sudden you can clearly hear the tire screech. What happens is a physics thing. Your mind actually knows that those gaps are missing, but it tries to fill in those spaces. Your ear detects those gaps, but in trying to fill in for those tiny breaks in the sound, your mind automatically hears those screeches a lot clearer. It actually pokes through. This doesn't work on everything, but on some things it helps out quite a bit, so that you can hear the sound you want to emphasize through the mix. I've used that on number of different things. Once you start tearing some of these techniques apart, you'll start hearing them a lot in movies and everything else. It's basically having your ear tune into something else, and all of a sudden, "Whoa! Where'd that come from?"

Learning surround sound is also very important, because all games are done in surround now. But before you try to mix stuff in surround sound, you first need to learn how to appropriately do a good mono mix. You should know how to properly do a mono mix of dialogue. Dialogue is a very good area to start, because learning how to make that dialogue fit in that pocket where other things can work around it is very important. For most of the dialogue in film and games, there's nothing below 150 or 200 hertz. It's just cut off.

Let's say you're going to do an interview with somebody over two days. Can you go in and clean up that dialogue and make it sound consistent, like a cohesive interview, between those two different days? Can you make it where the dialogue is clear, precise, and still has some dynamics and where I can understand every word in a mono mix? That's not even getting into doing sound design stuff. That's just a single dialogue and making it sound clean. It comes down to the basics, and it's the same thing that's applied in music. The best sound designers will ask, "How's this sound being used? What's it being used for? What's the context it's being used in?" This is because they know when they're doing their sound design, they need to know what things they need to emphasize, and it's all about the soundstage. Whether it's in movies, film, or games, it's still all about the soundstage.

Creating a game is probably about 500 percent more work than creating a feature film, and the reason why is because you make 500 percent more content. A film is a fixed event. Watching a two-hour movie is fine, but in games, we want you to play the game for 40 hours—or in the case of an MMO (massively multiplayer online game), it could be 200, 300 hours or more.

If you're paying $60 for a game, you want the full package that's emotionally engaging. When the audio is working well along with what you're watching and doing, it makes the game so much more immersive, and you actually feel better about playing it. You get a much better response out of the game than if it just has lousy little stuff in it. The game companies that just say, "Hmm, whatever" are going to be left behind.

I find that you cannot chase the competition. If you think the competition has this hot new thing in it, you can't all of a sudden, in the middle of the development of a new game, say, "We're going to put this hot new thing in our game." You need to be innovative and think of something that's not been done and think past it. When you approach things that way, you don't run into the problem of throwing things into the game because you're playing catch-up for the lack of creativity that you've had with your game designers.

Design should be designing with audio in mind, but it's really hard for many designers and game companies to design with audio in mind, because most of the time they never work with audio. They just think audio mysteriously happens. I think a lot of designers in game companies do not respect or grasp what a benefit audio can be to their designing capabilities if they bring in audio from the start, because audio can tell much of the story by itself. You get the best results when you have somebody who is designing the game and working with the audio person simultaneously to come up with the concepts and how things are going to work. When you see them do that in some games, the results are phenomenal.

Jerry Berlongieri

Credits include: Studio audio director at Treyarch. Game titles include Call of Duty 3: World at War, Descent 3, Spider-Man 3, *and* 007: Quantum of Solace. *See the Appendix for Jerry Berlongieri's full bio.*

Game audio has undergone a major evolution since its early days of beeps and bloops. I've been on this ride from those early days as a kid playing an Atari 2600, completely enthralled in the first generation of games, and as a result, I've developed a lot of respect for the creativity of the guys creating sound with those very limited resources. A lot of the music created for the early Commodore 64 games was really well crafted, very creative, using a limited palette. It's such an iconic sound; it's come to stand apart as a style that many musicians still explore.

When the game industry first started employing dedicated audio personnel, it was a jack-of-all-trades situation, covering everything from voice recording, sound effects editing, music...anything that would go in the game. Larger teams are common now, with specialized professionals assigned to certain roles. The credits in a AAA game [AAA is the term for a big-budget game] list audio roles that include casting and voice direction, foley recording, field recording, engineering and mix, composition, orchestration, arrangement and conducting, and any number of additional sound support roles both in-house and contract-for-hire. At some of our studios we have more than a dozen dedicated sound designers in house. The game audio industry is somewhat unique to film and TV in that sense, having a dedicated in-house sound team to help shape the audio from the very beginnings of production. That provides a wonderful opportunity to introduce sound as important to the narrative and also helps to influence and inspire the design. This is a relationship we're really beginning to see manifest throughout the industry, with sound playing a critical and integrated role in the storytelling.

While we look to film and television for inspiration, game audio presents a distinct and unique challenge. Film and TV production is linear; you've maybe two hours of story that dips and builds from west to east along your DAW timeline. In games, we're often dealing with a minimum of 12 hours and as much as 20 hours or more of presentation to cover with sound. So, to cover that much content, we have to think programmatically. We have to build sounds using techniques that will keep the sounds varied, modeling real-world behavior. We have to create not only a sound, but the tool and techniques that affect how that sound will play.

To give an example, in *Quantum of Solace*, when a computer monitor explodes and sparks, that is an event, an object, that appears in a lot of different areas throughout the game. Reuse is a major gameplay mechanic. So, how do we voice that in the game in such a way that it works with the visual but is also interesting and different every time it happens? We don't really know how the player is going to experience any event, so we have to think across a broader scope of how an event may be used over the course of a game. We don't often know where these items are going to be placed or what they may be placed with or set against. This goes along with what I was saying earlier, how it is very helpful to be involved at the beginning stages of a game's development. A level designer may decide to cluster 10 of those monitors together, which visually may look great when they all explode but sonically would cause problems. So, we take a look at the game environments as they are being mapped and try to encourage object variation and spacing. Further, art and design departments will have methods for creating and placing that exploding television. We have to tie into that so that sound gets carried along anytime that television is placed. The sound itself will likely consist of a set of disparate parts, each with several variations, combined with random pitch variation during playback, so that each occurrence is varied and unique.

Years ago, when we were creating an environment, we had to economize the size and fidelity of our sounds within the space limitations of the medium. Eventually, we were able to build more elaborate backgrounds so that in a game like *Call of Duty*, we could have a five-minute stereo file that was basically a composite of battle sounds, happening mid to distant in the world. Over the last few years, we've moved away from having a composite looping background and have moved more to separating and placing the separate background elements into the world. The problem with a stereo looping background file has to do with the fact that when the player is listening to the sounds of battlefield and turns, the stereo field turns with you, and you lose any real sense of direction. So now we separate the various elements and try to seat them in the world to achieve what we call *compass lock*. If you're playing *Call of Duty* and hear an air raid siren in the west, it is playing from a location in the map and is not baked into a stereo file. So when you turn, the sound stays in the west. You hear it move into the surrounds, you hear it move behind or around you as you turn. It retains compass lock, but it moves it across the panorama as the player turns. This dynamic style background gives a much better sense of depth.

When you are moving through a swamp in *Call of Duty*, it's not a static background. It's a stereo composite of bugs; it's all happening in the space. They exist in the world. We are working very hard to fill the space for the players, so they really get immersed and have a sense of their surroundings. The game engine is designed to place those sounds in the surround environment for us. Sound emitters exist in the world; whether it's a noisy computer monitor in the room that is chattering or a fire sprinkler that is going off, sound is emitting from that source, and as you pass it, it fills the sound field appropriately. We've begun introducing more complex obstruction and occlusion filtering into our games as well, so the sounds change as you move behind walls, and distant sounds in the game provide an even wider sense of space. Surround sound is incredibly important in a game environment. Rear speakers convey important information to the player. Surround is incredibly important in games, more so than in any other medium. You need to hear things that are coming from behind and get a sense of space in the world and where things are happening. You need to hear the enemy who is coming up behind you.

At the beginning of a project, we go out and record as much original source material as we can. We make every effort to build our proprietary libraries with each project and create unique assets from original source recordings. But we also use libraries, especially early on, to quickly seat a sound and get a sense of the textures that need to be there. We have access to a central server that includes all the main sound libraries from Sound Ideas, and we use them to drop in sounds and kind of block out our levels. But, as large as our libraries are, there are always new situations or game events that require a specialized session. Some tailored foley always fits best, when we can tune to our need and go and actually perform actions to what we have in the game. We have a recording booth in the office where we can bang around and record sounds as needs arise. We will go out in the field and record weapons or vehicles. We've recorded tanks for *Call of Duty*, and airplanes. It's a very busy, very vibrant experience for the audio department all the way through a project, from the beginning to the end.

Let me give you a quick idea as to how the development team as a whole works. The production department basically guides the game schedule throughout the development cycle. They will determine schedules and staffing, take a look at our game design docs, and make sure we maintain proper trajectory for our release date. Each department is assigned a producer who helps us coordinate with the needs of other departments. It's all about coordination. So, I have an audio producer who assists me in chasing an answer from art on the name of an effect, or we're having trouble determining why the game is crashing, or we're missing some important information or need to change something on the schedule and need to determine how that will impact other departments. Any time we encounter an issue or need some correspondence with other departments, they chase that down and make sure the game is progressing, that we're able to work.

The animation department handles player and character movement and cinematic cut-scenes—cut-scenes being the storytelling scenes shown between gameplay missions. These days the animators are also heavily involved in directing motion capture, which is the process of capturing live movement and attaching that natural movement data to our game characters.

Within the art department, we have teams who handle creating objects—anything from a soda machine to an air conditioner or a chair or whatever you see in the world. Another team within the art department creates all the visual effects—explosions, debris, powder, fire, glows, and dust. There is also a team who handles breakables—things in the world that break and the look and behaviors that occur, along with the visual change and effect.

The design department has level builders and scripters. The builders design the level environment and bring together all the pieces from the art department. They place those soda machines and chairs and objects within the level. The scripters work out how the action and events in the level will unfold.

There is, of course, the programming department, with many specialties. They cover everything from player controls to how the artificial intelligence behaves and reacts to the player. They help manage the engine that brings all the various artistic contributions together into one stable game environment. They help manage this engine from day to day; as all the various groups create and submit new content, there can be a lot of issues that occur. Just keeping it all working from day to day is an enormous effort.

The way music is used in the game is a critical part of the storytelling. And that can be challenging, because we're typically dealing with so many hours of gameplay, and we're dealing with music that will likely need to loop. Finding the right placement for underscore can be tricky—spots where loops can enter and exit or transition smoothly. There is a particular level in *Quantum Of Solace* where you're at an opera house, and you're hearing the music play as a sound coming from within the level. The music of that level is part of the world itself; what you're hearing is coming over the loud speakers. I think it is a very effective, rare case where music can serve as both underscore and sound effect.

We always employ a composer. Sometimes it's the same composer as the film, if it's a game based on one. Early on, we like to get the composer involved with what we're working on and play the levels for them so they can get a sense of the direction or what action or themes the level is going to be comprised of. They compose about 75 minutes or so of music to be spread throughout the game. Use varies—in a game like Bond, there is level-specific music, but there's also action music, stealth music…it depends. Each game is different depending on what its needs will be. In *Quantum of Solace*, the player can decide to stealthily move through the level, taking people out quietly, or come in with guns blazing, so the music has to support what approach the player has decided to pursue. We then had to have stems created that would kind of coincide with that and determine how to play it back.

The interactive nature of games has sort of created an opportunity to approach music in pieces and let the engine choose from a selection of possible combinations. With emergent delivery techniques, we have more opportunity to let music change, based not only on the player's decisions, but also on the variations in the game map or the type of enemy or area of the level that they are in. Sometimes it's a wonderful thing just to create an emergent environment that can surprise you with how it reacts to what the player is doing. It can also be quite a challenge to try and control sonically what you need the player to hear, and we're still developing the best methods for that…for music playback.

On *Quantum of Solace*, we had music delivered to us in stems. We had separate strings, brass, and percussion so we could mix layers where we needed to. We can take the composite track and sort of alter the layering to help support what the player is doing and suggest a pace. So if you're sneaking, you might just hear the tense strings down at the bottom. If AI [artificial intelligence] has alerted to your presence, you might hear the percussion layer come into the mix. Having the stems available gave us some flexibility to mix layers in support of the action.

We always try, as best we're able, to support what the player is experiencing in the game, the choices the player makes. If you decide to engage the enemy, as opposed to trying to sneak away, the music should respond to that, and that's difficult. In a movie, you can build to a scene. You can build to an explosion and have the music crescendo up to that point. In a game, we never know if the player is going to say, "I'm going this other way," while suddenly the music is crescendoing, and they just miss the event.

We try to account for those moments as best we can, and that kind of goes back to the beginning stages of the game design, when framing the scenes takes place. So, where the player may experience these big story events, we have to be aware of all the choices the player can make and have the right tools in place so the game can properly respond to the player's movements. There is a very technical side to what we do; it's incredibly exciting to see how far it's come and where we are right now. There's so much more there that we're going to be able do as we continue to evolve our tools.

The really cool thing about the game industry is the team and all the personalities and creativity in the team when you're working through a development cycle. The maturity of a game development team is very much like playing in a band, and at some point, when the band has been together for years, you can just jam, because you've really reached a point where you are familiar with each others' talents, and everyone is really contributing at the same level. You start to develop a sort of understanding of your group's style and way of doing things. You're able to continue to push the tools to get more out of what you're able to do, and really kind of perform as a group, and really create something that is creative and very natural.

There are games that I've played where I could feel that all disciplines came together really well like that, where the designers had time to put into it. A team that really knows the product they are creating and knows how to fill that world with interesting elements and events and can create something that's over the top—those experiences continue to inspire us.

Part of being in the game industry is playing games and watching what colleagues do in their projects. I'm friends with many audio directors, not only at Activision but throughout the industry, and we talk about what we're doing and share ideas and techniques as much as we're able. We all know we're facing the same challenges, so it's exciting when a great game comes out.

Whenever we see a game come out that the public gets really excited about, and it sells really well, and it's just a very well-done artistic product, it goes well for the whole industry. We are all striving for those products that the end user can truly enjoy and really feel like they had a great experience for the $60 they laid on the table. Whenever I play a game like that, it's inspiring.

MENTORING: GENERAL ADVICE

The question I probably get asked most from those starting out is, "How do you break into game audio?" That's always a challenge, because there are a limited number of game companies out there. Many have a relatively small department, and there is a very low turnover rate. When someone gets in here, they love it, and they are staying. Then again, there are more and more opportunities as new platforms, such as the iPhone, appear. We have a core in-house team, but we often utilize outside resources for additional support during busy times.

The thing that I always encourage kids to do is to not wait for employment to become a sound designer, just be a sound designer. Don't miss any opportunities to capture the unique sounds around you.

I remember some of the sounds I didn't get. There was a squeaky door to our bathroom in a college dorm that just had the eeriest moan. It used to creep us out every time we heard it, and I didn't record it. I always think back to that as one that got away. It was just a great sound! There are sounds that happen in our everyday experiences that, as a sound designer or sound recordist, we should always think about capturing and cataloging. Everyone has had a car with a muffler dragging. It's a sound that you can instantly recognize in your head—that muffler scrape on pavement sound. When you need the sound of a muffler dragging and you look in the sound libraries, there's nothing that would match. So I try to get students, kids starting out, to recognize when they encounter these sounds in the world, when these moments happen in life—don't miss them! If you get in the habit of doing that, you'll have those sounds when you need them. Build your library. At audio engineering schools, they will teach you how to mike a drum kit, but they seldom teach you how to mike a '97 Honda. That is a big part of what we do. It is figuring out how to go and capture these sounds. That's the kind of things I encourage these kids to do. Record your car. Record your toilet, your furnace, your washing machine. Record your life. Especially when something stands out with a unique sonic personality. That banging pipe that is driving you crazy, record it. While you're waiting to get a job in the industry, don't miss the opportunity while working at a shoe repair shop or working at the zoo or wherever you are. I have heard of all these interesting jobs people have had while they are waiting, and I say, "Go out and record all those sounds! You will never get them back!"

Chances are you know somebody who has an interesting job; you have a friend who works at the airport doing engine maintenance or a cousin who drives a garbage truck, and there are all these sounds out there that can be captured. Go out and record those sounds and start being a sound designer and creating these sounds right away. Don't lose out while waiting for the opportunity. Start creating!

Left column top to bottom: Dave Morgan @ Hollywood Bowl, Simon & Garfunkel show (photo courtesy of Dave Morgan) / Ben Folds @ Bonnaroo (photo by Rick Clark) / Los Super Seven @ Hardly Strictly Bluegrass Festival, Golden Gate Park (photo by Rick Clark). Right column top to bottom: Keyboard @ PLYRZ (photo by Jimmy Stratton) / Joey Burns of Calexico (photo by Rick Clark) / Osaka Pearl @ The Tone Chaparral (photo by Rick Clark) / keyboard @ PLYRZ (photo by Jimmy Stratton).

Guitar: Electric and Acoustic

It is almost impossible to overstate how important guitar has been in the world of popular music, whether it is rock, R&B, folk, country, blues, whatever. Sure, drummers, bassists, and keyboardists can all lay rightful claim to their essential roles, but somehow guitarists get the lion's share of the so-called hero-worship, whether it's quiet acoustic renderings, funky chicken pickin', or pure jackhammer, amp-blowing death rock.

It doesn't matter whether it is the amazingly fluid melodicism of Les Paul, Chet Atkins, or Tommy Tedesco; the psychedelic soulfulness of Jimi Hendrix; the tight, earthy groove of Steve Cropper; the dreamy fluid acoustic textures of David Crosby; the lyrical blues wailing of B.B. King and slide guitar expressiveness of Duane Allman; or the back-of-the-arena rock stylings of Jimmy Page, Pete Townshend, or Eric Clapton, it's hard to imagine most of popular music of the last 60-plus years without the musical contribution of the electric guitar.

The brilliance may start with the player, but behind the scenes in the studio is usually an attentive, resourceful engineer or producer, trying to catch sparks on tape.

For this chapter, we've got a who's who of contributors who know all about recording guitar: Jim Scott, Nick Launay, Russ Long, Stephen Barncard, Dylan Dresdow, Ronan Chris Murphy, Adrian Belew, John Jennings, Skidd Mills, Michael Wagener, and David Z.

Jim Scott

Credits include: Tom Petty, Wilco, Red Hot Chili Peppers, Sting, the Rolling Stones. See the Appendix for Jim Scott's full bio.

When I record electric guitars, I do what I call the "good mic, bad mic" approach for miking the amp. I'll use an expensive condenser, like a U 87, and a 57. I'll put the 57 on the cone, and I'll put the 87 out a little farther on the speaker. You just want to make sure you are making a good sound and not an out-of-phase sound. You have to be careful that when the 57 sounds good and you bring in the 87, the sound gets bigger, because it might not. You might have some phasing issues, or it might just be canceling out on that speaker.

You have to listen to each guitar cabinet. You almost have to go stand in front of the cabinet like you are standing in front of a painting and listen to it while it's just sitting there turned on, because it is going to make a noise. It's going to hiss or hum or buzz. It's going to have an ambient, at-rest kind of a sound when it is on. My theory is that that sound is what the amps sound like, so when you put a microphone on that amp and you don't hear that same hiss, then you are going to record something, but you aren't going to record what that amp naturally does, if that makes any sense.

If you actually put the headphones on and move the microphone around the speaker, it would go "shhhhhhhhhhhhhhhhwwwwwwwwwwwshhhh." Right on the cone it would be real bright, "whistley" and "sssssssssssss," and out on the cone it would be warmer and darker and more of a white noise kind of thing. But somewhere in between is the natural balance of what that amp sounds like. When you move your mics around, you can find a similar sound to the natural hiss, and that's where I try to put the mic.

The mic has got to be on the grill; otherwise, you are just inviting more phase issues. If you get it 2 inches back off the grill, it's got to go out of phase some amount or degree. So, I try to keep them close. Most guitar speakers are only 10 inches big, so those mics will be pretty close. The 2-1/2-inch phase plate of a 57, of an 87 and a 1-inch capsule, they are going to only be 3 inches apart. They are going to be side by side, but one's going to be on the cone, and one's going to be on the speaker. So that's how I would do my electric guitars.

For DI, I use Neve pres and probably use an 1176 compressor or an LA-2A compressor, if I feel like that is going to help the sound. That would be my A setup for an electric guitar. My B setup would be an RCA 77 mic about a foot away from the speaker. If I had one mic, I would just use a 77 and just hope for the best. [Laughs]

Stephen Barncard

Credits include: The Grateful Dead, Crosby, Stills, Nash & Young, New Riders of the Purple Sage, Van Morrison, David Crosby, Seals and Crofts, the Doobie Brothers. See the Appendix for Stephen Barncard's full bio.

In early 1970, before I started to record David Crosby's first solo album (*If I Could Only Remember My Name*), I had been working with a friend from Kansas City named Chet Nichols, who was a troubadour very much like Crosby, who played in open tunings and did these very beautiful, introspective, deep songs. Chet played with the same kinds of acoustic guitars that Crosby did—well-worn Martins and Guilds. Wally Heider allowed his employees to record acts during unbooked time, so Nichols's first record was produced by me on speculation, and it became my microphone-technique test bed.

At that point in time, I had decided to focus on acoustic guitar sounds. I realized early on that one of the things I liked about Crosby, Stills, and Nash were their guitar sounds, so I started focusing on real microphone theory, instead of my previous nonscientific approach.

There was a guy named Lou Burroughs who wrote a book called *Microphones: Design and Application* (Sagamore Pub. Co., 1974), now out of print. He was the guy who invented the Electro-Voice Variable-D series microphones. In the book, Burroughs goes into the concept of multiple microphone placement, close miking, phase relationships, M-S, and so on. Basically, it was the Bible of microphone technique for me, and I applied it in practice.

After I worked on *American Beauty* [the classic Grateful Dead album], I'm guessing David Crosby heard the acoustic guitars on that album and had communication with [Jerry] Garcia.

By the time Dave and I got into the studio, it all went pretty smoothly. My experimentation had paid off—Crosby was blown away by the attention I gave to the acoustic guitar. I ended up using a pair of AKG C 60s with the Omni capsules, which are basically the equivalent of the non-tube AKG 451 FET.

I would listen to David play, sit in the room for a few minutes and just hear him while he ran down the particular song of the evening. I noticed that a lot of cats don't listen in the room at all. They just throw up a mic, go back into the control room, and put an EQ on it.

After a respectful time to allow David to present the complete song—always the showman—I would have him play it again and then plug up one ear and move a single ear around in space until I found a sweet spot. Then I would look for another spot and put microphones in both places. If David was singing live, which he often did for basic tracks, I would probably get a Shure 546 Unidyne III or an SM56 for isolation. I also know CSN—have had a long history with this mic.

In the miking of acoustic guitars, there is usually a sweet spot off-center from the sound hole and another sweet spot up the neck or over the shoulder. I like to view the sound from the guitarist's perspective, because that's the area their attack and movements are reacting to—their biofeedback mechanism—through the headphones. You know it still needs to be pretty much what the guitar sounds like and not necessarily a little isolated spot in space that they don't hear. I try to get the best of both spots, and then I used to EQ and limit to tape often. The EQ was integral to the preamp circuit on the DeMedio consoles, a very short signal path.

I think I was pushing the envelope with the multiple mics. A lot of mixers didn't do that in 1969, because it was impractical and it wasn't speedy, but I considered it essential to explore all possibilities of what I could do with it later. It also helped that the industry had standardized on 16 tracks at this point, and all the possibilities of using those tracks. Over time I would learn the positioning for a particular guitar and store a catalog in my head of methods that work with other guitars. There is no universal setting for all guitars, as you probably know. They're all going to be different on different days because of humidity, temperature, and room acoustics, too. My goal was to find a positioning that sounded good immediately for each one and then work from there. A broken-in Martin D-45 is the sweetest sounding thing, or a Guild. But a brand-new Martin can sound terrible!

Usually I would print EQ and limiting to tape. There were many reasons to do that. The practice, in my opinion, contributed to a more cohesive final mix, and it allowed the reuse of the limited quantity of outboard gear available to the room. I think it made overdubs better, because in the headphones the artist is hearing what is building to be the final mix.

I didn't have much to work with as EQ, but it was fast and intuitive to use without looking. The 10k was actually left to right at −6, −3, 0, +3, +6, +9. Then there was a midrange that was switchable at 3k and 5k. The low end was at 100 and 50. The EQ used the famous 610 amplifier module designed by Bill Putnam and Frank DeMedio.

I limited the guitars aggressively with the 1176. Even though limiting on tracking and again on mixing, I used limiters judiciously. I worked on them for hours and found a sweet spot where they didn't pump too bad, but they made stuff sound big. My intention was to make the biggest acoustic possible. This was a direct result of my early experiments with Chet Nichols.

What I did was a variation on the trademark CSN sound, per Bill Halverson. I wasn't the first to do this with these guys. The EQ-heavy-limiting thing was a big part of their sound collectively. I just went a little more extreme and did it in stereo. Bill Halverson [who mixed and recorded the wonderful self-titled first Crosby, Stills & Nash and Déjà Vu albums and Stephen Stills' self-titled debut] used an intense compression, where you could hear the pumping, especially on a lot of Stills' guitar work. That was Stills' sound. Crosby needed a more dreamy, bouncy, blooming kind of sound, so I backed up on the release time and let it sit there a little bit and then come back. I like approaching his playing like that, because of slow-picking arpeggiated stuff. It does a nice thing. The compression just brings up the sound of all the other strings. So the idea is to emphasize the frequencies of the strings that are pleasing and de-emphasize ones that are bad or unpleasing. The compression also allowed the acoustic guitars to compete in the same sonic space as the drums. Today, with Pro Tools, I can really get to this place a lot easier with parametric equalizers and look-ahead limiters.

Russ Long

Credits include: Phil Keaggy, Sixpence None the Richer, Michael W. Smith, Dolly Parton, Steve Taylor. See the Appendix for Russ Long's full bio.

The mistake people make most often when they record electric guitars is failing to spend enough time ensuring everything pre-microphone is correct. The choice of guitar, amp, and cabinet, as well as everything in between, is crucial to achieving a great tone. And more important than that is the player. Good players lend themselves to good tone, where bad players, unfortunately, lend themselves to dodgy tone. The same guitar and amp with the exact same settings sound entirely different depending on who is playing.

In the world of guitars, tubes are always better than solid-state, so I try to make sure I'm always working with a good tube amp. There are occasions where a solid-state amp works, but they are rare. If I'm working with a session guitarist, I never have to worry about the gear; but if I'm working with a young band, I'll always check out what they have ahead of time, and if it isn't up to par, I'll borrow or rent something that I know will work. Regardless of the setup, I always use the Creation Audio MW1, which is a little miracle box for recording electric guitar and bass. I can't imagine working without it. Among other things, the MW1 lets me easily record a direct signal while continuing to record their guitar and/or bass tracks the same way I always do, giving me the option to re-amp tracks later. The box also has multiple isolated outputs, making it easy to simultaneously drive more than one rig. Best of all, though, the MW1 lets me insert +4 pro audio toys between the guitar and the amp, allowing me to use any of my pro audio gear in place of a bunch of $75 and $100 pedals.

I think the Royer R-122 is the ultimate electric guitar mic. It's what I use 90 percent of the time. I'm not married to any exact positioning, but my starting point is halfway between the speaker's center and its edge, about 1 inch off the grill, pointing directly at the speaker. I typically run it through a Gordon mic pre if I'm looking for a more natural sound or a Daking mic pre if I want a bit more color. As far as EQ goes, I'll usually use a Daking or a Neve 33114, and I nearly always use the Empirical Labs Distressor for compression. Occasionally, I'll use a Shure SM57 or a Sennheiser MD421 instead of or in addition to the Royer, but typically the sole Royer R-122 is the magic sound.

Another important factor is tuning. A potentially great guitar sound is quickly squelched if the instrument is out of tune. I always keep a line running out of the MW1's tuner output into a Peterson VS-R StroboRack so the tuning can easily be checked at any time. Session musicians automatically check their tuning every time they get a chance, but band members don't usually have that good habit.

Lastly, I try to make sure the musician is as comfortable as possible. If they are using a chart, I make sure they have a music stand and enough light to read it. I also make sure they have a pencil in case they have to make any notes. I even go as far as making sure their chair doesn't have armrests, which can restrict their movement.

Nick Launay

Credits include: Public Image Ltd, INXS, Yeah Yeah Yeahs, Midnight Oil, Gang of Four, Kate Bush, Semisonic, Supergrass, Nick Cave & the Bad Seeds, Eric Clapton. See the Appendix for Nick Launay's full bio.

A good guitar sound comes from a good guitar player, and anything you can do to get the guitar player to play better is what you want to accomplish first. If you're dealing with a young player, make sure they're playing their favorite guitar. You might make sure the neck is the right size for their hands. If it isn't, they're not going to play it really well; it's not going to sound very good. You've got to start there and make sure they're happy. Then get a really good amp.

If I have a trick at getting good guitar sounds, it is using a Beyer 88, which I put at a 45-degree angle on one speaker, as close as possible to the center of the speaker but off to the side. I then put an AKG 414 or an AKG C 12A [the one that looks like a 414, the black one] and just put that flat directly in the middle of another speaker.

Say you have a cabinet that has two speakers. I usually put the condenser mic at 90 degrees, straight at it in the middle, and then the 88 at an angle. This way, you've got two very different types of microphones with two different angles on it. The reason I don't put the Beyer 88 direct is you can get too much midrange. Basically, the idea is you have two different mics set at two different angles, and with these two different flavors, I can fade them in and out and work out what sound I want. I can put them out of phase with each other and get these good tones. And equally, once you've got that going on, you can back the 88 off and listen in the headphones, and as you're doing it, I can refine the sound even more. I basically use the phase difference between the two mics as my tool to getting the guitar sound I want. I get it as close as I can to what I want when I'm recording, but very often I'll print them separately, on separate channels, so that I can still refine this when I come to mixing. Using the faders, I can back one off and get a different tone, or I can EQ one differently, which affects the phase of the other.

I also record with a room mic, usually a ribbon, like an RCA 44 or a Coles ribbon, about 6 feet back. Ribbon mics work for capturing a room sound really well, and they have this honkiness to them that's so good...so wild and rock and roll–like. I find that with the combination of these three mics, I get the sound I want. Sometimes I like to just use the ribbon by itself.

Dylan Dresdow

Credits include: Black Eyed Peas, TLC, Wu-Tang Clan, Pink, Michael Jackson. See the Appendix for Dylan Dresdow's full bio.

I'll start with two mics on the front of the speaker. I usually use a Royer 122 toward the edge of the cone for low-end tone a couple inches back, and then I put a Shure SM57 where the dome meets the cone to capture the distortion presence right on the speaker grill. I'll put an IBP on the SM57 channel, flip the phase, and sweep the Phase Adjust knob until it sounds the most hollow. Then I flip it so it's back in phase and the two mics have a tight phase relationship.

For a bigger guitar sound, I put another SM57 toward the back of the cabinet and flip the phase on this. I have the guitarist play and the assistant move the mic around slowly. Once I hear it sound as out of phase as possible, I have the guitarist stop, which is the assistant's cue to lock in that mic placement. I then flip that channel's phase back in phase and add that into the signal with the other two mics, which are typically being summed to one channel anyway. So you actually have three different mics going into one channel. But since you've got the backup microphone behind the amp, it ends up taking a lot more space, and technically, it smudges up your attacks a little bit, which can be a good thing sometimes, and sometimes it's a bad thing.

When recording guitar, I will very often use Neve mic pres, or the Crane Song Flamingo with the Iron switch and the Fat switch engaged. Those both sound really, really good on an electric guitar to me. For compression, I really like using the Buzz Audio Potion, which is an FET compressor. I turn the mix up to 100 percent, and I turn the threshold down. The compression is much more aggressive than where I would typically keep it, and it's really just slamming this guitar part down, almost using it like a sustain pedal where everything just sort of stays in for a long time with a long release time. And then, after I've got it to where it sounds really aggressive and really apparent, I will turn the mix down to like 80 percent to 60 percent, and usually somewhere in there I'm pretty happy with the sound. And then sometimes I have to tweeze it back a little bit and make the compressions sound a little bit less heavy-handed.

From that, I take the output of that, and I usually use the A-Designs Hammer EQ, which works really great on guitar. And then I typically roll off all of the low end on guitar, anything below 60 Hz. I will also roll off some top end with maybe a 6-dB slope, so it's kind of nice and doesn't really take your head off as much. That's typically what I do with those. Sometimes what I'll do whenever I'm recording, if it's a rock project, I have the Little Labs PCP unit, and I keep that in the control room and just use that as a guitar matrix, so that I can go out to several different amp heads all at once.

It's a great way to dial in the guitar exactly how you want it, and you can switch very quickly between amps and determine which is best for the guitar part that you're doing. And then you can even dial in how much gain you want or even use it for re-amping during a mix. So, that's basically the main thing for guitar. Sometimes if I want more low end, if I'm using like a Mesa Boogie setup, like the Lone Star, for example, I will set up a Sennheiser MD421 mic, which tends to give me more low end. On all of these 421s, there's an M and an S knob that you can turn in the base of them. The S stands for speech. The M stands for music. I always keep them on the M setting.

Ronan Chris Murphy

Credits include: King Crimson, ProjeKct Four, Bozzio Levin Stevens, Steve Morse. See the Appendix for Ronan Chris Murphy's full bio.

When mixing a typical record, most of my energy is going into how I want to present the record and creatively approach a mix, whereas I find that with records done when guitars have been run through with digital amp modelers, most of my energy goes into trying to overcome how much those guitars are fighting everything else on the record. They tend to get to white noise pretty quickly, and they don't have the natural roll off that you would get from a speaker. You will also have the introduction of a lot of overtones that aren't harmonically related to the chord. A big part of the problem is that they just tend to smear, so all of a sudden the depth of your entire record will collapse. It's really amazing. If you put up a mix that has the guitars using amp modelers, you can mute the guitars, and you've just gained 20 feet of depth back into your drum track, and your lead vocal articulation just pushed forward and jumped out.

If you take a guitar plugged into a tube guitar amp and run it through five compressors in a series where it's not budging at all, it will not impart those negative qualities that the digital amp modeler will. A modern rock guitar sound coming out of the amp won't have much of a dynamic range, and the natural compression of all the tubes will actually keep everything pretty well in line.

Interestingly, I find that bass amp modelers generally don't suffer in such an extreme way. There's just something weird about guitars in digital guitar amp modelers, in particular, that are a big issue. You can run a keyboard, vocals, kick drum, and a number of things through one of those guitar amp modelers, and they don't seem to exhibit the same problems. It's just something about using one of those units for what they're designed for that imparts serious problems into a mix. They may become something different in a few years, but I'm not optimistic. There are ways to make a bad guitar sound work into a really exciting mix. There are times when there are ways to make those guitar sounds have interest and character, but I don't recommend using digital amp modelers.

Michael Wagener

Credits include: Skid Row, Extreme, Ozzy Osbourne, Metallica, Megadeth, Alice Cooper, Janet Jackson, Dokken, Testament, Queen, the Plasmatics, White Lion, X, Saigon Kick, King's X. See the Appendix for Michael Wagener's full bio.

There is an important relationship between amp output and speaker wattage. I subscribe to the theory that you have to push air to get your point across. That means I will always try to use an amp with more power reserves than the RMS wattage of the speaker cab. Of course, you have to be careful not to blow the cab to pieces. A tube amp of about 100 watts can have peaks around 250 watts, so make sure your cabinet can stand that occasional peak. Also, if you use a tube amp, that peak is liable to come smoother than or not as sudden as you would get from a transistor power amp. A tube power amp will probably give you a fatter, saturated sound, whereas a transistor amp will be cleaner with a bit of a harder attack.

Another very important part of the power amp is the output transformer. The output transformer can make or break the sound of an amplifier. Once, I had to exchange a blown output transformer of a great-sounding Marshall 100-watt top. I never got the original sound back.

The distortion doesn't always have to be generated in the preamp. Sometimes it's better to keep the preamp section fairly clean and get the distortion out of the power amp or the speaker. Speaker distortion is the smoothest distortion you can get. Unfortunately, because of the high volume, it also involves having a very good isolated studio, so the neighbors won't get distorted as well.

When you pick a speaker cabinet, there are a few considerations to be made. What kind of sound do you want to achieve? Are you looking for a clean sound or a distorted sound? Is the instrument going to be in the front or the back of the mix? Is it going to be doubled? Are you playing single notes, chords, or both? How powerful is your amp? Can your speaker cabinet withstand the power output from the amp? Is your speaker cabinet too "big" for the amp, so it won't push enough air? For example, a 4×30-watt cab would be a great, powerful cab for a 100-watt amp if you are looking for a fat, distorted sound. If you are going for a cleaner sound, you might want to try a 4×75-watt cabinet on the same amp. Make sure that the impedance of the cabinet and the amp match.

Make sure not to download the guitar output by hooking up a bunch of amps without a splitter. If you combine amps, it is important to look at the amp input as a resistor or load on your guitar. When you put two resistors in parallel, their value halves—think about two 8-ohm speakers switched parallel, resulting in 4-ohms. The smaller the resistor value, the more current [or power] gets drawn by it. Your guitar only has a very tiny amount of power available on its output, so if you simply Y-cord the guitar into two amps, you are liable to lose some of the pickup power of the guitar to the load of the two parallel amp inputs. The most noticeable side effect is probably a loss of high end or overall crunch.

The input impedance of a normal tube amp is around 1 million ohms, and the output impedance of a guitar is normally around 250,000 ohms. That is a pretty healthy relationship. If you combine two amp inputs, the input impedance goes down to about 500,000 ohms, which is a much higher load on your guitar output.

Sometimes, for creating sound options, it might be good to set up a few different amps and cabinets in different rooms—hard and soft, open and dampened. It also works well to have a certain amp just produce the upper frequencies and another one just for the low end. That way you can decide on the mix between the two from inside the control room. If you have enough tracks available, record them both separately and mix them later when you have a better idea about the whole sound of the song. If you record the [almost] same signal twice, you have to be careful not to get phase distortion.

Skidd Mills

Credits include: ZZ Top, B.B. King, Robert Cray, Audio Adrenaline, Big Star, Spin Doctors, Saving Abel, Skillet, Space Hog, Saliva, Third Day, Killjoys, Tetanus. See the Appendix for Skidd Mills's full bio.

First off, to me the most important element is the player. That is where most of the tone comes from. As far as amps go, I really like Matchless amps. I think they are really cool. I have recorded them a few times, and they've turned out really cool. Some of my favorites are also old Marshalls, Hiwatts, and old Fenders.

I almost always mike amps the same. I usually use two [Shure] 57s on a cabinet, a little off-center from the cone, right up against the grill. Sometimes, I will use a [Sennheiser] 421 or a [AKG] 451 with a 57.

I usually don't like to EQ my mics, especially separately, because when you're EQing separate guitar mics, you can get weird phase problems happening. If I'm going to do compression, EQ, or anything like that, it's almost always after the fact.

I rely more on the actual sound. I will stand out by the amp before I start to EQ anything on the board. I'll go out and stand by the amp and just make sure that it sounds good. If I do any EQ adjustments, I start first on the guitar amp itself. I won't add board EQ while I'm going to tape, because I really just want to get the sound of the amp. Sometimes I'll compress the guitar to tape, if I'm looking for a real heavy sound. One of my favorites is the Valley People 440. It has a lot of versatility to it.

For the most part, I don't like to slam guitars. When I'm standing in front of my monitors, I like to have the feel like I'm standing in front of the speaker cabinet. In other words, I'm pushing a lot of air.

You have to be careful with compression because you can squeeze the life out of a guitar sound until it sounds paper-thin. At the same time, you don't want to have the guitarist just strumming along and have one section come bursting out at you. When I'm mixing, I would say that my all-time favorite guitar compressor is the SSL compressor that is sitting in the board.

Initially, I work with the sound of the player and amp. I get all of that together before I start thinking about what mics and what compression I want to use. I listen to the playing and see whether the guitar and amp are most complementary to that player's style. Experimenting with different amps, guitars, and even picks can make a big difference. I usually like to have a lot of toys lying around, like a box full of distortion boxes and old vintage stuff. I like doing these things to achieve the best complementary tone for the player's style and the type of music, instead of having the guitarist merely plug in and mike it up and sit at the board EQing all day until I'm blue in the face.

David Z

Credits include: Kenny Wayne Shepherd, Jonny Lang, Fine Young Cannibals, Prince, Billy Idol, Lipps Inc., Etta James, Leo Kottke. See the Appendix for David Z's full bio.

The role of a funk guitar is almost like that of another percussion instrument. It's playing a polyrhythm. Basically, in funk music, everything is a little more percussive. Everything is more a function of the beat than in many other styles of music.

A lot of times, funk guitars are very clean, bright, and often intensely compressed, because the way funk is played is like a slapping, hard-picking technique to make it bite. It's usually a Fender guitar, because Fenders have a good short tone, meaning they have a quick attack and quick release on a note, as opposed to a smooth, long tone, like an acoustic or a Gibson or something.

With Prince, we used a Hohner, which sounded like a Tele, but it was 20,000 times brighter. It would come off with that "skanky" sound. There is also that Gibson or 335 sound for darker, funky chord sounds. Those are usually recorded pretty straight, with maybe a little chorus. They aren't real elaborate.

For compressors, I love the LA-2As or ones that grab you a little bit more, such as a dbx OverEasy or an Inovonics. Those grab hard. Sometimes that is what you want. Usually, I will have it set with a slow attack, to get the head of the note, and then slam it. Then I have a fast release. I usually have it set at a 4-to-1 ratio, but it depends. It's totally by ear. That's just a usual setting I might use.

Guitar amplifiers add some power, but they aren't a big part of the actual tone of funk guitars. You want to get that speaker tone, but the attack is a pretty clean tone. We are not looking for distortion. Recording blues guitar, on the other hand, is more a function of the guitar and the amplifier together because of the distortion factor. A lot of times, I will use a ribbon mic, like a Coles ribbon mic. A lot of times with blues guitar and also acoustic, I would take what I would call "multiple sources." For example, on the Big Head Todd and the Monsters record that I did, we had a lot of multiple sources. We ran through a Leslie, and we ran through a little Marshall. We miked the strings and then out of his regular amp all at the same time. We then had four different sounds going for the same part. Depending on what you pick and choose, you can get some pretty cool textures doing that.

Sometimes I will put what I call a "kamikaze" microphone focused on the bridge of the electric guitar. Sometimes I'll put that mic on a stand, or hang it from a stand, placed as close as you can get it. I mainly use an ECM-50 or ECM-150 lavalier mic, or the kind of Sony that newscasters wear on their ties. I might use a 452, or [Neumann] KM 84, a bright condenser mic, just to pick up the zing of the pick hitting the strings. You've got to roll off the bottom end. You're just trying to get some sort of high-end thing. Obviously, you have to put the amp in another room from the player, or you won't get anything worth using.

If you mix a little bit of that in with what he's playing, that adds a third dimension to it. You bring the sound into an even bigger arena, and you can spread it out. I like to do that, because in that way, you can actually make the guitar itself become much bigger sounding. I may not use some of those elements, but I will usually try to take multiple sources.

For Leo Kottke, we did a lot of multiple sourcing. We used a couple of mics, and we took a direct out of his pickup. We also used this guitar synthesizer that he had, a Roland VG-8. It added string sounds or other textures that played way underneath what he was playing. It gave the music a really eerie quality.

On Leo, I used the DI to get a little support and clarity. I had one signal running through a little Fender Champ in another room. I miked him with two mics, a 452 up on the neck and a 49 over the hole. Both were placed 2 or 3 inches away.

Acoustic guitars have some sort of a buildup in the lower-end areas, and it can really overwhelm you. I think the buildup is often around 150 Hz. You have to be kind of careful with compression and mic placement. A little roll-off and distancing of the mic helps. I tend not to compress very much.

Actually, the big acoustic guitars can be deceiving because they can be great-sounding live, but then the microphone picks up all of this boom, and it gets all screwed up. As a result, smaller guitars are sometimes the best. The player obviously can make a big difference.

Adrian Belew

Credits include: Talking Heads, David Bowie, King Crimson, Laurie Anderson, Joan Armatrading, Herbie Hancock, Mike Oldfield, Robert Palmer, Paul Simon, Frank Zappa, the Bears, and 17 solo albums. See the Appendix for Adrian Belew's full bio.

Before recording, I try to program most of my sounds into the multi-effects units the way that I want them heard, so there is little need for extra things to be done from the console, in terms of dynamic signal processing or EQ. Of course, there's always a certain amount of EQing that you will do.

There are always happy accidents or things that occur that I didn't plan on happening while recording. I always welcome those things, but most of the time it's important that I scientifically develop the sounds that I really want to use in a song in a way that allows me to reproduce them again live. I really concentrate more on my guitar setup and its abilities to generate those.

I like to build a single guitar sound out of several different guitar sounds. I may overdub three different guitars that are playing exactly the same thing but have different variations of sounds. It's important to me to create clean arrangements. In terms of sound, fewer parts are better.

I have several choices of amplifiers that I use in several different rooms of my home studio. I use a DC-30 Matchless amp, which has an incredibly good tube sound. I keep it in my studio's maple-floor room. I also have some other amps, like a Fender Twin, a couple of Jazz amps, and a Roland Jazz Chorus 120.

I mainly like to play through 12-inch speakers. I'll put up a couple of AKG 414s on them and maybe have a room mic, like a C 24, so there is a combination of close mic and room sounds to choose from. It just depends on what kind of sounds I'm going for. Sometimes, I'll just plug into the board and play straight into the console. Most of the time, I like to go through speakers.

If I'm recording guitar synthesizer stuff, I don't find that those sounds come out any better coming through a speaker and a microphone, so I generally just take the signal direct. I might go through a Tube-Tech to try to warm things up a little bit, if possible, and try to get the cleanest signal going right in to the board. If I'm going to go direct with a guitar, I particularly like the Eventide Harmonizers, because they have so many sounds.

I have four different synthesizers. In my rack, I have two that I use for all of my live sounds—they're the Roland GR-1 and the Roland GR-50. I also have the older GR-700, which has a lot of really nice analog-based sounds. I probably have designed about 200 sounds with that unit. It's a little hard to give it up, so I leave it in the studio. I also leave a newer model in the studio called the VG-8. It's not actually a guitar synthesizer, but it's yet another thing that I find works better for me in the studio than in a live application.

The VG-8 has some really nice properties. In particular, it allows you to use altered tunings. You can write in altered tunings, and the guitar sound is very realistic. There are many available guitar sounds, and you can play harmonics and get string noises, and you can really think that you are playing through a pickup, but you are actually not. In fact, you could use a guitar that has no pickups on it, as long as you're using the MIDI controller, and you would never know that you're not playing through pickups. Again, it's an excellent way to utilize a lot of different tunings, and that is one of the things that I mainly use it for.

John Jennings

Credits include: Mary Chapin Carpenter, Indigo Girls, Iris Dement, Janis Ian, Lyle Lovett, Bill Morrissey. See the Appendix for John Jennings's full bio.

For better or worse, I do have several default locations for placing mics. I like to think of them as good starting points, rather than rules. They work for me and may not work for you.

Go out on the floor and listen to what you're going to record. Don't just throw up a couple of mics and do your inspection from the control room. Mics and monitors can lie to you. If you're recording an acoustic guitar, listen with your face parallel to the face of the instrument. You'll want to be a few feet back from the guitar, and you'll want to move around a bit, mostly from side to side. You'll find the sweet spot, where all the elements of the sound are apparent and fairly well-balanced. Regardless of whether you're recording in stereo or mono, this is the zone you want to try to capture.

Once you have found a sound that you like, walk around the room a bit. Listen from behind the guitarist, from the side, and all over. There might also be another place you can add a mic that will help the sound overall. Sometimes you have to try fairly unconventional things to compensate for an instrument that is lacking in a particular area or to find a sound that fits a particular track. There are folks who will try to convince you, before you even try, that trying some unusual mic placement may not work. Having been guilty of this a time or two myself, I have reformed. I now say, "Whatever!" It only takes a few minutes to find out.

I personally prefer to record acoustic guitars in stereo, as I like wide images. I like to use matching pairs of mics and have a particular fondness for KM 84s. Point one toward the middle of the lower bout and the other at the 15th or so fret. Put them a foot or so from the guitar, with the capsule roughly parallel to the face, and adjust the distance to taste. You get that nice bottom end from the bridge and the articulation from the neck.

If you're recording direct, try to have a few options for DIs. It's always best to be able to tailor a sound to a particular track. As for recording electric guitars, I'm always searching for better ways to do it. I've become a proponent of the multiple-mic method. I really like to try several different mics on different speakers and move them around a good bit. Do yourself a favor: Buy a Sennheiser MD409 and use it in conjunction with an SM 57. I place the 409 about a foot from one of the speakers and point it toward the outer edge of the cone. I find the 57 useful in adding definition to the sound if the 409 seems a bit too soft. Nevertheless, there are many mics; try as many as you can. There are really useful microphones that are not very expensive, such as RadioShack PZMs.

When recording electric guitars, listen to the amp close up and at different points in the room. If the amp has multiple speakers, each may have its own character, no matter how subtle. Ask the guitarist where the spot is in the room that sounds good to him or her. If the guitarist is standing and has dialed in a tone that works from head height, try to make a provision for that. In other words, put up another mic!

Left column top to bottom: Richard Dodd (photo by Rick Clark) / Bob Clearmountain (photo courtesy of Bob Clearmountain) / Ralph Sutton (photo courtesy of Ralph Sutton). Right column top to bottom: Jim DeMain (photo courtesy of Jim DeMain) / Rick Clark & Russ Long (photo by Derrick Scott) / Tim Palmer (photo courtesy of Tim Palmer) / Jim Scott's PLYRZ Studios (photo by Jimmy Stratton).

Keyboards

From Charles Earland and Jimmy Smith funking up jazz on the B-3, to the Moody Blues' Mike Pinder with his densely orchestrated Mellotron atmospherics, to E. Power Biggs' grand pipe organ performances of Bach, to the amazingly subtle and musical application of analog synth on the Beatles' masterpiece *Abbey Road*, keyboards have always provided music with an almost endless array of colors and nuance.

It would take an entire book to adequately cover all the elements of recording keyboards. For this chapter, we enlisted Christopher Greenleaf, Cookie Marenco, Leanne Ungar, and Tony Visconti to offer their thoughts on recording everything from pipe organ and Fender Rhodes to accordion, synths, and Mellotron.

Tony Visconti

Production and/or engineering credits include: David Bowie, T. Rex, Morrissey, the Moody Blues, Gentle Giant, Adam Ant, Sparks, Boomtown Rats, the Stranglers, Kristeen Young. See the Appendix for Tony Visconti's full bio.

One of the most exotic keyboards to record is the Mellotron and its first cousin, the Chamberlin. They are not dissimilar in concept; they are both keyboard samplers that play prerecorded analog tapes. [Mr. Chamberlin left the Mellotron organization to start up his eponymous keyboard company.]

I started recording Mellotrons as early as 1968, after hearing that haunting flute intro to "Strawberry Fields Forever." In London, in 1968, you could actually hire that very same Mellotron the Beatles hired to play that very same flute sound and also that flamenco guitar run used at the beginning of "[The Continuing Story of] Bungalow Bill" [by pressing one key]. One could also request the sound effects library rack of tapes that the Beatles used for the jet airliner wheels squealing at touchdown at the beginning of "Back in the USSR." Even before hot string sounds were available on early ARP synthesizers, the Mellotron afforded the average Brit pop band a sleazy opportunity to have a string section on their record, and it wasn't synthesized—it was the real deal, real strings.

It isn't so strange to learn that the Mellotron was intended to be a home keyboard, an alternative to an electric organ. The mechanism that played a seven-second piece of tape at the touch of a key was not meant for heavy studio or road use. I have witnessed many times the contents of a Mellotron tape rack spewing its contents all over the control room floor. It was a gifted roadie who knew how to wind the tapes back onto their rack.

There are special ways to record a Mellotron. The Moody Blues were one of the first groups to get a reasonable-quality sound from this instrument. Justin Hayward confirmed to me that Mike Pinder used to smooth out the erratic wobble of the tapes and the limited seven-second playback by recording the same parts triple-tracked and playing slightly ahead and behind the beat so that the wobbles would smooth out a little by subsequent overdubs. In my early use of the Mellotron I did this too, with session players Rick Wakeman and others.

The only way to record a Mellotron was from its direct output, to get cleaner access to those tapes. It had built-in speakers, but they made the sound even more intolerably low-fi. The tapes were divided into three discrete tracks, so you had a violin, a cello, and a flute available on one tape rack. It was soon discovered that you could have a violin and flute sound simultaneously by jamming the tape playback head between settings. This is a physical procedure, not electronic switching. One can only assume that tape head azimuth was never a strong point of Mellotrons.

In recent years, the Mellotron has had a renaissance, and many of these old beasts have been resurrected from scrap heaps. In the late '60s it was apparent that the tapes were not getting any younger or fresher with constant use. I've heard that now there are enthusiastic Mellotron users who've found the original master tapes and are making copies for current use. This may be all well and good, but then there are the tape heads themselves, which are rutted almost beyond use on some units. In the '80s I realized that there will come a point when the last Mellotron [or Chamberlin] will fall sideways into the dust, so I decided to record and sample as many Mellotrons as I came across.

I first did this when recording with the Moody Blues in recent years. I produced the albums *The Other Side of Life* [featuring the single "Your Wildest Dreams"], *Sur La Mer* [featuring the single "I Know You're Out There Somewhere"] and *Keys of the Kingdom* [seven tracks]. The Moodies were reluctant to use their old Mellotron, kept in storage for more than a decade, because of its inherent unreliability. I coaxed their road manager to dust it off and fire it up, and I found the most exquisite string sample. Justin told me that they commissioned the string sounds themselves because they didn't like the original batch that came with it. I had my assistant engineer run a DAT as I played and identified each note of the chromatic scale. I then sampled only the best notes based on clarity and the least amount of "wow" and "flutter." Then I spanned them along the keyboard as Akai S1000 samples [a good, clear G# would also have to substitute for a wobbly G and A]. The results sounded better than any Mellotron on the planet. We used the results on tracks of *Keys of the Kingdom*, and of course I retained the samples for my personal sample library. The Moodies are using my sampled string patch on their live dates to this day. What is even more special about my samples is that I looped the notes very carefully so that I am not limited to the seven-second length restriction.

I was also fortunate to have a friend in Los Angeles who has an excellent Mellotron in his possession—Jan Paulshus, a salesman for Roland. He kindly allowed me to stick his instrument's output into my portable DAT recorder, and I played every note of every tape he possessed. Let's face it; these Mellotron tapes will never improve with age. They can't loop, either. My philosophy is this: A good Mellotron is a sampled Mellotron. As for the wobble of the tapes [wow and flutter], I intend to start resampling from my DAT originals and run these samples through my Pro Tools rig to even out some of the more vicious wobbles with my Antares Auto-Tune plug-in.

Here is my Mellotron credo:

A good Mellotron is a sampled Mellotron.

A good Mellotron sample is looped.

A good Mellotron loop is Auto-Tuned.

An obvious bonus to having a looped, optimum keyboard-scaled Mellotron patch is that it is MIDI-addressable—you can pitch bend, play dynamically, use a sustain pedal and add chorus effects, and so on. These enviable features are lacking in the standard, vintage Mellotron. The original, first-generation Mellotron players clamored for these features.

About other units, an electronic keyboard is a musical instrument, not just a playback machine. An engineer thinks nothing of reaching for outboard equipment, compressors, equalizers, effects boxes, and so on when recording guitars, drums, or vocals. With modern synths, sound designers give you their versions of onboard effects added to their patches, and in most cases they are not what you would want. I try to take the effects off by accessing them in the synths menu and then processing the dry patch according to what the song demands. For lead sounds, a fat tube compressor really toughens the sound. The best way is to actually play the synth through a hot guitar amp, mike it, and maybe blend it with the direct signal. A brass patch can benefit from being made punchier by putting a gate across the output and a compressor after the gate.

I'm currently finishing an album for a group called Rustic Overtones on Arista Records. Their keyboard player, Spencer Albee, uses vintage keyboards almost exclusively—a beat-up Hammond B-3, a Clavinet, and a Wurlitzer electric piano. For a crunchier sound on the Clav and the Wurlie, we put them through a SansAmp, the Swiss Army knife of guitar amp simulators. Sometimes the Clav actually sounded like a shredder guitar. Other times, we'd put these instruments through an actual Marshall or Soldano amp reserved for their guitarist. Of course, there is nothing like a dedicated guitar pedal to help spice up a keyboard. There are no rules that say you can't put a keyboard through a guitar pedal, and that's what we did on many tracks.

Leslie organ cabinets can be recorded many different ways. The usual stereo mic placement, plus a third for the low-end speaker, quite often negates the Doppler effect and makes the B-3 unusually wide for a rock mix. In the '60s, one mic was usually only used for the top of the cabinet, and this actually pronounces the Doppler effect more. For the Rustic Overtones B-3, we often added ambient mics to capture the sound of the room we had the cabinet in, and we were fortunate enough to record the B-3 in two great-sounding rooms—Studio A at Avatar in Manhattan and Studio A at Long View Farm in Massachusetts. This created a very warm, vibey sound on the quieter songs. For the loud songs, Spencer simply cranked the cabinet amps to the max, which almost slices your head off.

In the earlier MIDI days, synths and samplers were more monophonic and lacked onboard effects. Virtual keyboard tracks were unheard of, and a keyboard or sampler was recorded to tape. One way I made a monophonic source into a stereo spread was to double-track the mono patch with Varispeed on the multi-track, slowing the tape down a few percent, or by simply detuning the keyboard and playing back both tracks extreme left and right.

We did the tracking for David Bowie's *Scary Monsters* album at the old Power Station, now called Avatar. Studio A is virtually unchanged since the time we used it in 1979. We had the good fortune of having Bruce Springsteen and the E Street band recording in Studio B at the same time. We often met in the main reception area during meal breaks. Bowie drummer Dennis Davis casually leaned over to ask Springsteen what band he was in—that's how informal the atmosphere was then.

We borrowed Springsteen's keyboard player, Roy Bittan, for an overdub on a track that was later named "Ashes to Ashes." We adamantly decided that the intro of the song had to be played on a Fender Rhodes, with the vibrato on maximum. Unfortunately, one side of the Rhodes output had blown, and we were only getting on and off from one channel, no vibrato. We were too impatient to rent another Rhodes, but we wanted that rapid vibrato nevertheless. I had a bright idea, since the only other available keyboard that night was the grand piano. I sent the piano to an Eventide Instant Flanger and tweaked that thing until I was getting that long-sought-after vibrato. It was a better sound in the end than what we had hoped for. That electronically flanged piano is what made the final cut. So radically different was it from a normal "steam" piano that to this day people are still asking me what that instrument was.

Cookie Marenco

Producing and/or engineering credits include: Max Roach, Brain, Kenny Aronoff, Steve Smith, Tony Furtado, Tony Trischka, Dirk Powell, Rob Ickes, Charlie Haden, Tony Levin, Buckethead, Ralph Towner, Paul McCandless, Mary Chapin Carpenter, Pat DiNizio, Kristin Hersh, Ladysmith Black Mambazo, Mark Isham. See the Appendix for Cookie Marenco's full bio.

I used to be a keyboard player in a past life, and I still have about a dozen instruments around. There's been a renaissance in the last few years of the older, classic instruments like the Fender Rhodes and Hammond B-3 organ. I still haven't found a synthesizer that can duplicate their sound, let alone the feel and touch. Many synths can come close—or at least close enough to save your back when schlepping it around is an issue. In fact, my Rhodes was packed up and hidden in storage for 10 years until Myron Dove [bassist—Santana, Robben Ford] came in one day, found all the pieces, and put it together. I was shocked at how good it sounded.

There are two things that make my job of recording easier on keyboard. One is a great player who understands the nuances of these instruments, like the B-3, and the second is having an instrument in good shape. No easy feat. The B-3 can have problems like the percussion switch not working or the Leslie spinning at an odd speed—or not at all—and without a person who really uses those elements of the B-3, you'd never know there was a problem. But even a busted B-3 sounds better than any synth as long as it makes a sound.

For miking a B-3, I like to use three tracks whenever possible. A stereo pair on the spinning horns of the Leslie and one mic on the bottom. I've used three Neumann 87s a lot of times or two AKG C 12s as the pair and a Sennheiser 421 on the bottom. For Matt Rollings [on Jenna Mammina's record], I used two 414s and an RE20. I placed the mics about 6 to 8 inches from the horns on opposite sides to make the most of the Leslie spin. Matt is a master with the Leslie toggle switch and the volume pedal, which certainly makes my job easier.

The B-3 can be tricky if the headphones aren't just right, because the player will make adjustments with the volume pedal, like it or not. It's one of the more difficult instruments to get just right in the phones. It will affect level to tape, how the other players are hearing, and change the sound of the miking. It can ruin a whole session when it's not right. Even more difficult is when the B-3 player is using the bass pedals and functioning as the bass player. It takes real mastery of the instrument not to make a murky mess of the performance. Compression to the phones can help.

On rare occasions, I've been talked into doing a B-3 overdub, and this headphone issue plagued me so much that I've taken to setting a pair of Genelecs up on the instrument and not using phones. Fortunately, with the Leslie you can set it up to avoid bleed, but a lot of times I'll record regardless of the bleed. No phones just makes for a better performance if your recording allows it.

A special aspect that few people know is that touch can really affect the sound of the B-3. If you pull out all the stops and slowly push a key up and down, you can hear it go up the overtone series. A master musician will have the control to hit a key halfway or less to get a certain effect.

Another thing about B-3 is that there's a volume pot on the Leslie, by the tubes, that can adjust the volume being output. That's the "grit" dial. It's like turning a 50-watt Marshall up to 10 for a natural distortion. I don't try to hide room noise of the Leslie spinning. You can disguise it a bit by making sure the volume is loud enough coming out of the Leslie. It can be *really* noisy depending on the player, but with all the problems, there's nothing like that sound. You can amuse your friends and annoy your neighbors with that thing. I've done both.

And talk about annoying, one just assumes we're discussing the accordion! In the last month, I've recorded more accordion than piano. I keep one in the control room at all times now because you never know when you need protection. Rob Burger [Tin Hat Trio] was just in playing on Tony Furtado's new record. We used two mics, an 87 about 12 to 18 inches from the keyboard and a 414 about 24 inches from the bellows side. Most of the sound is coming from the 87. I've used three mics for Dirk Powell [Cajun multi-instrumentalist on Rounder]—stereo 414s about 12 to 24 inches back, over the keys, and an 87 catching the bellows. There can be a lot of key clicking and air moving, but it's part of the sound, so you just accept it.

The most fun I had recording the accordion was on an indie rock record for Terese Taylor. I was producing and decided to surprise her with an accordion part. So I dragged an 87 into the control room, ran it into a Princeton amp with the tremolo all the way up, and put a 57 on the Princeton. I turned up the speakers in the control room so I got lots of room bleed and proceeded to play the part myself. Okay, punching in was a problem, but I didn't really care. What I discovered was how good the drums sounded through the Princeton and the tremolo, which eventually became the basis of the song. That's the power of the accordion. It makes you do crazy things. Next is the stack o' Marshalls.

For synthesizers and electric piano, I prefer to mic the amp, but most of the time, convenience and time cause us to take a direct signal from those instruments. Typically, we'll take the line out and run it into our instrument input of our Neve preamps, Millennia Origins, or Manley VOXBOX...1/4-inch to 1/4-inch. The other method is to take the direct out and run into the Demeter Tube direct box or a Countryman direct box and then take the mic out from there and into our Millennia pres or other mic inputs.

That said, I will share an experience I learned early on: If you have a big synth session, you can blow up a console. Some small studios may not have all the DIs you need to separate all the tracks out, and you might find yourself using the mic ins instead of the lines. Make sure you have a 10 pad in, or you could cause serious problems. I have seen the light and smelled the smoke.

At a session with Wayne Horvitz and John Adams a few years ago, the SSL at Fantasy blew up twice on the same channel. We were running about 21 keyboard tracks live to tape (and 100 tracks internally sequenced), running the synths through amps and miking speakers, the works. To this day I'm not sure how it happened, but I was told that the assistant plugged an amp and speaker into the wall that caused some kind of voodoo to the channel. At some point, we noticed a funny smell. Electrical smoke can be a very bad thing in the studio.

Aside from the smoke, we had a great time running the synthesizers through various Marshall, Roland, and Fender amps and miking those speakers rather than taking the direct sound. It gives some "air" to the sound, some life, some character.

One thing I have discovered is how important great-sounding effects can make even the most mundane stock patch sound good. I rarely use onboard synth effects. Most of the time I head right to the 480L, 224XL, PCM-60, Lexicon Super Prime Time, or PCM-42 delays, Eventide Harmonizers, and AMS whatevers. Doctor it up with multiple effects, create the sound in the mix or print it to tape. I have a vintage Minimoog and a Prophet 5, which I still love. I own some digital synths like the M1 and Proteus, but they are pretty plain-sounding in comparison. Unfortunately, they are so easy when you just need to get a job done that they get used often.

For myself, I think I'm heading toward using more and more outlandish recording techniques, using hands-on effects to create loops live, miking speakers in odd places, and so on. And I'm finding that many of the young artists are not only willing but encouraging about it all. The bottom line is the song and the performance. If you've got that, even the most stock M1 patch can't destroy it—but it might come close.

Leanne Ungar

Credits include: Laurie Anderson, Carlene Carter, Leonard Cohen, Holly Cole, Janis Ian, Ray Charles, Temptations, Willie Nelson, Billy Joel, Elton John, Luther Vandross, Natalie Cole, Peter Gabriel, and the Paul Winter Consort. See the Appendix for Leanne Ungar's full bio.

When I started working in the studio in New York City in 1973, the Fender Rhodes was at the height of its popularity. It's still my favorite keyboard. It was standard equipment in every studio, along with a grand piano and a B-3.

When my client, keyboardist and producer John Lissauer [who did Leonard Cohen's *New Skin for the Old Ceremony*) would come in to record, he would call S.I.R. and rent a certain Rhodes by the serial number. He liked the distortion and harmonics of the low end on that particular keyboard. [Something not easily replaced by a sample!]

If I were using Rhodes on a basic track, I would take it direct, but when possible, I preferred miking the amp. It's a more aggressive sound. To bring out the attack and clean up the midrange, I generally cut at 400 Hz and boost 1.5 kHz on an API EQ.

There is no "art" to recording sampling keyboards, but some sound better than others. I always like the sound of the Synclavier. It had a richer, more lush sound. A sample is only as good as the sampler.

I was working with Laurie Anderson when she first got hers in 1982 or 1983. We were waiting one day for Phoebe Snow to come sing backing vocals. We were listening to her record to get in the mood. She called at the last minute to say she had a cold and wanted to postpone. We took the beautiful a cappella vocal stack from "Two-Fisted Love" [recorded by Glen Berger, to give credit where credit is due] into the Synclavier and tuned it down considerably, until the key was right. Phoebe was thrilled that she didn't have to travel with a cold, and she got credit and was paid as if she sang.

I was on the phone last week with the owner of a home studio, talking him through how to mike a B-3. I like to use a kick-drum mic for the low end, like an RE20, D 112, or 421, especially if I'm lucky enough to work with a great rhythm organ player like Jim Cox. Those mics can give low stabs a good punch. I'll usually use one or two large-diaphragm condensers on the high end, like 414s, for instance.

Don't give in to the temptation to mike the open back of the Leslie cabinet. The wind from the rotors can pop the mic capsules. Place the mics at the vents on either side (or just one vent works fine, too). If you are fresh out of expensive microphones, no problem. The drawbars on the organ are so expressive and so precise that you should be able to compensate and achieve any sound with the player's help.

For recording B-3, make sure that the sound isn't eating up the space in the midrange in your mix. If you are recording quiet passages, make sure you have enough signal to mask the rotor noise. And if things get loud, be alert for distortion—unless of course you want some. Don't forget to use the line in on the Leslie preamp for possible guitar, vocal, and so on effects.

Christopher Greenleaf

See the Appendix for Christopher Greenleaf's full bio.

People always ask for formulas, but there's nothing less useful than an imperfectly understood rote method. If I do have a rule, it is that each instrument and each acoustic setting and each performer determines my miking. While anyone who's been around the block approaches a given situation with possible miking approaches in mind, very few engineers or producers have an inalterable laundry list of setups.

Here's an example. I was recording two solo harpsichords built a year apart, after the same plan and by the same maker. I ended up using different mics at slightly different distances from the instruments and each other to achieve a comparable sound. For one harpsichord, I used fairly widely spaced [1.7m] KM 130s axially; for the other, I placed a pair of upward-angled KM 131s closer in and slightly closer together. The direct sound was virtually a match. There was no apparent disparity between the two instruments, though the very lively room came through slightly different with each array. Listening and experimentation, not formula, produced this result. I should add that, as with all my recordings, the performer and session producer had as much say in miking as I did. It'd be sheer arrogance to think I can do it all on my own, especially when a performer's ears can help me dial in aspects of the instrument I may not even suspect exist!

In approaching miking, I strive to establish a deeply musical balance between attack and warmth, clarity and richness, the performer's intentions and the eventual listener's enjoyment. I like the distance between main mics to be less than their distance from an instrument or ensemble; otherwise, the soundstage becomes disconcertingly broad. This is one of the two formulas I'm willing to pass on, the other being that there is always a dominant microphone pair [or, more rarely, a threesome of mics], whether I'm doing minimal miking or working with more involved arrays.

While I do go for sufficient proximity to perceive attack and the small beginnings of normal mechanical noise—because that's part of the true sound—I never rely solely upon the instrument's sound. This invariably brings the project into a room whose acoustic is more reverberant—sometimes startlingly more so—than a hall in which a musician typically would want to perform the same repertoire before his/her public. Needless to say, artists inexperienced in recording must be gently but firmly awakened to the fact that mics and the human ear perceive sound vastly differently, and that the aims of the recording process rarely duplicate those of live sound production.

Miking a harpsichord or piano extremely closely robs the instrument of its chance to interact with the air, to acquire the special coloration the lid imparts, to develop true power and breadth. You're left with white-hot attack. That may be very sexy, jazzy, and exciting, but such an approach makes it impossible to evoke the magic of acoustic bass or the singing vocal quality of middle registers. Virtually all the subtleties the instrument and room have to offer escape the recording process...*allora, ciao bellezza* [bye-bye, beauty].

With any other long-keyed keyboard instrument, there are three basic zones of sound production. There are also a number of areas relative to the instrument and room where the disparate elements that make up the sound come together.

What are these zones? One sound source is obviously piano hammers or harpsichord plectra (the two to three little tongues that pluck harpsichord strings for each note played). While these make a certain pitchless sound on their own, most of the tone production comes from the second sound-generating zone, the bridges and soundboard. The most interesting tone originates here, where the strings cross the soundboard and where the vibrating soundboard reacts most strongly to the bridge's movement; this may not be right at the bridge, but inches or feet away. One example of this is the justified popularity of miking a piano frame's open holes, which often have an amazing timbral character. The third source of direct sound is the reflection and refraction off the lid [and from the underside of an open-bottom acoustic instrument]. This last direct source helps establish the overall context and blend that make for an interesting keyboard sound. The instrument's maker spent a lot of time matching the lid's shape and angle to the rest of the instrument. Removing the lid or altering its angle is a common way of pulling a "different" sound out of the hat, but be wary of the sometimes drastic effect on the sound this approach can have.

For me, then, effective miking derives from finding the beauty of resonance and sustain, from unlocking the innate power and beauty of an instrument, from marrying the instrument's magic to the vibrant air of a world-class room. This is one way of describing the "classical" approach, as contrasted with the many others. To this end, I listen for and analyze the tone-producing elements of each instrument in the context of the room chosen for the recording. My aim is to achieve a sound that can be edited and released. Period. I happily reach for the many technical fixes now cheerfully lined up on the cyber-shelf when noise or odd acoustics require massaging, but I just do not record with the intent of relying on them to salvage a challenged project. That's not recording purism—it's just common sense for music in which beauty, clarity, and visceral realism are at stake.

I happily resort to gentle EQ and occasional dabs of assisting reverb when DSP will supply what the room and mics could not. A noisier-than-hoped-for session will require less ambient miking, so you 'verb it afterward. Persistent over-support of certain pitches in the instrument or room make a little EQ taming a logical part of post. But the best feeling in the world is to release exactly the sound we recorded, unchanged and vibrant.

I recently recorded Elaine Funaro, a fire-eyed harpsichordist in North Carolina, using the Earthworks omnis, Millennia tube preamps, and a Troisi A/DC. Just as important as the impact of the two very different harpsichords she used was the supportive, responsive acoustic of an all-stone, uncarpeted chapel on the Duke University campus. The resulting recording is a sizzler...it's almost scarily alive. I had also brought my Schoeps and Neumann omnis along, but once we'd heard the Earthworks QTC1s in this room and with these instruments, all the other mics stayed in their cases. I think the QTC1 is one of the major achievements in miking. It doesn't sound like any other mic I have ever heard. It is so unbelievably neutral that I don't hear a lot of the effects I normally think of as "audio." I merely hear good or bad miking, and that is what I want. It is strikingly transparent. In appropriate applications, it is as close to a perfect transducer as you can get. Needless to say, there are situations in which my Schoeps MK 2 has the edge, or rooms that fully respond only when the KM 130 or KM 131 listens in. While the B&K 4006 has its moments of glory, I find it sitting there in shockmounts for a session noticeably less than the others I've mentioned.

A microphone is in part a truth-sayer. But it is a coloring tool, like tinted glass. Its placement determines flavor and perspective. Some people will deem the Earthworks omni to be inappropriate because it lacks the coloration they're after. My cherished Neumanns and veteran Schoeps [including an original tube model] have their own beautiful take on things, and they often sound breathtakingly visceral, but for an amazing number of projects, this Earthworks omni is as close to the real thing as I've ever heard. In a very real sense, discovering how to use this new mic sound has been a private revolution. Because they are so transparent, truly fine mics help you punch through to things that you wouldn't be able to reach for with other mics. You learn to hear detailed, clearly defined sounds in your head and go for 'em. It's also loads of fun.

Music recorded with a superior microphone through radically good electronics has a different dynamic signature. That means that it has more life and air, more integration of vanishing, ephemeral details that add up to...being there. It can acquire a different kind of "life" when you put it through an exciter, but that's not same thing as experiencing that startling moment when mere speakers and living room disappear and the performer is there. It is because more of the acoustic cues from musician, instrument, and gorgeous room come through, and that is an unforgettable experience.

Let's get away from movable keyboard instruments. I've also used all these mics on pipe organs of all sizes. Bach once said that "the room is the most important stop on the organ." So it is sort of a no-brainer to state that a pipe organ in a bad room is utterly beside the point. The deep 16-foot and profound 32-foot bass don't come together unless the room is sizable and resonant. What you can get out of a top-flight, two-channel recording of a pipe organ in a good room simply defies belief. Most people would be stunned to experience the extent to which two [really good] speakers can reproduce what has been marketed to us as "surround sound." A properly made two-channel recording will survive surround processing well, but you lose both awesomely deep bass [produced largely by phasing differences between a pair of transducers] and the amazingly fragile timbral cues that communicate beauty and presence.

The Chapel at Holy Cross College in Worcester, Massachusetts, is a favorite miking challenge of mine. The four-manual Taylor and Boody organ there, a stupendous modern realization of Dutch and North German Baroque tonal schemes, embodies all of the unbelievable sounds that these instruments are capable of. The room, though beautiful, is a challenge since it is ferociously difficult to accurately reproduce on tape what the ear tells you is there.

There are countless delicate, finely shaded registers in this instrument, yet the gathered might of full organ is breathtaking. Marrying the instrument to its room is the great challenge, and it is here that each flavor of microphone becomes crucial. No post-production can cure miking inadequacy under these conditions, so one learns to be inventive and to write down every positioning when it's all working. In this room, I have variously used Schoeps, Earthworks, and Neumann mics, and each has captured a different splendor, a different credible soundstage. That's humbling.

For pipe organ, I often start with a pair of omnis 2-1/2 meters apart and maybe 10 meters from the organ [substantially closer in a smaller room]. If you become aware of the cancellation and reinforcement of certain frequencies in the room, which results in over- and underemphasized fundamentals, you allow for them by repositioning relative to the center line, to each other, and to floor-to-ceiling height.

One invariable phenomenon with spaced omnis, even in the case of a modest organ, is the great ease and authority of even very quiet low frequencies. Shoddily done, the sound is vague and soundstage-less. When nicely judged, such miking pulls in bass of great depth and power. Full organ, needless to say, is exciting as hell. When room, instrument, and repertoire want more upper voice clarity and location, I may add an ORTF or vertically spaced [20 to 30cm] pair of Neumann cardioids or the same firm's amazing subcardioids, placed just forward of a line between the omnis. I have no qualms about getting more room sound with an ambient pair of fairly widely separated omnis, provided the main mics have the principal say in the mix.

The sheer power of organ sound in a big room is nicely complemented by the gigantic dynamic range.... No wonder the recording world has long been fascinated with this special challenge.

As I said earlier, I like to use three clearly differing main mics, depending upon the application: the Earthworks QTC1, the Neumann KM 130, or the Schoeps MK 2.

The Schoeps preamp and capsule test better than almost any mic in the world. They were a bold design when they debuted decades ago, and they remain a standard to this day. They and the Earthworks QTC1 are about as uncolored as you can get. To them I add the challenging-to-use but very beautiful KM 131 omni and the KM 143 subcardioid. The latter boasts the useful virtues of a directional mic and the timbral honesty of an omni, as well as an omni's unparalleled ability to define room ambience.

The more transparent the transducer is, in a sense, the harder it is to use because the less it is capable of "lying." You are hearing everything. You have to be more careful than with lesser designs. Conversely, the more colored a mic is, the more you can get away with odd placement or mixing approaches, because the ear's built-in litmus test for verisimilitude doesn't apply to the same degree. We all use colored mics, like the stunning Neumann TLM 193 cardioid, for very special purposes and revel in their versatility, their relatively bulletproof resistance to strange positioning.

The QTC1 does have a few idiosyncratic characteristic colorations, such as a tendency to make strings and reeds recorded too closely sound breathily insubstantial. It also hardens or dries up rooms that have a small or harsh acoustic. This is not coloration in the standard sense, but it does mean that this microphone is inappropriate for overall ensemble pickup in an ungenerous room. It is a very alive-sounding mic as a main mic. As a spot mic [percussion, low brass and winds, piano tail], it blends into the main mix with absolutely amazing ease.

All omnis are proximity-sensitive. Moving twice the distance away is effectively moving four times the acoustic distance away, so they are not indiscriminate in what they pick up. For this reason, they make killer spot mics on loudspeakers and various keyboard instruments. Good mic placement obviates a lot of post. The old, proven saying in the classical music industry is, "Record well and long, post-produce cheaply and briefly."

For recording an electronic keyboard, I like to record the instrument directly [stereo only] and with two sets of speakers. I position two or three mics per speaker—one at a relative distance, even if there's risk of cross-bleed. Consider a just-off-axis mic as well as a standard off-axis mic. The two will pick up very different things. The options available from multiple miking of speakers are many. Mixing them together or in stereo opposition is an amazing tool for effects even before you're into post, thanks to the natural workings of phasing and mic proximity. It involves committing a greater number of channels, but your post-production time can be somewhat or significantly reduced, since there are so many options nicely synched up already. I'm prepared to be anally fussy about the quality of speakers and electronics I record. I would record dirty electronics for that specific effect, but only through top speakers.

In recording amplified instruments, I use absolutely audiophile amps and crossovers with extremely beautiful speakers. They don't have to be going very loudly to sound like heaven, but they do need to be away from coloring surfaces. I would naturally consider the color of the electronics and the speakers to be part of the instrument's recorded character. The most advanced home speakers are often better for miking than professional speakers because they are more fine-grained. They will stand the close scrutiny that modern audio permits. The old Celestion SL600, the stunning little ProAc One SC, and the world-standard Revel Salon [$14.4k/pair] are my picks.

As a session and post monitor, I always opt for the ProAc One SC, if available.

I would certainly urge performers and engineers who have a high-resolution sound source to experiment with omnidirectional mics for loudspeaker pickup. Omnis have the sweetest sound and the best dynamics.

I adore my Millennia vacuum tube mic pres, but I also am happy with my custom-configured API pre/mixer. When they've been available, I have often used tube mics and thoroughly enjoyed the result, but I am equally convinced of the musicality of the best non-tube contemporary circuit design. If you work in the real world, it is pointless [and impractical] to step firmly into one or the other camp. I greatly prefer an all-tube mic-amp chain for strings and woodwinds, reverberant rooms, banjo, guitar, lute, theorbo, and for the middle range of the piano. I like solid-state mics and a tube preamp for organ, string orchestra, French horn, deep bass winds, and low percussion. All-solid-state chains work superbly for the top and bottom of the piano...but so do all-tube systems. Each just sounds different.

Which approach you opt for is a matter for you, your client, and your—I hope!—stunningly competent session producer. The relevant commercial and aesthetic concerns may have gratifyingly more in common than you anticipate...if you mike well.

Live Engineering and Recording

You could do a book on just this one subject (and, in fact, people have!). Live engineering and recording presents a number of variables or situational wildcards that are out of the realm of typical studio work. Preparation is everything in a dynamic where anything can go wrong as you are trying to capture the fleeting moments of live performance in a way that helps performers feel comfortable giving their all, while bringing the best of those moments to the audience with clarity.

Dave Morgan is one of the most respected live audio engineers in the business. Here he shares some of his insights on how to approach this gig with the right spirit and level of professionalism.

Dave Morgan

Credits: James Taylor, Steely Dan, Paul Simon, Bette Midler, Cher, Stevie Nicks. See the Appendix for Dave Morgan's full bio.

A live show is such an emotional experience, and it's really impossible to re-create the energy generated in a full stadium by 50,000 people who are all focusing on one event. For this reason, most live shows don't translate very well as recordings. A really good studio record is always better than a live record. That said, I think some of the really bad-sounding live two-track bootleg recordings I've heard audience members make do a lot better job of capturing the energy at a live show than many of the recordings for which artists spend thousands and thousands of dollars. Although the concept is to capture the essence of a show, many artists proceed to overdub all the tracks because they are dissatisfied with their performances.

What often happens when live tracks are taken into a studio in an attempt to put them on a CD is that they are turned into a cerebral exercise, and thus they really become a translation and not a duplication of the concert experience. The raw energy of the stage is stifled by the artists and producers, and for that reason, I have never been much of a fan of live CDs. Most shows I have witnessed are so much more exciting than what you end up with once the tracks are crammed down to 16 bits on a plastic disc.

A concert is not a static experience. One of the greater challenges to capturing the essence of a concert in a recording derives from the fact that a concert is largely a visual and physical experience. It's not just about having speakers in front of you. You are in an environment with sounds bouncing all around you, but the experience is far more encompassing than the sound in the room. It's also about other people who are next to you and the energy you are drawing from all those fans around you and the excitement you draw from the band playing on the stage. Strong moods and emotions are simultaneously being created and controlled by the visual elements of the production. It is a holistic event.

A large part of the appeal for choosing to work in live sound as a career field came from the requirement to confront new challenges and come up with new solutions each new day and each new venue. Every listening environment is different, and one has to make audio decisions derived from compromises made with the physical conditions in order to produce the optimal experience for the listener. Dealing with the intimacy of the live performance dynamic and the immediate marriage of theory and practice has resulted in a very gratifying career for me. It is well suited to the nature of my personality.

Many engineers spend an inordinate amount of time and utilize too much technology making the board tape sound good—basically for job security...very simple. If the act listens to the show CD on the tour bus afterward and it sucks, you are going to get called on the carpet the next day.

Early in my career, I had that problem like anybody else, before I learned how to create consistency in the audio product, where the output of the console sounds like the output of the PA, which sounds like the playback of the DAT or CD machine. In other words, where it all sounds the same all through the audio chain, as it is supposed to do. Before I learned how to do that, I made some pretty rotten show tapes.

One of the first places where many mixers get in trouble is having the bottom end of the PA turned up so loud on the crossover output that, on the show tape, you don't even hear the kick drum or bass guitar. It's a common mistake. Another error is having the vocals up too loud, with the result that there is then this huge gap between the vocals and the band. That's not necessary; you don't have to mix that way. Vocal articulation comes from correct equalization and placement of all the inputs. You actually can make a show sound really good on a tape, in your cans [headphones] while you monitor, and out the speaker system; it can all sound the same.

Over the years, I have built up a system-tuning regimen via an ordered selection of songs that I play just off of CDs. I play tracks that excite the room at certain frequencies and allow me to balance the PA in such a way that I can create a monitoring environment in which everything sounds the same. I'll start tweaking things out in rehearsals, making recordings and playing them back. Most often I use a pair of Tannoy 12s as my monitors in rehearsals, and I know the EQ curve to put on them to give me the optimum output. It's amazing to go from cans to monitors to tape or CD and have it all be consistent.

During the tour I seldom alter the settings on the console. Instead, I massage the PA into giving me the matching output. I address the issues of speaker placement, speaker interaction, delay, equalization, compression, amplifier trimming, and relative volumes between the individual cabinets to create the optimum output throughout the room. I'm not just seeking a consistent audio output through the PA, but also an output that is consistent with what I am hearing from my console. When I learned how to do this, show tapes miraculously became masters. I have had quite a few of my cuts as bonus tracks on various CDs. Donald Fagen has a couple of them on his box set that came from our 2006 Morph the Cat tour. Paul Simon has included a few as bonus tracks over the years, too. It's cool to hear from the mastering engineers that the tracks were untouched other than normal tweaking and to be told that they sounded great right off the DAT tape or CD.

For headphones, I use ratty old Sony MDR-V6s. They have particular characteristics that lend themselves to doing a good PA mix. Where they are deficient is often what you need to retain. For example, where the high end rolls off in the headphones is something you'd want to keep in the PA anyway for articulation. Where the V6s get really thick in the 200 to 400 range is something you want to take out of the PA because that is an area that is so predominant in masking, hiding so many other frequencies and affecting the articulation of consonants and altering the overall clarity of the mix. When you hear a mix that is too heavy in the lower midrange, it's just ponderous and obnoxious.

I have never been a fan of one-note bass—you know, all the subwoofer cabinets tuned to 63 Hz. It's the classic rock-and-roll kick drum sound. It's that big thumping, hit-you-in-the-solar-plexus, stop-your-pacemaker kick drum sound. While it's appropriate for a lot of bands, it's not appropriate for James Taylor, Paul Simon, Bette Midler, Steely Dan, Lionel Richie...all the people with whom I have worked for a number of years. So I like to get rid of a lot of that big hump and try to smooth out the frequency response between 30 and 80 Hz. It's a more pleasing bottom end, yet it still retains good physicality.

I like to take a lot of that 200-Hz lower midrange stuff out so you get really good clarity and definition out of the PA. Eight-hundred Hz and 3 kHz are two other frequencies you really have to be careful about because they cause ear fatigue. A lot of people don't realize it, but after a half hour of being exposed to a badly equalized PA, your hearing may be shot if you haven't taken ear fatigue into consideration. You have to create a listening environment for yourself that can be bearable for two and a half to three hours so that you are able to do the same job at the end of the show that you were doing at the beginning of the show. This, of course, requires a working knowledge of physiology and audiology. I don't see a lot of people really addressing the ear fatigue issue or the general physical fatigue of being assaulted by subwoofers all the way through a show. I don't mind a good, solid hit in the solar plexus once in a while, but to have to listen to it for two and a half hours is physically deadening, and you actually become exhausted.

There is an immense amount of calculation, consideration, and preparation that goes into doing a live show, and I would like to see more done more often. It's not a lot to ask that you have a working knowledge of acoustical physics before you get behind a console. It's not a lot to ask that you are really, really familiar with all the microphones that you use before you throw them up on the stage and then try to compensate for bad choices through radical EQ on your console. It's not a lot to ask that you are familiar with the catalogue of the speaker manufacturer whose products you're listening to. This is just simple preparation.

If more engineers take the time to really study what they are doing rather than thinking of themselves as artists first and technicians second, I think we would have better concerts overall. I don't know about you, but I don't go to a lot of shows that I walk out of and say, "That was a great-sounding show." I do go to a lot of shows that I quickly walk out of to protect my ears because they are being mixed much, much too loud.

I know there are no standards for mixing. There is no test you have to pass to determine whether or not you know what you are doing, but there is an implied, if not explicit, contract with the ticket buyer that you have to maximize and optimize their experience. A live sound engineer isn't just there to please himself or herself. You are out there as a representative of the artist who is on the stage, and you have to realize that you are the creative medium through which the artist's performance is translated to the audience, and you have to be as conscientious in your re-creation of the artist's vision as you can possibly be.

Choosing to deviate from what is being played on the stage just because you're having fun with your devices out at front of house is not acceptable. That action is imposing the idea that your judgment is better, that you are a better producer than the artist on the stage. There is quite a bit of hubris implied in that kind of approach. Instead, you have to make sure that you have a good understanding of what makes each song work and why the artist has chosen the arrangements by which he or she has presented those songs.

Alternatively, there is nothing wrong with going to a musician and saying, "Can you change your sound a little bit, because, in a big hall like this, that part is not coming through?" That is not being egotistical or rude. That is doing your part to help make sure that their arrangement is translated. So communication is paramount, and having a good, trusting working relationship with the principal artist or artists working on the stage is absolutely essential.

During the first days of rehearsals I will quite often sit on the stage in the middle of the band and not even go near the front-of-house setup. I just find the sweet spot on the stage where I can hear everybody playing and try to find out what's making each arrangement work. With Paul Simon I used to sit on the corner of the drum riser between Steve Gadd and Bakithi Kumalo, the bass player. I would just sit there for hours and listen to the interaction of the two of them, to the band playing around me, and to what sounds Paul had woven into a musical tapestry before going out to attempt interpreting it out front.

It's total folly to turn the PA on immediately, thinking you already know it all, and just throw a mix up. That behavior does not lead to developing that very special and necessary relationship of trust and confidence between artist and engineer. When the band sees you sitting on the stage and actually listening to what they are playing, that makes them feel like you are really interested in what they are doing and that you are doing your homework. Homework does not stop when you graduate from college. It goes on forever.

My training as a musician has helped me tremendously. I started in the business a guitar player and singer. I did everything from playing jug-band music to being a solo folk performer to playing in a punk metal band. I guess I've done a lot. I started piano lessons at six years old; I started performing for money at 14. Through amazing good fortune, I've never had any other job other than music; I managed to survive for 45 years in this business, and I'm extremely grateful. There aren't all that many of us who have been granted a similar opportunity.

There is a certain aspect of mixing of which one must always be conscious. What are the elements that actually make an arrangement work? It's like finding the hook as a songwriter or finding the right melody line as a composer. There is always something about an arrangement that is the glue. Whether it's the relationship between the bass and the drums, a repeating guitar line like the Rolling Stones' "Satisfaction," or a horn hook, there is always something that the audience can latch onto. I have always tried to find that one piece that connects everything and makes the experience something organic rather than something cerebral. I have really tried very hard to make music and the performance of music guide everything that I do. It isn't about the budget or available technology or whether I am using a microphone because George Massenburg did. I am always trying to make music the determining factor in all my choices.

My biggest responsibility is always to the person in the audience. I want the show to sound just as good for the guy in the back row of an arena as it does for the high rollers up front. I want everybody to walk out happy, knowing they have heard the songs that they love and that they have been able to embrace those performances with their hearts and their minds. I am very conscious of that aspect of the unwritten contract with the ticket buyer. I am also very aware of the fact that I am not just doing this show for the here and now; I am doing this show as an advertisement to persuade the audience to come back the next time the act comes through this city. If this artist does not do well on the road, get great reviews, and generate great word of mouth, there is not going be another tour—and if there is not another tour, I don't make a living.

It's very simple. If the audience doesn't have a good time and they vote with their wallet not to come back, all of a sudden I am out of the job. So I take that part of the contract extremely seriously, not just because I respect the ticket buyer, but I want to keep working. [Laughs] There is a purely selfish motivation in there. I simply want to keep doing the job that I love. That overall motivation for putting out the best possible product I can every night determines pretty much everything I do during the preceding part of the day, beginning as soon as I walk into the venue.

I go into the building early in the morning, and I'm right there with the PA crew and the riggers to determine where the PA is going to go up, how it's going to go up, and how much we will be able to put up. I want to know all these things. I don't want to walk in with the band at sound check and say, "Why hasn't this been done this way?" My responsibility is to make sure it already is that way. That's not somebody else's job. That's my job! I am the audio engineer.

I have always gone in at rigging call, and I have always left at the end of load out. I load the trucks with the guys, and I do the whole gig. A long time ago, when I was a kid, someone said to me to never ask anybody to do anything that you are not capable or willing to do yourself. That particular statement really resonated with me, and I felt that was always a good way to live your life. If you want people to follow, you have to show them that you are not only capable of being a leader, but that no job is too dirty for anyone to do. If I am asking you to do this, then I am going to do this with you. If it means putting up a difficult PA system in the rain, then I am out there doing it with you. If it means doing an awful load out in 30-degree weather, I am there with you doing it. It's just something where I feel the camaraderie and the teamwork aspect is just as important as the creative aspect of the job.

If we didn't have to protect James Taylor's hands, he would come in and work with us and change his own strings and load in band equipment. He has never developed any sort of elitism at all. After all these years, he is still the same guy who used to load into the Troubadour and handle all of his own gear. That's wonderful to see, and because of that, we are all willing to go the extra mile for him.

It's just an illustration of what I am trying to say. He definitely shows that he is one of the guys, and by him being one of the guys, we are all completely dedicated to doing our best job for him. It's leading by example.

Even before we get the PA up, I'll sit in the arena or the stands and listen to what the room itself sounds like. What does it sound like when you roll a case over a plywood floor? What does it sound like when you drop a shackle on the stage? What is the low-end resonance of the trucks at the truck dock? You can hear all these things. Can you hear the words being spoken when the riggers are up on the high steel and are yelling to people down on the ground? Can you actually understand everything they are saying? Where are the articulation problems? Can people talk at a normal voice and be heard, or do they have to yell and scream and repeat themselves five or six times in order to get a concept across? When you are in a building with intelligibility issues like that, you know you are going to have a problem later. While doing this critical listening, I have to start thinking about what compromises I am going to make or what compensations I am going to take to get some sort of intelligibility out of the PA system. Sometimes you have to sacrifice certain elements of your optimum mix in order to maximize intelligibility and instrument separation.

There are compromises that you have to consider every single day. If I am in a really bass-heavy building, then I am turning those 18s down, and I am not going to allow a huge boom to overcome the rest of my mix. I might lose some of the physicality or rock feel of the show, but the overall satisfaction of the ticket buyer comes into play here. Can they understand the lyrics my artist is singing? Can they hear all the parts that they need to hear so that they realize they are listening to that incredible song they have fallen in love with over the years? People who try to impose their will on a building tend to lose. Less experienced people often attempt to fight that dynamic by just trying to turn it up so loud that they overwhelm it. The result is usually a disaster—a lion roaring against the sea.

Live sound, especially with a larger band—say, like Paul Simon—could commonly have 80 or so separate inputs from the stage. The Bette Midler show I am currently doing in Las Vegas has 84 inputs. At this point, you are talking about the interaction of microphones, then you're talking about leakage management, and then you're talking about placement and polar response. Once again, you get back to homework.

Are you choosing the microphone that is best suited to not only the instrument you are miking, but also the other microphones around it? How is off-axis information going to sound coming into this microphone? How well does it reject adjacent instruments? What is the frequency response characteristic at 180 degrees off axis? How does it interact with stage monitors? So choice, placement, and application—the concepts are the same in the studio as in live settings, but in live you also have the intrusion of speaker systems and the room. Most studio rooms are pretty controllable, while most live environments are far more out of control and tend to speak into the microphones more than in a nice padded studio room.

There is an interaction and a symbiosis that occurs on a live stage that demands a really thorough knowledge of all the aspects of each microphone that you use. That's why I am saying you never choose a microphone because Engineer B is using it in the studio. You choose a microphone primarily because you have tried it, and it works for the specific application. But you also choose a mic because it can handle riding in a truck, getting bounced around for a few hundred miles while withstanding temperature extremes, and still work for the show. A live mic has to handle going from 120 degrees in Las Vegas in the summer to −50 degrees in Edmonton, Canada, in the winter and still be fully operational. So there are a lot of parameters that you have to know about.

The really great engineers are still around because they love what they do. It's not a job; it's a life. It's not just a profession. It's a gift, and I think that most of us have to be really, really grateful that we have been given this opportunity to listen to music for a living. And I get up every day, and I try to say thank you for all the events and experiences that have led me to this point where I now realize that my next job is six more weeks on the road with James Taylor—a great band, a great group of guys on the road crew, and where we produce wonderful shows from which people walk out smiling. It can't get any better than that.

Left column top to bottom: Andy Leftwich at House of David Studio (photo by Kate Hearne) / Allen Sides at Ocean Way Recording (photo courtesy of Ocean Way Recording). Right column top to bottom: Mark Evans (photo courtesy of Mark Evans) / Kirby Shelstad (photo by Rick Clark) / Big Star's Jody Stephens (photo courtesy of Ardent Recording, John Fry).

Mastering

Mastering is the final refinement that helps give a finished recording the best sound it can have. A good mastering job can make a well-engineered recording sound perfect on the radio and audiophile systems. Listen to Dire Straits, Steely Dan, Sting, U2, or any number of classic releases to underscore that point. Mastering can also help restore and present very old recordings in their best light. That said, some "remastered" classics have been ruined by over-limiting originally dynamic classics...but that's another story. For this chapter, I've invited Bob Ludwig, Andrew Mendelson, Greg Calbi, Gavin Lurssen, and Jim DeMain to offer their insights into mastering, from technical issues to interpersonal client perspectives.

Bob Ludwig

Credits include: Radiohead, Madonna, Bruce Springsteen, Guided by Voices, Paul McCartney, Rush, Pearl Jam, Nine Inch Nails, U2, Bee Gees, Dire Straits, Jimi Hendrix, Nirvana, AC/DC, Bonnie Raitt. See the Appendix for Bob Ludwig's full bio.

Mastering is the final creative step in the record-making chain. The purpose of mastering is to maximize the inherent musicality on a given master recording, be it analog tape, Direct Stream Digital, hard drives, DVD-ROMs, or a digital download. The recording and usually the mix engineers have struggled to get their part of the recording as good as it can be, and a good mastering engineer has to have the knowledge and insight to know whether preparing the recording for the pressing plant and iTunes requires doing a lot, very little, or even nothing creatively to the master.

I have often said it is difficult to give awards to mastering people for a particular project, as no one but the artist and producer usually knows exactly how much improvement came from the creative input of the mastering engineer. I worked on an Elvis Costello master engineered by Geofrrey Emerick [one of the engineers on Beatles recordings] that was so good all I could do was get out of its way and let it just be itself. On the other hand, I once mastered a recording that needed so much help, literally 20 dB of level changes during the course of the album and lots of equalization and judicious use of compression. This particular recording won a Grammy for its engineer for Best Engineered Record - Non-Classical...not even a thank you for me! So even having the best job in the world does have its peaks and valleys.

Only a few years ago, recording and mix engineers all tried to make the very best-sounding mixes they possibly could. This culminated in making audiophile analog or high-resolution digital surround sound recordings. We were finally leaving the quality of the compact disc behind and ascending to new audio quality heights. Then the iPod and iTunes were introduced to the world a month after 9/11.

Sony's invention of the Walkman cassette player and MDR-3 headphones broke ground in 1979. In 15 years, Sony sold 150,000,000 players. This allowed people to hear a cassette of a Mahler symphony and get emotional goose bumps while hiking on top of a mountain. The cassette contained the equivalent of a single vinyl LP.

In less than seven years, between October 2001 and September 2008, Apple sold 173,000,000 iPods, the most successful audio player ever. The single 80-GB iPod, smaller than the Sony Walkman with better quality, could hold the equivalent of an entire record collection, a stack of vinyl records over 16 feet tall. This revolution of convenience over quality quickly took hold. The quest for high-resolution audio and, for me, the extra musical emotion that a system like that can yield went quietly away. Now the average consumer sound quality was less than a compact disc. We now hold the compact disc as the gold standard of sound quality because everything else has fallen beneath it. This is a shame.

Partially due to the instant A-B comparisons everyone now makes on their iTunes software and with disparate sources fighting to be heard next to each other on the iPod Shuffle, many producers and artists have been pushing harder and harder to have their recordings be as loud as or louder than other recordings. If it isn't already as loud as a commercial CD, some A&R people will reject an otherwise perfectly musical mix submitted from a great engineer. It is as if the mastering process is being ignored. People decided they no longer wanted to turn their volume knob clockwise to enjoy a dynamic mix with a low average level. Now many world-class remix engineers will mix a recording and do the musically suicidal act of compressing it to death before sending it to the mastering stage. This insanity comes out of paranoia that non-loud mixes will be rejected in the marketplace, and the world-class engineer might find himself not working as much. Most of the world-class mixers do not fall into this trap, but there are actually so few truly excellent mixers that if even one of them succumbs to this pressure, it turns the fun part of my job into an annoyance, as I have to figure out what to do with what they have given me. I have nothing against a loud CD that makes sense musically. It is just that every CD is different, and some benefit from loudness, and most benefit from dynamics.

In the days of vinyl disk cutting, there were a handful of really great disk cutters who were also creative sound mastering engineers. When the CD was invented, some people asked me, "What will you do now that there is no more mastering?" They did not understand the finesse and importance of the mastering stage that had nothing to do with making a good cut. Now there are thousands of people who call themselves mastering engineers who convince clients they are audio artists. Most of them only know how to do one thing well—how to turn a limiter knob clockwise until the music is squished as loudly as a commercial CD.

Mastering is the last chance to make something sonically better. The first rule of mastering is like the doctor's "first, do no harm" credo. There is nothing worse than a mastering engineer doing something to a mix that doesn't need anything just to earn his fee. An ethical engineer will tell a client if they have submitted a perfect recording. Fortunately for the mastering profession, even with excellent mixes one can usually make a valid musical contribution that will in fact make it sound better. A well-honed mix may need only a small amount of correction to really make it shine. Some artists, like the Indigo Girls or the late Frank Zappa, are so in tune with their music that they can accurately perceive the smallest EQ change, something that would escape even most musicians. These subtle changes mean a lot to them.

So there is much more to mastering than making something loud—it is finding the sweet spot between something that sounds impressively loud and something that sounds impressively dynamic. The engineer often contributes to determining the spacing between the songs and the rebalance of the internal levels of each song, adding or subtracting equalization as each song requires. In short, the engineer wants to make a great-sounding record that a consumer can put on and not feel the need to change their playback level or adjust their tone controls while listening.

WHAT TO SUPPLY TO A MASTERING ENGINEER

When mixing a recording, it is wise to make the best balanced mix you can and then supply an additional mix with the vocal track raised perhaps 1/2 dB and even another one with the vocal raised a full dB. This can make life much easier if an A&R person decides that your vocal level wasn't quite loud enough. In addition, if there is an issue with the vocal after mixing, one can edit from a vocal upmix to fix a word or phrase that wasn't quite intelligible. Sometimes, an engineer will supply us with a vocal stem as well as the TV track, which is the rest of the music minus the lead vocal. This allows the mastering engineer to rebalance the mix himself. This would seem ideal, but most mastering engineers do not want to get into the mixing business. Mixing a record is a very different "head" from mastering a record, and it can be difficult to stop a mastering session, go into "mix mode" with the stems, and then try to get refocused into mastering again.

THE EVOLUTION OF MASTERING

For the approximately 90 years between the invention of the phonograph record and the invention of the compact cassette, disk cutting was the only medium one needed to deal with while mastering. The quality of the cassette became suitable for music reproduction and eventually outsold the vinyl LP due to portability at the expense of quality. The cassette was, 95 percent of the time, mastered exactly as the vinyl disk was. In fact, it was made from the identical cutting masters created for international vinyl cutting. A vinyl disk can cut 15,000 Hz at a high level, but only for a few milliseconds; otherwise, the cutter head would heat up from the massive amount of energy it was being fed from the cutter head amplifiers. The cassette tape was simply not capable of recording 15 kHz at a high level, so the overload characteristics of the cassette were different from the LP. Sometimes we would need to make specially done masters for cassette duplication that had the sibilance especially reduced.

When the compact disc was invented, for the first time we could concentrate totally on the musicality of a piece of music and not have to worry about any technical considerations of skipping grooves or the inability of the medium to reproduce high frequencies, et cetera. The *Brothers In Arms* album I mastered by Dire Straits was one of the first albums mastered with the CD totally in mind. No compromise was made for the vinyl disk cutting process at all. Plus, it was long, to take advantage of the longer playing time of the CD versus vinyl. The original release had an edited, shorter version for the vinyl. It was the "killer app" for the compact disc, and it sold big numbers and was highly regarded.

Of course, when I started mastering, everything was analog; there was no digital. I mastered my first discs that were cut from a digital source in 1978: a Telarc classical disc.

The theory behind digital recording has been around for quite a while. Pulse-code modulation, the system we generally use to record and play back digital music, was patented in 1937. The earliest examples of digital music were created on big computers by feeding it stacks of punchcards and letting the computer crunch the numbers overnight. Most of the results were disappointing, in retrospect. The world was waiting for computers to get fast enough to process the amount of data necessary to record music and play it back in real time. The first digital tape recorder was invented in 1967 but was not suitable for music. In 1976, Tom Stockham and his Soundstream company made some of the first digital recordings that still sound good today. He also invented the ability to sample-accurate edit digital audio on a computer. Some think this qualifies as the first DAW [digital audio workstation]. Then a plethora of non-standard digital machines came into common use. Mastering studios either needed to rent these expensive devices or own some of the more widely used ones. There were no standards at first for the sampling rates of the recordings; only 14- or 16-bit dynamic range was available. Digital recorders included the Sony and JVC recorders operating at 44.1 kHz and 44.056 kHz. The 3M digital machine originally ran at 50 kHz. The Mitsubishi X-80 ran at 50.4 kHz. Then sampling rates became fairly standardized at 44.1 kHz and 48 kHz. When the CD was invented, mastering studios needed to re-outfit themselves with very expensive Sony PCM-1600, then 1610, then 1630 ADC and DAC boxes that recorded on 3/4-inch U-matic tape recorders that were all expensive to buy and to maintain. Expensive digital editors and tape checking devices, as well as machines to author the CD with the proper PQ and ISRC codes, needed to be bought.

Mastering was revolutionized again in 1987, when Sonic Solutions, which came out of the 1985 Lucasfilm DroidWorks project [that also created Pixar], created the first digital audio workstation as we know them today. It did non-linear editing as well as CD creation and NoNoise™ digital de-ticking and de-hissing. This changed everything. As chief engineer of Masterdisk, we bought the first Sonic Solutions on the East Coast. Originally, digital recorders and editors were made to mimic analog tape machines as closely as possible. Early Sony and JVC digital editors mimicked tape machines with their ability to "rock" a virtual tape to locate an edit spot. The Sonic Solutions suddenly transformed digital recording with non-linear editing, the ability to make sample-accurate edits with one's eyes as well as one's ears, and the ability to repair defects in recordings that were otherwise thought to be unfixable.

Mastering then evolved with the invention of digital domain consoles and signal processors that could be used with these new machines. Many outboard boxes were digital devices. The early Sonic Solutions workstations contained digital equalizers and compressors, parts of which were easily surpassed in quality by standalone hardware boxes by Daniel Weiss, Lexicon, and other early pioneer digital manufacturers.

When Pro Tools came on the market in 1991, they quickly grabbed market share from the then-ubiquitous Sonic Solutions by opening their architecture to third-party developers. Sonic stuck to trying to make everything themselves, but Digidesign [makers of Pro Tools] soon had a plethora of different digital plug-ins that sold a lot of machines for them. Sonic still led the way with being the first digital workstation to operate 24-bit with 96 kHz and then 192 kHz, then even Direct Stream Digital 2.8224 MHz, but Pro Tools finally caught up at least with high-resolution PCM. Of course, other digital workstations came on as competitors.

The present state of mastering, due to cheaper memory, hard drives, and blazing multi-processor chips, has finally created a situation where the digital workstation can now have plug-ins that finally start to rival any standalone hardware box. The fact that it is all highly automatable and perfectly repeatable for recalled mixes makes it a highly compelling way to operate. For now, mastering in a hybrid mode of both analog and digital has big advantages. It can allow the mastering engineer to remain in the right—creative side—brain and have a minimum of switching into technical mode by needing to use a mouse to click on a button a few pixels wide, et cetera. But soon digital workstations will have virtual touch-screen interfaces that can look like an analog console or anything one desires. Touching the screen can have exactly the same result as moving actual knobs as one does today. Equalizers will have so much DSP that they will be able to equalize based on harmonic structure of the music being played into them, perhaps even moving with the chord changes—who knows? As prices drop and DSP becomes even more plentiful, the gap between professional and consumer gear will pretty much disappear. Already, anyone who owns a Pro Tools rig considers himself a mastering engineer. It takes years of constant learning to become a really good mastering engineer, a lot of patience and people skills. I feel I am still learning every day, and I've been doing this a lot of days!

Andrew Mendelson

Credits include: The Rolling Stones, Death Cab for Cutie, Emmylou Harris, Garth Brooks, Mariah Carey, Dixie Chicks, Kings of Leon, Mötley Crüe, Van Morrison, Willie Nelson, Kenny Chesney, Ricky Skaggs. See the Appendix for Andrew Mendelson's full bio.

Today's recording industry is rapidly changing, and the role of the mastering engineer is changing with it. The decentralization of the recording business, as well as new techniques and production standards, has made the role of the mastering engineer more difficult to define than it once was.

The first step I take when approaching a new project is to determine the most effective role I can play. Many projects I work on have teams of producers and engineers who have spent countless hours working with the artist, picking apart every detail of the music. Through their efforts, they often come very close to or completely realize their vision. Other projects come from musicians who have done their own recording and feel apprehensive about the results they were able to achieve. These two situations will often require different sets of skills and tools. Additionally, there are many desirable sonic possibilities for any given piece of music. Understanding what is appropriate in a given style and what your client wants, even when they are unable to express it, is a necessary skill set to develop. Accurately determining the role your client wants you to play and the role the source material requires you to play is fundamental to successful results.

The mastering stage is essentially a bridge between the studio world and the consumer world. My primary goal is to make sure the vision of the artist and the producer will translate as intended outside the production world. This is one reason my mastering room at Georgetown Masters is set up to feel like a listening room you can work in, rather than a workroom you can listen in. The room consists of two sides. When facing one side, you have the mastering console in front of you, along with a pair of near-field monitors. When you turn around, you face an audiophile-quality listening chain with nothing between the listener and the speakers—the ultimate environment for listening with minimum sonic and mental distractions. In addition to its sonic benefits, this type of setup promotes a different way of listening from that of a typical studio—one more conducive to someone enjoying a song rather than creating one. I listen in a different way than my recording and mix engineer counterparts. I can listen to songs as entities in and of themselves, never having been intimately involved in their creation. This provides me with an important vantage point to find flaws missed by the tunnel vision that can be created by being too close to a project.

To become a successful mastering engineer, remember that you are collaborating with people, even if you never meet face to face. In my experience, people tend to want to work with somebody they feel they can relate to. Building strong relationships with your clients will lead to not only repeat business, but also more successful sessions. The first thing I do prior to starting a session is to ask the client about their recording philosophies, their desires for dynamic range versus apparent volume, and any other subjective opinions they may have. Although these opinions may change over time or from project to project, working with somebody with whom you have a strong long-term relationship can give you greater insight into their beliefs and may greatly enhance everyone's ability to achieve their goals.

Mastering is among the most exciting yet misunderstood processes in music production. Mastering is both an art and a science, drawing upon musicality and emotion, technique, and methodology. The creative stage of mastering, in its simplest form, involves taking what are essentially completed songs and then primarily utilizing elaborate but similar controls to those used daily by music listeners on their own playback systems, extracting the full potential of each song's musicality. The difference is that the tweaks I make are allowed to become a part of the music's identity, rather than simply a personal playback preference. If my concept of musicality translates and resonates with those who created this music and those for whom this music was created, I am successful in my job. For all intents and purposes, I am a professional music listener—pretty good work if you can get it.

Greg Calbi

Credits include: Paul Simon, John Lennon, David Bowie, Bruce Springsteen, Norah Jones, Beastie Boys, Bob Dylan, John Mayer, the Ramones, Talking Heads, Patti Smith, Pavement, Dinosaur Jr., Brian Eno. See the Appendix for Greg Calbi's full bio.

TWENTY-FIRST-CENTURY VINYL MASTERING

Imagine for a moment that the oil crisis caused a jump in the use of the horse and buggy. That's the best way I can describe the phenomenon of the vinyl record album's comeback in our time. The skill I developed mastering LPs for 20 years between 1972 and 1992 is suddenly back in demand, and after mastering thousands of albums, I hope to offer some advice to producers, engineers, and record companies, which these days are often the same person. Because the techniques used to record and mix albums—or sound files, as they are currently known—have morphed into something entirely different since the vinyl era, understanding the complexities of the vinyl LP is essential to making a great-sounding product. The vinyl LP, like the horse and buggy, provides unique pleasures, but it takes a commitment to excellence to make the experience truly worthwhile.

There is no way to assess the correct technique for cutting a master lacquer without an analysis of the technical aspects of the project itself. In their heyday, albums were cut from analog tapes assembled with razorblade and splicing tape on A-side and B-side reels. The assembled mixes passed through analog equalizers and limiters into an amplifier and cutter head, and then they were cut into an acetate. Today, the vast majority of projects begin as digital files of various word lengths and get mastered for CD duplication. These Red Book 16-bit/44.1 files, in turn, frequently get converted to compressed digital files as they are purchased and stored by consumers. The most commonly asked question by clients today is, "Can I use the CD master to cut the vinyl?" Here's the not-so-simple answer: "That depends...."

As with any product, the manufacturer needs to determine what he is selling and to which market he is selling. You don't see Rolex displays in college bookstores, nor does Tiffany carry hoodies. The most important technical question that needs addressing is, "Is the LP simply a transfer of the sound of the CD on a different medium, or does it stand alone as a translation of the mixes into the vinyl form?" The simple transfer of the CD can be accomplished at a much lower cost, as the mastering cost has already been absorbed in the CD budget. However, if the desire of the producer is to make maximum use of the sonic potential of the LP, additional steps need to be taken at a not insignificant cost—one that could boost the sales price of the LP or cut into its profit potential. To complicate matters further, the LP now exists in the music world as a special product. Many artists are using them as loss leaders to reach a niche market, one that in many cases includes bloggers who eagerly respond to the great sonics of the LP—an anti-MP3 of sorts. These factors will all determine how the LP mastering should be accomplished.

CUTTING FROM DIGITAL MASTERS

Let's begin by outlining some of the factors in turning digitally mixed albums into LPs. At present, this would include more than 90 percent of the albums we master at Sterling Sound.

1. Have the mastered levels of the CD compromised the intended dynamics, or are they an essential part of the sound of the production? Has competing in the level wars diminished the impact of the mixes? This is a key question, and had the dynamics been compromised, it would require a separate mastering for

making the best-sounding LP. The mastering engineer and the producer should discuss this prior to the mastering, as generating a separate digital LP master would take much more time when done at a later date.

2. Can the LP master be generated as a high-definition file (88.2 to 96K) during the CD mastering, considering the techniques of the mastering engineer? Again, this could add to the amount of time used and can add a bit to the budget. At Sterling Sound, our cutting room has a high-resolution digital-to-analog converter (DAC), which can significantly improve the sound of the LP.

3. Huge amounts of low end will eat up space on an LP, sometimes causing the level of the LP to be lowered significantly. If so, an analysis needs to be done with the engineer in relation to the total length of the sides of the LP. More than 21 minutes of music could result in a decision to cut some of the ultra low end, again requiring a separate LP master to be generated. Of course, this decision could be made by the eventual LP cutting engineer, with a much less degree of control by the producer.

4. Brittle, intense highs will overload a cutter head causing distortion and put greater demands on LP playback systems, which are often misaligned. Again, problematic top end can be filtered by the cutting engineer, but greater control of highs can be accomplished by generating a separate LP master during the CD mastering stage.

5. A cutter head does not do well with ultra-wide stereo information. It causes extreme vertical movement in the head, resulting in light or actually missing groove depth. This causes skipping and will either be rejected by the pressing plant or undiscovered by both the plant and the cutting engineer, causing buyers to return their LPs because they skip.

   A separate cutting master can be generated using mix narrowing in the workstation to allow for a safe cut. This is sometimes impossible to do at a later time by the cutting engineer.

6. Most of these problems can be solved by the cutting engineer simply lowering the level of the cut, but as the cut gets lower in level, the surface noise becomes a major factor, and the LP can lose its immediacy. Furthermore, for some reason, louder grooves just sound better. There is some physical element in disc playback that seems to fatten and widen with the louder cuts. There were always level wars for LPs in the '70s, but they resulted in better-sounding product, not worse-sounding as in the CD era.

As you can see, it is important to control costs and expedite the process to determine in advance whether the project will be released on LP. Unfortunately, until now, this has not been the case, and many times the client will grudgingly agree to use the CD master to make the LPs. Again, I repeat that this is not always undesirable, but in many cases is not the best way to make a great LP.

CUTTING FROM ANALOG MASTERS

To analog purists, vinyl records cut direct from analog tape represent the highest evolution of music playback. However, for those not experienced with this workflow, there are a number of factors to consider.

When cutting from analog masters, the engineer uses a specially configured "preview" tape machine with two sets of playback heads and two sets of output electronics. On playback, the tape first passes over the preview head, which feeds the disc-cutting computer. Then, after going over an additional roller that creates a delay, the tape passes over the audio head, which feeds the cutter head.

1. The songs need to be assembled on reels. This is impossible if the mixes were done at different speeds or with different alignment, as was a constant problem in the LP era. However, in those years many projects were done with one producer and in one studio; this is frequently not the case now. Any of the mixes done digitally would have to be copied to analog tape and inserted.

2. Crossfades are extremely time consuming in the analog domain. Three analog machines are needed, with two sets of faders and an extremely patient and deep-pocketed client. Any album that relies on crossfades to have the right mood would need to be budgeted accordingly.

3. If an excessive amount of EQ and limiting needed to be done to the mixes, and the songs needed a very different mastering approach from song to song, the mastering engineer would be limited as to just how much he could process them, as AAA cutting requires changes to be done on the fly between songs.

I would add that very few projects recorded and mixed in this era would qualify for an AAA cut, and that decision should always be discussed with the mastering engineer. Generating a high-definition digital master would be an effective alternative.

In conclusion, I must stress that producing a great-sounding LP will require a financial and artistic commitment, but one that would have tremendous rewards for the vinyl lover. An experienced cutting engineer with a quality DAC, lathe, and cutter head can make a fine vinyl cut from a 16-bit/44.1 CD master. The additional steps I have outlined here can further enhance the cut and expand the market for the LP. Next time you rifle through a bin of old LPs at the local antique center, realize that albums you see were recorded in professional studios with budgets 8 to 10 times higher in real dollars than the average budget today and were transferred to vinyl with no digital conversions whatsoever from original master tapes. They were probably recorded by professional engineers who spent years as studio assistants, and the only way to listen to them on demand was to buy them or have friends who did. If you see one by an artist you like, and it's less than 10 bucks, I would recommend you buy it and a turntable to play it back. The sound might surprise or even shock you.

Gavin Lurssen

Credits include: Elvis Costello, Tom Waits, Quincy Jones, James Taylor, Alison Krauss and Robert Plant, Leo Kottke, Social Distortion, Guns n' Roses, Rob Zombie, Lucinda Williams, Queen Latifah, Diana Krall. See the Appendix for Gavin Lurssen's full bio.

Listening to music is an intensely subjective experience. We all hear things a little differently, depending on the frequency range within which we function. What may be too bright or too loud for me may be just right for you. Experienced audio engineers can—and should—give advice, but the final sound that really counts is the sound that the artist wants. It is essential for all of us in the recording industry to understand that fact so that we can give our clients the best product possible, the one that really captures their vision and opens a connection between the artist and the fans using current-day formats of audio storage. The best way to achieve that goal is by clear communication. I have learned over the years that one of the first important steps for me as a mastering engineer is to communicate with a client at a human level and to leave the technical stuff until later.

Communication with artists and producers—even with fellow mastering engineers—can be quite an art inside a mastering studio. And, of course, it is an art outside the studios in media such as the trade press. I have written a number of articles, and one of the best received was about the use of compression. I tried to relate the subject to everyday human experience, and I found to my pleasure that people seemed to like that approach.

At Lurssen Mastering, our first objective is to sift through the spoken and body language to decipher precisely what is wanted and to help the client reach a point of understanding of what is technically desirable and possible. Unless the engineer observes and listens carefully, it can be quite easy to understand something differently than the way it was intended. This is one of the reasons why regular clients are so valued. We get a feel for what people want, and they know what we can provide. There is a comfort level based on experience and achieved results. But a comfort level can be quickly established with first-time clients too, based on a clear level of communication. Once that level has been found and a good back-and-forth rapport established, we can get down to work.

I work within a frequency spectrum. I mix with frequencies, and I do it using analog equipment. I use equalizers, compressors, limiters, analog-to-digital converters, digital-to-analog converters, and carefully planned gain structure in the interaction of all the equipment to accomplish all of this. There are either customized or stock line-level amplifiers in every step of the stage and of particular importance on the front end of an analog-to-digital converter and on the back end of a digital-to-analog converter. It is crucial that the gain structure of what is feeding the A-to-D or what the D-to-A is feeding is properly integrated in the chain of events. Only with very careful attention paid to the gain structure of all these devices working in concert can we achieve a fully professional sound—this along with two decades of training and sensibilities learned on the job and during my time at Berklee College of Music.

Sometimes I open up stem mixes and do the blends in the mastering studio, which is a step closer to the mixing process. As studio environments have been set up in compromised environments, clients rely on me more and more to open stem mixes and work from them. Stem mixes are a two-channel blend of drums or guitars or vocals or whatever else can be imagined, blended into two tracks so that two tracks of drums and two tracks of guitars and two tracks of vocals can all be further blended and mixed. This process can open another can of worms because a summing bus amplifier needs to be used in order to properly integrate the blend of frequencies into the rest of the signal chain.

Everything involved in the interaction between a mastering engineer and the client, which can consist of the artist, the engineer, the producer, the manager, and the A&R person, is like mastering a record itself. We are paying attention to a lot of detailed aspects, which include communication both ways, the use of equipment and the way it all interacts along the signal chain, and the way songs sound using our sensibilities in these areas to create one big, successful picture. A happy artist and a good sounding product....

And it is all done for the fans.

Jim DeMain

Credits include: John Hiatt, Lambchop, Vince Gill, Kris Kristofferson, Nanci Griffith, Michael McDonald, Jimmy Buffett, Albert Lee, Marty Stuart, Steve Earle, the Iguanas, Billy Joe Shaver, Jill Sobule, Shazam. See the Appendix for Jim DeMain's full bio.

Part of the mastering engineer's job description is creative problem-solving. The following are several issues that seem to crop up regularly.

One of the biggest issues I have concerns having to address over-compressed mixes. I'm sure I'm not the only mastering engineer to have this problem. If I get something that's way over-limited, it's really hard to achieve satisfying results. No matter how much you do, it will never be as good as if the mix was right in the first place. I've found the easiest way to address this is to request a non-limited version of the mix. A lot of my clients do this for me. That way, I really have control over the final compression/limiting.

It's strange to me that, with the extended dynamic rage that the virtually bottomless noise floor of digital has afforded us, we have gone completely in the other direction to make everything as loud as possible. It's truly unfortunate that more artists don't take advantage of that extended dynamic range, instead of being part of this constant push to make louder and louder over-limited CDs. I believe we are really doing a disservice to the recorded music during this time period by the destructive properties of over-limiting. It doesn't just destroy the dynamics; it also really skews the harmonic overtones of the instruments. So not only do we lose the natural rhythm, but it all starts to sound like white noise. There really is a difference in the way music that has not been over-limited fills the room. It's much more interactive. Could this trend of over-limiting possibly be a reflection of the increasing noise in the world around us?

Another issue many mastering engineers encounter concerns receiving poorly or non-labeled projects. I can't stress this enough: Label everything clearly and date it! You may think you'll remember what was on such-and-such disc, but in two weeks' time, chances are you won't. It sounds crazy, but I sometimes have received projects in the mail or FedEx packages containing only a silver disc with no label, notes, and even sometimes no name.

One last problem I regularly encounter is tracks with lots of tiny pops and clicks as a result of not setting an edit crossfade during vocal comping. They're almost always either right before or right after a vocal line. Please make sure you've really addressed this in the mix before you send it to mastering. It's no big deal to fix these things, but it can be very time consuming.

When I work, I sometimes do everything in real time through all the outboard gear; other times I work "in the box"; and then there are those times when I'll do a combination of both. It really is all about the project. I usually spend the first hour or so just trying out several different signal paths. I'll try analog only, digital only, combinations, et cetera, to see what flatters the mixes the best. I can usually tell pretty quickly what will work. Sometimes, just the combination and sequence of the gear can make a big difference before you even start turning any knobs.

Obviously, having an accurate, reliable monitoring setup is the most important thing you can have as a mastering engineer. You can have all the latest bells and whistles in compressors and EQs, but if you can't hear what's really happening in the recording before you, then all that other stuff doesn't really matter. Ultimately, you're making final decisions on people's work they've spent hours and hours working on up to this point.

Concerning my work methodology, I'm not a guy who's like, "It has to be all analog through a console!" Now, there's no argument that a good mix done through a console sounds phenomenal. The front-to-back depth and the height and width of a mix through a console is still pretty hard to beat in the box. But I have heard really good recording and mixing that was done all in the box. I think it really comes down to the people who are doing the recording, using their ears.

Ultimately, your ears are the most important piece of gear you own, and learning to truly listen is the most important thing you can do. It is a disservice to say, "When we do things a certain way, through this or that piece of gear with this method, we always produce great results." You have to be constantly listening. I sometimes think that with all of computer monitors in front of us, maybe we are looking at the music a little more than we're listening to it.

I don't really have a lot to complain about concerning my line of work. After all, I could be carrying bricks up a ladder for a living. That said, I do have a couple of observations about trends in the recording industry that concern me. One is I feel like we may be compromising art in pursuit of convenience. Art shouldn't necessarily be easy. You shouldn't just push a button and get art. But I think with the convenience of digital workstations, we are on our way to servicing that delusion. I just hope we can keep things in perspective. Having all these great tools can really be a double-edged sword. I'm not sure that it's such a great thing that we have the ready facility to make somebody who can't sing sound like they can sing, or somebody who can't play an instrument sound like they can play. Fortunately, that sort of stuff usually works itself out in the long run. But, on the other hand, I'm bothered more when I encounter talented artists who actually can play or sing having recordings where every fluctuation in the performance is perfectly straightened out on a grid and every note auto-tuned. Let's be careful not to trade personality for convenience.

Mixing

If you ask most consumers what drives them to purchase certain albums, chances are the way an album "sounds" figures in almost as much as the artist's elements of songwriting, playing, and singing. If you ask almost any mixer to state a mixing philosophy, he or she will probably tell you that it is to be as transparent as possible, allowing the artist's vision to shine through.

The average music listener might be content with the idea that the artist naturally "sounds" the way he or she does on record, but what would the Beatles have sounded like without George Martin? Would the Righteous Brothers' "You Lost That Lovin' Feeling" or "Unchained Melody" have the same transcendent power had Phil Spector not imbued them with his Wall of Sound? Surely, some of the most appealing qualities of Sting's music come from the sonic detailing, impact, and space revealed in Hugh Padgham's mixes.

None of this is meant to discount the very real talents and artistic statements made by those artists, but even the most "transparent" mixing by a great engineer has a way of enhancing the magical elements of a performance—elements that might otherwise have been hidden in less capable hands.

Those who obsessively check out album credits will often find the same names appearing on many of their favorite albums. It's a great argument for the value of the right mixer with the right project, and almost anyone reading this will certainly recognize names such as Tom Dowd, Chris Thomas, "Mutt" Lange, Tom Lord-Alge, Creed Taylor, John Potoker, Don Was, Eddie Kramer, Bruce Swedien, Brian Eno, Daniel Lanois, Steve Lillywhite, Glyn Johns, and Eddie Offord.

Mixing might merely be a matter of, as one producer put it, "turning up the good stuff and taking out the bad," but it takes great ears and a sure command of the tools of the studio to know what to enhance and what needs eliminating to create the most emotional impact.

Bob Clearmountain

Credits include: Bruce Springsteen, Bryan Adams, Roxy Music, the Pretenders, Chic, the Rolling Stones, David Werner, Squeeze, the Rezillos, Elton John, Kiss, INXS. See the Appendix for Bob Clearmountain's full bio.

Mostly everything I do these days deals with music that I haven't heard prior to the mixing session. It doesn't matter what kind of music I have before me, if I'm unfamiliar with the music, I might listen to the lyrics as I'm putting together a really quick rough mix. Of course, in the case of something I have produced, I don't have to listen to the lyrics. I know it inside and out.

There is no systematic way that I go about putting together this rough mix. I don't automatically start with drums and go on to bass and guitars or anything like that. I put up all the faders and begin working on the first element that grabs my interest.

Usually, I will work out the pans first. I may go into the guitars and try to figure out what should be panned to the left and what should be panned right. I'll start to set up the soundstage and try to picture everything visually and see where everybody is standing. Once I kind of get a visual thing happening, I will start going into individual sounds. I often work on the vocal sound pretty early in the mixing process. At this point, I will usually figure out what effect I want on the vocal in the context of this sort of rough mix that I have going. Sometimes I won't put on any effects.

Once I have a perspective on the vocal, I will start basing the rest of the mix around it. To me, the vocal is the most important thing in pop or rock music. After I have the vocal approximately where I want it, I start working on the drum sounds and do whatever has to happen with the drums and bass. After that, I usually begin to work on the individual guitar and keyboard sounds. I really don't have a systematic way of doing this, I just go back and forth between each musical component. I might work on keyboards a little bit and then work on the drums a little bit more and then go work on some guitar sounds or background vocals. It is almost random, but very instinctual.

When I am monitoring, I listen at an average level, usually quietly. For my monitoring setup, I use Yamaha NS-10Ms, KRK-E7s, and a pair of Apple powered computer speakers. The NS-10s are a bit ugly sounding, but for some reason they make me do a certain thing that seems to translate onto other systems. Unfortunately, they kind of roll off very quickly on the bottom end, so it is really hard to tell about anything happening on the bottom. The Dynaudio BM 15As are quite a bit more hi-fi sounding and a lot more fun to listen to. I usually set up the mix on the Yamahas and at some point switch to the Dynaudios. I will switch back and forth and make sure that everything is translating between the two. I also use the Dynaudios for surround mixing.

I was mixing the Pretenders with Chrissie Hynde, and she said, "Hey, do you have some little mono speaker we can listen on, just like a car radio?" I said that I had these Apple self-powered speakers that I got free as part of a promotion at CompUSA. I plugged one of them in and put the mono mix through it, and it was fantastic. I could hear everything so clearly. It is just one of those speakers that hangs off the side of your computer monitor. It's got two speakers in it, so it has got enough bottom end that I can tell exactly what is going on with the mix. I use them in stereo, although they sit on top of a rack off to my left, and they are about a foot and a half apart. They really offer an objective perspective. Too bad Apple stopped making them!

One of the common problems I encounter concerning mixing vocals is harshness on the track. It may be a case where the engineer chose the wrong mic for the singer. Sometimes I find people will go through great pains to be esoteric, just for the sake of being esoteric. It's like job protection. They will put a vocal through some really bizarre, very expensive preamp and use a very expensive old tube mic and some very exotic compressor, when really they could've ended up with a better vocal sound by using a newer mic that is in better shape, through an SSL preamp, which actually sounds pretty good. There have been times when I've gotten some amazing vocal sounds from a nice new U 87 through an SSL preamp and an LA-2A or an LA-3A, or something like that.

Some singers think they have all this mic technique. They think that if they sing really loudly, they should move away from the mic. It is something that many vocal coaches teach. Moving back from the mic might work well live on a stage, but the more the singer moves around, the more the tones are going to change. When a singer moves away from the mic, the voice gets really thin and harsh. If he or she moves in too close, it gets warm and wooly sounding. When there are these loud notes that get all harsh and shrill and quiet notes that are all warm and muddy, getting a pleasing vocal sound becomes difficult. If the singer had just stayed in one place, it would have been great. There's a great gadget that can help with this problem—it's the DPR-901 by BSS. It's a dynamic equalizer. You find the offending frequency, as you would on an EQ, and it attenuates just that frequency as it hits a threshold, like a limiter.

I know a lot of mixers who end up with all of the faders pushed to the top. Don't keep pushing stuff up. Turn stuff down. Figure out what is in the way. If you are not hearing a guitar part, figure out why you are not hearing it. What is covering it up? The same is true with the bass. It is all about getting the right balance. If you are not hearing the bass, ask yourself why not. Is there something getting in the way? Sometimes it is an EQ dip on some instrument that will clear another instrument. It also might free up more room for the voice.

Proper balance with EQ is often what it takes to create the right space around the voice. A lot of people don't realize that EQ isn't just adding top and bottom. It is actually balancing the frequencies in the overall mix. Sometimes it is a matter of dipping some frequencies out of the guitar to make room for something else.

Sometimes you go nuts trying to EQ the bass, and you just can't get it right. Really what is happening is something else in the mix is clouding it. I will solo the bass with various instruments, like the keyboards and the guitars, and listen to what it sounds like. If the sound gets muddy when I put in another instrument with the bass, I'll start rolling out bottom on that instrument to make the bass guitar clearer. You might have this big, warm acoustic guitar sound, and if you thin that out a bit, suddenly the bass comes shooting out, and it sounds really clear.

Generally, I find that the bottom end affects the compression more than anything in a mix. First of all, I usually compress the bass guitar if it needs it. I won't compress the bass if it has already been done.

I really get particular about the way the bass drum sound blends with the bass. It should become part of the bass, rather than have a sound on its own. The bass and the bass drum should ideally sound like one thing. Hopefully, the players are playing tight enough to where that is possible. If they are not, then that is a whole other problem. [Laughs] If I put a sample on the bass drum, the intention is to make the kick work with the bass more effectively.

Again, I must emphasize that I believe the most important element is the vocal in a song, and all the music has to complement and work with the song. I don't dissect the drums and work on a big bass drum sound first and then go work on a big snare drum sound. I have found that if I just sit and work on the drums by themselves, I will get what I think are pretty cool sounds, but the end result may be out of proportion when put in the context of the song. Everything has to be in the context of the song. I suppose part of it is that listening to soloed instruments all day gets kind of boring!

The most important thought that I like to get across to aspiring mixers and producers is to always keep the song in mind. At every stage try to step back, listen to the song, and ask yourself, "Is this actually helping the song? Is this something that makes the overall thing better?"

Think of it from the point of view of a listener who isn't paying attention to all of those little tricks and doesn't care about that fancy flange you put on the hi-hat or whatever. The average listener is listening to the vocals and possibly the lyric and hopefully the performance. All those little extra things that you are doing may be fun and interesting, but are they distracting from the song? Are they taking anything away?

If one of your fancy sound tricks is distracting, then forget it or bury it or do something with it to make it work with the song. I think that people get carried away with their drum sounds and this sound and that sound and their tricky things. Sometimes the best thing to do is nothing. That is why on some of my favorite mixes that I have done, the vocal is totally dry. I have done absolutely nothing, and there are very few effects in the mix. Those are the ones where you know, first of all, that the song and the performance are strong enough to carry it.

One mix that I used to judge my own work by was "Refugee" by Tom Petty. Shelly Yakus mixed it. There is something very special about that mix. There is nothing fancy happening, but everything is so incredibly clear and perfectly well balanced, and it all works with the song. Every element is complementary to every other element. It is fantastic. In contrast, "Killer Queen" by Queen [which was produced by Roy Thomas Baker in the '70s] is one of the trickiest mixes ever, but it serves the thrust of the song too—in a different way. Another song I'd love to mention is "Tempted" by Squeeze. It is one of those records that I think is absolutely perfect. There is nothing tricky happening in the mix—the song gets the full emphasis. Roger Bechirian and Elvis Costello produced it.

Having just made a case for simplicity, I'd like to add that I'd rather receive a cluttered multitrack than one that doesn't have the necessary ingredients. I have had more frustration with tapes that were under-produced, where you get to the outro and there is this rhythm section where nobody is singing, and there is no melody or solo. Where's the rest of it? That's frustrating. I would rather have something cluttered and have to weed through a bunch of junk and find something that works and have to take things out. You can always take stuff out.

In the end, my favorite records I've mixed are usually because of the music, more than what I did in the mix. I can't do a good mix of something that is garbage. To me, the reason a mix turns out well has to do with what's in the recording. Even though I did the mix, I have trouble separating what is the mix and what is the overall record. If I did a good job, it is because of the music.

Richard Dodd

Credits include: Tom Petty, Wilco, Clannad, Dixie Chicks, Roy Orbison, Joe Cocker, Traveling Wilburys, Ringo Starr, Boz Scaggs, Del Shannon, George Harrison, Red Hot Chili Peppers. See the Appendix for Richard Dodd's full bio.

There are no wrongs, and if there are, I make sure that I don't know them. I have one thing that I take with me whenever I mix, and it is not a piece of equipment. It is an attitude of "I'm going to make this thing work. I don't carry monitors, and I don't have a favorite room. I'm looking for something that I haven't done yet."

[When Dodd does bring along a complement of outboard gear, the setup often consists of Urei 1176s, MoTone, EQ 3D, and SPL Transient Designer.]

I like Urei 1176s, especially the black-faced ones. I like their distortion. Distortion and noise have never bothered me.

Basically, if you put your mix up and it sounds a bit dull, why go through 24 equalizers when you can put the whole thing through one stereo one, brighten them all up in one go and all in phase with each other? I hope that you could play any of my mixes in mono and still enjoy the balance. That is a criterion that I have.

The most important thing to me is to understand the song and know what is wanted. Generally, I like to start the mix with something that represents the song, something with the chord structure, like a couple of guitars if any are there. You've also got to get a clue from something other than the drums about what the drums are going to sound like, in my opinion. I very often attempt to balance the whole song before I consider what things will sound like.

It really makes me feel sad—superior really, I guess—when I see an engineer about to commence a mix, and he lifts up the mics closest to the kick drum and snare and reaches for every piece of equipment he's got on his hands to try to make it sound like a drum with a mic 2 or 3 feet away. A few faders off are the overheads, and that is where his drum sound is. If he listened to that, he would know what he's got. Very often, all he would need those close ones for is to give the feeling of where the time is and where they are in the stereo picture.

I also encourage mixers to consider the unintended colors that mic bleed presents as an asset. Throwing various mics in and out of phase or shifting their time is a favorite way I expand my sonic palette.

Just because a fader says "kick" doesn't mean it is just a kick mic. There is a little bit of hi-hat there as well, unless it came out of a machine. The drums all interact, and they are all miked for each other.

People tend to like the manual mixes more, because they have fewer options. If they see you sweating like that, they are more reluctant to say, "That word 'the' on the second verse—could it have just been a tenth of a dB louder?"

They don't say things like that when you are doing manual mixes. They are more inclined to say, "That felt great," or "Did the voice feel loud enough?" They refer to feeling. When I am working on a computer, they refer to things by tenths of a dB—ridiculous.

I spend most of my time in the digital world now. It is the way the industry—forced by the need to lower cost and make up for less talent—has gone. Instead of saying, "No, I don't like the way it sounds," I now say, "Okay, I'll have to do this to make it sound right."

To help put some tone back, I always use my MoTone. It helps the finished product to sound less sterile.

Dave Pensado

Credits include: Beyonce, Pink, Earth, Wind & Fire, Mary J. Blige, Nelly, Christina Aguilera, Destiny's Child, Justin Timberlake, Bell Biv DeVoe, Shakira, Backstreet Boys, Whitney Houston, Mariah Carey. See the Appendix for Dave Pensado's full bio.

I think teaching mixing from a visual perspective, in terms of color and composition, is not as dark and mysterious as teaching from a hearing perspective. If you look at the painting "Las Meninas" by Velázquez, he manipulates your eye around that canvas masterfully to different elements, and then all of a sudden you find yourself seeing this little girl, who is the real subject of the painting, and then you notice this dog to her right. A good mix should have that same effect. A good mix should have layers, where each time you hear it, you experience something new and interesting.

The brain tends to not notice something visually in a room unless it moves. When it comes to a mix, you've got to move things around once you notice them. You need to manipulate levels in such a way that it keeps an interest going.

I believe the brain likes to process three hooks simultaneously. When it's processing two hooky things, it's okay. If it is processing one or none, the brain just shuts off, so I always try to provide three cool things to process and experience.

In visual arts, such as painting, photography, and design, there is a term called the *Rule of Thirds.* If you divide your canvas into three spaces vertically and horizontally, the points where those lines intersect are primary areas where the human brain and eye like to see their focal points.

For instance, if you take a picture of your kid, and his eyes are perfectly centered in the photograph, it's just unpleasant or uninteresting to the eye. But if you set your kid's eyes on the upper-left node, where those lines intersect, then you have something interesting happening that's more pleasant to the eye. The ear is the same way.

I apply the Rule of Thirds to mixing. It can be interpreted in a number of ways, but one way of viewing our "thirds" are simply left, middle, and right. To me, those have always been the three most sacred spots in the mix, and you've got to have an incredibly good reason to put something in those three spots.

If you listen to my mixes, I don't pan my stereo effects returns hard left or hard right. I don't clutter that area, because it's sacred territory. It's noble. You've got to think that way.

Say you've got a guitar, and you want to put reverb on it. Don't just have the reverb come back hard left and hard right. Have your guitar come back a little left and your reverb come back a little right. What's wrong with that? Now you've preserved that area for the most important things. Same thing goes for the center.

Traditionally, we put the vocals, kick drum, snare in the center. Sometimes you can spread the bass, with like a Dimension D, to get it out of the center, which helps keep things clear, because there's nothing more important than the vocal. When you've got a lot of programmed instruments in your track, your vocal takes on new importance, not just from a harmonic standpoint, but also with your dynamics.

To address that, I sometimes treat vocals like they are tom fills. For instance, if I've got a vocal line going from the verse into the chorus, I might yank up those notes like crazy and change the EQ on them, maybe add some midrange, and put on a drum reverb just for those six notes and treat them like a tom fill.

If you listen to my mixes, you should be able to just drop the needle down in any chorus and any verse and within two bars know where you are. That's how the production should be done, and that's how the mixing should be done. I ride my master fader on every mix, so by the time we get to the last chorus, it's the loudest part of the song. I'm probably at that point 2 dB louder than the first verse. I'll go up a little bit for the first chorus and then bring it down a hair for the second verse.

There are two types of bridges. There's the bridge where it's the loudest part, and then when you get out into the vamp, it's more like a tapering off of energy and settling down. Then there's the other kind of bridge where you bring everything down, like in a live concert, and then you come back with the PA wide open, and the sound of the drums through the PA is like thunder, and you go into that last chorus, and people wet their pants. That's the other kind of chorus. You can do that individually with each fader, but I try to think what I would do, if I was playing live, to get that emotion in there. If I'm programming drums, I'll manipulate them like a live drummer would perform.

If you look back at mixes of the music you like, there's always a skeleton or a backbone to the song, and that's what the song is built around. It varies from song to song. Sometimes it's a loud tambourine. Sometimes it's a Farfisa or a guitar. There's a reason for that, and the reason is that you need a reference to compare the loudness to. "Loud" in the mix world doesn't have a meaning. It's all relative. Let's say I've got a Rhodes, a guitar, drums, and a vocal. If the guitar is the loudest thing in the mix, it's a rock song. If I can hardly hear the guitar, the vocals are up there, and I hear a lot of Rhodes, maybe I've got an R&B or pop song. The manipulation of the main elements relative to each other is everything, and obviously, that's why we call it mixing—and that statement is about as simplistic as you can get.

By not over-compressing the elements on the front end, you're allowing yourself to react emotionally as a mixer to point the finger at the dynamics to direct the way you want the listener to go down that path with you. That said, I'm always amazed at the greats and how they compress and how they do it. I don't use any stereo bus compression.

I like to work with the same mastering engineers, like Eddy Schreyer, Big Bass Brian, Herb Powers, and Tom Coyne. All the Sterling Sound guys are good. I've worked with them for 20 years, and they do a better job at compression than I do. So why do it? Just so that I can say that I did it? The guys that start their mix off with compression and are really good at their mixes evolving underneath that umbrella of compression have learned how to manipulate that into their sound over the years. I just let my dynamics go and give my mixes to one of that handful of great mastering guys. It's like Christmas for them, because it has not gone through that extra processing. As a result, they get to really do what they do well. Sometimes they're so used to having it the other way that I'll get it back over-compressed, but most of the time we're on the same page.

I think having a personal relationship with a good mastering engineer is very important. Good mastering is hard to find because tastes are involved and different genres are involved.

Dylan Dresdow

Credits include: Black Eyed Peas, Wu-Tang Clan, Michael Jackson, will.i.am, Ice Cube, Nas, TLC, Bone Thugs-n-Harmony, Usher, Madonna, Ricky Martin, Macy Gray. See the Appendix for Dylan Dresdow's full bio.

Here are a few pointers that would make every mixer's job much easier. Not labeling tracks is terrible. It's very frustrating whenever I get sessions, and they are all labeled Audio 1, Audio 2, and so on. All of that stuff should be cleaned up before it comes to the mix. This is something any engineer should know to do.

Whenever you're mixing, all you want to focus on is the mix. You don't want to be distracted with editing, comping, auto-tuning vocals, and Beat Detectiv-ing drums. None of those things should be done during the mix stage.

When the mixer has to spend time on things like tuning vocals and comping tracks and all of these different things that should've been done before the mix, suddenly jumping over to the creative side from the mechanical side of your brain can be very difficult to do. You should get all the technical stuff taken care of before you get to the mix; then you know you'll be focusing directly on the mix.

Another thing that I run into very often is phase problems with live drums or impedance mismatching when it comes to drum machines. A lot of times people will take the direct out of a synthesizer or drum machine, and they won't match the impedance correctly for that instrument, which can negatively affect the signal path. For most drum machines, you should take the drum machine output and go into a DI, and then out of the DI into a mic pre. That's how you should be sending your signal to the DAW.

Also, engineers need to be careful trying to get the hottest levels they possibly can. In theory, it would seem like that is a good thing because you're getting ultimate bit resolution and everything. The problem with that is if you record right to zero, and I want to boost 5 dB at 600 Hz of the snare drum to give it more of a wood knock, I have no room to do that. You have to make sure you give your mixer enough headroom so the engineers can do their job.

Poor tuning techniques are another big problem. If your tuning is supposed to sound like a vocoder, that's one thing, but typically you should make pitch correction sound as transparent as possible. If you can hear things getting squirrelly and jerky and sounding like a robot, you haven't done your job properly.

For correcting drums and things like that, make sure that you have your edits and any crossfades that you need to do done properly and that you solo the tracks and make sure that there aren't any clicks or pops that might not necessarily be audible until you put a certain degree of compression on it, which brings those artifacts out.

Another simple thing that can help a mixer concerns keeping all your drums side by side track-wise, instead of having them all over the place. All of your background vocals should be side by side, too. It should typically go drums, percussion, bass, guitar, synthesizers or any sound effects, then lead vocals, then background vocals. People often keep all of their aux and aux returns to the far right so that they can quickly go down and scroll to the right and they can adjust all of the effects returns as they need to.

Whenever I get a mix, I will typically listen to the song a few times. Sometimes I write down notes; sometimes I just try to vibe and get injected into the song as much as I can. Now, if I dislike the song, it is going to be more difficult for me as a mixer to make the thing sound good. If I'm not into it, it's hard to do that. Sometimes, quite frankly, you get stuck with songs that just aren't that good, and you have to find a way to make them work. What I'll do with that is I'll pull up my reference CD that has a bunch of different songs on it. The first half are songs that I think just have the best mixes ever. The second half are just songs that I plain love—Beatles, Led Zeppelin, A Tribe Called Quest, Slayer—songs that are going to get me excited about working on music. Once I crank the music on the mains and get excited, I really quickly try to rush into the song that I don't like as much that I'm working on that day, so I will have the excitement level of it for reference and will inject that into my mix.

This is a service-based industry. If I was a barber, and someone came in and sat down on the chair and said, "I want a mullet," I would have to give them a mullet haircut. Now, I'm going to try to make that mullet as creative as I can and make it look cool and not let the person look like an idiot, but in a service-based industry, I have to give these people what they want. As a mixer, sometimes it's difficult to identify what the people want, but the longer you work with people, the more helpful that is in achieving the best results. When I've worked with new artists, I usually go as far as I can and do exactly what I would normally do to the extreme. Most of the time they enjoy that and then that becomes part of their sound, because I never mix records exactly the same.

It can get frustrating, during a mix, when a producer references a Nas, Common, Black Eyed Peas, or Michael Jackson song I've mixed and says to make the snare drum sound like the snare on one of those tracks. I feel we should look at making the snare drum sound our own thing and something new, because hopefully five months from now, someone is going to say the same thing about that record.

The better mixes that I've done have been with producers with a solid direction, but who leave room for us to push off each other. Sometimes I might have put an effect on something, and I'm just patting myself on the back and then the producer comes in and says, "Why don't we put a flanger on that?" That will turn on a new dynamic, and we just push and push and push. For example, will.i.am and I have always done a good job of challenging each other back and forth *sans* ego, and at the end of the day, I think the product ends up becoming better because of it.

A lot of times I'll hear a song on the radio, and it sounds great, but I would do something completely different because I think they missed an opportunity to sell the song or set something up. I think most artists and producers should ask themselves, "Would I know what the song title was after the first time I heard it?" If you don't know the song title, it's going to be much more difficult for the consumer to track that down—either online or in a record store. That's a big part of the selling point for popular music. When you heard Led Zeppelin's "Whole Lotta Love," you knew what that song was called after the first time you heard it. There are exceptions to that rule, if you could call it that. That's just something that I think, production-wise, people need to seriously consider.

There are things mixers can do, like drop out all the instruments on that one key line, to make sure that the song is instantly recognizable by the person who is listening to it for the first time, and at the same time give the listener something special. Whenever you do those things as a mixer, I think the songs have more longevity and stand up to the test of time. I want to make sure that it's something that truly adds a musical element to the mix. If I'm doing an effect for my own glory, there's no purpose in doing it. It all goes back to the artist and being true to the song.

At the end of the day, people are not buying records because there are great mixes on them. It can help translate and it can help make things sound great, but I don't know people who are buying records because they think a great mix was done on the album. I just don't think that's why people buy records. I don't even think that the consumers care how we make records, for the most part. They just want to enjoy them at the end of the day. And that's what I try not to lose focus of whenever I'm working on a console or in the box.

Ken Kessie

Credits include: En Vogue, Tower of Power, Tony! Toni! Tone!, Celine Dion, David Foster. See the Appendix for Ken Kessie's full bio.

The foundation of R&B and hip-hop are kick and bass. The Holy Grail is a fat low end that shakes a club or Jeep system, while at the same time sounds clear and punchy on a small radio or TV speaker. To help accomplish that, I sometimes use a lot of fader multing, which is a twist on bi-amping.

What I do is mult the kick onto two different faders. The first fader gets the low end and without too much punch. I usually add some slight compression (SSL or dbx 160X) and lots of Pultec boosted at 100 or 60 dB.

The other fader is set for maximum punch, heavy compression (again using SSL or dbx 160X), harder EQ (SSL, API Graphics), boosting upper mids, and cutting speaker-distorting low-mids. I then mix the two faders 'til I get a kick drum that booms on big systems but doesn't distort the NS-10s.

Another trick for removing those pesky low-mids is a BSS DP-904, set to remove 200 to 400 Hz on kick impact only, restoring them after the attack has passed. I use a similar multing process to achieve the ideal bass tone.

I go for the lows on one fader, using Pultecs or my pet Moog parametric. On the other fader, I use SSL filters to take out a lot of the bottom and a bit of the high end, until the bass pops out of an Auratone speaker at low volume. For bass compression, I will use either the dbx 160X, SSL, LA-2, LA-3, Dynamite, Summit, or Tube-Tech. I often chorus the bass slightly with a TC 2290 (preset 85) to fill out the sides of the mix.

I don't hesitate to employ snare samples. In dealing with the flams, muddy bottom, hiss, and completely filled-in midrange found in the obligatory sample loops, I often use an API 560 graphic to boost or cut desired frequencies.

Sometimes I spread a loop using a short delay (14 milliseconds), then pan the original to the left and the delay right. This can prevent clog up in the center of the mix.

For vocals, I'm a firm believer in clear, bright, more personality than effects, Motown-style vocal. The vocals are the most important element in a mix, so they get as much attention as other key elements. Vocal and groove combined get about 70 percent of my mixing time.

For male lead singers, Urei 1176s seem to work best for compression, while I prefer to use API or Massenberg EQs to address the top end with a Pultec or Focusrite for warmth. I use a dbx 902 de-esser if necessary.

Female singers generally require a more complex outboard chain. On the last En Vogue album, a typical lead vocal went through an 1176, an EQ, a dbx 902, and a dbx 165.

To give a lead vocal some ambience and help it punch through the mix, I may use a couple of delays and some reverb. Delay #1 might be very short, usually a thirty-second or sixteenth note, and EQ'd very brightly to make the S's and other consonants bounce slightly. Delay #2 would probably be set for an eighth or a dotted eighth and EQ'd to give a subtle trail to the singer. For reverb, I use AMS Ambience [480 Warm Plate, Zoom 9300 Clear Plate] set for pre-delay to keep the singer up front.

If your lead vocal isn't bright enough, you don't necessarily EQ the vocal itself, because you might start thinning it out. Add an effect to the vocal that is very bright, and that way you get to keep the body and tone of the original vocal, but you have added the high end that you need. That works great on background vocals, too.

Unlike many mixers, I start loud on the mains and then switch to NS-10s, with only occasional moments back on the mains.

Many pop mixers remove bottom from a mix until they can crank up the NS-10s without distortion. This would be too thin for a good R&B mix. I leave in a little bit of low-end breakup when the NS-10s are loud. As the mix goes on, the volume gets quieter. Just before printing, I am switching between near-fields, a mono Auratone, and headphones. I use the headphones to check for any left-right imbalances or unwanted noises, and to ensure seamless transitions between all sections.

For the transfer from console to two-track, I like using an Apogee A/D, before going to DAT [for rock], and I use the A/D converters of the Panasonic on R&B/hip-hop. I usually print a variety of mixes to cover any possible situation— vocals up and down, no lead vocal for TV, an instrumental for single and editing purposes, a cappella lead and background for sampling and digital editing, and any other variations that might be desired.

Phil Ramone

Credits include: Billy Joel, Tony Bennett, Rufus Wainwright, Elton John, Luciano Pavarotti, Luther Vandross, Ray Charles, Paul Simon, Barbra Streisand, Frank Sinatra, Rod Stewart, Paul McCartney. See the Appendix for Phil Ramone's full bio.

I have two monitoring levels that I set in the room, and I don't veer away from them. I'll mix extremely soft, almost to the point that people can hardly hear it. Once I've got a reasonable soft mix that I am comfortable with, I'll mark that on the fader. I'll then do the hype playback, which is playing it back big. For that, I go to the big speakers to see where I am, just to make sure that I haven't veered off.

You have to start with something for a reference. You should bring a a selection of music that you love, and you should play those recordings you brought with you at two different levels. Maybe one level would be putting out at 80 or 90 dB on near-fields, which is plenty loud. The other setting might be at 65 or 70 dB. That would be a level that would stress your brain and ears to have to hear little nuances that you can't hear in a normal world. If you want that little bell to cut through lightly with a shaker, you will never know this if you are listening too loud all the time. I can work much longer hours because I am not forcing myself to burn my eardrums. I take ear breaks when I have worked for two or three hours.

I tend to print mixes very quickly. I don't leave them in the computer for someone to say, "Ah, what was Take 2 like? You never played Take 2."

Within the hour that I start, I have put a mix down. I will then go to a couple of other rooms, or I will set up a pair of self-powered monitors with a player out in the lounge, which is another way to listen. This way, you can get a picture of where you are going. I'll then go back to that original monitor level setting, and I don't change.

I beg all my assistants, if I am physically doing the mix, that whenever I walk into the room, the level is set where I left it. When I say, "Now play it at the other level," it comes back exactly at that level.

I still listen to my mixes in the car. Roy Halee taught me that a long time ago, when I went to watch him make a mix. He used to transmit it from the mix room down to his car on a little cheap transmitter. When he put his own compressor on it, he got a true feeling of what the record mix was about. I always thought that was a cool idea. We used to do that between our cutting room and our mix room at A&R Recording when I worked there. We could broadcast from two rooms and see what was going on. You listened on your favorite little portable radio. Overall, I think you have to test your music on about four different systems to know whether the mix really works.

By the way, when I go to master, I don't have levels that go all over the place, because I've been consistent in maintaining a set listening level during the mixdown.

Sometimes, if the artist is in the room, I might hand him a pair of headphones so that he can hear it with all of the subtleties he wants to hear. Some artists, however, like to crank it up, and that can cause problems and interrupt your creative flow in a mix. If you are going to do surgery, and it is microsurgery that you are dealing with, you have got to concentrate. If you are there to make a great record, you shouldn't be interrupted.

I generally have an open mind about what the mix process is. I tend not to come to the table with the same thing every time. I've been in situations where I didn't have much equipment, and I still made it work. I think it is in the hands of the mixer. Putting all the right tools in front of a monkey might get you a mix, but it may not be the one you want. [Laughs]

It is nice to have a couple of pieces of equipment that you feel secure about. I know there are guys who really feel strongly about having an old Fairchild limiter in the chain somewhere. That's fine. Old tube equipment keeps coming back like antiques. Some of us who remember that equipment don't always fall in love with it, because it was painful when it made noise or was crumbling, or it was sounding like bacon and eggs.

I do think that tubes bring you warmth, but I think that it is your ears that bring warmth. The so-called cold sound of digital is purely something that is poorly recorded, without thinking about where to place the mics, as well as how to use your tonal controls. In this day and age, it is inexcusable not to make good sounds.

Ronan Chris Murphy

Credits include: King Crimson, Steve Morse, Los Gauchos Alemanes, Chucho Valdes and Irakere, ProjeKct One through ProjeKct Four, Bozzio Levin Stevens. See the Appendix for Ronan Chris Murphy's full bio.

As a mixer I have one of the coolest jobs in the world, but there are three things that will really make me feel like I work for a living, and they are getting projects with really hot levels into the digital recorder, guitars recorded with digital amp modelers, and drums that are tuned or performed inappropriately for the music or vision of the album. For almost everything else there are usually cool workarounds, but those are the big three things I really have to wrestle with.

The one thing that I see done poorly so often concerns really hot levels in a digital recorder, where they're clipping or the meters are not clipping but the signal is distorting the analog input stage of the converters. Super-hot levels are probably the one thing I find consistently to be a trouble spot, to the point where you can sometimes lose performances. It can really be a showstopper for a mix, when the levels are so hot that they've induced really ugly distortion to the point where you can't really use or manipulate the track.

For example, I can deal with a guitar that isn't bright enough. If I would've liked a little more presence on something [such as a close mic instead of a distant mic placement], I can find a way to integrate that and work it into the mix, but the hot levels thing is the one thing that's made a few recordings unusable. This is always a big heartbreak, because there are ways to work around almost everything else except that.

Now I'm just talking about the levels in digital. With analog, it's a completely different deal. This is just something that is very specific to recording in digital mediums. There are some people who think you should record as hot as possible to get maximum resolution, and the truth is that the sweet spot of most gear isn't right at the top of it. It's actually quite a bit below.

Let me give an example. It's not an ideal situation, but if something showed up for me to mix an album, and all of the levels were peaking at about –40 dBfs, my take on it would be, "Man, I'm going to need about an extra 20 minutes to sort this out," and that would be the end of the trouble. It's completely usable and workable. Now, if I have a track where the levels are right at the top and peaking and messing things up, it might be a point where I have to say, "I'm sorry, but I can't mix this record. I can't get it to a quality level where I'd want to put my name on it, because the converter or digital distortion is so bad and inappropriate for the music."

When it comes to the argument for recording really hot levels to digital, you can get into esoteric arguments about whether that makes sense, but the potential downsides are so vast that I think they far outweigh any potential benefits, because if you're recording at 24-bit and your levels are at –20 dBfs, you've already far exceeded the resolution and dynamic range of a commercial audio CD. So it's the kind of thing where if your levels are hitting –6 or even –18 dBfs at the loudest point on the whole record, then there is, in my opinion, absolutely no downside to that. None whatsoever. You've lost a few dB of resolution of a signal that's probably already exceeding the dynamic range of almost all of your recording gear.

If you get a record that shows up and the guitar sounds are really terrible on a record, then you can think, "Well, I can mix this record so that the excitement and the energy is in the drums, the keyboard, and the vocal," or "Wow, that's the worst kick drum sound I've ever heard," but we've got some techniques to salvage that. We can fly in some samples or whatever.... There are ways to get around that, even if the vocal has this weird analog distortion on it because they really pushed that preamp too hard. Then it's like, "Let's mix it like a Strokes record," or something where that crunch is part of the sound. The one thing that is a showstopper is really hot levels peaking out and messing up to your digital recorder. Some sounds will survive the super-hot levels, but others can get totally ruined by it.

There's not as much of a defining line between artist and recordist as there used to be. A lot of artists are recording themselves now, so the guitar player is the engineer, or their buddy has learned a little bit and they're just going to spend four months recording with him, rather than working with somebody more experienced. A lot of times, that's where people really start getting into trouble.

Usually some of the best self-recorded records I get to mix are situations where the band decided to record themselves, and they were just too nervous to do anything fancy. They're like, "Yeah, we just put a microphone up and made sure our levels weren't distorted and moved it until it sounded good. We were too scared to do anything else...." Those records are a joy to mix because they haven't really done anything to impede the mix options, and if they've moved the mics around until they actually like the sound of it, it's really easy for me to go in and do compression and EQ or even to apply some of the fancier techniques that they've heard about and want in there for creative reasons.

As odd as it sounds, I think a lot of people just don't really listen to their tracks. I'll get something to mix and push up the faders and listen to the kick-drum track, and it's hard to imagine that anybody would have listened to that track and thought it in any way, shape, or form an acceptable or interesting drum sound. Especially when the band starts talking about the records they love—"Oh yeah, we would really love it to sound like this Tom Petty record"—and then you pull up the kick-drum track and you wonder if they ever listened to their kick drum or a Tom Petty record and thought that this was in any way acceptable to get to their end goal. Often, they could have just moved the microphone around—you know, where they go, "That's just not good at all; let's try and move this," or "Let's try and dampen the kick drum," or "Let's try taking off the damping on the kick drum," or whatever that end goal is. It's not rocket science, but I find a lot of people don't take the time to critically listen. For the artists who are recording themselves, one of their greatest luxuries is the time to experiment and listen.

I've probably made a few-hundred more records than they have, but it's sort of like if they have converted their living room into a recording studio for the next six months, they have the time to bring the drummer over and say, "Let's screw around with mic placement for Saturday and move it around until you can push up that fader and go, 'Man, that's actually pretty cool; we like that.'" I don't think people take the time to experiment and actually just listen.

A lot of times when you're mixing a record and you have something that has technical problems in the recording, there are sometimes a limited number of options available to try and actually salvage that sound in particular. In those cases, the answer is to rethink the perspective and the priorities on the mix. Even if it's a hard rock band, and the electric guitars aren't really happening, those acoustics might sound pretty great. Maybe pull up the acoustic guitars to drive some of the energy in the mix. Sometimes it's like, "Well, the drums aren't really happening. They just sound murky and dull, and there's no definition, but, you know, we do have a pretty great-sounding conga track." So there are ways to change the perspective around to make it exciting and powerful or whatever the end goal is, but it's not always exactly what you thought it was at first.

Bill Schnee

Credits include: Steely Dan, Barbra Streisand, Dire Straits, Neil Diamond, Whitney Houston, Carly Simon, Natalie Cole, Boz Scaggs. See the Appendix for Bill Schnee's full bio.

I really feel the best mixing engineers are born and not bred! It's much like the difference between a natural musician and a learned one—anyone can learn the science of recording (or playing an instrument) and become a reasonably good recording engineer (or musician). But even today, with the help of automation and the importance of effects, a person's intuitive sense of balance is still what will separate a great mixing engineer from a good one.

I don't think there's a finite answer to what constitutes a balanced mix. To me, a good mix captures the mood, energy, and spirit of the music. It emotionally moves the listener to the place the artist was trying to go with his vocals, instruments, et cetera. Not only will what it takes to accomplish this vary from song to song, but there's always more than one way to skin a cat. I've always thought an interesting experiment would be to give the same multitrack recording to maybe five great mixing engineers and tell them to have fun. My suspicion is that you would have five great mixes with different "flavors," if you will. Also, sometimes what we think should work in a mix in fact doesn't. Any experienced engineer can tell you of mixes where they thought there should be more bottom on the record [for example]. But after adding more bass, the mix actually didn't feel as good as before!

When I get a song to mix, I usually ask for a rough mix to see where the producer and artist think the song belongs. This helps me save time in getting the mix going, unless they want a completely fresh approach, which some producers do want.

People usually hire a mixing engineer for the specific talent he brings to the mix, and therefore I never feel shy in offering my ideas...musical and otherwise. The amount of creative input I personally feel I should give to a mix varies with the type of music being mixed. With a jazz record, I start with the basic assumption that what is on tape is the record they want—not a lot of effects, et cetera. But with a pop or R&B record, I feel I have a lot more freedom to try different ideas—effects, rearrangement ideas, or whatever—as long as the experimenting that takes place doesn't cause one to lose sight of the overall picture. All too many times in a complicated mix with a lot of experimentation, the musical "forest" is lost for a bunch of effects or idea-driven "trees"!

Even though I've always felt engineers should have at least a basic knowledge of electronics, I truly feel mixing is a right-brain function. Like the musician doing a solo, where he needs to forget all the technique he's spent years developing so he can give an inspired performance, so should an engineer ultimately feel and not think his way through a mix.

When I am recording a project, I try to get everything on tape as close as possible to how I want it in the end. This means levels—the old "yardstick" approach—and may include effects, although not usually reverbs. But since I mostly mix other engineers' recordings, I come across all kinds of recording philosophies. I love getting a song where everything is organized and ready to go. I have never liked the concept of fixing it in the mix. I would just as soon not have to fix things that could or should have been dealt with during the recording process and save my energy for more creative efforts. Of course, there are certain situations that are best left to be dealt with during the mix. My rule of thumb is: 1) If it ain't broke, don't fix it! 2) If it is broke, try to fix it before you mix it! Of course, there are times when the kick or snare should be replaced or augmented, and I'm grateful for sound replacement plug-ins at those times. Then there are times when I'll try running a track through a guitar head or amp to change the sound radically. These kinds of creative efforts are where I would like to spend mixing time instead of fixing problems—or comping vocals, for that matter!

I grew up sonically in the world of hi-fi—tubes and such. As a result, I've always gravitated toward consoles that are more transparent—with an open or natural top end—and have good punchy bottom. I suppose in this category you find old Neve, API, and Focusrite consoles—although I constantly found myself going for studios with one-off custom-made consoles with minimal electronics in them.

When I committed to opening my own studio [29 years ago], I decided a console of this type was a must. I designed the console with Toby Foster and Steve Haselton. It uses discrete amplifiers, tube mic preamps, and a tube stereo bus amp. Since every amplifier—even resistor or capacitor—in the audio chain acts like a piece of gauze through which you listen, my philosophy is "less gives more!" I would rather have to make extra patches or find a more creative way of accomplishing a certain signal flow for events that take place 5 percent of the time in exchange for less electronics that you listen through 100 percent of the time. What does any of this sonic purity have to do with getting great mixes? Very little, to be sure. But since this kind of fidelity is so hard to capture and so easy to lose, I would rather not have to fight the console to get it. Note that in many types of music or in certain situations, you might not want extended fidelity, but it's much easier to throw it away when unwanted than to get it, when desired, if it's not there.

My analog console has GML automation, which for me is a necessary evil! I say necessary because with 48 tracks or more of music and only two hands, there's a need. I say evil because I much prefer to do all the mixing myself—in real time. In fact, one of my favorite things to do is live-to-two-track—or direct-to-disc in the old days—where you have to mix or "perform" on the spot. I don't like having to need to use automation, but in most cases, I'm afraid I do. The good news of automation is how it allows you to perfect subtleties in a mix. The bad news is there's not as many last-minute right-brain moves or accidents in a mix (a.k.a. spontaneity!). As a result, I usually get the mix to a reasonable state before I even turn the automation on, having most of the EQ, effects, and reverbs set. Then I fine tune with the computer making the fader moves. When mixing, I love to create dynamics in various parts of the song for added impact. The automation definitely lets me do more of these moves more precisely, but hopefully not at the expense of spontaneity!

These days I now am forced to mix in Pro Tools. This is because virtually every artist, producer, and A&R man wants the ability to make changes—oftentimes very small ones—to a mix. The bad news is mixing in Pro Tools doesn't sound as good as mixing on the console with analog EQ and compression. But I've done everything I can to make it sound the best it can. I use the mixer in the box with all the EQ and compressor plug-ins. I use the echo sends in the box as well. I come out of PT with 24 tracks of stems, so no bus in PT has very much information on it. I sum these stems with the reverb returns [for the analog EMT plate and the digital hardware reverbs] and a few analog effect returns. This comes out of the tube stereo line amp in my console and can then go to an analog compressor and is printed to a 24/192 digital recorder on a DVD for mastering. This chain has worked very well for me sonically for the last few years.

The big monitors in my room are the same ones at the Mastering Lab—a custom system with an EV tweeter, Altec midrange horn, and two Utah woofers. However, what I use mostly for mixing are Tannoy 10-inch Golds with custom enclosures and crossovers. I use modified Yamaha 2200 power amps, which I have found to match up great with the Tannoys. These are anything but true hi-fi speakers, but they are very accurate for me. I've never liked mixing on speakers that sound too good, even though I love listening to music on them. I find I don't work as hard on those types of speakers because everything tends to sound so good. The most important thing is that the engineer relates to his speakers so that a mix done on them sounds reasonably good on a multitude of other speaker systems. I mix at a medium level (about 80 dB). I decided years ago to ensure longevity in my career by not blowing my ears out! I had no idea eyes would be as important as ears in mixing with the importance of computer screens!

Kevin Shirley

Credits include: Aerosmith, Judas Priest, Journey, Iron Maiden, the Black Crowes, Led Zeppelin, Rush, HIM, Metallica, New York Dolls, Dream Theater, Joe Satriani. See the Appendix for Kevin Shirley's full bio.

Everyone hears things a little bit differently when they're mixing. I'm always amazed by how people hear things. I like to be kicked by the music, always. The way I mix for a lot of artists, I start very often with the vocal, and then I fit the other elements around the vocal as opposed to starting with the kick drum and building up a world of individual sounds to make it total.

I usually like vocals to be proud, present, and clear, but sometimes I like to bury them in the mix. There's no real formula. There are a couple of guys out there that mix all of the radio songs. They are terrific mixes, but it's a mix formula, mixed to compensate for radio compression or MP3 compression or however people listen to these things. It's not very audiophile. I like sonics. I'm not really about the loudest thing on the radio at all.

Every mix you do creates a different feeling. It elicits different emotions in people. Some make you dance; some make you lie back and have a glass of wine. Some dissipate anger; some create energy. Some are just happy. Music is all about that. I do different things depending on the song. You know, maybe you want people to turn it up and get a little angry, so you'll tuck the voice back in the mix a little bit. It might not sound the same when everyone is doing Shuffle mode on the iPod, but everything is meant to do different things.

The singers I work with are very much character voices, in a way. Steven Tyler [Aerosmith] has a unique voice. Steve Perry and the singers who have followed him in Journey have distinctive voices. So, you know you're starting off with big, hall-type ambience on a Journey record, because that's just trademark of the stadium-rock sound that they've created. You bury that a little bit from band to band, depending on the emotion that you want to create, but I try to create it like a unique space for each artist so that they sound different. It's kind of predetermined by which band the person is in and where they are in the stature of the band.

Personally, I really like dry vocal sounds. I love having a nice, crisp, compressed, dry vocal. Sometimes a little tail on it will stick it to the track a lot better. One of the cool things about the early '60s recordings and early '70s recordings was that things really did stick together. There was a glue in those mixes that you sometimes don't get now. Sometimes I'll use a little slap to stick stuff to the track so it doesn't sound that separate.

Certainly an analog tape slap works, but I'm not opposed to using a digital slap now, especially if you roll with some of the top-end stuff that actually sounds like an analog tape slap. The slap doesn't need to be a high-quality thing. In fact, the higher quality, the less effective it is with all the top end being repeated. I'll normally put a low-pass filter on them anyway, so you get rid of the sibilances and create some depth to the voice. The brighter it is, the more transient the slap, and then it becomes more like an effect, as opposed to functioning as glue.

Compression is the most important thing for me, in creating that glue and depth. One of the things that it will do is bring up the natural reverb or the slap in a room. I definitely use slap, but they're pretty generic pieces.

Of the compressors I like, the 1176 LA Audio Classic is my favorite, which I use on drums. I like the SSL compressor. Then there are these Peavey VCLs, which I kind of have really been digging. They're like my pseudo-Fairchilds...my secret Fairchilds. They're inexpensive compressors, and they're great.

I try to think of drums as one instrument. Very often I will end up having the entire drum kit sub-grouped on one fader controlling the group. I like to get the drums sounding like they're kicking you, and then I adjust them as one instrument. For me, it's not like kick drum down or snare drum down. Bring the whole lot down together. I treat them very much the same when it comes to reverbs. You'll mostly find that when I put a reverb on, I'll put it on a room microphone rather than put them on individual drums and things like that. It kind of makes them easier to fit together.

I don't really get off on hearing a lot of separation. As much as I love to hear Steely Dan's clinically perfect recordings, I would never do that myself. In fact, I never use a hi-hat microphone in a drum mix at all, because it's all about the whole sound of the drum kit. It's not all about the sound of the individual instruments.

Sometimes I'll just put the whole set through a compressor and compress the whole set as one instrument and have nothing else hitting that compressor. Also, if you compress drums like that, you don't get pulsating in the other instruments. You can get them pumping on their own, and you can layer a vocal on top of that and not have it reacting to the dynamics of the drums in such a way that it pulls them into them.

For guitars, I often use the Peavey Kosmos, which is a spectral enhancer. I use it to put the guitars beyond the wings of the speakers. It's almost like the phase thing happening in the middle where it gets wider. It allows me to get more room for the drums and the vocals. So, you kind of carve out the middle and push them aside a little; I find it works very well. The Kosmos isn't a phase device. There is a phase quotient to it. If you listen to just that signal in mono, you'll see that there's plenty of out-of-phase information when you're only using one source. You don't hear it in the track. Actually, you feel it in the track, and that makes it go wider. Not like QSound, though. It's different from QSound.

There is always the issue of where you deal with placing all of the instruments, but you have to find space for them, whether it's in the pan field or whether it's in the three-dimensional depth field. All of those things are just as important. When you have conflicting frequencies, you make an allowance for them where you'll find a place for each one. So, if you have a guitar and a vocal biting the same place in the upper midrange, you may move the guitar higher or the vocal lower. You'll change the nature of them, depending on the sound.

In my productions, I like to make sure I've put in enough stuff for audiophiles to enjoy, as well as be accessible and enjoyable for listeners with a boom box or iPod. Also, radio has always had its own kind of compression and limiting, too, that affects things. It's important to consider all these things.

Tom Tucker

Credits include: Prince, Chaka Khan, Lucinda Williams, Jonny Lang, George Benson, Mavis Staples, Big Head Todd and the Monsters, Tuck & Patti, Joan Baez. See the Appendix for Tom Tucker's full bio.

It is important to stay in the tune when you are mixing and never kid yourself, "Is this magic? Do I have goose bumps, yet?" If I am not getting goose bumps, then I should ask, "What is wrong?" I try to keep it exciting, and sometimes that means starting over or regrouping.

I guess the biggest lesson I have learned is not to get carried away on any one thing. If the snare drum is driving me nuts, and I find that is all I can think about, then I may blow the whole mix.

I very much like to put in a long day, like 12 hours, and then leave the mix up and come in with a real fresh head in the morning. I want to make sure that I am not kidding myself about there being magic there.

You can't make a performance be magical if it isn't there in the tracks. That is something that all young engineers should know. I quit trying to do that years ago. You can enhance things in a mix, but I learned that you have to work with quality people, or you may just be kidding yourself.

Particularly in R&B, the groove itself should be magical. By that, I mean that the groove should be hooky, before you even hear a single note of the song. I look to put all of that together, so that it is all meshing together very well.

Paul Peterson [Prince's bassist] plays a five-string that really growls around 40 Hz, which is really nice. Prince became fond of that, so between the Moog basses and the five-string basses being able to get the real deep thing going on, I don't think there is a record that I have done in the last five to six years that doesn't have a lot of 40 Hz on it, for example.

In the old days, we couldn't do that because they couldn't cut it on vinyl. Now with CDs, we don't have to be afraid of bottom end, and I really like to pound that on. I limit it pretty heavily going in with tube limiters, like the Summit, and then, in the mixing process, I like to use the Neve 33609, which I hit pretty hard. I am also very fond of Avalon EQ. It is very common for me to use Pultec or GML on the program, but the Avalon stuff is just unbelievable. It is 50-volt bipolar, it goes down to 18 hertz, and it has the high frequencies up to 25 kHz, so you can put a lot of air on the top and really get the bottom to be big, too.

My technique of equalization is normally subtractive. I begin my mixing with subtractive EQ. It is less phasey to do that as well, versus additive EQ. It is a little more difficult technique, but once you learn it, you can build holes in the musical spectrum, all the way from 1.5 kHz down to 150 Hz, opening those areas for the other instruments to speak through. I think it very typical that the lower midrange is the "mud" area. Often keyboards, like Rhodes sounds, are all lower midrange. By opening the window in the other instruments, the vocals can speak through there.

I love the really great-sounding EQs for additive EQs, like the API, the old Neves, and Pultecs. If I use any additive EQs, it is usually that. If I want something to be crunchy, I use SSL EQs, like for drums. However, I use a couple of different EQs for the bottom. I will use the SSL EQ in the 80- to 150-Hz range, because it is kind of punchy, and then for the deeper stuff, where I really want the subs to be pure, I will go to an Avalon or Pultec.

The API is very clean and pristine. It can get harsh, though. If something is already a little harsh, I might opt to add the Neve for the additive EQ or a Pultec, which has a very soft top.

I don't gate anything while I record it. You can really screw things up. It really bothers me when anybody does that. There is really no reason to gate something while you are recording. I pretty much always use Drawmer gates, like on the toms, snare, and kick, when I am mixing, because they are frequency selective. If I am in a studio that doesn't have Drawmers, I will use Kepex, but I will key them off of an EQ, so that they are frequency selective. That is very critical.

Toms will ring and put a rumble through everything. It is like a big low-grade cloud, so the gating process is really important in the mixdown situation.

If I have any say over the mastering and I know that it is going to go to radio, I probably will ask that some of the real deep low end get knifed off, just because it isn't going to translate, and so that it won't grab it too hard. I think for radio, if it sounds a little crunchy, it's better.

I naturally go for a very even, natural sonic spectrum. The kick drum, the snare and the bass, and the lead vocal are probably all at equal levels. Those particular instruments won't get in the way of a lead vocal either. The lead vocal can feel really loud, and those things will not clobber the vocal, in terms of hearing the lyrics.

Matt Wallace

Credits include: Faith No More, X, Burning Spear, John Hiatt, the Replacements, Michael Franti & Spearhead, O.A.R., Maroon 5, Blues Traveler, Train. See the Appendix for Matt Wallace's full bio.

For me, when the concept of building a mix is mentioned, my approach tends to be backwards from some of the folks I know who do a lot of mixing. I tend to start from the vocal and the guitar and kind of build down to the drums, instead of starting from the drums and building up. For me, most songs tend to "live" between the voice and an acoustic or electric guitar or some kind of keyboard.

As I build the voice, guitars and keyboards, or whatever, I will get the balances set and then I will mute the lead vocal and listen to the play between the instruments to make sure that the EQs are right and that sort of thing.

To me, it has been easy to get the drums to sound good or big. In the past, if I got things sounding good and massive from the drums up, it might be like, "Where does the voice fit?"

The problem I had, building a mix up from the drums, was that you'd find yourself EQing the voice to be heard in the mix instead of EQing the voice to sound wonderful. I think that is slightly backwards. The voice is really the reason we listen to most songs. I try and get it to sound really great and then build around it.

I've had a lot of success in the past mixing with a lot of compression, but over the years I've learned to use less and less stereo bus compression. Stereo bus compression can be like an instant shot of heroin. You can push it on, and all of a sudden, it is like, "Wow, this mix sounds like the radio." The problem with that is that it tends not to force me to focus on what is or is not working in a mix. If you put enough compression on it, you can pretty much make anything kind of stand up and work.

You can actually start fighting compression in a mix because you get to a point where you've got to turn up your voice a little louder, and you push the voice up, and suddenly the compression from the kick or the entire mix will start to suck it down. It really opened my eyes when I was mixing. One day, while I was mixing, I went, "What the heck? I'll turn the compression off." My mix sounded horrendous. It was like, "Oh my God! What is going on here?" It was really unbalanced.

Now, I may mix for six or eight hours, and once I really feel that the mix is in its place, I will go, "Okay, now with the addition of minimal compression, it should actually help and give things that extra sheen or gloss that kind of glues everything together." It has certainly made me work a lot harder as a mixer and try to make things work on a more organic level. At that point, compression is kind of the icing on the cake, instead of the main spice or ingredient.

Conceptually, the major questions in starting a mix are, "What am I going for? Am I going for something that is loose and slightly sloppy, or am I going for something really polished and hi-fi, or do I want lo-fi? What kind of feeling do I want the listener to have at the end of the day? Should it be very together and tight and well performed and mixed, or should it be a little more organic-sounding? Should the listener be impressed with the technical prowess of the musicians, or should people be moved to tears by the feeling of the performance?" All those things are in the forefront of my mind. You can mix a song any number of ways. You can bring things to the forefront that will draw you in or things to the forefront that are really aggressive and impressive. It really depends on where you are going with it.

I also have a theory that a good mix really isn't necessarily the same as a perfectly balanced or EQ'd mix. It is really all about the emotion and feeling. For the most part, I think that perfect mixes can be boring. I like it when things are slightly odd or interesting or flawed. When it gets down to it, with all of the equipment that we have these days, with automated mixes and delays to put things in time, with harmonizers and putting things in Pro Tools, you can actually create a technically perfect recording and mix pretty much anyone off the street. But does it actually move someone, and is it something that is a little unique? When you listen to some of those Jimi Hendrix mixes, there are phase anomalies where you can barely hear the drums at all. Everything is swimming in the mix, and occasionally the tom toms will jump out of nowhere. From a rhythmic technical perspective, they are horrible, but from an emotional spiritual place, they are outstanding. You listen to that stuff and go, "Oh God, I must be on some awesome drug here. What this guy is putting across has got me in his sway."

An emotional mix can enable me to remove myself as a professional and go, "Oh my God!" Maybe for five minutes, I have forgotten about my bills and life and everything. When I actually get an emotional response, I want to go jump in my car and go buy that record and listen to it a million times. It is just wonderful, and that is what it is all about, whether I am speaking as a fan or as a professional.

Jim Scott

Credits include: Tom Petty, Red Hot Chili Peppers, Wilco, Sting, Ride, Dixie Chicks, Lucinda Williams, the Rolling Stones, Pete Yorn, Foo Fighters, Counting Crows, Matchbox Twenty, Weezer. See the Appendix for Jim Scott's full bio.

It's important to be a decision maker. There are a million reasons why people don't decide. A lot of it is bad habit, a lot of it is time management…might be better for me to do it than for them to try and do a bad edit. Then you spend all your day taking clicks and ticks and pops out of bad edits that they didn't properly create when they were doing their file management.

If someone sends me a track, and they haven't comped the guitars, and there are five guitars, I can comp that guitar as fast as you can play back those five tracks. I'll know where the good stuff is and how to put it together. It might be one whole take, it might be 10 edits in between all five tracks, but I'll decide if that's what they want me to do. I will do that, and I will do it really quickly and decisively.

There were decades where people would expect you to do 30 mixes of a song—vocal up, vocal down, guitars up, guitars down, guitars up, vocal down, guitars up, bass up….Every combination geometrically increasing in number of mixes per change… I feel sorry for all those wasted hours now and all the tape that went into the landfill, because it's just not important. It's not necessary. To have that minutiae and the details that people thought they were experiencing in those moments was probably real, but 10 years later, 10 days later, 10 minutes later, none of that means anything.

Nowadays, when I mix I just do a couple of options. I'll do a vocal up, because I really like the vocal up. I'll do one mix where I think it's really right, and then I'll do one with the vocal a little louder, and I'll do one a little quieter in case someone thinks I've just stepped on the pedal to hard. But that's about it, plus a TV mix and an instrumental mix.

On Wilco's album, *Sky Blue Sky*, there was one mix of every song, because we mixed the record by hand. There was no computer involved. It was on tape. It was a performance sort of situation where you started the song at the beginning, and you did all the rides on one go at one performance. When you got it right, and Jeff Tweedy agreed that it was right, the mix was done and that was it…period. Thank you. Done. There was no instrumental mix, no TV mix, no vocal up or down or guitar loud. It was like that's a performance from everybody—from the band, from the mixer guy. It's a great record, because the music that was recorded was good, and it all comes down to cool guys singing a cool song with a cool band playing it. Why is there so much fear and mystery? Why do we have to have all these options? Why don't we just have what it is? It is what it is. "Is the bass really too loud?" "No." "Is it really too quiet?" "No." "It's fine. I hear it." "How does that snare sound?" "Fine! I guess…it's a fine snare sound." "Does it have to have more crack or more reverb on it?" "No. It could…but why? It sounds great this way." That's how we talked about it. That's how we wanted it. I like it. You like it. The artist likes it. If you went home and played it for your girlfriend, she'd like it. If she played it for the girls at the office, they'd like it. Why are we even talking about this anymore? It's good music.

Left column top to bottom: Inspirational music books (photo by Rick Clark) / Jim Dickinson (photo courtesy of Mary Lindsay Dickinson) / Marty Stuart's American Odyssey, XM/Sirius Satellite Radio at Eastwood Studios (left to right) Eric Fritsch (owner, chief engineer), Rick Clark (producer), Marty Stuart (chief visualizer) (photo by Tzuriel Fenigshtein). Right column top to bottom: 5.1 and The Secret Teachings of All Ages (photo by Rick Clark) / Studio charms at Jim Scott's PLYRZ Studios (photo by Jimmy Stratton) / Calexico's John Convertino - Los Super 7 sessions (photo by Rick Clark) / Calexico's Paul Niehaus - Los Super 7 sessions (photo by Rick Clark).

Recording Strings and Orchestras

There is nothing quite like the sound of a great string section or orchestra. A magic performance of a great symphony, concerto, or chamber piece is arguably every bit as powerful as any inspired rock, R&B, or jazz performance. Since the advent of popular recorded music, orchestras and string sections have been appropriated to elevate the emotional delivery of a recording or live performance. In some cases, the integration of symphonic or chamber elements to a band track have been nothing more than sweetening. In other cases, such as the Beatles' "A Day in the Life," it has been an essential part of the composition's integrity.

For this chapter, I talked to experts who have recorded orchestras and chamber groups for serious classical music projects, as well as those who have primarily worked within the popular music contexts. I've given them some space to share some important ideas on how to do it right. I would like to thank Milan Bogdan, Richard Dodd, Ellen Fitton, Bud Graham, Mark Evans, and Tony Visconti for their generous gift of time and insight for this subject.

Richard Dodd

Credits: Tom Petty, Dixie Chicks, Wilco, Boz Scaggs, George Harrison, Traveling Wilburys, Roy Orbison, Clannad, Francis Dunnery, Sheryl Crow, Red Hot Chili Peppers, Green Day. See the Appendix for Richard Dodd's full bio.

There are so many factors, other than the technical side, that make for a good string sound or recording. To focus on the method of recording strings and just to talk about microphones and that sort of stuff would be very remiss. If there's an art for me, it's in encouraging the people to be at their best, which gives me an opportunity to be at mine. That's the only art involved, really. The rest of it is a series of choices, very few of them wrong. The microphone is almost irrelevant. In fact, if mics were invisible, it would be the best thing in the world.

Nevertheless, if you have a pretty good quality microphone, used in a pretty conventional, orthodox manner, it is hard to mess things up if all the other factors are right. Sometimes people can drop into a session while you are recording a big 60-piece orchestra, and it will sound amazing, and they think you are great; but truthfully, it is sometimes easier to record an orchestra than to record a solo guitar and voice. It really is.

You have 30-odd string players out there, and it doesn't matter if three of them don't play at their peak all of the time. The spectacle and what they produce can be quite amazing.

It really comes down to the caliber of musician—I can't emphasize that enough—and that musician having something worth playing, and the person next to him doing his job, too. If they respect the leader and the arranger, and they don't mind the music—it's very rare they are going to like it in a pop commercial world—then you're onto a good thing. Give them some fun and compliment them. Everybody likes that. After all, they're human, and there are a lot of them in an orchestra.

Here's one little tip to make things better. I used to go around the studio—especially in the summer in England, when it was dry—and spray the room with a spray gun (the kind used for plants) before the musicians would arrive. I would go around and soak the cloth walls, and the humidity would gradually leak into the room. It just made things better. I found that I preferred the sound of a wet, humid environment to a dry environment. I think it makes the sound more sonorous. I observed that when it was raining, it sounded better than when it wasn't. Not having air conditioning helped the sound—but not the players—because it wasn't de-humidifying.

I also think it adds more of a psychological effect than anything. If you see someone taking care, it tends to impress you. There is a comfort factor as well. If someone isn't comfortable, then he isn't going to play well, so imposing the humidity was a good thing. It made people think that you cared and in turn would give you an edge.

You know, you can have the best players in the world, but if they don't like the arranger, the engineer, the studio, or the person sitting next to them, they are not going to play their best. Even though they might try, it just won't happen. Yet, if they have a smile on their face, it comes through. You should try to make them comfortable, and try not to take advantage of them, and treat them with respect. It's the best thing you can do. They deserve your respect, because they have trained very hard to be where they are. If you do that, you can have some great days with them.

There are numerous recording strings tips, in terms of indoctrination, that I could share. My first session around string players happened when I had been assisting maybe about two weeks. Unbeknownst to me, the engineer had arranged for the lead violinist to teach me a lesson that I wouldn't forget. He told me that I must walk carefully when I walked around the players and the instruments. Make my presence felt. Speak firmly and clearly so people would know I was there. And don't creep up on anyone, because some of the instruments they are holding are worth thousands and thousands of dollars. You don't want to have an accident. So the engineer set me up to adjust a mic on the first fiddle, at the leader's desk, and I had done everything he had told me to do. As I stepped back to make my final tweak on the microphone, he slipped an empty wooden matchbox under my foot. The sound of crushing wood under your foot is something you never forget. [Laughs] It was very clever and a good education. You can tell people all you like about being careful, but there is nothing like that adrenaline rush of "Oh my God, there went my career before it's even started." You remember things like that.

Ellen Fitton

Credits: Wynton Marsalis, Firehouse, Dionne Warwick, Bee Gees, Chaka Khan, Jessye Norman, Yo-Yo Ma, Kathleen Battle, Chicago Symphony, Philadelphia Orchestra, New York Philharmonic. See the Appendix for Ellen Fitton's full bio.

Classic music is all editing. It involves hundreds of takes and hundreds of splices. That's how classical records get made. You usually are talking about maybe 200 takes for the average record, but we did 15 Christmas songs for a Kathleen Battle record, and there were 2,000 takes. When I say *take*, it's not complete start-to-finish recordings of all of the material. It's little inserts and sections. There might only be several complete takes. Then they record a section at a time or a movement at a time, or there might be a series of bars that they play eight or nine times until they get it right. It's that sort of thing.

The function of the producer in a classical record is kind of different than in a pop record, because they're really sitting with the score, listening to each take, and making sure that each bar is covered completely by the end of the session or series of sessions. They have to make sure they have all the right notes that they need, and then they have to come up with an edit plan to put it all together. There's no drum machine or sequencers. So that's how classical gets it right.

The producer has to keep track of tempo, pitch, and how loudly or softly the orchestra played each section. The producer also has to know that if the orchestra plays the piece with a different intensity, then the hall reacts differently. When that happens, the takes don't match.

It is important to familiarize oneself with the piece of music being recorded, so you will know instrumentation-wise what you have, how much percussion there is, and whether there are any little solo bits by the principals in the orchestra. Then you start laying out microphones. We prepare a whole mic list before we go wherever we're going. We take specific microphones, specific mic preamps out with us when we go. All of the recording is done on location, in whatever hall we choose, and we take all of our own gear with us. Tape machines, patch bays, consoles—everything gets put in a case and packed up and taken with us.

For the most part, you want a fairly reverberant hall, but you don't want it so reverberant that it starts to become mush. A good hall should have at least a couple of seconds of reverb time.

Normally what we have is a main pickup, which is usually what we call a *tree*. It contains three microphones set up in sort of a triangular form, and they are usually just behind the conductor, about 10 feet up in the air. Some are 8 feet, some are 12; it depends on the hall. We use B&K's 4006s or 4009s because they're really nice omnis that are really clear and clean. They have a nice high end and give you a good blend.

The goal with classical recording is to try to get it with that main pickup, and the input from all the other mics is just icing on the cake. If you end up in a really bad hall or a hall you don't know, then you end up using much more of the other mics.

Bud Graham

Credits: New York Philharmonic, Philadelphia Orchestra, Boston Philharmonic, Cleveland Symphony. See the Appendix for Bud Graham's full bio.

My feeling of string miking is quite different than normal pop miking. I like to mike from much more of a distance. It is a question of taste. My feeling is that if everything is miked close, the strings are kind of piercing and sharp. I prefer a mellower string sound, and that is the way I like to do it. It is my style. Again, it is a classical sound, as opposed to a pop sound, where everything is close miked, and people desire a more biting sound.

I like the natural room ambiance, but I am more constrained by a good or bad hall. If you are miking close, and it is not a good hall, you are not really hurt by it. If I am miking at a distance, and it is a bad hall, it is going to sound bad. It has to be a good hall for my type of miking to work. It has to have ambiance, and it has to have a high ceiling.

Some of the great halls—Carnegie, the Princeton University Hall, the Concertgebouw in Holland—are hard to get because they are booked well in advance. You have to book many months in advance to get a good hall.

I favor B&K 4006s for violins to cellos. For bass, tympani, French horns, tuba, and other brass, I like Neumann TLM 170s, which are great mics for darker-sounding instruments. For vocal choruses and harp, I choose Schoeps MK 4s. Neumann KM 140s work well for percussion.

While I've done many projects that involved a combination of many close and distant mics, I feel that the proper application of a minimal number—like a couple of omni-directional mics placed out front—can achieve some of the most ideal results.

On occasion, it works very well to work with two microphones, usually placed at 7 or 8 feet behind the conductor with the two microphones placed at 7 or 8 feet apart. Depending on the hall, though, it might be 12 to 15 feet high.

The placement and focusing of the microphones is important. At one time, an engineer said to me, "What difference does it make, because you are using omni-directional microphones?" I said, "Well yeah, but it may be only omni-directional at certain frequencies." The focusing is extremely important. It isn't just something that you put up and aim in the general direction of the orchestra. It has to be properly focused, or you will get too dark of a sound.

In order to focus, I would focus between where the first and second violins meet on the left side. I would try to aim it down so it was kind of cutting the strings in half, between the first and second violins. The one on the right side would be doing the same thing, aimed where the violas and cellos would come together. The leakage from the brass would come in and give it distance and provide a nice depth view. If I aimed too far back, then the strings would get dull, and they would lose their clarity. It may also get more brass than you wanted. By focusing the mics at the strings, with the brass coming in, it gives the recording a lovely depth of field.

I found that when the two mics worked, and you listened to it, you could hear the difference between the first horn and the second and the third, with the first one being slightly left of center. The second one would be left of that, and the third one would be left of the second. It gives a wonderful depth and spread.

I once heard a CD where the horns sounded like they were not playing together at all with the orchestra. It was a recording where all these multiple microphones were used. Every one of them came at a different time factor, so that what actually happened was that it sounded like a badly performing orchestra. Actually, it was because of the lack of clarity that was created by all of this leakage. You were hearing the instruments coming to the picture all at different times. The problem wasn't the orchestra; it was the miking process.

While many engineers still favor analog for recording, I feel that digital is more than fine and just requires a little rethinking, as it concerns mic placement to achieve that warm sound.

Digital is a cleaner medium than analog, and now that we are using 20-bit, there is a noticeable difference. Analog is like a window that has a little bit of haze on it. When you put it to digital, you clean up that window, and it gets to be a little too crisp and sharp. We then learned that we had to change our techniques a little bit. What we had to do, when we started moving in from analog to digital, was to not mike as close. As a result, the air did some of the softening or mellowing that analog would do.

Tony Visconti

Credits: David Bowie, Morrissey, T. Rex, the Moody Blues, the Strawbs, Gentle Giant, the Move, Sparks, Thin Lizzy, Caravan, Boomtown Rats, Dexy's Midnight Runners, U2, Adam Ant. See the Appendix for Tony Visconti's full bio.

Recording strings is a huge subject. It must be looked at as both a recording technique and a writing technique. I've heard a string quintet sound enormous at Lansdowne Studios in London in the late '60s. I asked Harry, the engineer, how he managed to make them sound so big, and he humbly replied, "It's in the writing, mate!" That was probably the biggest lesson I've ever learned about recording and writing for strings. I've also heard big-budget string sections sound small and MIDI-like due to the unimaginative writing of the novice arranger. I also must stay with strings in the pop/rock context because there are certain things that apply here only and not in the classical world, with which I have very little experience.

The violin family is several hundred years old, more powerful descendants of the viol family, which used gut strings and not the more powerful metal strings we're used to today. The violin family [which includes the viola, cello, and bass] have a rich cluster of overtones that make them sound the way they do, and there are many ways of enhancing these overtones in recording. When used in a pop context, the huge hall and sparse mike technique of the classical world won't work with the tight precision of a rock track. Especially nowadays, when we are getting fanatical if our MIDI strings are two ticks off center. The reverberation of a huge room is often anti-tightness. Recently, I did some live recording in a large London room with a singer, also playing piano, accompanied by a 40-piece scaled-down symphony orchestra. When I counted in, I had to leave off the number four because the reverberation of my voice leaked onto the first beat of the song. I know—it's every engineer's dream to record strings in a huge room, but no matter how huge the room is, artificial reverb is added in the mix anyway. Recording pop or rock is not reality! You could never record a loud rock band and a moderate-size string section in the same room anyway.

Ideally, I like to work with a small section consisting of minimally 12 violins, four violas, three celli, and one double bass. I like them to be in a room that would fit about double that amount of players, with a ceiling no lower than 12 feet. I have worked with the same size ensemble in smaller rooms with great results too, because the reverb is always added in the mix anyway. But the dimensions of the room help round out the lower frequencies of the instruments. I like to close mike to get the sound of the bow on the string. If a string section is playing to a rock track, you must hear that resin! So I will have one mic per two players for violins and violas, always top-quality condenser mics! For the celli and bass, I prefer one mic each, aimed at one f-hole and where the bow touches the strings. Then I place a stereo pair above the entire ensemble to catch the warmth of the ensemble, and I use these mics about 50 percent and the spot mics 50 percent in the mix. If I record a smaller group, I use more or less the same mics. A string quartet gets one mic each, plus the stereo pair for the ensemble sound. If I had a larger section, I'd use one mic per four violins, et cetera. Of course, with lots of mics, a phase check should be carefully made—it's the same problem as when you are miking a large drum kit.

In a perfect world, I love to record each section on a separate track, dividing the violins into two sections and the ambiance on separate tracks too. Often I have fewer tracks than that, and sometimes only two tracks are left for the entire string section. Then it's a careful balancing act with more lower strings in the balance than what appears to be normal. When using strings with a rock track, there is a lot of competition in the low end, and the low strings seem to disappear.

I don't approach strings as something from another, more aesthetic world. If strings are to go over a tough rock track, then they must be recorded tough. I've seen many a cool rock engineer intimidated by the sight of a room full of middle-aged players and $30,000,000 worth of Stradivarius. If the track is loud and raucous, then the strings should be recorded likewise. It's also quite appropriate to record with a fair amount of compression so that the energy matches that of the guitars and bass [also stringed instruments].

Headphones also changed the way strings are recorded. When I first started writing for strings in London, the players refused headphones. I had to wear them and conduct furiously to keep them in time. Often we had to play the backing track in the room through a speaker for them, which would lead to leakage problems. That was sometimes a blessing on the mix, but often not! In the early '70s, the younger string players knew that their elders were always chronically behind the beat, and so they "invented" the technique of listening to half a headphone—the right ear is listening to the track, and the left ear to the fiddle. Remember, those things don't have frets!

As for writing, my Cecil Forsythe book on orchestration—my bible—has over 60 pages devoted to the violin alone. I won't go into this deeply here, but the writing of some classical composers is worth examining when writing for a rock track. Beethoven comes to mind. Because the violin family doesn't have frets, you must have the minimum of one or three players per part. Otherwise, the tuning will be abominable! It is impossible for two players to play in tune for any length of time. One player can only be in tune with himself. But with three, according to the law of averages, one will be in tune, one will be sharp, and the other one will be flat. This will temper the tuning of the part. With a small section, I don't write in the very high registers—a few instruments will sound squeaky up there. With very high writing, I almost always have half the violins playing the same part an octave lower.

There are so many ways of playing a violin. For more warmth, they can clip a small lead weight on the bridge, and this is called a *mute*, or *sordino* in Italian. This works well against acoustic guitar–based tracks. For pizzicato [plucking the strings with a finger], the volume often drops considerably. This can be addressed two ways. Warn the engineer so that he can push up the faders on pizzicato passages or ask the players to stand up and play, putting them closer to the mics. For col legno, in a concert the players tap the strings with the wood side of the bow; in the studio, a pencil sounds much better. Try col legno sometimes instead of pizzicato— you'll be surprised.

A final word on professionalism when recording strings: A room full of string players is very, very expensive. Each player is being paid hundreds for three hours of work. You should set up and test all mics and headphones the night before or at least two hours before the session. [String players start arriving an hour before the session time.] You don't want to be setting up with 20 temperamental musicians underfoot—not to mention the odd violin, which is very easy to step on. With mic stands, allow room for bowing [the right elbow]. Give each two players one mic stand to share. Check for squeaky chairs and replace them! Because you have to get a sound very quickly on such an expensive section, ask every section to play the loudest section of the arrangement several times. In other words, if you are using three mics for six first violins, have each pair of players play separately from the other four. When your mic levels and EQ are achieved [EQ the first mic and match the other two with the same settings], ask them all to play at once to check that the three mics are truly capturing six musicians equally. These are mixed to one track, so get it right, dude! Then do the same with the rest of the players. This should take about 10 minutes tops, and then you can get on with the pleasures of recording 20 highly trained experts!

Milan Bogdan

Credits: Marvin Gaye, KC and the Sunshine Band, Funkadelic, Merle Haggard, Barbara Mandrell. See the Appendix for Milan Bogdan's full bio.

There is a lot to cutting strings. It isn't just setting up the microphones. If you want to do it right, it takes a lot of time, and the setup is all-critical. You have to know the room you are in and what its characteristics are. Is it heavy at 400 cycles, and should you turn that down? If so, then you don't want to put the lower strings in that area of the room, because it will muddy up the whole thing. It is the technique of listening to the whole room and then knowing where to stick the microphones and the instruments in that room.

Sometimes, we will dampen the room down. We might put carpet down on the floor, if it is too live. My preference, however, is for a more live kind of room.

Even though I like a live room, phasing can be more of a problem. You may encounter reflections coming back from a wall that may be almost as loud as the original source signal. You can get an echo effect that causes the strings to lose their presence. That now comes into the microphone technique of where and how far away it is from the instrument.

Omni microphones are always the flattest and the best sounding and more preferable than a cardioid pattern. In some instances, I have to switch to a cardioid pattern to knock out some of the reflections in the back, if they get too loud.

To me, the high-voltage mics always sound better than just the phantom-powered mics. That is why I like the Neumanns—the 47s, 67s, and 87s—and the high-voltage B&K and Schoeps mics with the power supply on the floor. The 4000 Series high-voltage B&Ks, especially for violins, are magnificent. They are mind-boggling. They are probably my favorite for miking the room and miking the strings.

For smaller sections, it obviously is a smaller, more intimate sound right away. Usually, I will mike each instrument by itself and get a closer, more up-front, present kind of sound. I will usually use a couple of B&Ks in the room. I am paying more attention to each individual instrument than I am to the overall room sound. When there is less of a phasing problem, then it is easier to make the whole thing work.

For solo cello, I like to use an Audio-Technica 4041A. I would mike it fairly close, but that would depend on the room and how live it is. I would mike it fairly close to the large part of the body of the instrument, because that mic is so bright.

For bass fiddle, I would use a 47 tube and put it toward the body in front of the instrument, either slightly below or slightly above where the bow is actually touching the strings.

For violin, I usually mike overhead, but here is also certain amount of sound that comes from under the instrument itself. It depends on what you are trying to get. You get a fuller sound underneath. If you are miking from both sides, the producer might say, "I don't like [the bow side sound]. That is too scratchy." A lot of times, it isn't that it is too scratchy. You are just getting too much of the bow. So I just turn that mic down and bring the other one up. All of a sudden, the producer likes it, and I didn't change the EQ, and I didn't have to change the mic.

I very seldom EQ strings as I record. There is no way to duplicate that. I would rather put some on later. I am so busy dealing with the mix and the blend and the phasing that I don't have time to mess with the EQ. That is why I pick good mics and just do it right that way.

Mark Evans

The following contribution by Mark Evans pertains to his specific approach to recording the Prague Symphony Orchestra for Kevin Kiner's score for the George Lucas movie, Star Wars: The Clone Wars. *See the Appendix for Mark Evans's full bio.*

I'm a close-mike guy. It's a little annoying to record an orchestra and not have at least some kind of real control in the mix. I don't like the sound of an orchestra with the cellos and basses just kind of spread everywhere and when there's just no focus.

When you hear soundtracks like *The Bourne Identity*, there is a lot of edge and impact in the orchestral sound. You can't get that without close miking the instruments. Of course, samples might be employed to get some of that sound, but whenever you can, it is nice when you can get that impact with the real instruments. I will usually put 10 mics on 10 cellos and six mics on the six basses and basically just bus them to a stereo panning array.

For recording Kevin Kiner's score for George Lucas' *Clone Wars*, we used a 100-piece orchestra in Prague. I had 50 mics in, plus a Decca Tree,* as well as a set of U 87s as surround mikes set in the middle of the room. I have two sets of custom cardioid mics built by a good friend of mine, Howard Gale of Zentec. I always use them in an ORTF array on the front of the Decca Tree (these are the most important mics in the room) and the U 87s in omni on the left-rights.

*The Decca Tree mike technique employs three usually omni-directional microphones placed in a triangle, with one microphone in front, closer to the sound source. Decca Tree is most popular for orchestral and large string section recordings in large acoustically designed rooms or halls and is commonly used in Hollywood film soundtracks. The advantages of the Decca Tree are similar to the M-S mike technique over AB in the fact that you have the ability to adjust the center microphone, thus adjusting the power and central pull of the sound. AB Stereo Microphone Technique is sometimes criticized for lacking a central pull and being too wide a stereo image when placed close to a sound source. The Decca Tree began as a modified AB, adding the center forward spaced microphone. Original size of the T or Triangle was 2 meters wide and 1.5 meters deep. (Definition courtesy of WikiRecording.)

I used the Earthworks QTC50 mics as overheads on the violins. They are incredible microphones. There is a certain warmth and silkiness these microphones possess that works out great on the violins. It's not so much you hear it as you can feel it.

I wound up using KM 84s all the way across the basses and the cellos, and it gave the sound the kind of urgency I was looking for, and it ended up sounding great.

I've seen so many guys mike French horns from the front [the bells are facing the other way], or I've seen guys mike them really high, from the back. One of the big qualities Kevin Kiner wanted with the French horns on the *Clone Wars* score was for them to be really in your face. We had eight French horns in the section, and I close miked them from the rear, about 3 feet away. I had two A-B stereo arrays behind them. I used four TLM-103s, which I like to use on the brass. It's a very good-sounding mic. It's bright, and it really can stand some high sound pressure. There actually wasn't much room to mike them from the rear. I was really taking a chance, but I just had to do it. The Studio in Prague had a baffle around the French horns and was just relying on the reflection of the sound, which in the end made the horns sound behind the beat to me. I also miked them from the front with the RØDE X/Y stereo microphone. This is because we used Wagner horns on some of the cues. They are actually played with the bells facing forward. The combination of X/Y microphone and the close mics sounded great on the French horns. It really worked very well.

When you're miking an orchestra, you don't really have a chance to say, "Hey, hold it there guys! It's not working, sorry. We're gonna have to stop!" [Laughs]

I know Kevin Kiner's writing really well. I knew what he was going to go for; he wants things to be rocking! We call it "The Rock and Roll Orchestra Sound."

It's always a challenge to make the percussion sound as good as a sample library. The sample libraries that are out there now are incredible because they have so much definition. It's just in your face, and you can't really do that with a bunch live guys in one room. We had six percussionists in the orchestra; with all those wide-open microphones, it was really hard to get the definition on any of the percussion, but I think I was able to do it. It's always a challenge when you have everyone playing live in one room.

I usually like to give the soundstage mixers enough stems so they'll have options and can actually do something with the orchestral elements. Close miking the strings really helps the stems. As a result, they actually had control over the urgency of the strings; although in the case of *Clone Wars*, not one thing was touched on the orchestral score mix. When I went to hear the playback of the final mix, the mixers told me they wound up not doing anything to my mix. That felt good.

Left column top to bottom: Stephanie Smith Mabey at East Iris Recording (photo by Rick Clark) / Sam Taylor playing a 200B Wurlitzer at PLYRZ Studios (photo by Jimmy Stratton) / Piano shot (photo by Rick Clark) / Flaco Jimenez, Los Super 7 sessions (photo by Rick Clark). Right column top to bottom: John Deaderick (photo by Rick Clark) / Jaymar toy piano and Mellotron at PLYRZ Studios (photo by Jimmy Stratton) / Ronan Chris Murphy (photo by John Rodd).

Percussion

When most people think of drums, they think of the traditional trap set that contain the usual snare, toms, kick drum, hi-hat, and cymbals. Rock and roll, country, and rhythm and blues may be great American musical forms that express many rich sides of our rhythmic sensibilities, but most records in those genres offer little more than a drum kit, tambourine, and shaker of some type in the mix.

There is a world of countless exotic percussion instruments that subdivide time and define the rhythmic "pocket" with subtlety, amazing complexity, and earthy directness. This chapter attempts to touch on recording and mixing a very small part of all those things that add richness to our music.

For this chapter, I have enlisted four highly regarded engineers—Mike Couzzi, Rik Pekkonen, Eric Schilling, and Allen Sides—who have certainly done their share of accurately capturing the spirit of great percussion performances.

Mike Couzzi

Credits include: Santana, Christina Aguilera, Gloria Estefan and the Miami Sound Machine, Rod Stewart, Shakira, Juanes, Pet Shop Boys, Frank Sinatra, Ricky Martin, Art Blakey & the Jazz Messengers. See the Appendix for Mike Couzzi's full bio.

In dealing with recording most Latin music, I have the challenge of recording obscure and exotic percussion instruments from around the world. A lot of the percussionists I work with travel all over the world and bring in some really bizarre instruments. A lot of this stuff is so primitive that it's like prehistoric recording. It isn't just bringing in a shaker and a conga.

With some of these instruments, you don't know where the sound is going to come out. You hear it in the room, but you can't just stick a mic anywhere. The most important thing with recording percussion is listening to the sound in the room. You've got walk around and put your ear close to the instrument and far away and see where you really hear most of the sound and the harmonics taking place. The sound of the room, of course, is very critical. I look for a live, neutral-sounding room usually, and I will always use an ambient microphone and vary the distance for effect. A very dead room will work also, providing it adds no ugly coloration or standing waves.

Most of the time, the artist wants a fairly acoustic natural sound without a lot of processing. For miking a large drum, like congas, I might use one mic close and one ambient overhead. If there are three congas, I use an XY setup, usually three feet directly over the drums. Congas sound best placed on a wooden floor. I usually use Neumann TLM 193s or AKG 414 TL IIs, which are also my favorite mic for small handheld percussion. Both of these new-design mics sound great and have a wide dynamic range and frequency response. If I know the instrument is to be the primary percussion holding the groove together, I'll use some compression with a dbx 160 to add slap or attack. With congas, that is what most percussionists want to hear. Sometimes on small hand drums I'll use a Sennheiser 421, boosting between 4 kHz and 10 kHz.

Recently, I recorded some udu drums and Moroccan hand drums and an instrument called the box [also known as a *cajón*], which the percussionist sits on and hits with his hands like congas. It looks like a big speaker cabinet with a hole in it. I miked it in the back, outside the box hole, to get all the bottom end, but I put the mic close enough to the hole to get a lot of punch out of it, too. I put the front mic about 2 feet away to catch the slap of the hands. Both mics were Sennheiser 421s. On the udu drum, I placed a 421 in the hole and used an AKG 414 overhead. You can get a very deep sound, almost like a huge drum, just by changing the mic blend.

A batá drum is a two-headed drum that is worn around the neck and played with sticks. One side of the drum is bigger than the other, and the player hits both sides all of the time, making a rhythm. The larger head gives you more of a low impact, and the high one will give you more of like a flap sound. You can't really put a mic in the middle and get all of that. I found that for the most impact, it is better to mike both sounds, because it is kind of like two drums. You put one mic on each side, but when you do that, you usually get some low-frequency cancellation, so you have to flip one of the mics out of phase to put it back in phase, so you can get all of the low end out of it. If you don't, it will sound really small.

The same is true with the bombo, which is like a huge Andean bass drum that is played with a muffled rawhide mallet. You have to mike both sides, because they are hitting it with a mallet on one side, and you are getting that big thud on one side, and on the other side you are getting a boom coming out the back side, like a double-headed kick drum. In order to get the "boom," it is good to mike it from the back. It just gives you a big low-end sound.

A berimbau is like a tree branch with a gourd attached it with steel strings coming out of it. You play it by striking the strings with this other tree branch that looks like a bow with steel wire wrapped around it. You tune it by sliding this other prehistoric-looking piece of wood up and down the neck. It sounds like a huge Jew's harp, and it's really loud.

For that, I use a really good tube condenser microphone overhead, like a Neumann U 47, between where the musician was striking the instrument and the gourd, about 3 or 4 feet away. You are catching the room, and you are trying to get the whole instrument. If you close mike, all you will get is this weird stringy noise. You've got to get an overall picture.

When I close mike an instrument, I'm prepared for a percussionist to start wailing on his drums, so a mic with a huge dynamic range and some compression is essential for analog tape. I don't really like to overload transients on analog tape, because I find that with a lot of percussion, the sound starts to get dull, even with the new formulation tape.

As far as mixing goes, sometimes the percussion should be in your face, so I'll EQ it and compress it a lot. Sometime I'll auto-pan a shaker or other single instruments that are really thin or bright. Panning is very important, and I usually try to keep percussion as far left and right as possible—the reason being that if there is a singer or lead instrument, the percussion isn't going to fight with it.

For more ambient sounds, I'll use an AMS "room" program, which is very natural, or I'll use the newest software for the Lexicon 480 Ambiance programs. Sometimes I'll use heavily gated reverbs for impact and blend in a room or bright plate.

Rik Pekkonen

Credits include: B.B. King, Joe Cocker, Joe Jackson, the Crusaders, Dixie Dregs, Ry Cooder, Neil Young, T-Bone Burnett, Roy Orbison, Ringo Starr, Randy Newman, Iggy Pop, Garth Brooks, Ziggy Marley. See the Appendix for Rik Pekkonen's full bio.

A percussionist used to always be a guy who could play vibes and marimbas as well as all the toys. Victor Feldman was a percussionist, in the old sense of the word, who was not only a great piano player, but played vibes and all the percussion instruments. My favorite microphones for marimbas and vibes would be KM 54s. They are very smooth-sounding old tube mics with these wonderful highs.

Schoeps mics will work well, too. They would probably be brighter, but the KM 54 has this really nice smoothness to it, but with lots of highs and presence. Vibes can be very percussive. You can literally get too much percussion on them and be in your face too much. That is why you should move the mics away, maybe 3 feet above the instrument, and use a smoother-sounding mic on them. That way, you can get a much more even sound out of the instrument. In fact, for all the instruments that "speak" and have all this super clarity to them, the Neumann KM 54 smoothes those guys out and gives you a much more usable signal.

Also, unless you are going for a special effect on vibes or marimbas, I wouldn't record with compression or limiting. I have a rule of thumb that I never compress it, because the producer might change his mind about the direction of the song or arrangement; and if you had compressed it originally, you might be in trouble because you can't undo it.

I used tympani on a Bonnie Raitt track that is a version of the Traveling Wilburys's song "You Got It." It was for a Whoopi Goldberg movie called *Boys on the Side.* Jim Keltner played the tympani on it. I used a Neumann M 50, at least 6 or 8 feet up above the kit. That was an omni pattern. The tympani has so much sound that to capture the entire instrument, you have to get the room "working" for you.

Andy Narell, a steel-drum artist on the Windham Hill label, is someone I worked with. He likes to use two KM 54s and a transformerless AKG 414. The mics were maybe 3 feet above the drums. He got the stereo from the two KM 54s, and he filled the middle with the 414. It worked very well.

The KM 54 is also good for instruments like chimes, timbales, and glockenspiel. For tambourines, a Neumann M 50 is an ideal omni mic for capturing the instrument in a room. The Shure SM57 is one solid choice for a closer in-your-face recording.

Bongos are so bright and percussive sounding that they will cut through anything. You can put on almost any mic, and you can get a decent bongo sound.

For gongs, a Neumann U 47 FET, which is a cardioid mic, would probably be my first choice. It has a nice clear midrange with a lot of bottom to it. It also has pads, so you can pad it down. A U 67 is also a good alternate choice. I would probably put the mic a little bit to the side, instead of putting it directly at the instrument.

I think what is interesting about this whole thing is that there are no rules, no clear-cut way. Even if you started every rhythm base the same way, you will find that you will have to change up here and there because of what is going on in the song.

Eric Schilling

Credits include: Gloria Estefan, Julio Iglesias, David Bowie, Janet Jackson, Natalie Cole, Jon Secada, Elton John, Natalie Imbruglia, Shakira, Chayanne, Cachao, Arturo Sandoval, Frank Sinatra, Crosby, Stills & Nash. See the Appendix for Eric Schilling's full bio.

When I started to work with Gloria [Estefan], I was exposed to a lot of beats and instruments I hadn't heard before. I came from a place where I did a lot of rock, so there was a certain period of time where I had to rethink my approach, because there were no drums [trap sets] in some of this music. I also had to learn that you don't balance them the same way that you would a drum kit.

With dance and rock stuff, the kick drum tends to be very up front. Whereas in the real Latin music, you tend to put it way back, because that part of the beat is not something they want you to hear a lot. It isn't emphasized.

Only one song on the [Grammy-winning *Mi Tierra*] album [by Gloria Estefan] had a trap set on it, and it was used in a very background way. Normally, you would build your mix around the drums and bass and then piano and so on. In this case, I started with congas and timbales being the main part of the song. That is where you start your mix. Then I will start working on the bass and then the piano. After that, I may start to work on all the hand percussion. It takes a while for you to rethink your approach.

Timbales are a special recording challenge, due to an extremely wide range of dynamics and sounds. You have to think about how you are going to cover the whole drum, because it is going to go from some fairly soft stuff, with the drummer playing on the side, to playing extremely loud fills or cowbell. You've got to capture this all at the same time. What I tend to do is put a Sennheiser 421 in the middle of the bottom side of the two drums facing slightly toward the rim of the shells. That way, I capture the ambiance of the wood coming through the bottom of the shells and the tapping on the sides. I feel that dynamic mics are preferable to condensers when recording that close to the drums.

I will then put one tube mic, probably a Sony 800 set in a cardioid pattern, 4 to 5 feet above the kit, facing straight down at the cowbell, so I will get a lot of the top skin and get a more even sound. If I get too close, I won't get a good blend between the two side shells and the cowbell and, say, a crash. Sometimes, if the mic is up 6 1/2 feet or so, I might move it out 2 or 3 feet in front of the kit. It is just something you have to play around with, because each guy's kit has a certain sound, and he will play it a certain way.

I really like to use compression on timbales. Generally, I would use a Urei 1176. It has the attack and release time, so you can fine tune it and get what you want. I might set it for a medium attack and a fairly fast release time. You don't want something that is too fast, because if the attack is too fast, then you hear it too much. It sounds very stepped on.

I normally use an API "lunchbox" for EQ. I would tend to mix the two mics, compress them, and then EQ the whole thing, so I work on the sound more as a group, as opposed to one EQ on the low mic and another EQ on the top mic.

For congas, most players come in with three drums—a high-tuned one in the middle and two lower drums to the side. I will tend to catch a lot of it with one microphone. If a large part of what he is playing is on the high drum, I will put the mic so that it is facing the high drum, but it has got a wide enough field so that it can get the low drum that tends to be quite loud, as well as the medium drum. If one of those drums feels too far away, I will throw in a 421. I will use that to fill in the blend.

If they want to have a stereo sound, especially if it is for part of a song that is sparse, with only a shaker and a timbale, then I will use two mics of a matched pair. I generally use the same mic that I use for timbales, the Sony 800. In some cases, I will use a Neumann U 67, two cardioids at 90 degrees. I will just move them around until I get a good spread.

For congas, you can't be as drastic with compression. I tend to use a different kind of compressor on them. I will a Compex, which was manufactured by Audio Design Recording. The Compex was the stereo version of the Vocal Stresser. It is a compressor that you can tune a lot, in terms of the ratios, attack time, and gain.

The Urei has got more pumping to it, and it tends to make the drum feel, when you hit it hard, more exciting to hear. It's great for timbale, but on a conga drum, the Urei would tend to pull down the attack a little too much for me and make the sound seem a little too small.

I really like to get warmth from congas, and I will work a long time to achieve that. I don't tend to like those drums sounding real bright. Congas are probably the most work for me to record. I am always trying to find a balance. I want to hear some nice "air" on them, and I want to hear some nice snap and attack, but I don't want them to sound thin. It is a matter of finding a balance of trying to make the drums feel fat but still have some attack up at the top. If you dial in a lot of 5 kHz and 10 kHz and all of that, then it will sound thin. On congas, I tend to do from 12 kHz and above for "air." I might just do a notch of 3 to 5 kHz, just to give a little snap to the attack. I probably wouldn't do more than +4 dB on any of those settings. At that point, if it still isn't sounding good, I would be saying that probably isn't miked right or I didn't use the right mic.

In the case of the Cachao album, I had one piece where we didn't use congas and timbales. We totally abandoned that and went for a more street-level instrumentation. There was one guy who played a hoe, the same thing that you use in your garden. He had a steel rod and was playing the subdivision part of the beat, so I had to mike a hoe. You might say, "How do you mike a hoe?" Well, basically, you take an AKG 414 and get about 2 feet away and point it at the hoe. He held it in a way that didn't dampen the steel part of it. He was hitting the metal part, so that the hoe had a really live sound. It was great.

For mixing Latin music, I have found that where the percussion tends to be very dense, you kind of have to pick what is going to be wet and what is going to be dry. It can't all be one thing. You have to create a contrast. The toughest part—especially if you have 10 things, like congas, timbales, guiros, shakers, cowbells, and so on—is to create a space for all of this stuff. You kind of have to pick what is going to have a long reverb and what is going to have a short one. It is really a question of contrast. Typically, the stuff that is playing a lot of fast time is going to tend to be drier. Stuff that is a lot sparser I will make more wet.

You have to look at Latin percussion in a very different context than you would philosophically approach a trap set in a mix or production. See, you really can't say that it is just one part. You have to look at all of them. You can't really say that a certain drum is the equivalent to a snare. That would be simplifying things too much. In an orchestra you might have crashes and tympani and maybe someone playing a glockenspiel, but you have all of these guys making the whole piece, and that is the way it is with Latin percussion.

Allen Sides

Credits include: Beck, Green Day, Eric Clapton, Ray Charles, Frank Sinatra, Duke Ellington, Joni Mitchell, Frank Zappa, Ry Cooder, Phil Collins, Faith Hill, Alanis Morissette, Count Basie, Ella Fitzgerald. See the Appendix for Allen Sides's full bio.

I am very big on stereo with percussion, particularly things like shakers. They sound so cool when you have a shaker in a space with a pair of great microphones. It can create such a presence, where a mono recording would not. It makes such a difference in size and space. If I want to position something, I will basically have the musician move toward the left or right of the mic. That way, I can have a true perspective rather than panned mono.

My microphone of choice for cutting most percussion is the Neumann KM 54. The KM 54 has tremendous punch and presence. It doesn't matter if you are using bells, congas, vibes, anything you can think of, KM 54s are stunning. It sounds big, and in the dialogue of recording, the only thing I always listen for is size. It is easy to make something small, but it is really hard to make something bigger-sounding.

If I can't get some KM 54s for recording percussion, then I will use a pair of Schoeps cardioids, which are among the most impressive phantom-powered mics I have ever heard. If you have never heard a pair, they have an effortless top end that is very present and clear. It isn't harsh. The KM 54 is similar, but it is silkier-sounding. There is a certain richness to it that goes beyond the Schoeps.

Another mic that I like, particularly on timbales, is the AKG C 12A. Sometimes in a busy, thick track, you can hit a timbale and all you hear is the sound of the stick and the top, and not the tone of the drum itself. The AKG C 12A helps because it has a lot of low-end proximity, and it tends to make things sound fuller.

Sometimes when you hear a very busy, thick track, with certain very dynamic percussion instruments placed in that mix, you will only hear the peaks—the floor or quieter parts just disappear in the mush. Often what I do, rather than just compress the instrument I'm recording, is to take a mult and compress that and add it back into the uncompressed signal. This allows me to keep all the punch and fill in the bottom.

When recording percussion as an overdub or on film scores or more symphonic-style sessions, I like to record suspended cymbals, snares, tympani, and concert bass drums using two or three Neumann M 50s in somewhat of a Decca Tree configuration. If it's going to be straight stereo, I would only use two M 50s. I will move the percussion forward or backward in relation to the microphones to determine what level of presence I am looking for. The point of all this being, I am trying to not sound as if it was an overdub, but as if the percussion were played live with the orchestra. Also, this type of percussion sounds much bigger at a distance.

Cookie Marenco and Jean Claude Reynaud @ The Vibe sessions at The Site (photo by Rick Clark) / Steve Wilson of Porcupine Tree (photo courtesy of Steve Wilson). Row 2: Kevin Shirley (photo by David Shirley). Row 3: Millennia HV-3D 8-channel mic preamplifier and the B&K 4003 mics used at The Site's Live Chamber (photo by Rick Clark).

Engineering Philosophy

Audio engineering, as practically anyone reading this book knows, is more than just throwing up a mic or twisting an EQ knob. As any great engineer, producer, or seasoned musician or artist will tell you, one of the hallmarks of an engineer who makes a real difference comes from a highly developed ability and trust in instinct to "read" the dynamic between all the parties involved in the session and act on solving potential problems before they become problems. An engineer who understands the difference between a good sound and the right sound for a project and who can aid a producer and a band in arriving at the desired vision is priceless.

When I was sorting through the mountain of interview transcripts for this edition of the book, I realized there were a number of things shared that weren't really production philosophy observations. Though some were really close, they weren't exactly the kinds of mullings that neatly landed in a chapter about recording drums, for example. Hence this chapter, which features Dave Pensado, Nathaniel Kunkel, Ryan Freeland, Ronan Chris Murphy, and Jim Scott providing their insights.

Dave Pensado

Credits include: Beyonce, Pink, Earth, Wind & Fire, Mary J. Blige, Nelly, Christina Aguilera, Destiny's Child, Justin Timberlake, Bell Biv DeVoe, Shakira, Backstreet Boys, Whitney Houston, Mariah Carey. See the Appendix for Dave Pensado's full bio.

I think the best thing a young engineer can do is just to totally immerse himself in music. I probably listen to more music than just about anybody I know. Listening to lots of all kinds of music helps you gain a musical vocabulary. If I want to give a rock song a little bit of hip-hop credibility, then I add an 808, which is like a vocabulary "word" I would've acquired from listening to and studying everything I heard. If I want to imply surfer music, then I'm going to take my Fender Telecaster and run it through a Fender Twin with a little bit of vibrato and spring reverb. It's not that a Telecaster through a Fender Twin sounds good, but over the years that's what our brain has established as "the sound," and there are trillions of sounds that have become part of the vocabulary of music.

I think that a good engineer should explore that concept and understand how it works. When you have enough immediate "words," then you can start constructing "sentences" into musical paragraphs. You have to have the vocabulary. Once you have that vocabulary, you start building on it. The next thing you know, you can mix a record, produce a record, or track a record.

For instance, how can you set up some drums and mic them if you've never heard the song before or have any understanding of what is needed for that style of music? I've seen it done. How can you do that? I've seen engineers start a mix without ever having heard the song. They just immediately pull up the drums and start EQing. That would be like putting a can of tomato sauce in pot, and you just start adding spices. What the heck are you cooking? Don't you think you should kind of know what the dish is before you start adding spices?

Nobody wants to be a tracking engineer anymore. Nobody wants to dedicate their life to getting live drum sounds. Everybody wants to be a mixer. I guess everyone wants to be a director in the movie profession. I personally think that it takes greater skills to be a really topnotch tracking engineer than it does to be a mixing engineer. I'd like to see the schools and the recording community really emphasize and focus on creating great tracking engineers. Do they exist any more?

If I mention some famous person in the recording world as a great tracking engineer, it would be an insult. They would write to you and say, "I'm not a tracking engineer; I'm a producer." Calling oneself a tracking engineer is no longer cool, and nobody wants to be it. I'd love to see an emphasis and a shift on that because, like we're saying, if you take the sheer amount of time that goes into the making of a song from the time that it's conceived to the time that it's on the radio...let's just make up a number...85 percent of that's the tracking guy. Ten percent is the producer, if they're two different people, and 5 percent is mixing. I'll do maybe 250 to 300 mixes a year, and it's extremely rare—maybe 20 times during the year—that I get something I feel was tracked really well.

So where did we get this concept that track engineering isn't key? Tracking has gotten so bad that much of my mixing is now repairing, and the guys that are good at repairing are considered great mixers. Ten years ago, I'd typically spend about 20 hours on a mix. Now I average around 12 hours, and of those, I spend a good six repairing, four hours getting sounds, and maybe two hours mixing.

Nathaniel Kunkel

Credits include: Lyle Lovett, James Taylor, Carole King, Graham Nash, Jimmy Buffett, Linda Ronstadt, Little Feat, Neil Diamond, Ringo Starr, Heart, Nirvana, Elton John, Billy Joel, Jackson Browne, Barbra Streisand, Crosby, Stills, Nash & Young, Morrissey, Sting. See the Appendix for Nathaniel Kunkel's full bio.

To acquire the skills you need to be able to effectively manipulate audio, you first need to learn to sit and listen. The process of record production or engineering is being quiet within yourself, hearing music, having an opinion about the music, having a feeling about what you need it to be, and seeing that in your mind's eye. Then it's a matter of going to your skill set, pulling out the skills that you need to do it, going to your toolbox, manipulating those tools with your skill set, and applying it to the audio you hear...before you lose your perspective. It's important to be able to work fast, because the process has to be very transparent and intuitive, and it has to be on the back side of what your emotional responses are to the music. I don't know how you can acquire the ability to hear a piece of audio, know what you wish it to be, and understand what tools are going to make that vision happen as quickly and efficiently as you need it to occur without having years and years of listening experience.

LOUD-LEVEL PRODUCT

I don't personally know one engineer who loves mixing only over-compressed tracks. He just needs to pay their mortgage, and he knows certain clients will reject his mixes if they're not loud. Another thing a lot of people don't realize is that if they mix really dynamically and then let mastering compress it to within an inch of its life, the balance changes. If you want something to sit all the way at the top, you have to make it 5 dB or so louder than you would if it was a dynamic mix, because you're not going to have any transient response. You need everything to get out of the way of the snare drum, or you're not going to hear it. You need to do 5 more dB of vocal de-essing, because you're going to pick up those high-frequency artifacts with all of that peak limiting. So, you've got to pick a horse, and you've got to ride it.

Okay, so let's make a loud record! That means it's going to leave this console with half a dB of dynamic range, because then I know what my mix is. It all comes down to what George Massenburg told me: In the end, all these excuses, all these feelings, and all these late nights aren't going to matter. All that is going to matter is that your name is on the back of the record, and it's going to sound a certain way. That's all that matters. At that point, you aren't going to be able to put a Post-It note on the back of each album saying, "Really sorry this is so over-compressed. I didn't want it to be this way, but the A&R guy was a jerk. He wouldn't listen to me. Blah, blah, blah, blah, blah! Hope you enjoy it anyway." You can't do that! On the back, it'll say it was recorded and mixed by me! It has half a dB of dynamic rang, and it's like, "Whose fault is that?" It's mine, and my name is on the record, so you have to make everything sound good. No matter what the client needs from it....

In truth, I think we're going to look back in the coming years at all of these highly compressed records, and there's a good chance we're not going to like them as much as we do now. Even with drastic compression on Beatles records, they still allowed those recordings to be dynamic, open, interesting, woven pieces of music where you could hear new things every time you listened to them.

When was the last time you heard a Pink Floyd record and thought, "Jeez, this isn't loud enough." It just doesn't happen! When you hear Pink Floyd, you say, "Damn! I forgot how amazing Pink Floyd records were!"

My immense frustration these days is that we're not making records as good as we once were. Not only that, but they're not selling, and we still continue making them not as good. The definition of insanity is expecting a different response from the same action, and yet that's what most of us are doing.

Ryan Freeland

Credits include: Aimee Mann, Mose Allison, Bob Seger, Christina Aguilera, the Corrs, Duffy, John Fogerty, Loudon Wainwright III, Son Volt, Crowded House, Brett Dennen, Jewel, Liz Phair, Paul Westerberg, Joe Henry. See the Appendix for Ryan Freeland's full bio.

There are more right ways to record and mix music than wrong ways. Engineers spend a lot of time thinking about what the perfect drum, bass, vocal, guitar, or piano sound is when such a thing does not exist.

Gear does matter. It's like a painter's choice of acrylic or oil paint, canvas or cardboard—or how a cinematographer's choice of lenses and filters radically affects the final product. We make choices to capture a moment and present a mood for each record. Like how different New York City looks in Martin Scorsese's *Taxi Driver* compared to Woody Allen's *Manhattan*—though they were filmed in the same city only a couple of years apart. Or Pablo Picasso's Cubist view compared to Gustav Klimt's Art Nouveau movement—they were contemporaries, but each made radically different choices. The tools we use do define our sound, and our aesthetics reside in 19-inch rack spaces, 2-inch reels of tape, gold-sputtered capsules, and computer hard drives. Your gear choices are a big part of what defines your sound and your statement as an engineer.

Giving too much credence to studio precedents, like analog tape, three-microphone drum techniques, and vintage gear, can distract one from making a meaningful recording. Analog tape sounds great, but recording with digital will most certainly not ruin the entire project. The Glyn Johns drum recording technique is amazing, but it won't work on every drummer in every room. The Neumann U 47 is one of the world's truly great microphones, but it's not always the right choice for every situation. I think it's an easy trap to fall into—trusting precedent and concept over reality and your own sound judgment.

Performance matters, but it is not everything. I've read often that the key to getting a great sound is to start with a great player. And while I love to work with great musicians, it can be equally fun to make a great recording with an average band. And an average band with an amazing or interesting recording can be much more emotionally effective than a great band whose performance isn't thoughtfully captured by the right engineering. It doesn't really matter how great you play if no one can hear it. Great recording with a great engineer can make all of the difference.

There are no absolutes. Even if you could go into RCA Studios, record to analog tape, and use only vintage microphones, your recording is probably not going to sound like Sam Cooke's *Night Beat*. The other big problem with that, besides the obvious problem of not being Sam Cooke, is that borrowing concepts from the past is a good thing, but straight imitation removes your artistry from the equation. The Beatles made amazingly great records, but I don't want to limit myself by thinking of that as the gold standard—comparing everything I record and mix to some other record. The band and the songs almost always tell you how they are supposed to sound in order to best get their point across. You can get extremely lost by trying to force a song to a sonic place it doesn't want to go. Just let it be what it is; don't ruin it by trying to make it something it's not.

The way the public listens to recorded music is ever changing—from vinyl, to compact discs, and now compressed files playing on phones and laptops. Every change offers the engineer a new set of problems to deal with and solutions to benefit from. My mixes need to compete with the end user's entire music catalog on random shuffle. During the days of vinyl, the consumer got up every 20 minutes to change the record and usually adjusted the volume, bass, and treble levels for each record they put on. Now everything runs in a random shuffle of singles with no adjustments made. It certainly changes the way one thinks about mixing and sound in general.

Mix notes have also changed drastically, as people are mostly listening on ear buds and laptops. It seems like fewer and fewer people actually have decent sound systems in their homes anymore. One of the benefits of this is that the degradation created when you compress a sound file is less obvious when you listen through laptop speakers. So the current music playback technology has kept pace with the compressing of the sound file—it's all pretty mediocre. It's sad that no one else will ever hear the record you just slaved over in all of its hi-fi glory. The upside is that you, too, can bring your entire music catalog with you wherever you go. I've got a large collection of songs that travel everywhere with me on my phone. I end up listening a lot more to a larger variety of things. And the main thing I've learned from all this listening is that there are a million ways for records to sound—from big and dark to thin and bright, from loud and compressed to soft and dynamic. And what this constantly reinforces is that more of it sounds good to me than bad—or at least it sounds interesting. It shows that there is no one way to make a great record. There are as many ways to approach sound as there are people in the world.

I now feel like there are a lot more right choices to be made while recording than wrong choices. The important thing is that the entire record sounds right to my clients and me, not that the kick drum sound I got holds up against every kick drum sound ever recorded. Kick drums don't exist in a vacuum. They belong as part of a whole, as a vehicle to create a vibe for a particular song. You could drive yourself crazy trying to achieve a perfect kick drum, only to realize that particular sound doesn't work for the next record you record or mix. Let it be what it is. Better to focus on the emotional impact of the entire recording as opposed to focusing on the technical aspects of just one of its elements. There is no wrong answer when it comes to these sorts of things, only differences. Is this mic better than that mic, is analog better than digital, and is tube gear vibier than solid state? I say use it all, abuse it if necessary, and swap it out if it's not getting you what you need—even if it is a Neumann U 47.

Ronan Chris Murphy

Credits include: King Crimson, Steve Morse, Chucho Valdes and Irakere, Bozzio Levin Stevens, Willie Oteri, ProjeKt One, ProjeKt Two, ProjeKct Three, ProjeKt Four. See the Appendix for Ronan Chris Murphy's full bio.

As great as a Pink Floyd record sounds, and as great as the engineering was on those records, David Gilmour's guitar tone doesn't send shivers up my spine because of the compression they used or the dithering scheme they used on the remaster. It's because the magic happened before the microphone, and it seems some people don't really pay enough attention to that fact. It's like they are busy thinking, "What can I do down the chain, after the microphone, to try and convert this into magic?" It's a really easy place to fall into, even as a more experienced producer and engineer. Sometimes I've gotta smack myself and go, "Wait a second; if it's not getting me excited without any of my stuff, we're not where we need to be yet."

I can do things to manipulate or enhance for creative purposes or mitigate problems, but it doesn't matter what I have if it isn't sounding great on the floor. It's really easy to fall into that trap of "Let me scroll through my plug-in selection and see what might make it sound good," when a lot of times there are just changes they could make before the microphone.

The difference between two esoteric preamps is far less significant than changing the gauge of your guitar pick or rolling back the volume knob on your guitar amp about 20 percent, so there are all these things that happen before the mic that are all of these night-and-day differences. Switching the preamps from Soundcraft to Neve is not going to change the character of who that person is as an artist or even change the feel of the music. People get obsessed about the fact that some transformer has a little bit more steel content in it than nickel content, but I'm way more interested in what is happening with the guitar in that guy's hands.

One of the big mistakes people make is they completely obliterate the space between the notes in the music. The reason so many of those classic records sound amazing over the years is the space in between. You can hear the separation and the detail. *Dark Side of the Moon* was 16 tracks, and they didn't really use up all the tracks. Something like a David Gilmour track will sound so great because, one, he's playing it, and two, there isn't much else going on when he's playing. It's all big guitars, and you hear the detail and practically hear the coils on the pickups and the subtle decay trailing off. *Back in Black*, to this day, is pretty much the benchmark hard rock album, but those guitars are clean and arrangements are sparse and there's tons of space.

Now you have people recording to their DAW, piling up tracks and filling all of the space with sound. It seems crazy to me having mixes show up with 150 tracks. I see these bands wanting to have this powerful sound, and their recordings are all layered up and they are wondering why their record doesn't have the impact of *Back in Black*.

With the introduction of the DAW and seemingly infinite track count, people now throw on layers of guitars, voices, and keyboards and say, "We'll just figure out what we like later," but what you've done is reduce the joy of mixing to a file-management nightmare, sorting out tracks and almost ensuring the magic of the performance will never materialize. You'll have the product of too much thinking that's just ordered tonalities with a beat and little soul.

Some people will say they want their music to sound just like their live show, but for it to be just like that live show, the playback would have to be at about 120 dB SPL, and you'd have a couple of beers in you, and there'd be a light show and so on. It's a visceral experience. Somebody listening to your album in their car or at home doesn't have that, so it's all about finding ways to actually get the listener closer to a specific space, because you don't just have that live, visceral, multisensory experience.

Often you might want to change the perspective from trying to reach the people back in row ZZ and make things a little bit more intimate, like you're performing to someone three feet away. That even applies to heavy-metal bands. What you're going to want is to create a really tight relationship, which is why it's quite common to back off the amount of distortion you have on an electric guitar for the album versus the live show, because what you're trying to do is get that to be a little more articulate and immediate. A super-overdriven guitar will feel a little bit distant. When you start to bring elements like guitars and kick a little closer to the listener, it makes it really exciting to somebody in the car on the expressway or sitting back in an audiophile listening environment. It's all about finding ways to create that unique experience.

Jim Scott

Credits include: Tom Petty, Red Hot Chili Peppers, Wilco, Sting, Ride, Dixie Chicks, Lucinda Williams, the Rolling Stones, Pete Yorn, Foo Fighters, Counting Crows, Matchbox Twenty, Weezer. See the Appendix for Jim Scott's full bio.

What I like to do is get four, five, or six guys who play great in the same room at the same time with a great song and a great singer, and have somebody count to four and see what happens. If you've got those ingredients, something good will happen and usually pretty quickly. It will happen for them, and it will happen for me on the engineering side.

You can dial in a great tom tom, snare, bass, and other sounds, but until they all play together, you don't really know if that sound is the good sound or the right sound. You can get a sound that isn't distorted and doesn't buzz and hum and doesn't distort the speaker, if that's your goal, but until everyone plays together and you actually hear music, you don't know if there's going to be a balance or any kind of fidelity or any sort of interesting noise that's being made. If you get great guys playing a great groove, the record is 80 percent done in the first three minutes of work. It's kind of the hardest work, but it's also the easiest work because if you really hit it, that's the most fun.

Great players know how to supply the tone and usually will have it in their first two or three passes. If you're brave enough to just let them do it without grabbing a bunch of EQs and compressors and trying to force a mix, and you let the musicians listen to themselves, you'll discover that the guitar player makes a subtle change. He moves the kick back closer to the bridge and gets a sharper sound, or the bass player will throw away his pick, play with his thumb, and get a deeper sound. Maybe the drummer figures out which tom tom speaks out, so he plays his fill on the tom toms that sound good to him. The next thing you know, you are hearing stuff that all sounds better. The musicians will make it happen.

If you want to jump in and start having everyone chasing their tails, then go ahead and start EQing the bass while he's trying to change the bass and play with his pick. While you are dulling down his sound, he has changed to his thumb, and now it's too dull. It gets a little out of control until someone decides to wait, and usually that's me. I'll just wait for a take or two and have them come in for a little playback. The experienced musicians will know exactly what they need to do to make a good sound, as long as you provided an environment for them to be comfortable to play and gave them a good sound to start with.

My approach is to get as many people going live as I possibly can and keep it all, because that is the heart, soul, and core of a record. If it feels good at that moment, it will always feel good. Even if you take everyone out and just listen to the snare drum or just the rhythm guitar, it still is going to feel good, because it felt good at that moment.

Where is the inspiration, if you are over-dubbing everybody to quantized tracks? To me, that's just counting bars and beats and doing it by the numbers. Where is the "go for it"? Where is the "I'm going to try to do something here across this crazy change and this thing where it really speeds and goes into the solo"—whether it speeds up or not, it might feel like it should. Personally, I like that excitement, the action and the mystery that happens from people taking chances playing together in a room.

When it comes to fixing things, Pro Tools is just another way, but it can be a bad drug because it's easy to abuse that. In the old days, you could cut tape, and you would stay up all night. At the end of it, if you cut something together that felt good, you knew that was a good night's work. You created something where there was nothing, and that was just one way of fixing things. People sang out of tune before there were pitch-correcting devices, and there were ways to fix that, too. You slowed the tape recorder down and copied the offending part over and flew it back in at a different speed—a long note, a short note. Or you could put up a "smoke bomb"—put a power cord on top of that weak part or put a piano note on top of it. There were ways to disguise flaws and put a little makeup on things that didn't sound so good, but the computer has made all of that the norm. Fix everything...and I think that way of doing things is really unhealthy for the music.

Nowadays, a band can suck, and they will go into the studio, and some poor recording engineer pushes a button, and it comes out sounding in time. No one said it was good, but it's in time and it's in tune, and they think, "Geez! It sounds like everything else on the radio. We are great!" If young bands learn the hard way and experience the realization of, "We have worked all night long and our track still sucks"—well, next time they go into the studio, they will have rehearsed a lot, and they may be ready and sound like a unit.

When I trained at the Record Plant in Los Angeles in the early '80s, preparation was everything. That was when studio time was expensive. In those days, it wasn't all 12-hour-a-day lockouts. There were some three-hour sessions and six-hour sessions, where it was downbeat right at session time. That meant at 10 a.m., it was the countdown to start recording, "1, 2, 3, 4, go." And you hit Record, and the band was ready right then to play. What this meant was that all the mics, mic cables, headphones, extensions...everything had to be tested, working, and ready to go before that session downbeat started at 10 a.m. or 2 p.m. or 6 p.m.

As an engineer, the preparation for a session has always been really important. You have to know what kind of music you are recording. People are paying you to be ready. You make a few phone calls; you get the plan before they arrive. "How many different guitar amps does the guitar player have? On this one song, a horn section comes out." That's good to know, so that you can put some more mics out. "On this song we have three background singers." Good to know...we can put mics out for the background singers. If you didn't care, and the background singers arrived with no place to sing, you would look terrible and never get hired again. You have to prepare, communicate, and then use your experience to make it all look like it's really easy. I hate people running around and not being ready, especially me. That's why it's nice to be prepared, and it's nice to know how to do it. It's a great feeling to know that everything in the room is working. I'll go in Sunday night for a Monday morning session, because I want the Monday morning session to be great. I don't want to be sweating. I want to be the calmest one in the room on Monday morning. That's preparation, and that's what you need.

There is a little science and physics to recording. You can anticipate how loud a guy might hit a snare drum, and you can set the mic preamp at a level that at least gets you close. Whereas, if you don't get a really long time to do your sound check, at least you'll be in the ballpark at what would be safe to not distort the tape, not distort the mic preamp, or not distort the Pro Tools when the session starts.

If you have some experience you can set up the room and be ready when the musicians walk in, so it's not like, "Gee, how do I record a floor tom today? Where should I put the mic? What level should I set the mic preamp at?"

Hopefully, at some point, there is an experience level where you can have everybody almost ready to go and almost have the sound dialed in on things before the players even sit down to track. Some of that comes from habit, some from experience, and some from using something that worked in the past that will probably work again in the future. That's my experience with it. I don't feel like it's experimenting, recording school every day.

Some people come to me and say, "I really like the guitar sounds you got on that band. I really like the drum sounds you got on that band." And that's why they are there, because they want something kind of like that. I feel it's my job to give them something kind of like that. Not to say, "Yeah, yeah, I don't do that drum sound anymore. Now I record all my drums in the park with one mic. So we are going to the park today." That's not what they want. They want a big fat rock drum sound. So you approach it that way, and if you can, use the same drums. Use the same drummer if you can. Give them what they want. That's what I try to do with mixing, with service and tracking and everything. The musicians will be happy if they hear something that they want to hear, and so will the record company. If you give them what they want, they are going to be happy. They will call you back next year and give you another try. It shouldn't be that hard, but some people make it harder than it needs to be. I try to keep it as simple as possible. Keep everyone happy and create an environment of safety, love, good vibes, and good music and invite the best players that I can up here to play. That's how I try to get it done.

Left column top to bottom: Ryan Freeland's studio setup for Ray LaMontange sessions (photo courtesy of Ryan Freeland) / Rick Trevino (photo by Rick Clark) / Lynn Adler of Adler & Hearne @ House of David Recording (photo by Kate Hearne) / Karel Van Mileghem and Rick Clark @ The Tone Chaparral (photo by Derrick Scott). Right column top to bottom: The Fabulous Superlatives (left to right) Kenny Vaughan, Harry Stinson, Marty Stuart, Brian Glenn @ Eastwood Recording / Porter Wagoner & Marty Stuart @ Omni Recording / Eric Fritsch, Rick Clark, Marty Stuart, David Haley @ Eastwood Recording (photo by Tzuriel Fenigshtein) / Jose Manuel Blanco @ The Vibe Sessions, The Site (photo by Rick Clark).

Production Philosophy

This is probably the most open-ended chapter in the book. The subject at hand isn't so much how one captures instruments on tape or builds a great mix, and yet this is the heart and soul of this whole undertaking.

In the world of recording and producing music, it is easy for some to get caught up with the latest gear and what it does or focus too much on cleaning up extraneous noise on tracks and achieving some kind of idealized sonic clarity. In other words, it's easy to focus on the details so much that one can't see the forest for the trees.

We are trying to capture magic in those fleeting moments where brilliance happens—not sand it out of existence.

I really believe that art generally happens in spite of artists, and the function of great producers and engineers (and really everyone on the staff of a good studio) is to assist the artist to be in the self-actualized moment of creating and being. That is where truth happens.

It is important for producers and engineers to remember that they, too, are equally susceptible to letting too much "thinking" get in the way of paying attention to the intention of the flow. A true pro knows his or her craft enough to let go and be in the moment.

Over the years, I've been blessed with many wonderful ponderings from some of the most amazing talents in the recording industry. The following production-related insights come courtesy of Tim Palmer, Csaba Petocz, Roy Thomas Baker, David Briggs, David Kahne, Norbert Putnam, Tony Brown, Jim Dickinson, and Joe Boyd.

Among the longer contributions is the section from the late, great David Briggs, who produced Neil Young's greatest rock albums. This might be the only place you'll get to read any extended comments from one of rock's production legends. Another legend and friend who passed away as I was assembling this edition of this book was Jim Dickinson. Like Briggs, Dickinson's passion for producing bordered on spiritual in a theatrically earthy kind of way. Both of them were good teachers, and I'm grateful to have them in this book.

Basically, the ruminations in this chapter run the gamut on everything, from what is a producer, to tricks to get something extra out of performers, to the state of the industry, to a few war stories and a lot of attitude thrown in for fun.

In the spirit of what I just shared, this chapter is intentionally fluid, so just go with the ride. Something might shoot sparks in between the words and notes that you'll carry with you for a long time.

Tim Palmer

Credits include: Pearl Jam, James, Live, Tears for Fears, Robert Plant, Ozzy Osbourne, U2, Rancid, the Cure. See the Appendix for Tim Palmer's full bio.

What really defines producing a record? Who the heck knows? The only thing we do know for sure is that it is an ever-changing scenario. If it had a job description, it would be very hard to pin down.

Sometimes when working with an extremely creative and proficient group, producing is quite an easy occupation and very enjoyable; other times, it is a pain from beginning to end.

There are many psychological aspects to producing a record. Aside from making the record you want to make, you have to be best friend and confidant to the artist, and of course the record company. This, you may think, is a conflict of interests, and you would be right. Your job is to sort through the chaff, listen to both sides of the argument, and hopefully come to the right conclusions. There is no point in pissing off the record company to keep the artist happy and in the end having no push from the label in the marketplace. Conversely, if you toe the company line and don't have any feeling for the artistic vision, you won't last more than a couple of days in the studio. Don't forget to be proud of your work. If you don't have any confidence in what you do, it will be hard to convince others.

It is probably worth being careful in your choice of reference points. This can be explosive to your artists. If you are trying to get them to like an idea, telling them it reminds you of Kajagoogoo will not help if you are producing Motorhead. Firing a musician is a very touchy subject. Choose your words extremely carefully. In the past I have actually received death threats from thwarted musicians who took their dismissal very badly. As it happened, this wasn't even my decision, but the producer gets the flack.

Being a technical wizard in the studio or at the computer is obviously a plus, but if you are going to create a piece of work that has no emotion or feel, then you are wasting your time. We have all heard too many wonderfully engineered, yet terribly drab albums. If you have a lousy song, then you are off to an extremely bad start. I was always told that you cannot polish a turd. Pro Tools has created an amazing aid to recording, and as a creative tool it is phenomenal, but don't forget that the listening public never demanded records that were more in time or more in tune. Don't waste countless hours making dull, lifeless recordings. Leave some mistakes in; they may turn out to be your favorite bits.

Pre-production is a great opportunity to find out some of the parameters of how you will make your project work. You are looking for ways to create the most comfortable and creative environment in which the project can proceed. Sometimes it is just making it work any way you can. If a band likes to record underwater eating bananas, then that's probably your best plan. Don't forget that being a producer is a bit like being a juggler.

Your basic overview is to ultimately create a valid piece of work that has something credible to offer. You should aim for at least one redeeming quality. This can come from many directions—maybe the artist writes great lyrics, maybe the music is aggressive, maybe the band writes great pop songs. Decide this early on so that when you are burned out trying new ideas, you don't lose sight of your original plan.

Accept the fact that you will sometimes have to be a father to your groups. Many times I have had to actually go in, wake a band up, make sure they have eaten, and drive them to the studio. In one instance I had to carry a singer out of a Los Angeles bar over my shoulder to stop him from drinking any more vodka. Of course, I hadn't drunk anything!

You may have times when you haven't worked for six weeks and you feel you are over. Don't let your crushed ego get the better of you. Overall, don't forget: "If you can't take a joke, stay out of the music industry!"

Roy Thomas Baker

Credits include: Queen, the Cars, Journey, Foreigner, T. Rex, Free, T'Pau. See the Appendix for Roy Thomas Baker's full bio.

My whole thing is this: The more unique you can sound from anything else around and still be commercially successful is great! I hark back to that philosophy over the years. Back when I did "Bohemian Rhapsody," who would've ever thought of having a single with an opera section in the middle?

The first Cars record was totally unique. Even stuff I did when I was going from second engineer to engineer, like T. Rex's "Bang A Gong (Get It On)" or Free's "All Right Now"—they all had a different twist on what was basically the same thing. Now nobody wants that different twist. They all want to sound like each other. It is very odd.

Now I have all these bands come in with their little CDs and say, "I want that snare sound," and "I want that bass sound," and "I want that guitar sound."

I'll go, "Hello! These guys you are playing to me have already done this. Why do you want to do it?" It has totally gone backward.

They want to look like each other, and this might be a throwback to the late '80s, where everybody had to look like each other and they all had to wear the same leather bracelets and they had to have the same haircuts. We ended up with every record sounding the same. It was so generic, and I hated it. I drove away from the business in the States for a little bit and went to Europe and worked with T'Pau and people like that.

Over here, it was getting silly. Everyone was going to the same mix engineers to get the same drum sound, which used the same snare that everyone was using with the same echo on it, with that horrible sound. Every record was interchangeable. It didn't matter who the band was. They might've thought they were different; Pepsi and Coke are different, but who cares? The stuff is still cola. It's not champagne. [Laughs]

I stay clear of that. It is funny how many people put down the '80s, but the early '80s were great. You had the Cars and the Pretenders and Joe Jackson and Elvis Costello.

To sell records, you don't have to be the people who are also selling records on the charts. In fact, if you can sell records by doing something different, then you have found a little niche for yourself, and you can be around for years. It is the ones who sound like each other who are the one-hit wonder bands that come and go. When that scene is over, it goes like it went from horrible glam heavy metal to alternative overnight.

Where did all of those bands go overnight? They were all okay bands, as far as being able to play their instruments. They just vanished! Nirvana and Pearl Jam came along, and what happened to all of those other bands? They were all carbon copies of each other. They said they were alternative bands, and yet there was a time when if I saw another pair of checked shorts and everyone walking around saying they were from Seattle.... It was very weird. Luckily, that has gone, too. Alternative became generic as well, because everyone was copying that thing.

Then it goes on to the next thing, which now seems to be pop. I have no problems with pop. I'm not too cool to admit that I liked ABBA in the '70s. I thought they were a really good band. I do like pop songs, but I do like a different type of pop song. I don't like generic pop songs.

Selling yourself as something different is the root of where everyone should go.

In one respect, most bands don't want to sound like each other. I agree with that, but I don't believe that selling records is selling out. Communicating with the most people you want to communicate your message to is the whole point. Anyone can sit around in their bedroom and twiddle around with their guitar and not communicate with anyone. Duh! Everyone who is sitting in front of a video game is doing that!

If you want to communicate with the most people, you have to go out there and communicate. Communicating, in a sense, is selling records, and what is wrong with making money? There is nothing wrong with making money as long as you don't sound like the next band along. A lot of these bands that say, "I don't want to sell out," sound like some other band who did sell out. [Laughs]

When it actually comes down to it—and this is going by what people are willing to accept—a great song recorded on a 4-track Portastudio stands a better chance than a lousy song recorded in a real recording studio. That is because people will communicate with that. That has been proven time and time again. There have been far more hits out of lousy-sounding good songs than there have been with great-sounding bad songs.

Every time a band either raises the money or gets a contract with a major label—or even with an independent with some means—the first thing they do is look at the back cover of all of the favorite producers they want to work with based on what they like. They do that whole guilt-by-association thing, which is, "I don't want to work with that [producer] because of that artist. I want to work with him, because he worked with this artist." Using these criteria is very strange. They get into a situation where they expect perfection from everyone around them, except themselves.

So what happens is if they think they can surround themselves with the right producer in the right studio with the right technical abilities, it will make them sound a million times better. But the old proverb about "you can't polish a turd" still applies. Somewhere you've got to turn that turd into a piece of gold and then it can be polished.

It all ends up in this situation where there are thousands and thousands of bands out there with these really smooth, great, generic-sounding records that nobody gives a toss about. Then somebody like Beck comes along, and he hits a can and sings about being a "loser," and he gets a number one, and who knows what that was recorded on? [Laughs] And who cares? I loved it! So that is all that matters to me. For all I know, Beck might've spent a year trying to make that sound like it was really crappy. I doubt it.

The other thing that keeps coming out—and it has to do with A) the artist and B) the record companies—is that every band would like to produce its own records. That, to me, is a bit like someone wanting to be their own lawyer in court. It doesn't matter that, even if you are a lawyer, you shouldn't represent yourself in court. I think even if you are a great producer who happens to be an artist, and you are great at working with other artists, you should never produce yourself. I think you still need the element of somebody else kicking you in the butt to make sure you get the best out of yourself, because you can't be in two places at once. You need that extra brain on that.

A lot of artists will often go to an engineer, who is probably a great engineer, but as of that stage has not produced anything. But you know there is more to a production than getting a nice, polished sound, and people will still not go out and buy a nice drum sound if the song isn't there.

I came up with an engineering background, and some of my favorite producers have come up with an engineering background. But engineers have got to realize that producing is totally different from engineering. The first thing I did when I took up producing was to give up engineering. I can still engineer, and it is a great tool for me. I can still talk to whomever I have as my engineer and talk to them on a technical level, but I don't actually physically engineer myself anymore. I might go over the shoulder and twiddle a little bit, and on mixing I do some of the rides, but I abandon that, too.

I think a lot of people confuse the role of the producer and the role of the engineer.

If an engineer decides to get into producing, I would hope that he would automatically have an engineer working for him. Producing has its own difficulties, and twiddling knobs is only a means to an end. It isn't an end in itself. Get another engineer and train that engineer so he can become a producer.

I haven't seen a single band that can work out a budget and stick to it. The first role of a producer is to get the budget together. [Laughs] Most bands are totally useless at that. Even if I was to become an artist tomorrow, I wouldn't produce myself. [Laughs] I have to be out there being creative. Meanwhile, the producer is trying to kick me in the butt to make me stay on track and make sure that I go to the level beyond the level I thought I could go to.

When the first Cars record was Number One on the charts, I was driving on Sunset in Hollywood with Ric Ocasek. We drove past the billboard for the Cars record, and he said, "If someone had told me a year ago that I would be driving along Sunset Boulevard with Roy Thomas Baker looking up at a billboard of my record that is Number One, I wouldn't have believed him."

That is a classic example. When Ric Ocasek does his own records, he doesn't always produce himself. He lets other people produce him. Yet, Ric is a very good producer, and he has produced some hits himself, like Weezer. Ric is a classic example of somebody using his brain. "Hold on! I need someone to kick me in the butt in the same way I kicked that other artist in the butt!" [Laughs]

The thing is, everyone thinks, "It's in the mix. It's in the mix!" But that is like saying, "A movie is in the editing." It is not strictly in the editing. Yes, a bad editing job can screw up a good movie. Yes, a great editor can enhance a great movie. If it is a lousy movie, you can't get anyone to edit that to be great. It just can't be done. The same thing applies to music. Yes, a bad mix can mess up a great song. And yes, a great mix can enhance a great song. But a great mix can't make a bad song a hit or make it sound great for the radio otherwise.

People need an identifiable sound. They want to know that when the song is being played on the radio, people can hear who it is, even without the DJ mentioning it.

All the great bands have that quality. When a Stones song comes on the radio, even though they have had a lot of different changes of sound, you can hear instantly who they are, regardless of the period of music they are in. You can hear exactly who it is, and you don't need a DJ to tell you, "That was the Stones." You can hear it. That rule applies for every great band of the last 30 years. That is the thing that people are missing. If you don't have that identifiable sound, you are getting merged in. If the DJ isn't mentioning who it is, then nobody will know who it is. It will just be another band, and nothing is worse than being anonymous. That is exactly what you don't want.

Csaba Petocz

Credits include: Elton John, Metallica, Oingo Boingo, Camper Van Beethoven, Vince Gill, Ted Nugent, Stanley Clarke, Etta James, Kenny Chesney. See the Appendix for Csaba Petocz's full bio.

Tom Dowd once told me, "If you're a recording engineer, go out and be a recording engineer." I think that he was very firmly of the opinion that you can't wait to work with Aretha Franklin every week, because there are not that many Arethas in the world. Those generational artists are brilliant because they only come around so rarely, so you can't just sit there and wait to work with Aretha Franklin. You've got to go out there and work and go, "You know what? This band might be just a fairly okay band," but what you can do is make them the greatest recording of their artistry that you possibly can. There's validity to that.

You know the interesting thing about making records? It's so not about what box you have—and by the way, if you have the same box that everyone else thinks is the best box, you're just making another version of a box. Get your own thing, get an opinion, find something you like, and go for it.

A great producer I worked with once said something that I'll take with me to my grave. He said, "If you make a record and play it to 10 people, and 10 people like it, you have a Budweiser commercial." The object of the game should be if half the people passionately love it and half the people hate it, you've got a record.

I've been doing this for 30 years now, and I'm kind of talked out about gear and microphones and stuff. It's truly so uninteresting to me—or gear being great. It's just knobs and switches and capacitors that we use to capture performances. The whole idea that there is a best microphone, or a best preamp, or a best anything is kind of ludicrous. There's so much technology out there, and while I'm a huge proponent of Pro Tools and all the great things it can do, I don't really care which one of the

800 preamps out there sounds the best. It so doesn't matter at this point. If you get one of George Massenburg's preamps, or any one of the 12 superb preamps out there, it will more than amply handle the job. If you can't get good sounds with that, the problem isn't your equipment. The thing that truly interests me most is the psychology behind making music.

I would like to think I'm a good producer and a pretty great engineer, but I'm a mediocre musician. I rely on the record being not the sum of my talent, but the sum of all the talent I can utilize from the pool of musicians that I've selected. If it works, then the record can be greater than even the sum of their talents multiplied.

I don't have enough years left in my life to learn what George Doering knows about playing the guitar or understand what Vinnie Colaiuta understands about playing the drums.

My production is based on the fact that I think I have the credibility and reputation to where these guys will follow me down whatever path I ask, and that I have enough respect for them not to make them perform like trained monkeys.

Vinnie Colaiuta, for example, can give you more focused energy in six minutes than most people can give you in a day, and you've got to respect the fact that he's not a machine, that what he just did was fairly unbelievable, and that you can't keep asking for it. When you hit Secretariat [a legendary Kentucky Derby racehorse] on the rear end, you've got to understand what that horse is going to deliver.

This is true when working with the greatest players. It's not fair to ask them to do that all day, because of the sheer amount of intensity and processing that takes place. This is one of the single greatest production lessons I've learned.

If you have integrity, people will follow you anywhere as long as you don't take away hope. If they play something great and you don't acknowledge to them that it was great, or at least let them know that you understand what you just witnessed, it'll evaporate so fast. When I work with musicians, I'm really specific with my requests. If I have a take I know is great, and I go, "Guys, I need one more as a safety for such and such a reason," they'll do whatever I ask, as long as I acknowledge the moment I was just given and give a good reason why I want another take. Don't ever just randomly go, "Yeah, that was really good. Let's do another one," because those guys at some point will stop trying for you. You have to respect that moment.

It's amazing how generous the great ones are. It's almost always that the most generous guy in the room tends to be the most talented, and conversely, the guy whose headphones never fit, his cables are always broken, and he doesn't like the reverb on whatever is always the guy who's struggling to keep up.

I try not to engineer my own tracking dates when I'm producing. I want to be focused on capturing the moment. I'm lucky I'm good friends with some of the world's best engineers, and I hire guys I know I don't have to say anything to. They're going to make everything sound great. I can be working with Joe Chiccarelli, and we'll be reaching to change the same knob at the same frequency on the same instrument, but I know Joe's going to get it.

My favorite engineers of all time are Joe Chiccarelli, Bruce Swedien, Chris Lord-Alge, and Mick Guzauski, who basically taught me most of what I know. Mick is so good, it's really humbling to watch him work, but at the end of the day you look at his console, and it's not like there's any radical different thing than anyone else does, but his taste is so exquisite.

Early in my career, I butchered a good few records trying to sound like Mick Guzauski or Joe Chiccarelli, and it wasn't until I stopped trying to sound like someone else that I started hopefully making good records. The only thing I have to offer the creative forces out there is to try to be the best me I can be.

Chris Lord-Alge has got unbelievable ears and taste, and that's what he pays attention to, and then whatever the system is that he has going. I've given him some of my work to mix, just because I want to hear what Chris would do, and he is ungodly fast. I just like walking in and reacting to what he does. His chops are so good, and his taste level is so exquisite. I might go, "Chris, can you favor the acoustic instead of the electric," or whatever. It's just tiny little taste factors. You sit there, and anything you have to say about the mix, he can accomplish for you in 10 or 15 minutes because he really has got it dialed in so well.

Here's something to consider: If you walk into a mix session and you're talking to the guy for more than 30 minutes about what needs to be accomplished, you've probably got the wrong mixer. When Mick Guzauski mixes something for me, it's like, number one, this is absolutely gorgeous, and anything I do to change this will just be my personal little predilections—and that's fine, but it's not going to sell one record more based on the changes I've been making. What he does is absolutely beautiful.

Both Chris and Mick do the most wonderful, adventurous, opinionated mixes, and their mixes speak volumes. It's not just some kind of passive arrangement of what you've given them to where you can hear everything. It will really have an angle.

Quincy Jones said something once—I thought it was one of the greatest lines ever. I believe it was a paraphrased version of, "If it was easy, everyone would do it." It's not supposed to be easy, and some of the records that I look back on that continue to mean something to me were not easy, but they were rewarding. I did this record years ago that achieved some kind of notoriety, but I still get work from it today, and people still revere the record. It was *Key Lime Pie* for Camper van Beethoven. That was my first involvement with producer Dennis Herring. To this day, what I think is great about it is that record doesn't sound dated. It's still really valid from a musical and sonic perspective. It was a life-changing experience, and I wouldn't swap that for all the easy, non-memorable, cotton-candy stuff that I've done, as we have all done.

I think the worst thing that Pro Tools brings out is the fact that great art is never made from limitless possibilities. Great art always comes from limits, kind of by definition. There's the Sistine Chapel. Paint it. It's a pain in the butt. Figure it out.

These people who never comp tracks and just hand it to mixers! Guys, make a choice somewhere along the way. So few great records are made now because you don't have to make a decision. The whole idea of never having to commit to some kind of vision—that it's always just another endless stream of possibilities—I think is not good for making records. The technology is phenomenal. It's great that you can tune people and shift beats around, but we've also got a generation of so-called artists who can't really perform or play, and that's not interesting to me.

That said, one of my pet peeves right now are guys my age sitting around whining about how the '80s or '90s aren't coming back. As painful as this transitional period is with the Internet and iTunes and all that stuff, something better is going to come out of this, and I really believe it's an incredibly exciting time.

Norbert Putnam

Credits include: Dan Fogelberg, Jimmy Buffett, New Riders of the Purple Sage, Joan Baez, Dobie Gray, Jerry Butler, Eric Anderson. See the Appendix for Norbert Putnam's full bio.

There is an emotional aspect to the arts that many people seem to lose sight of. Rick Hall, with his four-channel Shure mixer and Fender bassman monitor system, was completely adequate for the emotional brilliance of the legendary Arthur Alexander. Willie Mitchell didn't need the latest console or the microphone for those records he did with Al Green. Al Green could sing the phone book, and people would love it.

When I lived in Nashville, they used to always talk about the songs. Of course, Nashville is run by publishers, but to me it has never been "the song." A great song is a wonderful thing, but you take an artist like Al Green or Elvis Presley, and you can give them a very trite lyric, and they can sing it with such emotion and power that will give you chill bumps. It's not the lines; it's the artist. So I totally disagree with all those people who peddle the idea that the song is the thing. If you take those songs and put them on a sheet of paper and read them, you'll know that the song is not the thing. Elvis Presley definitely proved that me.

What we sell in this business is emotion. When you have a purveyor of emotion, like Al Green or Elvis Presley, then you have magic. That is the beginning and end of it. It is never the equipment. It is not the SSL, Neve, Mackie, or Trident console. It is not the snare drum or the reverb. And I would've argued this point years ago, but it is not the bass line. [Laughs] It really is the artist. People hear the artist, and they hear the emotion. They either buy it or they won't. I think it is a quick study.

I had a friend who was president of Elizabeth Arden cosmetics. He said, "Norbert, we just sell boxes. We sell these beautiful decorated boxes, and when a lady walks by the perfume counter, she glances at the boxes, and the one that catches her eye, she buys. And we probably have a 5- to 10-second window to capture her imagination."

When you and I are listening to the radio, we may not even give it 5 or 10 seconds. We lock on a station, and we may hear three or four seconds and then we pass on to another station. So it is a magical thing that a good artist does with his or her voice that attracts us or sends us away. That is really what this industry is all about. Anything else is disposable art. It is like a piece of candy that is good for a few moments, and it's gone.

David Kahne

Credits include: Tony Bennett, Sublime, Imogen Heap, Wilco, k.d. lang, Paul McCartney, Sugar Ray, Dionne Farris, Bangles, Fishbone, Shawn Colvin, Matthew Sweet. See the Appendix for David Kahne's full bio.

I can tell when something is right when I am kind of scared of the person I'm considering signing or producing. I'm always looking for that little fear in myself when I try and decide. I think that is where the greatness is going to come from. If I know what they are going to do, it is not going to be good enough. [Laughs] I'm not the artist.

When people are really good, you've got to know what you are doing and what you are talking about. You've got to be able to hear and listen, because you are going to be challenged. If you don't, you are just going to be ignored.

It is very important to understand that A&R is more than just signing someone who can make a great record. I mean I've made records that I thought were really great, but I found out that the artist couldn't really follow through on being a recording star. I'm not just talking about looking good for the video. I'm talking about having the energy and the kind of thing to go out and be somebody who is going to be an image for a lot of people.

In the last few years, it has become so easy for someone to make a record. A lot of people get record deals and put out albums way before they should. They might have a good song, but you can feel the boundary very quickly on what is going on.

In the '60s, the best bands had the best drummers, and there weren't that many good drummers around. If you had a good drummer in your band, and you sucked, eventually he would be quitting and joining a better band. Nobody has to go through that gauntlet anymore. You can just get loops or machines. Even though I love using loops, I love more than anything making loops with a great drummer.

That whole thing of being able to make a pretty good-sounding record with less rehearsal and less performing and weight and depth in your experience is a pretty weird thing. It not only affects the bands, it also affects the A&R people. There are a lot of A&R people who don't know how vast it is. If they did, they would run screaming from music. Once you sign somebody and make the record, it is like "Whoa! What is going on?" It just gets wider and wider and wider. You push on music, and it is completely malleable. You are building something out of nothing.

Bands go in, and they'll have something that feels pretty engaging, but then you go in to record and try to blow it up into the space of a real record, and there isn't enough to become a real record...a full album. I think a lot of people are disappointed in buying albums and not finding whole albums there.

At my apartment in New York, I can look out and see the CBS building and the Time Warner building, where Elektra and Atlantic and all that stuff is. One day I was listening to tapes that people had sent me, thinking about me producing a record. I was into about my tenth tape, and every one was, "This is really not good, not good, not good, not good." Then I was playing this song back, and it had this chorus, and there was this really cool thing going on, and I was thinking, "God, this is really great."

I started thinking how music is so private and it is so perverse and when you are in recording, you might've been working for three weeks and nothing is coming together, and in a split second there is something there that has meaning and it has tone. My feeling from that is that the artist always lets a secret out, and that secret and that moment always shows up on tape. It is this invisible thing that you can't really pinpoint in time and space. You just happen to be recording, and you set this whole track up, and someone may be out there singing. All of a sudden, there is shape to the music and a center to the song.

Anyway, I was listening to this song, and I thought that when I hear something that really works, it is kind of a miracle because it kind of defies gravity. It is like, "Why does this sound mean something and all of these other sounds don't mean very much?" While I was listening to this, I turned around and looked out the window, and I looked up at these buildings and saw this inverted pyramid of this giant corporation and this little teeny song with this big corporation on its back. [Laughs] And I was thinking, "These songs are struggling to save these giant companies. That is really what it is about." It has gotten more and more that way, I think. "Is music really made to support this whole thing?" Well, in a certain way, I don't think it was.

A hundred years ago, a guy would've been sitting in a village with his guitar playing at a local wedding, and it was probably what popular music was at the time. Now it's been amplified, and the whole distribution of it is huge. Nevertheless, it still begins with somebody with this little secret that slips out. That is the part of it that I love. I love being there and hearing it come together and going, "A second ago this wasn't music, and now this is music." From that point outward, it is all kind of a mess. [Laughs]

I think that trying to save these huge worldwide companies with these little songs is sometimes humorous, and sometimes I really despair over it. Because it affects the people playing the music, and it just changes the values of it.

I'm not a purist by any means. I'm not saying that music shouldn't sell. But I think that it is harder to operate in that environment, and I didn't think that it used to be so much that way.

The companies are bigger and they are worldwide, it takes more and more energy to keep them going, they need music faster, and it is just kind of an odd relationship between the two things. Still, you know a record is not going to be good, unless a guy sits in a room and that weird little thing happens.

As a producer, I take everybody individually, but I think my one sort of guiding principle is that I don't like to make an album without at least one single on it. By "single," I mean not necessarily something for the radio. I just mean that I always have to have a place to start from, and it is usually based around a song where I feel I really can get the essence of everything about the band or artist into that one song.

I've noticed that whenever I can leave an album, and I have a track like that on the record, the record tends to do well and take the band to another level. That was true with the Bangles, Sublime, and Sugar Ray.

When you listen to someone like Cream or R.E.M. or anyone who has ever had a career, and you listen to their first record, you always hear a song that has that thing on it. On R.E.M.'s first album, it was "Radio Free Europe." It wasn't a hit, but it was definitely a single. It got airplay on certain formats, and it kind of coalesced the energy around the band. They had that one song on that record that got on the radio, and it had a great melody and release on it.

It is something that I have to hear from the artist. That has really been the thing I have followed in my whole career. I'll do whatever it takes to get a song to be the point at the end of the spear.

When I was working with Sugar Ray, I heard "Fly" in the rehearsal room. It was just barely started, but I heard Mark singing in a lower register, and I thought, "I know I could make a great record out of this song."

It is important to build up a song and create a tone so that you can hold somebody's interest for three or four minutes without one single tiny glitch. Somebody has got to know, from that first measure, where they are, and you've got to keep them there until you are ready to let go. I still do that today.

The thing about A&R versus production—there are some people who have this A&R philosophy of just signing stars. I think that is great, but there has to be some sound on the record that has to be a start, too.

Tony Brown

Credits include: Lyle Lovett, Steve Earle, Reba McEntire, George Strait, Barbra Streisand, Joe Ely, Nanci Griffith, Vince Gill, Patty Loveless, Jimmy Buffett, Marty Stuart, Mac McAnally, Wynonna Judd, Billy Joel. See the Appendix for Tony Brown's full bio.

If you are producing a session and there is one person in the room who is holding things up, you've got to move them out of there. How you do it is as important as deciding to do it. It can be done. You can either completely close down a session or deal with it in a smooth kind of way, where nobody knows it happened, but it happened.

I've seen one person completely start shutting down a tracking session. I just know it, and everybody in the room knows it. That's when it becomes the producer's responsibility to take care of that problem. It is not the artist's responsibility. That's a hard job to take care of, and an artist shouldn't have to deal with that. He needs to be creative. He shouldn't have to worry about that. I think that is when a lot of musicians look at a producer, and they see you do that and they respect you for doing it.

You have to do it just right. You can't make a scene. If it is a scene, then you have blown everything. It may take you 30 minutes to get the nerve to do it, but you can figure it out. There are all kinds of ways. You can pull them out of the room or have them sit in the control room. You have to give them a reason. Nine times out of 10, depending on their ego control, they will usually say, "Have I got time to run an errand?" [Laughs] That means, "I'm embarrassed. I'm out of here." They might say, "I'll be at this place. Call me if you need me."

At the time that it happens, artists will look at me with fear in their eyes. I just say, "Listen, this is business. No problem." Then two hours later, I realize that they have already forgotten about the incident. Maybe they'll ask me about it later on, but at the time, I think they think it can't be done.

I find that great musicians even know when they are not cutting it. That's one thing I learned years ago with Rodney Crowell. Rodney would have no qualms about saying to me, "Hey, Tony. Your part is sort of messing up the groove. Let's overdub you." I was fine with that because I just wanted to be a part of this record-making process, even if I didn't play a note. That's the way I felt. Rodney picked up on that. I figured that whenever it was right, it was right. You need to learn how to deal with the record-making process and learn that you've just got to be in control of your ego.

For Rosanne Cash's "Seven Year Ache," I played that for seven hours, but then Emory Gordy ended up playing the piano part on the record. He ended up playing all the staccato eighth notes. The only place that I exist on "Seven Year Ache" is somewhere in echo return, if I bled into somebody's earphones. [Laughs] Otherwise, I'm not on that record.

Emory was sweating it, saying, "Ah Tony. You can do it." Meanwhile, Rodney would say, "Emory, I like the way you do it. You play those eighths better than anybody." He did, and Rodney was right. When Emory played them, it was just different.

I learned from all that to just suck it up and learn. It is crucial to learn that when you have the access to anybody's talent in a room, maybe even the engineer could play that part. Whatever! Who cares! You've just got to learn how to make records. If you are there, then you are part of it.

Joe Boyd

Credits include: Pink Floyd, R.E.M., Fairport Convention, Nick Drake, the Incredible String Band, Richard Thompson, Billy Bragg, Toots and the Maytals, Linda Ronstadt, 10,000 Maniacs. See the Appendix for Joe Boyd's full bio.

Everyone talks about how much the recording process has altered in the past 30 years. And it's true that digital recording has changed the game tremendously. But for me, the essentials remain the same. I believe in getting as much of a live feel as possible, while maintaining a high-quality sound that permits achieving a mix of the highest quality. That means getting as much of the track recorded live as possible. It also means using rooms that are live, that have character, and that reward an approach that takes risks by forgoing isolation in most cases.

It is important that musicians have a sense of occasion and danger in recording. Putting down tracks or vocals with endless opportunities to correct and perfect accomplishes the opposite of what I look for in a recording. I can usually tell when a click track, or one-by-one tracking has been involved—the results are usually clean, correct, and lifeless. When there is one track left on a 16-track machine for vocals, for example, the singer and the producer have to choose after each take whether to go for another or erase the last pass. This puts everyone on edge and forces great performances out of singers.

People sometimes comment on the depth and warmth of the recordings I made with John Wood at Sound Techniques in the 1960s. Recording in modern small, dead rooms cannot accomplish this. To me, many, if not most, modern recordings sound shiny and two-dimensional. Attractive, perhaps, on first listen, but without the durability to endure repeated listenings....

You could say that two-track recording is the purest form of record making. Four-track, eight-track, et cetera through the present limitless expanse of possibilities on Pro Tools have all been steps backward in terms of making recordings that will endure the test of time.

David Briggs

Credits include: Neil Young, Neil Young and Crazy Horse, Spirit, Royal Trux, Alice Cooper, Grin, Willie Nelson, Nick Cave and the Bad Seeds. See the Appendix for David Briggs's full bio.

Production is an art form, or it is the world's highest paying babysitting job. It is kind of like coaching sports. You've got to know when to kiss butt, and you've got to know when to kick butt. You can't do them both at the same time, and you can't do the wrong one at the wrong time, or you will just ruin everything.

As a producer, the one thing I always remember is I am not making David Briggs' records. I am making other people's records. Even though everybody leaves a little piece of themselves behind, I try and stay as invisible as possible on my records. No matter what genre of song it is, it is all the same music to me. You listen to the songs, and there is a performance, and I just try to lay out the context as clearly as possible so that no side roads present themselves to the artists as they go toward their art. If you can do that, then their art will stick through and it will stick on tape.

I actually don't like to work in studios very much. Most studios are so sterile. If you give me a chance, I'll take a remote truck and record in this hotel room and get a better sound than most people get in a studio. I would rather record in a house or a barn, a high school gym, or any place other than a studio.

If I have got to work in a studio, I want to work in a giant room or soundstage. There are a few good studios, like Criteria in Miami or Bearsville in New York. Bearsville has a really great room. Criteria has got a huge playing room, and they've got a great old Neve 80 Series console.

The reason I like to use the big rooms is because I prefer live recording. You can't do it in a little room, at least not with the bands I work with. They all play at such big levels, and to work the way I work, I need a huge room. I don't use any baffles, and I use a full PA in the room. It is enormously loud when I work, so I have to have a big room to be able to keep the sound from coming back in on me. Basically, that is it. Most people use baffles to keep it in. I use baffles and hang things to keep it from coming back.

On the last record I did with Neil [Young], I used a soundstage. I rented lights and set them up. I set the band up like they were on stage and put a full PA in there and let it rip.

I mike the amps. I mike the drums. Of course, I mike all the vocals, because they are all live vocals as well. Then I also mike the room, and I use that as well. It is in the swims where the spook lives. That is exactly what it is. It is like everything sounds like records, until you start to bring that room up and then it is just like, "Who the heck knows what it is?" It sounds like something different. [Laughs] It doesn't sound like you are in a studio anymore. That is for sure.

I look for the spook in the swim. The swim is what happens when you've recorded the space in the room and all the instruments you put into any volume of space—whether it is Madison Square Garden or House of Blues in Memphis—get dumped into the mix. That is the swim.

The spook is the weirdness, the strange unpredictable stuff that you'd never know if you just tight-miked everything. If you haven't done this, then you ain't living. [Laughs] You might be living, but you are living safe. You are not skating out on the edge. When you start using rooms and things like that, and the big sound, strange things happen. They really do. If you know how to control it and you know how to focus your tight-miking and how to make your tight-miking work with you instead of against you, you can do some great stuff. Otherwise, it will sound like a mush. Obviously, great mic technique is a key.

One of my aims is to take the "studio" out of the sound. With the Neil Young stuff, a lot of his records—like *Rust Never Sleeps*, for instance—were all recorded live. The only difference between *Rust Never Sleeps* and *Live Rust* is *Live Rust* has the crowd in the mix and *Rust Never Sleeps* has the crowd stripped. That is the only difference.

All of the electric stuff was cut at the Forum and Madison Square Garden and you name it. It was all over the place. I took the truck with me. I did *Rust Never Sleeps* and *Live Rust* at the same time. I used all the same performances, and I just stripped the crowd. When you listen to the record again, you know what you are hearing is a performance in front of 15,000 people. When I digitally stripped the crowd out, it sounded like the studio stuff except that it had the performance energy of playing in front of 15,000 people. That is a big difference.

The reason I personally like to record like this is that I am lucky, or unlucky, enough—I don't know which one it is—to have been making records for a really long time. I can remember when Little Richard or Ray Charles made records. They made them by everyone going into the studio, and they all played at once. They would all get their tones on the spot, and they would all play at 75 percent of their abilities all together, and it would make a 100-percent record. It would sound really great. There was no introspection or nitpicking and pulling things apart, like wings on a fly.

When you work like that, the most critical part of it is that instead of the vocal coming in later and shoehorning itself into what a bunch of other people have decided is the dynamic of the song, you have a band playing to the vocal's dynamic. That is where the magic is.

You would be amazed at how little bleed I get in my recordings. I use what everybody else uses. When people come in and iso up my tapes, everyone is always shocked. They go, "There is no leakage. Why is it so clean?" Well, you just have to know where to place the mics.

When I did [Neil Young's] *Ragged Glory*, we cut it in a barn. I had mics 6 and 8 feet away from Neil's guitar, as well as up close. I had four or five microphones on the amplifiers, including ones that were 5, 6, and 7 feet away. I also had a full PA in the room, plus everything blasting and we put them [the mics] all in the right spots and got it. If you don't put them in the right spots, you get this big wash of crud. It is the same with drums.

When you are live recording drums, for instance, if you focus the mics back at the snare drum, then you don't get phase cancellations, and the ones that you do cancel out leakage and stuff like that, as opposed to loading up all the leakage on the drums. I will tell you that even in cases where I have to redo the vocals, for instance, I don't ever have to compromise the room for it because of leakage, because it is not there. You never hear the leakage.

I like [Neil Young's] *Ragged Glory* a lot. I got seven of the songs on that album all in one pass, all in one night. We just went straight through song after song after song. We just doubled the background vocals, and that's what we did. It was the night of an earthquake, and nobody felt it. We just played right through it. The ground was shaking, and we thought it was us. [Laughs] Any time you can get even finished masters in one night, you know you are doing something right.

Producing the Royal Trux was five days, from the day I walked into the studio door until the day I walked out with the rough mixes. It took a day and a half to cut all the songs. I spent a day overdubbing and three days mixing. It was all there right from the start. That is the kind of thing I like. You walk in the door. Nobody is working. It is not hard. There is no effort. You walk out the door and seven songs are done, and you go, "How did I do that?" The first blush is, "They can't be any good. Anything that easy can't be that good." It is a philosophy I see repeated in the bands and record companies and everybody. "It can't be any good. It's too easy. Anything that you can do in two days can't be any good." Not! Two years is when it is not any good. I love things that just get up and go and have their own life to it.

When I did Neil Young's *Tonight's the Night*, we started that record off in L.A. in the studio and then one day I fired the studio and tore it all down and went to some studio rentals and a rehearsal room, kicked a hole in the wall, put a truck outside, and started recording. They would come in and play and bash around and have fun every night, and I would just take notes. Every time when something happened that I thought was extraordinary, I would walk to the truck and mix it on the spot. Then I would walk back in. Five minutes would go by, and they would be out having a cup of coffee, and they wouldn't even know I was out doing mixes. When we finished the record all up, I remixed the entire record three times in every studio known to mankind and remixed it and remixed it and remixed it, and finally I got so bored with it I said, "I don't want to work on this record anymore." I totally lost interest in it, and Neil totally lost interest in it.

Two years later, he played it for the band, and they played my original rough mixes and they went, "What record is this?" He had just played them *Homegrown*, a record he was going to put out. They said, "Oh, *Homegrown* is great, but what record was that you just played?" So three years after I did it, it came alive again and was released.

I like *Tonight's the Night*. It has got the edge, balls, and attitude. There is no fear in those takes. "Tired Eyes" is one of Neil's most underrated performances, with that talking voice. It is so spooky. The spook was in the swim on that night. There is no doubt about it.

It was like one of those things where it was so easy, and everyone just played and had fun. Nobody ever said, "Let's work music." They all said, "Let's play music." A lot of people do work music, but I like to play music. Anything that comes like that is almost always inevitably good.

I think when you are looking too much at what you are doing, all you see are the "blue" spots. You don't see the shine and the magic. When you do it layer by layer by layer, you never have a chance to see the magic of the whole picture until you are somewhere on down the road. This way you see it immediately. Immediately! If the band delivers something that is great, they walk in the door and they listen to what is close to a finished record. It is a big difference.

I couldn't tell you the year I met Neil [Young] if it was on the calendar, but I know how I met him. I was driving my Army Personnel Carrier down the road, and Neil was just walking down the road. I just thought I would give the hippie a break and pick him up. Give the hippie a lift, you know. [Laughs] It was the beginning of a long relationship. "Nice truck!" [Imitating Neil] Neil and I have a lot in common. We both like cars a lot. Cars and guitars. We don't do it so much anymore, but we used to drive a lot. We used to love getting in the car and just going. It didn't matter where. I still love to do that.

Every time when we finish a project, and we have got a four- or five-day jump, I always drive home. Any time I can drive somewhere, I'm happy. I like to sit there and blast the tape as loud as I can with the windows down and the air rushing by. It's great. Anybody that doesn't do that doesn't have a musical soul. People that really love music love to get in their cars and drive.

When I am done at night, even at three in the morning, I get in my car with my tape from the day and drive until I hear it all, even if I have got 30 minutes of work on it and I live eight minutes away from the hotel. I have been that way since I have been a kid, and I still feel that way. That is where I hear music.

For my rent-a-car, I found out about four years ago that the Cadillac Seville had a sound system that I fell in love with. The graphic equalizer and how the speakers are placed are great. In all honesty, it has been my ghetto blaster ever since. I rent that Cadillac Seville. I have spent thousands and thousands of dollars renting this ghetto blaster. If I had just gone out and found this ghetto blaster that had a good tone, I probably could've saved myself ten grand or something in the last four years. I like the sound of that car. I just get in that thing and go.

Jim Dickinson

Credits include: The Replacements, Big Star, Screamin' Jay Hawkins, Toots Hibbert, Ry Cooder, the North Mississippi Allstars, Bob Dylan, the Rolling Stones. See the Appendix for Jim Dickinson's full bio.

Somebody once asked me down at South by Southwest whether I felt my obligation as a producer was to the company or the artist. I replied that I felt my primary obligation was to the project itself. That said, I tend to be more sympathetic to the artist than the company, but that's just a personality flaw. It keeps me from getting work. [Laughs] I do think that the vision belongs to the artist, even though he or she may not be aware of it. Huey Meaux once said, "You gotta keep the artist in the dark—that way his star shines more brighter." You know? [Laughs] It may not always be, you know, to the advantage of the outcome of the project for the artist to know what's going on.

I do think that the record kind of preexists in the collective unconscious. I try to hear what's in the artist's head and figure out how to get that space between the notes on the tape. If you think about what you do visually, there's a big difference between high-contrast production and what you could call earth-tone production.

I think that contrast is at the basis of all art. It's in the contrast between motion and stillness, sound and silence, and light and darkness where the sparks of artistic realization are born. I want to show the artist how to use the studio rather than be abused by it, and that's what I try to do with any artist who's interested in that. If they're not interested in that, I try to eliminate the problems that are between them and a successful recording.

Back before I produced the Replacements' *Pleased to Meet Me*, I literally never talked to A&R people. I was always hired by managers or groups to protect the artists from the company. Then after the Replacements' record, I started getting hired by A&R people who had "problem" bands. So I sort of inherited the socalled "problem" groups. [Laughs] Yeah, I think I've had my share of them.

I think that, in the case of many young bands who can remain nameless, the more they compromise, the more they eliminate the very thing that they might have had that could have gotten them across more meaningfully to an audience.

I have a reputation with companies. They'll say, "Oh yeah, well, Dickinson, he goes for the quirks." That's right; I do go for the quirks. And they say that as if that's bad. I think the quirks need to be magnified, because music—good music—shoots sparks. And I try to catch those sparks. I try to turn 'em up to where they're in your face, maybe a little more obvious than normal, because I think a record has to be bigger than life. I'm not a documentary producer. I try to capture the moment and enlarge it to where it's more obvious.

I look for the overtones, the squeaks and squawks on the strings, and the human element that many engineers and some producers try to eliminate. I know engineers and producers who go back with the computer and systematically remove the breath from the vocal performance. Well, when you take away the breath, it seems to me obvious that you are destroying the life. Obviously, that's what's alive is the breathing. When I record horn players, I'm very aware that there's always that breath before they play, and I always try to get it because I think it sounds alive. No musician I've ever heard breathes out of meter, you know.

I do try to consider why it is specifically that people come to me. I mean, I think it's hard to get in touch with me, so they have to really want to seek me out, and that's part of it because I think some of 'em should be eliminated, you know. As I told one A&R person in a situation that didn't turn out well for anybody, "Be sure you want it. Don't ask me for it if you don't want it, 'cause I'm gonna give it to you. I'm gonna put it on ya, and it's not for everybody."

Some labels that approach me aren't interested in integrity as much as they are interested in manipulation. There are producers who do that, you know, but it's just not my long suit to go in heavy-handedly and fire members of the band and reconstruct things musically. That's just not what I'm good at, and I do try to make sure that whomever it is that I'm working with understands that.

I used to hear that if you are coming into a new job as an executive, the first thing you should do is fire somebody and then promote somebody to prove you can. There are producers who do this as a rule of thumb. They fire the drummer because it is easier to bring in another drummer. They also set out to make someone feel important. I know that I tend to "produce" certain members of a group more than others. There are always members that require more production.

When you lose a band member, that is a casualty. I've had band members quit, and that can be devastating, too. It's like the run of a play. A chance camaraderie develops that is part of the production process. There is enough of a trance bond that happens in the studio from playing the songs over and over and listening to them back that it really becomes a little sub-family unit. Tensions and casualties are very serious to me in a recording project.

I grew up watching and learning from these old blues men—Fred McDowell, Bukka White, Furry and John Woods, Nathan Beauregard, and Reverend Robert Wilkins—who provided a different understanding of the realities of the music business. I learned some very important life lessons about survival and how not to take things personally.

In this business, rejection and humiliation are literally daily occurrences. You can't ask an artist not to be sensitive. It just doesn't make sense. At the same time, if you do take it too personally, it will kill you and your art.

I had this coach in high school who told me and a friend of mine—when we were considering joining the Marines as an alternative to being drafted—"If you do this thing, you've got to remember that they're not doing it to you…they're just doing it." I didn't apply that to the Marines, but I have applied it to the record business, and it has true meaning for me. They are just doing it. They're not doing it to you. It's happening, you know. It's falling on you, and it's falling on your art, but you can't take it personally.

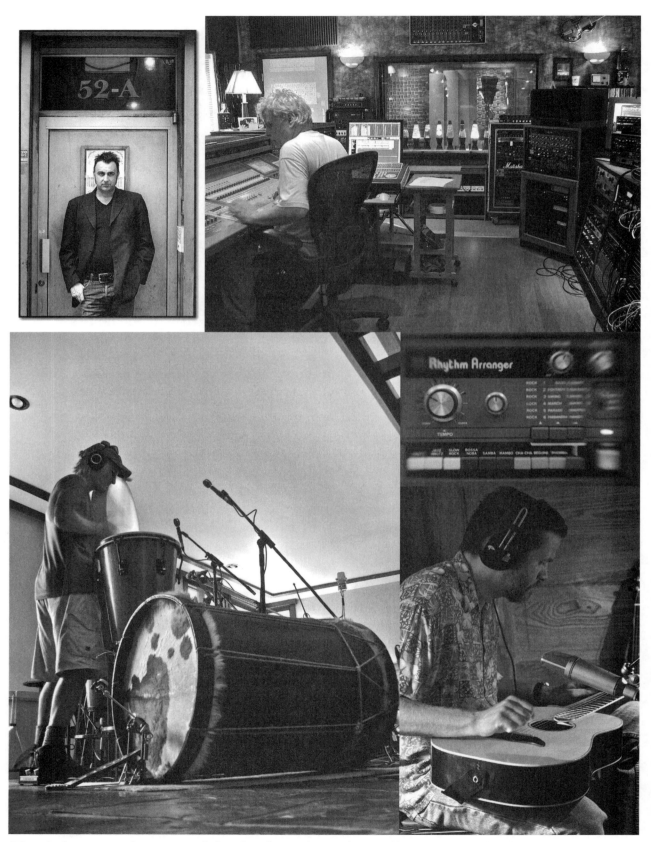

Tim Palmer at Electric Ladyland (photo by Asko Kallonen) / Michael Wagener at Wire World (photo by Rick Clark). Row 2: Kirby Shelstad (photo by Rick Clark) / Rob Ickes (photo by Rick Clark).

Piano is one of the most amazing creations in the universe of musical instruments. It is capable of some of the most delicate melodic expressions, as well as delivering brute percussive attacks that are startling in their immediacy. It has been a vehicle for timeless classics, such as Beethoven's haunting "Moonlight Sonata," the playfulness of Chick Corea's "Spain," and Count Basie's swinging minimalism. Rock and roll, blues, and R&B's finest moments have been served well by the piano, thanks to Jerry Lee Lewis, Charles Brown, Fats Domino, Allen Toussaint, and many others.

Capturing piano on tape is an undertaking that requires a good understanding of the instrument at hand and its effect on the room in which it is being recorded. I rounded up four experts on the matter of recording piano, two of which are professional pianists. The points of view range from classical to rock and roll, and from philosophically seeing mono as the best way to present the instrument, to the virtues of dead strings. I would like to thank Jim Dickinson, John Hampton, Richard King, Cookie Marenco, and Ralph Sutton for their insight and enthusiastic participation in this piece. Ellen Fitton and Michael Omartian also deserve thanks for their input.

Richard King

Credits include: Yo-Yo Ma, Riccardo Muti, Filarmonica della Scala, Los Angeles Philharmonic, Philadelphia Orchestra, Yefim Bronfman, Emanuel Ax, Murray Perahia. See the Appendix for Richard King's full bio.

Two main elements needed are a good piano and a good hall. After agreeing on a recording venue, the producer and artist will choose a piano, out of many pianos, so they are really deciding on what piano sound they want, based on the instrument. I only use two omni-directional microphones, and I really rely on the piano sounding exactly the way the artist and everyone is expecting it to sound. From that, I try to duplicate exactly what we are getting in the hall. Very rarely will I add any additional mics to enhance the hall sound.

For mics, the B&K 4009 is my choice, which is a high-powered 130-volt input mic that has been matched at the factory. People would probably be more familiar with the 4003, which is a powered omni. The 4009 is a matched pair of those. They match them throughout production, choosing pairs of caps and other elements to build them. They are a true stereo pair. The serial numbers are an A and a B. B&K 4006s are good, too.

On a number of occasions, I have also used the Schoeps MK 2, which is again an omni with a high-frequency shelf. The B&K has a peak way up high, around 18 kHz. So it has more of a sparkle on the top end, rather than the brightness characterized by the Schoeps. The B&K is a little tighter on the low end than the Schoeps.

I will use outboard preamps and go straight to tape, so there is no console involved. I have used with great success fully discrete Swiss-made preamps made by SONOSAX. They are solid state, and they are very fast. The extension to the low and high end is very good. Like the B&K mics, they are incredibly quick, which is a sound that I like.

I've also used the Millennia preamp, which is very good. It has a 130-volt input on it, so I can use the high-powered B&Ks without their own power supply, which I think is inferior. I can go straight into the Millennia with a 130-volt line, which is kind of nice.

We have customized the input gain stage to 1 1/2 dB steps, on the Millennias, in order to optimize level to tape. Millennia did the mods for us.

The other thing that I've done on occasion is put my A/D out on the stage with the piano and then just run an AES snake back to the control room to the tape machine, so that I am converting digital onstage, so the analog line is getting pretty short.

We record two tracks. We've used the Nagra digital tape machine with great success. It is a four-track machine, but I just put stereo down on it twice for redundancy. Lately, we've been experimenting with 96-kHz/24-bit stereo, which we also store across four tracks of the Nagra.

We've also used the Sony PCM-9000, which is a magneto-optical recorder, and also the Prism setup with the PCM-800, which is the same as the Tascam DA-88. It'll do four tracks at 24-bit, but I'm just printing two mics again. So I just put the two mics down twice for redundancy.

I tend to prefer a more live hall. For my mic positioning, I could be anywhere from 4 feet to 8 feet away from the piano. The mics are set, from the audience's perspective, somewhere around the middle of the longest string on the piano, halfway down the instrument. The mics will be pointed, however, toward the hammers and are normally set up parallel to one another.

For spacing the mics, I sometimes tend to go as tight as 18 inches apart, and I've been as wide as 4 or 5 feet. The mic spacing directly correlates to the desired image of the piano recording. The deciding factor depends on the repertoire and the sound that the producer and the artist want. It is always subjective.

I just did a record with Arcadi Volodos in England of all piano transcriptions, which means that orchestral scores were reduced to being played on a piano by one player. For that, it seemed right that we had a much larger piano image, so there was a much wider spread on the microphones. Prior to that, I did a record of Prokofiev piano sonatas, where I really wanted a good solid center image, so I went with a tighter mic spread.

Obviously, with omnis, you can't pan them in at all, because there will be phase cancellation, so I always leave them hard left and right. In fact, I'm not even going through a console most of the time, so it really is just left and right. If I want more of a mono image, I'll place the mics closer together.

If the hall isn't so great, then I will also go a little tighter with the mics and add a little reverb. But generally, it is all natural recording, if I can get away with that.

When I need to apply reverb, I like the Random Hall setting found on the Lexicon 480L. I also like the Small Random Church [setting]. Between the two of those, I usually can find something that I can work with. I always change the parameters and customize the settings. They are just the settings I usually start with.

I tend to pull down the Random Hall in size to around 31 or 34 meters, depending on the recording. Again, I am trying to bring in something that matches the existing hall sound, because these recordings are never dry. I try and sneak in something where you can't actually tell that I've added additional reverb to, so I am very careful to match the characteristics of the existing room reverb.

On a 480, I find that the Shape and the Spread controls offer a lot of flexibility. There is also a high-frequency cut-off that actually enables you to change the basic overall sound of the reverb without actually running an additional EQ stage.

I only do this if the hall isn't so adequate. Most piano records that I have done have just been two mics and that is it—no EQ and no additional reverb.

Sometimes, if a grand piano sounds a little "covered," I'll extend the stick [the prop that holds up the lid]. I'm always on a full stick [the piano lid prop fully extended] anyway, but if I want the piano to sound a little more open, I'll bring a piece of wood that is maybe another 4 inches longer than the regular stick and put the lid up slightly higher. I've used a pool cue with great success, because of the rubber base of the stick and the felt tip. It doesn't damage the piano, and it gets the lid open a little bit more.

Concerning panning, I always go with the image of the lower notes to the right side and the high notes coming out of the left, so it is always audience perspective for me. There are usually some telltale extreme low notes usually coming from the right, and extreme high comes from the left, but the main sound of the piano comes from the middle. I think that most people in jazz and pop do the opposite panning, which is from the player's perspective.

My absolute favorite hall to record in is on the east coast of England. It is called Snape Maltings. It used to be the malting place, where they created the malt that then would get shipped out to the brewery. It is an old brick building with a wooden roof, and it has a really great reverb. Even the higher notes of the piano ring into the room with a great sustain, but it is still a very warm sound.

My favorite pianos are Hamburg Steinways. I think they record the best. For classical, the Hamburg Steinway has a better balance of low and high notes. The Hamburg Steinways also seem to be a little better for me than the New York Steinways. I find that Bösendorfers sound great, but for some reason, I've had real trouble recording them. It is kind of a wild instrument. The Steinway sounds the most even over microphones. I've used Yamahas for pop and jazz, and they are really great for that, but for classical, I find they are a little too bright.

Cookie Marenco

Credits include: Mary Chapin Carpenter, Charlie Haden Quartet West, Ladysmith Black Mambazo, Brain and Buckethead, Mark Isham, Turtle Island String Quartet, Philip Aaberg, Steve Swallow, Carla Bley, Glen Moore, Ralph Towner, Oregon, and Clara Ponty. See the Appendix for Cookie Marenco's full bio.

One of the hardest things to find is a good piano in a good studio. At my studio, I have a 7-foot Steinway that was built in 1885. A lot of people from all over come to play on it. As a player, I like the Steinway for the touch and because there is a roundness to the sound that I prefer.

We keep the piano brighter than most Steinways. We don't voice it down as much as a classical instrument for a concert, but it wouldn't be as bright as a Yamaha, which tends to be a brighter-sounding instrument. Personally, I'm not a big fan of Yamaha.

You can hear the difference between the various pianos, once you get familiar with all of them. You can hear a recording and tell whether it is a Yamaha, Steinway, or Bösendorfer.

Sometimes, Steinways get a little muddy in the midrange, between the octave below middle C and the octave above it. That is the only thing you have to watch for in a Steinway.

Usually, when I record a piano, I'll use two B&Ks [the 4011s or the 4012s], placed in sort of a V position, about 8 or 9 inches apart, with one mic pointed toward the keyboard and one pointed toward the back end of the piano. They'll be placed at more of a 45-degree angle, somewhere in the center of the instrument, where the midrange is, about halfway up, between the piano lid and where the strings sit. If I do that, I get a lot of clarity in the middle.

If I am doing more of a classical session, the mics may be backed off more—not even inside the piano—to get more of the room. It depends more on the sound that the artist is looking for.

If I were in a situation where I didn't have B&Ks, then KM 84s would be another choice. The Schoeps mics work well, too.

You really have to listen, because every player attacks the piano differently. Even slightly different positionings or placements in a room can change the phase relationships.

On a lot of the 9-foot pianos, I'll even put up a couple of other floor mics, as sort of "insurance" mics, to capture the range of the instrument.

I'm a big fan of stereo piano. Mono piano drives me crazy. I know a lot of classical engineers will record with one mic, but if there aren't two tracks of piano, then what's the point? [Laughs]

You know what drives me nuts is that whole low-high issue, with the bass of the piano on the left side and the treble end of the piano on the right. When I get that in reverse, my whole world goes bananas.

Sometimes, when you do this miking in the center like this, it is actually tough to tell. A lot of other engineers don't seem to care, so I will have to make the record, and the stereo image will be reversed. Something will be wrong, and I won't know what it is. It almost always turns out to be the piano in reverse. There is nothing wrong with it; it is just me psychologically. I just can't handle it.

Unless it is a solo piano record, I rarely hard pan left and right. It depends on the instrument and the instrumentation, because I don't necessarily pan at 10 and 2. If I have a lot of guitars going on, I might do an 11 and 5.

When I am laying down tracks, I try not to EQ anything. I try to go flat. Almost always, I am using Dolby SR.

I prefer everything analog. With digital, I find that the transients are compromised. I don't like the sound of what digital does to an instrument like a piano or any kind of plucked or attacked instrument. Every generation of digital gives you more unpleasantness on the top end.

Jim Dickinson

Producing credits include: Ry Cooder, the Replacements, Big Star, Toots Hibbert, John Hiatt, Mudhoney, Jason & the Scorchers, North Mississippi Allstars, G. Love & Special Sauce, Screamin' Jay Hawkins. Session credits: The Rolling Stones, Bob Dylan, Aretha Franklin, Primal Scream, Los Lobos. See the Appendix for Jim Dickinson's full bio.

First off, I want to dispel some mythology, which is that you should mike the piano from the inside. I've gone back to recording piano mono. I did record stereo piano for years, which I now think is incorrect, because you simply don't listen to the piano with your head inside it.

The whole idea of stereo piano, which is a '70s idea, is totally incorrect. You can create a kind of false stereo, if you are interested in the horrible idea of separating the left hand from the right hand, which of course no piano player would want to do. You are trying to create the illusion of one big hand anyway.

When you sit behind the piano, you do hear the treble in your right ear and the bass in your left ear, but no one else does. It really depends where you think the piano image goes in the stereo spectrum. If you see the stereo spectrum as 9 o'clock to 3 o'clock, I think the piano goes at 1:30, for instance.

The lid of the grand piano is designed to project the sound out horizontally to an opera or concert hall, and the sound of that piano actually focuses about 10 or 12 feet in front [meaning the audience side of the piano that the lid is open to] of the instrument, toward the audience, which is why it is idiotic to put the mic inside it.

The best textbook example of concert hall grand piano recording that you could ever want is found in a documentary from the late '50s of the Glenn Gould Columbia sessions. There are microphones all over the room, but they are recording in mono. There isn't a microphone any closer than 8 feet. There are some microphones considerably farther away. They are recording with no EQ and no compression, and when they wanted more top end, they simply turned up the microphones that were close to the top end. It was just a beautiful thing to watch. They were recording with a mono unit and a stereo unit, which was really a safety, because the needles were moving in unison on both tracks.

Even with the multi-microphone approach, these old-school Columbia recording engineers were making a blending of the different mics. That is what a grand piano sounds like.

Much of vintage rock and roll is an upright or a spinet piano, which is, of course, a vertical harp, rather than a horizontal harp, in a whole different miking technique. The Jerry Lee Lewis records were cut on a spinet piano, with a microphone placed behind it, because on an upright or a spinet, the sound comes from the back of the soundboard. There is a place between the struts there, to the treble end of the keyboard, behind the third brace, where there is a sweet spot on any upright or spinet piano. That is where I mike it.

The Jerry Lee Lewis piano recordings were interesting in that part of the piano sound was coming through the back of the vocal mic, as well.

On my recordings of old blues musicians, I like to mike the front of an upright piano, so I can get the sound of the fingernails on the keys. That is a subtle thing, but to a piano player, it makes a big difference. Some guys click louder than others. It adds personality. It is a question of what you think you are recording from a keyboard player.

On the movie soundtrack for *The Border*, we had an old piano that came out of Amigo Studios, and it had a sticker on it that said "This is the property of the Los Angeles County School System." It had been painted white with house paint. Nobody used it except for us. Nobody cared what I did to it, so I could cover the strings with duct tape and tinfoil and whatever else I wanted to use. The strings were all really dead, so there weren't any overtones, which is what I wanted it for. I wanted the piano that way to ensure that its sound would not interfere with the guitar's tonalities.

Someone might wonder why I would choose dead strings. Why not just EQ out the clashing frequencies on the piano? Well, I would rather listen to signal than EQ.

The overtone series of a piano is very complex. The longer the strings, the more dominant the overtones are going to be. With dead strings, the first thing that goes is the overtones. The deader the strings, you primarily end up with the principal frequencies. With Ry, the guitar is a dominant instrument, so it is imperative that the piano is out of the way. Conversely, if was I making just a piano record, I would want a strong representation of overtones from a piano.

My personal favorite piano is an old white Bush & Gerts that was made in Chicago before World War II, that I took out of Stax Recording. The best piano that I ever put my hands on is Willie Nelson's sister's full-sized grand piano at Arlyn Studios in Austin, Texas. I can never remember the name of it. It was just this fabulous instrument that made a Bösendorfer sound like a Kimball. It is exactly the kind of instrument I normally don't like, but this one is wonderful. I have known that piano for 15 years, and it has gotten better. Steinways are really best suited for classical players.

There is a piano down on Beale Street in Memphis that is absolutely whipped; but yet every time I sit down and play it, I enjoy the experience. Here is this old piano that Mose Vinson and God knows who else has played since Year One, and you can feel the humanity through the ivory keys, which is something that plastic can never convey.

You can be "Save the Elephants" and all that, but I'm sorry, man, give me ivory keys. [Laughs] I like elephants as much as anybody, but I hate to put my fingers on plastic keys. It feels like a synthesizer. [Laughs] Ivory feels so much better. You can feel the ivory, the wood, and the felt on the hammer and the metal on the string. It is all part of what is in your hand, and it is a wonderful feeling. Now that is a piano, and there is not a real piano player on Earth who won't understand what I'm saying.

John Hampton

Credits include: B.B. King, Travis Tritt, the Replacements, Vaughan Brothers, Lynyrd Skynyrd, Robert Cray, Alex Chilton, Little Texas, the Bar-Kays, Gin Blossoms, Afghan Whigs. See the Appendix for John Hampton's full bio.

A piano was meant to be heard phase coherently. When you listen to a piano, you're hearing the piano hammers hitting the strings and the sound reflecting off the lid and coming to your ear. It's all pretty phase coherent, out there where you're standing, because it's all hitting your ears at the same time.

Now, there are a lot of people who'll put one mic on the bass strings, and then about 3 1/2 feet away, place another mic on the top strings. Now you've got your low end happening in one speaker, and you've got your top end happening in one speaker, but what about the strings in between, which is the main part of the piano where most people play? You've got the sound meeting these microphones at all these different timing intervals, and it's totally not coherent. In a mix, if you pan it left and right, it sounds like it's coming from behind your head. That's not correct.

There are several ways to obtain a phase-coherent piano recording. If you want the low end of the piano on one side and you want the high end of the piano on the other side, that's fine; but there are a lot of ways to obtain that and still have phase coherency to where the strings in between don't sound like they're coming from behind your head. One of them is M-S stereo, or mid-side stereo. I love mid-side stereo. An M-S recording of a piano can give you a truly phase-coherent, left-to-right picture of the piano without all the weird phase distortion on the keys in between the low and the high.

The best microphone I have found for that application is the Shure VP88. Put the mic over the hammers, but not too close, because you don't want the mid-strings to be louder than the low strings and the high strings. Pull it back a foot or so from the hammers and put it on the M setting, which is a medium M-S picture. If you do that, then you will have a phase-coherent picture of the piano. You also don't need to EQ the VP88, because it is such a natural-sounding microphone.

There is a French method of miking a piano, which is called ORTF. It was developed back in the '70s. That is where you take a couple of mics, like KM 84s, and put them in an X-Y setup with the capsules 7 centimeters apart. That's the magic number. It's actually not phase coherent on the frequencies that are 7 centimeters long, but it gives a fairly phase-coherent picture of a piano low to high.

My favorite method, believe it or not, is to put two PZMs back to back. Just tape them together. I will put them 12 to 15 inches above where the hammers hit the strings. They need to be the kind of PZMs with the high-frequency boost. With those, you never need to EQ the piano.

Those are the three ways that I have recorded piano that I have consistently experienced the most satisfying results.

Ralph Sutton

Credits include: Stevie Wonder, Lionel Richie, the Temptations. See the Appendix for Ralph Sutton's full bio.

Stevie Wonder owned two Bösendorfers—one 7 footer and a 9-foot concert grand. The concert grand sounded spectacular in the room, but it is a beast to record because it's just so big and broad. It is an excellent piano if you are recording it solo or in a trio setting, like piano, upright bass, and a trap kit. But anything outside of that, it was just too big, so I personally preferred the 7 footer. Now for me and my personal engineering and production taste, I like the Steinway Model C-227 and the Yamaha C7, which are both 7-foot, 6-inch pianos and perfect for true R&B and soul music recording.

When I mike the piano, I typically like to use a pair of Schoeps CMC 5s with the MK 4 cardioid capsule or SE 4s set to cardioid about 4 to 6 inches off the strings.

For the treble section, I like to place the microphone right above the hammer shank, and the mic placement is over the A, B, C strings. Note that this is a starting point for getting good R&B piano attack that will cut well and give you the ability to place this hand or treble section anywhere in the mix and get very good distinction and clarity. If you want to keep distinction and get a smother sound, slide the microphone back away from the hammer shank. Be careful that you do not point your microphone directly at the hammer flange and main action rail, because you will pick up noise.

For the tenor section, I do the same thing except I start with my microphone behind the hammer flange and main action rail and adjust accordingly.

For the bass section, I like to use a large-diaphragm condenser—either an SE Z3300A or a TLM 49. With the bass section, I like low-end warmth, so I place my microphone about 4 to 8 inches off the strings and 1 to 1 1/2 feet behind the hammer flange and main action rail over the C, D, E strings. For me, one of the best ways to get a great recording is to adjust the microphone based around the song, track, and instrumentation.

Very rarely, if I want a more ambient recording, I might place a stereo pair of C 12s [about 3 feet apart and 5 feet high and arranged in a high–low configuration] outside the piano, but if you are planning on adding other instrumentation, you'll find you start losing the detail of your overall sonic picture, and the detail is the key, especially with R&B, blues, and soul music. The piano is very important and should not have to compete with the bass and the drums and whatever synthesizer or Rhodes we are using. So typically, the ambient information is just not heard.

I record literally right over the mallets. A little back off of them, starting at 2 to 8 inches back from the hammer shank. I like this sound; it helps me get the resonance of the strings and the attack of the hammer. This gives me the ability when I'm mixing to actually get that piano up in the mix where the listeners can hear it and enjoy it without me having to do too much to it EQ-wise.

If you've put the microphone where it's supposed to be, and you've selected the appropriate microphone for the application or the instrument, you will have to do very little EQ. When needed, I use high- and low-pass filters. I very rarely add anything, because I find that everything is there once you filter off everything you don't need. So if you are addressing the mic located on the right hand of the piano, then I don't need the low end on there, so I will filter up into the 80- and 90-Hz range. Conversely, on the low end, or the left hand, I'll filter what I know I'm not going to hear. I find immediately that this opens things right up, which gives me the clarity and distinction that I am listening for. That's pretty much how I like to EQ acoustic piano. I always filter away what I don't need and listen. And then if I'm still missing some top or some mids, I will definitely move that microphone before I start messing around with EQ. I have always believed that EQ and compression are an effect. A lot of new engineers and producers may or may not realize that, but they are. Once you plug the microphone to the cable and into the mic preamp, anything after that is an effect.

Christopher Boyes, Skywalker Sound (photo by Steve Jennings, Skywalker Sound). Row 2: Jacquire King (photo by Rick Clark) / Neumann M 50s (photo by Rick Clark) / Cookie Marenco (photo by Rick Clark). Row 3: Cregan Montague of Osaka Pearl (photo by Rick Clark) / Plug-ins (photo by Jimmy Stratton).

You've worked seemingly endless hours in the studio trying the produce the ultimate single that you think has a real shot to make a splash at the top of the charts. You are thinking that this is the pop music shot in the arm that will cause a zillion listeners to go into an appreciative trance and head over to the nearest music store.

It all comes crashing down the first time you hear your local nationally consulted radio outlet squash the life out of your pop opus, right as the first chorus makes its big entrance. Even that magical moment where the singer delivered the heart-breaking hook was lost in a sea of swimmy effects. What happened?

While it is a good bet that many of the most formative musical moments in our lives arrived courtesy of tiny transistor boxes, single-dashboard-speaker car radios, and other less than ideal audio setups, none of us as kids realized the degree of processed sonic mangling stations employed to deliver those magical sounds.

I knew I hit a hot topic when producers, engineers, and mastering engineers lined up to speak their minds. The following are a number of those very folks—names most of you know quite well—taking their turn with solid advice, horror stories, and the occasional dig at those broadcast mediums that have caused us as professionals to pull our hair out with frustration, while having to admit that our lives would be very different without them.

I would like to thank John Agnello, Michael Brauer, Greg Calbi, Richard Dodd, Don Gehman, Brian Lee, and Benny Quinn for their generous gift of time and insight for this chapter.

John Agnello

Credits include: The Breeders, Dinosaur Jr., Redd Kross, Screaming Trees, the Grither, Dish, Buffalo Tom, Triple Fast Action, Bivouac, Lemonheads, Tad, Gigolo Aunts. See the Appendix for John Agnello's full bio.

Obviously, before music television, a lot of people mixed for radio, and a lot of those records were mixed for radio compression. There are a couple of different schools of thought. One is that you make it sound slamming on the radio, and when people buy it and bring it home, they get what they get. Another school of thought is to not really concern yourself with the radio. Then there is the guy in the middle, which is what I think I try to do. At least back when I was really concerned with radio, I tried to make a record sound kind of punchy on the radio, but not like a whole different record when you brought it home and listened to it on a regular system without the heavy radio compression.

For me, I just like the sound of bus compression on the mix anyway. I am a big fan of that stuff. When I was mixing more for radio, I would have the whole mix up and basically sit there with this really hard line compressor that was cranked at 20 to 1. I would check vocals and work on the mix, so I could tell what the radio might do, while monitoring through the compressor. This would help you tell how much of the "suck" you would get from the radio.

In fact, I would go to tape with the compressor, but not at 20 to 1. I would go back to more of a normal setting. MTV is here, but most people still listen to TV on a little mono speaker. Phasing is a main concern. If your snare drum is out of phase and it comes out on MTV, there is not going to be any snare in that mix. Phase cancellation is the correct term of what has taken place.

I use the Phase button more than I use the EQ button, especially on drums and things like that. Also, check the phase if you have a bass DI and a microphone, or if you are running a bunch of different mics on a guitar amp. You should always check the phase on those. If you are really careful about that kind of stuff, you can actually mix for maximum rock, as opposed to constantly EQing something that is screwed up on a different level.

I think that it is really important to regularly reference your mix in mono, if you are really concerned that your records really slam on MTV or any kind of music television. You can really tell how well your vocals are going to come out if you work in mono at lower volumes, and referencing on different speakers is also a good way to get a sense of your mix.

Michael Brauer

Credits include: The Rolling Stones, Bruce Springsteen, Jackson Browne, Billy Joel, Luther Vandross, Stevie Ray Vaughan, Michael Jackson, Jeff Buckley, Tony Bennett, Eric Clapton, David Byrne, Coldplay. See the Appendix for Michael Brauer's full bio.

Over the past few years, the approaches to mixing for radio and for albums have become almost the same. This is because of the need for the recorded signal to be printed on tape or digital as loud as possible, with the possible exclusion of classical and jazz music, because those musical forms are so pure, and compression would be heard immediately. No compressors of any kind were used for my Tony Bennett *Unplugged* mixes.

The mixer accomplishes this task by using an array of compressors to keep the audio dynamic range down to 2 to 3 dB. The mastering engineer takes over and has his own custom-made toys of A/D converters and secret weapons to make the CD as loud as those little 0s and 1s can stand.

Radio stations have their own limiters and EQs with which to process their own output signal, in order to make things as loud as possible. The less you do to activate those signal processors, the better your song will retain its original sound. The potential problem is that you can end up with a mix that has no dynamic excitement left to it. It's been squeezed to the point of being loud, but small.

Over the years, I've found ways to get the most dynamic breathing room possible within the 2- to 3-dB window. I break down my mix into two or three parts instead of putting my mix through one processor. The bottom part of the record (A) includes bass, drums, percussion. The top part of the record (B) includes guitars, keys, synth, vocals, et cetera. The third part (C) is sometimes used for vocals or solos only. I assign my reverbs to A or B, depending on their source.

The dynamics of the bottom end (A) of the record are no longer affected by the dynamics of the top part (B) of the mix. Once this concept is understood and executed, you then experiment by getting A to effect B, B to A, or C, et cetera. When done properly, the bottom of the record pumps on its own, independent of the top end of the music.

The problems I used to have with just using a stereo compressor became a vicious cycle. If I wanted a lot more bottom, the compression would be triggered and work harder, causing the vocals to get quieter. If I wanted more vocals or more solo instrument, my drums and bass suffered. By the second or third chorus of a song, the dynamics need to be coming to a peak. You don't want the compressor holding you back. Ten years ago, the use of a stereo compressor was less of a problem, because the dynamic audio range was smaller. TR-808s and Aphex changed all that.

My mix of Dionne Farris's "I Know" is typical of this style of mixing. The bottom end just keeps pumping along as the vocals and guitars have their own dynamic breathing room, all within that little dynamic window. The complete album, video, and radio mixes are all the same.

Greg Calbi

Credits include: Paul Simon, John Lennon, David Bowie, Bruce Springsteen, Norah Jones, Beastie Boys, Bob Dylan, John Mayer, the Ramones, Talking Heads, Patti Smith, Pavement, Dinosaur Jr., Brian Eno. See the Appendix for Greg Calbi's full bio.

In a very petty sense, people are very conscious of their records being louder than everybody else's records. Everyone wants their mastering to be louder. We are having a lot of problems with that, because people are cutting these CDs so hot that they are not really playing back well on cheaper equipment, and a lot of people have cheaper equipment.

Many mastering guys have gotten disgusted because it has really gotten to a point of diminishing returns. Why are we making them as loud as this? It is because musicians and producers all want a more muscular sound, but if they were all taken down a couple of dB, they might sound a little cleaner.

This is an example of almost like a lack of confidence. Everybody wants that little extra edge. If they feel volume is one of those edges, then that is something that I can give them, because all I do is turn the 0 to +1, and it is all of a sudden louder. The fact of the matter is, if you give radio something, and their compressors hit it the right way, and you have it tweaked up right, it is going to sound loud anyway. If your record is bright and clean, it will cut through a small speaker on a car. If it is really busy and dense, you will get that muffled quality.

Someone recently talked to a guy on radio who said that he likes to get stuff that is real low level off the CDs, so his compressors at the station can kind of do their thing. He felt it made stuff sound better than stuff that was really hot. We always thought that the hotter you cut it, the hotter it was going to sound on the radio. Well, suddenly, here was another twist on that debate. I thought, "Now this really takes the cake, because I've heard everything."

I have a feeling that things sound great on the radio, more on how the parts are played and the whole thing is thought out from the get-go. The other day, I heard a Springsteen song, "Tunnel of Love," on the radio. It sounded great, and it was so simple. The bass was down there playing the part. Guys like Springsteen and Bryan Adams write and arrange songs that are in the range that are made for radio. They give you one thing to digest at a time. There aren't all these layered parts conflicting with each other. These are some basic tenets of arranging that kind of hold up on a little speaker. In my opinion, I think it comes more from the conceptual stage.

Richard Dodd

Credits include: Tom Petty (solo and with the Heartbreakers), Dixie Chicks, Boz Scaggs, the Traveling Wilburys, Wilco, Robert Plant, the Connells, Clannad, Green Day. See the Appendix for Richard Dodd's full bio.

Here's an analogy. We have a pint glass to fill, and with reference to mixing to radio, the broadcast processing makes it a point to always keep that glass full. If we under-fill it, their system will fill it. If you overfill it, or attempt to, it will chop it off. That only leaves us with control over the content of that glass. It can be filled with a few thousand grains of sand, a few small rocks, or a mix of both. Those are the parameters we have to work with. We make those decisions.

The stronger the song, the stronger the performance, the less we need. If the song or performance is perhaps lacking, we tend to go for the denser, thicker (more sand) approach. That is the control we have, but basically, there is still only so much that can fit in the glass. That is just the way it is.

If you want a voice and guitar at the front of the song to be ×6, and when the band kicks in to be at least 0, you are never going to hear it like that on the radio. The nature of the compressor is to bring the quiet things up and the loud things down. But, if you use that facility correctly, then you can get the radio compression to remix the song for you.

I'm not going to make music for the type of processing radio thinks sounds right today, because tomorrow they are going to think something else is right. Then every piece of music that I made today is wrong. So I don't mix for the radio, but I do mix with the radio in mind.

Even though you can't have the dynamic, there are ways to create that sense of dynamic on the radio. I take things out. I turn the band down. It is under-mixing. Otherwise, without witnessing what happens through a second set of limiters, you don't stand a chance.

A slower-tempo song can be apparently louder than an up-tempo song. If you have a drummer bashing away at 100 miles an hour, it is going to eat up all the space, and there won't be room for anything. Remember that whatever is bad about a mix, the radio is going to emphasize it and make it worse. If you have something that is really laid back, with all the space in the world, that allows time for the effects of radio to recover before they act again, that can also be an effective dynamic, which you otherwise wouldn't have gotten with the fast, busy track.

By extracting from the content, you can compensate for the lack of dynamic in a song. Less is more, basically, and extraction is part of the trick. It is in taking away, even if it is just using the facility to bring what you took out back again.

We all want to fill the glass to the top, but the only facility we can affect is content density.

Don Gehman

Producer credits include: Tracy Chapman, R.E.M., John Mellencamp, Hootie & the Blowfish. See the Appendix for Don Gehman's full bio.

I think the key to a great-sounding radio mix is to get your balances correct. I'm not just referring to the correct balance of basic core elements, like snare, vocal, bass, and guitar, but the frequencies within them are what have to be balanced as well. That way, everything hits the compressor with equal power.

I used to always use bus limiting, like on an SSL or this little Neve stereo compressor I have. For many years, I just let that thing fly with 8 to 10 dB of compression and just flatten everything out. When it went into mastering, I would have people sometimes complain that it was a little over-compressed, but they could work with it. They might say they couldn't bend it into the frequency ranges that they needed.

I have been working with Eddy Schreyer over at Future Disc Systems, and he has encouraged me to use less limiting and more individual limiting and get my balances right. It has taught me a valuable lesson.

What we are doing now is I'll try and contain that bus limiting to 2 to 4 dB, just enough to give me a hint of what things are hitting at. It is kind of a meter of which things are too dynamic. I'll then go back and individually limit things in a softer way, so that the bus limiter stops working. Then I can take it in and put it on this digital limiter, which is this Harmonia Mundi that Eddy's got, which is invisible. It doesn't make any sounds that are like bus limiters that I know. We just tighten it up just a little bit more to give it some more level to the disc. That results in something that doesn't sound compressed. It is very natural.

You can hit a radio limiter and have something that is very wide-open sounding, if the frequencies, like from 50 cycles to a thousand cycles, are all balanced out, so that they hit the limiter equally and your relationships aren't going to move. They are all going to stay the same, but you've got to get that all sorted out before it goes into that broadcast limiter.

The way you do that is by using some example of it, to kind of test out. I use a bus limiter to kind of show me where I am hitting too hard, and then I take it away and get rid of it and let the mix breathe. That is the trick that I am finding more and more in helping get your balances just right.

With the whole practice of frequency balancing, I know you can have tracks that seem dynamic on radio. Green Day's "Longview" is a great example. That chorus slams in, but it is balanced out well enough that when the chorus hits the limiter, it just adjusts the level and doesn't gulp anything else up.

If you have bass frequencies that come in too loud and aren't balanced in the midrange, the limiter "sees" whatever is loudest and puts that on top. If the low end is too loud, then everything will come out muddy when it hits. If all the frequencies are balanced, the limiter will equally turn down the balances, with them all staying intact, and life goes on just as you intended.

Brian Lee

Credits include: Janet Jackson, Pearl Jam, Ozzy Osbourne, Gypsy Kings, Lou Reed, Gloria Estefan, Charlie Daniels, Cachao. See the Appendix for Brian Lee's full bio.

It is very important to check for phase problems by referencing to mono regularly in the mix stage.

When you mix, you should definitely be listening in mono every now and then, so you know that when it goes to mono, it will still sound just as good and in phase. I believe that the fullness of the overall sound when you are in stereo can cause you to pay more attention to the instruments and effects than to the vocal.

Interestingly, a lot of people use phase for weird effects. We have done heavy metal albums that are really out of phase. They especially like to put a lot of effects on the vocal. Maybe they just didn't think it was going to get played on the radio, but some stuff was totally out of phase, and if you pushed the mono button, everything just went away. We could've put everything back in phase, but I think they would think it would ruin the effect that they wanted.

It is important for producers and mixers to print mixes with vocals and other desired elements with higher and then lower settings, so as to allow the mastering engineer more flexibility in attaining the ideal presentation.

We do suggest that you get a mix the way you think it should sound and get a few different passes, like vocal up and vocal down. Mixing is very expensive, and you should get as much out of it as you can. If you are going to the Hit Factory or some studio like that, that is a lot of money a day. You don't want to have to go back and rebook time and remix the whole thing just to get the vocal right. When you are mixing, you should also do your instrumental TV track and versions with lead and background vocals up and down.

If you have the time and patience to do that, you will be in great shape, because when you get to this stage of mastering, you can actually sit back and reflect and say, "I need more vocal on this particular section," or, "I think this particular vocal is overshadowing this part of the song. I think it needs to be brought down." Then you can do edits at that point.

When you are traveling around from studio to studio, listening and mixing, you may think a mix sounds great until you hear it on another system, and for some reason things sound like garbage. You may find yourself going, "What is going on here?" Usually, mastering is a third party's subjective opinion about the whole process. That is one thing that the whole mastering process is about. We know our speakers very well, and when you bring your work in here, hopefully we will have some frame of reference for you to get it right.

Benny Quinn

Credits include: Eric Clapton, Elvis Presley, Aaron Copland, dc Talk, Johnny Cash, Isaac Hayes, Alabama, Dixie Dregs, Indigo Girls, Bela Fleck, Bob Seger, Cracker, Widespread Panic, Amy Grant, Boston Pops Orchestra, Willie Nelson, Nanci Griffith, Shirley Caesar, Lyle Lovett, Reba McEntire. See the Appendix for Benny Quinn's full bio.

Mastering for radio is like a dog chasing its tail. It's really a losing proposition in that you'll never get there. Each radio station is different and processes their station differently than the one next door in the same building that's playing the same music.

What most engineers—especially new mastering engineers—are not aware of is the fact that in FM broadcast, the FM standard requires an HF boost on the order of 15 dB at 15 kHz, and a complementary roll off in the receiver at the other end. What does that mean? It means that as we push more high frequencies onto the discs, the more the broadcast processors limit and roll that off.

Also, as we push the levels harder, with more clipping and smash limiting, we end up with more distortion that the processors interpret as high-frequency energy and roll it off even further.

The sequence is sort of like this: The processors measure the HF content and apply the pre-emphasis curve to see how far over 100-percent modulation the signal would be. Then, the overall level is turned down to allow that to fit in the station's allowed transmission bandwidth. [100 percent is the legal limit.]

So, let's say that the CD is mastered such that there needs to be a 5-dB level drop for everything to fit. Then the multiband processing is added, then transmitted. At the radio end, there is no information that says, "Oh, by the way, this song has been turned down 5 dB." It just sounds duller, maybe smaller, and not like the record you mastered. The producer hears this on the radio and says, "Hey, it's not bright enough or loud enough. Next time I'm really going to pour on the highs and limit and compress it." Guess what happens? The next record sounds even worse.

What's the answer? Well, if you listen to an oldies station that plays music from before the mastering level wars started, those songs sound great. If you listen at home to those same recordings, they have life, sound natural, have dynamic range, and are easy to listen to. Mastering for radio should be mastering for great sound. That's what works for me.

Here are some more specific pointers to consider. Everything has got to be very clear sounding. You have to make sure that everything is distinguishable, as far as the instrumentation is concerned, and that can be done with a combination of EQ and limiting.

The low end is what will normally grab and kick a compressor or limiter at a station. If you have too much low end, and it is too cloudy and big, then all you will hear are the station's compressors grabbing the low end and moving everything up and down with it.

While I typically don't cut off the bottom end, I do try to make sure that the bottom end is clean and present. Normally, you will find frequencies in the low end that are rather cloudy. This changes from song to song and mix to mix.

You can often find one or two frequencies that may create more cloud than distinction. You may be rolling off at that frequency, using a really broad bandwidth and then possibly even adding back a very similar close frequency, maybe even the same one, using a very narrow bandwidth. What you do is take that cloud and that woof out of the low end. That usually helps significantly, as far as radio processing is concerned. The top end doesn't seem to hit the station's signal processing as hard as the bottom end, and radio compression doesn't seem to hurt the top end as much as it does the bottom end.

Most rock stations compress more heavily than other station formats do. When something is out of phase, it causes very strange sounds in the reverbs. You will hear more reverb on the track, while played on the radio, if the phasing problem is with the original signal and not with the reverbs on the tracks themselves. The original signal will want to cancel, and the reverbs won't, making things sound even more swimmy.

Studio Design, Room Tuning, and Wiring

Great recordings have been made in situations where mics were thrown up with little consideration other than capturing the magic of the performance moment. Great mixes have happened in environments that were designed for anything but mixing. However, these are exceptions to the rule. Anyone who is serious about creating a recording facility with a rep for putting out consistently good sounds needs to have the tracking spaces and control room set up to enable the engineer and mixer to have the most control over the sound. The facility must also provide a level of security that allows the engineer and mixer to know that what they are hearing is an accurate reflection of the actual sonic character of the final mix.

For this chapter, we have four well-known leaders in the areas of room tuning and studio design and one studio owner/engineer/producer to provide some thoughts and methodologies on what can make the difference between a facility that develops a waiting list of loyal clients jazzed on the great sound and a place that finds itself struggling to keep the doors open because word has gotten out that there are too many anomalies in the sonic profile of the room.

George Augspurger

See the Appendix for George Augspurger's bio.

There are essentially two schools of thought concerning the art of tuning a room: one that believes the proper alignment of a room's sonic characteristic should be addressed purely from an acoustical design perspective and one that is comfortable addressing the situation with electronic equalizers.

You will obviously get two camps of philosophy. There are some people who say, "No, you should never apply electric equalization to the speakers. Any problem should be taken care of with room acoustics." On the other hand, you will also find today that those of us who still very often use electronic equalization will still say that the best EQ is the least EQ. I would certainly say there are twice as many bad-sounding rooms that have been ruined by too much EQ as the other way around.

The first thing I do, if it is a new room that I am setting up, is listen to the selected speakers on music. In setting up the speakers, I play with their location and probably with room surfaces, with no thought of electrical EQ as any part of that first go-around at all. The first thing you have to do is find out what it takes to make a given set of speakers sound right in a given room. Once you get them to sound pretty good, then you can come back and use EQ as frosting on the cake.

Bob Hodas

Clients include hit mixer David Pensado, producer Rob Cavallo, composer John Debney, and recording artist Stevie Wonder. See the Appendix for Bob Hodas's full bio.

With soffit-mounted speakers, the first thing I do when I go into a room is think, "How can we fix things acoustically? What can we do as far as trapping and diffusion or absorption?" Each situation is different. It depends on what is going on in the room. I really look at the acoustic problems first. As far as I am concerned, getting the room as close acoustically as possible is number one. That way, you wind up with a nice big sweet spot. In a room with freestanding monitors, I have a different approach. Seventy-five percent of the outcome will be achieved by finding that one spot where the speakers and listening position produce the smoothest frequency response. Once we accomplish that, then I look at the acoustic solutions to further improve the room.

These days there are many people out there selling acoustical treatment products. There is a wide range in effectiveness, so my philosophy is not to use a product unless I've measured the results in a room. In the realm of sound absorption material, compressed fiberglass or "spin glass" is still the most commonly used material for first-order reflections. Homemade panels can be just as effective as expensive premade items or foam products. The cost is really all about the look you're trying to achieve. These days I'm using a lot more of the recycled cotton panels instead of fiberglass. They have pretty much the same absorption coefficients as fiberglass and are a lot more pleasant to work with. Plus, they're environmentally friendly.

Diffusion is a great tool for opening up the perceived size of small rooms. It stops the signal by breaking it up and spreading it out in time. So most of the original energy is maintained, and the room still sounds alive. I can't stand walking into a room that has been over absorbed and hearing my voice come out of my chest. One tip for diffusors is don't let anyone sit too close to them; otherwise, it sounds really weird, like a comb filter.

The science of bass traps has come a long way, and my approach these days is more about surgical bass treatment with tuned membrane absorbers than the broadband-absorption approach. It's difficult because the traps must be placed where the problem frequencies have the most energy, and that requires time spent on mapping out the pressure zones in the room. But the results are well worth it. The broadband trapping approach requires a lot more real estate, something that is typically at a premium in studios. With bass, there always seems to be some give and take.

I think symmetry is the most important factor for successfully tuning a room. You need symmetry in construction, speaker placement, and gear placement. Without symmetry, the speakers will have different frequency responses, and the acoustic treatments that work for one speaker won't work for the other. When I have issues with symmetry, the first thing I try is to integrate subwoofers into the system. A subwoofer has a lot more flexibility in placement than a pair of monitors. No imaging to worry about, for one thing. Subs are difficult to get right in a room and won't sound good unless you get proper phase integration with your mains. I wouldn't do it without my analyzer.

Sometimes, due to budget considerations, construction or expensive treatments restrict some of the acoustic approach. At that point I'll say, "Now what can we do electro-acoustically through equalization to finish solving the problem or to create a curve that is conducive to making records?"

A minimum-phase parametric is really my equalizer of choice. That is a parametric that can address minimum-phase problems, which are problems of boundary loading. By using a parametric as opposed to a graphic equalizer, I can shape the equalization to perfectly fit the problem, as opposed to tuning around the problem, because I am restricted with fixed frequency centers and fixed cue. Room problems are not third-octave issues, and they are not all at these fixed frequency centers the third octave provides you with.

Nobody has got a flat room, or nobody really likes flat, in my experience. Flat is not necessarily conducive to making records. Of all the rooms I have tuned, which must be at least a thousand, I have found that people tend not to like flat. If I was going to make a generalization to apply to the majority of the rooms, I would say from 80 cycles to 5 kHz is generally the area people like to have flat, then with some kind of roll-off from 5 kHz on out, with a slight low-end boost somewhere around 50 hertz, just as a fun factor. It varies from room to room, although the hip-hop guys always want the low end jacked way up. The amount of high-end roll-off can also vary greatly, depending on the crazy dB levels some of these engineers work at. I have a lot of clients who I think will be deaf in five years.

Some speaker systems are not linear with respect to amplitude. In other words, as you turn them up or down, the frequency response changes. So when I am tuning a room like that, I have to be careful to make sure that I tune it within the general volume that it is typically being used. Room acoustics can dictate how the bass feels at certain volumes as well, so I take that into account when tuning, too.

Recording studios spend more on coffee than on control-room monitor maintenance. It is true, and that is the sad part of it. People have sort of let the large monitor systems in their rooms fall by the wayside, which is a real scary thought to me because that is what the recording studio is supposed to be all about. It isn't about the latest digital delay or effects box. It is about good sound. We, as an industry, have sort of ignored the sounds of our rooms and gone after the toys to make those sounds, and that is the part that bothers me the most.

Bret Thoeny

See the Appendix for Bret Thoeny's bio.

People have even tried setting up speakers in meadows and mixing, and it doesn't work. You have got to relate to how the music is going to sound being played back in your car, home, or wherever. That is why some people run out to their cars to hear something. That is why some studios have portions of the backseats of cars with cassette players, so they can listen. You have got to look at it all in the same environment.

The [control] room size is determined by the function of the room and then by the criteria of the selected monitors that the client chooses, whether they are medium, high, or super-high power. You can't put a small near-field monitor in a huge control room. It is not going to load the room. You are not going to get the sound pressure.

Even speaker manufacturers, when they design a control room monitor, will say that this monitor works within 6,000 or 7,000 cubic feet to 10,000 cubic feet. They give you a parameter. All they are saying is that the type of drivers, the components, and the speaker in that room can excite that volume of air to get a 90/95 in optimum range of that speaker, so you are not overloading it. You are not pushing the speaker too far, so that it starts to go into distortion. That is what happens. You can put little speakers in a big room and crank it up, and the speaker will be working beyond its optimum range and will start going into clipping and distortion, which is bad. That is what they are telling the consumer, and that is what the designers should take into account when they design a room.

I just ask, right off the bat, "What kind of speaker and what range are you going to be using in this room?" Even if they don't know the model, even if it is going to be double 15s. Is it going to be a near-field? What's going on? How do you like to work? A lot of composers like to work in a very small space with near-field speakers. They don't need soffit-mounted speakers.

Of the soffit-mounted speakers, I like Quested, ATC, and Westlake Audio. For near-fields, KRKs and Genelec Golds.

The Genelecs are self-powering. That is a really good trend, and I am glad to see that. You don't need to over-amp it or under-amp it when you buy a package that is designed to be totally competent. It is great. JBL has done that for their industrial speakers.

We did a room for Bob Clearmountain, and I consider Bob probably the premier mixer in the world. He uses no soffit-mounted speakers. He goes back and forth between NS-10s and the smaller KRK—I think it is the 7000—which he puts up on the console.

While many people are primarily using near-fields, I definitely feel that good soffit-mounted speakers are ideally used for really hearing what is going down during tracking.

The reason for a soffit-mounted speaker is usually for a tracking situation. When you are putting up the drums, you can hear the kick and get that energy punching right at you, as if you were sitting right in front of the drum kick. That is the reason for it.

If you can get away with it—if the low end can get out of the room—it is much better than trying to control it. Some of the rooms that sound good are sometimes rooms that are built very minimally, meaning that sound can actually go through the walls. That is a much better circumstance than containing it. The low end goes right through the wall so it doesn't load in the room. It goes out into open space. Many old studios were great because they allowed the bass to escape.

If you build a block house like a vault, everything is going to stay in there. You have to dissipate it with elaborate traps and diffusers and all the elements just to get the room back to sounding natural. Typical rooms that we are used to are usually ones where the low-end sound can go right through the walls.

You can't always do that, however. In multi-studio complexes, you've got to use good detailing and good acoustical analysis, as well as walls and floors that work, and that is kind of what separates the boys from the men. You don't have a choice. In a nice freestanding building, you still want to control environment.

In tracking areas, live sound is pretty much what people have been wanting. Ten years ago, things were so dead because there was so much isolation and everything was individually miked. Now the engineers are back with much better tools and much more sophisticated knowledge of how to work a live room. Electronics have improved too, so they can work a live room and get a much more natural sound.

I believe that wood is the best material for recording space. Wood has the most warmth to it. You can make it bright, but it doesn't get edgy or unnatural. Some studios will put in concrete block, and the sound is much too harsh with the way it sounds and the psychological aspects. If you make a room too high tech, it kind of goes against the grain of musicians and what they like to be surrounded with.

Anything in large-scale acoustics, you need a lot of one element to make a difference. You need a lot of wood to really let the wood respond to the room. Throwing up some diagonal slats of redwood that you get at the lumberyard doesn't quite do it. If you dabble it here and there and drywall everywhere else, the room is going to sound like the drywall and not like the sound of the wood.

It is really the percentage of the area that you cover with a particular material that gives it its character. If you have a hardwood floor and you have large splays and diffusers out of wood, you are going to be getting into that area. People say they have wood rooms, and if they have really put down carpet and a lot of drywall, it is not going to sound the same.

Chris Huston

Credits include: Van Morrison, Todd Rundgren, Blood, Sweat & Tears, Patti LaBelle, the Drifters, Led Zeppelin, the Who, the Fugs, Wilson Pickett, James Brown, ? & The Mysterians, the Rascals, Eric Burdon.

THE SOUNDSTAGE: HOME LISTENING ROOM VERSUS STUDIO CONTROL ROOM

A couple of months ago, I was involved in an Internet forum discussion about the differences between the acoustics in the home and those of the recording studio. The various responses to the thread, on the audioasylum.com-sponsored Rives Acoustic Forums, were diverse and very interesting in that they underscored what an extremely subjective thing listening to music can be.

As a recording engineer, on more than a few occasions, I have been reminded of this subjectivity in some very amusing ways. For instance, one evening, after a full day of mixing, I was invited to visit some friends in the Hollywood Hills on the way home. Just stop by and say hello. As I had a cassette of the mix that I was working on with me, I asked if I could play it on their system, which consisted of Macintosh components and JBL speakers. A very nice system at that time—the mid 1970s. As we sat on the couch facing the speakers, I was horrified by what I heard! My mix sounded nothing like the well-defined track that I'd spent the better part of the day in the studio crafting. The bass was out of proportion, loud and boomy, and the relative balances between the instruments and voices seemed way off from what I remembered from an hour or so before. I started to apologize, saying that it was just a rough, unfinished that I was taking home to evaluate, all of which was true. But my friend, who was a fine musician himself, waved me off, saying that it sounded really great to him. He said that he knew his speakers and offered to put on some other records for comparison, which we did. Over the years, I've since learned that you can adapt to pretty much anything. That is, you can train your ears to get used to a certain pair of speakers and the room that they are in. This has proved useful because many of the professional studio control rooms that I've worked in, all over the world, have left much to be desired with respect to the sonic accuracy of their playback systems. I usually carry a few of my favorite CDs around with me for comparison and to get a quick start on evaluating control room playback speakers.

There is a difference between the acoustic environment in which music is mixed and the acoustic environment in which it is listened to for enjoyment. In a 1981 publication called *Studio Acoustics*, Michael Rettinger gives a classic definition of the control room as a working environment:

> *Control rooms for music studios are for the purpose of regulating the quality of the recorded program rendered in the studio.... The operations may involve level adjustment, the addition of a reverberatory note to the renditions, tonal modifications by means of equalizers, the use of limiting, compression, or expansion of various passages and other checks and modifications.*

THE LISTENING ROOM ENVIRONMENT

By contrast, the listening room is usually designed for no other purpose than leaning back in a comfortable chair and enjoying music. If I had to single out one area in which the relative differences were greatest between the control room and the listening room, I would have to say that it was in the soundstage. Whenever we talk about the soundstage, we are talking about what can be a very complex and convoluted subject, one that can involve everything from the relative diffusion and reverberation time of a room and also the interaction of its modes. Talking about diffusion and reverberation time might be explained by the fact that audiophiles invariably use the room as a creative part of their listening experience, certainly to a much greater degree than their counterparts, the recording engineers. This is because the audiophile is seeking to add to his musical experience, enhancing and broadening the musical soundstage, sometimes beyond the intent of the original recording; whereas the recording engineer does not really have the freedom to do this. The recording engineer—or mixer, as he or she is sometimes referred to—tries to keep the musical soundstage within the confines of the information coming from the speakers, eliminating, or at least desensitizing, any acoustic artifacts that might artificially enhance or otherwise adversely color what they are listening to and evaluating. The reason for this must be obvious. If the room is providing the reverberation—and with it the illusion of depth—or any other complimentary aural quality, then the engineer might not feel that he had to introduce it himself, thus seriously affecting the final outcome of the mix.

REVERBERATION AND ECHO

Reverberation and echo are used in the mixing of music primarily to separate instruments and vocals and to give an overall feeling—illusion—of depth and size to the performance. In this context, reverberation is used to counter and make up for the recording techniques sometimes employed while making records. By way of explanation: Studios are, for the most part, usually tightly controlled environments, designed specifically to record instruments in close proximity to each other. Studio acoustics have changed drastically since the advent of multitrack recording. Studios were originally designed to complement and acoustically enhance musical ensembles (groups, bands, or orchestras, et cetera) playing live, with their performance being documented on either mono or, later, stereo tape. Today, studios are more like workshops where musical performances are, in many instances, no longer documented, with all the musicians playing together in the same room as a norm, but created instrument by instrument, track by track. Rather, they are recorded piecemeal. More common is that instruments are recorded just for tracking purposes—getting the structure of the song down—and replaced later, with more concentration being paid to the musical performance. The caveat to this is that in order to have control over the instruments and record them on separate tracks with as many musical options as possible, the studio acoustics must be controlled and can be quite dead, sterile, and lacking in kinetic energy—in other words, excitement. It is not hard to imagine the sound of one or two 100-watt guitar amplifiers, a bass amplifier, and a full drum set all in the same room. If that room was live—that is, without any acoustic treatment—the sound would probably be uncontrollable, albeit exciting, depending on your point of view. To counter this, many studios have what are called Iso [Isolation] rooms or individual smaller sound-isolated rooms within the studio area in which to put instruments to ensure that they can be recorded with a high degree of acoustic isolation from other instruments. In mixing, the separate instruments are recombined to make them sound like they were playing live in a huge room without acoustic damping.

TAKING A LOOK AT THE SOUNDSTAGE

Having described the basic methodology behind the recording process as it is today, together with a few of the reasons for the controlled acoustic environment, let's look at what a soundstage is with respect to the control room and the listening room. In general terms, the soundstage might be said to be the area in which the listener sits and the speakers perform. Also, by extension, it can extend to anything that has an acoustic influence or an aural effect on that area. For instance, if the walls of the listening room are dead, without reflection, and the floor is carpeted, then the soundstage will be relying on, for the most part, only the sound coming directly out of the speakers themselves. This will be particularly true at lower volumes, where the room is not significantly involved in the reproduction of the lower frequencies. By this I mean that the various room modes—relative to the primary physical dimensions of the room—are not being excited and reinforced, because of the low playback volume. As the volume is increased, the room modes become excited and can become major contributors to the low-frequency response curve, which can be good and/or bad. So far, this description is common to both the control room and the listening room. At this point the relative philosophies part ways, as the engineer and the listener require different sound-stages. As mentioned earlier, the engineer does not want his soundstage to be overly live or reverberant, as it could prevent him from hearing, or at least [cause him to] misinterpret, certain musical and aural nuances of the performance. The listener, in contrast, might want to create a stage—literally.

The best of acoustic soundstages are, to me, ambient but diffuse. Diffuse is the key word here. I want my early—first order—reflections to be spread out, not concentrated on just one small area. Live areas that rely on singular or low multiples of acoustic reflections tend have adverse and harsh coloration when compared to areas that have as their source multiple and closely spaced first-order spectral reflections that do not converge directly on any one listening position in the general area. Small rooms tend to be harder to work with as far as creating well-diffused soundstages. This is because the boundary walls, hence the reflective surfaces, are so close and more easily overcome by loud music. This is one of the main sources of adverse reflective coloration. One of the biggest victims of this type of reflective coloration is the human voice—voice intelligibility.

ACOUSTICS

We've all been in halls, churches, or rooms where the acoustics have reduced voice intelligibility to zero or thereabouts. Churches are prime examples of environments that have been designed primarily to enhance speech, and as soon as a sound rein-forcement system is powered up in it, as is the fashion, those beautiful acoustics are overpowered, and all bets are off. Likewise, most older concert halls were designed to acoustically enhance orchestral performance and other unamplified events. It is interesting to note that the RT-60s [Reverberation Time] of some con-cert halls have extensions of one to two seconds or more, when measured in the critical bandwidth of the human voice [500 Hz to 5 kHz]. Listening rooms and even studio control rooms can suffer the same fate if not enough attention is paid to their acoustical treatments. Although smaller than churches and concert halls, they are nevertheless bound by the same laws of physics, just on a different, albeit less grand, scale.

One way to counter the closed-in effect of small rooms is to deaden the walls. Stop the mid/high frequencies from reflecting before they start. This is really a brute-force method and not an altogether ideal or advisable approach. It is often used in smaller control room situations where a more controlled listening area—soundstage—is usually preferred. It is also useful in some instances, in the smaller home listening room, when other more diffusive acoustic treatments are precluded because of room size or budget, et cetera. The effect of diffusion, as stated earlier, is to produce multiple and closely spaced [spectral] acoustic reflections that can, if correctly designed and implemented, enhance the listening area by adding dimen-sion, excitement, and kinetic energy to the musical soundstage.

KINETIC ENERGY AND BASS TRAPS

Kinetic energy, in an acoustic context, can best be explained as follows: When low frequencies travel around in a room, they will eventually reach their physical poten-tial, which are the boundaries of the room, the walls, ceiling, and floor. This is the point of maximum excursion and least velocity. After striking these boundaries, much of the acoustic energy—depending on the construction of the room—is turned back into the room and proceeds to complete another full cycle, relative to its wavelength, until it naturally dies away, having expended all its energy. As they move through the room, multiple low frequencies are continuously modulating the air, moving it around in complex patterns and forms. In this way, all the sound energy in the room is in constant flux, and this is sometimes referred to as *kinetic energy*. I like to think of it as musical excitement. In a room that is too heavily damped, the low frequencies can be overly absorbed, causing them to have less or no acoustic energy when they are returned from the room's boundaries. This can cause the mid/high frequencies to travel in more or less straight lines through the room, in basically unmodulated [unexcited] air, and the resultant sounds can be fatiguing, harsh, and unpleasing to the ear. In this way, the low-frequency characteristics of the room can and do act upon the soundstage—the critical listening area.

There is a myth about so-called bass traps…that they should act so efficiently that they totally remove the effects of the modal reactions in the room and cure all low-frequency problems. This is not going to happen, as the modal habits of sound in any environment are governed by physics. Anyway, the idea is not to remove all the bass from the room. This can take all the musical excitement and energy out of a room. Rather, it is to allow the bass to reach its full physical potential naturally, without undue and adverse reinforcement of the bass, due to modal influences, thereby allowing the overall musical performance as originally intended in the mix.

Live End/Dead End (LEDE)

Having come this far, it is only fair to mention that there is a school of thought that supports a different kind of soundstage, one that has the immediate area around the speakers dead and in the rear of the room, behind the listening position, live. It is the LEDE concept that was developed and championed by designer/acousticians Don and Carolyn Davis. LEDE stands for live end/dead end, and it was, funnily enough, initially intended for studio control rooms. I first had a chance to mix in an LEDE control room in the mid '70s. The studio was one of four or five studios belonging to Wally Heider, who had far and away the hottest studios in both Los Angeles and San Francisco in the late '60s and early '70s. Wally refurbished one of his control rooms and, wanting to stay on the cutting edge, incorporated the LEDE design into it. The studio did not get rave reviews as Wally had hoped. Just the opposite, and he quickly changed it back to a more conventional acoustic design.

The philosophy, as I mentioned, was to have the front of the room acoustically non-reflective, literally dead, and to rely on reflections generated by diffusive acoustic wooden arrays on the back and, sometimes, the rear side walls. I found it extremely hard to mix in it and could not really get used to the feeling of the room at all. In thinking it through, I realized that I didn't want to rely on reflected sound from behind me when listening to a stereo mix in front of me. Apart from feeling alien, I started to see some potential pitfalls in the concept. For instance, while for some it might work quite well in a smaller control room, what would happen if the depth of the room was, say, 25 feet or more? That would mean that the sound had to travel past me to the back wall and then be reflected back to my position at the recording console. In a 25-foot-deep room, say 23 feet to the back wall [if the speakers are a little off the front wall] plus the distance back to me, sitting behind the recording console, say 14 feet. That equals a path of 37 feet, round trip. It is not hard to see how these reflected signals could really be in conflict with the original signal. At that distance, it is starting to become problematic. Any longer, and the signal path would be in real danger of becoming a discernable echo to the initial signal, rather than being easily integrated into it by the brain. This condition would fall afoul of the Haas effect. The Haas effect states that the human brain has the wonderful ability to integrate sounds that arrive at the ear up to around 35 to 50 milliseconds. After that, instead of being perceived by the brain as part of the original sound, such late reflections would be heard as an echo, reverberation, or an addition to it. This causes ear-brain confusion and loss of clarity in the sound.

I hope this has helped explain some of the differences between the control room and listening room environments and the reasoning behind them. Simply put: One is for creating a reproduction of the musical performances, and the other is for enjoying them.

Cookie Marenco

Producing and/or engineering credits include: Max Roach, Brain, Kenny Aronoff, Steve Smith, Tony Furtado, Tony Trischka, Dirk Powell, Rob Ickes, Charlie Haden, Tony Levin, Buckethead, Ralph Towner, Paul McCandless, Mary Chapin Carpenter, Pat DiNizio, Kristin Hersh, Ladysmith Black Mambazo, Mark Isham. See the Appendix for Cookie Marenco's full bio.

Gone are the days of ignorant bliss! When I laid down some hard-earned cash to start my studio a generation ago, I had done all my research about the mics, recording device, mixing console, et cetera, never really thinking about how it was going to be put together. I left the pile of gear with my band members as I trotted off to meet my relatives from Italy for three weeks. I'm not really sure how it happened, but, fortunately, one of the guys in the band did soldering for a living and knew that we needed to buy wire. Good call. Unfortunately, his wiring chops were the worst in the group. Someone in the band knew to buy a spool of Belden wire, label the ends, and we were off to the races.

When I returned from the month with the relatives, the new studio had been wired, the cheapest mic cables bought, and I was looked at sternly and told, "Now, *you're* going to learn how to work this stuff!" Thus began my recording career.

We had a patch bay made of mini ins and hardwired out. Soon, we had to buy more patch bays and ended up with 1/4-inch ins, because mini bays weren't made anymore. If there was a kind of end, we had a patch bay for it. At some point, we added another mixing console and wired it to return effects. Having an outside engineer come into the room was not on the agenda in those days. Patching was an incredible exercise in dealing with limitations. We knew every suspect input and potential problem, track by track, channel by channel, and still, with all these limitations, learned how to make recordings acceptable by the acoustic music audiophile community.

Lesson One: You're only as good as your weakest link. No matter what you put in it, if it's got to go through a mini plug, that's as good as it gets. Now, all is not lost. You can learn about gain structure and stressing your system to the point of giving out and then back down. You'll be ahead of 90 percent of the others who don't know how to maximize the system and shove as much signal through as you can. This tactic keeps the noise floor down.

When we stepped up our mixing console, we went to Tiny Telephone patch bays [TTs]. Our tech assured us that Belden was good enough. We didn't have the time or money to rewire, so we tied the new board to our system with the old wire, promising that we would rewire someday. Then we built a new control room; didn't have time to rewire; carefully carried the board, patch bay, et cetera, in one swoop with 20 hands on board; set it in place; and started the recording session.

A pop here, a fizzle there, a "what the heck is going on?!"—it was always the cable. As much as we wanted to blame the $1,500 mic or the capacitors in the board or the new piece of gear, it was the cable 99 percent of the time. After 10 years of nonsense, I decided I would never take cabling lightly.

Finally, the moment of truth came when I got the bid on our next upgrade—another new console, bigger, better, faster, mo' money. I bought the board used from a well-known industry vet who was moving to LA. I called my tech for an estimate of the wiring. This time, I wanted no mistakes. We were starting fresh, new cable, no one in my staff would solder. I wanted accountability; I wanted the best wiring job possible. I never wanted to have another wiring issue.

Something in your life changes when you realize you're going to spend three times more for the wiring than you're going to spend on a new console. It's not the cable; it's the labor. Since I never wanted wiring to be an issue, I paid the price. Our tech asked if we wanted to install Mogami instead of Belden. At this point, the $2,000 additional cost was pretty small, so why not? I never wanted to do this again. Our tech told us that we probably wouldn't hear the difference. He didn't really believe in all that cable hocus-pocus. He thought it all sounded the same.

Wrong! Three months later, we ran our first signal through the system. Even bypassing the board, the sonic difference was incredible. Suddenly, highs and lows—definition I had never heard. Clients who hadn't been in the studio for six months could hear the improvements and were amazed. We had been swapping out mic cables for Mogami and Canare for a while, but now all other brands were physically tossed out of the studio. It was a revelation. There was a *huge* difference in sonic quality. How could the myth of cable being all the same have permeated the industry? Those of us who were believers seemed like a lunatic-fringe clan. I kept thinking, "Doesn't anyone ever actually do a comparison test?"

I was okay at this juncture, satisfied I had made the $2,000 upgrade, because I *never* wanted to do that again. Rewiring your room is a nightmare; just accept it. Using even the best technicians, it takes months to suss out the problems, and there will be problems!

At this point, I was pretty happy, and I didn't want to upset the apple cart by changing anything. In 2004, after starting Blue Coast Records, I had a production partner, Jean Claude Reynaud, who introduced me to the world of the audiophile. His father, Jean Marie, is a well-known speaker manufacturer in France. Jean Claude began speaking about the silver cable his father built for the French aerospace industry. They use it for their speakers' internal wiring and sell it as speaker cable for their customers. Jean began reciting unbelievable specs for mic, line, and speaker lengths. Yeah, yeah, yeah...I really didn't want to hear about it. I was happy about the Mogami swap—that was enough for me. I really didn't want to hear about new cable or the thought of even swapping out a speaker cable to check it out.

Then one fateful day, after a bottle of wine and some heated words, I agreed to let him take the cable out of the NS-10s and put in the silver cable in. (Yes, NS-10s—sorry, it was the lowest denominator I would agree to.) As much as I didn't want to hear a difference, there it was—undeniable extended frequency response in the highs and lows. The image of the stereo expanded; it sounded like cotton had been taken off. From Mogami to the silver, yes, there was that much difference.

We began making 100-foot cables and swapping out the usual suspects with stunning results. We cultivated a product that uses topnotch ends, silver solder, and is tested for strength. Our entire microphone stock is silver—with a couple of Mogami left around for headphones and the occasional time when the silver is just *too* transparent. (You know, like an SM57—sometimes nothing else will do but lo-fi.) We've heard RF from Mogami, swapped, and it's gone. Amazing. The shielding is incredible.

We've modified the design for the iPod, which is amazing. Bass players say it makes them feel faster. For us, it's like the difference between mics or preamps. Sometimes, you just want to take it to another level of clarity.

Since joining the audiophile movement, I've discovered there are all kinds of wacky cables. I don't really have the time or money to try them all out! It's amazing that pro audio hasn't adopted some of these other cable choices. Give it a try, open your ears, learn to listen, and be flexible to change.

Michael Rhodes

Clients include: Echo Mountian Recording, Ocean Way Nashville, Warner Brothers Nashville, Blackbird Studios, as well as personal rooms for Marshall Mathers (Eminem), Clint Black, Vince Gill, Kenny Alphin, Jewel, and the White Stripes's Jack White. See the Appendix for Michael Rhodes's bio.

There are so many important details to consider that affect how a studio should be designed. Trying to narrow all of those details down to pinpoint the needs of the client boils down to, first off, identifying the studio's special purpose. Who will use the studio? Will it be a commercial room or a private space for a band or producer? The single best question to ask is, "What does the client want to do in his/her new studio?" Mainly track? Mix? Overdub? That is also the point in time they should consult with a professional.

Too many times I get calls from people after they get too far into a project. They often end up having to then spend even more time and money redoing something that could have been thought out and solved from the start. There are plenty of great, honest, and knowledgeable people out here, so it is a smart thing to consult a professional. A professional has already been through this process many times and will be able to see and avert pitfalls before they happen.

When I am asked to lay out a studio, there are really three main studio situations that I run across regularly, not including mastering rooms. The main three are:

✤ Commercial studios (for rent) (full, overdub, or mix)

✤ Private studios for an artist or band (full, overdub, or mix)

✤ Small private studios for an artist or songwriter (overdub only) (small overdub and songwriters' rooms)

There are a lot of things in common with all three. In all three, planning is the most important step.

If you are going for a commercial studio, the approach is different than, say, a privately owned complete studio or even an overdub/mix space. In building a commercial studio, you have to think of everything that someone might do in a session, possibly years from now.

For example, there was a very cool API room in North Carolina. The owner told me the band that did the initiating burn-in session used every input of the console and just about everything else. During the planning of the studio, they originally wanted fewer lines running up to this huge live room upstairs from the studio. We talked about it and decided to double the mic lines to 48 and add more interconnects. The band who did the test run really loved cutting up there, instead of the tracking room. The tracking room is a fantastic room, but the room upstairs is this huge live space where they could all play together. It worked out great for that session. Thank goodness we decided to build in 48 mic lines, among other things, to accommodate that possibility. Once again, it illustrated the need to plan ahead.

A commercial studio has to be much more flexible than the private studios because of all these variables that can happen from session to session. Unfortunately, that means more connections. We would all love there to be no connectors inline and for everything to be hardwired. It would sound better, but that isn't the world in which commercial rooms reside. We have patch bays to save time in routing. In a commercial studio, the person renting the studio will have to be able to access the patch bay if he has large racks of his own gear, which might mean a set of Elcos or DLs connectors to a guest patch bay or something along those lines. The tape machine/hard drive flavor of the week needs to have a way of interfacing to the console as well. Machine-room patching is great for that. Use of standard pin-outs is very important. Those who know me know that I am insane about the wiring standards!

In a private studio, there is a much more tailored approach. The best way is to have the client walk you through a typical session the way they like to work. Depending on what they want to accomplish, you can tailor to their needs, but it is wise to think ahead and consider what their future needs may be. With only a few people using the space, you don't have to be quite as flexible as with a commercial facility. You can do more normaling in the patch bay to make it easier for that person or band to work, and that also means you can hardwire more things directly into the patch bay. That means there will be fewer connectors to fail or make noise because of bad or dirty connections. Special setups just for that person can be done with things like normaling keyboard gear or vocal chains. When I say normaling, I am speaking of the normal state of the patch bay before any patch cables are plugged in it.

I just rewired a room for a local songwriter. He wanted all of his keyboard gear to go into certain gear, so we set it up to be normaled into that gear.

There are many ways to set up a patch bay for someone. If it is for only them, it makes sense. If other people will use it, standard is better.

Private studios also lend themselves to more mods on gear. In a commercial studio, no one wants to rent a studio and then have 10,000 switches to learn how to use. They spend half of their day saying, "What does this button do?"

The people already know how to use their own personal gear and how it sounds. You *can* use that switch that changes it to a half-powered British overdrive super retro gigamahoo.... In a commercial studio, an 1176 needs to sound like an 1176. Mods that make the gear have a lower noise floor are great, but mods that change the color or sound of the gear are not.

In a private studio, anything goes mod-wise.

Small overdub and songwriters' rooms are the last type. They are really just small versions of private studios, which we have already talked about. You still tailor the room to the client, but just on a smaller level. They usually have a small format desk with just a little outboard. There still should be enough room to get behind everything to patch directly. Usually, these types of small studios need either a vocal chain or an instrument chain of some kind for their main recording path. Because of the price drop and increasing quality of the gear, pro-level studios are in reach for a lot more people, but these are the people who usually can't believe their wiring costs are so high. It still costs the same to wire a $50,000 16-channel Console A as it does to wire a $4,500 16-channel Console B. The number of points is the same. It is, however, a much larger percent of the overall cost. The layouts are usually very similar for both consoles. It's the labor that runs up the final cost.

This leads me to emphasize this: Know your budget! Always try to budget appropriately according to your needs. It really shocks most people to find out how much it costs to wire a studio correctly, if they have never built one. Yes, you can buy cheap cables, and they will pass audio, but is *passing* audio enough—especially if you are wanting excellent sounds and results? As our ears learn how to listen, good enough is not good enough. Once you hear something clean and transparent, it's really hard to go back. With the wiring done right, you can have a much lower noise floor and much cleaner, wider-sounding audio.

Many times I meet people who buy gear with every penny they have and then spend nothing on the sound treatment or wiring. When they take the cheap way out, I hear things like (in a whiny voice), "My C 12 sounds like crud; it must be broken," or even, "My SM57 sounds better than my C 12." In reality, the SM57 is doing a great job of rejecting the sound of their bad-sounding room. The C 12 not so much, and you hear it....

Also needing emphasis is proper gear and installation. Whenever I wire a studio, there are things in common with all of them. Start with good monitoring, so you know what you are listening to. As we all know, it all starts with the sound of the room acoustically and good, clean, transparent monitors. That is not to say it has to be sonically perfect, but you should be able to trust what you are hearing to be able to make informed adjustments. I've seen people who have a $12,000 microphone through a $5,000 preamp, only to listen through a set of $300 speakers with a $200 cruddy-sounding amp. That isn't going to provide very accurate listening.

Great-sounding gear is the next step. Again, it's about trust. Trust your ears—unless of course it's late in the day, and your ears are shot. In that case, trust your ears tomorrow.

Some examples of details that are often overlooked are things like electrical power, wire runs, types of connectors, and even the wire itself. They all make a huge difference.

As far as power is concerned, hire an electrician who is familiar with the challenges of a recording environment, especially with grounding.

The audio wire runs should be as short as possible with a service loop. Service loop is the amount of wire used to pull a piece of gear out and work on it. You—or someone—will have to get into it to change or fix something later. I remember getting a console into a studio that someone had to use a hacksaw to cut off of the floor because the wiring was so tight. We had to rewire the entire patch bay. A few connectors and a service loop would have saved them a lot of time and money.

Always put in more pipe space than you need. There will always be things that were not thought of until later. You never want to be surprised with, "Wow, wouldn't it be cool if we could...." If you have to go back later, it's usually much more expensive. If you build a little more than you need, it could cost as little as some extra pipe. Always give yourself room for expansion. More pipes, more outboard points, et cetera....

It's nice to know that if you get a new piece of outboard gear, you have a place to plug it in without rewiring the whole setup. You know the setup will change over time. Be ready. Again, no brainer, but I see it all of the time.

Connectors make a big difference. The biggest pitfall in connectors is the patch bays. Think about it: It's 96 jacks plus the harness. Half of your connections. All of your audio in most studios goes through a patch bay. It drives me crazy to see people try to skimp and buy the cheapest patch bay they can find. These are the same people who will spend money on gold contacts for XLRs and then buy a used patch bay off of eBay and then try to make it work. Patch bays have come down in price. I cannot stress enough the value of having good patch bays. As with all connectors, higher-quality contacts last longer under heavy use and corrode less over time. Less corrosion means clear audio and fewer problems later.

You know who you are, and you have been warned....

The wire used also makes a huge difference. Many people go with Mogami because it is perceived as the standard. There is a good reason why people call a standard a standard. A standard is a consensus of a lot of different people who have decided that a certain thing is the best for a certain task. For myself, I use Mogami not only for the sound, but also for the ease of use and durability. It does cost a little more. You don't know until you listen for yourself or you are shown. There are all kinds of esoteric wires out there that sound more transparent. It's your ear and price, among other things, that will make the determination of what to use. Some wire, like Alpha, sound great but are totally impractical for most people. It takes twice as long to wire. It's a single solid-strand wire. It's also bulky and not very flexible, but it does sound more transparent. I think it worked out well inside the walls. For harnesses and such, outside the walls, not so much for all of the reasons listed. It does sound more transparent, but at what cost?

If you have the budget and desire to build or create an uncompromising facility like Blackbird in Nashville, Tennessee, the difference in sonic improvements is palpable, but the cost to achieve that difference is steep.

Surround Sound Recording and Mixing

For decades, audio specialists have been trying to expand the sense of space and point of origin in recorded music. Reverbs and delays can only do so much sonic trickery in mono and stereo recordings to provide the listener with a sense of space. In the early '70s, the music industry introduced quadraphonic sound to the consumer market. It was too early; for various reasons, the format was a bust. Obviously, the motive behind quad was to place the listener in the middle of the audio experience. Almost 40 years later, the industry is ready to go after the consumer surround music experience. Much has changed since quad. The introduction of digital technology and the proliferation of home surround systems for television have sent an encouraging signal to the industry that the public might be ready and willing to buy into surround sound.

While the CD hardly held a candle to a well-recorded, well-pressed vinyl album on a good system, the average CD and CD player sounded better than most beat-up home turntables and scratchy records. The convenience of the CD helped hasten the demise of the LP, along with the fact that the industry was determined to kill the vinyl record.

From the '90s through to the mid-'00s, there was a concerted push to bring a high-quality surround experience to consumers. However, there was conflict and indecision about what format to commit to for surround. There were formats like DTS, SACD, and DVD-Audio, as well as different players to play a specific format. In the end, it was all very confusing to the public. Certainly, the days when we just had vinyl as a universal format seemed so simple. It's not surprising that vinyl has made a resurgence, but that's another discussion.

In the last few years, it's been gratifying to discover people who haven't given up on surround audio and have been part of some extremely satisfying surround listening experiences. Obviously, the public has embraced surround audio in film. A masterful surround audio mix in a film can take a rather average viewing experience and turn it into a transcendent overall experience.

Personally, I still think surround audio is something worth pursuing. I've heard the argument many times that people just will not sit still between speakers and listen like they once did. But I think that if you give them a compelling experience, they will gladly sit and repeatedly listen. One natural listening place for surround audio is automobiles. I have several hundred surround releases, and the best ones have even surpassed the original stereo experiences, bringing new meaning to the music. As technology evolves, I believe surround audio will find a way into our homes and cars.

While the bulk of the surround work is originating from preexisting classic stereo catalog releases, increasing numbers of people are working in the creation of new music that considers surround from the outset.

For this chapter, seven very knowledgeable contributors discuss surround: Chuck Ainlay, Stephen Barncard, Steve Bishir, Doug Mitchell, Kevin Shirley, Steven Wilson, and Cookie Marenco. Along with a number of other people I've talked to, they are still keeping the surround discussion alive with great work.

Steven Wilson

See the Appendix for Steve Wilson's bio.

When I first approached surround sound, I thought, "Ahh, this is going to be great! We're going to put the drums in all four corners. We're going to have the dry drum sounds at the front and all the room reflections at the back." But when I tried it, it sounded horrible. It didn't work at all. It was like hearing two drum kits, neither of which sounded good, coming unglued. So, I learned by trial and error how certain things don't work. The surround field seems to come together best with the drums and the bass anchored pretty much at the front. However, some of the things that do really work fantastically in surround are keyboard details, harmony vocals, and acoustic guitars. Also, when you start to work on recording albums with the knowledge that you're going to be mixing in surround, you start to think, "Well, let's track this four times," whereas previously you might just double-track a guitar twice—left and right. Then, you have the option to put one guitar in each corner, and it sounds amazing. That said, it's really a question of always working from the stereo up for me, so the surround mixes usually will take only a few hours more. Ninety-five percent of the work on a surround sound mix is in actually creating a good stereo mix first. At that point, you have all of the sound processing in place—EQ, compression, reverb, and delays—as well as basic levels and volume rides. While these may need adjustment in the surround picture, it's unusual for that to be the case, so creating a 5.1 mix simply becomes about moving things into a more three-dimensional space.

When stereo first came along in the '60s, engineers were doing stereo mixes where they positioned the whole band on one side and the vocals on the other. When you listen to the Beatles, you're reminded how odd some of the early stereo mixes are. I think some of the early surround mixes kind of went a similar way.

When I first started with surround, I listened to a lot of existing 5.1 releases and didn't like a lot of them because I thought they were too gimmicky. It was like, "Hey, you know what? We can have the guitar whizzing around the room, we can have the drums over there, and we can have the vocals flipping back and forth between the center and rear speakers. It's gonna be great!" The trouble was that it wasn't something you would want to listen to repeatedly. Why would you create a mix like that any more than you would create a stereo mix where things were bouncing backward and forward between the left and right the whole time?

Years ago, I think the whole thing about mono versus stereo was that, ultimately, people were looking at stereo as a way to make the music have a little more spatial dimension. To me, surround is the same approach. You just have an extra dimension, and you're not looking to be gimmicky. You're not looking to be distracting with the mix.

The first two Porcupine Tree album surround mixes were done with Elliot Scheiner. I was very lucky to be able to watch him, see how he worked, and figure out how he approached things. So, I started to develop my own vocabulary for mixing in surround, which seems to have gone down well with the people who like that format. But I really just approached it from a very intuitive perspective, trying to make the whole listening experience more immersive. I didn't want to make it feel like it was just showing off the whole time.

When Robert Fripp was approached about me doing the King Crimson catalog in surround, he was also of the opinion that it was some kind of gimmicky thing, and he really wasn't interested. But I suggested that I take one album and mix it anyway, as an audition of sorts. I knew that if it was done properly, he would like it. I picked *Discipline* because of the interlocking guitars, and as soon as he heard it, he was jumping up out his chair and saying, "All right, we're going to do the whole catalog!" I truly believe that almost any musician could be won over given the chance to hear a sensitively done 5.1 mix of their music. I like to think I could win over even the most skeptical person. Nothing to do with me or the way I do it, but simply because if it's done even half-decently, it's a revelation. It's like you can never go back to mono or stereo after you've heard your music in surround.

For me, there's certainly a style of music that suits surround sound absolutely perfectly: the art/progressive rock tradition. Any album where the production has so many layers to the sound—Pink Floyd and King Crimson are perfect examples. When they are in the studio, they are not bound by the conventions of live music. They're experimenting with sounds and instrumental relationships that couldn't necessarily be reproduced live. Because of that, we as listeners don't have any preconceptions about how the sounds should or should not be positioned in space. That's perfect for surround, where you can approach those different layers in the production in a similarly experimental way.

Fortunately (and unusually), the great thing about King Crimson is that Robert Fripp, the leader of King Crimson, actually owns all of the rights and the master tapes. We were able to have the tapes baked and transferred. We used UK companies FX and Universal Tape Archive to do the actual transfers. The tapes, some of which were 40 years old, were in very delicate condition; they had to actually hand-wind them in some cases. It was very laborious process.

Along the way, I found a whole bunch of stuff on the tapes that had never been mixed, so the other thing I was able to do was stereo mixes of never-heard-before alternate takes and do new stereo mixes of the actual album tracks themselves.

We had no original recording notes at all, so I was lining up a copy of the existing CD and comparing literally every few bars to make sure I was being faithful to the original mixes. In some of the early tapes, there are many alternate overdubs that are not in the mix or that kind of pop up in the mix for a few moments, then disappear again, so it was a long process to re-create the original mixes in stereo.

I grew up in the '80s, but I was always listening to music from the '70s because the music that was around me in the '80s just didn't appeal to me at all. I got into the world of recording at the very beginning of digital recording technology. I didn't really ever have the opportunity to learn how to do things in a "vintage" way, but all the sounds I liked were on records that were made using analog equipment, so I ended up teaching myself how to make those sounds using digital technology. If I had to pick one thing that I would say is my strength, that would be it. Sometimes, people don't believe that the records I make are completely mixed inside a digital environment, but if I'm good at anything, it's making digital things sound warm because those are the sounds I like and naturally aspire to. That's the vocabulary that I want to speak in, even though I don't have access to the tools those guys had then, and I wouldn't have a clue how to use them anyway.

I'm using Logic with the Digi TDM engine, so I'm able to use all of Pro Tools' plug-ins. I rely a lot on the Focusrite d2/d3 compressor, the Line 6 Amp Farm and Echo Farm, and D-Verb, which is a reverb plug-in that comes free with Pro Tools. I think a lot of people don't use it simply because it's the free Digidesign one, but I think it's terrific because it's so flexible and quite transparent when you need it to be.

Echo Farm does a great job of simulating the old vintage tape slap, and I love being able to add the tape warble to make it sound even more authentic. I also have no qualms about getting plug-ins that are not supposed to sound old to actually sound more vintage. Digital is probably more faithful in the sense that it reproduces more of the top end and the low end, but there's certainly something special about the sound of those classic vintage recordings. If you have digital plug-ins, put filters across them, and emphasize more of that middle, to my ears you get more of that vintage sound—for example, putting low-pass and high-pass filters on reverbs to take out a lot of what people might associate with being high fidelity. I do that with a lot of the digital plug-ins. This was essential for revisiting the King Crimson albums since they were putting mono plates on a lot of the sounds. So many modern reverbs seem to think it's their job to sound fantastically impressive in their own right, with vast, shiny stereo reflections. But I think that a lot of times, mix engineers are looking for a more practical application of a reverb as being something that you hardly know is there. It just adds a kind of "halo" around the instrument and makes it sit better in a mix.

With a lot of the King Crimson stuff, a lot of the effects were printed to tape. Compared to the way most recording is done now, it's a very different way to work. When I started working with these tapes, I was very impressed with how much was committed to tape and how good it sounded. I'm sure this is true of a lot of the recording during that classic period—it's the economy in the use of over-dubbing. They made decisions and committed them to tape. Not only did they make decisions, they got incredible tones that didn't need to be tracked four times to sound impressive. I think that's becoming a lost art. We now live in a recording era where it's very easy to track something eight times and make it sound huge. You know, "We've got a guitar and unlimited tracks, so let's get an OK sound but track it eight times." Back in the '70s, those guys couldn't work that way, so they made sure that one guitar's tones were just huge. There's that whole thing about necessity being the mother of invention, which is absolutely right. If you're limited to 16 tracks or eight tracks, then you have to know how to get incredible tones that will sound good without tracking them.

In the Court of the Crimson King, King Crimson's 1969 debut album, was recorded on eight tracks. "21st Century Schizoid Man" is one pass on eight track tape, but most of the other tracks on the album were bounced down several times before they had a complete master, so the first bounce would be to reduce the chosen take of drum, bass, and guitar from the backing track session to two tracks on a second reel. Then, they'd fill up the remaining six tracks with Mellotrons before bouncing down a second time in order to track the vocals. By the time you get to creating a stereo master, those original drum, bass, and guitar takes could have been through four or five generations of tape, with all the extra hiss, grime, dropouts, loss of transients, and other audio characteristics that this entails. Fortunately, we were able to go back and resynchronize the various session reels. This was important for 5.1, anyway, where we needed to be able to control, move, and work with isolated instruments. Although it was kind of a byproduct of those 5.1 mixes, the idea to also create and release new stereo mixes naturally came up. I was referring to the original stereo mix, and I could hear that the difference was huge. Rather than using second- or third-generation drum or bass tracks, we had first-generation tracks for the first time ever to mix from. It was too hard to resist the chance to produce a definitive stereo master using the new multitrack session that we'd built and that no one had ever had available to them before.

Effectively re-creating the original stereo mix as faithfully as possible became step 1. In the case of King Crimson, I'm very familiar with the originals. I'm such a fan of them that I'm reluctant to change anything, and if there's anything different on the King Crimson remixes, it's probably because Robert said he'd like to change something or felt it was never right in the first place. Even then, I think you need to be careful because the quirks and inaccuracies of mixes become familiar to people over a period of years; even if it's not quite what the artist intended, that's how people know it. To correct it can sometimes make it unfamiliar and break the spell, so creating the new stereo mixes did involve a fair bit of discussion. If I felt Robert was asking for changes that I felt were not somehow faithful to the spirit of the original, then I would certainly say so, but there were other changes that definitely made sense to me.

It's only at the point that everyone is happy and agreed on the stereo that I start to break the mix out into the three dimensions of 5.1. Once you have an idea about what does and doesn't work in surround, it's actually quite easy and a lot of fun to be suddenly sitting inside the music that until then has only been coming at you from the front.

Stephen Barncard

Credits include: The Grateful Dead, Crosby, Stills, Nash & Young, New Riders of the Purple Sage, Van Morrison, David Crosby, Seals and Crofts, the Doobie Brothers. See the Appendix for Stephen Barncard's full bio.

My first surround mix release was *Another Stoney Evening*, a show from the Crosby & Nash tour of 1971. During that time, Rubber Dubber, a famous vinyl bootlegging label, put out this two-disk pressing called *A Very Stoney Evening* based on one of the nights of that tour. I don't know how they recorded it, but it was a fairly decent–quality live recording from that tour.

Unbeknownst to Rubber Dubber, David Crosby and Graham Nash had decided to record the whole tour. They got Bill Halverson, who was a remote recording heavy, to go out with the Wally Heider truck with the famous Frank de Medio eight-channel tube console. It was one of the first modular consoles with these big rotary faders and module strips with the UA 610 amplifiers and great electronics and not much EQ.

Eight tracks were a viable medium to record this tour because it was just two guys with just enough tracks to add a pair of stereo audience tracks, a Wally Heider specialty. This was usually recorded with a far-placed stereo mic pair placed far away in a sweet spot that really captured the expanse of the audience, and as little of the PA as possible.

At this distinguished venue in 1971, audiences were still polite. There was no shouting and rude "Where's Stephen?" calls. When David Crosby did "Guinevere" or "Where Will I Be?" they were a respectful, listening audience. The recording was done on October 10, 1971, at the Dorothy Chandler Pavilion in Los Angeles, which was a classy place, normally a place for classical and theatrical events. David's dear mother was even in the house that night.

During that tour, Crosby & Nash were so loose and so high and so funny and so good! Both of them had their best batches of songs from both Nash's and Crosby's first solo albums, and they did all of these tunes from these great records in a very casual way—just the two of them, two guitars, and a piano.

Thanks to the Wally Heider crew, I had great audience tracks to work with and could build the foundation of the surround mix by placing them in the back channels. Joel Bernstein and Robert Hammer had taken a hundred excellent photos of the show, and I had studied the setting and the positioning of the mics. Looking from the audience, Graham was on the left and David on the right, and you could hear them sitting in their chairs, moving around, and talking. I was influenced by the loose format of the Grateful Dead's live records and wanted the project to have a casual, vérité feel. A lot of it was really funny. They had great comedic timing that you couldn't script, and there was an overall dynamic that was staggering. There was also a lot to cut out. That had to wait for the Crosby, Stills & Nash box set and, later, digital editing.

We really didn't discover this tape that would become *Another Stoney Evening* until 1991, when Nash called me and asked me to work on the CSN box set. They had all of these tapes in storage, including some instruments they had packed away and forgotten about. Graham Nash loves history and spelunking for old tapes with undiscovered performances. In one of the boxes, we found this series of eight track 1-inch tape reels recorded on the Crosby & Nash tour of 1971. When I saw this, I thought, "This might just be great a future release of some kind." The recording was pristine—a fantastic live recording by the master live recordist Halverson. So, in 1997, I made an independent deal with Grateful Dead Records for a stereo version, and after DVD-Audio surround was finally standardized in 2002, this all led to contact with DTS, who wanted me to mix a surround version of *Another Stoney Evening*.

The transfer session for *Another Stoney Evening* was done at dBTechnologies in Burbank. They did the transfers from eight-track 1-inch to digital, and then gave me the files in 96/24.

I had my monitors measured and set up to the NAB/AES standards. I had and currently have the five speakers set up in a very small surround circle—as small as I can make it to fit around the tables that I'm using. I call it near-field surround mixing, which is basically putting the speakers as close of a radius as possible for one person while maintaining appropriate speaker positioning. This approach has worked well for me.

When I did the surround mix for David's record *If I Could Only Remember My Name*, I had transfers of some eight-track and 16-track reels of the sessions. I was able to go back to first-generation elements and found some of the eight tracks had been later bounced to the 16 tracks for further overdubs. I was doing this so the mixes would all be using first-generation tracks and sound better.

I got to get really deep into the acoustic guitar sound on the mixes. In fact, I spent most of my time on the guitars because that's what David's album is—a great guitar album (dominated by acoustics) with David's beautiful vocals. To try and keep the vibe of the original, which was well known to the fans who had heard the stereo version over the years, I would always keep the original stereo version alongside the multitracks to listen to and compare at any point in the song.

I tried to re-create the echoes and expanded the concept to surround. I tried various digital echoes, but ended up liking these stereo stock echo plug-ins that come with Pro Tools. I liked the idea of being able to tune the channels a little more, so I made this little matrix, and once I got these little echoes tweaked up and in surround, I had this blob that I could re-create that almost sounded like the various Wally Heider live chambers. At Heider's in San Francisco, we had four real acoustic chambers that consisted of shellacked, non-parallel walls where some of them could sound like the Taj Mahal. It took a couple weeks to get the virtual chamber space I created tuned in, but it worked great and I was working totally in the box. I tried to use a control surface, but it was such a pain that I just ended up moving faders on the screen.

During the making of *If I Could Only Remember My Name*, I had this experience of sitting on a stool in the studio while they were jamming, running tracks down. If you put up the surround mix and play it in a big room, you can walk around and you're right there in that space. You're in the musician's perspective.

On the track "Cowboy Movie," there are two Jerry Garcias playing lead on it. I placed each Garcia in the left and right surrounds (rears) alone, so you can go over and stand by one side and just listen to Garcia wail, you can go to the other speaker and listen to the other Garcia do the reply licks, or you can go and listen to the acoustics in another speaker and David's vocal in the center.

I usually kept David up in the front speakers and guests and percussion in the back, but on "Orleans" there were many chiming and picking parts. If there were three parts, then I spread them out in a triangular pattern; if there were four parts, I made a quad. There was a melodic thing that he plays at the end—of multiple acoustics and harmonies—and that was fun. Every song was an absolute joy to invent a sound space for.

I didn't hold onto any conventions that the center channel had to carry any special instrument in the surround mix. For most listeners with average systems, the bass instruments below 80 Hz were going to be spread by bass management anyway, but in some cases I would move the high-end ticky-tacky part of the bass into the center channel for clarity.

On *If I Could Only Remember My Name*, I didn't use the LFE (low-frequency effects or .1) channel at all because I couldn't find anything in that range on any of the songs that made it worthwhile to attempt it. I had attended several surround conferences and seminars where the participants were divulging their techniques and giving master classes talking about the LFE—the low-frequency effects. LFE was put there by the movie people for rumble stuff like earthquakes, but I don't think it was intended to be a thing to just add more bass in the mix. Almost all consumer systems have bass management, which is not LFE. Many mixers still don't get that bass management takes the low-frequency content from all of the surround channels, filters at about 80 Hz the feed to each of the five amplifiers, and mixes a sum of the five to mono, filters all above 80 Hz, and puts that in the sub woofer. The LFE channel is added on top of that, is under the control of the mixer, and goes directly to the subwoofer. But end users may have differently calibrated systems, and a LFE signal may just get in the way—the listener ends up with too much or muddy low end. With that in mind, I felt it was more important to focus the mix toward five full-sized speakers with very occasional use of the LFE channel for impact.

A surround mix gains body and depth by starting in a stereo realm that is already known. This has proven to be more efficient than starting in surround and then folding back into stereo. Once the stereo mix is established, I spread the instruments into a wider soundstage and then further expand with ambience.

There are basically two ways to approach a surround mix. One is with the players in front, as if on a stage, with some kind of ambiance swirling in the back, and we're the audience sitting in our seats. I think that method is boring.

The other method is filling all corners of the room with instruments, well, separated. There's motion and activity all around, and surround can truly get you about as close sonically as possible to the real thing. That dance is what this record was about, and if there were any record that would have the deep and interesting sonic sources to draw from, *If I Could Only Remember My Name* in surround was it. I wanted this to be a "killer app" recording that would help sell the idea of surround to the masses.

Kevin Shirley

Credits include: Aerosmith, Judas Priest, Journey, Iron Maiden, the Black Crowes, Led Zeppelin, Rush, HIM, Metallica, New York Dolls, Dream Theater, Joe Satriani. See the Appendix for Kevin Shirley's full bio.

Surround adds such a dimension to music. I had my dad in in my studio yesterday. He's a classical music aficionado, and I played him "Kashmir" from Jimmy Page and Robert Plant's *No Quarter: Jimmy Page and Robert Plant Unledded*. My dad has never been a fan of anything non-classical. He sat and listened to this, and he had tears in his eyes. He was shaking his head and saying, "I can't believe it. It's unbelievable." To experience immersive sound like that puts you in a different world. It can transport you.

Certainly, on *No Quarter*, the picture has some relevance to the sound source, but when you're in surround, there's so much you can do creatively.

If the surround mix you are doing is a concert, like *No Quarter*, then you need to feel like you're in a concert, whether you decide to be in the front row or in the center of the mosh pit. The nice thing is you can really place the listener in the sound field. I think surround sound in live applications like that is incredible.

Outside of live concert applications, music is always meant to be about energy or relaxation or fun or anxiety or anger—all these things. Surround sound is so much fun. It's just fantastic to listen to it and be in that world with things going on all around you. It's like being in the forest; it's birds and streams all around you, but only when you stop in one place and really listen, you go, "Wow, this is so fantastic. Why don't we have this in all our iPods?" That's why I love it. It's just so much fun.

My surround monitors are set up a little higher in the rears. It's a little tighter in the front. The center speaker is really important because it can be really bad. It's pretty much bent; it hits me pretty hard. I make sure that if there's anything coming out of the center speaker, I'm not going to be bothered about it being hard.

One of my biggest issues about all things audio is the thought that there has to be a disparity between cinema and music. We have different configurations for surround sound in music and different configurations for when we send stuff for movies. It doesn't make any sense to me at all. Surround is really cinema. That's what it is! You don't really mix surround without cinema because you focus on the picture. I just think that there should be one format for cinema and music. It should be the same.

For anyone who owns a CD and DVD collection, at most you'll watch DVDs like twice, but you may listen to a CD 50 times, so there's no doubt that the audio triggers a whole different set of emotions and responses in you than the visual does. You see those visuals, and you kind of analyze them at a much more basic level: "I know what's going to happen next." Once you've been there twice, it usually doesn't draw you into many repeated viewings, whereas with audio, you just enjoy it. So why wouldn't you have that enjoyment as part of your visual experience? Why would you limit that?

You can watch a movie on an iPod, and if you have big sound, it seems much more real. I love what they do with movie audio. Some of these movies, like *Apocalypse Now*, just sound phenomenal. That's what I'm striving for. In my surround now, I'm saying, "Forget all the conservative thinking out there about what effects should be in the front and should be in the rear and how much to track from that." I want my surround audio mixes to play like movies. I want them to be like that—fun, exciting, and explosive, you know? I wish we could just deliver them in a much easier way, so people could actually bother listening to them. That would be great!

I remember my first meeting with Jimmy Page. I discussed with him the architecture of surround and how to place things within the box given that these speakers were giving you this 360-degree space that you can put anything, anywhere, in. I've since refined that a little bit in my way of thinking. The subtlety gets lost, and I think that unless you're in a dead environment like this studio, where you have point-source sound, even then stuff can get lost in the crossfire of all these things. That point-source material is much more effective than some of the subtle things. I find when you can bypass that—rather than putting one audience mic there, one audience mic at 75, one audience mic at 50 percent—it's almost more effective if you have them in the four corners, like it's literally coming out of each specific speaker as opposed to being panned somewhere in the middle. I find that there's a natural convergence anyway that happens in any room.

Chuck Ainlay

Credits include: Mark Knopfler (solo and with Dire Straits), Trisha Yearwood, Vince Gill, Steve Earle, Lyle Lovett, Wynonna, and George Strait. See the Appendix for Chuck Ainlay's full bio.

I got interested in the idea of doing surround sound production after hearing quad recordings in the '70s. They gave me my initial impressions, as well as hearing films in surround at movie theaters later on. I don't think I actually thought about doing a music mix in surround other than the work for film tracks that I had done because, at the time, there wasn't any delivery format that I was aware of. When I was approached by Tony Brown of MCA Records about doing Vince Gill's *High Lonesome Sound* for DTS in 5.1, you can only imagine that I leapt at the chance.

When I started, the first roadblocks I encountered were primarily due to the fact that we were forging new ground and little was known. Speaker setup, bass management, and how to monitor in 5.1 on consoles not equipped to do so were some of the technical problems. There were also ideological questions as to what to do with the center channel, what to pan to the rears, and how much to engage the listener with a music-only surround mix.

A lot of my concepts about mixing for surround had to do with how ultimately the casual listener might come into contact with a surround mix, and I realized that most of the conditions would probably be less than perfect. The center channel speaker being a different voicing than the left and right speakers, rear channels intended only for ambience, being underpowered, and having insufficient bandwidth, bass management levels, and car systems were also some of the unknowns.

So far, my experience is with 5.1 only. I haven't done anything for formats above that, and, really, I think that it is unlikely that the consumer will allow any more speakers in their home. Formats like 6.1, 7.1, and up are for movie theaters and special venues. The formats of music I have done in 5.1 have been delivered on Dolby Digital, DTS, DVD-Video, and DVD-Audio.

Even before I started working with surround, I think the way I've always understood mixing was in a three-dimensional environment. The picture I have always tried to create was three dimensional, but the tools I had to create that environment only allowed for a three-dimensional perception within a two-dimensional stereo space. So, I had to create the perception that there was depth, although in reality it was a flat space with tricks to make the mind's eye view depth.

Personally, I don't think the thought process I use for mixing 5.1 is really different than when I'm creating a stereo mix. The uninitiated mixer shouldn't get scared jumping into a 5.1 mix. You are probably already correctly thinking all the things you need to think. The techniques of doing some things are different, but with experience, it'll become easier and quicker to do. You're just within the sound field as opposed to looking at it.

With 5.1, we can now actually create a cubicle or an expanse that surrounds the listener, and the vision that was originally perceived for the stereo mix actually can now be expanded in a three-dimensional realm around the listener.

It's the difference between looking at a canvas and looking at a holographic image. You can get a sense of depth when you are looking at a canvas, but that perception of depth happens only when you look at it one way. With a surround mix or a holographic image, you can walk around that image, or you can be within and look at it from many different angles. Obviously, you can sit in the middle of it, be within that landscape or that painting, and have it surrounding you. You can also move to the edges, look at each corner of it, and see the picture from so many different angles. I think what's interesting about surround mixing is that it can take on so many different appreciative points of reference.

If you have a picture on the wall, you can look at it straight on, or you can walk over to the side of it and look at it, but it doesn't really change all that much. You see what the painter had in mind by trying to fill your whole peripheral vision or create depth, but it's always going to be one landscape that never really changes, no matter how you walk around it to get a different sense of the painting.

With a holographic image or 5.1 mix, you can actually walk around it and see the rear or front of it. You can sit in the center of it, which is the reference perspective, but you can also move about within that landscape and get a different mix of instruments. You appreciate the musical event in a completely different way. You may be able to concentrate more on one instrument than the whole if you're off to one corner.

As a mixer, I think it's important to understand that the listener may be hearing this from more perspectives than that one central location, and it is important to accommodate the variety of listening positions by making that mix compatible with many different listening situations. I think that will be the ongoing challenge for people mixing in surround.

There is a real need to create tools that can fine tune signal placement of discreet elements better. That said, it's almost as if we need to be able to have one of those kind of units on every channel, so that you could take a discreet element and put it through a multi-channel processor that would create the space that you had in your mind. If you had that kind of setup, you would be able to accurately put the discreet element where the sound would be initiated. That way, you could create all the appropriate early reflections and reverberant fields around that within that 5.1 box to accurately reproduce that locale, rather than take a dry element and just put it in the surround field.

Let's say, for example, you place the signal to the left rear, and then use lots of different reverbs, delays, and so forth to kind of imitate what would happen in a real situation or even an artificial situation that you'd expect to hear.

Let's say I want a background vocalist to appear from behind me over my left shoulder. If I were to merely pan it, you would be feeding all the speakers the same thing in just slightly different proportions. The problem with that is our ears have trouble with the phase relationship of those different point sources. It's actually coming from five different places, not one that's just over our shoulder, so if there is any movement by the listener, there is a comb filter effect. It works fine in stereo because our ears understand the two points where the sound is coming from, and they create the appropriate phantom image. When you have more than two sound sources, the ear gets confused.

What I propose is to feed all speakers something slightly different. That way, it tends to limit the comb filter effect at the listening position. It may be that I feed the front speakers a delay of close proximity, like 10 or 20 milliseconds of delay from the original source. That way, it's actually something slightly different. It might have some harmonizing to it, or chorusing. That tends to pull the source off the left rear speaker, but it's a unique element that's fed to the front speakers.

The way I actually go about doing it is that I set up delays and harmonizers for the front and rear. Then, I can feed those effects varying amounts to create the desired ambient space.

When I'm doing surround remixes, things that may have worked in the stereo mix may not work when they're exposed in this new setting. An example may be a single delay on a guitar solo that may have created this sort of illusion of sustain and distance in a stereo field. Nevertheless, when the effect is exposed in the surround mix, you may actually hear that single delay in a different light—it sounds like a gimmick. In that situation, you may have to rethink the application of that single delay. Maybe it's a dual front/back delay that bounces between front and back speakers, rather than the individual delay that was used in the stereo mix. In surround, it's always more interesting to hear things with movement that utilize this expanded soundstage.

If the album you are remixing to 5.1 is a classic that is held dear by many listeners in stereo, those listeners may feel cheated when they hear the surround if the whole conceptualization has changed too dramatically.

Monitoring is definitely a huge issue in 5.1. It's important that the monitors be as full range as possible in 5.1. We can get away with small monitors when working in stereo because they're generally set on top of the console and have an increased bass response due to coupling from the proximity of the console surface.

Since the 5.1 setup will be a midfield speaker arrangement, you have to be careful about the way you handle the bass. There is a very real trap that many 5.1 mixers get caught in when trying to deal with low end. You may be just pumping a lot of low end into the subwoofer channel that, when reproduced on a full-range system, would create an exaggerated low end. It is therefore important to use bass management.

Bass management is a system where the feed to the five speakers is crossed over so that the low end of each channel is combined with the subchannel to feed the subwoofer. As a result, the subwoofer takes over the very-low-end frequency range of the entire speaker system.

When monitoring to see whether the bass in the mix is properly balanced, I occasionally mute the sub feed to make sure that what I'm doing with the bass is necessary.

I think artists and writers are beginning to think about surround sound from the creation stage. I can't wait until Mark Knopfler and I make a record together where we're doing the sounds in surround and conceptualizing the music in surround from the very beginning of the project. One of the main reasons Mark wanted to do this 5.1 remix of *Sailing to Philadelphia* was to start understanding what 5.1 is.

When we did Dire Straits' *On Every Street*, it was back when QSound was available. Mark had been approached to do the album in QSound, but at the time it was just a distraction to Mark because it wasn't discreet like 5.1. When he first heard 5.1, his comment was, "Well, nobody's done it right yet, but I can see the potential." I think that was the same thing he felt when we did this surround remix of a stereo album. With the remix of *Sailing to Philadelphia*, I think Mark felt somewhat limited in that we were doing a recall. The effects had already been established in stereo, and we were simply expanding everything into 5.1. I know he's really more intrigued by the idea of conceptualizing something in 5.1 and taking it from beginning to end. I think that's when 5.1 will be at its most interesting. You will not limited by the whole conceptualization of the original stereo event.

Steve Bishir

Credits include: Michael W. Smith, Steven Curtis Chapman, Amy Grant, Third Day, Mercy Me, Garth Brooks, Aaron Neville, Travis Tritt, Asleep at the Wheel, Martina McBride. See the Appendix for Steve Bishir's full bio.

For this book, I was asked to give my thoughts, tips, et cetera as they relate to surround mixing. I think the best way for me to do this would be to approach a hypothetical mix and take you through it. It may be a bit stream of consciousness, but I usually work that way anyway. Some of these things were learned the hard way, some through reading books like this, and others through the "ah-ha" moments that I have when playing around with stuff or discussing things with peers.

I'm going to make a couple of assumptions up front: that we are already familiar with the terms of surround mixing, like fold-down, divergence, LF, LR, C, LS, RS, and LFE. Or at least there's a glossary handy somewhere else in this book.

Let me start with the mechanical aspects of the mix. That would include room setup, speaker setup, gear, et cetera.

In stereo, one has a relatively simple setup: two speakers and maybe a subwoofer. The speakers need to be relatively balanced, and the sub as well. The mix decisions are limited to left, right, a combination of the two, and volume. We just push up some faders (or in the case of "in the box" mixing, pictures of faders) and there we are—genius! The phantom images appear between the speakers, and everything is beautiful. We can easily have more than one set of speakers, we can have some headphones, or we can make a CD, pop out to the car, and check it out. If the bass isn't quite right, the vocal feels too loud, or overall it's too bright or dark, we come back and make tweaks. We can throw it into iTunes and check out how it rocks the little computer speakers and how it compares with all the other songs in our library. Simple.

None of this is quite as straightforward when we move to surround. We can't easily throw up another set of speakers, we can't just pop out to the car with a CD (usually), and we can't just throw on some headphones (usually). The monitoring environment, which includes the room, the speakers, and the interaction between the two, necessarily must be pretty on the money it terms of imaging and frequency balance. We have to know that when we set the EQ just so and place that cowbell just there, that is exactly what the mastering engineer will hear as well.

Who hasn't put up stereo speakers out of phase before? It's pretty easy to tell—your head twists unnaturally, and you might have a nosebleed.

So, we flip the phase on the input to one of the speakers. It might not achieve correct absolute phase, but the speakers are in phase with each other, and we can get our work done. In surround, this is a bit trickier; the relative phase difference might not be so readily apparent between, say, the left front and the right rear. Use of positive pulses and a phase checker would be recommended. For correct speaker placement, there are diagrams and measurements dealing with radii of circles, angles of deployment, distances between speakers and subs, et cetera.

The levels for all the speakers and the sub for the LFE must be set as well. Surround setups benefit from a calibration disk and an SPL meter to check for accuracy.

We need to check all the other things in the signal chains as well—the routing from the bus outputs, the sends to whatever device is capturing the mix, the sends to the speakers and sub, the sends and returns from external effects, et cetera. This may seem basic and unnecessary, but anything wrong here will be magnified later.

All this setup may seem like a pain, but it will make things work more smoothly as we move on to the mix.

Okay, we have the speakers set and the measurements made. Now what?

Now the concept questions begin. What kind of surround mix are we making? Is it a live project? If so, where are we, the listener? Are we on stage with the band? Are we in the seventh row, center? Are we at the back of the hall? Is it to film, where we have to track panning, FX, and music to what is happening on screen? Is it a studio project, where there are no rules for anything? Where you can have the guitars fly through your head? All of these approaches are valid and have their place, yet are pretty different in their uses of divergence, panning, and balance.

Since we are suddenly dealing with a sound field that surrounds us, as it were, there are things that we need to consider.

In stereo, there is basically one place for a phantom image to appear: the space between the two speakers. In surround, we now have the phantom image between the front speakers, the center and left, the center and right, the front left and rear left, the front right and rear right, the rear left and rear right, the front left and rear right, the front right and rear left, and the center and everything else. (Wow.) Intimidating as that seems, it's really a lot of fun. If we want that snare to be in our lap, so be it. The trombone can be hitting us in the back of the head if we want.

Let's say that our mix in this instance is going to be a live concert. I tend to opt for the seventh-row-center approach here. This means the band is going to be laid out in front and maybe a bit to the sides of us, and the ambience and audience mics are going to fill out the rear.

The band will be panned as if on stage—not only left to right, but also front to back.

How that works in surround is that we are going to be panning things mostly statically among the five speakers. For example, we want the lead vocal to be pulled out from the plane of the front speakers; we want the singer to be hanging in space in front of us. Now, we could pan it to the center speaker only, but that would pin it down in the front and nowhere else, that speaker would be doing all the work, and the center bus would be delivering all the level. If we then want to pull the vocal toward us, we would need to add a little bit into the rear speakers to bring the image forward. This is fine, but a better use of the bus headroom would be to divide the load across all the speakers, maximizing the amount of volume (everything these days is supposed to be loud, right?) before running out of bus headroom.

Using our divergence control, we can add a percentage of the signal into the left and right and/or front and back channels to let some or all of the speakers share the load. If we look at the bus meters now, instead of the center bus being the only bus showing level, some or all of the meters (depending on the setting) will be showing level. They will all be at a lower amount for the same volume at the listening position. This means we can increase the overall bus output and achieve a higher volume without resorting to limiting and without clipping. We get to have volume and dynamics.

Now, if we start out with the vocal out a bit from the center, it means we have room behind the vocal to put stuff. The 3D panning is one of the things I really love in surround; I can not only put stuff side to side, I can also put it front to back. With an orchestra, I can pan and place it in the correct relative position on the imaginary stage.

Once we are happy with where we have everything placed, we can look at another control labeled something like "LFE Send." The low-frequency effects channel is the .1 in 5.1. This is a potentially dangerous thing in surround music mixing. In film mixing, it is used for explosions and such. In music mixing, I tread lightly here.

I use it to round out the bottom end of kicks, bass, toms, maybe some snares—anything with some low-end content. I don't put anything only in the LFE channel, but I don't ignore it, either. The danger arises when the project is mastered and out in the real world. If someone who loves big explosions and has their LFE channel cranked way up gets our mix, and we put the kick and bass mostly or only in the LFE, structural damage followed by complaints may occur.

When it comes to balances, it is really easy to get carried away. If the project is a studio, no-rules mix with extreme panning, and things may be flying around with automated panning, balances that sound kind of cool in surround may be weird when folded down to stereo or mono. I do quite a bit of listening through a fold-down matrix in stereo and in mono. I've found that when things stay balanced when folded down, the full surround mix usually sounds better, too.

Doug Mitchell

See the Appendix for Doug Mitchell's bio.

So, you want to get on the audio bandwagon and do some music mixing in surround? You'll be glad to know that you are in good company, and you'll also be glad to know that there are many inventive possibilities with very few rules—in fact, many are being made up as we go along. Additionally, the tools and techniques for mixing in surround are improving at a radical pace to allow you the most creative freedom in your mix.

However, you must first be aware that there is some history to the world of surround music mixing. The first attempts in this arena occurred more than 50 years ago. It was in 1940 that Walt Disney Studios released the movie *Fantasia*. *Fantasia* utilized a sound reproduction process known as "Fantasound." The Fantasound experiments included the placement of three horn loudspeakers across the stage and two horn loudspeakers in the rear corners of the auditorium. The panoramic potentiometer (now known as the "pan pot") was developed as part of the Fantasound process, allowing two optical tracks on the film: one to be delegated for the center loudspeaker, and another to be divided among the four separate remaining loudspeakers. After experimentation, another pair of loudspeakers was added to the side walls of the theater, and another loudspeaker was added to the ceiling.

Following Disney's experiments, additional multi-channel formats were developed for wide screen–format film in its competition for viewers with television. Then, the debacle of quadraphonic sound occurred in the late '60s and early '70s. Mercifully, the quad era only lasted a few years. The market was unprepared for quadraphonic technology, especially in terms of technological delivery. The numerous competing formats also helped to seal its demise. Multi-channel music delivery would have to wait another 20 years for an appropriate technological delivery medium to be in place.

Blockbuster movies in the late '70s, including *Star Wars*, *Apocalypse Now*, and *Close Encounters of the Third Kind*, ushered multi-channel sound for picture into the public mindset. The soundtracks for these and most other films released throughout the late '70s and into the '80s relied on Dolby Cinema technology. Dolby Laboratories developed cinema sound processors that borrowed from previous quadraphonic ideas so that the discrete left, center, right, and monophonic surround channels could be matrixed onto a two-channel optical film soundtrack. In the theater, the two channels are decoded back to the four channel locations. It wouldn't take long for additional enhancements to bring this type of delivery into the home with Dolby Pro Logic and THX home audio systems in the early '80s.

Of course, the new delivery formats are in the digital domain, both at home and in the theatre. The Dolby AC-3 specification for digital film sound was introduced in 1992 with the release of *Batman Returns*. The data reduction technique developed by Dolby placed digital information between the sprocket holes on the film for each of the sound channels (left, center, right, rear left, rear right, and LFE—low-frequency effects). The release of the DVD-Video specification in 1995 allowed for both an increase in the amount of data that could be stored on a CD-style disc and a specification that called for AC-3 coding of the discrete digital audio channels representing a full 5.1 channel listening environment. Two new formats—Super Audio Compact Disc (SACD) and DVD-Audio—are intended to make high-performance audio systems capable of playing back multi-channel audio mixes. Neither of these systems utilizes aural data compression. However, both are intended as primarily music-oriented release formats. Both formats are being developed to allow the inclusion of navigation systems and may include text, artwork, and brief video material as well.

An appropriate place to begin with multi-channel music production may be at the recording end. Just how might you begin to record material that is intended for multi-channel release? As multi-channel music production matures, undoubtedly there will develop new sets of production standards, similar to the conventions presently utilized in two-channel stereo work. However, those who are currently engaging in multi-channel music production are developing their own standards and adapting previously proven techniques. There have been a number of microphone techniques proposed for recording up to 5.1 channels of information, but these continue to be developed. I'll relate a few of the documented techniques here. However, keep in mind that in this arena there are few rules, and if you think of an idea that might work, try it out!

To begin our discussion of microphone techniques for capturing a multi-channel soundfield, it might be prudent to indicate that the conventions utilized for stereo two-channel microphone technique are applicable, if not more so. Obviously, any technique utilized should minimize phase error to prevent phasing and comb filtering between two or more channels. It might also be a good idea to check the downmix performance of the technique being attempted. Keep in mind that not all consumers of your multi-channel mixes will have the capability of playing them back in full in a 5.1 monitoring environment. We'll discuss more on the area of downmixing when we examine surround monitoring. Another item to keep in mind is that just as it is certainly appropriate to record certain instruments or amplifier cabinets with a single microphone for stereo mixes, it may also be appropriate to do the same for a multi-channel recording. In fact, monophonic sources in a surround mix are easier to pan to specific locations within the room. Jerry Bruck of Posthorn Recordings has proposed the use of a purpose-built multi-channel microphone technique utilizing Schoeps microphones. The system utilizes a Schoeps sphere microphone combined with two Schoeps CCM 8g bidirectional microphones mounted at the sides of the sphere. Schoeps now markets this arrangement as the KFM 360. The Schoeps sphere microphone is 18 centimeters in diameter. Its pickup response simulates the natural pickup of the human head (like a dummy head microphone) and also relies upon pressure-zone response due to the positioning of the omnidirectional elements on the sides of the sphere. Two bidirectional microphones are mounted on the sides of the sphere in the same positions as the omni elements. A mid/side matrix of the resulting pickup allows the engineer to derive both front and rear left/right outputs. The center channel is derived from a separately matrixed and filtered sum of the two front channels. Schoeps separately markets a preamplifier/matrix decoder called the DSP-4 Surround. This unit also allows for the alteration of the resulting front directional pattern from omnidirectional to cardioid to figure-eight. The rear-facing directional outputs may exhibit the same pattern as the front, or a different pattern may be derived to suit the acoustical balance.

Another multi-channel microphone technique has been proposed by John Klepko. This microphone array is composed of three directional microphones representing the left, center, and right channels. The surround channels are represented by pickup from a dummy head microphone. Each of the three front microphones is spaced 17.5 centimeters apart. They are positioned 124 centimeters in front of the dummy head. Each of the five microphones employed utilizes the same transducer element (condenser/large or small diaphragm). The left and right microphones are configured for super cardioid pickup, while the center is configured for cardioid. The elements used in the ear molds of the dummy head are configured for omnidirectional pressure response.

Curt Wittig and Neil Muncy developed the double M-S microphone technique while they taught courses at the National Public Radio Music Recording Workshops in the 1980s along with David Moulton, Paul Blakemore, and Skip Pizzi. It was developed for two-channel stereo as a solution to the problem of making stereo recordings that could be set up quickly with a minimum of fuss and visual clutter when making live and recorded classical music broadcasts for NPR.

The front M-S microphone pair is utilized primarily for direct sound pickup. The rear M-S microphone pair is placed at or just beyond the critical distance of the room (the position where the power of direct sound equals the power of reverberant sound), facing away from the front pair and into the reverberant field.

The multi-channel application of this technique might be to place the output of the front pair in the front left and right, while the outputs of the reverberant field M-S pair are directed to the rear left and right. The matrix describes no center channel information, although it is easily derived by feeding the output of the front-facing cardioid microphone to the center speaker without the benefit of the M-S matrix. Curt has successfully used this arrangement for a number of years. He also describes a variation of 5.1 stereo by modifying this setup with a sixth captured overhead channel that creates a tangible (and very stable) three-dimensional stereo surround illusion.

Michael Bishop has developed a modified version of the double M-S surround array technique. He uses both the Neumann KU 100 dummy head and laterally positioned M-S pairs. He describes the setup as thus: "The M-S pairs are positioned 3 to 8 feet behind the dummy head and are usually placed about 6 feet apart from one another on each side. For the M-S pairs, I use the Sennheiser MKH50 and MKH30 microphones. When I matrix the M-S pairs, I may have to pan the cardioid microphone to fill the sides. It's very touchy to get the panning and imaging correct, especially with panning across the sides. Prior to the recording, I'll have an assistant go out of the room and walk around the microphone array while I listen to the decoded M-S matrix. In order to get the surround microphones to breathe, I place them perhaps a few feet back or even farther if the acoustics of the hall call for it."

The SoundField MKV microphone is uniquely suited to multi-channel recording. This microphone design consists of four separate microphone elements arranged in a tetrahedron (three-sided pyramid) in the capsule. The outputs of these four separate elements are matrixed in multiple M-S pairs in the SoundField MKV controller unit to form four discrete channels. These channels, called "B-format," are termed "X" for depth, "Y" for width, "Z" for height, and "W" for omnidirectional pressure.

The SoundField microphone and the corresponding surround system called Ambisonics were developed in the late 1960s by Michael Gerzon of the Mathematical Institute in Oxford, UK, Professor Peter Fellgett at the University of Reading, and others.

In 1992, Michael Gerzon, working with Geoff Barton of Trifield Productions Limited in Britain, proposed a 5.1 version of the decoder. The resulting technique was presented at the 1992 AES convention in Vienna and is now referred to as "G-format."

SoundField Research now produces a 5.1 G-format SoundField microphone decoder that allows users of SoundField microphones to produce 5.1 outputs from the microphone.

Two Tonmeister students from Germany, Volker Henkels and Ulf Herrmann, developed the ICA-5 multi-channel microphone technique following research they performed comparing various multi-channel microphone techniques. The design calls for five matched dual-diaphragm condenser capsules mounted on a star-shaped bracket assembly.

The front-facing microphones are positioned at 90 degrees to one another and mounted on spokes 17.5 centimeters from the center. The left and right surround microphones are positioned at 60 degrees to one another and are 59.5 centimeters from the center.

Two German companies, Sound Performance Lab (SPL) and Brauner Microphones, collaborated to produce the Atmos 5.1, a commercial version of the ICA-5 system. The Atmos 5.1 utilizes Brauner ASM 5 microphones developed by Dirk Brauner. The bracket allows for adjustable positioning of all microphones in the array. The second component of the Atmos 5.1 system is the controller/preamp produced by SPL. Although the ICA-5 defines the use of cardioid microphones, the Atmos 5.1 system allows for continuous polar variability to accommodate a variety of acoustical environments.

Another development that has gained attention for recording in 5.1 is the Holophone microphone system developed by Mike Godfrey. This football-shaped microphone captures a full 5.1 surround soundfield and may be utilized with wireless transmitters to aid in the portability of the system. This technique has already been used with a high degree of success at major sporting events, including the Super Bowl.

Although most of the techniques described in this article might be most ideally suited for classical or jazz multi-channel recordings, there are certain situations where any engineer might try any one of these arrays. This experimentation is perhaps the most exciting aspect of the process of recording for multi-channel: there are few rules to go by, and we get to make them up as we go along.

ESE Recording and the Vibe: Rick Clark

The following is the audiophile surround recording adventure of producer/engineer/all-around entrepreneur Cookie Marenco. It deals with her ESE surround recording project and her efforts to present this to the public.

The dusk outside The Site was magical with deep reds, oranges, and grays, as the clouds and mists from the California coastal overcast drifted around the Marin County Redwoods outside the studio tracking room windows. Inside, Glen Moore, of the legendary acoustic fusion band Oregon, was improvising his own magic on his 300-year-old string bass. The rich tonalities filled the room, while an impressive complement of precisely placed microphones captured his performance. When I walked into the control room, it sounded like I was still out on the floor listening to Moore live. It sounded like Moore was in the middle of the Neve console, and when I walked around the room, the bassist's position hadn't changed. There was a clear sense of place. Standing outside the array of JMR Speakers were producer/engineers Cookie Marenco and Jean Claude Reynaud. After listening for a few minutes to Moore's emotive bass playing, Marenco exclaimed, "No bad seats!" She was right.

What I had been listening to were the fruits of almost two years of work, in which Marenco and Reynaud pursued the realization of a surround production approach that would truly bring to life performance-oriented recording in a fashion that was simultaneously intimate and expansive. They called their trademarked technique ESE, for Extended Sound Environment.

Marenco, no stranger to audiophile-level production and engineering, has worked with some of the music world's most creative talents and has been consulted by a number of the recording industry's more innovative manufacturers. She also worked as A&R at Windham Hill, during the label's glory days, where five albums she produced earned Grammy nominations. Marenco's other producer credits include Oregon, Turtle Island String Quartet, Tony Furtado and Alex de Grassi, and others. As an engineer, she has recorded many notable artists, including Mary Chapin Carpenter, Ladysmith Black Mambazo, Charlie Haden Quartet, and Max Roach.

Marenco's odyssey, which led her to these sessions at The Site, began a few years earlier, when she had grown frustrated by what she saw as a record-industry malaise increasingly accepting of overly compressed recording and compressed MP3 audio. She took a three-month break from everything, trying to figure out what was going to make her happy and whether she even wanted to go back into the studio.

"I knew that I had to go back in with a partner," says Marenco. "I needed somebody who would motivate me and make me want to be in the studio again."

It was a 2002 trip to attend a wedding in France that changed things for the frustrated Marenco. It was there that she spotted some Schoeps microphones placed over the drum set at the reception party and became curious about who would utilize such fine mics for such an application. Who Marenco discovered was another equally frustrated producer/engineer named Jean Claude Reynaud.

"I had learned a very classical kind of recording from great old-school engineers in France, and it seemed that everything I had learned was being thrown away by digital sound," says Reynaud.

Reynaud (whose father manufactured the audiophile JMR Speakers out of France) and Marenco immediately realized they shared many of the same feelings and soon found themselves checking out surround audio at the 2002 AES show. What they found happening with the format at the show was disappointing, and soon they began visualizing a way to make multi-channel recording something that satisfied them.

They booked time at The Site in December of 2002 and began a series of experiments. They were aided by the generous help of manufacturers such as Sony, Millennia, Manley, JMR, and Didrik de Geer.

After trying out many mic and speaker configurations, they realized that the ITU layout most ideally suited their goals. Not only did they utilize the ITU setup for the listening environment, they also echoed it exactly with microphone setups in the tracking space and in The Site's 19×13×17-foot Live Chamber. Additional close miking was applied for the musicians.

The session proved to be very enlightening, motivating the team to reconvene at The Site in December 2003.

"The ESE technique uses a combination of mic placement in the tracking room that is an ITU configuration in front of the musicians, in addition to close mic positions for a more 'direct' sound from the instrument. We find the combination of close and room miking more pleasing than using one and not the other...as well as providing an alternative to surround listening," says Marenco. "Surround listening offers only one 'optimum' listening position, which is in the center of the five channels.... Our ESE technique is designed to be able to have a three-dimensional approach to multi-channel listening and offers the listener the ability to listen outside the speaker circle as well as walking 'through' the speakers and in the center."

One of the themes of The Site dates was "no compromise"—an aesthetic that was followed all the way from selection of gear to the players involved.

"The results are dependent on the quality of the microphones, speakers, preamps, speaker cable, recorder, and FX used," adds Marenco. The team determined for their purposes to record to 2-inch analog (Studer A-800 2-inch W/24 track and 16 track heads) with Dolby SR for the multitrack format at 15 IPS and mix down the 5.1 to Sonoma 1-bit DSD system, which was provided by Sony for the mixdown. The two-track format for mixdown to stereo was 1/2-inch analog (Studer A-80 VU 1/2" with two and four track heads) with Dolby SR at 15 IPS, as well as backups to the Sonoma system for two-track editing.

The Site's Neve 8078 console had 72 inputs (plus 32-channel jukebox) and was modified for surround mixing. The signal was bussed out to Sonoma with Ed Meitner converters, recorded in DSD 1-bit, and returned to the console with a six-channel monitor section monitored out to Nelson Pass amps, which were wired with JM Reynaud silver cable to Offrande JM Reynaud speakers single-wired and a JM Reynaud Furioso self-powered subwoofer.

"Because of the delicate phase issues created, we use one track for every mic used in the recording, and for our initial experiments have intentionally kept the ensembles to duos and solo performances, with no option for overdubs," says Marenco. "This led to our choice of exceptional musicians capable of great live performances and interactive dynamics. The use of headphones is not an option at this time."

"The choice of 1-bit recording and avoiding the use of PCM digital also led us to choose *not* to use digital effects in the process, instead choosing to use the chamber for additional reverb," Marenco adds. "We miked the chamber in the ITU configuration with two to four speakers placed inside with individual sends from the board. We did use very minimal compression on some of the direct mics on mixdown only; however, we realized the issues created with compression and only used it sparingly, if at all."

For the tracking room, Marenco and Reynaud used 5 DPA or B&K 4003 to the Millennia 8-channel HV-3D mic preamp. All the mics used to capture the room sound were set facing up about 45 degrees and to the outside walls. The mics that were used for close miking the guitars were DPA 2 4041s placed about 8 inches from the guitar, pointing 45 degrees from the sound hole. Didrik de Geer mics with Neve preamps from the console were used for vocals and set about 24 inches from vocalists. Only one B&K 4041 mic was used on guitars when a vocal was also being recorded. For dobro, a B&K 4011 in an X/Y configuration about 24 inches above the instrument was employed. For Glen Moore's acoustic bass, they also used a B&K 4041 on top with a Didrik de Geer mic on the bottom. In this case they used the Millennia pres.

The subsequent mixdown of the session was done at Skywalker on a Neve 72 88R surround console. The 80×60×30-foot scoring stage was used as the reverb chamber, and the ITU was enlarged to accommodate space.

The feedback from the players involved was most gratifying.

"I think what gave us the most gratification were remarks from musicians who would say that the recordings really sounded like them. It was not the sound of a guitar. It was the sound of *my* guitar. It wasn't the sound of a voice. It is the sound of *my* voice," says Reynaud.

Marenco agreed, enthusing, "After four albums producing Tony Furtado, he came in and said, 'Cookie, you finally got my banjo sound!' I thought, 'Was this what I had to do to get your banjo sound?' [Laughs] That was amazing."

Even though the team was committed to the concept of no compromise, that also ultimately meant working in service of the most important aspect of the whole undertaking—the highlighting of the emotional spirit of the event. In that light, the striking intimacy and enveloping ambiences of the ESE recordings were most interesting in that they seemed to highlight the existence or lack of chemistry between the players even more so than before.

"You are capturing that moment in time, and that moment in time is about the vibe," enthuses Marenco. "We tried putting great musicians with each other who didn't have that friendship of years and years and years of playing together, and it didn't quite work. We realized that they needed to be friends on a musical level, because our technique was going to enhance that dynamic or lack of dynamic. When it worked, it was an amazing experience to see it come to life."

"I had my moment at the end of the sessions, where I realized that we had really captured the vibe and that we were recording respect for the sound and respect for great musicianship and respect for the long-term relationship that each of the players had with each other. With the depth immediacy of sound that ESE provided, I felt that we were recording more than music. We were recording respect for the sound and respect for great musicianship and respect for the long-term relationships of the people involved in making the music and who have supported us over the years."

"Most people haven't heard this kind of sound in so long, and even when we bring out our two-track stereo mixes of these sessions, people go, 'Wow.' It forces people to listen," continues Marenco. "It seems that people have stopped listening, and it is part of the reason that the music industry is in a shambles. The way much of the music is recorded now, it is not providing emotion. The current fashion is to be over-compressed and to hit everything as loud as possible. It is horrible, and we don't want it anymore. We see ESE as an opportunity to bring back the real sound...the real emotion, and that comes from dynamics."

Starting a Label...and a Movement: Follow-Up Observations by Cookie Marenco

It might be of interest for the readers to know what happened to The Vibe sessions after Rick's incredible article. I believe an honest assessment is valuable for those of you thinking that there is ever an Easy Street in this business. Even after 20 years in the business, it was very difficult to create a new identity. Here's my account of all the trials and tribulations that come with pursuing a dream.

In December 2002, Jean Claude Reynaud and I entered the studio without really knowing what we'd find or where it would lead. From the experiments of that first session, we knew there had to be more. It was on the third day, during Keith Greeninger and Dayan Kai's performances, that Gus Skinas from Sony said, "I hope you're making this into an album!" Without hesitation, I exclaimed, "YES!" Did I know what I was getting into? NO!

At a time when the record industry was beginning to collapse, it seemed crazy to consider having a limitless budget to experiment with an acoustic 5.1 surround recording, but the results from this first session were too good to think otherwise. I was encouraged by potential investors. Jean Claude was willing to move to the USA, and the second sessions in December 2003 were scheduled. The investors never came through, the long and expensive process for getting Jean Claude a work visa was tackled, and I refinanced my house to have the limitless budget. This isn't something I'd suggest to those who have a low tolerance for risk. But, for those of you pursuing a career as an engineer or producer, get used to risk or get out now.

In December 2003, Rick Clark was kind enough to come to the sessions and document the process, which even after 20 years of recording was a new and exciting experience for all of us. It was magic, as Rick wrote so well about. We still had no name for the label, and through a long process of research, we found a name that had meaning to us—Blue Coast Records (fortunately, just before his article came out in *Mix*). We completed the mixes in May 2004 at Skywalker Studios and mastered with David Glasser at Airshow Mastering.

For anyone who is a musician, engineer, or producer, after the finished product is when you *really* start the work. Jean Claude had made the decision to return to France and work with his father in the speaker business. I continued developing the Blue Coast brand with logos, establishing art, writing content, and searching for investors. If you think you've spend a *lot* of money producing the disc, figure it will cost four times more to do a bare-minimum job promoting your project.

By 2005, my limitless budget hit the limit—no investors in sight, but incredible response about the quality of the recording. I made the decision to return to work as a producer at my studio, OTR Studios, after a three-year absence. The music business was beginning to dissolve, recording studios were dropping by the wayside, and I had an unbelievable high-end product on my hands with no money left to manufacture SACDs or promote the label. Life was pretty dismal right then.

I made a thousand five-song promotional CDs in white paper sleeves and gave them away free at the AES show. One disc got into the hands of John Johnsen of NHT, who used the disc to demonstrate their speakers at the CES show. Without knowing that the disc was being used for that purpose, John called me to say that they had won the Ultimate Audio Award at CES using the disc and wanted to co-brand a release for giveaway with all their speaker sales. It gave me hope that a quality product still meant something to somebody. I didn't know John until then, except from a business card I had stashed away, but that event led to a lifelong friendship with him and NHT.

NHT ordered 2,000 units of the disc directly from Blue Coast Records. I now had the money to manufacture the SACDs—or so I thought. Mastering the SACD proved to be another ordeal to face. The test pressing proved to have problems that couldn't be traced without spending huge sums and delaying the project for months. We made the decision to release a CD to get it done sooner.

Keep in mind this was now 2006; CD sales were in strong decline, and MP3s were taking over the world. All music discs were reduced to $9.95 at Walmart. Even audiophile labels were offering artist deals at $1 per record and not selling through 700 units. At that rate, I would never have a chance to recoup costs, so I posted the CD for sale at the Blue Coast website for $30 per unit, figuring it wasn't going to sell anyway, so I might as well keep the price high!

Meanwhile, in France, Jean Claude sent the disc to a renowned magazine called *La Nouvelle Revue du Son*—the premier audiophile magazine in France. I had no idea about this, and in fact conventional wisdom would have me ask him *not* to do that without the chance to get it into stores. This was a happy accident. In July 2006, a most stunning five-star review came out about the CD, hailing it as the new standard for acoustic recording. I might never have known about the review except that we suddenly were making sales by the hundreds in France. So I called Jean Claude to find out if he knew anything. He sent me a copy of the review. I was overwhelmed.

I would have given up on the SACD and surround release, except that Jean Claude convinced me that the recording was too spectacular to not make at least 1,000 units. Also, the premier online audiophile store would not sell a CD, only SACD. Armed with the wonderful *Mix* article that Rick wrote, the review from France, hundreds of supporters, and Patrick O'Connor (my new GM, webmaster, and graphic artist), one year after the failure of the first SACD manufacturing, we tried again. The problem proved to be a glitch that was discovered, and the master was re-cut. Although the music was now four to five years old, it was still timeless in its quality. The work on the logos, branding, and promotional materials was all starting to make sense.

By 2007, the music industry was in a shambles, but we were feeling pretty confident. Despite our distributor's reluctance to put such a high price tag on the disk, we decided to release the disc at $40 per unit and go against logic of the times. We now had the disc on Amazon, but most of our sales were word of mouth at our website. We collected the PayPal names and began our fan base. Our first thousand SACDs sold in the first six months online. We decided not to sell the CD any longer.

I made a call to the online audiophile store, Acoustic Sounds, in 2007, about one month before the Stereophile Show in New York, and spoke to Chad Kassem, the owner. He thought I was out of my mind when I offered the discs at twice the normal wholesale price, in quantities by the hundreds and paid in advance before shipping. Unheard of in the music business! Chad did know who I was and didn't care, but he was kind enough to give a listen, and it happened that the package was on his desk. We had the disc packed with reviews, coordinated brochures, postcards in a wonderful folder. He called back within a day and ordered the first hundred. The quality spoke for itself, and I wouldn't give in to pressures of what the rest of the industry was experiencing.

Let me say that starting a new brand is not only hard work, but it's humbling. At this point in my career, I had known just about everyone I wanted to know in the professional recording world, but the audiophiles couldn't care less who I was. Patrick and I first attended an audiophile show in France with Jean Claude and began to meet many of the manufacturers and others in that world. Within a few months, we tackled the Stereophile Show in mid-2007 giving away hundreds of discs to manufacturers for them to use as demos. Our disc made their equipment sound good! They had to have it. Meanwhile, we'd leave brochures for fans to take and purchase the disc.

Perhaps most amazing in this is that our sales grew at Amazon, and orders began to come in from traditional retail with no effort on our part. We had given up on traditional sales with our high prices, so it was a bonus. While we continued to nurture sales and take on distribution outside of the USA, we managed to attract a very crucial distribution partner in China. Reviews continued to pour in worldwide, and I learned to use the Google translator.

By 2008, the recession in the USA had really taken its toll. Blue Coast Records was still far from being able to support itself. The fans and distributors were asking for another recording. Fortunately, Jean Claude and I had a beautiful recording of solo piano we had made with Art Lande. We wanted to keep with our tradition of releasing the SACD, an expensive adventure. Being short on cash during the recession meant refinancing or loans were *not* options, so Patrick and I pursued high-resolution downloads of at least 44.1/16 or CD quality to avoid manufacturing costs. We found no company that would support us on this, so we developed a proprietary system of electronic delivery that we now call Downloads NOW!

With the American economy in a mess, we saw no value in releasing any of our recordings in iTunes or MP3 format. Instead, we chose to stream entire songs at 192 Kbps and offered the digital download at the same price as the CD, more than twice the price of an MP3. We announced to our fan base that we would sell the downloads of the new disc, and through sales of downloads, we made enough money to pay for several thousand SACDs of the new recording.

Now in the habit of thanking each fan who purchases online, I noticed a sudden flurry of activity back in March 2008. I asked the fan from France how he heard about us, and he responded, "From a forum in France." He sent a thank-you note on my behalf, and suddenly hundreds of sales were made that day. I saw the power of the Internet and used the translator to get onto the forum and thank them directly. With each new entry came sales. To this day, that is our one of our top referral sites, and analytics are my friend. (If you don't know Google analytics, you need to learn.)

In April 2009, we brought in Keith Greeninger (vocals and guitar), Brain (drummer Primus/Guns N' Roses), and Chris Kee (bassist Houston Jones) to the studio for a quick recording and special event—record and upload to the Internet 96-kHz files within three hours. We recorded two songs, uploaded 96-kHz files to our site, went to dinner, and when we returned, we had hundreds of sales at $3 per single. Since that time, our 96-kHz downloads have exploded, outselling the 44.1 downloads nearly 20 to 1. Our eyes were opened. Regardless of what the media was telling us, we saw that people around the world came to our website for high-resolution downloads.

Our next project is a 24-Karat Gold Collector's Edition of the Blue Coast Collection as requested by our Chinese distributor. We will probably release vinyl and 1/4-inch tape formats as well. Coming soon will be DSD files and more SACD titles, along with Blue Coast World, a new distribution company specializing in high-quality recordings and high-resolution downloads.

It's been nearly eight years since the first chance meeting with myself and Jean Claude. Not only has the music business changed, but the world economy has shifted. I've got a long way to go to recouping my costs, but I'm here to encourage any of you to follow your dreams wholeheartedly. If you can't give 200 percent to make it happen, get a job somewhere else. Quality and commitment still have a place in this world. I've got thousands of fans around the world to prove it. You can, too. Don't give up or give in.

Faders (photo by Jimmy Stratton) / Skidd Mills (photo courtesy of Grant Craig, Skiddco Music).
Row 2: Ken Lewis (photo by Rick Clark) / Osaka Pearl sessions: Russ Long, Cregan Montague,
Ben Trimble, Danielle Tibedo, Rick Clark, Kima Moore (head) (photo by Dick Richards).

Tracking: Notes on Ensemble Recording in Two Locations

For the purpose of this chapter, I'll describe the setup for two different session situations to show the similarities and differences to recording in two polar-opposite recording studio environments. I asked Chuck Ainlay (who I consider to be one of the finest engineers in the business) to share his thoughts on his process with a couple of very different projects. One setup was for recording a Mark Knopfler solo at British Grove, which is the artist's own studio. British Grove is a dream recording environment for any artist, producer, or engineer wanting to be surrounded by the best of the best. The other album project Ainlay addresses is in a more limited studio situation, in terms of space and range of available gear, but it benefits greatly as an inspirational place, thanks to its geographical setting.

You not only can hear Ainlay's work on Mark Knopfler solo albums and Dire Straits albums, but you can also check out his work on recordings by Emmylou Harris, George Strait, Lyle Lovett, Peter Frampton, Lee Ann Womack, Taylor Swift, Vince Gill, and Sugarland.

Chuck Ainlay

Credits: Mark Knopfler (solo and with Dire Straits), Trisha Yearwood, Vince Gill, Steve Earle, Lyle Lovett, Wynonna, and George Strait. See the Appendix for Chuck Ainlay's full bio.

For Mark Knopfler's new solo album, we have been recording in London at Mark's own studio, British Grove Studios. Mark built the studio amidst an ever-declining studio market because he believes in preserving the institution of making records in a great recording environment. For his efforts, the studio just received an award for Best Studio by the Music Producers Guild, and in my many years of recording, I must say, it's the best studio I've ever worked in. While making some of Mark's previous albums, he and I would talk about the different studios we've worked in and what was great about them, what wasn't, and what we'd do differently. We then sort of laid out on a napkin how we would do a studio, and that's where it all began. The studio is so great because there just aren't any limitations to what you can do. It accommodates all the ways I like to work by offering isolation yet having large room acoustics. There's also the best of British, German, and American, analog and digital, tube and transistor recording equipment, as well as unbelievable musical instruments. It's amazing to work in this studio, but when I finish here, I'm flying to Key West to record the next George Strait album.

As with the previous two albums for George, we've recorded at Jimmy Buffett's tiny Shrimpboat Sound studio right off the docks there. It was an old storage building for the shrimp fisherman. Everyone is squeezed into one room that's so small we have to use the truck that brought all of the musicians' instruments down from Nashville to put the guitar and steel amps in. Even still, George's last album that was recorded there [*Troubador*] won a Grammy for best Country Album, and what a great thing it is to walk out the door on a break and look at the water and boats and tourists walking by. I say all this because making music is not an exact science. You have to improvise and be creative and most importantly be spontaneous. Great songs, a great artist, and great musicians are also key. I try to not get in the way and just be positive and make everyone feel as comfortable as possible. Of course, my goal is to make the highest-quality album that I can, and I take great care, regardless of the situation, to use the appropriate microphones and recording chain to get that end.

To begin, with the drum setup at British Grove, I allowed for an aggressive style of drumming as well as the possibility of a more intimate style, as I knew we would encounter both while making Mark's new album. I was prepared to have both an AKG D 112 and D 12 through Neve 1081 modules, to go inside the bass drum, as well as a Neumann FET 47 and a Sony C500 through Neve 1073 modules a few inches away from the front head. The D 112 and FET 47 combination was used for the more aggressive stuff. On the snare drum, I had three microphones. On the top head, I had both a Shure SM56 and a B&K 4011 [current version is branded DPA] run through Neve 1081 modules and combined together on one track. On the bottom side of the snare drum, I used another B&K 4011 through a Neve 1073. On some of the more aggressive songs, I moved the top head 4011 out to the side of the snare drum, and instead of the Neve module, I ran it through a channel of Mark's EMI TG MK 3 console and compressed it considerably. In this situation, I separated the mic to a separate track to allow for more mixing possibilities. An interesting note about this TG 3 is that it was the console that Paul McCartney used to record *Band on the Run* and is the console type that Chandler has copied to make their current outboard equipment.

For each of the rack toms and floor toms, I miked the top head with either a Sennheiser MD421 for the aggressive performances or a Sony C-37 for a more natural sound, and on the bottom head I used an EV flipped out of phase. All the tom mics were run through Neve 1073 modules and mixed together to a stereo pair of tracks. For overhead microphones I used a pair of Schoeps CMC 6 with MK 4 cardioid capsules, on a stereo bar, as a spaced pair. Farther up, I had a fairly rare Neumann KM 53. The hi-hat mic was also a Schoeps, and all the overheads and hat mics were recorded separately through Neve 1073 modules. The drums were placed in the large recording area that I miked with a wide-spaced pair of Neumann U 67s, up high and compressed heavily through the TG 3. In the middle of the 67s, I had a Coles 4038 ribbon mic also through the TG 3. Varying the compression for the different styles of tracks really made an impression on the room sound for each recording.

For the drums on George's album, I won't be as blessed with the amount of space, rare microphones, or channel paths, but I will have my own equipment that I take almost everywhere I work [with the exception of British Grove] and Shrimpboat Sound's Neve 8068 recording console. The setup will be similar, with exceptions being I'll not have an FET 47 for the outside of the bass drum, so I'll use an Audio-Technica 4047. I'll not have the Schoeps mics, so instead I'll use DPA 4011s on the overheads and a Shure KSM141 on the hi-hat and underneath the snare. The room mics will be a pair of Shure KSM44s with a Royer 121 in the middle, and high up over the drums I'll use one of my more vintage microphones, an

Altec M11 coke bottle. Instead of having the TG 3 for compression, I'll use my 1176s, but all the microphones will be recorded the same using either my Neve modules or the channels in the Neve desk.

I've always been a fan of the Neve sound for drums. I guess it's the transformers that tend to absorb the transients and, to me, make the drums sound more musical. I also like the EQ, and it is the drums where I do the most EQ. In fact, I don't track with much EQ otherwise, and I rely on mic selection and positioning. The general EQ I do on drums, you could almost apply to any session, as it's meant to deal with the proximity effect of having the mics so close to the drums and the fact that most people will never listen to a record as loud as the drums are naturally. Therefore, it's mostly about cutting a bit at between 350 to 480 Hz and adding a bit at 60 or 100 Hz on the low end and maybe some at 5, 10, or 15 kHz on the top. Actual application would take too long to discuss here, so have a go and try for yourself. At Shrimpboat Sound, there will be a lot of bleed into other instruments, so consideration must be taken because everyone is in the same room—or in the case of the fiddle and acoustic guitar, they may as well be, since the booths only reduce the leakage a bit. Really, I can't ever get over how well it works to record there, but that really attests to the musicianship, since there are very few punch-ins to correct mistakes.

On both Mark's and George's albums, a good bit of the albums will be recorded using electric bass, but there's also upright bass on some of the songs. I'm fortunate here as well, since the same musician plays for both artists. Glenn Worf is certainly one of the best bass players I've had the great fortune to work with, and he's proficient on both instruments. He also has great instruments and knows how to get a great sound out of each. I say this because as with all instruments, it's so much about the musician and his instrument, but particularly so about the bass. I also believe that a great-sounding record begins with a great-sounding, uncluttered bottom end. At British Grove I used a Telefunken V72 for the electric bass that was adapted to be a direct box, which was run through one side of a Fairchild 670 compressor, while the Ampeg V-15 amp was miked with a Neumann M 49 and run through a channel of Mark's EMI Redd 51 console and then through the other side of the Fairchild. British Grove built a panel so that the two channels of the Fairchild can be linked, and that's how I had it set.

Another interesting note is that the British Grove EMI Redd 51 is one of the very few remaining consoles of the type left, on which all the early Beatles records were made. And due to the fabulous technical staff at the studio, it is in perfect working condition. I used the Redd to record some of the acoustic guitar, electric guitar, and piano tracks as well, where I wanted that beautifully warm and rich character of the tubes. The upright bass was recorded using a Neumann M 49 about 8 inches straight out from the bridge and an AEA R88 up by the fret board to get more of the percussion. Both mics were fed through a pair of Martech mic preamps and then into a second Fairchild 670. For a more aggressive sound on a few of the songs, I put a Shure SM55 up close to the f-hole and fed that through a stomp box–type compressor and ran it into a small Fender amp. I simply miked that with a Shure SM57 to add in. We even ran that mic through a Leslie for another effect. Remember, there are no rules to recording, and if you imagine it, you should try it.

For George's album, I'll use my Millennia TD-1 on electric bass for the direct, and we won't record an amp. I'll have a Neumann M 147 near the bridge of the upright and a Royer 122V on the fingerboard. I'll run both mics through a pair of UpState Audio 20/20 preamps and lightly compress them with a pair of Anthony DeMaria ADL 1000s. A note on the UpState Audio preamp is that I have serial number one here with me in England, but Al Schmitt, Michael Bishop, and myself have been testing prototypes for the past four or five years, and it's got to be the best-sounding preamp I know of for just plain purity. They will just now be available for purchase by the time this book gets released, so you owe it to yourself to check them out.

The piano at British Grove is a big 9-foot Bösendorfer, which is somewhat uncommon in recording studios. You will almost always encounter a Yamaha C7, which is what Shrimpboat Sound has. I've tried a number of different mics on the Bösendorfer, from AKG C 12s to Neumann KM 56s, Neumann KM 83s, Schoeps...and the best thing so far is a pair of Neumann KM D digital microphones with the omni capsules that I had here on loan, to test for a METAlliance certification. (I have a side business with Al Schmitt, Ed Cherney, Elliot Scheiner, George Massenburg, Phil Ramone, and Frank Filipetti called METAlliance, which we formed to help promote awareness of audio quality through product certification and education.) This totally amazed me, as I wasn't convinced that a digital mic could best some of the truly great vintage mics I had tried. I also tried the KM D pair on the acoustic guitar with equally great results. In many cases I also recorded an AEA R88 stereo microphone positioned outside the lid of the grand piano. All piano mics were run through channels of a Creation remote-controlled mic pre. In some instances I used the Fairchild or a Neve 2254 compressor for effect.

On the Yamaha at Shrimpboat Sound, I'll either use a pair of DPA 4041s or a pair of Audio-Technica 4060s. I really like the AT mics on piano, which might surprise some readers, but they just work. I'll use the UpState Audio preamps and maybe do some slight compression with a Crane Song STC-8. Since the piano is in the same room, what I do is use a drumstick to lower the lid on, as it creates the minimum opening while still allowing me to get some distance with the mics. I'll then drape packing blankets over the lid and down the sides of the piano to isolate it as best I can. I also put baffles around the piano, and with all that, it works surprisingly well to keep the drums out. This technique deadens the piano a good deal, but a bit of top EQ, roll out a little bottom, and add a little reverb in the mix, and you've got an acceptable piano recording.

As you might have noticed by now, British Grove is blessed with a great microphone collection. I selected a pair of Neumann KM 56s to record most of the acoustic guitars and bouzoukis that Richard Bennett played on Mark's record. I set one on bidirectional, which was aimed head to body in front of the sound hole, while the other was set to cardioid, aiming straight ahead in as close of proximity to the bidirectional mic as possible to create an M-S pair. I ran each mic through the UpState Audio preamp and did the sum and difference setup on channels of Studio A's main recording desk [Neve 88R] and bussed them to a pair of tracks. Richard's electric guitar tracks were recorded using a Shure 57 and a Neumann U 67 through the EMI Redd. On occasion I used a Coles 4038 and miked the back of an open-back cabinet. Of course, this mic was phase-flipped. Mark's electric guitars were recorded using the same setup of a 57 and a 67 but were run through Studio 2's API channels. [British Grove has two identical control rooms with a 5.1 set of ATC 300 speakers—the only real difference between the two being the main desk, with Studio 1 having a Neve 88R and Studio 2 having an API legacy.] At times, I recorded a direct of Mark's electric so that at a later date, I can re-amp his guitar for the purpose of adding in room ambience. Mark's acoustics were mostly recorded with a U 67, but for tracking I was using the new DPA 4099 clip-on mic to get really great rejection of his tracking vocal. I used a pair of Neve 1073 channels on the acoustic with a bit of bottom pulled out on the DPA.

The acoustic guitars for George's album will be played by Randy Scruggs and Steve Gibson, when he's not playing electric, and I intend on using a pair of DPA 4011s in both cases in an X/Y array. I'll run them through my 1073 modules. The electric guitars will be a Shure 57 and a Royer 121 on both Brent Mason's and Steve Gibson's amps, and each mic will go through the studio's Neve desk.

Mark's vocals were recorded using a Neumann U 47 through a Neve 1073. He spent a lot of time trying different mics and preamp combinations to arrive at this. For all of George's albums over the years, we've always used a Neumann U 47, but the last couple were done using Jimmy Buffett's mic that was overhauled by Bill Bradley. I've tried different preamps, but the last album was obtained using the UpState Audio preamp, and I prefer that.

From here, the similarities of instrumentation depart, and suffice it to say that the same attention to detail was maintained. You can also take from this that where possible, I've used the shortest signal path by avoiding the recording desk's bussing and gone directly to the recording device. In the case of Mark Knopfler's album, we recorded to dual 16-track Studer 800s synced to a 64-channel Nuendo DAW using Prism converters. The analog takes were transferred to the DAW, and comps of the takes were done to create the master take. For George Strait's album, we'll record directly to Nuendo at 96k using 48 channels of Apogee converters, as is in my current system. My approach has always been to utilize what is available, reach out to try new things so that I stay current; but not dispatch of the old vintage gear and techniques, because they contribute to sonic reference of past recordings. I love what I do with a lot of passion, and I think you must to continue to do this job for such a long time. Each project presents new obstacles and challenges, but that's what makes each one unique. The idea is to look for new ways to make a great recording, but always be mindful of the techniques that have created those cherished recordings of the past. Also, you must listen—it's all about what you hear, not what you see on a computer screen.

Redd Volkaert (foreground) and Paul Niehaus (background) tracking, Austin, TX (photo by Rick Clark) / Danielle Tibedo (photo by Rick Clark). Row 2: Didrik DeGeer mic used during The Vibe sessions, The Site (photo by Rick Clark) / Dave Pomeroy's hat (photo by Kate Hearne).

If you look at the classic popular vocal recordings that have endured over the decades, the primary element that has helped get the magic across was not a cleverly gated, million-dollar drum sound, but rather a vocal performance that communicated something essential that touched countless listeners.

A great vocal performance often contains qualities that transcend mere technique. Great engineers and producers are those who are hip to the sometimes fleeting moments when art is happening—almost in spite of the artist—and genius is realized.

We enlisted 10 engineers and producers whose credits run the gamut of artists, including King of Leon, Gloria Estefan, the Rolling Stones, Metallica, Norah Jones, Willie Nelson, Bob Dylan, Bonnie Raitt, and Iggy Pop. We also invited a highly regarded vocal coach and producer to offer extra input. Finally, we would like to thank Lisa Roy and Susan Zekovsky for helping facilitate the realization of this chapter.

Although this chapter addresses microphones, mic preamps, and outboard gear techniques, each of these contributors underscores the essential importance of providing the right psychological support to the singer. Great mic technique can salvage a bad recording climate, but some of the most powerfully immediate vocal performances have been caught in the most primitive of recording situations, where everyone felt in sync with the truth of the moment.

Ed Cherney

Credits include: The Rolling Stones, Bob Dylan, Jann Arden, Bonnie Raitt, Jackson Browne, Bob Seger, Iggy Pop, Bette Midler, Buddy Guy, Eric Clapton. See the Appendix for Ed Cherney's full bio.

To me, a vocal is the hardest thing to record. It is harder than a hundred-piece orchestra or a three-piece rock-and-roll band. That is probably because it is a very literal instrument. Typically, on a recording, a voice sounds like what a voice sounds like, unless you are filtering it or doing other things to it to make it fit into the music. It is also the most dynamic instrument there is. It goes from being really soft to being really loud, and you need a microphone that can deal with that.

After about a dozen records, the Audio-Technica 4050 is the first mic I put up for most singers. I used it on Jann Arden and Richie Sambora, as well as a lot of the Rolling Stones record I just did. The Audio-Technica is smooth, very clear, and open sounding, and it has a lot of headroom. It is also a very consistent-sounding mic.

That said, mic selection changes for every vocalist and situation. Sometimes, I may get stuck with a microphone, not necessarily because of the way it sounds, but as a result of the way the music is tracked. I might have an artist who likes to sing live vocals out in the room with the musicians playing, because he or she likes to feel the immediacy of the energy and groove in that shared space. In that kind of situation, I have to consider the mic's rear rejection capabilities and how tight the mic is when I put the singer into the room. I also may not be familiar with the singer's voice, so I'll put up a microphone and get a really great take and 75 percent of that vocal performance may be a keeper, but I'll have to go back and match it up to punch in the lines that I need. As a result, I'm stuck using that microphone and that particular set-up to get the vocal to match. Then later, in mixing, I will try and get it sounding the way it probably should.

I rarely use the mic preamps that are on the newer consoles. I have a rack of old Neve 1073s that I carry around with me. I really love the way the old mic preamps sound. They have plenty of headroom, and they are typically really rich and open at the same time.

To get singers to sing great is mostly psychological. A great performance will always transcend a less-than-great sound on a vocal. I think that everything that you do has to be designed around making the singer feel comfortable, and for me that means getting it quickly. The first time that singer is sitting in front of a microphone, I hit record and get everything they do.

Part of it, too, is letting them sing and staying off the talkback. I let them sing the song five, six, or seven times. That may entail building a slave reel so you have plenty of tracks to comp and do your vocals.

It is all about creating that environment—making sure that the temperature is nice in the studio. If the lights are right, the headphone balance is perfect, and the singer feels that you are working with them and you are not trying to bust their hump, then they sing better. I also always try to have the singer's principal instrument in their hands when they are singing.

Also, as a producer, you have to understand that it may not be a great day for the singer, so you go on to something else.

Of course, you try and plan out the session like you are going to have vocals recorded on this day, but "vocal" day is like putting all of your eggs in one basket. It is the added pressure of "Well, I have to do it now. It is now or never." I never want to create that situation.

You should have the option of singing a song any time you want. If you feel it now, well, the mic is open, so go get it. I even do that when we are mixing a song. If I feel there is maybe a phrase or a line or verse or something that can be phrased better and you are looking for that thing, I just want to be sure that everyone is free enough to go do it when the moment happens. I want to make sure that I have tape on the machine and I have the tools ready to go in and get it. I want to be there to document these great moments that happen because you never know when they are going to come and I want to be ready for them, as an engineer and as a producer.

Phil Ramone

Credits include: Billy Joel, James Taylor, Ray Charles, Aretha Franklin, B.B. King, Paul Simon, Elton John, Bob Dylan, Chicago, Madonna, Frank Sinatra, Rod Stewart. See the Appendix for Phil Ramone's full bio.

Some people create a track and then have the vocalist come in to sing afterward. They make this enormously wonderful track, and then the vocalist sometimes doesn't work. The best way to know what you are doing is to have a pilot vocal that is there to build the arrangement around. By doing this, I have some place to go, even with the worst scratch vocal happening. With a pilot vocal, you can ascertain if the guitar player's and the piano player's parts are going to stay in the correct range with the vocal.

If you have a double line going on in the background that is heavy, big, and powerful, you've got to make its EQ work around the voice. You are kidding yourself if you don't because, in the end, the band will hate you because they couldn't hear what they played, and the singer will hate you because you drowned him out.

I think that you make the singer sound great, and then you take the singer out of the equation and listen to where the band is. If it is all nasal, somewhere in the making of the record, you either missed the boat by not expressing that or recording it properly.

Concerning EQ, you can be very tough with a vocal. There are a lot of things that you can do with a vocal that, if you listen to it solo, it may not please you, but you can really get it to sit in a track.

If you are making a vocal album, you have to remember who is paying the bill, in the sense that the front cover tells who the artist is. If you get the vocal to sound great, it will work in almost every track if you are consistent in the way you record.

You should get the sound of the singer right early. It shouldn't be a last-minute, wait-until-we-get-to-the-final-mix-room logic. That is why I am happy to carry an equalizer, a preamp, and a limiter in the recording process. I get it right from day 1.

You know what? Half the time, what I put in my final vocal comps comes from the rehearsals. Many times, when an artist is running it down, the vocal is incredible. I'm not going to sit there and say, "You know if I had used a compressor, I could've recovered this or fixed that." That is just stupid. If you come to the gig, and you are going to race the car, you better be ready.

Don't sit around and say, "Oh yeah, in an hour I'm going to have a sound. By the way, I'm switching mics." I switch mics before I am ready. If I am going to use an Audio-Technica mic, I kind of know by looking at and hearing that person that this is the right mic. I'm about being ready. If the singer loves their voice on the first playback and says, "This is the way I feel I sound," then you have done it. You and the engineer are then on an easygoing course.

You should record singers every time they sing, even when they are doing overdubs. I always keep a track for looseness while they are warming up. You might pick up six or eight lines that are just incredible because they weren't overanalyzing what they were doing. They might go, "I'm not in voice yet. Let me warm up. I can't hit those high notes." Suddenly, these high notes come pouring out of them because they are not thinking that you are recording. Without being ready with a good setup, where do you go?

Renee Grant-Williams

Vocal coach credits include: Huey Lewis, Bob Weir (of the Grateful Dead), Linda Ronstadt, Charlie Daniels, Tim McGraw, Lyle Lovett, Jill Sobule, Kim Wilson (of the Fabulous Thunderbirds), the Subdudes, Sonny Landreth, Doug Stone.

One of the things that is important to keep in mind is that the singer is a living organism, and the quality of the vocal will depend on how healthy and resilient and well-prepared that organism is. One of the things to take into consideration is scheduling. Sometimes, the singer will wear out their voice singing rough vocals with the tracks 2 or 3 days in a row, and then the next day final vocals may be scheduled and there is nothing left. It is important to remember that while the voice is a very resilient thing, it can get too thin and lose its elasticity and resilience.

It is important to give the singer time to re–warm up and reestablish his technique, and be aware that it is like a runner running short sprints. It is very important that the runner limbers up, not just run hard and then get cold and then run hard again. You always have to take waiting-around time into consideration.

I very highly favor a microphone position that is fairly low.

There is a tendency for some engineers to hang a microphone high, but if you have to stretch your head up or hold your chin up, it puts tremendous strain on the voice. The best position is right at lip level or slightly below, so you can kind of contract into your body support with your head tilted slightly forward. Think about the classic Elvis position—the way he cocked his head over the microphone, then kind of looked up from underneath. That allowed all of that sound to resonate up in his head instead of putting a strain on his neck and shoulders. Support, which is the way the body powers the sound, is very important.

Perfectly normal people, who wouldn't be caught dead running around town with their hands behind their backs, will do that when there is a microphone in front of them. Suddenly, it is like, "What am I going to be doing with these things at the end of my arms? Let's stick them behind the back." Well, that robs you of a lot of support.

The body language from people in the control room is very important. A lot of times, people don't realize that while they are having a laugh about something totally innocuous in the control room, someone singing out on the floor, who can't hear what is going on, can become sensitive and misconstrue things. Many singers, on some level, imagine that it must be about them. It is important to create an atmosphere that is helpful to the singer.

People tend to creep up on the mic as time goes by. That is why you need to put some kind of tape marker on the floor.

Give the singer a choice of headphones to listen through so they can find what helps them the most. If the vocal is too high in a headphone mix, the vocal will tend to go flat. If the vocal is too low in the headphone mix, then the singer will often tend to push things and go sharp.

I have a problem when I hear people telling a singer to relax. It is the one statement that I find makes a singer uptight. Nobody wants to think that they are not relaxed. There was a studio in Canada that had a sign that stated, "Try to relax, or we will find someone who can." [Laughs] The point of that is it is a terribly intimidating thing to tell someone to relax. Everybody likes the kind of magic that doesn't exist anywhere else.

Oftentimes, singers have trouble figuring out what they did well during a vocal performance while they are out on the floor singing with their headphones on. I think it is important for a production team to be specific. I've been in sessions where the production team is making a singer do something over and over again, and only offering statements like "That's not getting it. Let's do it again." If the singer doesn't specifically know what aspect of the performance needs to be addressed, it can be very frustrating. Again, encouragement has more to do with getting a good performance than anything.

Eric Paul

Credits include: Willie Nelson, Waylon Jennings, Johnny Cash, Townes Van Zandt. See the Appendix for Eric Paul's full bio.

We are taught to be purists in one sense when recording voices, but the right compression while recording is great. Compressors work better off live signals than off tape because a reproduced signal is never as strong and pure and never has the same kind of transients that it does when it is coming off a live microphone preamp.

I am very careful not to overcompress. I never use more than a couple dB of compression when I am recording a vocal.

If I am in a studio where I don't have access to a good LA-2A, my favorite low-end compressor is the Composer by Behringer. The mass public has access to those, and they are in a lot of demo studios across the country. The reason that I like it is that it is transparent, it will hold back the vocals from getting out of control, and you can't "hear" it.

While I prefer the LA-2As, it depends upon the tubes. My favorite tubes are the old GE tubes, if you can find them. You take any piece of tube gear, compressors, microphones, and if you put a good old GE tube in there, it will sound so much better than anything else. I've done many comparisons.

I have a Sony C-37A that is the sweetest vocal microphone on a female voice that you have ever heard. Daniel Lanois used my C-37A on Emmylou Harris for the *Wrecking Ball* album. Again, the trick to the whole deal is old GE tubes, which greatly improved their performance.

For male voices, I generally like the U 47, but my favorite overall microphone for voices is the Shure SM5B.

For mic preamps, the API 312 is my favorite, bar none. Peavey makes a dual tube microphone preamp that sounds great. The combination of the Peavey microphone tube preamp and the Behringer Composer is an accessible, affordable combination for most people that is great. If they can't get a Shure SM5, they can get Shure SM7s, which are still available.

With analog tape, you have to be really careful not to hit the tape too hard with the vocal because it can really do terrible things to it. In the same manner, it is important not to get too low of a level. I usually like to have my vocal peaking out at 0 on a VU meter. It depends on what tape you are using and how you have it set, but I am in this case referring to 499 set at +5 over 250, which is what most everyone uses now on 499 and the new BASF 900, which I personally like better because it is quieter and has more energy to it. It sounds like old tape to me. There is something right that the old tape had that BASF has figured out, and Ampex is not doing it.

Csaba Petocz

Credits include: Elvis Costello, Etta James, Lynyrd Skynyrd, John Michael Montgomery, Stevie Nicks, Metallica, Concrete Blonde. See the Appendix for Csaba Petocz's full bio.

I don't think there is any such thing as the perfect vocal mic. There are just different mics for different people. You should just understand what each different mic sounds like and how it changes the sound of the human voice, and obviously select the mic that enhances the sound of the voice.

You should go out on the floor and hear the person sing, hear what it is that they do, and see what parts of their voices are really special. Obviously, if the person is worth recording, there is a uniqueness there and you should really try and highlight that aspect of the vocal. Over the years, I have gotten to where I can hear a singer and know within one or two mics which should work.

If you've tried out three very expensive tube mics and you aren't happy with any of them, then the next step should immediately be something at the other end of the scale, like an SM7. I will almost always guarantee you that if the expensive mic doesn't work, an SM7 will. You have to mess with EQ a little bit, but for some reason some people sound better on them.

I think that 80 percent of getting a good vocal is in giving the singer a good headphone mix. If you can make a singer enjoy singing and really hear what is going on with the small nuances in the voice by giving them a great headphone mix, you can get the artist to do 90 percent of your work. This is especially true if you can get them to be attuned to what it is that you would really like to hear. Most singers get challenged by it. Artists really get into the fact that you care enough to make it that 2 percent better.

More than anything that you record, the human voice is the one that reacts most to small changes. You can really make a vocal sound significantly better by changing variables minutely.

Having been in country music for about 5 years, the most hi-fi aspect of country music has to be the vocals. You can take a lot of liberties in country music, but taking liberties with the vocal isn't one of them. Country is not the genre to do that in—it just doesn't work.

After going through so many years of doing alternative rock records, it is kind of nice to record something really well. I know that may be unhip to say, but I get off on the purity of it. Also, without any disrespect to any of the other musical forms, I think country and R&B have some of the most accomplished singers, and it is a lot more fun recording with someone who is a great singer.

Most recordings get 95 percent of the way there. The challenge is to get that last extra percentage, and that is what separates great vocal sounds from everyone else's. It is more than just putting an $8,000 microphone into a $2,000 preamp. That 95 percent is just meat-and-potatoes good recording, but the last 5 percent is about how to relate to this human being in front of you singing, who is incredibly vulnerable and trusts you enough to go in there and work hard enough to get that last 5 percent of the vocal that makes them sound just that much different than every other artist out there.

No one cares about any vocalist or performer until they are touched by them. The record doesn't become great until it's not the artist's song, but the listener's song. Once it becomes the listener's song, that's a record. I don't care about Patsy Cline. I care about the fact that when Patsy Cline sings, that's my story, or that's me relating to my wife or my first love, or what have you. It's like watching people act.

The greatest actors and actresses are the ones who don't appear to be acting. The worst actors are cringe-worthy because you know you're watching somebody act. It is the same when people are "singing." It's the minute I get the sense that they're "singing"—"Watch me weep," or "Listen to me yell and scream"—and suddenly I'm bored out of my mind. As soon as it becomes melodrama, you're done.

Where does it transition from being breathtakingly, heartbreakingly moving to a Broadway-schmuck parody of someone being sensitive? It's almost impossible to verbalize, which is what makes producing vocals interesting to me. I think in pulling that out of singers, you can only ask them to do two or three things to internalize. I think the minute you get into the fourth concept, you're wasting your time. "What you need to do is be more in pitch. Second one is to be farther back. You're flat on the seventh note on the..."—it just becomes rambling noise at some point. You have to be economical and have laser-like precision with your input. We've all heard the joke of the producer saying, "Make it a little more blue." That's nonsensical to me. You have to provide something specific. Saying "Make it better" isn't production.

Concerning Auto-Tune, I don't think the crazy "in-tuneness" of today's records comes from the public wanting it to be the way. I think it comes from producers and record companies being so insecure and having such a lack of vision and focus that it's like, "Well, I'm not going to be made to look stupid. You know what? If this record fails, it won't be because it's not in tune."

One of my favorite singers in the world is Neil Young. On a scale of 1 to 10, I'm sure he would be the first one to tell you his vocal is a 2, but the way he uses it is so beautiful. As far as I'm concerned, he's one of the great singers.

Eric Schilling

Credits include: Gloria Estefan, Jon Secada, Babyface, Crosby, Stills & Nash, Barry Manilow, Julio Iglesias, and Cachao. See the Appendix for Eric Schilling's full bio.

When you work with someone who is singing, it tends to be a one-on-one process. The whole key to me is to keep a rhythm so the singer never loses the flow. If you are working and they say, "Let's go back to the verse and do lines 2 and 3," you want to be fast enough that it happens in a seamless way. The moment you start going, "Oh no, I've got to figure out where I am, and I've got to fix some EQs," they start drifting. Recording voices is one of the most fun things for me to do, and I love it when that "flow" is going.

When you are working with someone who has a really "pure" voice, it is harder for them when it comes to the issue of pitch because there are fewer harmonics in their voice. You easily hear it when things fall from pitch. Just to make a crude example, Karen Carpenter had to be really in tune because she had a very pure voice, but Bob Dylan, who has a kind of gruff voice, can move the pitch around a whole lot because his voice has a very wide spread of overtones.

It is funny how you can find an album of someone like Dylan who has that kind of voice, and though you hear some pitch stuff, you don't really mind it. On the other hand, if the voice is really "pure," it can be very grating if it isn't really in tune.

Concerning pitch correction, I think it has a use, but it is my preference that it is the last thing that you do, not the first thing. I still like to see a person who is going to come in, work on the voice, and not sing it through twice and say, "Well, you can fix it." I don't believe in that. I'll use it to fix some minor things on a vocal performance that may have a great overall vibe, where the singer feels that he or she can't top that level of performance again. Utilizing pitch correction at that point is probably fine.

It's funny—sometimes, when you pull it too far in tune, it doesn't feel right and it takes away the character of the performance. I don't believe that music is meant to be a perfect thing. When you sing, you don't always sing exactly on the beat or exactly in pitch all the time, like if you were playing a fretless bass or anything else where you have some room to move. You have to be careful when you tamper with the recorded performance.

Generally, I am a big fan of the John Hardy mic pres, which I think are real neutral sounding. I also like the Millennia and API. My first choice of compressor is a good LA-2A, if I can get my hands on one. Another compressor I really like a lot, which you don't find that much anymore, is a Compex. It is a British-made compressor that used to be called a Vocal Stressor.

I always cut flat, mainly because if they are going to come back and change a part, or we recorded a month earlier and they want to recut some lines, I find that it isn't as hard to match the sound.

With many older mics, you have to be very careful about the room you are in. If you are in too small of a booth, you will actually start to hear the sound of that booth, especially in the lower frequencies. They essentially behave like omnis in the lower range. So, if I have somebody who is working on a tube mic and they are in a small room, I am going to have them about one hand width or 5 inches away. I generally use a pop screen instead of a wind screen to keep the spit off the microphone, and it keeps people from getting too close. I can always tell when they can't hear enough in the phones because they start to push the pop screen in closer to the mic.

Concerning singing with large groups, I guess I come from the school of putting up one microphone. When I came down to Florida, my old boss was doing the Eagles records. He would put up an omni, and they would stand around it and work until they got the balance.

I am not a huge fan of flying vocals in and that kind of stuff, but some people I have worked with will say "Great, I'll sing it once, and you can fly it all in." Nevertheless, if I can get them to sing the whole song through, that is my preference. I like doing it this way because the emotion changes. I just think there is a kind of stride that you hit as a background singer that also plays into the song from an emotional point of view. If you listen to a background track that is sung the whole way, next to a sampled track with the vocals flown in, the sampled track will sound static. As a result, the music will tend to feel more static, too. I see why people fly vocals in, but there is an emotional side to this that they are missing.

Dylan Dresdow

Credits include: The Black Eyed Peas, Michael Jackson, TLC, Wu-Tang Clan, Ice Cube, Madonna, will.i.am, Macy Gray. See the Appendix for Dylan Dresdow's full bio.

When I'm recording vocals, I'll often set up three to six microphones and have an assistant solo each one of the mics as the singer sings. I don't want to know which one is which, so I don't look at them. I just listen to the sound and find what sounds best for their voice until we arrive at the most appropriate microphone. The mics that I set up are typically a Sony C-800G, a U 47 tube mic, a C 12 tube mic, a U 67 tube mic, a U 87 tube mic, and a Shure SM7B mic, which is like a $300 mic. Sometimes, to my surprise, that $300 mic beats out some mics that cost many times more.

I really like the SM7B mic for people who have converted their closet into a vocal booth. Because it's a dynamic mic, it doesn't pick up as much of the boxy room tone as a large-diaphragm condenser mic, which will probably sound better in a big, open live room. Many times, you get more of the vocal out of the dynamic mic if you're in a small confined space. Knowing which mic is going to pair best with the vocals and whatever room they are in is something that's really important for people to learn. After we determine which microphone is the best, I typically use a Crane Song Flamingo mic pre, or sometimes a Neve 3408 or Groove Tubes ViPRE. Those are typically the pres I will start with when recording vocals.

For compression, a lot of my decision for choosing the right compressor really depends on several things. For example, the C 12 microphone does a great job on most female R&B vocalists because it captures their top end really well, better than one like the Telefunken 251 mic. A C 12 captures all of the top end detail really well, but sometimes it sounds a little bit too bright. It just doesn't sound like it has enough depth to it, so a lot of times I'll use the LA two-way compressor. There's a sweet spot on that compressor that I think most engineers know is somewhere around 5 dB of gain reduction that just sounds killer on vocals. When you dial it in, your lead vocal will instantly sound like it has a pocket within the mix. If you try putting more LA two-ways in your background vocals, it won't work the same because, basically, you have everything fighting for space with the same coloration within the mix. Many times, when I'm mixing a song, I look at it the same way I look at video, where if someone is standing right in front of me, someone is standing a couple feet behind him, and someone is standing a couple of feet even farther behind him, I can adjust the lens so that I can focus on everyone at one time. Or, I can use a shorter depth of field and focus on just the person in the middle, so the person directly in front of me and the person in the very back are distorted and blurry, and the person behind them will be blurry, but the person in the middle is focused and clear. To accomplish this, it's not merely about "Let's turn the bass down 2 dB," because sometimes the bass is at the perfect level, but you just want to smudge the audio a little so that it's not as in-your-face and clear as everything else. Tubes are great for smearing up the audio and making things sound less focused. That's a great way to put some things in the background and put everything in its correct place perceptively.

"Fixing" a mix is a term that should never be used. It should always be fixed initially, typically from the source. If you start with a great source, it's going to sound great all the way down, and all of that stuff you do later on is audio sweetening, as opposed to audio bandaging. I think a great way for artists to go into the studio is to think about things like "I'm going to fix things at the source before turning to audio gear and transistors and plug-ins to fix it for me." One of the unfortunate things about all of this great technology we have is that people are overusing it.

Personally, if a singer can't get it in 10 takes, quite frankly, he needs to spend more time with a vocal coach. Again, this goes back to the idea that "If they can't sing this stuff in the studio, how will they ever perform live confidently?" Unfortunately, a lot of artists are lip-synching these days. It is impossible for some of these artists to pull off their choreography and still sing without huffing and puffing their way through it, so I understand why they do it, but I think that music should be the primary focus, and the dancing and everything else should be secondary.

Jim Scott

Credits include: Tom Petty, Red Hot Chili Peppers, Wilco, Dolly Parton, Black Sabbath, Sting, Dixie Chicks, Foo Fighters. See the Appendix for Jim Scott's full bio.

I try to get a live vocal with the band that I'm recording. I encourage almost everyone to sing live. Sometimes, the guy is going to play guitar or piano and sing at the same time. Of course, with Tom Petty, I would put a C 12 on his vocal and an 87 and 452 on his guitar. The vocal and guitar became one thing. Even though they were printed on separate tracks, it became one sound because of bleed and who he is and how he plays. You might as well have recorded it all on one track. There really wasn't any rebalancing. If you turned the vocal up a little louder, then the guitar wasn't loud enough. If you turned the guitar up a little louder, then the vocal was too ambient and too sketchy. They became a natural balance.

Lately, I've been using Shure SM7s because they are very directional, and they are warm and clear and very, very tough. They are a low-output microphone, so you have to turn the mic preamp up an extra click or two just to get them to speak out, but it's been a great choice. It's a good mic for men to sing on. John Hiatt likes to use one, and I use one on Anthony Kiedis (Red Hot Chili Peppers). Anthony is a loud singer, and he gets close on the mic. I compress him pretty hard, and that's how he gets his sound.

For compressors, I would use an LA-2A on the right singer, but an 1176 brings a smile and a sparkle. To my ear, even when they are compressing hard, they still sound musical and loud. Even when they are compressing really hard, they are holding it up instead of holding it back.

For female singers, I have had good luck with U 87s, just because they are warm. U 67s are also a great choice, which is what Natalie Maines used with Dixie Chicks.

Jacquire King

Credits include: Kings of Leon, Modest Mouse, MUTEMATH, Buddy Guy, and Tom Waits. See the Appendix for Jacquire King's full bio.

Once I've established what a basic track sounds like in terms of the instrumentation early in the tracking process, I look at fitting the vocal into that picture. The vocal is a primary element in popular music, and there are several things that I have to weigh in making the choices for recording a vocal sound. I like to set up a situation where I've gathered up as many microphones as possible, even the ones that aren't typically thought of as vocal mics. I do this because everyone's voice is different, and there is a lot to capture.

My process starts by recording the vocalist singing a verse or a chorus over the basic track. I audition the microphones that way because I want to find one that accentuates their voice in a way that fits into the music. I use the same mic pre to compare all the mic choices. This way, I automatically get to hear which mics are doing some of the equalization without ever touching an EQ. After all the mics are heard, a few choices are then clearly identified. The next step is to audition a number of different microphone preamplifiers because of the various colors and influences they bring to the sound. Once I narrow it down to a microphone and a preamplifier, auditioning some compressors comes next. I can continue to have the singer work with me or just insert the compressor choices on the recorded track. It's not always great to have someone sing for a long time when you're making these listening comparisons. I know I have to move quickly and be considerate, but it is also a great chance to get comfortable with one another without it being "the take" (I don't ever erase anything vocally that I've recorded because it just might have some magic on it).

When all the right choices have been made and a flat vocal sound has been found, there won't be too much I'll have to do in terms of EQ or dynamic management. The vocal sound will always work well when it comes time to mix. It's funny—quite often, a microphone that you would not have even thought would be a great vocal mic ends up being the one that is used.

One of the mics that I like to use is an SM7—it is actually often a good choice for rock vocals. I like the U 67 and U 87, and the RE20 can be a good choice, too. These are wonderful places to start. Actually, sometimes a Shure SM58 handheld microphone can do a good job for the personality of a vocal. I recently did a project with Pictures and Sound where we used a 421 for all the lead vocals and then used a Sony C-37A for the doubles. That actually makes me think of when I record vocals in a more ambient space, maybe a few feet off the microphone. In doing that, I get a more reverberant performance of a vocal part, and it is almost like a performed effect. You can add texture to a lead vocal, and even go for a different vocal approach by having the vocalist sing louder or even shout doubled parts. It adds interest and texture in a unique way. Another mic I enjoy is the Neumann M 49—it's really about what is useful. I've used some of these mics specifically with various artists. For example, Tom Waits is an M 49, Caleb Followill (Kings of Leon) is an SM7, James Robert Farmer (Mother/Father) is a TL2 (which is an AKG 414 with a C 12 capsule in it), and Isaac Brock (Modest Mouse) is a Stephans tube microphone, a custom-made microphone that uses a C 12 capsule.

In thinking about a vocalist's reaction to a microphone, it is always interesting to observe them hearing their voice coming through all these different choices, seeing how they respond to certain kinds of sonic clarity and balance. You will get different amounts of excitement because of the way vocalists hear themselves. It becomes inspiring, and that is an important part of recording an extraordinary vocal performance.

That is indeed the job of a producer, making sure the artist's experiences are enhanced as they are recording. One of goals as a producer/engineer for me is to capture an inspired moment of art and overcome the technical hurdles involved in the studio process. Sometimes, the recording environment creates anxiety, especially with newer artists who have waited and worked for the moment of recording for a long time. It all happens very quickly and very intensely, and the pressure for it to be the absolute best is always there. Making sure they are having fun and that it sounds genuine to them adds to the excitement of what we are doing. If I don't have an artist's enthusiasm, I won't have a recording with much depth to it.

Gail Davies

Credits include: 15 albums as an artist. Vocalist on records with Neil Young, Glen Campbell, Emmylou Harris, Ralph Stanley, Hoyt Axton, Lacy J. Dalton, Rosie Flores. See the Appendix for Gail Davies's full bio.

A difficult aspect of producing can be the vocals. I've been asked by other producers to come in and help them get the vocals right as this is probably my strongest suit. I learned to produce from Henry Lewy, who recorded all the early Joni Mitchell albums. We were once listening to a playback of a song I'd recorded with him, and he asked me if I was singing in my head while I was listening (which I was). That, he pointed out, was canceling out what I was listening to. Things like that may sound really simple, but they help to separate yourself, especially when you're producing your own music, so you can listen objectively.

Another point, if you're trying to move through a project quickly and don't have a lot of studio time or money, is to make sure you've got at least three good vocals that you can put together at the end. Sometimes, producers will concentrate solely on the music, thinking they'll get the vocal later, but then find they can't get the vocals and they're in vocal hell for the rest of the project. I was once called in to help a budding young producer, who later became quite famous, on a project he was doing with a friend of mine. He had spent all his energy getting the band to sound great, with wonderful guitar overdubs and so forth, but ended up at the end of the night with his vocalist sitting on the bathroom floor crying because she was too tired to sing.

My suggestion for the future was once you've decided on the track you're going to use, let the musicians take a short break and have the singer take two more passes straight through the song. Then, if you find yourself in a bind later, you'll have three vocal tracks where the vocalist has the same amount of phlegm in their throat, attitude, feeling, and approach to the song. If I'm really under the gun, I'll do this while laying down another acoustic guitar track as well.

If I'm working with a good singer, I try to get the vocal in the first or second take as that's usually the best one. After a while, they tend to start doing what I call "over-intellectualizing" every note, and then you're dead. I like spontaneity, so I'll go on to another song and come back later if I can hear the singer thinking too much instead of just singing.

To me, emotional content is extremely important in the vocals. I don't want to hear music that's perfectly in tune, unless it's a symphony that has no feeling. I can live with a few dodgy notes if there's emotional content (e.g. Janis Joplin). I try to get singers to think beyond the microphone in front of them, to the lover or person they'd be talking to. That's what makes the vocal meaningful to the listener.

Russ Long

Credits include: Dolly Parton, Sixpence None the Richer, Osaka Pearl, Gary Chapman, Swag, Michael W. Smith, Phil Keaggy. See the Appendix for Russ Long's full bio.

I think that there are three important factors in capturing an amazing vocal performance. The first is choosing the correct mic, the second is the signal path, and the third (and most important) is making sure that the singer has been provided with an artistic environment that will yield the best possible performance, both technically and creatively.

A simple mic shootout is the easiest way to select a mic. I usually throw three or four mics up and have the vocalist sing the tune, or at least a verse and chorus, down through each mic. My go-to vocal mics are the Sony C-800G, the Brauner VM1 KHE, the Blue Cactus, and the Mojave MA-200. The Coles 4038 gets used a lot, too, and depending on the vocalist, I'll often give a dynamic mic like the Beyer M88, the Heil PR 40, or the EV RE20 a shot. If I'm recording vocals on a project that I've also been tracking, then I will already have tried several potential vocal mics, so I will already have a good idea what will or won't work. If I didn't track the project, I'll listen to the tracking guide vocals, and if they sound good, I'll talk to the tracking engineer about the vocal mic so I can make sure I have the same mic included in the shootout. I'll also talk to the vocalist about what they've had good or bad results with in the past. A lot of artists have a good idea of what does and doesn't work on their vocal. The tricky thing about vocal shootouts is you don't want to burn the singer out with long, drawn-out experimentation. Shootouts aren't too inspirational, so the quicker you can make a decision, the better. I'll always keep every pass, too. Sometimes, a vocalist sings a pass during the shootout that later becomes the keeper vocal.

Choosing the correct signal path is tremendously important. I usually use either the Gordon or the LaChapell Model 583s mic pre. Both sound amazing, but they are very different. The Gordon provides a clean, uncolored sound that lets the mic's true color shine through, while the vacuum tube LaChapell colors the sound very musically. The 583 has separate input and output controls, which makes it easy to control the amount of tube saturation. Another great feature of the 583 is the easy tube access, which allows the use of vintage Telefunken, Mullard, RFT, or Philips tubes for additional sonic flexibility. If I use EQ, I'll almost always use it before the compressor. I don't like frequencies that I'm pulling out to key the compressor, so that's my preference. I'll use either the GML 8200 or the Empirical Labs Lil FrEQ EQ. The 8200 works better for a transparent sound, while the Lil FrEQ has a bit more color. The FrEQ has a great de-esser built in as well, which I'll occasionally use. If I'm using the GML and I need a de-esser, I'll use the dbx 902. I usually use the de-esser right after the mic pre, but sometimes I'll put it last in the chain—it just depends on what sounds best along with the other elements in the chain. I usually compress the vocal twice during tracking. I run through the Tube Tech CL-1B first. It's amazingly transparent, allowing me to wrangle the dynamics without coloration. I follow the CL-1B with a compressor with a lot of color, usually the Empirical Labs Distressor, but sometimes the RCA BA-6B or the dbx 901. The Distressor has extremely precise attack and release times, and its ability to emphasize second- or third-order harmonics works wonders when tracking to digital. The RCA doesn't work well 90 percent of the time, but when it does work, nothing can touch it. It's aggressive as hell and works miracles on rock vocals. The 901 loses top end the more it compresses. This is not ideal for most situations, but some vocalists tend to get a bit shrill as their volume increases, so the 901 can be a perfect match in these cases.

Lastly is the environment where the singer tracks their vocals. It's important to realize that there are no die-hard rules regarding this. The big trick is getting inside the singer's headspace and trying to see what inspires them and what doesn't. I like to record vocals in relatively small rooms. Usually, something in the 10- by 10-foot to 14- by 14-foot range is about right. Rooms much larger than this can be intimidating, and if they are much smaller, it can be claustrophobic. Flexible lighting is important, too. Some singers like minimal lighting, and many like no light at all. Singing a lead vocal puts the vocalist in a state of vulnerability, so they often don't like any visitors around, and many times they may not even want their bandmates in the room. Most of the vocals I've recorded include only the producer, the vocalist, and myself. There are always exceptions to this rule, though. I've recorded plenty of singers who need an audience to feel inspired. Typically, candles or incense help create an inspired ambiance, but many singers despise heavy aromas, so it's important that you check with them before filling the studio with scent of Nag Champa.

Contributor Bios

GREG ADAMS

Since 1970, Tower of Power has carved a name for itself as one of the best, most powerful horn sections in the world. From its inception until 1994, Greg Adams served at the lead arranger and trumpet player. Adams' and Tower of Power's work has appeared on more than 1,000 recordings, including work with Elton John, Santana, Eurythmics, Little Feat, Rod Stewart, the Grateful Dead, Luther Vandross, the Rolling Stones, B.B. King, Madonna, Bonnie Raitt, Terence Trent D'Arby, Huey Lewis and the News, Michael Bolton, Phish, and Linda Ronstadt. You can hear Adams' collaboration with Paul Shaffer on the opening theme of the *Late Show with David Letterman* and on musical score arrangements on numerous films.

Since 1994, Adams has put out the solo *Hidden Agenda* (co-produced with Ken Kessie), which stayed at the number-one position on the R&R NAC charts for five weeks, and other successful albums, such as *Midnight Morning* and *East Bay Soul*.

Adams' deep commitment to music education and the art of contemporary music is shown through his continued involvement in our public schools through seminars, clinics, performances, and development of new artists. He strongly believes in music programs at all levels of education.

Having served three terms on the Board of Governors of the Los Angeles Chapter of The Recording Academy® - National Academy of Arts and Sciences, Adams participates in Grammy Camp, a national outreach program that provides insight to high-school students about careers that are available in music and direction on how to prepare for them. He's also actively involved in the Entertainment Industry Foundation's National Arts and Music Education Initiative to help increase public resources available for education in the arts for children and young people.

JOHN AGNELLO

Starting his recording career as an assistant engineer at the Record Plant in New York, John Agnello worked on several legendary early-'80s albums, including John Cougar Mellencamp's *Uh-Huh*, Aerosmith's *Rock in a Hard Place*, Scandal's *The Warrior*, Twisted Sister's *Stay Hungry*, Cyndi Lauper's *She's So Unusual*, and John Waite's *No Brakes*. After Agnello went out on his own, he enjoyed a string of successes recording albums with the Hooters, the Outfield, Patty Smyth, and Sophie B. Hawkins.

Over the years, Agnello has earned a reputation as a producer and engineer with extensive credits in the modern rock and alternative music world, including the Breeders, Dinosaur Jr., Jawbox, Buffalo Tom, Alice Cooper, Redd Kross, Screaming Trees, Grither, Social Distortion, Dish, Triple Fast Action, Bivouac, the

Lemonheads, Tad, Gigolo Aunts, Mark Lanegan, Patty Smyth, Jay Farrar, Dar Williams, Jimmy Eat World, the Murder City Devils, the Sammies, Burning Airlines, and many more.

BRIAN AHERN

Brian Ahern made his first big mark as a producer when he discovered Canadian artist Anne Murray and produced her hugely successful hit "Snowbird," as well as 11 albums. Ahern also discovered Emmylou Harris in the early to mid-'70s. Together, they created a sound that drew from the best elements of traditional country, folk, and pop and (coupled with a knack for finding great songs) forged a timeless body of work represented in more than 20 album releases that have earned multiple Grammys. Ahern's production credits also include Johnny Cash, George Jones, Ricky Skaggs, Rodney Crowell, Billy Joe Shaver, Marty Robbins, David Bromberg, and others. Ahern has also been deeply involved in surround audio, producing critically acclaimed surround albums for Harris and Cash.

CHUCK AINLAY

Chuck Ainlay is regarded as one of the finest engineers and mixers in the audio world, particularly in country music. He's been recognized by the National Academy of Recording Arts and Sciences with multiple Grammy nominations for his critically and commercially successful albums. Ainlay's country music credits include George Strait, Lyle Lovett, the Dixie Chicks, Waylon Jennings, Patty Loveless, Marty Stuart, Wynonna Judd, Emmylou Harris, Willie Nelson, Rodney Crowell, Steve Earle, and many others, but he's also done extensive work outside country music, particularly with Dire Straits and Mark Knopfler's solo releases.

Ainlay is also one the audio world's most respected mixers for surround audio, with acclaimed releases for Knopfler, Vince Gill, Peter Frampton, and others. Along with Knopfler and Bob Ludwig, in 2006, Ainlay collected the Grammy for Best Surround Sound Album for Dire Straits' *Brothers in Arms*.

GREG ALLEN

Known throughout the game industry as an audio guru, Greg Allen is audio director for Ubisoft. His work in the gaming industry as a sound designer and audio director includes time as creative director at Apparatic and senior audio director for Sony Online Entertainment and Electronic Arts (EA) Chicago, where he oversaw all aspects of audio for the organization's games and projects. During his time at EA, Allen grew the audio department, created a full production studio, helped create the award-winning *Fight Night Round 3*, *Def Jam: Icon*, and an unreleased Marvel fighting game. He also spearheaded the Motion Picture Sound Editors award–winning game *GoldenEye: Rogue Agent* at EA Los Angeles. Allen helped build the *X-Men Legends* franchise when he was working at Activision. He spent 7 years as an audio developer with Interplay, where he worked on legendary titles like *Baldur's Gate*, *Fallout 1* and *2*, and *Descent*. During his time there, Allen helped push for audio improvement from the days of 8-bit DOS to the Nintendo 64. Afterward, he moved to Hamburg, Germany, and worked at a startup company called C&G

Entertainment, where he oversaw production for games, TV, film, and recording artists. During his career, Allen has touched many games, worked on several foreign TV/film projects, produced music for several artists, won several audio awards, and worked with some of the most talented people in the industry. He has worked on every platform from the days of DOS to the latest Sony PlayStation 3, Nintendo Wii, and Microsoft Xbox 360.

KENNY ARONOFF

Since the early '80s, some of rock's most distinctive sounds have been the cracking snare and solid grooves of Kenny Aronoff. His exciting style has restraint and taste, while conveying an ever-present sense that something explosive can happen just around the corner. Among the many artists whose albums bear Aronoff's trademark artistry are John Mellencamp, the Smashing Pumpkins, Bonnie Raitt, Santana, Trey Anastasio, Alice Cooper, Meat Loaf, Rod Stewart, Alanis Morissette, the Rolling Stones, Elton John, Lynyrd Skynyrd, Joe Cocker, Melissa Etheridge, John Fogerty, Bob Seger, Bob Dylan, Lisa Germano, Jann Arden, and Jon Bon Jovi. Aronoff was named the top pop/rock drummer and top studio drummer for 5 consecutive years by the readers of *Modern Drummer*. He has played on more than 30 Grammy-nominated recordings.

GEORGE AUGSPURGER

George Augspurger is best known in the audio industry as an expert in studio design through his consulting firm, Perception, Inc. Many of North America's most prestigious studios proudly boast "Augspurger-designed" rooms and monitors. Before striking out as an independent consultant, Augspurger spent more than a decade with JBL, starting in 1958. He began as JBL's technical service manager and was later responsible for establishing and managing the Professional Products Division. In 1968, Augspurger became technical director for JBL, a position he held for 2 years before deciding to move on to independent consulting.

ROY THOMAS BAKER

Roy Thomas Baker has produced some of rock's most audaciously distinctive recordings of the last 40 years. Baker started at Decca Records in England at age 14. Later, he moved to Trident Studios, where he worked with people such as Gus Dudgeon and Tony Visconti. One of Baker's best-known productions is Queen's enduring hit, "Bohemian Rhapsody." Baker has also produced artists such as Guns N' Roses, the Who, the Rolling Stones, David Bowie, the Cars, Foreigner, Journey, Pilot, Ozzy Osbourne, Mötley Crüe, T. Rex, Devo, the Stranglers, Dusty Springfield, Starcastle, T'Pau, Yes, Cheap Trick, Gasolin', the Smashing Pumpkins, and the Darkness.

STEPHEN BARNCARD

A San Francisco Bay Area producer/engineer and part of the legendary Wally Heider Studios staff, Stephen Barncard is probably best known for his work producing two classic albums: the Grateful Dead's *American Beauty* and David

Crosby's *If I Could Only Remember My Name*. His credits also include the New Riders of the Purple Sage, Brewer & Shipley, the Doobie Brothers, Graham Nash, Crosby & Nash, Seals & Crofts, Van Morrison, Graham Central Station, the Ozark Mountain Daredevils, the Tubes, and the Rave-Ups. Barncard's work in surround, particularly on *If I Could Only Remember My Name*, places him among the most respected in the field.

ADRIAN BELEW

Adrian Belew is one of the most innovative guitarists in rock history. Frank Zappa, who first heard Belew playing in a Nashville club in 1970, gave Belew his break, inviting him to play in Zappa's band. Since then, Belew has recorded and toured with David Bowie, the Talking Heads, and King Crimson. He's appeared on numerous albums by other artists, including Nine Inch Nails, Paul Simon, Tom Tom Club, Tori Amos, and Herbie Hancock. Belew has put out 17 solo albums and several albums with the Bears and the Adrian Belew Power Trio.

JERRY BERLONGIERI

Jerry Berlongieri is senior sound designer for Activision Blizzard. As one of the game world's top audio experts, his credits include such hugely successful titles as *007: Quantum of Solace, Call of Duty: World at War, Spider-Man 3, Call of Duty 3, Tony Hawk's Downhill Jam, Ultimate Spider-Man, Alter Echo,* and *Descent 3.* As a composer, he has been credited with creating the soundtracks for *Descent 3* and *Alter Echo.*

DAVID BIANCO

Grammy winner David Bianco has enjoyed a long, multifaceted career. As a mixer, he's helped craft records for a diverse array of artists. Bianco has mixed records for heavy rock bands like Coal Chamber, U.S. Crush, Danzig, and Failure. He has also worked with more mainstream artists, such as AC/DC, Ozzy Osbourne, John Hiatt, Mick Jagger, Del Amitri, Teenage Fanclub, and the Posies.

STEVE BISHIR

Nashville-based recording engineer Steve Bishir has been working on recordings, primarily in the contemporary Christian genre, for more than 20 years. Working alongside legendary contemporary Christian producer Brown Bannister, he has worked on albums by Michael W. Smith, Steven Curtis Chapman, Amy Grant, Third Day, MercyMe, and many others. His other credits include albums by Garth Brooks, Aaron Neville, Travis Tritt, Asleep at the Wheel, and Martina McBride.

MILAN BOGDAN

Milan Bogdan is one of Nashville's best engineers. Besides recording many TV and film orchestral dates, Bogdan has done string sessions for many of country music's finest artists and R&B dates for Motown artists like Marvin Gaye, Diana Ross, and the Temptations.

JOE BOYD

During the mid-'60s, Joe Boyd got his start in music working as a production and tour manager for George Wein in Europe, where he traveled with Muddy Waters, Coleman Hawkins, and Stan Getz, and at Newport, where he supervised Bob Dylan's electric debut. In 1966, Boyd opened the UFO Club, London's psychedelic ballroom. His first record production was four tracks by Eric Clapton and the Powerhouse for Elektra in 1966. From there, Boyd went on to produce work by Pink Floyd, R.E.M., the Incredible String Band, Soft Machine, Fairport Convention, Nick Drake, Nico, Maria Muldaur, Kate and Anna McGarrigle, James Booker, Jimi Hendrix, Toots and the Maytals, Richard and Linda Thompson, Billy Bragg, ¡Cubanismo!, Taj Mahal, Sandy Denny, June Tabor, Joe "King" Carrasco and the Crowns, and 10,000 Maniacs.

As head of music for Warner Brothers Films, Boyd organized the scoring of *Deliverance*, *A Clockwork Orange*, and *McCabe & Mrs. Miller*, and made *Jimi Hendrix*, a feature-length documentary. He later went into partnership with Don Simpson to develop film projects. Boyd helped set up Lorne Michaels' Broadway Pictures in 1979–1980, and then started Hannibal Records, which he ran for 20 years. He is also author of *White Bicycles: Making Music in the 1960s*.

CHRISTOPHER BOYES

Christopher Boyes started out in his teens wanting to work in movie making. For years, he thought his calling was camera work, until he realized the creative freedom one could have in the realm of sound field recording, sound design, and mixing. Boyes' "banzai" dedication to field recording and sound design inspired renowned sound designer and mentor Gary Rydstrom to call him the "Indiana Jones of effects recordists."

Today, Boyes is arguably one of the most successful sound designers and mixers in film. Based at Skywalker Ranch in northern California, Boyes has won four Academy Awards and in 2007 was nominated for another two for his work on *Pirates of the Caribbean: Dead Man's Chest*. He has worked with directors such as James Cameron (*Avatar*, *Titanic*), Peter Jackson (*Lord of the Rings*, *King Kong*), and Clint Eastwood (*Million Dollar Baby*). Other film credits include *Iron Man*, *The Weather Man*, *Mystic River*, *Pearl Harbor*, *Armageddon*, *Con Air*, *The Lovely Bones*, *The Taking of Pelham 123*, and *Minority Report*.

MICHAEL BRAUER

Michael Brauer is truly one of popular music's greatest mix masters, having created hit soundscapes for Bruce Springsteen, Aerosmith, the Rolling Stones, Sade, Eric Clapton, Bob Dylan, Ben Folds, Wilco, Paul McCartney, Travis, the Enemy, My Morning Jacket, KT Tunstall, Tony Bennett, Luther Vandross, James Brown, Billy Joel, Stevie Ray Vaughan, Michael Jackson, Jeff Buckley, and David Byrne. He has earned Grammys for his work on John Mayer's *Continuum* and Coldplay's *Parachutes*.

DAVID BRIGGS

Regarded by some as one of the greatest non-technical rock-and-roll producers in the industry, David Briggs pushed musicians and friends to the very limits of their capabilities and utilized a low-tech, highly emotional, lively approach to bring out the best in every artist.

On any number of Neil Young's finest albums—including *Neil Young, Everybody Knows This Is Nowhere, After the Gold Rush, Tonight's the Night, Zuma, Rust Never Sleeps*, and *Ragged Glory*—you will see Briggs listed as a producer. The two met in 1968, when Briggs picked up Young hitchhiking. It can be easily argued that Briggs was the production force behind Young's best albums, and certainly the ones that rocked the hardest and possessed the most emotional tension.

In addition to his work with Young, Briggs produced the brilliant swan song by the original lineup of Spirit, titled *Twelve Dreams of Dr. Sardonicus*, featuring "Nature's Way." He also worked with Nils Lofgren, Grin, Murray Roman, Alice Cooper, Tom Rush, Nick Cave and the Bad Seeds, Royal Trux, Crazy Horse, Willie Nelson, and Merle Haggard.

TERRY BROWN

Terry Brown is best known for his production work on several Rush albums, including the classic platinum-selling *A Farewell to Kings, Hemispheres, Permanent Waves, Moving Pictures*, and *Signals*. Brown scored a number-one hit with the first Cutting Crew record, "(I Just) Died in Your Arms." He has also produced Blue Rodeo, Voivod, and (among his more arcane production credits) the three Klaatu albums.

TONY BROWN

Tony Brown is one of Nashville's greatest, most successful producers and record men. Brown started out in the '70s as a gospel pianist, even playing on stage as part of the Stamps Quartet with Elvis Presley in Las Vegas. He later became part of Emmylou Harris' legendary Hot Band, but by the end of the '70s he chose to do A&R for RCA. Brown's early signings were Alabama and Deborah Allen. By 1983, he was doing A&R for MCA, where he would remain for many years. Brown not only had a knack for signing and producing huge mainstream country artists, but he also pushed the envelope by working with artists like Lyle Lovett, Steve Earle, Joe Ely, Nanci Griffith, and Todd Snider. His mainstream successes include George Strait, Reba McEntire, Vince Gill, Rodney Crowell, Wynonna Judd, Patty Loveless, and the Mavericks.

GREG CALBI

Greg Calbi started in the mastering business in his early 20s at the top—the famed Record Plant, where he worked on such '70s classics as John Lennon's *Mind Games*, David Bowie's *Young Americans*, and Bruce Springsteen's *Born to Run*. In 1974, Calbi joined the staff at Sterling Sound, developing one of the most wide-ranging mastering résumés in the business, including the Ramones' *Ramones*, Bill

Frisell's *This Land*, Patti Smith's *Easter*, and Paul Simon's *Graceland*. Calbi's associations with an eclectic variety of genres and producers continued through his 1994–1998 stint at Masterdisk, where he worked with such avant-rockers as Sonic Youth, Bardo Pond, and Yo La Tengo. Calbi has mastered literally thousands of albums in his career, including releases by U2, the Talking Heads, Eric Clapton, Yes, Dire Straits, Lou Reed, Brian Eno, James Taylor, the Rolling Stones, Van Morrison, R.E.M., Tom Petty and the Heartbreakers, Bob Dylan, Lenny Kravitz, Luther Vandross, and Dr. John.

BENJAMIN CHEAH

With more than 30 features to his credit, Benjamin Cheah's field recording, sound design, and sound re-record mixing work has graced films and TV shows like *Adventureland*, *The Wire*, *The Royal Tenenbaums*, *The Big Lebowski*, *Fargo*, *Big Night*, *Casino*, *Sleepy Hollow*, *Bowfinger*, and *Get Shorty*.

ED CHERNEY

Producer/engineer Ed Cherney's discography includes a number of legendary and critically acclaimed artists, including Bob Dylan, Elton John, Bonnie Raitt, Bob Seger, Iggy Pop, Eric Clapton, Ry Cooder, Ringo Starr, Lyle Lovett, George Harrison, Little Feat, Jackson Browne, the Goo Goo Dolls, Barbra Streisand, the Rolling Stones, Fleetwood Mac, and the B-52's.

Cherney has amassed six Grammy nominations in his career, with three wins. He engineered 1992's Record of the Year, Eric Clapton's "Tears In Heaven," and won 1994's Best Engineered Album for Bonnie Raitt's *Longing in Their Hearts* (he remarkably recorded and mixed three of the five albums nominated in that category). Cherney has also been honored with seven TEC award nominations, with three wins, and three Emmy nominations for his work on Bonnie Raitt's broadcast of *Road Tested*, the Rolling Stones' *Live from Madison Square Garden* on HBO, and Eric Clapton's 2004 *Crossroads Guitar Festival*.

BOB CLEARMOUNTAIN

In the world of mixing, Bob Clearmountain is a superstar. His extensive credits include Bruce Springsteen, the Rolling Stones, Chic, Bryan Adams, David Bowie, Rufus Wainwright, INXS, the Cure, Peter Gabriel, Crowded House, Tina Turner, Nine Inch Nails, Sheryl Crow, Roxy Music, Robbie Robertson, and the Pretenders.

Since the mid-'70s, when he first made his name at New York's Media Sound and Power Station, Clearmountain's mixes have expanded the possibilities of dimensionality and nuance on the popular music musical soundstage—for example, his mixes of "Tougher than the Rest," from Springsteen's *Tunnel of Love*, "Hymn to Her," off the Pretenders' *Get Close*, or the title track from Roxy Music's *Avalon*. Clearmountain's mix of Chic's dance classic "Good Times," blended the song's visceral R&B bass and drum punch with an almost otherworldly atmospheric string and vocal sound; it perfectly suited the heady spirit of disco escapism.

Clearmountain could also get incredibly raw, as evidenced by his mixes on the Rolling Stones' *Tattoo You*. "Neighbors" benefits from one of the trashiest snare sounds ever committed to tape. Fine examples of his earlier work include David Werner's self-titled 1979 Epic album or the Rezillos' *Can't Stand the Rezillos*. Clearmountain's wonderful 5.1 re-imagining of *Avalon* is a great example of his work with surround audio.

Clearmountain has been nominated for four Grammys and won a Latin Grammy in 2007 for Best Male Pop Vocal Album for his engineering work on Ricky Martin's *MTV Unplugged*. He has also been nominated for an Emmy and has won seven TEC Awards for Best Recording Engineer, two TEC Awards for Best Broadcast Engineer, the Les Paul Award, and a Monitor Award for the Rolling Stones' *Voodoo Lounge* pay-per-view show.

PETER COLLINS

Peter Collins has produced an amazingly wide range of critically and commercially successful projects, including work by Rush, Alice in Chains, Bon Jovi, Tracey Ullman, Queensryche, Jewel, the Indigo Girls, Alice Cooper, Billy Squier, Brian Setzer, Elton John, and LeAnn Rimes.

MIKE COUZZI

Mike Couzzi is one of south Florida's most successful independent engineers. A native of Los Angeles, Couzzi worked at Wally Heider's studio in the '70s before relocating to Florida in 1980. Besides working with artists like Jaco Pastorius, Herbie Hancock, Rod Stewart, and Jermaine Jackson, he has done extensive work recording Latin- and African-influenced music. Couzzi's work can be found on many award-winning albums, including Paraguayan harpist Roberto Perera (1993 Billboard Contemporary Latin Jazz Album of the Year for *Dreams & Desires*), Arturo Sandoval (nominated for six Grammys), and Vicki Carr. His other Latin credits include work by Julio Iglesias, Gloria Estefan, Jose Feliciano, Chayanne, Roberto Carlos, and Jon Secada.

GAIL DAVIES

As a singer, Gail Davies' voice (described by jazz critic Nat Hentoff as "brilliantly evocative") has earned her numerous nominations from the CMA and ACMA, as well as the coveted Best Female Vocalist award from the DJs of America. One of the few artists to have received a standing ovation on the Grand Ole Opry, Davies is a consummate performer who has played venues from the Ryman Auditorium with Del McCoury to Great Britain's Royal Concert Hall with John Prine. She has appeared on *The Today Show* and *Good Morning America*, as a guest of the CBS television special *The Women of Country*, the TBS documentary *America's Music: The Roots of Country*, and the BBC series *Lost Highway*. She has been featured in *Newsweek*, *Rolling Stone*, and *USA Today*, and was described by *No Depression* magazine as "one of Nashville's most iconoclastic performers."

In 2002, Davies received an IBMA award and Grammy nomination for her duet with bluegrass patriarch Ralph Stanley. She was also nominated for an Americana Award for her production work on *Caught in the Webb*, a tribute to country legend Webb Pierce that featured George Jones, Emmylou Harris, Willie Nelson, Pam Tillis, the Jordanaires, Dwight Yoakam, Charley Pride, the Del McCoury Band, Crystal Gayle, Dale Watson, Allison Moorer, Guy Clark, Mandy Barnett, and BR549.

EDDIE DELENA

Eddie DeLena has worked with many of the world's top artists, including Stevie Wonder, Tom Petty, John Mellencamp, Mick Jagger, Michael Jackson, Black Sabbath, Kiss, and Devo.

JIM DEMAIN

Jim DeMain is one of Nashville's most in-demand mastering engineers. His sensitivity to artists and their music has created a loyal client base that comes to his facility, Yes Master. His clients include Patty Loveless, Sonny Landreth, Audio Adrenaline, Billy Joe Shaver, Steve Forbert, Jill Sobule, Peter Cetera, Jimmy Buffett, Will Kimbrough, the Iguanas, Jim Lauderdale, Al Anderson, Phil Lee, Swan Dive, Keith Urban, John Hiatt, Lambchop, Michael McDonald, Todd Snider, Marty Stuart, Bill Lloyd, Andrew Bird, Albert Lee, Duane Jarvis, Nanci Griffith, Webb Wilder, Dan Dugmore, and Tommy Womack.

JIM DICKINSON

To those who knew Jim Dickinson, he was someone who celebrated regionality— specifically, Memphis, the northern Mississippi Delta, and the Texas Hill Country. At the beginning of his career, Dickinson was a recording artist on Sam Phillips' legendary Sun Records label. He approached his productions as part philosopher, part theater director, and part musician, and held a deep respect for the sanctity of each artist's gift. Dickinson, who passed away in 2009, guided and produced many artists' most meaningful work. As a musician, his credits include work with the Rolling Stones, Aretha Franklin, Bob Dylan, and the Flamin' Groovies. Dickinson's production credits include work with Ry Cooder, the Replacements, Willy DeVille, Screamin' Jay Hawkins, Toots Hibbert, the North Mississippi Allstars, Mojo Nixon, Alex Chilton, Big Star, and Mudboy and the Neutrons. Honored by his local NARAS chapter with the Board of Directors' Governor's Award in 1992, Dickinson won Producer of the Year seven times before retiring his name from the competition.

RICHARD DODD

The career of engineer, producer, and mixer Richard Dodd has taken many interesting twists and turns over the past three decades. Since the early '70s, when he was recording hits like Carl Douglas' "Kung Fu Fighting," Dodd has worked with artists such as George Harrison, Roy Orbison, Boz Scaggs, Wilco, the Dixie Chicks, Green Day, Steve Earle, Delbert McClinton, Robert Plant, the Traveling Wilburys, Clannad, and Tom Petty and the Heartbreakers (as well as Tom Petty's solo work). Dodd has won five Grammys and received five other nominations for Best Engineered Album, Recording, Mixing, and Mastering. His consistently detailed and creative work has also earned Dodd multiple platinum and gold records and a legacy of hundreds of top-10 credits.

JERRY DOUGLAS

Jerry "Flux" Douglas is a contemporary American dobro player well known in bluegrass circles for playing with bands such as the Country Gentlemen and Alison Krauss & Union Station. He has also been part of such notable groups as the Whites, the New South, and Strength in Numbers. He has also continued to explore and expand the vocabulary for the dobro as a solo artist. In addition to his 14 solo releases and countless special projects, Douglas' stellar playing has graced more than 1,700 albums, encompassing a wide range of musical styles. As a sideman, he has recorded with artists as diverse as Ray Charles, Peter Rowan, Béla Fleck, Emmylou Harris, Phish, Dolly Parton, Paul Simon, Ricky Skaggs, Bill Frisell, John Fogerty, Nanci Griffith, Tony Rice, Elvis Costello, and James Taylor. He also performed on the landmark soundtrack for *O Brother, Where Art Thou?* As a producer, he has overseen albums by the Del McCoury Band, Maura O'Connell, Jesse Winchester, and the Nashville Bluegrass Band.

DYLAN DRESDOW

Grammy winner and multi-platinum tracking and mixing engineer Dylan "3-D" Dresdow has worked with such artists as Ice Cube, Coolio, Redman, Method Man, TLC, and the Wu-Tang Clan. In 2002, he gained more notoriety when he contributed to the cover of "Lady Marmalade" performed by Christina Aguilera, Pink, Mýa, and Lil' Kim, which won a Grammy (out of three nominations) at the 2003 Grammy Awards and was also nominated for a TEC Award. The next year, he worked on the Black Eyed Peas' *Elephunk*, which was nominated in the Album of the Year, Record of the Year, and highly coveted Best Engineered Album, Non-Classical categories.

In 2009, Dresdow was again nominated for several Grammys with the Black Eyed Peas, including Record of the Year, Album of the Year, and Best Dance Recording. He also mixed a single on Flo Rida's *R.O.O.T.S.*, which was also nominated for Best Rap Album.

Dresdow's Paper V.U. Studios is located in the Burbank/North Hollywood area of California. He has mixed work for many hit artists there, including Michael Jackson, Mariah Carey, Rihanna, the Game, Nas, Ciara, Talib Kweli, Macy Gray, Bone Thugs-n-Harmony, Herbie Hancock, Chris Brown, Fatlip, Ricky Martin, Cheryl Cole, and the Tree Brains.

STEVE EBE

Over the last 25 years, Nashville-based drummer Steve Ebe has performed or recorded with numerous artists, including rockabilly legend Carl Perkins; fusion guitar wunderkind Shawn Lane; roots rockers Sonny Landreth, Sonny George, and

Webb Wilder; country artists Marty Stuart, Tanya Tucker, and George Ducas; Anglo pop rocker Tommy Hoehn; and soul music king Steve Cropper. Ebe was also part of Human Radio, which recorded an album for Columbia Records.

MARK EVANS

Los Angeles–based Mark Evans has been the go-to guy for film and TV composers who are seeking immediate-sounding audiophile-quality orchestral recording for their scores. A great example of his recording work is Kevin Kiner's score for *Star Wars: The Clone Wars.*

ELLEN FITTON

Ellen Fitton's recording career has included R&B (Chaka Khan, Dionne Warwick, and the Bee Gees), jazz (Wynton Marsalis), and rock (FireHouse), but her most extensive credits are in classical. She has recorded the Chicago Symphony Orchestra, the Philadelphia Orchestra, and the New York Philharmonic, as well as artists like Jessye Norman, Yo-Yo Ma, and Kathleen Battle. Among Fitton's favorite places to record strings are Royce Hall in Los Angeles, Myerhoff Symphony Hall in Baltimore, and Symphony Hall in Boston.

PAT FOLEY

By the time Pat Foley began working for Slingerland Drums as director of custom products a number of years ago, he had already amassed an impressive list of credits as a designer of unique drums sets for the stars, including sets for Gregg Bissonette for the David Lee Roth tours (which looked like they were exploding), sets for the Jacksons' 1984 Victory Tour, the garbage can–looking trap set for Twisted Sister, and sets for Bernard Purdie, Jim Christie (Dwight Yoakam), and Taylor Hawkins (Alanis Morissette). Foley's drum tech credits include Faith No More, Los Lobos, and Mötley Crüe.

MARK FREEGARD

If you listen to the Breeders' brilliant *Last Splash*, Madder Rose's *Panic On*, or Dillon Fence's *Living Room Scene*, a name that pops up on each is Mark Freegard, a resourceful British producer/engineer who, in the realm of creatively treated sound, was to those albums and others what Steve Lillywhite was to the early to mid-'80s world of distinctive production. Freegard's other credits include Ride, Del Amitri, the Sisters of Mercy, Erasure, the Manic Street Preachers, Marilyn Manson, Ultravox, Marillion, Pete Townsend, and Bluebird.

RYAN FREELAND

Since veteran engineer/mixer Ryan Freeland went out on his own in 1997 (after 3 years working under legendary mix master Bob Clearmountain) and established Stampede Origin Studio in West Los Angeles, he has become one of the most in-demand engineers and mixers for producers and artists who seek a unique take on organic soundscapes. Freeland's credits include Aimee Mann, Joe Henry, Grant-Lee Phillips, Ingrid Michaelson, Amy Correia, Liz Phair, Paul Westerberg, Counting Crows, Jewel, Brett Dennen, Son Volt, Chuck Prophet, Ian Axel, the Weepies, Jim White, Loudon Wainwright III, Alana Davis, Jonatha Brooke, and Christina Aguilera.

Joe Henry has brought a number of projects to Freeland, including Mose Allison's *Let It Come Down*, the Carolina Chocolate Drops' *Genuine Negro Jig*, Loudon Wainwright III's *Recovery*, Mary Gauthier's *Between Daylight and Dark*, and Rodney Crowell's *Sex & Gasoline*. In 2010, Freeland received a Grammy for Best Traditional Blues Album for recording and mixing Ramblin' Jack Elliot's album *A Stranger Here*. Freeland's credits also include work on the movies *Knocked Up, I'm Not There, Moulin Rouge!*, and *Coyote Ugly*.

DON GEHMAN

Don Gehman was among the most successful producers of the '80s and '90s. His rich heartland sound is most familiar to audiences through his collaborations with John Mellencamp, R.E.M., Tracy Chapman, and Hootie & the Blowfish. Gehman's other credits include Nanci Griffith, Better Than Ezra, River City People, Blues Traveler, the Divinyls, Pat Benatar, Treat Her Right, and Eric Carmen.

RICHARD GIBBS

Richard Gibbs was the keyboard player for the New Wave band Oingo Boingo from 1980 to 1984. He was also a session player, performing on more than 150 albums for artists as diverse as War, Tom Waits, Robert Palmer, and Aretha Franklin. Gibbs also started the band Zuma II with Michael Jochum, which had an eponymously titled record released by Pasha/CBS Records. He has appeared live with Korn, the Staple Singers, and Chaka Khan, and his production credits include Korn and Eisley.

Like his former Oingo Boingo bandmate Danny Elfman, Gibbs embarked on a life of scoring movies and television shows. He has written scores for more than 50 films, such as *Dr. Dolittle, Step into Liquid, Say Anything...*, and *Queen of the Damned*. He has also acted as musical director and composer for various television shows, including *Muppets Tonight, The Simpsons*, and *Battlestar Galactica*.

BUD GRAHAM

Over the last 30 years, Bud Graham has been one of the most highly regarded engineers for serious symphonic recording. He has recorded renowned orchestras (Philadelphia, New York, Cleveland, and Boston) in some of the world's greatest concert halls. Graham, now retired, has earned six Grammys.

RENEE GRANT-WILLIAMS

Since the mid-'70s, Nashville-based vocal coach and producer Renee Grant-Williams has helped numerous singers develop artistically. Her clients have included Miley Cyrus, the Dixie Chicks, Faith Hill, Kenny Chesney, Huey Lewis, Bob Weir, Linda Ronstadt, Charlie Daniels, Tim McGraw, Lyle Lovett, Jill Sobule, Kim Wilson, the subdudes, Sonny Landreth, and Doug Stone.

CHRISTOPHER GREENLEAF

Christopher Greenleaf has extensively recorded work with acoustic instruments under "classical" conditions. He is respected in audiophile circles as an engineer of exceptional recordings.

PAUL GRUPP

Since 1972, Paul Grupp has been one of Los Angeles' most in-demand engineers/producers. He has worked on many big sessions since that time, including work for Roger McGuinn, the Little River Band, Rick Nelson, REO Speedwagon, Sammy Hagar, Quarterflash, Charlie Daniels, Pure Prairie League, and Michael Murphy.

JOHN GUESS

Over the years, John Guess has been one of the hottest producers/engineers in Nashville. He has worked with numerous mainstream pop and country artists, including Suzy Bogguss, Michelle Wright, and Linda Davis. Since the late '80s, Guess has been in demand as an engineer and mixer for such country stars as Vince Gill, Rodney Crowell, Reba McEntire, Marty Stuart, Patty Loveless, Wynonna Judd, and George Strait.

Before moving to Nashville, Guess worked on gold and platinum pop projects by Rod Stewart, Donna Summer, and Kenny Loggins, as well as projects for artists as diverse as Captain Beefheart, Michael Omartian, Funkadelic, Luther Vandross, Frank Sinatra, Jeff Beck, Stevie Wonder, and John Fogerty.

ROBERT HALL

Journeyman drummer and drum tech Robert Hall has handled the studio fine-tuning percussion chores for producers like John Hampton, Jim Gaines, Joe Hardy, and the legendary Jim Dickinson. Since 1987, Hall has teched R.E.M. in the studio and periodically on the road, and has worked with Little Texas, Chris Layton (Stevie Ray Vaughan), and Mickey Curry (Tom Cochrane). Hall also founded the Memphis Drum Shop, a full-service operation that has attracted business from drummers all over the country.

JOHN HAMPTON

Over the past 30 years, John Hampton has made his name as a producer, engineer, and mixer. His credits include work with Alex Chilton, the White Stripes, the Raconteurs, the Gin Blossoms, Lynyrd Skynyrd, Audio Adrenaline, B.B. King, the Afghan Whigs, Todd Snider, Jimmy Vaughan, the Replacements, ZZ Top, Robert Cray, and the Cramps. Hampton's mixing skills on numerous country projects, including work with Travis Tritt and Marty Stuart, have helped put some attitude into that genre's sound, too.

JOE HARDY

Joe Hardy is responsible for helping ZZ Top achieve their legendary gritty crunch. Besides engineering and mixing their multi-platinum albums like *Afterburner* and *Eliminator*, Hardy's producer/engineer credits include the Georgia Satellites, 38 Special, the Jeff Healey Band, Steve Earle, the Hooters, and Tom Cochrane. Hardy's engineering and mixing credits include work with Booker T. & the M.G.'s, Ry Cooder, the Replacements, and the Staple Singers.

ROGER HAWKINS

Over the last 30 years, some of the greatest records of all time have benefited from Roger Hawkins' brilliant, sure-footed pocket. His credits include work on such classics as Percy Sledge's "When a Man Loves a Woman," Aretha Franklin's "Respect" and "Chain of Fools" (in fact, most of her biggest records), the Staple Singers' "Respect Yourself" and "I'll Take You There," Paul Simon's "Loves Me Like a Rock" and "Kodachrome," Bob Seger's "Old Time Rock and Roll," and Traffic's "Shoot Out at the Fantasy Factory."

BOB HODAS

Since 1993, Bob Hodas has traveled the world, tuning more than 1,000 rooms. His clients include engineers, producers, and studios. Notable clients include hit mixer David Pensado, producer Rob Cavallo, composer John Debney, and recording artist Stevie Wonder. His work has taken him from Tokyo for Sony Music Entertainment to London for Abbey Road. Stateside, he has tuned rooms for NRG Recording Services, the Record Plant, Blackbird Studio, and Lucasfilm.

CHRIS HUSTON

Chris Huston's credits as an engineer or producer include work with Van Morrison, Todd Rundgren, Blood, Sweat & Tears, Patti LaBelle, the Drifters, Led Zeppelin, the Who, the Fugs, Wilson Pickett, James Brown, ? and the Mysterians, the Rascals, and Eric Burdon and War (he earned a Grammy for *The World Is a Ghetto*). Since the early '80s, Huston has traveled the world as one of the finest acoustic consultants and room designers in the business, including major recording facilities and home studios for artists, as well as home theaters and listening rooms for audiophiles.

DENNIS HYSOM

Dennis Hysom has enjoyed substantial success as a producer, composer, musician, and field recordist for numerous environmentally inspired audio CDs that feature his extensive field recording work and evocative compositions. Of particular note is his series of releases for the Nature Company, inspired by the Nature Conservancy's Last Great Places program to protect wilderness habitats of rare and endangered species. The titles include *Cloud Forest*, *Glacier Bay*, *Caribbean*, *Prairie*, *Ocean Planet*, and *Bayou*. Hysom has also recorded many award-winning children's albums, including the *Wooleycat* series on BMG Kidz and worked on Mel Gibson's film *Apocalypto*.

WAYNE JACKSON

Mention the legendary Memphis Horns to anyone who has avidly listened to and loved popular music of the last 30 years, and the raw, sensual immediacy of classic Memphis recordings by Al Green, Sam & Dave, Otis Redding, Rufus, and Carla Thomas readily come to mind. Wayne Jackson and Andrew Love, founders of this revered two-man ensemble, created a sound that has been the blueprint for what makes a great track greater with inspired horn charts. Since the Memphis Horns' classic mid-'60s dates, Jackson and Love have played on more than 300 number-one hits, including releases by Elvis Presley, Aretha Franklin, Rod Stewart, Sting, Jimmy Buffett, the Doobie Brothers, Fine Young Cannibals, Neil Diamond, Dionne Warwick, and Willie Nelson.

JOHN JENNINGS

Producer, multi-instrumentalist, and solo artist John Jennings' production credits include nine albums by Mary Chapin Carpenter and releases by BeauSoleil, John Gorka, and Janis Ian. Jennings has played acoustic, electric, slide, lap, steel, and baritone guitars, synthesizers, organ, piano, and percussion, sung background vocals, or produced albums for artists such as the Indigo Girls, the Rankin Family, Cheryl Wheeler, Iris DeMent, George Jones, Robin and Linda Williams, and Auldridge, Reid & Coleman. As a recording artist, he has five albums to his credit.

DAVID KAHNE

Grammy-winning producer David Kahne has worked with a wide range of artists, including Tony Bennett, Stevie Nicks, Sublime, Bruce Springsteen, the Strokes, Fishbone, Cher, Sugar Ray, k.d. lang, Human Radio, the Bangles, and Paul McCartney. Kahne is also notable for his role as in-house producer and engineer at 415 Records, the first American New Wave label, and for his subsequent roles as vice president of A&R at Columbia Records and Warner Bros. Records. Kahne has also produced songs for *Vanilla Sky*, *Orange County*, *The Beach*, *Clockstoppers*, and a variety of other films and television shows.

DAVID KERSHENBAUM

With more than 75 international gold and platinum albums to his credit, David Kershenbaum's production credits include work with Joe Jackson, Tracy Chapman, Cat Stevens, Supertramp, Bryan Adams, Janet Jackson, Joan Baez, Peter Frampton, Graham Parker, Marshall Crenshaw, Kenny Loggins, and Duran Duran. While at A&M Records, Kershenbaum was known for being a true artist development executive. In the current digital music world, Kershenbaum has formed Music Pros Hollywood to help new artists find their way to stand out from the thousands of daily uploads on the Internet and get their music heard and remembered.

KEN KESSIE

Ken Kessie has made a name for himself as one of the finest, most in-demand engineers and re-mixers in the recording world, particularly in R&B and dance. His gold and platinum credits include work with En Vogue, Whitney Houston, Céline Dion, Tony! Toni! Toné!, CeCe Peniston, and Stacy Lattisaw, as well as mix projects for MC Lyte, Herbie Hancock, Jody Watley, All-4-One, Regina Belle, and Tower of Power. Kessie's production credits include the platinum debut by Brownstone, as well as co-production of former Tower of Power arranger Greg Adams' acclaimed solo album *Hidden Agenda*.

JACQUIRE KING

Jacquire King is a Nashville-based producer/engineer whose career includes recordings with Tom Waits, Norah Jones, Modest Mouse, Kings of Leon, MUTEMATH, Clinic, Pictures and Sound, Sea Wolf, Annuals, Archie Bronson Outfit, Buddy Guy, and many others.

RICHARD KING

Richard King has traveled all over the world, from La Scala in Italy and Abbey Road in London to China, recording serious symphonic, small chamber group, and solo piano music. As a senior recording engineer for Sony Music Studios in New York, King has worked with Yo-Yo Ma, Riccardo Muti and the Filarmonica della Scala, the Los Angeles Philharmonic, the Philadelphia Orchestra, and many classical pianists, such as Yefim Bronfman, Emanuel Ax, and Murray Perahia.

WAYNE KRAMER

Guitarist, singer, songwriter, producer, and film/TV composer Wayne Kramer came to prominence in 1967 as a co-founder of the Detroit rock group the MC5, whose first album, 1969's *Kick Out the Jams*, remains one of the most influential records of the era, laying the groundwork for the rise of punk a decade later. Over the years, Kramer has released 11 solo albums. As a film and TV composer, his work can be heard on the Will Ferrell comedies *Talladega Nights: The Ballad of Ricky Bobby* and *Step Brothers* and the HBO comedy series *Eastbound & Down*; Fox Sports Net's *5-4-3-2-1, Spotlight, In My Own Words*, and *Under the Lights*; the Emmy-nominated series *Split Ends*; HBO's controversial 2006 documentary *Hacking Democracy*; and the ITVS/PBS documentary *Narcotic Farm*.

CRAIG KRAMPF

Over the last 30 years, Craig Krampf has played drums on more than 200 albums, including 60 top-40 hit singles, and many movie and TV soundtracks, such as *Clueless*, *The Breakfast Club*, *Flashdance*, and *Rocky III*. These efforts have garnered more than 60 gold and platinum awards, and several Grammy-winning and -nominated songs for various albums. Krampf's hit session credits include Kim Carnes' "Bette Davis Eyes," the Motels' "Only the Lonely," and the Church's "Under the Milky Way." He has also appeared on a diverse range of releases by artists such as Son Volt, Steve Perry, Alabama, Alice Cooper, and Santana. Krampf's production credits include Melissa Etheridge, Disappear Fear, Ashley Cleveland, Janis Ian, Cassino, Angela Kaset, the Dee Archer Band, Gretel, Jane His Wife, the Features, Laws Rushing, and Greg and Rebecca Sparks. As a songwriter, Krampf won the prestigious BMI Million Broadcast Performances Award for co-writing Steve Perry's number-three hit "Oh Sherrie" and won a Grammy for the *Flashdance* track "I'll Be Here Where the Heart Is," which he co-wrote with Kim Carnes and Duane Hitchings.

BOB KRUZEN

Jerry Lee Lewis, G. Love & Special Sauce, Mojo Nixon, the Radiators, and God Street Wine are a few of Bob Kruzen's credits, many of which he shares with producer Jim Dickinson. Kruzen, a lover all things with big tubes and vintage gear, has worked in Memphis, Nashville, Muscle Shoals, and New Orleans. As a live recording engineer, he has also recorded Live Aid, Hall & Oates, and the Neville Brothers.

NATHANIEL KUNKEL

Los Angeles–based producer, engineer, mixer, and 5.1 surround mixer Nathaniel Kunkel has earned a reputation for sonic excellence that has brought him plenty of industry recognition, including Grammys for his work with Lyle Lovett, B.B. King, the Trio (Emmylou Harris, Linda Ronstadt, and Dolly Parton), and comedian Robin Williams; Surround Music Awards for his work with Graham Nash, James Taylor, and the Insane Clown Posse; and an Emmy for his recent work with Sting. Kunkel's credits also include Morrissey, Fuel, Good Charlotte, Barbra Streisand, John Mayer, Julio Iglesias, Diana Ross, Nirvana, Van Morrison, Crosby & Nash, Everclear, Little Feat, Heart, and Linda Ronstadt.

Kunkel is also known for his "studio without walls" concept, which provides mobile recording and mixing services to take the studio to the client, including residences (Sting's Malibu home is one notable example), hotel rooms, soundstages, garages, trucks, or anywhere else that he likes and where the client can feel comfortable and be creative.

NICK LAUNAY

Nick Launay got his first break at the legendary Townhouse Studios, where he worked as an assistant engineer on albums including the Jam's *Sound Affects*, Peter Gabriel's self-titled third album, and XTC's *Black Sea*, assisting producers John Leckie, Tony Visconti, Steve Lillywhite, and Hugh Padgham. His first production credit was Public Image Ltd's influential *Flowers of Romance* in 1981. Launay's blend of fearless experimentalism, refined song sense, and good instincts for capturing great performances have helped him amass an impressive body of work with artists like Nick Cave and the Bad Seeds, the Yeah Yeah Yeahs, Arcade Fire, Kate Bush, the Talking Heads, Gang of Four, Grinderman, INXS, Midnight Oil, the Cribs, the Posies, Semisonic, the Living End, Silverchair, Lou Reed, and Supergrass.

BRIAN LEE

Brian Lee has worked at Gateway Mastering Studios since 1992. Working hand-in-hand with chief engineer Bob Ludwig, he has worked on many mastering projects, including work by Rush, John Michael Montgomery, Gloria Estefan, the Gipsy Kings, Emilio, William Topley, the Bee Gees, Wilco, Billy Bragg, Xscape, Alejandro Fernandez, Janet Jackson, Juliana Hatfield, and Kenny Chesney. As Gateway's DVD designer and authoring engineer since 1998, Lee has worked on DVD projects for artists including Bruce Springsteen, Madonna, Frank Sinatra, Eric Clapton, Nine Inch Nails, the Blue Man Group, Roy Orbison, Paul Simon, Jonatha Brooke, and Prince.

RUSS LONG

Nashville-based producer, engineer, and studio owner Russ Long has recorded country greats Dolly Parton and Neal McCoy, and he's also known for his dynamic work with rock, pop, gospel, rap, and film soundtrack projects. His credits include work with Wilco, Allison Moorer, Osaka Pearl, Chagall Guevera, Phil Keaggy, Carolyn Arends, the Kopecky Family Band, PFR, Hotspur, Relient K, Swag, Jim Brickman, Paul Rodgers, Newsboys, and Leigh Nash, as well as Sixpence None the Richer's Grammy-nominated tracks "Kiss Me" and "There She Goes."

BOB LUDWIG

Grammy-winning mastering engineer Bob Ludwig began his professional career in 1967 at A&R Recording as an assistant engineer working with Phil Ramone, Roy Halee (who worked there for a short time), Don Hahn, Roy Cicala, Shelly Yakus, Elliot Scheiner, and other staff engineers. He learned the art of vinyl record mastering at A&R with Ramone as his mentor. Over the years, Ludwig has worked as vice president at Sterling Sound and vice president/chief engineer at Masterdisk, and eventually opened his own Gateway Mastering Studios in Portland, Maine. His mastering credits read like a greatest hits of legendary albums by artists such as Led Zeppelin, Jimi Hendrix, the Band, Neil Diamond, Janis Joplin, U2, Sting, the Police, Bryan Adams, Barbra Streisand, and Dire Straits. Ludwig was the first person to be honored with the Les Paul Award when it was established in 1991. He's also won numerous Pro Sound News Mastering Awards and the TEC Award for Outstanding Creative Achievement, Mastering Engineer, an unprecedented 13 times. Gateway Mastering Studios has won the TEC Award for Mastering Studio nine times.

GAVIN LURSSEN

Hollywood-based mastering engineer Gavin Lurssen owns Lurssen Mastering and has mastered recordings by Tom Waits, Sheryl Crow, the Who, James Taylor, Linda Ronstadt, Quincy Jones, Guns N' Roses, Mötley Crüe, B.B. King, Lucinda Williams, Loretta Lynn, Matchbox Twenty, T-Bone Burnett, and Mose Allison. His Grammy-winning work includes Alison Krauss and Robert Plant's *Raising Sand*, *Martin Scorsese Presents the Blues: A Musical Journey*, the soundtrack for the Coen brothers' film *O Brother, Where Art Thou?*, and Oscar-winning and -nominated films like *Slumdog Millionaire*, *Transamerica*, *Cold Mountain*, and *A Mighty Wind*.

COOKIE MARENCO

With more than 20 years in the music industry, Cookie Marenco's creative and technical skills have touched almost every aspect of the business. She has engineered or produced five Grammy-nominated records, several gold records, and an Oscar-winning documentary. Her credits include work with Max Roach, Brain, Steve Smith, Tony Furtado, Tony Trischka, Dirk Powell, Rob Ickes, Charlie Haden, Tony Levin, Buckethead, Ralph Towner, Paul McCandless, Ernie Watts, Mary Chapin Carpenter, Pat DiNizio, Kristin Hersh, Brad Mehldau, Matt Rollings, Art Lande, Ladysmith Black Mambazo, and Mark Isham. Her production and engineering skills can be found on projects for the Monterey Jazz Festival, the Telluride Bluegrass Festival, Rock Marinfest, MIDEM, the Hard Rock Cafe, Windham Hill Records, Verve, Rounder Records, Om Records, Sony, and Warner Bros.

Marenco was an early pioneer in Internet audio, being the part of the Liquid Audio team offering the first copy-protected music downloads in 1997. She was a producer and A&R representative at Windham Hill Records, working on more than 100 projects during her tenure. Marenco's production company, Cojema Music, oversees her work as an independent producer and the operations of OTR Studios (her commercial San Francisco Bay Area studio), Blue Coast Records (a high-quality acoustic music label), and Goddess Labs (a silver cable company).

ANDREW MENDELSON

Andrew Mendelson is the owner and chief mastering engineer at Georgetown Masters, one of the world's top mastering facilities. His mastering credits include the Rolling Stones, Death Cab for Cutie, Kenny Chesney, Emmylou Harris, Mötley Crüe, Ozzy Osbourne, Mariah Carey, Van Morrison, AC/DC, Neil Young, Ricky Skaggs, Osaka Pearl, Adrian Belew, McCoy Tyner, Johnny Cash, Joe Cocker, Mark Knopfler, Yo-Yo Ma, Willie Nelson, Dolly Parton, Pete Seeger, Take 6, Derek Trucks, and Bruce Hornsby.

SKIDD MILLS

Producer/engineer Skidd Mills started in Memphis working at the legendary Ardent Studios. While there, he developed a reputation for knowing how to capture heavy rock with clarity and immediacy. His credits there include ZZ Top, B.B. King, Skillet, Space Hog, Third Day, Saliva, Robert Cray, Saving Abel, the

Spin Doctors, the Killjoys, and Joe, Marc's Brother. Mills later formed SkiddCo and relocated to Nashville, finding success producing Saving Abel, Tetanus, Brent James, and Deepfield.

DOUG MITCHELL

Doug Mitchell has been a professor in the field of sound recording for almost 20 years. In addition, he is a technical writer for a variety of periodicals in the professional audio trade, having written hundreds of articles and reviews on recording audio. As a freelance recording engineer and producer, Mitchell has worked in many types of music, but he has a particular interest in sound for film and video. He has worked extensively as a sound designer, Foley artist, and on-location sound recordist.

DAVE MORGAN

TCA Award–winning engineer Dave Morgan is one of the most respected front-of-house engineers in the world of live sound. Among the artists who have employed Morgan are James Taylor, Paul Simon, Steely Dan, Bette Midler, Cher, Stevie Nicks, and Simon & Garfunkel.

RONAN CHRIS MURPHY

Ronan Chris Murphy works around the globe as a producer, mixer, and guitarist. His eclectic discography spans hundreds of albums, and he has gained a reputation for working with some of the most noted musicians in the world, including King Crimson, Robert Fripp, Terry Bozzio, Tony Levin, Alexia, Steve Morse, Steve Stevens, Martin Sexton, Chucho Valdés, Ulver, Teo Peter, and Nels Cline, as well as projects that have featured members of Wilco, Tool, and Weezer. In addition to his global production work, he operates a commercial studio in Los Angeles called Veneto West and runs a series of recording education workshops called Home Recording Boot Camp.

CLIF NORRELL

Clif Norrell began his studio career at the legendary Ocean Way Recording in Los Angeles in the mid-'80s. Throughout his years there as staff engineer, Norrell honed his skills working with superstars like Bruce Springsteen, Prince, the Beastie Boys, and Van Halen. He has produced or engineered work for many other artists over the years as well, including Faith No More, Rush, Weezer, the Beastie Boys, John Cale, the Cramps, John Fogerty, Tom Petty and the Heartbreakers, the Replacements, John Hiatt, the Pixies, Iggy Pop, Queens of the Stone Age, Rancid, Ry Cooder, Echo and the Bunnymen, Natalie Cole, R.E.M., Brian Wilson, Henry Rollins, Kiss, Paul McCartney, and Jeff Buckley. Norrell has also mixed songs for popular movies such as *Man on the Moon, Speed, Brokedown Palace, Singles,* and *So I Married an Axe Murderer.*

Norrell owns Casa Zuma Studio in southern California, where he does much of his work. He is also the CEO of Supersonic Music, where he partners with his wife Michelle in music supervision for film, TV, and advertising. They have worked on many projects together, including commercials for Honda, McDonald's, Toyota, Nissan, and Sapporo, and trailers for many films.

MARK O'CONNOR

Multiple Grammy–winning violinist Mark O'Connor has enjoyed a career that has enabled him to follow his artistic muse from bluegrass to jazz/rock fusion to more classically oriented undertakings. He was named Musician of the Year by the Country Music Association 6 years in a row (1991–1996). His "Fiddle Concerto" has received more than 200 performances, making it one of the most performed concertos written in the last 50 years. He has composed six violin concertos, string quartets, string trios, choral works, solo unaccompanied works, and a new symphony.

O'Connor, once one of the Nashville session world's most in-demand players, has worked and recorded with a wide range of artists, such as Chet Atkins, James Taylor, Michelle Shocked, Alison Krauss, David Grisman, Tony Rice, Béla Fleck, Renée Fleming, Stéphane Grappelli, Patty Loveless, the Dixie Dregs, and Wynton Marsalis.

EDDY OFFORD

Since the late '60s, Eddy Offord has amassed a discography that has included blues, jazz, pop, rock, and practically any other type of music that comes to mind. His work with '70s art and progressive rock bands elevated him to legendary production/engineering status. Offord worked on the first four Emerson, Lake & Palmer albums and produced classic Yes albums, from *The Yes Album* (amazingly, his very first production) to *Relayer*. He has also worked with John Lennon, the Police, the Dixie Dregs, Andy Pratt, Levon Helm & the RCO All-Stars, Wet Willie, David Sancious, John McLaughlin, Utopia, Tim Hardin, Thin Lizzy, and 311, and has worked on films such as *The Last Waltz* and *Zabriskie Point*.

TIM PALMER

Tim Palmer has enjoyed a lengthy career that has covered a wide range of rock and pop. His credits include work with Pearl Jam, James, Live, Tears for Fears, Robert Plant, Ozzy Osbourne, U2, Rancid, and the Cure.

RODGER PARDEE

Rodger Pardee specializes in sound-effects editing and design for feature films, as well as production sound, re-recording mixing, and sound editing. He is an assistant professor of recording arts at Loyola Marymount University in Los Angeles. His film credits include *To Live and Die in L.A.*, *Waterworld*, *Men in Black*, *The X-Files*, *Geronimo: An American Legend*, *The League of Extraordinary Gentlemen*, *Pacific Heights*, *Red Heat*, *Rambo III*, *Apt Pupil*, and *The Flight of the Phoenix*.

ERIC PAUL

Austin-based producer and engineer Eric Paul has made a career out of knowing how to tap into the heart of great American country and folk artists like Willie Nelson, Waylon Jennings, Emmylou Harris, Townes Van Zandt, the Flatlanders, Billy Joe Shaver, John Gorka, Johnny Cash, Don Walser, the Highwaymen, Shelley Laine, and Big Sugar.

RIK PEKKONEN

Since 1965, when he started as an engineer in Los Angeles, Rik Pekkonen has carved out an impressive track record that includes work in jazz and fusion (the Crusaders, the Dixie Dregs, Freddie Hubbard, Jeff Lorber, and young jazz singer Jamie Cullum), R&B and blues (Booker T. & the M.G.'s, B.B. King, Peabo Bryson, and Sly and the Family Stone), country (Willie Nelson, Waylon Jennings, and the Nitty Gritty Dirt Band), rock and pop (Brian Wilson, Ringo Starr, Was (Not Was), David Crosby, Guns N' Roses, Neil Young, Nancy Wilson, Iggy Pop, Joe Jackson, the B-52's, Roy Orbison, and Jackson Browne), and more undefinable artists (Bob Dylan, Leo Kottke, Ladysmith Black Mambazo, and T-Bone Burnett). From T. Rex's *Electric Warrior* to Joe Cocker and Jennifer Warnes' Grammy-winning "Up Where We Belong," Pekkonen has worked on hundreds of albums and dozens of film soundtracks, such as *Backbeat*, *An Officer and a Gentleman*, and *Brewster's Millions*.

DAVE PENSADO

Los Angeles–based Dave Pensado is one of the most successful mixing engineers of the last 20 years. Pensado honed his audio skills during the '70s and '80s in Atlanta's club and hip-hop scene, engineering in both live and studio settings. In 1990, he moved to Los Angeles, hoping to hit the big time, and within 3 months mixed the number-one hit "Do Me!" for Bell Biv DeVoe. Since then, Pensado has mixed an impressive string of chart-topping hits and platinum releases, sometimes with multiple number-one hits in the same month by different artists. Among the artists who have benefited from his mixing are Beyoncé, Christina Aguilera, Pink, Brian McKnight, Justin Timberlake, the Pussycat Dolls, Missy Elliott, Destiny's Child, Keyshia Cole, Mýa, Lil' Kim, the Black Eyed Peas, Warren G + Christina, Ice Cube, Mary J. Blige, Nelly Furtado, India.Arie, Yolanda Adams, Macy Gray, Bone Thugs-n-Harmony, Seal, Céline Dion, Hilary Duff, Mariah Carey, Ludacris, Jamie Foxx, and LL Cool J.

CSABA PETOCZ

Csaba Petocz is not only a great engineer, mixer, and producer, but he also imbues his work with a special passion, creating a studio dynamic that helps artists get to their emotional core. His wide-ranging list of credits includes work with Elvis Costello, Camper Van Beethoven, Elton John, Etta James, Cracker, LeAnn Rimes, Stevie Nicks, Metallica, Quiet Riot, Al Jarreau, Stanley Clarke, the Temptations, Vince Gill, Brenda Russell, Larry Carlton, MUTEMATH, Ben Folds, Eisley, Miley Cyrus, Korn, Mark Knopfler, Jeffrey Osborne, Oingo Boingo, Kenny Chesney, Poco, and Concrete Blonde.

JEFF POWELL

Memphis-based producer/engineer Jeff Powell's love for music with earthy immediacy has attracted artists like B.B. King, Susan Marshall, Alex Chilton, Big Star, Lucinda Williams, the North Mississippi Allstars, Jackie Johnson, Wilco, Alvin Youngblood Hart, the Afghan Whigs, Jolene, Bob Dylan, Primal Scream, Stevie Ray Vaughan, 16 Horsepower, Beth Orton, Tonic, Rob Jungklas, and the Memphis Horns.

NORBERT PUTNAM

Since the early '60s, Norbert Putnam's career has taken him from being one of Nashville's most in-demand session bassists to multi-platinum producer. His studio player credits include work with Elvis Presley, Henry Mancini, and Linda Ronstadt. As a producer, Putnam's credits include work on Dan Fogelberg's and Jimmy Buffett's biggest records, as well as the New Riders of the Purple Sage, Joan Baez, Dobie Gray, Jerry Butler, and Eric Andersen.

BENNY QUINN

Benny Quinn is one of Nashville's most prominent mastering engineers, with mastering credits covering genres such as symphonic, rock, country, gospel, R&B, and jazz. His credits include work with Eric Clapton, Elvis Presley, Aaron Copeland, DC Talk, Johnny Cash, Isaac Hayes, Alabama, the Dixie Dregs, the Indigo Girls, Béla Fleck, Bob Seger, Cracker, Widespread Panic, Amy Grant, the Boston Pops Orchestra, Willie Nelson, Nanci Griffith, Shirley Caesar, Lyle Lovett, and Reba McEntire.

PHIL RAMONE

With 14 Grammys (33 nominations), a Technical Grammy for his lifetime of innovative contributions to the recording industry, an Emmy, and numerous other honors and accolades to his credit, Phil Ramone is one of the most respected, prolific music producers in the recording industry. His impeccable list of credits includes collaborations with artists such as Burt Bacharach, Bono, Ray Charles, Chicago, Natalie Cole, Bob Dylan, Gloria Estefan, Renée Fleming, Aretha Franklin, Etta James, Quincy Jones, B.B. King, Madonna, Paul McCartney, Liza Minnelli, Sinead O'Connor, Luciano Pavarotti, Peter, Paul and Mary, André Previn, Carly Simon, Paul Simon, Frank Sinatra, Phoebe Snow, Rod Stewart, James Taylor, Bruce Springsteen, Bonnie Raitt, Gladys Knight, Sheryl Crow, Chaka Khan, Nancy Wilson, Dianne Reeves, Queen Latifah, Ruben Studdard, k.d. Lang, Keith Urban, Wynonna Judd, the Dixie Chicks, Michael Bublé, Dave Koz, John Legend, Juanes, and Stevie Wonder.

A passionate fan of all forms of entertainment, Ramone has numerous concert, film, Broadway, and TV productions to his credit, including *A Star is Born, August Rush, Beyond the Sea, Flashdance, Ghostbusters, Midnight Cowboy, On Her Majesty's Secret Service, Passion, Seussical the Musical,* Simon & Garfunkel's *The Concert in Central Park, Songwriters Hall of Fame Awards, The Score,* VH1/BBC's *Party at the Palace: The Queen's Jubilee Concert,* and *The Good Thief.*

MICHAEL RHODES

Michael Rhodes is a highly respected studio designer from Nashville. His clients include Echo Mountain Recording, Ocean Way Nashville, Warner Brothers Nashville, and Blackbird Studio. Rhodes has also designed personal rooms for Eminem, Clint Black, Vince Gill, Kenny Alphin (Big and Rich), Jewel, and Jack White.

NILE RODGERS

During the late '70s, Chic was unquestionably the most elegant band with the deepest R&B grooves in disco. A key component in Chic's artistic vision was producer/guitarist Nile Rodgers. Aside from Chic, Rodgers has produced for some of the biggest acts in popular music, including Madonna, Peter Gabriel, Duran Duran, Power Station, the Vaughan Brothers, Paul Simon, Al Jarreau, Sister Sledge, and David Bowie.

ELLIOT SCHEINER

Elliot Scheiner has worked with many of the most successful and influential acts in pop and rock. His credits include a string of platinum artists: the Eagles, Fleetwood Mac, Foo Fighters, B.B. King, Van Morrison, Beck, Jimmy Buffett, Aerosmith, John Fogerty, Billy Joel, Toto, Boz Scaggs, Stevie Nicks, and Steely Dan. He has earned six Grammys (23 nominations) and multiple Emmy and TEC Award nominations. Scheiner's surround mixes are among the most impressive in the industry, such as his surround mixes for Beck, Steely Dan, R.E.M., Diana Krall, Donald Fagen, Van Morrison, Queen, and Lenny Kravitz.

ERIC SCHILLING

One of the most successful artists to synthesize Latin American musical sensibilities and mainstream American pop is Gloria Estefan. The man who has recorded and mixed 16 of Estefan's albums (solo or with the Miami Sound Machine) is Eric Schilling. The Miami-based engineer/producer has also recorded Jon Secada, Natalie Cole, Elton John, Natalie Imbruglia, Shakira, Julio Iglesias, Chayanne, Cachao, Arturo Sandoval, and new artist Anthem.

Since 2000, Schilling has garnered three Grammys and seven Latin Grammys. Two of his Grammys were for Best Latin Pop Album: in 2000 for Shakira's *MTV Unplugged* and in 2003 for Bacilos' *Caraluna*. In 2003, he was honored at the Florida chapter of NARAS' Heroes Awards gala for his contributions to both NARAS and the state of Florida.

BILL SCHNEE

Mention Bill Schnee's name to any engineer who's been around, and that person will no doubt offer some major respect. Schnee's been an icon in the Los Angeles recording industry for decades. His production, engineering, and mixing credits include work with Barbra Streisand, Marvin Gaye, Miles Davis, Dire Straits, George Benson, Billy Joel, Take 6, Captain Beefheart and His Magic Band, Rod

Stewart, Barry Manilow, the Pussycat Dolls, Ringo Starr, Carly Simon, Pablo Cruise, Steely Dan, Boz Scaggs, Chicago, Al Jarreau, Teddy Pendergrass, the Jacksons, the Pointer Sisters, Neil Diamond, and Mark Knopfler.

JIM SCOTT

Los Angeles–based producer/engineer and mixer Jim Scott likes the sound of real musicians playing off each other and, if that is happening on the tracking floor, he's one of the best at catching the sparks and turning up the rockets. Scott, a multiple Grammy winner, has an impressive list of credits, including work with the Red Hot Chili Peppers, Wilco, Tom Petty, Neil Young, the Rolling Stones, the Finn Brothers, Robbie Robertson, Sting, Santana, Seal, Jewel, Johnny Cash, Matthew Sweet, Foo Fighters, Matchbox Twenty, Slayer, Ride, Jack Cadillac, Weezer, Jason Mraz, John Fogerty, the Dixie Chicks, Black Sabbath, and Will Hoge.

KEN SCOTT

Ken Scott has been part of the some of the greatest popular music recordings of the last 50-plus years, including Elton John's expansive "Tiny Dancer," Lou Reed's unforgettable "Walk on the Wild Side," the Mahavishnu Orchestra's hyper-driven "Birds of Fire," the Beatles' explosive "Help!" and David Bowie's glam master-piece "Ziggy Stardust." Scott started at age 16 working in the tape library at Abbey Road Studios and soon became a recording engineer working with such acts as the Beatles (*A Hard Day's Night, Beatles for Sale, Help!, Rubber Soul, Magical Mystery Tour*, and *The Beatles*), Jeff Beck, Pink Floyd, the Hollies, and Procol Harum. He moved to Trident Studios, where he worked with such artists as Elton John, George Harrison (*All Things Must Pass*), Harry Nilsson, the Rolling Stones, and America. As a producer/engineer, Scott's credits include David Bowie (*Hunky Dory, The Rise and Fall of Ziggy Stardust and the Spiders from Mars*), the Dixie Dregs, the Mahavishnu Orchestra, Supertramp, Missing Persons, Kansas, Devo, Billy Cobham, Stanley Clarke, and Level 42.

TONY SHEPPERD

Tony Shepperd is a Los Angeles–based producer/engineer and mixer. His credits include Queen Latifah, Faith Hill, the Backstreet Boys, Lionel Richie, Whitney Houston, Kenny Loggins, Flora Purim, Elton John, Boyz II Men, Barbra Streisand, Madonna, Take 6, Chicago, Yolanda Adams, BeBe Winans, Michael W. Smith, Neil Diamond, and Melissa Etheridge. He also worked on *Handel's Messiah: A Soulful Celebration*, which featured Patti Austin, Tevin Campbell, Stevie Wonder, and Quincy Jones. Shepperd's film and TV credits include *Sister Act 2: Back in the Habit, House Guest, General Hospital, The Wedding Planner*, and *A Walk to Remember*.

One of Shepperd's other passions is mentoring. To that end, he helped found Techbreakfast, a professional forum that covers topics including Pro Tools, Logic, and DP, as well as separate forums for producers, engineers, musicians, mastering, legal, schools, and publishing.

KEVIN SHIRLEY

Malibu-based Kevin Shirley spent his early years producing and engineering records for many successful artists in his native South Africa, such as Robin Auld, Juluka, Jonathan Butler, Lesley Rae Dowling, Steve Louw, and Sweatband, as well as performing and recording with his own band, the Council, which featured legendary South African singer Brian Davidson.

In 1987, Shirley moved to Australia, where he continued working with the Hoodoo Gurus, the Angels, Cold Chisel, Girl Monstar, Tina Arena, the Screaming Jets, and the Baby Animals. After the worldwide success of Silverchair's debut album *Frogstomp*, which he produced, Shirley moved to the United States. He has continued to produce successful albums for some of the biggest artists in American rock music, including Aerosmith, Journey, and the Black Crowes, and for international hard rockers like Iron Maiden, HIM, Slayer, and Jonny : Black. He also worked on the hugely successful retrospective *Led Zeppelin* DVD and has produced several albums for American blues-rock guitarist Joe Bonamassa.

ALLEN SIDES

Allen Sides is not only the owner of Ocean Way Recording, but also one of the most respected engineers/producers in the music industry. Sides began his distinguished recording career in 1968 and opened his first studio, Ocean Way, in Santa Monica in 1973. In 1977, he purchased the renowned United Recording and relocated to Hollywood. In 1979, he acquired Western Recording and consolidated both venerable operations into Ocean Way. Record One became part of the Ocean Way family in 1988. In 1997, Ocean Way Nashville opened on famed Music Row. As an engineer/producer, Sides has recorded more than 400 albums and won two Grammys. The artists with whom he has worked include Phil Collins, Green Day, Eric Clapton, Alanis Morissette, Faith Hill, Trisha Yearwood, Wynonna Judd, Beck, Mary J. Blige, Ry Cooder, Joni Mitchell, Frank Sinatra, Ray Charles, Count Basie, Duke Ellington, Ella Fitzgerald, John Williams, Jerry Goldsmith, Tom Newman, André Previn, and Frank Zappa.

LELAND SKLAR

Leland Sklar is one of the best known, most influential bassists of the last 40 years. Sklar and his distinctively melodic playing first came into the limelight during his work with James Taylor. In the 1970s, Sklar worked so often with his bandmates with James Taylor—drummer Russ Kunkel, guitarist Danny Kortchmar, and keyboardist Craig Doerge—that they eventually became known as "the Section" and recorded three albums between 1972 and 1977. Over the years, Sklar has contributed to thousands of albums as a session musician, including Crosby, Stills & Nash, Carole King, Jackson Browne, Randy Newman, Ray Charles, Phil Collins, Donovan, Art Garfunkel, Vince Gill, Hall & Oates, Lyle Lovett, the Manhattan Transfer, Reba McEntire, Roger McGuinn, Dolly Parton, Linda Ronstadt, Rod Stewart, Stephen Stills, Barbra Streisand, Donna Summer, and Warren Zevon.

RALPH SUTTON

Ralph Sutton has a well-established background in the music industry as a recording engineer and music producer. Over his more than 28 years of experience, he's worked on many Grammy-winning projects with elite musicians such as Stevie Wonder, Prince, Lionel Richie, and Marvin Gaye. During the '00s, Sutton relocated from Los Angeles to Memphis to re-open the legendary House of Blues Studios and focus on the music of the Deep South and Delta regions of the United States. During that time, Sutton served as chairman of the Memphis chapter of the Recording Academy's Producers and Engineers Wing and was a board member of the Folk Alliance to mentor musicians and artists in the region. Recently, Sutton was lured back to Los Angeles, where he engineers at Stevie Wonder's Wonderland Studios.

BRUCE SWEDIEN

Bruce Swedien is a multiple Grammy–winning engineer, mixer, and producer especially known for his work with Quincy Jones. He recorded, mixed, and assisted in producing the world's all-time best-selling album, Michael Jackson's *Thriller*. He was also the primary sound engineer for Jackson's studio recordings from 1978 to 2001. Over his career, Swedien has recorded and mixed for jazz and blues artists such as Count Basie, Duke Ellington, Dizzy Gillespie, Stan Kenton, Lionel Hampton, Quincy Jones, Muddy Waters, John Lee Hooker, Dinah Washington, Oscar Peterson, Herbie Hancock, and Jeff Oster. His work in pop includes artists such as Patti Austin, Natalie Cole, Roberta Flack, Mick Jagger, Jennifer Lopez, Paul McCartney, Diana Ross, Rufus, Edgar Winter, Chaka Khan, Barbra Streisand, Donna Summer, and Sarah Vaughan. He also worked on the scores for *Night Shift*, *The Color Purple*, and *Running Scared*.

Swedien is notable for pioneering the Accusonic Recording Process, which involves pairing up microphones together on vocals and instruments when making recordings. This process achieved an enhanced roomy ambient sound, some of which is evident on albums produced in collaboration with Quincy Jones, such as Jones' *Sounds...And Stuff Like That!*, George Benson's *Give Me the Night*, and several Michael Jackson albums.

SAM TAYLOR

Producer, multi-instrumentalist, and composer Sam Taylor's work has earned the respect of many in the industry, particularly his production work on the first four critically touted, award-winning King's X albums. Much of Taylor's work synthesizes the sophisticated arrangement sensibilities of his mentors George Martin and Geoff Emerick, with an assertive progressive and hard rock attitude. A native Texan, Taylor has also produced albums for Third Day, the Galactic Cowboys, Atomic Opera, Jack Cadillac, and Annapurna. As a film director, editor, and producer, he has shot documentaries around the world and created numerous music videos. Taylor's compositional work can be heard on Sam Taylor & the Moons of Jupiter's *Callisto*.

DAVID THOENER

David Thoener started his career in 1974 as an assistant engineer at the Record Plant in New York. He learned his craft working on such seminal albums as Aerosmith's *Toys in the Attic*, Bruce Springsteen's *Born to Run*, David Bowie's *Young Americans*, John Lennon's *Walls and Bridges*, and Electric Light Orchestra's *Face the Music*. Over the last 30-plus years, Thoener has enjoyed a long run of hit records, including classic records for AC/DC, John Mellencamp, John Waite, the J. Geils Band, Matchbox Twenty, Sugarland, Heart, Bon Jovi, Cher, Cheap Trick, Kiss, Bob Seger, Courtney Love, Meat Loaf, Bob Dylan, Faith Hill, and Jason Mraz. In 2000, he won two Grammys—Record of the Year and Album of the Year—for recording and mixing "Smooth," by Santana featuring Rob Thomas.

BRET THOENY

Bret Thoeny (with his company, BOTO Design) has designed some of the finest facilities in the recording world, more than 250 in all. Among his accomplishments are Hans Zimmer's Media Ventures (Santa Monica), Electric Lady Studios (New York), Paisley Park Studios (Minneapolis), Britannia Row Studios (London), Westlake Audio (Los Angeles), George Massenburg's "The Complex" (Los Angeles), Pacific Ocean Post Sound (Santa Monica), Todd-AO/Glen Glenn Studios (Studio City), and private recording and mixing studios for Don Was, Bob Clearmountain, David Tickle, Jackson Browne, John Tesh, and Giorgio Moroder.

BRENT TRUITT

Brent Truitt is a master of many stringed instruments, as well as a producer and engineer. He has recorded or mixed more than 250 records with musical styles including rock, Dixieland, and bluegrass. His credits include Grammy-winning work with Riders in the Sky, the Oscar-winning film short *For the Birds*, and work with Alison Krauss, Kathy Chiavola, Holly Dunn, Sweethearts of the Rodeo, Jon Randall, Gail Davies, Tom Roznowski, and David Grier. He's also worked with the Dixie Chicks, James Taylor, Dolly Parton, the Nitty Gritty Dirt Band, and the Lonesome River Band, and has recorded tracks for films including *Monsters, Inc.*, *Toy Story 2*, and *The Grave*.

TOM TUCKER

Tom Tucker has been engineering and producing recordings since 1974. He has received a multitude of gold and platinum credits for artists as diverse as Jonny Lang, George Benson, Prince, Soul Asylum, and Chaka Khan. Tucker won a Grammy in 2003 for co-producing Lucinda Williams' *Essence*, which he also tracked and mixed. In addition to his engineering experience, Tucker has helped build and operate several of the Minneapolis area's premier recording facilities, including Metro Studios (1985–1990), Prince's Paisley Park Studios (1990–1996), and MasterMix Studios (1999–2007).

LEANNE UNGAR

Leanne Ungar is a producer/engineer with 30 years of experience in records, films, and television scores. She is also an associate professor in the Music Production and Engineering Department at the Berklee College of Music. With technical skills that encompass both analog equipment and digital applications, Ungar has produced or engineered seven albums for Leonard Cohen, and she worked with the avant-garde artist Laurie Anderson on three albums, *Big Science*, *Mister Heartbreak*, and *United States Live Parts I–IV*, and a concert film, *Home of the Brave*. Ungar's list of credits also includes the Temptations, Fishbone, Holly Cole, Guster, Joe Henderson, Willie Nelson, Luther Vandross, Natalie Cole, Vonda Shepard, Carlene Carter, the Paul Winter Consort, and Tom Jones.

Since her career began in the early '70s, Ungar has worked in both New York and Los Angeles, and she has had a hand in the creation of many historic recordings, including works by James Brown, the Brecker Brothers, the Manhattan Transfer, Cat Stevens, Loudon Wainwright III, and Janis Ian. Her film score credits include *Kafka*, *Pump Up the Volume*, and *The Limey*. Her television scores include *Thirtysomething*, *The Wonder Years*, *Full House*, and *Family Matters*. She recorded music on location for the films *Matewan*, *Passion Fish*, and *The Underneath*, and was involved in live recordings for the Leonard Cohen albums *Cohen Live* and *Field Commander Cohen: Tour of 1979*.

TONY VISCONTI

Unique artists have always gravitated to Tony Visconti, a native New Yorker who has been associated with some of the finest records and artists to come out of Great Britain and the United States. In 1967, Visconti was "loaned" by his publisher Howard Richmond to British producer Denny Cordell "to find out how the British do it." Somehow, the agreed-upon 6 months stretched to 23 years. Under Cordell, Visconti assisted as a producer, engineer, and orchestral arranger for Procol Harum, the Move, Denny Laine, and Joe Cocker, including the classic song "With a Little Help from My Friends."

Two key artists came into Visconti's life in 1968: David Bowie and Marc Bolan of Tyrannosaurus Rex (later T. Rex). Between 1969's *Man of Words/Man of Music* and 2003's *Reality*, Visconti has produced 14 albums with Bowie, including *The Man Who Sold the World*, *Diamond Dogs*, *Young Americans*, *Low*, *Heroes*, *Lodger*, and *Scary Monsters*. With Bolan and T. Rex, Visconti's production yielded a handful of brilliant albums, including *Electric Warrior*, a slew of huge hits in Great Britain, and the worldwide hit "Bang a Gong (Get It On)." Visconti's production credits also include work by Badfinger, Iggy Pop, John Hiatt, Gentle Giant, Sparks, the Moody Blues, the Alarm, Wings, Kristeen Young, Tom Paxton, U2, the Strawbs, Osibisa, Thin Lizzy, Bert Jansch, and the Boomtown Rats.

BIL VORNDICK

Bil VornDick is one of Nashville's finest engineers for making great recordings that feature acoustic instrumentation. He has engineered or had production credits on eight Grammy-winning projects and 42 albums that have been nominated for

Grammys. His many credits include Mark O'Connor (including the Grammy-winning *The New Nashville Cats* and *Heroes*), T-Bone Burnett, Jerry Douglas, Edgar Meyer, Béla Fleck, Doc Watson, James Taylor, Alison Krauss, Claire Lynch, Maura O'Connell, and Ralph Stanley's *Clinch Mountain Country*, which features Bob Dylan, George Jones, Vince Gill, Patty Loveless, Hal Ketchum, the Rayburn Brothers Band, and Diamond Rio.

MICHAEL WAGENER

Michael Wagener's credits reads like a who's who of hard rock and heavy metal. His odyssey from his native Hamburg, Germany, began in 1979, when he met Don Dokken, who was touring the country with his band. Dokken invited Wagener to Los Angeles, and by the next year he was working as a maintenance engineer at Larrabee Sound Studios. Wagener's first production was Dokken's first album, which went gold. From that point on, Wagener produced, engineered, and mixed work by several very successful rock bands, including Mötley Crüe, X, Great White, Extreme, Accept, Poison, Metallica, Megadeth, White Lion, Testament, Alice Cooper, Skid Row, Queen, Black Sabbath, Ozzy Osbourne, Warrant, Saigon Kick, and Janet Jackson. Wagener, who works out of his Mt. Juliet, Tennessee, studio called Wire World, continues to work with bands and artists from around the world who love the immediacy and audiophile quality of his work.

MATT WALLACE

Matt Wallace started his career in music as a musician, playing and singing original songs in various San Francisco Bay Area bands. Although he never achieved fame as a musician, singer, or writer, the experience gave Wallace the understanding to help bands with arrangements and chord choices, as well as occasional co-writes. Over the years, he has been able to apply those musical sensibilities to a wide range of artistry, including the hugely successful eccentric hard rock of Faith No More, John Hiatt's rootsy rock, Susanna Hoffs' bright Anglo pop rock, the reggae-influenced Michael Franti & Spearhead, and the funky jam rock of the Spin Doctors. Wallace also had the special skill to take the Replacements' raw big star–meets–garage punk and fashion it into their biggest record, *Pleased to Meet Me*. His other credits include O.A.R., Train, Blues Traveler, and Chagall Guevara's self-titled major label debut, probably the best rock album to ever come out of Nashville.

STEVEN WILSON

Steven Wilson is a producer/engineer and multi-instrumentalist. He is best known as the leader of the critically acclaimed British band Porcupine Tree, which incorporates elements of progressive and art rock but has more song sense than many bands in those genres. Wilson is involved in many other bands and musical projects as a musician and producer (including No-Man, Blackfield, and Ephrat), as well as his own solo career. Wilson is also a major player in keeping the fires going for surround audio, accompanying Porcupine Tree and solo releases with surround mix versions. As a result, he has increasingly become a go-to person for creating emotionally involving surround mixes, including the King Crimson catalog.

SHELLY YAKUS

Shelly Yakus has engineered successful recordings such as John Lennon's *Imagine* and U2's *Rattle and Hum*. More than 100 million records with his work have sold, equaling more than $1 billion in sales. Yakus was nominated for induction into the Rock and Roll Hall of Fame in 1999. His credits also include the Ramones, Tom Petty, Van Morrison, Alice Cooper, the Band, Blue Öyster Cult, Dire Straits, Don Henley, Madonna, Stevie Nicks, the Pointer Sisters, Lou Reed, Bob Seger, Patti Smith, Suzanne Vega, Warren Zevon, B.B. King, and the Raspberries.

DAVID Z.

David Z. is one of those producers/engineers with the good fortune of being able to defy pigeonholing. His credits include work with dance music divas Jody Watley and Neneh Cherry, Prince, blues-rockers Kenny Wayne Shepherd and Jonny Lang, Fine Young Cannibals, and the Freddy Jones Band. Most recently, he has been working with the alternative insurgent country-rock scene, a genre in which he is very comfortable. After all, the movement's late icon, Gram Parsons, was his friend and co-songwriter.

Index